MEAT AND BONE
BY KAT VERHOEVEN

FOREWORD
BY KEVIN CZAP

It will be obvious once you start reading this comic, but I wanted to emphasize that Kat Verhoeven is an amazing cartoonist. She's made it very easy to get swept away with the story, but I'm asking you to slow down while you read and take notice of the craft when you can. When you take a moment to soak in the page, you start to see how Kat brings a sense of design to every single panel. There's not one boring composition in the whole thing – that is rare even among other cartoonists of her calibre. Every centimeter is considered, every line arcing up and out like a song. Rereading it once again, my lavish praise continues to be just as called for today as it was when *Meat and Bone* first began as a webcomic in 2012.

As far as I'm concerned, Kat was already a world class illustrator when we met at the Toronto Comic Arts Festival, back in 2011 or '12. At the time, she was running a food illustration blog and making formally explosive mini-comics that telegraphed the serious skill at her disposal. She was making work to salivate over in every sense. Just at the first moments of my own career, it was validating to discover a peer making comics in a way that made me so excited about the medium.

This was my frame of reference when Kat decided to take all her considerable talents and put them to use on a long-form, deeply personal project. As *Meat and Bone* pages started to appear online, I joined the ranks of fans rapt over where this gorgeous strip would lead. We immediately became enamored with Anne and were captivated by her friends, the restaurant their lives revolved around, and the stunning Toronto backdrop that Kat captures with such familiarity. Then there's Marshall… surely everyone's problematic fave. I still care deeply about these characters, especially at the points when there's no guarantee it will all work out. *Meat and Bone* never shies away from digging into the difficult topics at its heart, and it gets difficult. I have to applaud Kat for her measured hand guiding everyone though.

Circling back to the craft – wielding an ensemble story like this takes chops. That the artwork elevates already-great writing to such a degree is remarkable. I could write another intro entirely about Kat's use of colour, but let me just mention how courageous she is with her choices, sticking the landing each time. She takes chances and they pay off, creating a warm identity for this world that is varied yet cohesive. Adding to the list of things I'm inspired by, the colours in *Meat and Bone* helped shape my own artistic development, without a doubt.

As I said, Kat's an amazing cartoonist, because she really shows how all the different elements work in harmony. It takes many varied skills to pull off comics like this, and Kat has long been in possession of them all. I'm proud to have been reading from day one, but I'm equally excited for the new readers who get their introduction with this fully realized edition. It is my honour to tell you that this comic is the complete package – a beautiful testament to friendship and to Kat's place as one of the greats of our time.

Bon appétit.

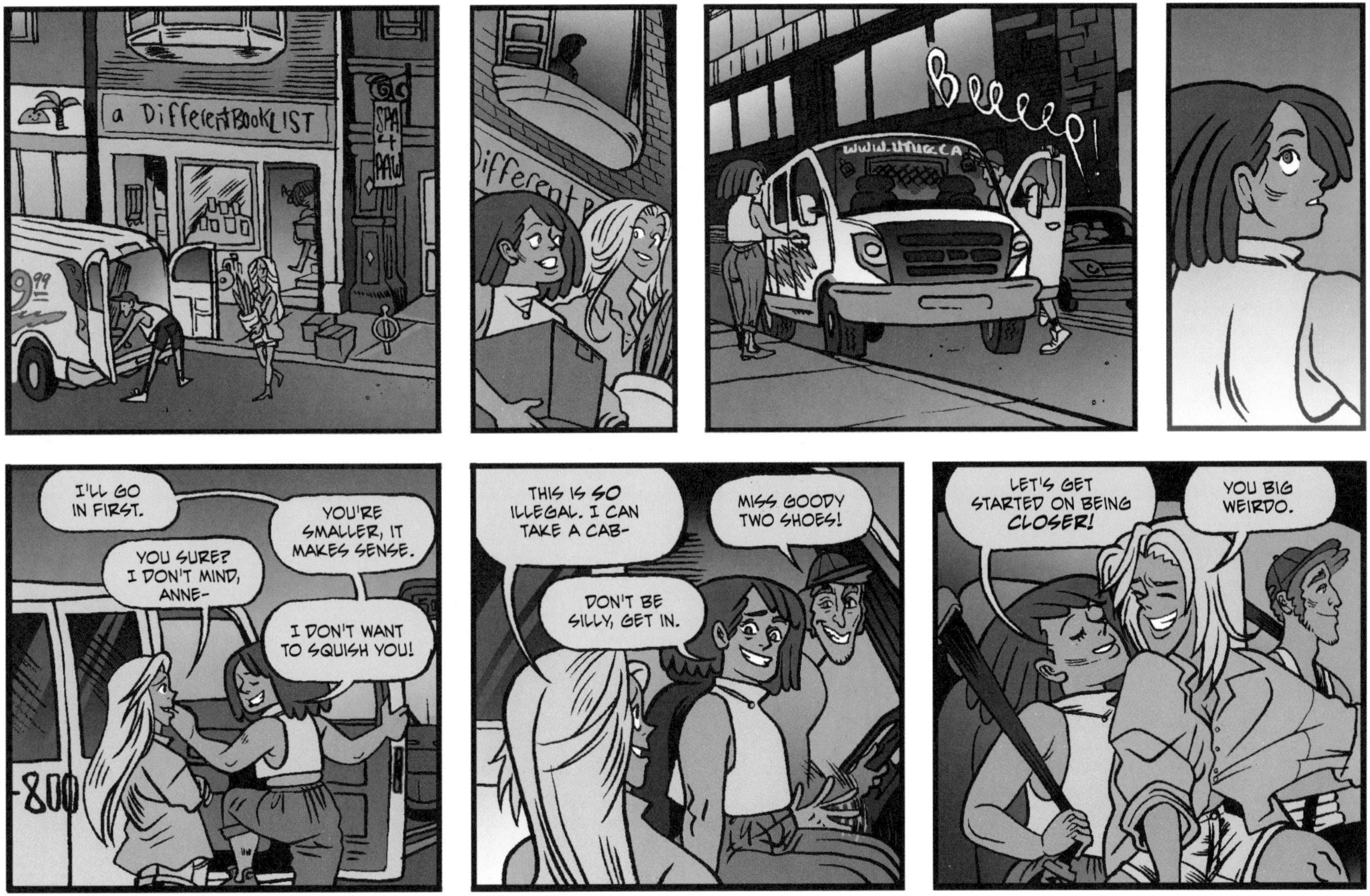
a DifferentBOOKLIST
SPA 4 PAW
Beeeep!
I'LL GO IN FIRST.
YOU SURE? I DON'T MIND, ANNE-
YOU'RE SMALLER, IT MAKES SENSE.
I DON'T WANT TO SQUISH YOU!
THIS IS SO ILLEGAL. I CAN TAKE A CAB-
DON'T BE SILLY, GET IN.
MISS GOODY TWO SHOES!
LET'S GET STARTED ON BEING CLOSER!
YOU BIG WEIRDO.

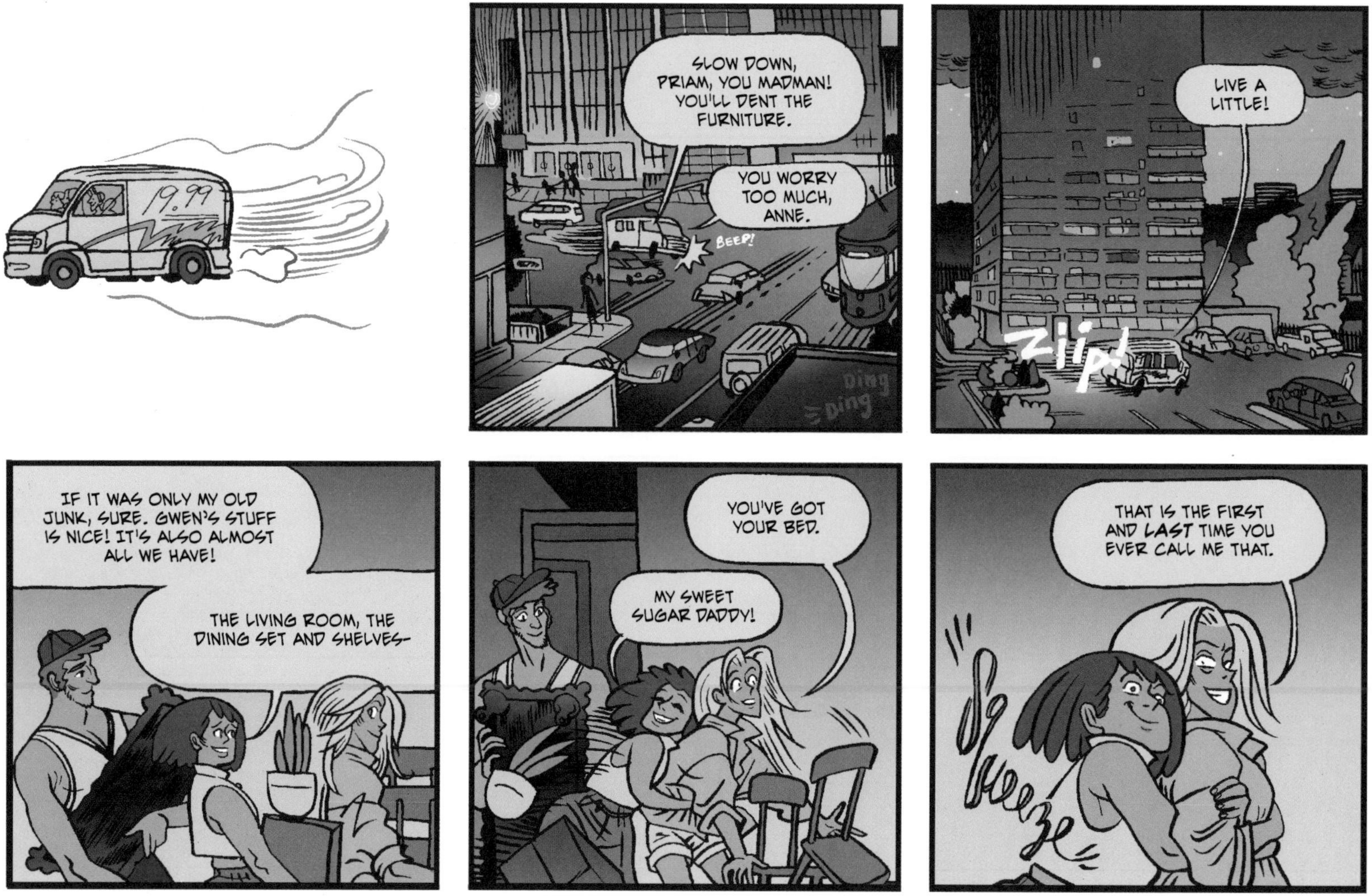
SLOW DOWN, PRIAM, YOU MADMAN! YOU'LL DENT THE FURNITURE.
YOU WORRY TOO MUCH, ANNE.
BEEP!
Ding Ding
LIVE A LITTLE!
Ziip!
IF IT WAS ONLY MY OLD JUNK, SURE. GWEN'S STUFF IS NICE! IT'S ALSO ALMOST ALL WE HAVE!
THE LIVING ROOM, THE DINING SET AND SHELVES-
YOU'VE GOT YOUR BED.
MY SWEET SUGAR DADDY!
THAT IS THE FIRST AND **LAST** TIME YOU EVER CALL ME THAT.
Squeeze

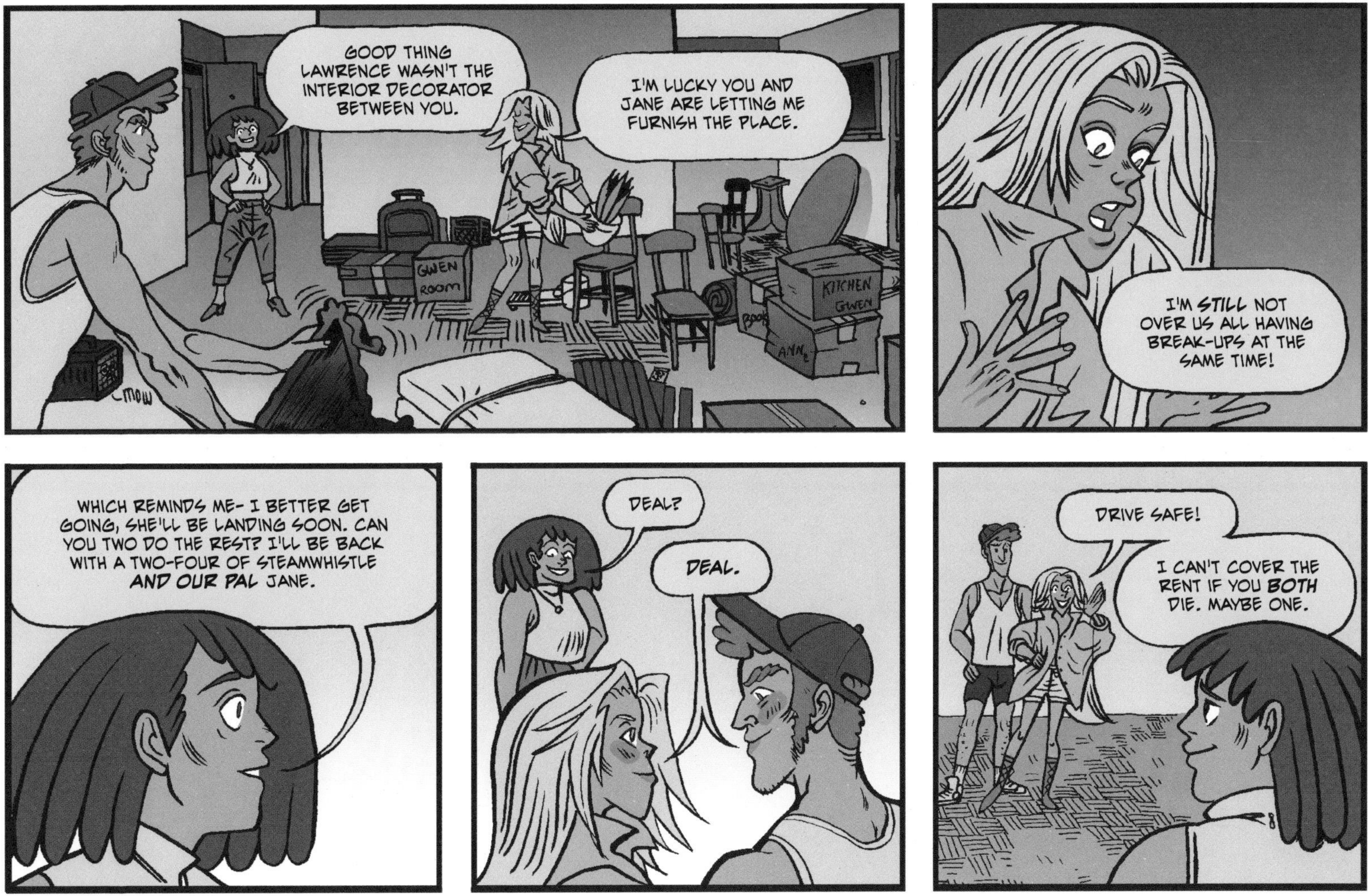
GOOD THING LAWRENCE WASN'T THE INTERIOR DECORATOR BETWEEN YOU.
I'M LUCKY YOU AND JANE ARE LETTING ME FURNISH THE PLACE.
GWEN ROOM
KITCHEN GWEN
I'M STILL NOT OVER US ALL HAVING BREAK-UPS AT THE SAME TIME!
WHICH REMINDS ME- I BETTER GET GOING, SHE'LL BE LANDING SOON. CAN YOU TWO DO THE REST? I'LL BE BACK WITH A TWO-FOUR OF STEAMWHISTLE AND OUR PAL JANE.
DEAL?
DEAL.
DRIVE SAFE!
I CAN'T COVER THE RENT IF YOU BOTH DIE. MAYBE ONE.

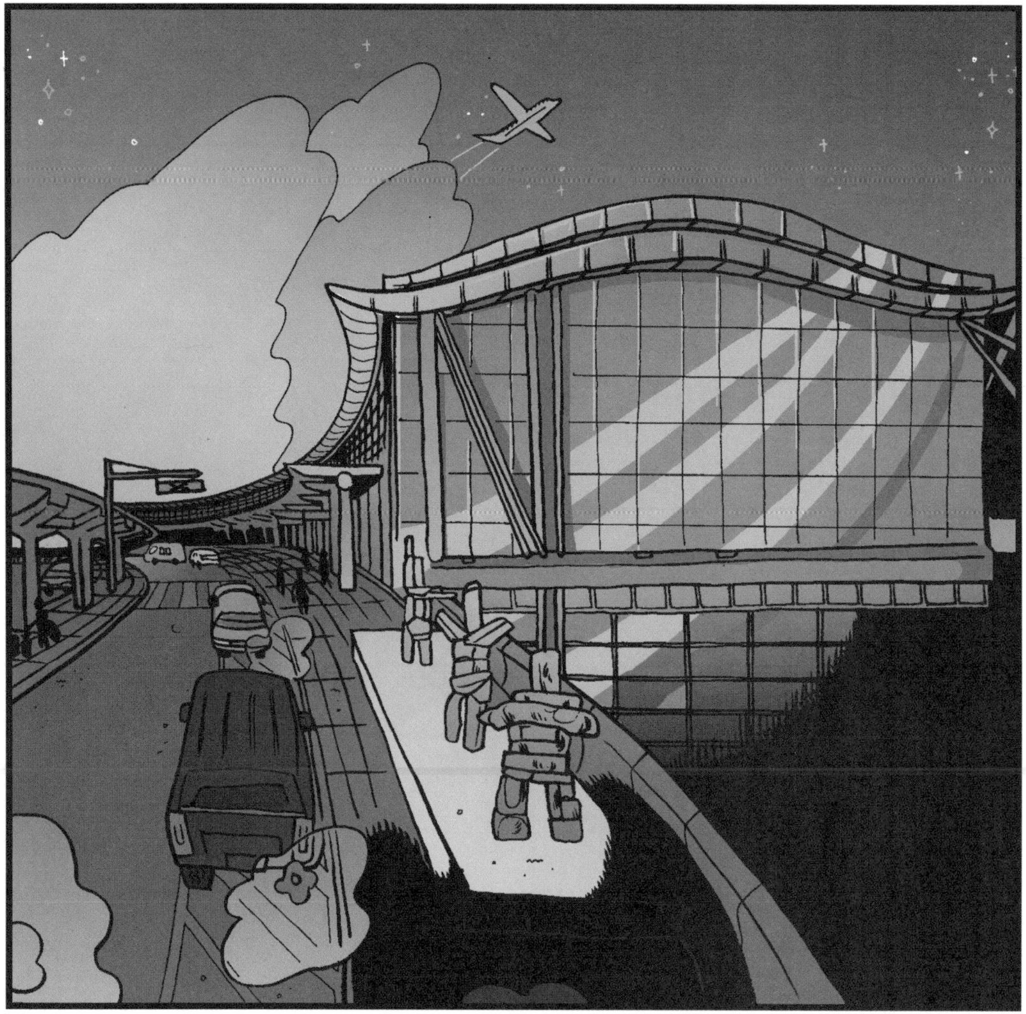

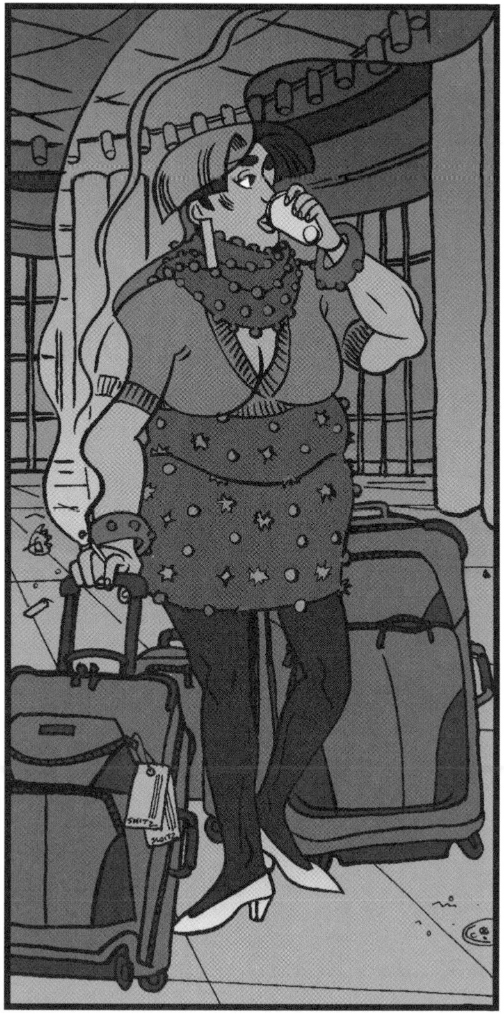

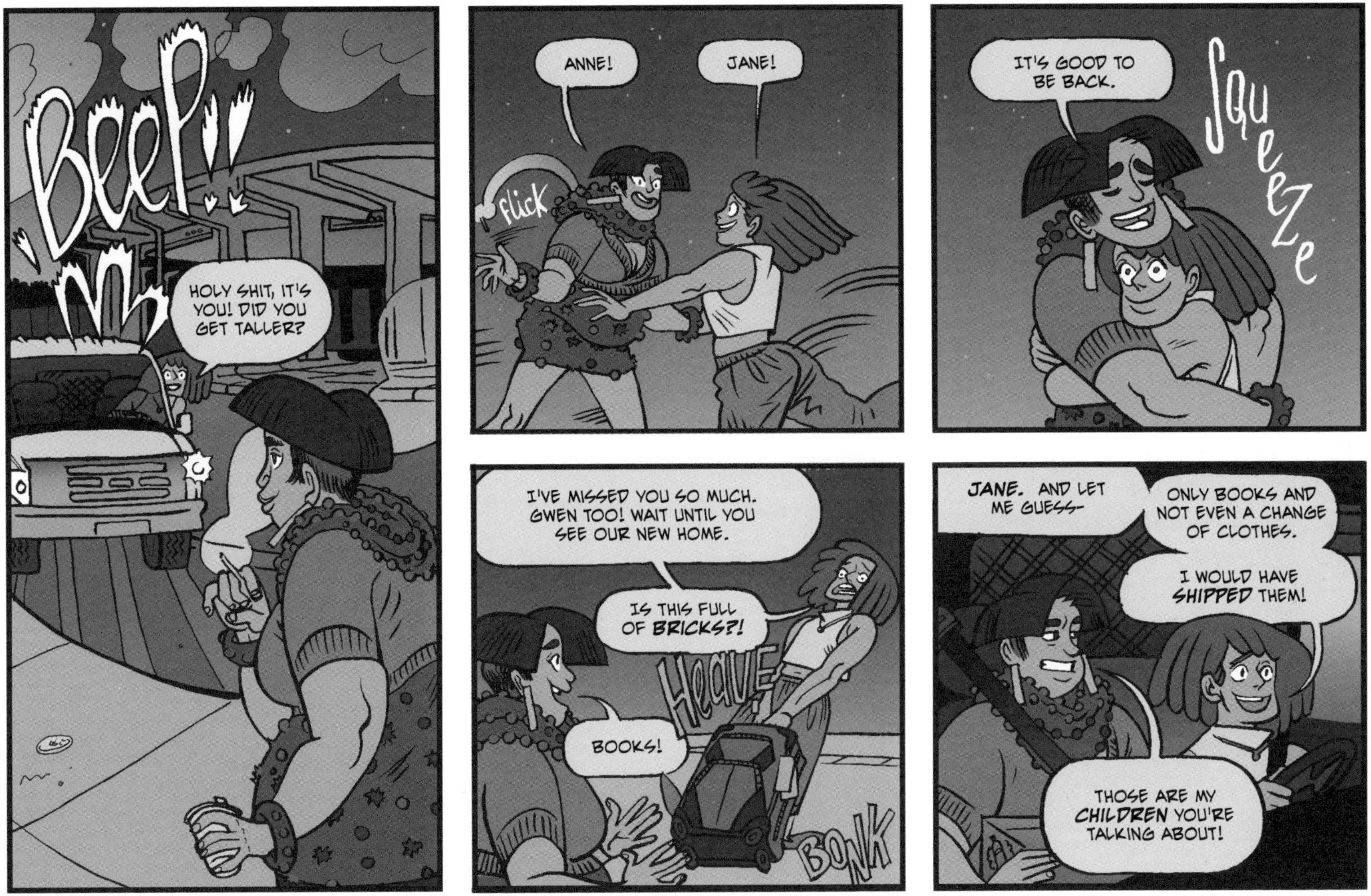
BEEP!!
HOLY SHIT, IT'S YOU! DID YOU GET TALLER?
ANNE!
JANE!
flick
IT'S GOOD TO BE BACK.
Squeeze
I'VE MISSED YOU SO MUCH. GWEN TOO! WAIT UNTIL YOU SEE OUR NEW HOME.
IS THIS FULL OF **BRICKS?!**
HEAVE
BOOKS!
BONK
JANE. AND LET ME GUESS-
ONLY BOOKS AND NOT EVEN A CHANGE OF CLOTHES.
I WOULD HAVE ***SHIPPED*** THEM!
THOSE ARE MY **CHILDREN** YOU'RE TALKING ABOUT!

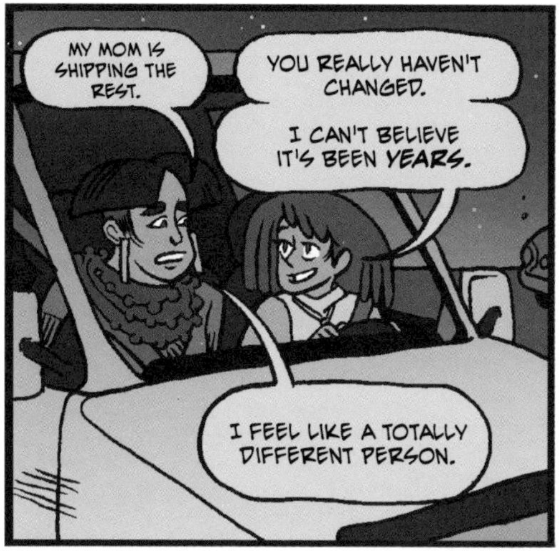
MY MOM IS SHIPPING THE REST.
YOU REALLY HAVEN'T CHANGED.
I CAN'T BELIEVE IT'S BEEN YEARS.
I FEEL LIKE A TOTALLY DIFFERENT PERSON.

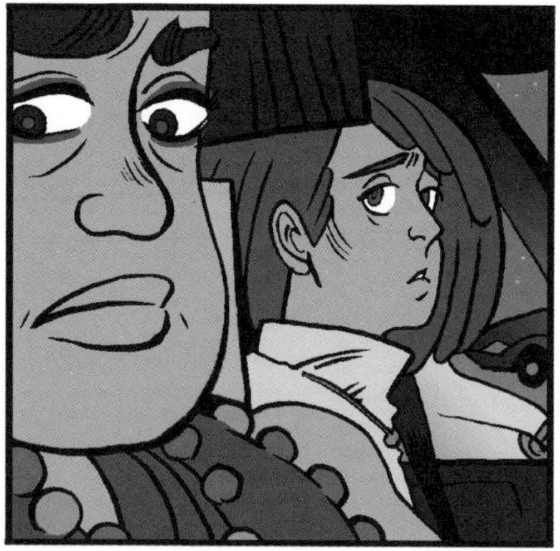

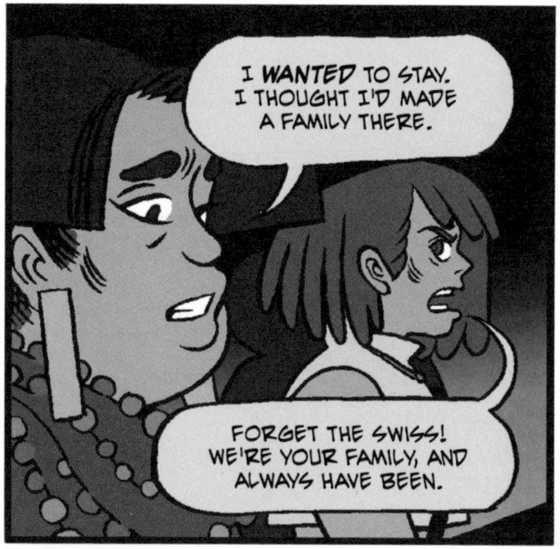
I WANTED TO STAY. I THOUGHT I'D MADE A FAMILY THERE.
FORGET THE SWISS! WE'RE YOUR FAMILY, AND ALWAYS HAVE BEEN.

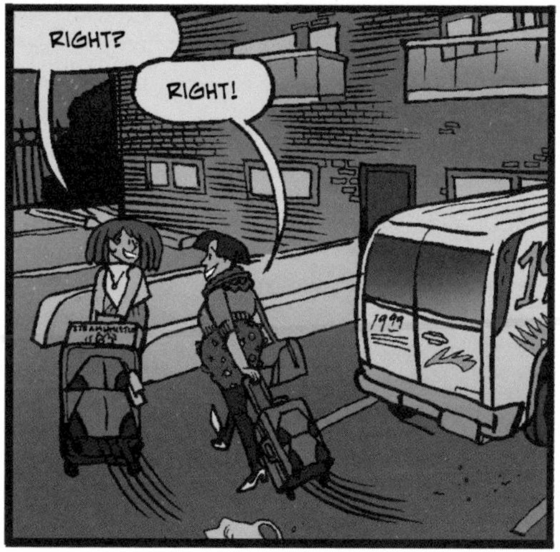
RIGHT?
RIGHT!

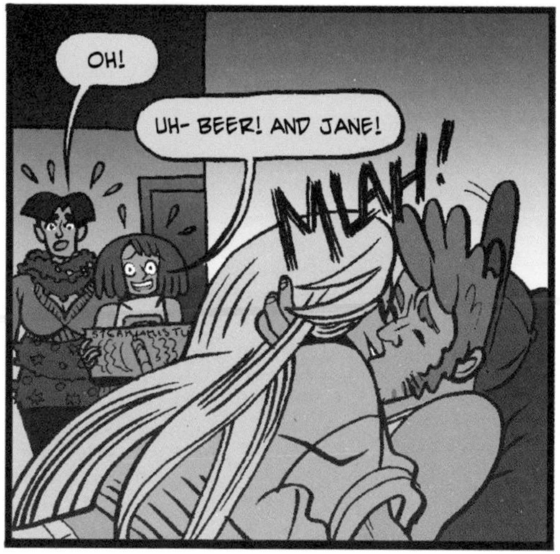
OH!
UH- BEER! AND JANE!
MLAH!

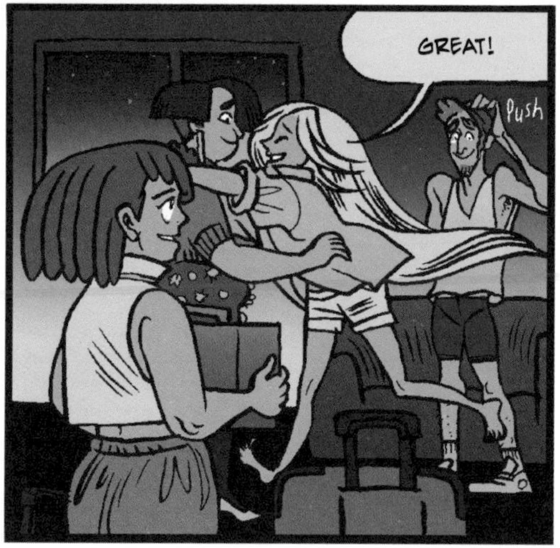
GREAT!
Push

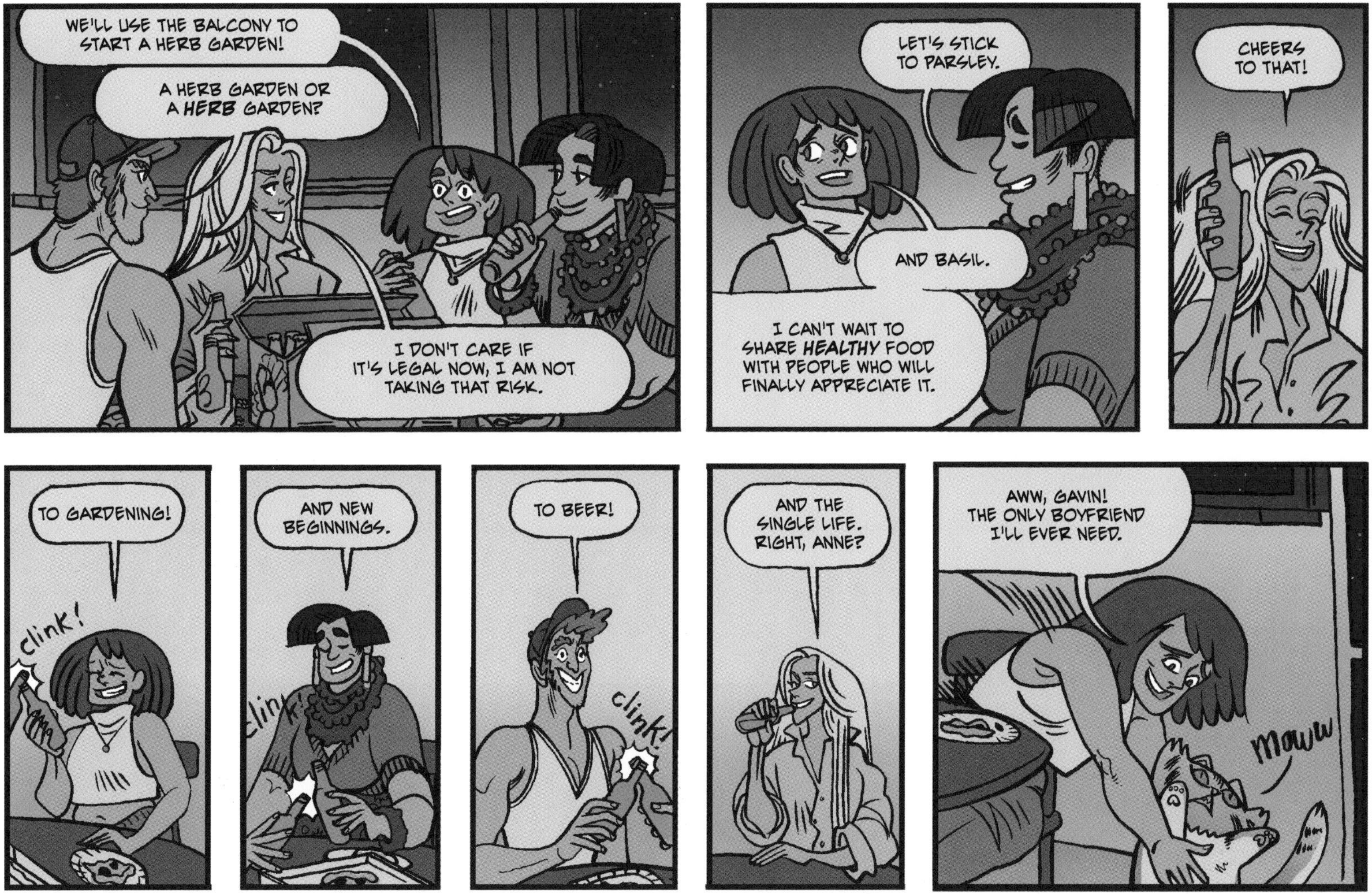
WE'LL USE THE BALCONY TO START A HERB GARDEN!
A HERB GARDEN OR A **HERB** GARDEN?
I DON'T CARE IF IT'S LEGAL NOW, I AM NOT TAKING THAT RISK.
LET'S STICK TO PARSLEY.
AND BASIL.
I CAN'T WAIT TO SHARE **HEALTHY** FOOD WITH PEOPLE WHO WILL FINALLY APPRECIATE IT.
CHEERS TO THAT!
TO GARDENING!
clink!
AND NEW BEGINNINGS.
clink!
TO BEER!
clink!
AND THE SINGLE LIFE. RIGHT, ANNE?
AWW, GAVIN! THE ONLY BOYFRIEND I'LL EVER NEED.

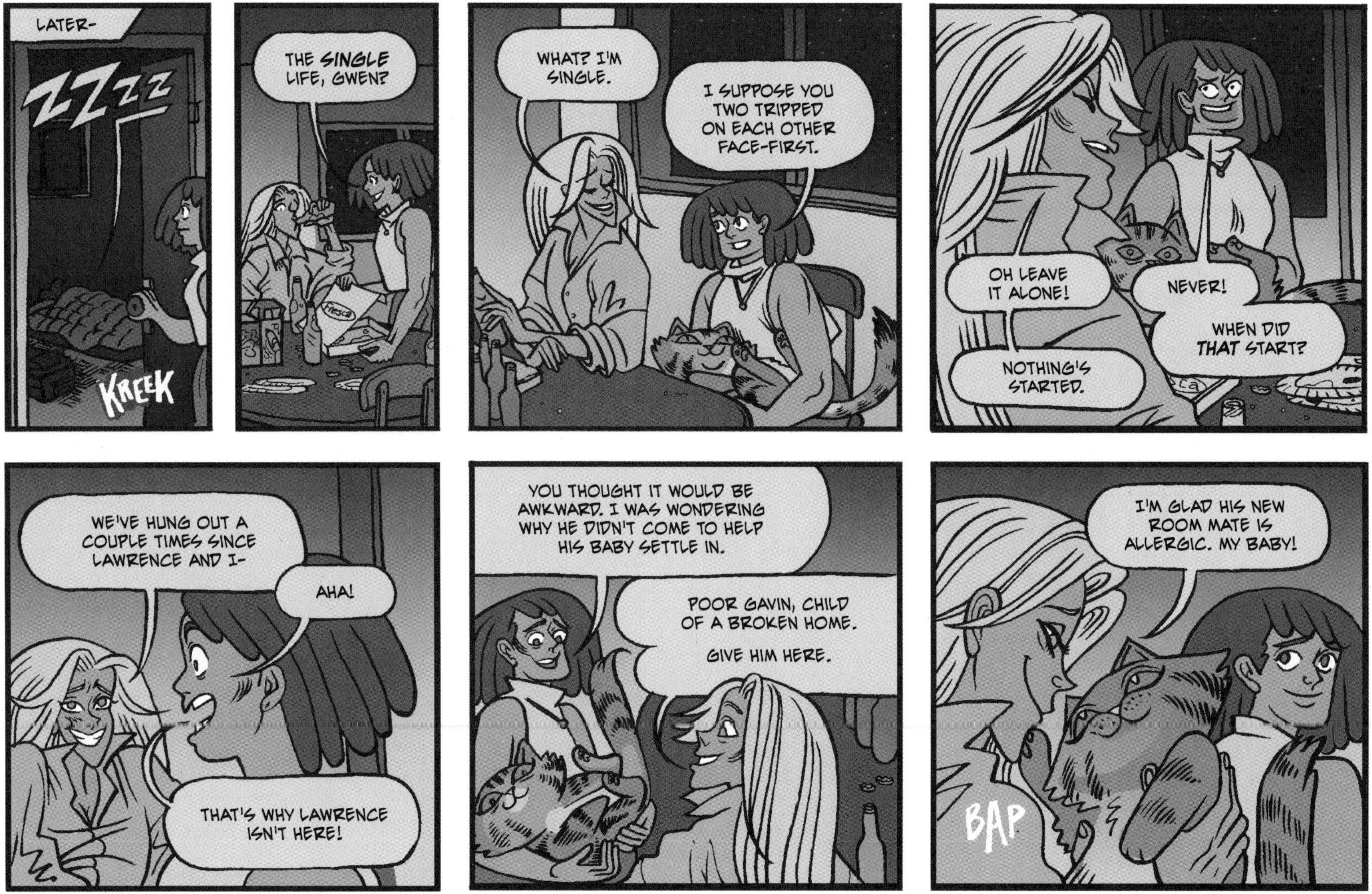
LATER-
ZZZZZ
KREEK
THE SINGLE LIFE, GWEN?
WHAT? I'M SINGLE.
I SUPPOSE YOU TWO TRIPPED ON EACH OTHER FACE-FIRST.
OH LEAVE IT ALONE!
NEVER!
WHEN DID THAT START?
NOTHING'S STARTED.
WE'VE HUNG OUT A COUPLE TIMES SINCE LAWRENCE AND I-
AHA!
THAT'S WHY LAWRENCE ISN'T HERE!
YOU THOUGHT IT WOULD BE AWKWARD. I WAS WONDERING WHY HE DIDN'T COME TO HELP HIS BABY SETTLE IN.
POOR GAVIN, CHILD OF A BROKEN HOME.
GIVE HIM HERE.
I'M GLAD HIS NEW ROOM MATE IS ALLERGIC. MY BABY!
BAP

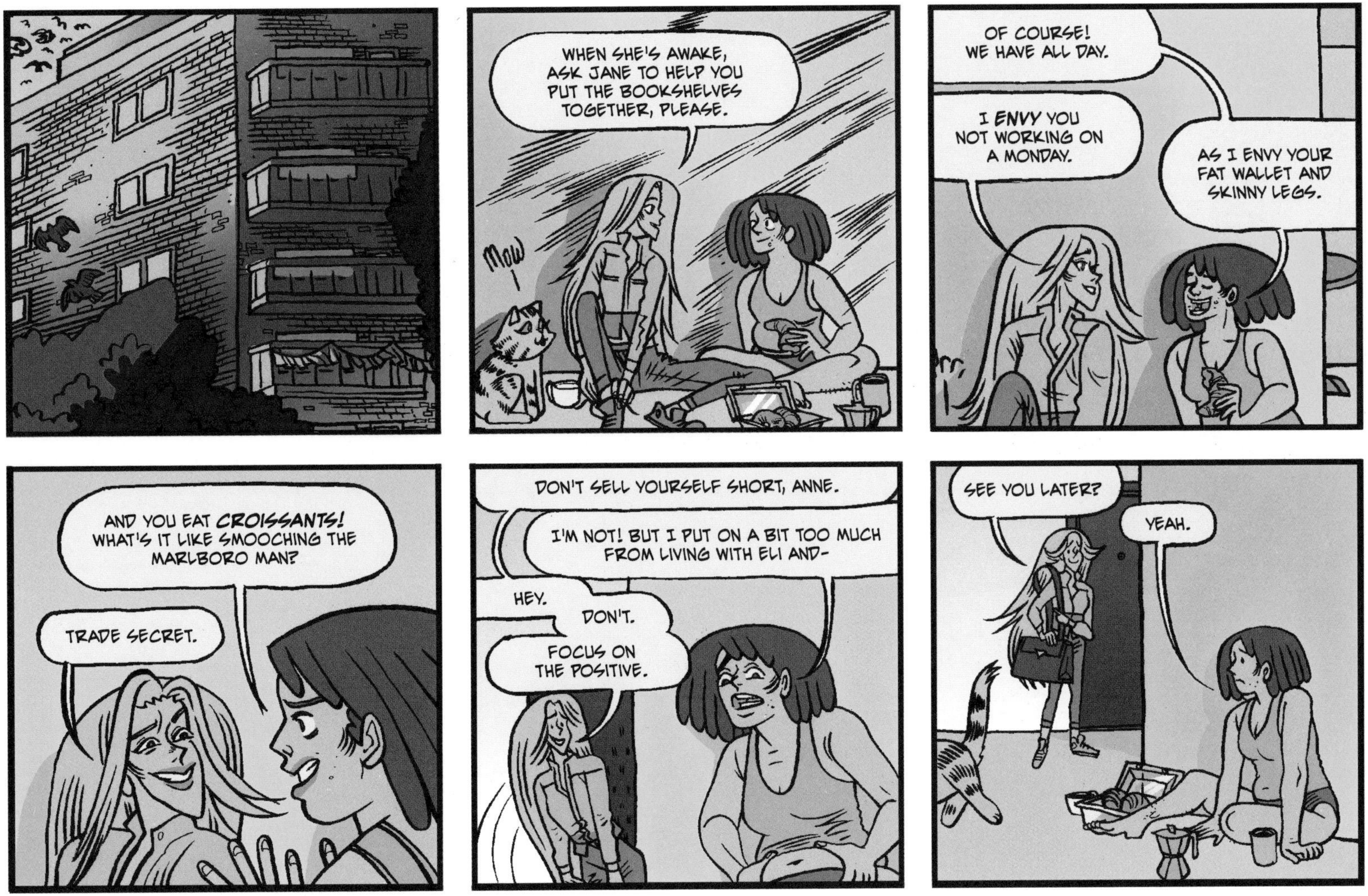
WHEN SHE'S AWAKE, ASK JANE TO HELP YOU PUT THE BOOKSHELVES TOGETHER, PLEASE.
MOW
OF COURSE! WE HAVE ALL DAY.
I ENVY YOU NOT WORKING ON A MONDAY.
AS I ENVY YOUR FAT WALLET AND SKINNY LEGS.
AND YOU EAT CROISSANTS! WHAT'S IT LIKE SMOOCHING THE MARLBORO MAN?
TRADE SECRET.
DON'T SELL YOURSELF SHORT, ANNE.
I'M NOT! BUT I PUT ON A BIT TOO MUCH FROM LIVING WITH ELI AND-
HEY.
DON'T.
FOCUS ON THE POSITIVE.
SEE YOU LATER?
YEAH.

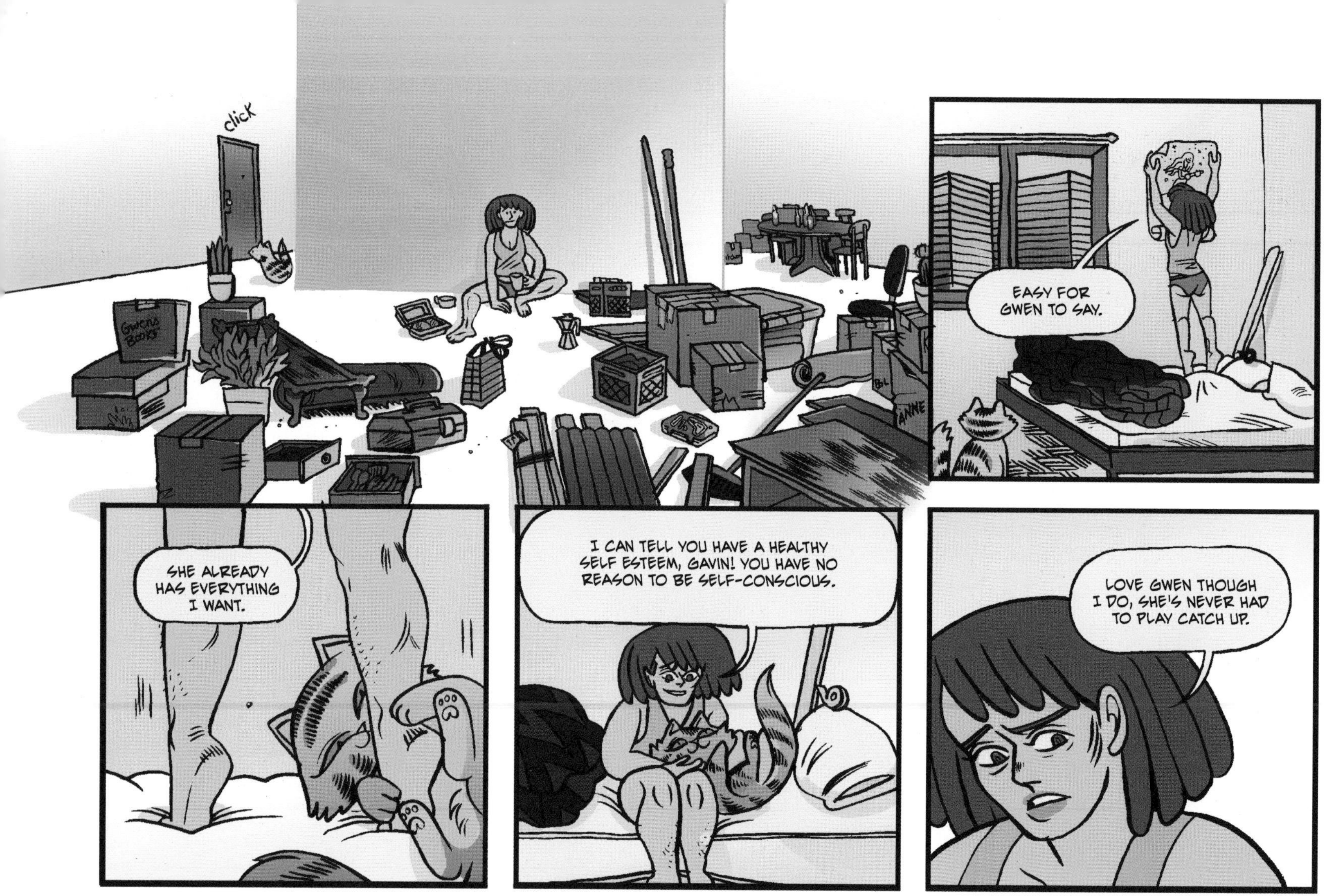
click
EASY FOR GWEN TO SAY.
SHE ALREADY HAS EVERYTHING I WANT.
I CAN TELL YOU HAVE A HEALTHY SELF ESTEEM, GAVIN! YOU HAVE NO REASON TO BE SELF-CONSCIOUS.
LOVE GWEN THOUGH I DO, SHE'S NEVER HAD TO PLAY CATCH UP.

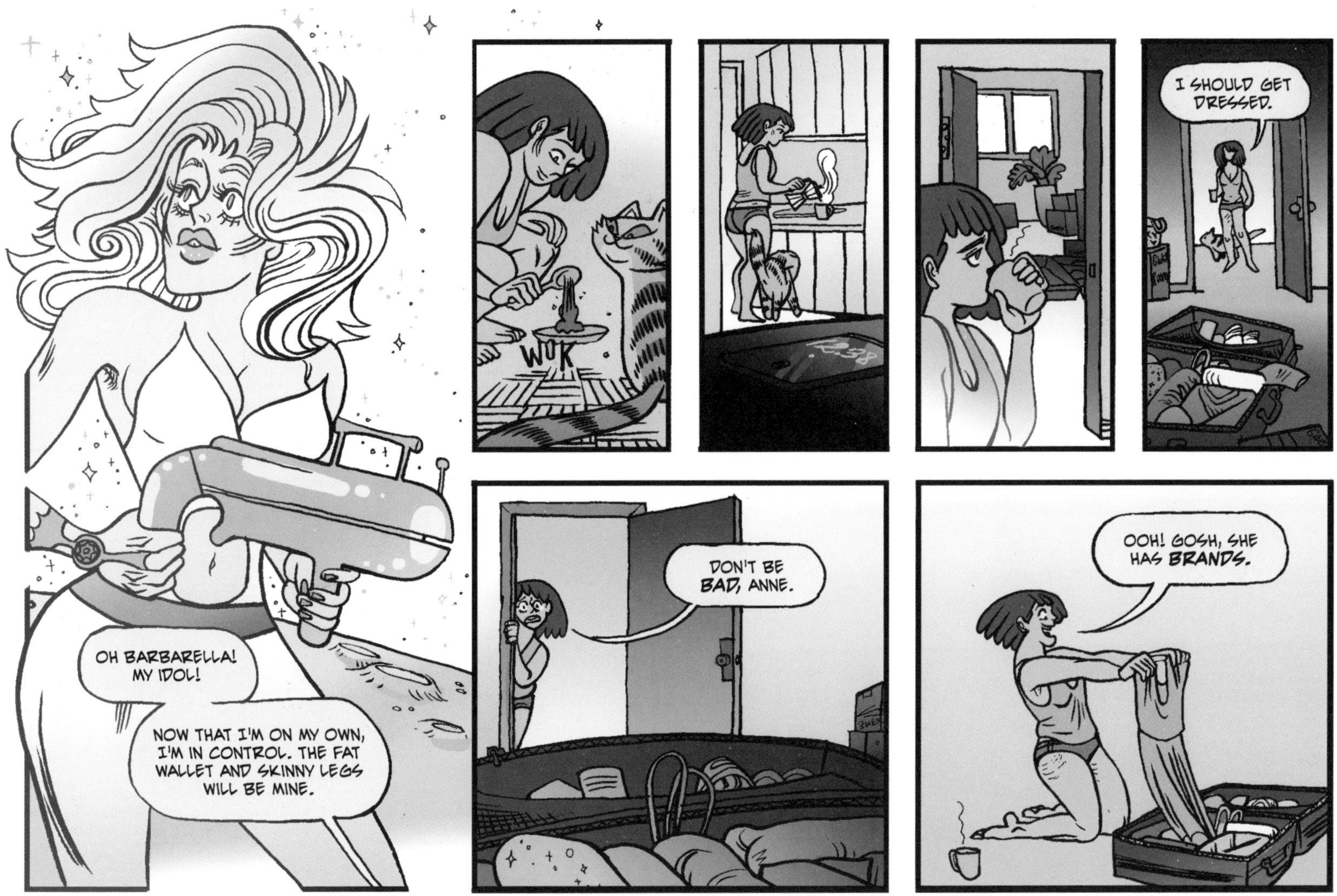
OH BARBARELLA! MY IDOL!
NOW THAT I'M ON MY OWN, I'M IN CONTROL. THE FAT WALLET AND SKINNY LEGS WILL BE MINE.
WOK
I SHOULD GET DRESSED.
DON'T BE BAD, ANNE.
OOH! GOSH, SHE HAS BRANDS.

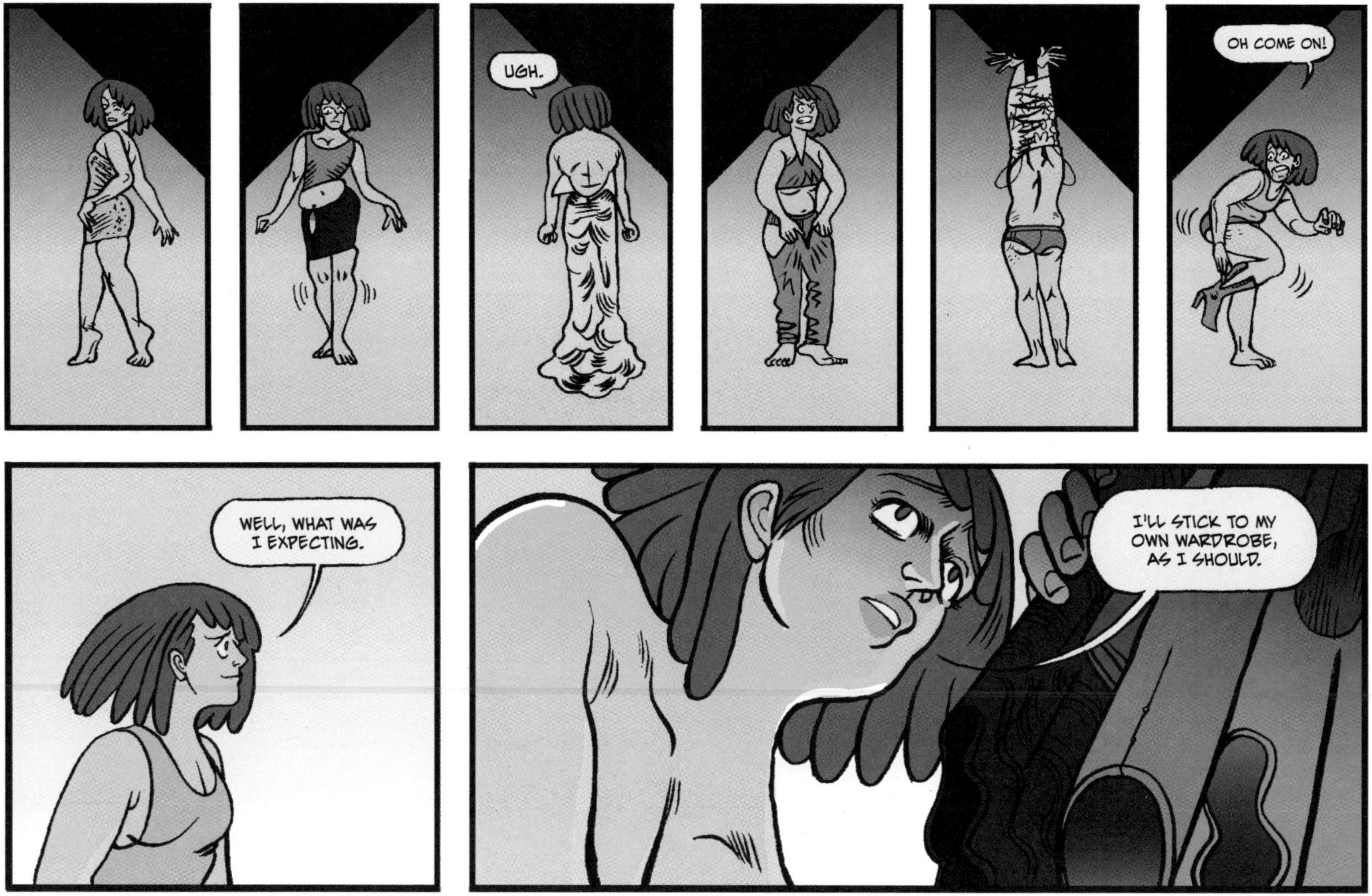
UGH.
OH COME ON!
WELL, WHAT WAS I EXPECTING.
I'LL STICK TO MY OWN WARDROBE, AS I SHOULD.

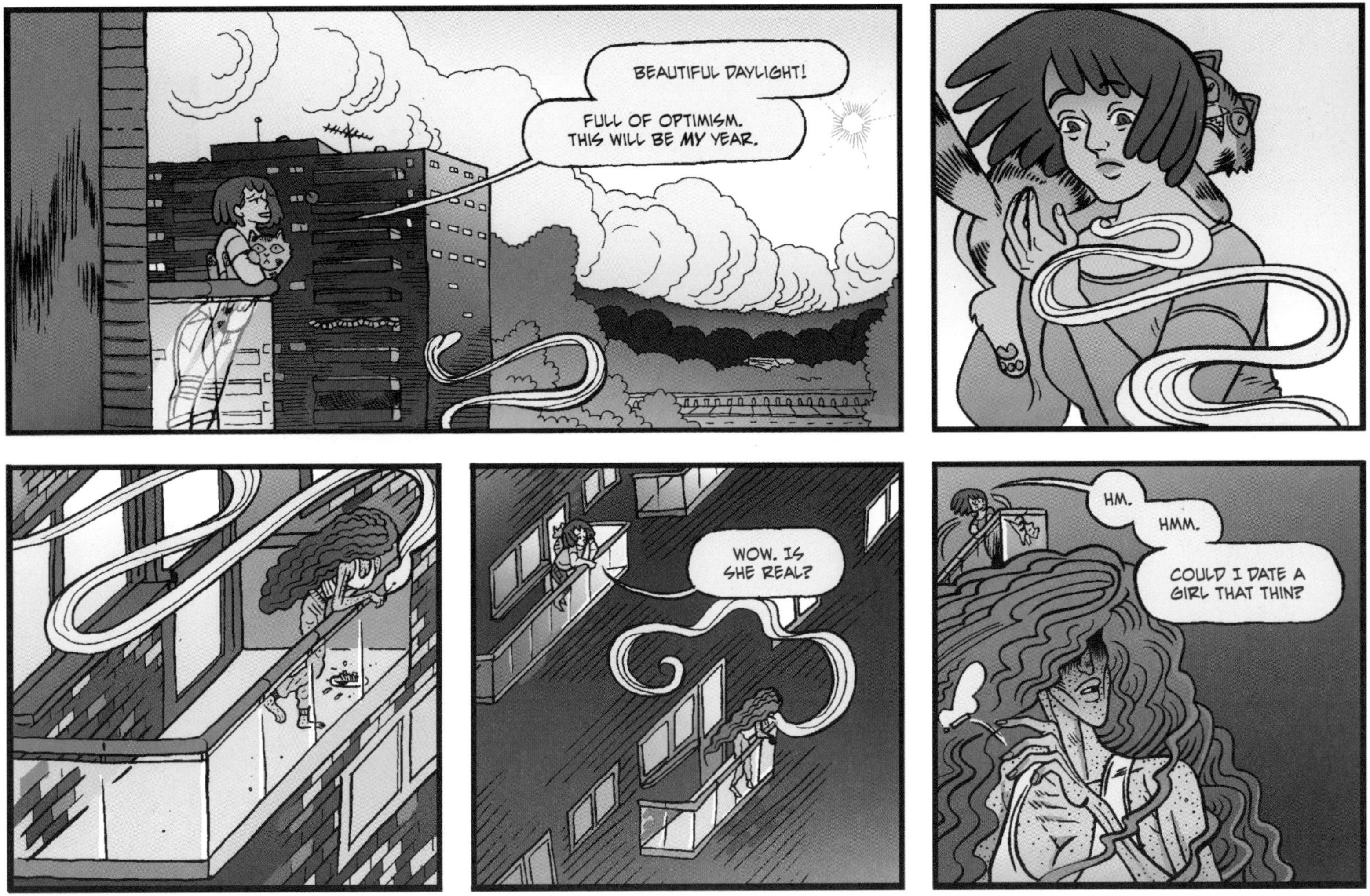
BEAUTIFUL DAYLIGHT!
FULL OF OPTIMISM. THIS WILL BE MY YEAR.
WOW. IS SHE REAL?
HM.
HMM.
COULD I DATE A GIRL THAT THIN?

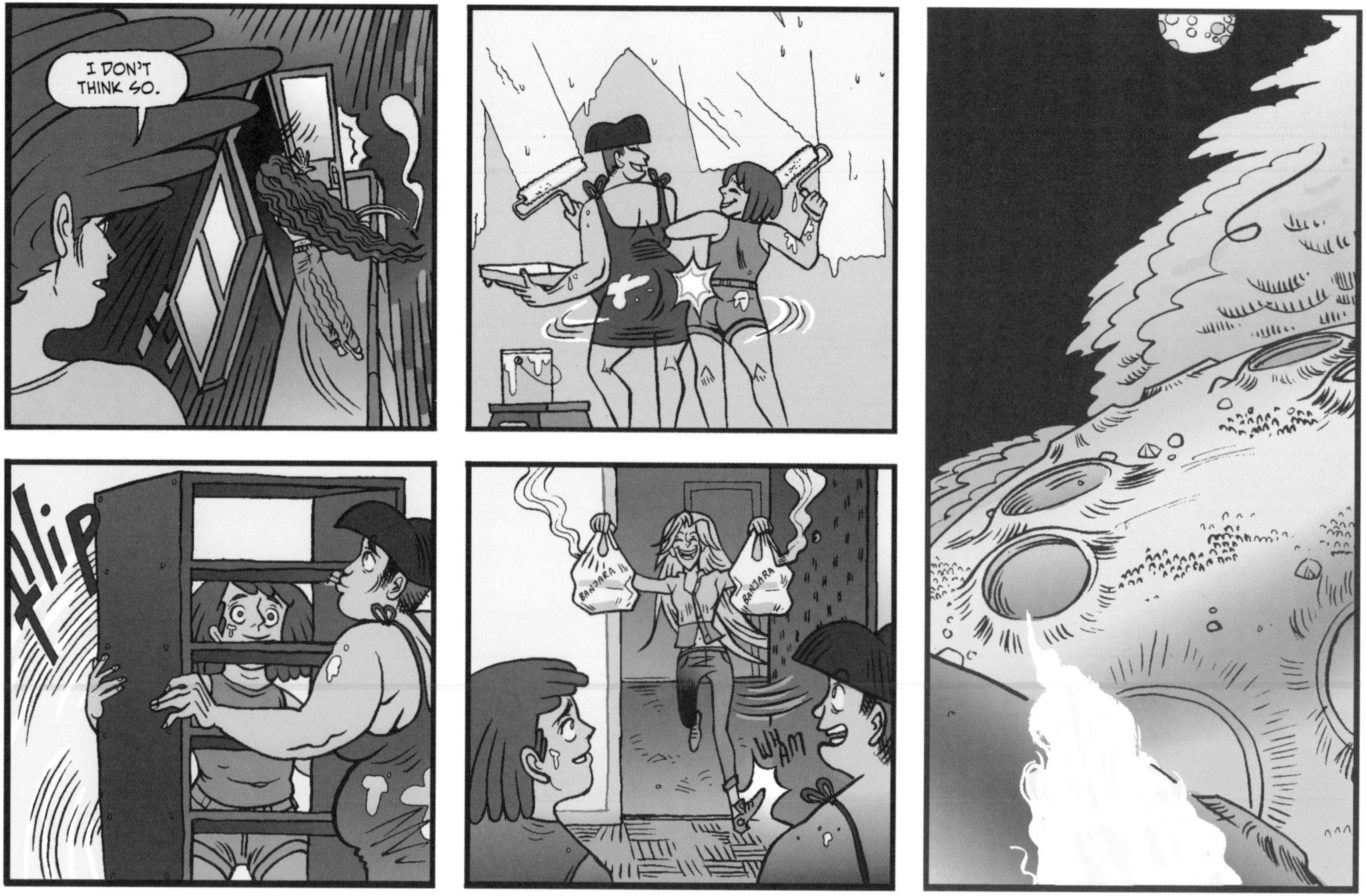
I DON'T THINK SO.
flip
BANJARA
BANJARA
WHAM

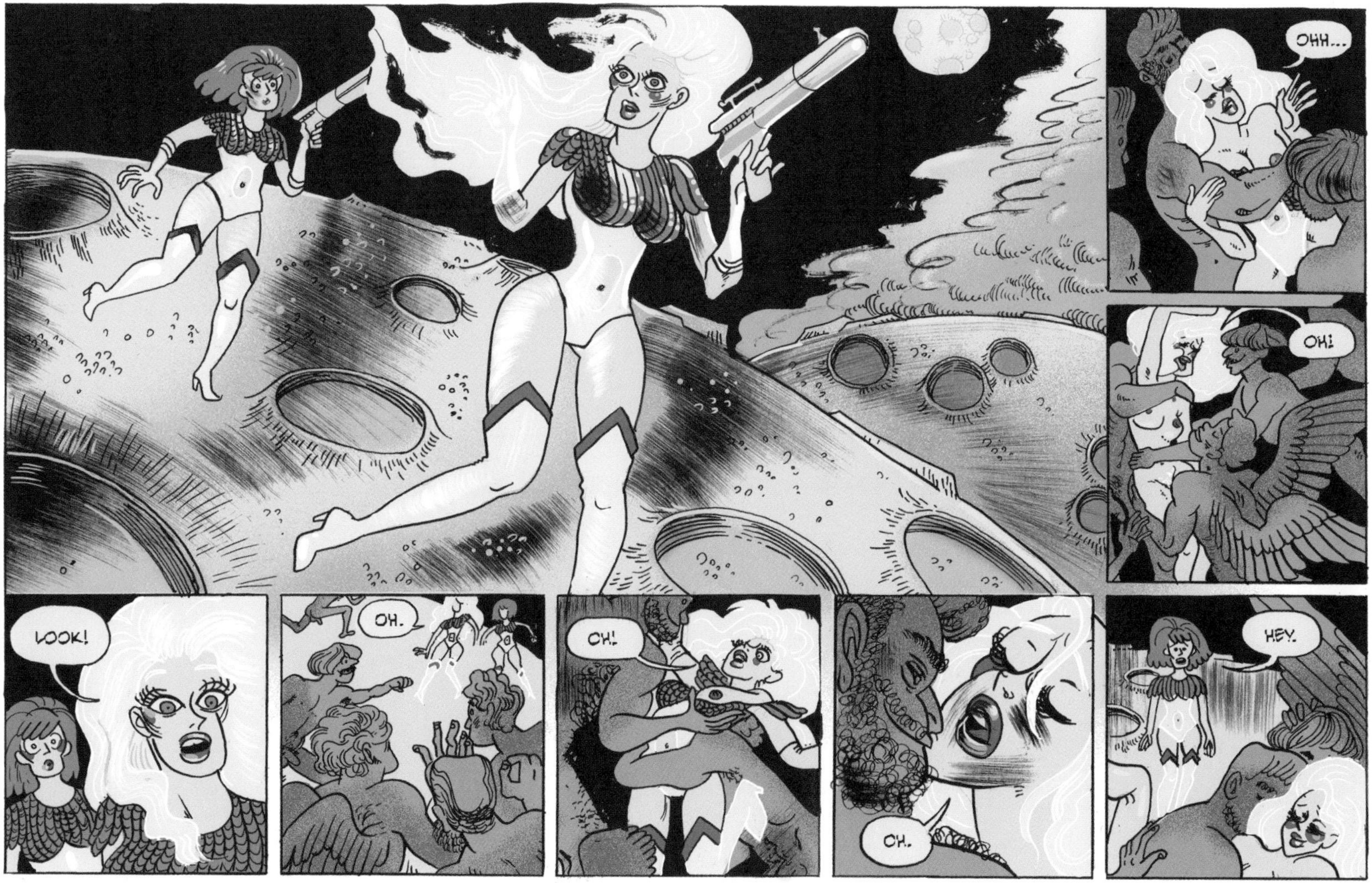
OHH...
OH!
LOOK!
OH.
OH!
OH.
HEY.

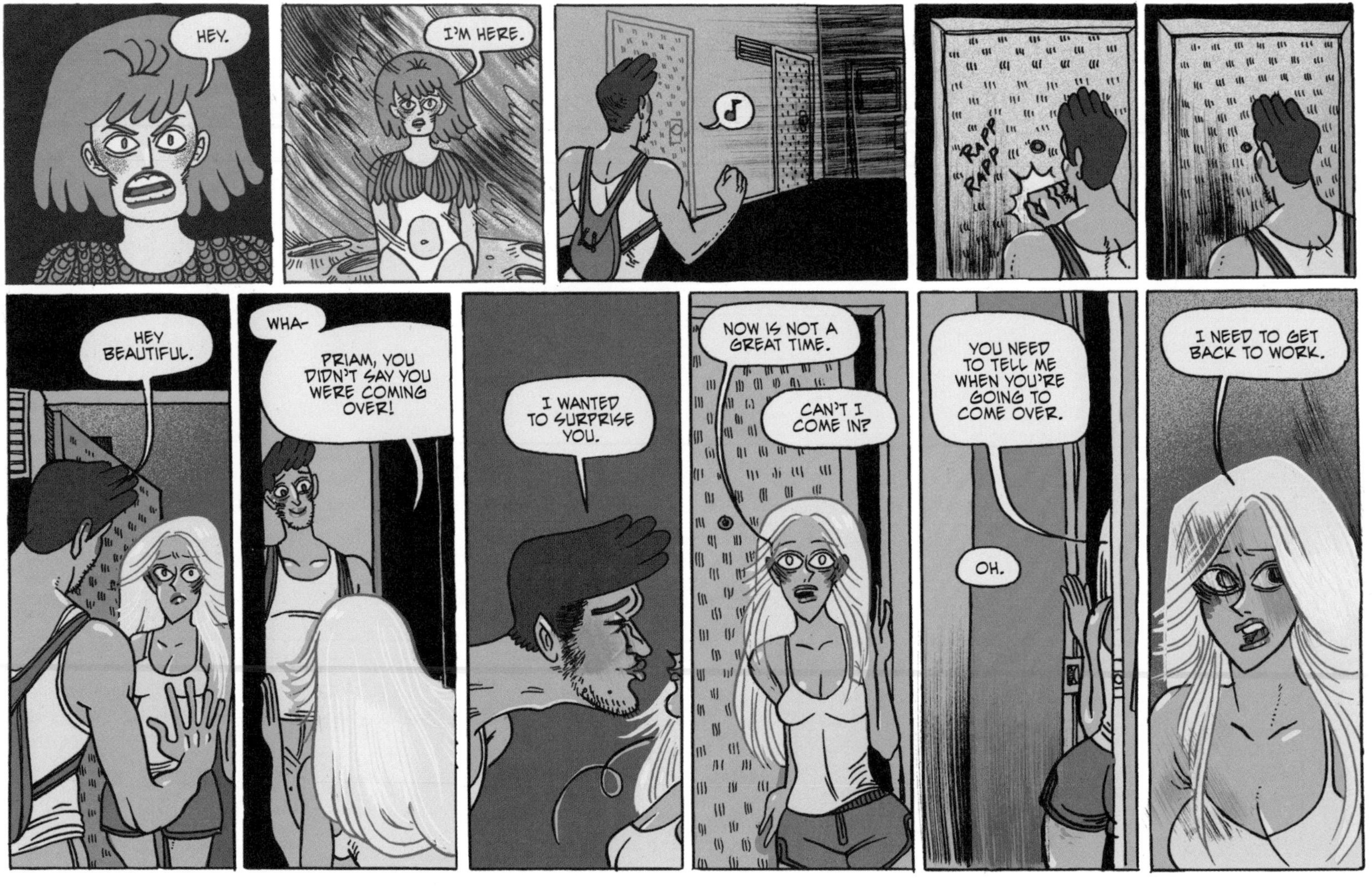
HEY.
I'M HERE.
RAPP RAPP
HEY BEAUTIFUL.
WHA-
PRIAM, YOU DIDN'T SAY YOU WERE COMING OVER!
I WANTED TO SURPRISE YOU.
NOW IS NOT A GREAT TIME.
CAN'T I COME IN?
YOU NEED TO TELL ME WHEN YOU'RE GOING TO COME OVER.
OH.
I NEED TO GET BACK TO WORK.

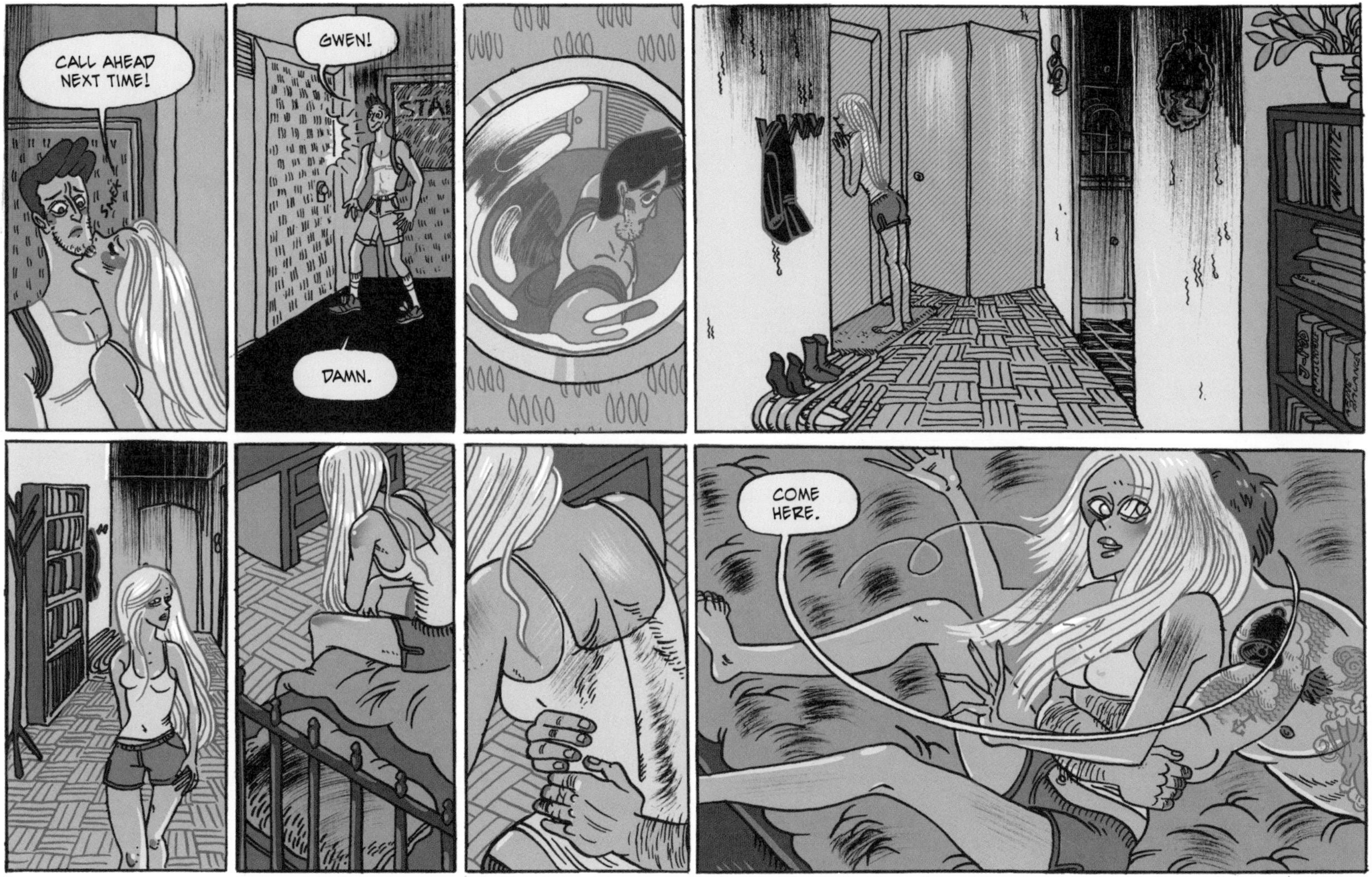
CALL AHEAD NEXT TIME!
SMEK
GWEN!
DAMN.
COME HERE.

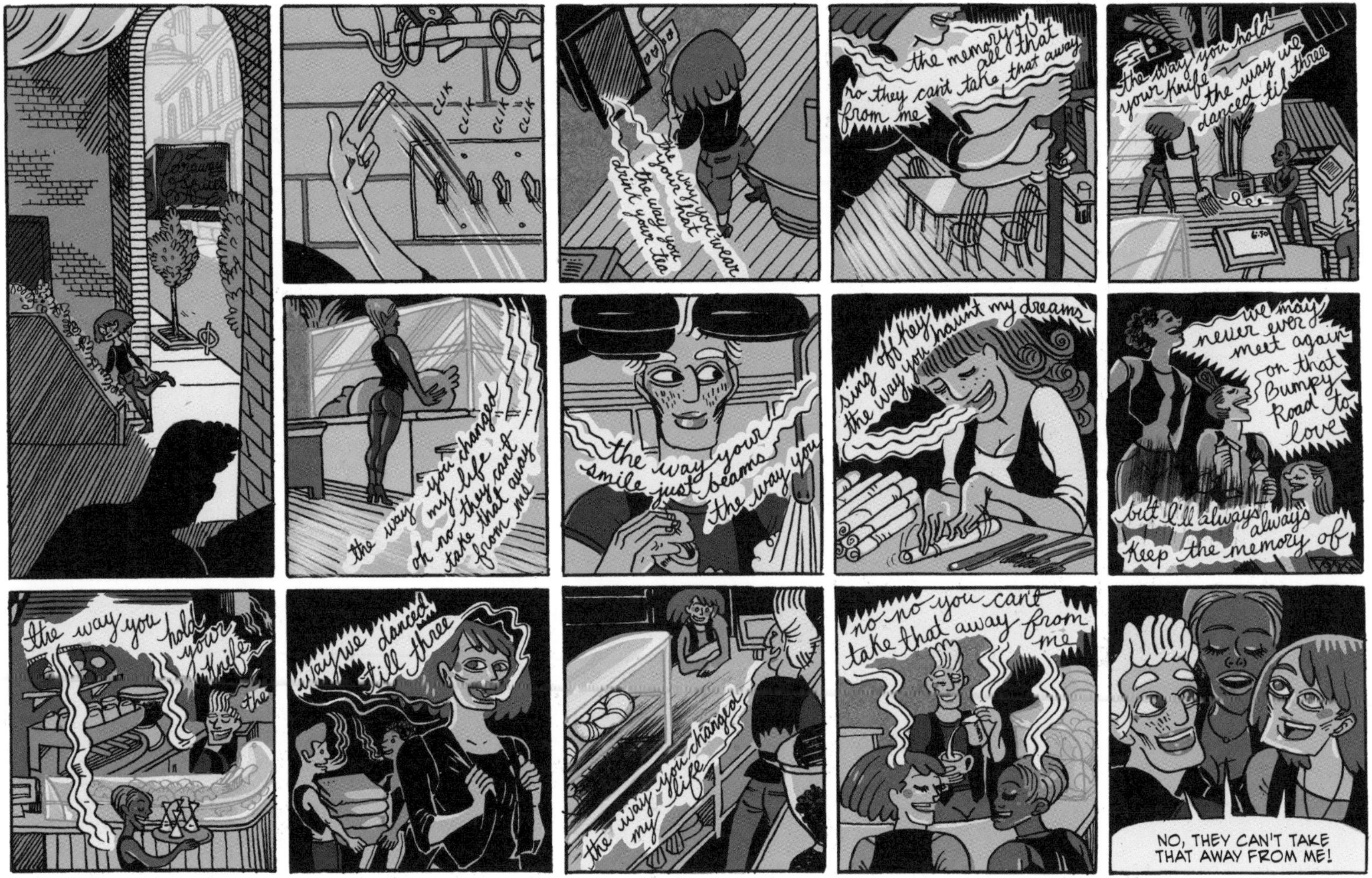
CLIK CLIK CLIK CLIK CLIK
the way you wear your hat
the way you drink your tea
the memory of all that
no they can't take that away from me
the way you hold your knife
the way we danced til three
the way you changed my life
oh no they can't take that away from me
the way your smile just beams
the way you
sing off key
the way you haunt my dreams
we may never ever meet again on that Bumpy Road to love
but I'll always always keep the memory of
the way you hold your knife
the
way we danced till three
the way you changed my life
no no you can't take that away from me
NO, THEY CAN'T TAKE THAT AWAY FROM ME!

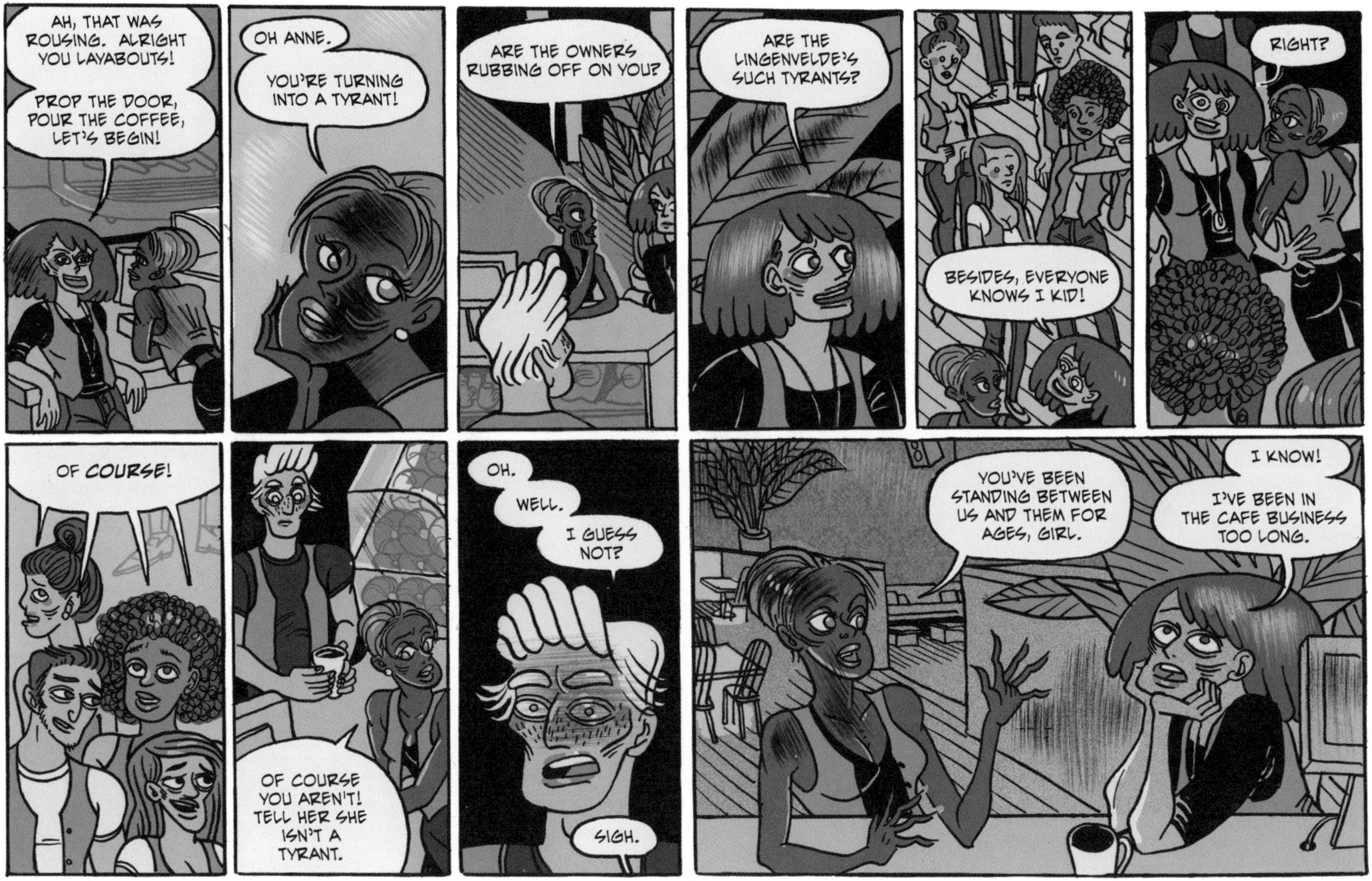
AH, THAT WAS ROUSING. ALRIGHT YOU LAYABOUTS!
PROP THE DOOR, POUR THE COFFEE, LET'S BEGIN!
OH ANNE.
YOU'RE TURNING INTO A TYRANT!
ARE THE OWNERS RUBBING OFF ON YOU?
ARE THE LINGENVELDE'S SUCH TYRANTS?
BESIDES, EVERYONE KNOWS I KID!
RIGHT?
OF COURSE!
OF COURSE YOU AREN'T! TELL HER SHE ISN'T A TYRANT.
OH.
WELL.
I GUESS NOT?
SIGH.
YOU'VE BEEN STANDING BETWEEN US AND THEM FOR AGES, GIRL.
I KNOW!
I'VE BEEN IN THE CAFE BUSINESS TOO LONG.

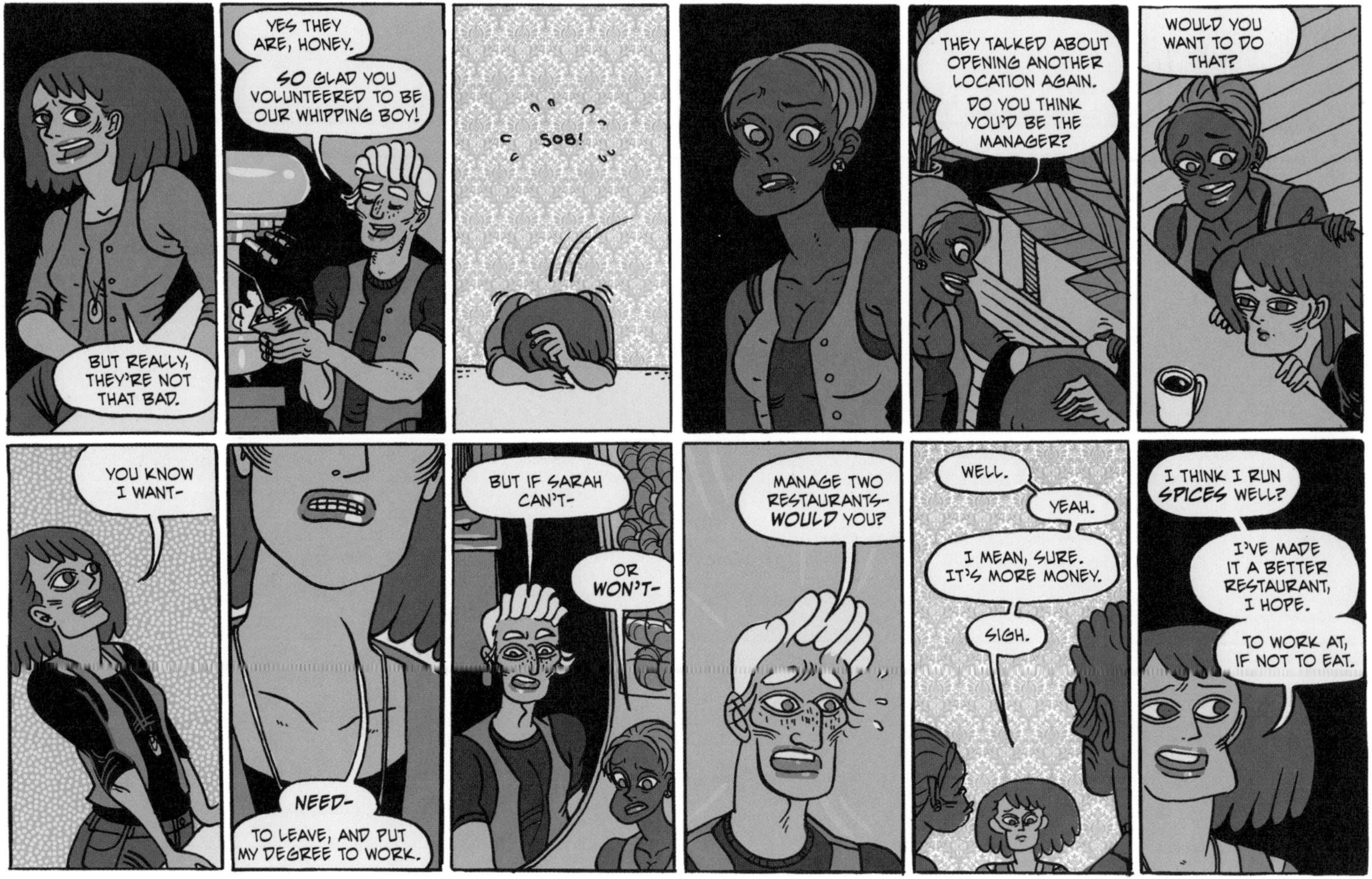
BUT REALLY, THEY'RE NOT THAT BAD.
YES THEY ARE, HONEY.
SO GLAD YOU VOLUNTEERED TO BE OUR WHIPPING BOY!
SOB!
THEY TALKED ABOUT OPENING ANOTHER LOCATION AGAIN.
DO YOU THINK YOU'D BE THE MANAGER?
WOULD YOU WANT TO DO THAT?
YOU KNOW I WANT-
NEED-
TO LEAVE, AND PUT MY DEGREE TO WORK.
BUT IF SARAH CAN'T-
OR WON'T-
MANAGE TWO RESTAURANTS-WOULD YOU?
WELL.
YEAH.
I MEAN, SURE. IT'S MORE MONEY.
SIGH.
I THINK I RUN SPICES WELL?
I'VE MADE IT A BETTER RESTAURANT, I HOPE.
TO WORK AT, IF NOT TO EAT.

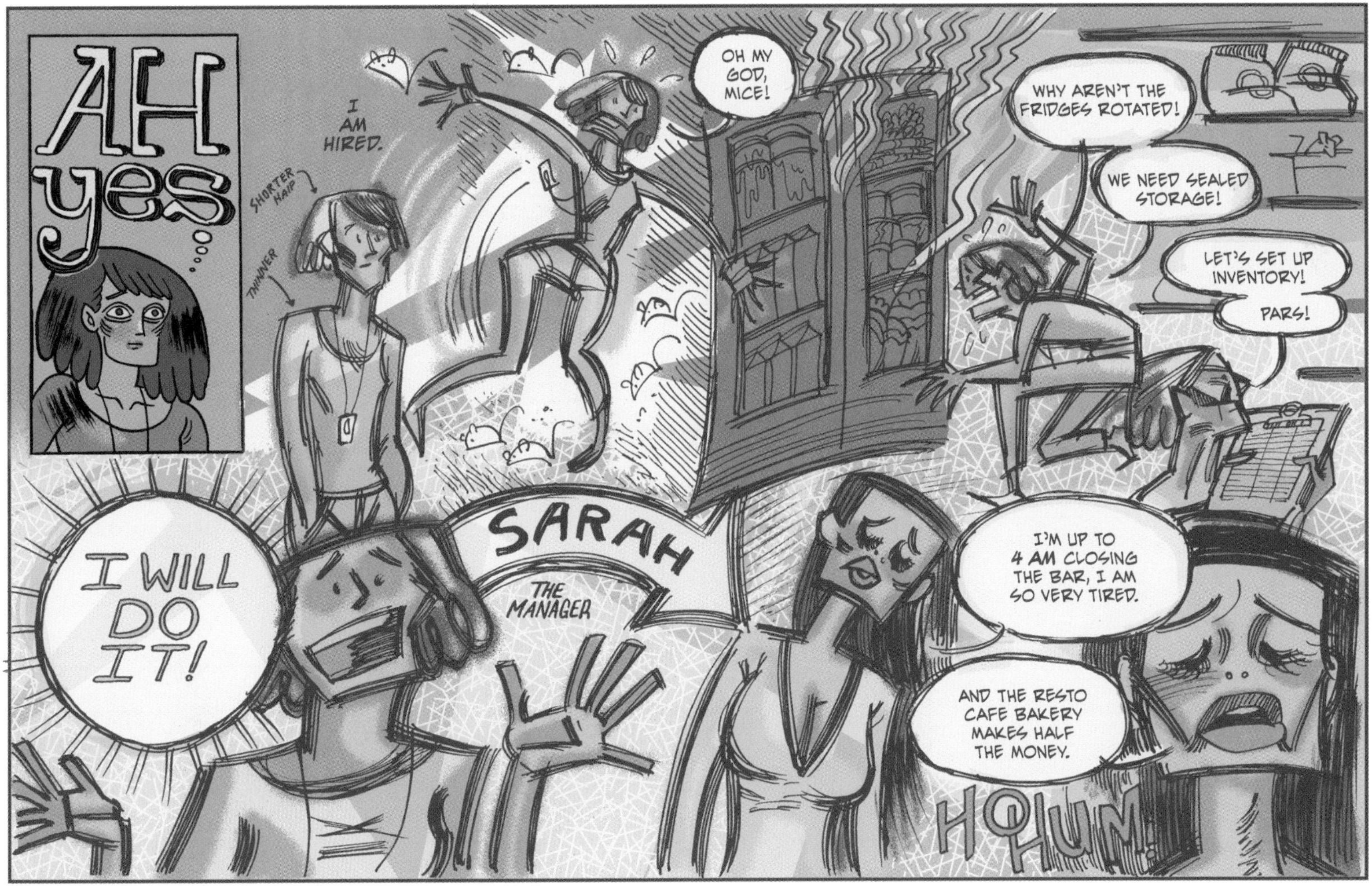
AH yes
I AM HIRED.
SHORTER HAIR
THINNER
OH MY GOD, MICE!
WHY AREN'T THE FRIDGES ROTATED!
WE NEED SEALED STORAGE!
LET'S SET UP INVENTORY!
PARS!
I WILL DO IT!
SARAH
THE MANAGER
I'M UP TO 4 AM CLOSING THE BAR, I AM SO VERY TIRED.
AND THE RESTO CAFE BAKERY MAKES HALF THE MONEY.
HO HUM!

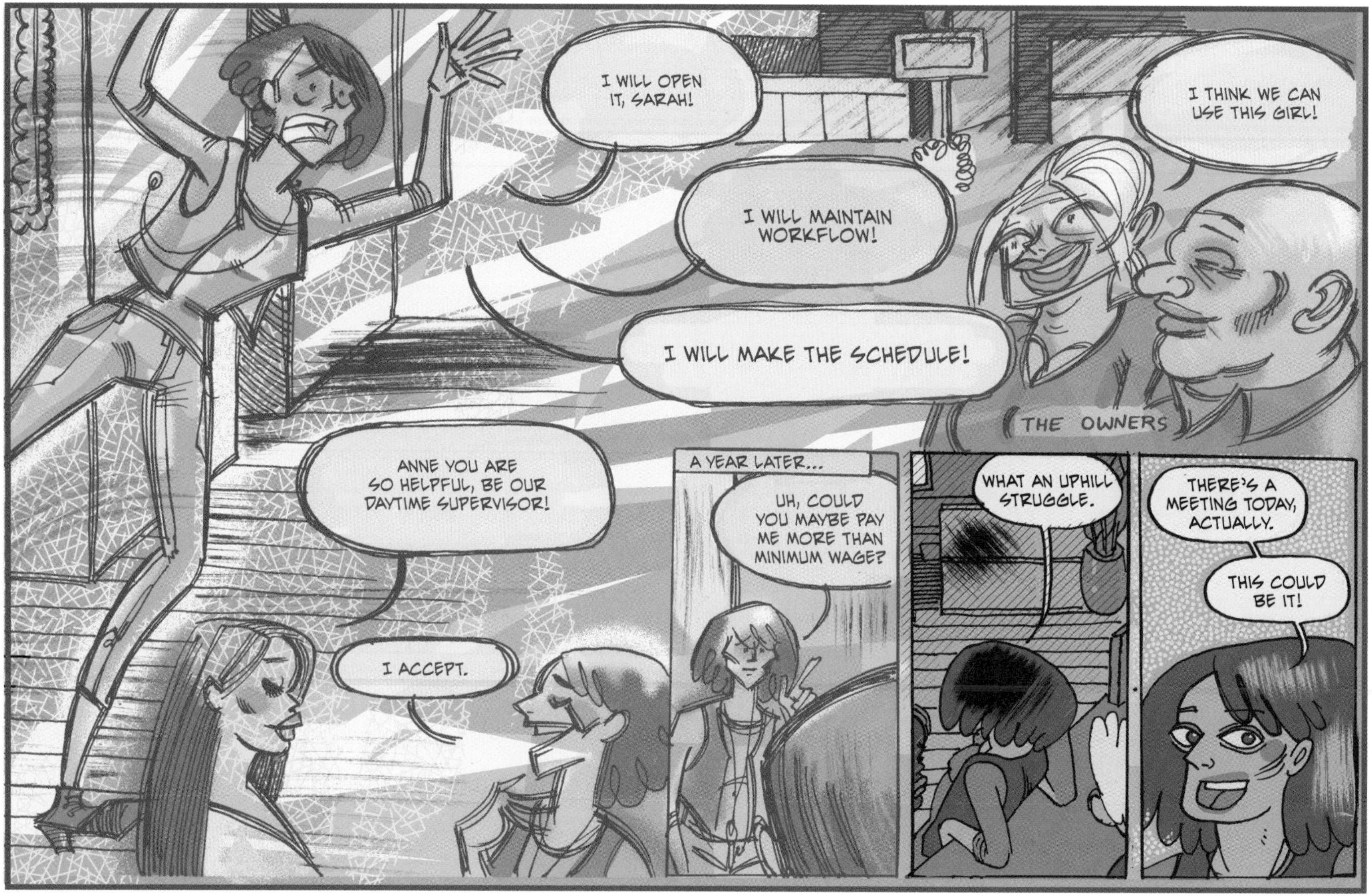
I WILL OPEN IT, SARAH!
I WILL MAINTAIN WORKFLOW!
I WILL MAKE THE SCHEDULE!
I THINK WE CAN USE THIS GIRL!
THE OWNERS
ANNE YOU ARE SO HELPFUL, BE OUR DAYTIME SUPERVISOR!
I ACCEPT.
A YEAR LATER...
UH, COULD YOU MAYBE PAY ME MORE THAN MINIMUM WAGE?
WHAT AN UPHILL STRUGGLE.
THERE'S A MEETING TODAY, ACTUALLY.
THIS COULD BE IT!

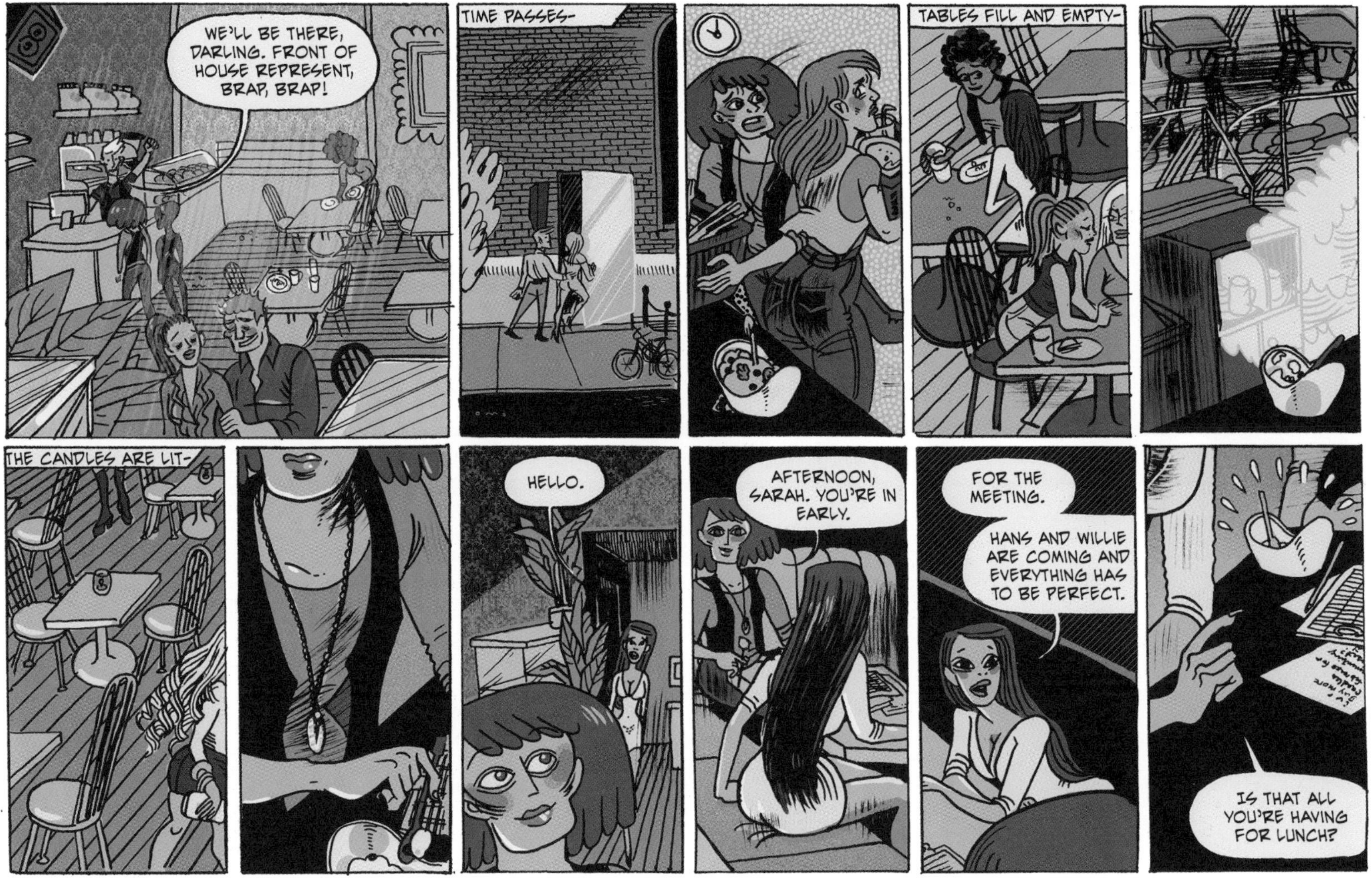
WE'LL BE THERE, DARLING. FRONT OF HOUSE REPRESENT, BRAP, BRAP!
TIME PASSES-
TABLES FILL AND EMPTY-
THE CANDLES ARE LIT-
HELLO.
AFTERNOON, SARAH. YOU'RE IN EARLY.
FOR THE MEETING.
HANS AND WILLIE ARE COMING AND EVERYTHING HAS TO BE PERFECT.
IS THAT ALL YOU'RE HAVING FOR LUNCH?

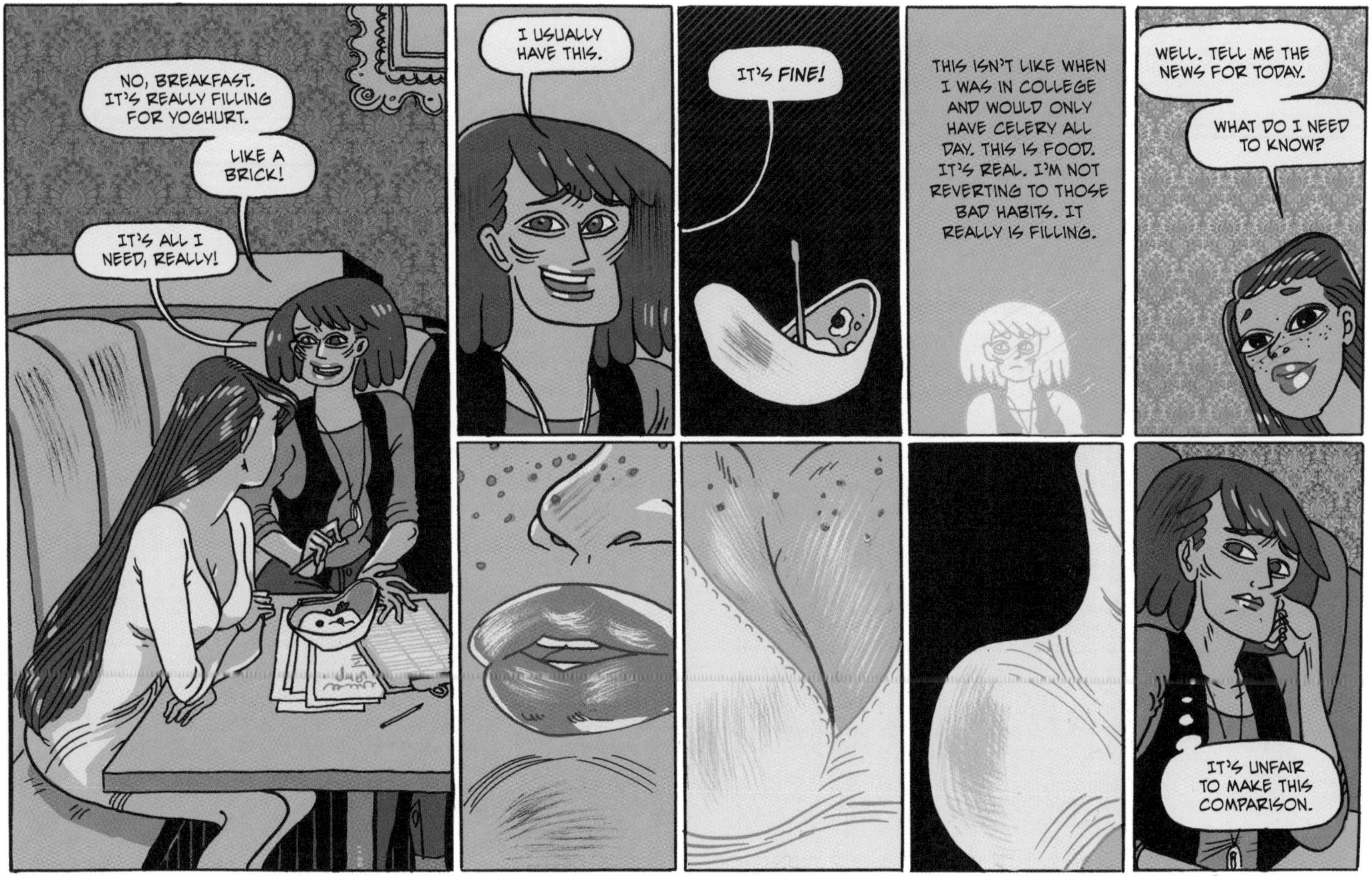
NO, BREAKFAST. IT'S REALLY FILLING FOR YOGHURT.
LIKE A BRICK!
IT'S ALL I NEED, REALLY!
I USUALLY HAVE THIS.
IT'S *FINE!*
THIS ISN'T LIKE WHEN I WAS IN COLLEGE AND WOULD ONLY HAVE CELERY ALL DAY. THIS IS FOOD. IT'S REAL. I'M NOT REVERTING TO THOSE BAD HABITS. IT REALLY IS FILLING.
WELL. TELL ME THE NEWS FOR TODAY.
WHAT DO I NEED TO KNOW?
IT'S UNFAIR TO MAKE THIS COMPARISON.

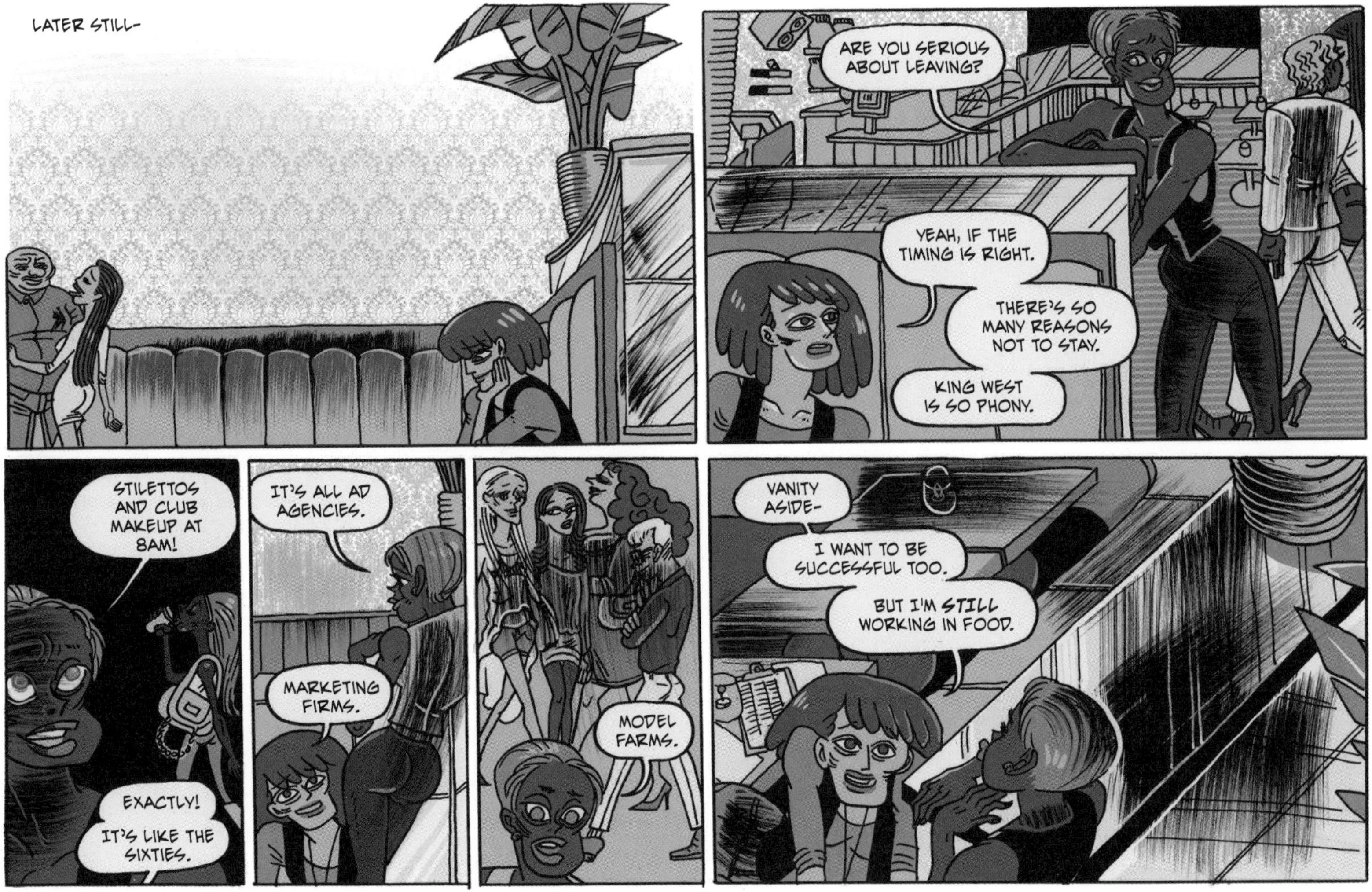
LATER STILL-
ARE YOU SERIOUS ABOUT LEAVING?
YEAH, IF THE TIMING IS RIGHT.
THERE'S SO MANY REASONS NOT TO STAY.
KING WEST IS SO PHONY.
STILETTOS AND CLUB MAKEUP AT 8AM!
EXACTLY!
IT'S LIKE THE SIXTIES.
IT'S ALL AD AGENCIES.
MARKETING FIRMS.
MODEL FARMS.
VANITY ASIDE-
I WANT TO BE SUCCESSFUL TOO.
BUT I'M STILL WORKING IN FOOD.

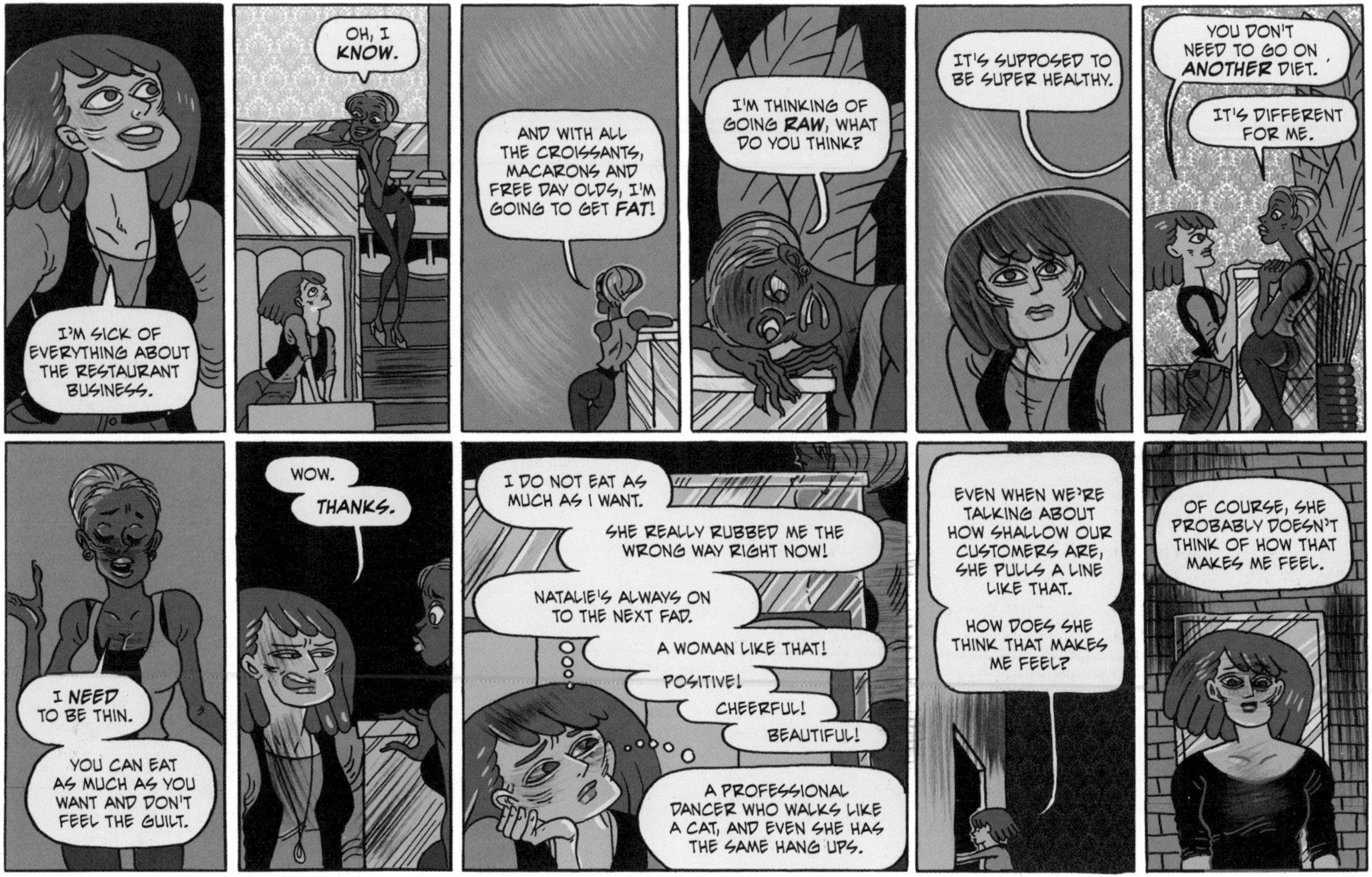
I'M SICK OF EVERYTHING ABOUT THE RESTAURANT BUSINESS.
OH, I KNOW.
AND WITH ALL THE CROISSANTS, MACARONS AND FREE DAY OLDS, I'M GOING TO GET FAT!
I'M THINKING OF GOING RAW, WHAT DO YOU THINK?
IT'S SUPPOSED TO BE SUPER HEALTHY.
YOU DON'T NEED TO GO ON ANOTHER DIET.
IT'S DIFFERENT FOR ME.
I NEED TO BE THIN.
YOU CAN EAT AS MUCH AS YOU WANT AND DON'T FEEL THE GUILT.
WOW.
THANKS.
I DO NOT EAT AS MUCH AS I WANT.
SHE REALLY RUBBED ME THE WRONG WAY RIGHT NOW!
NATALIE'S ALWAYS ON TO THE NEXT FAD.
A WOMAN LIKE THAT!
POSITIVE!
CHEERFUL!
BEAUTIFUL!
A PROFESSIONAL DANCER WHO WALKS LIKE A CAT, AND EVEN SHE HAS THE SAME HANG UPS.
EVEN WHEN WE'RE TALKING ABOUT HOW SHALLOW OUR CUSTOMERS ARE, SHE PULLS A LINE LIKE THAT.
HOW DOES SHE THINK THAT MAKES ME FEEL?
OF COURSE, SHE PROBABLY DOESN'T THINK OF HOW THAT MAKES ME FEEL.

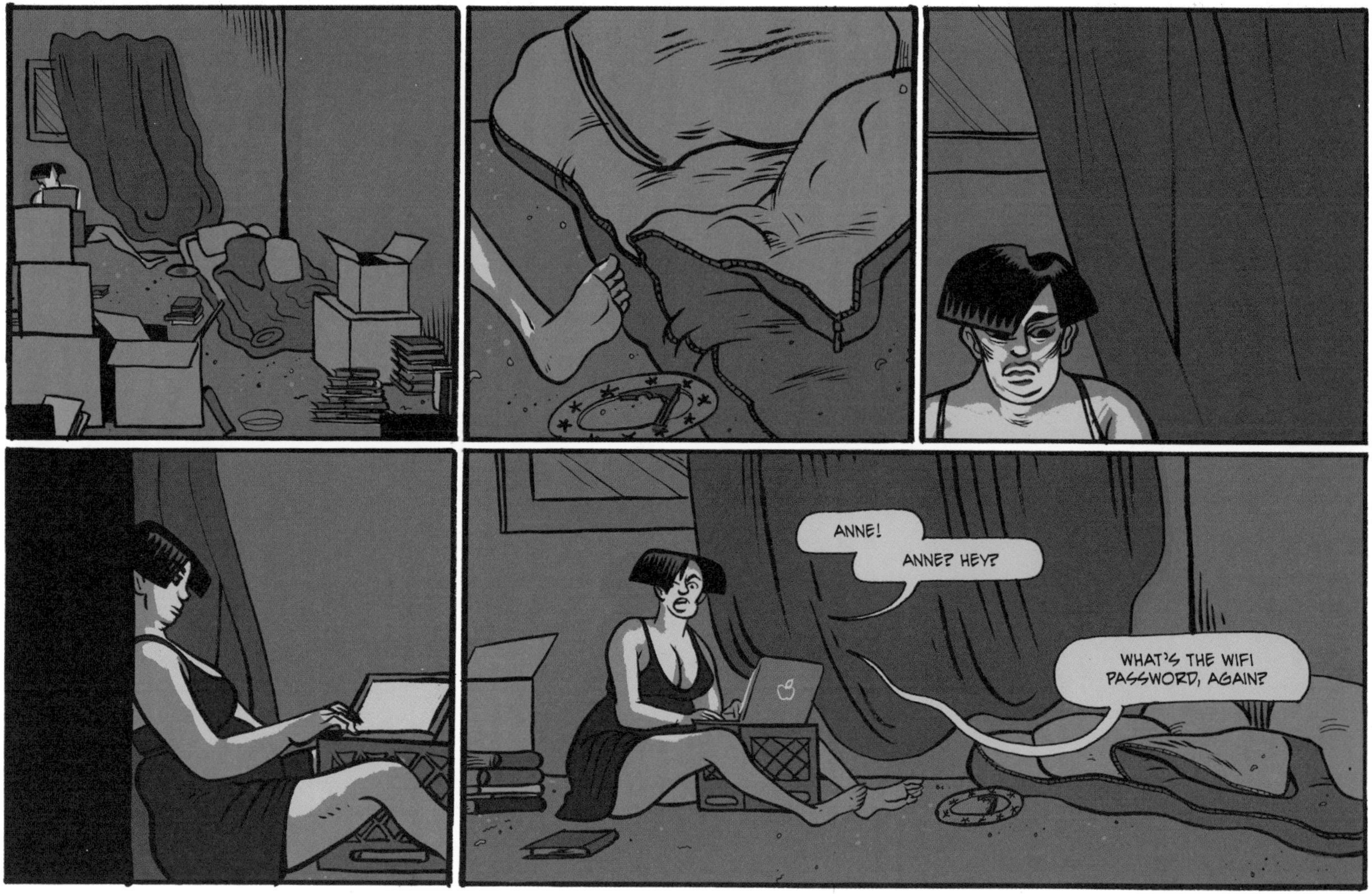
ANNE!
ANNE? HEY?
WHAT'S THE WIFI PASSWORD, AGAIN?

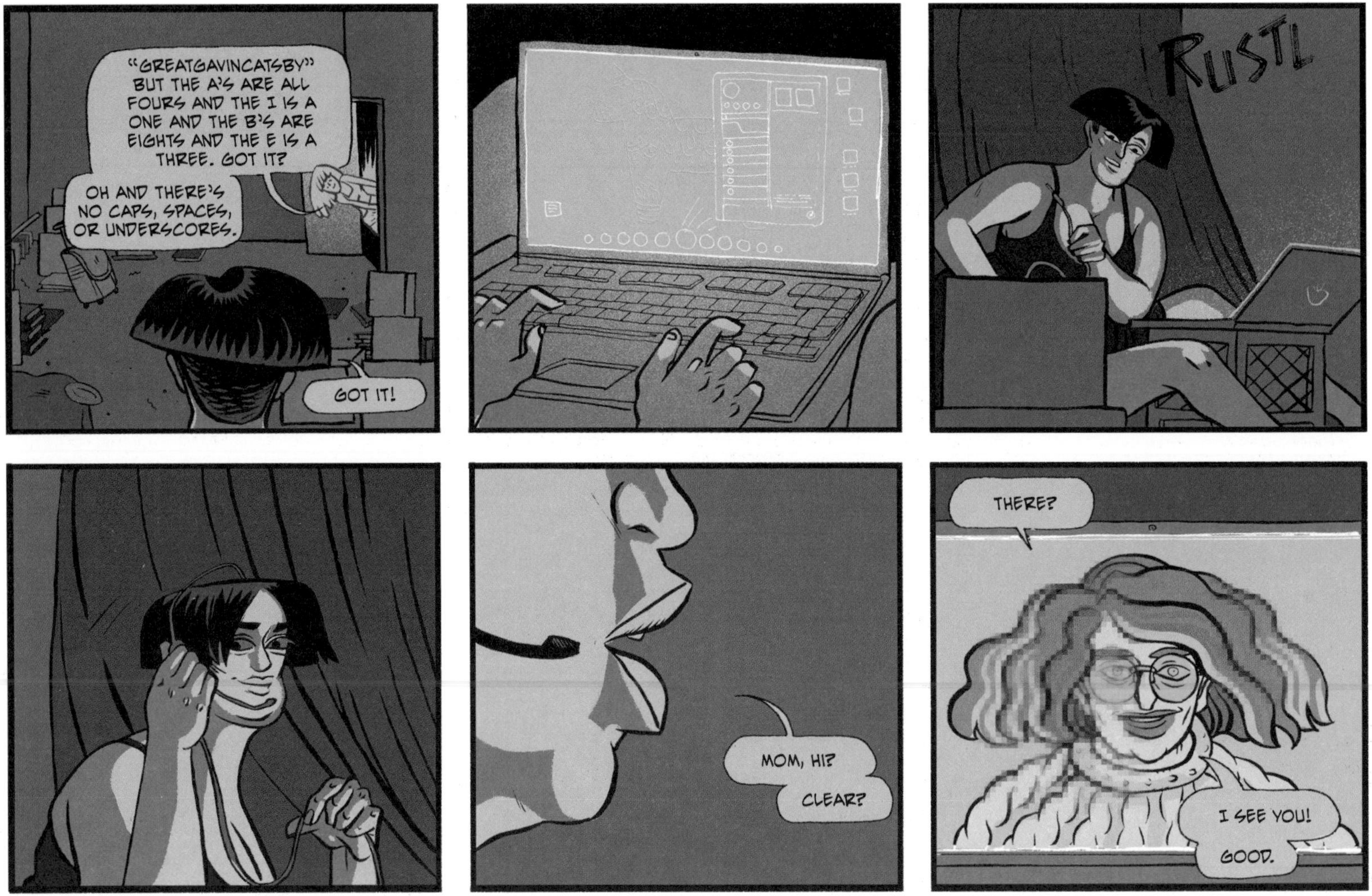
"GREATGAVINCATSBY" BUT THE A'S ARE ALL FOURS AND THE I IS A ONE AND THE B'S ARE EIGHTS AND THE E IS A THREE. GOT IT?
OH AND THERE'S NO CAPS, SPACES, OR UNDERSCORES.
GOT IT!
RUSTL
MOM, HI?
CLEAR?
THERE?
I SEE YOU!
GOOD.

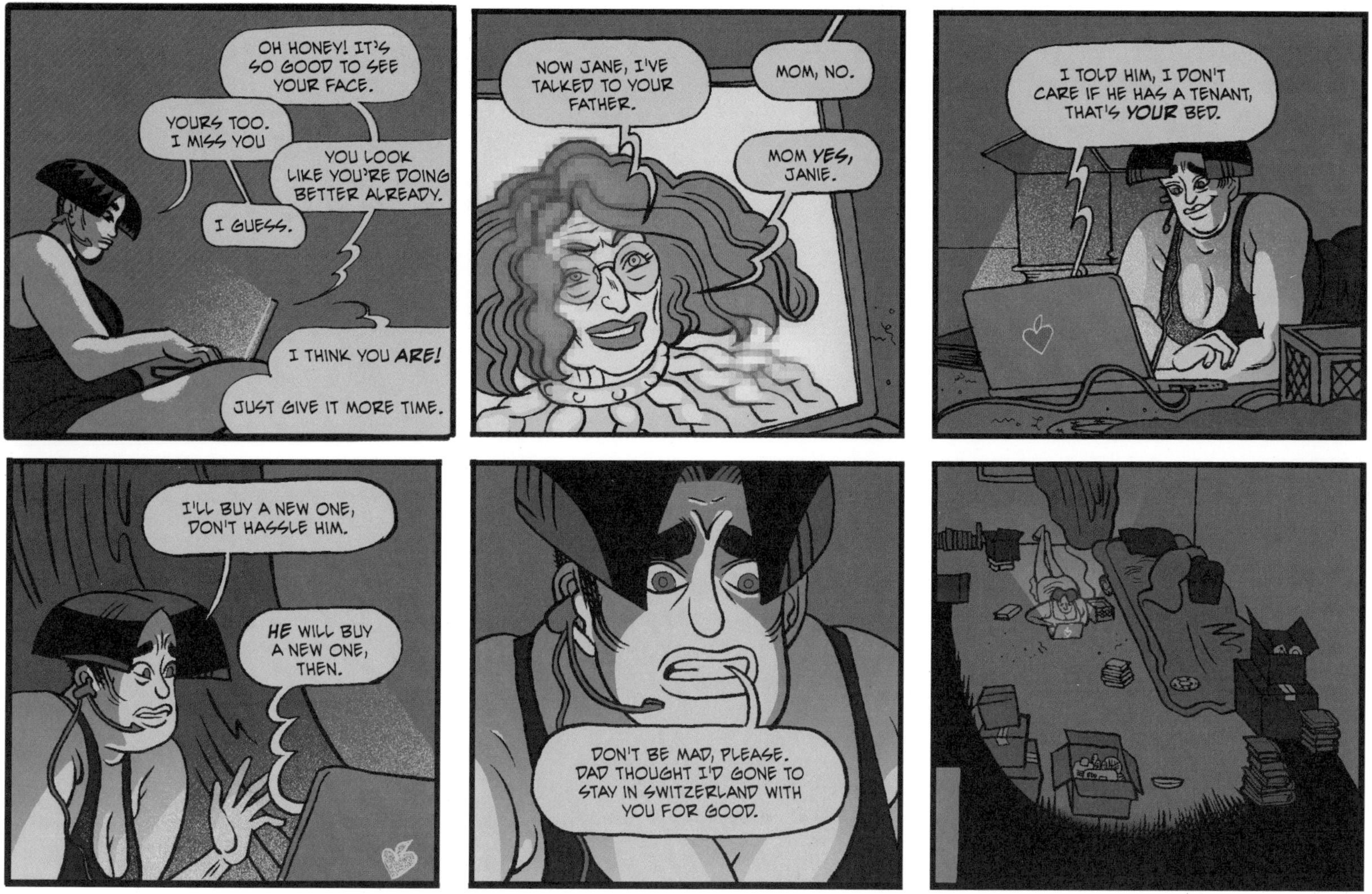
OH HONEY! IT'S SO GOOD TO SEE YOUR FACE.
YOURS TOO. I MISS YOU
YOU LOOK LIKE YOU'RE DOING BETTER ALREADY.
I GUESS.
I THINK YOU **ARE!**
JUST GIVE IT MORE TIME.
NOW JANE, I'VE TALKED TO YOUR FATHER.
MOM, NO.
MOM ***YES***, JANIE.
I TOLD HIM, I DON'T CARE IF HE HAS A TENANT, THAT'S ***YOUR*** BED.
I'LL BUY A NEW ONE, DON'T HASSLE HIM.
HE WILL BUY A NEW ONE, THEN.
DON'T BE MAD, PLEASE. DAD THOUGHT I'D GONE TO STAY IN SWITZERLAND WITH YOU FOR GOOD.

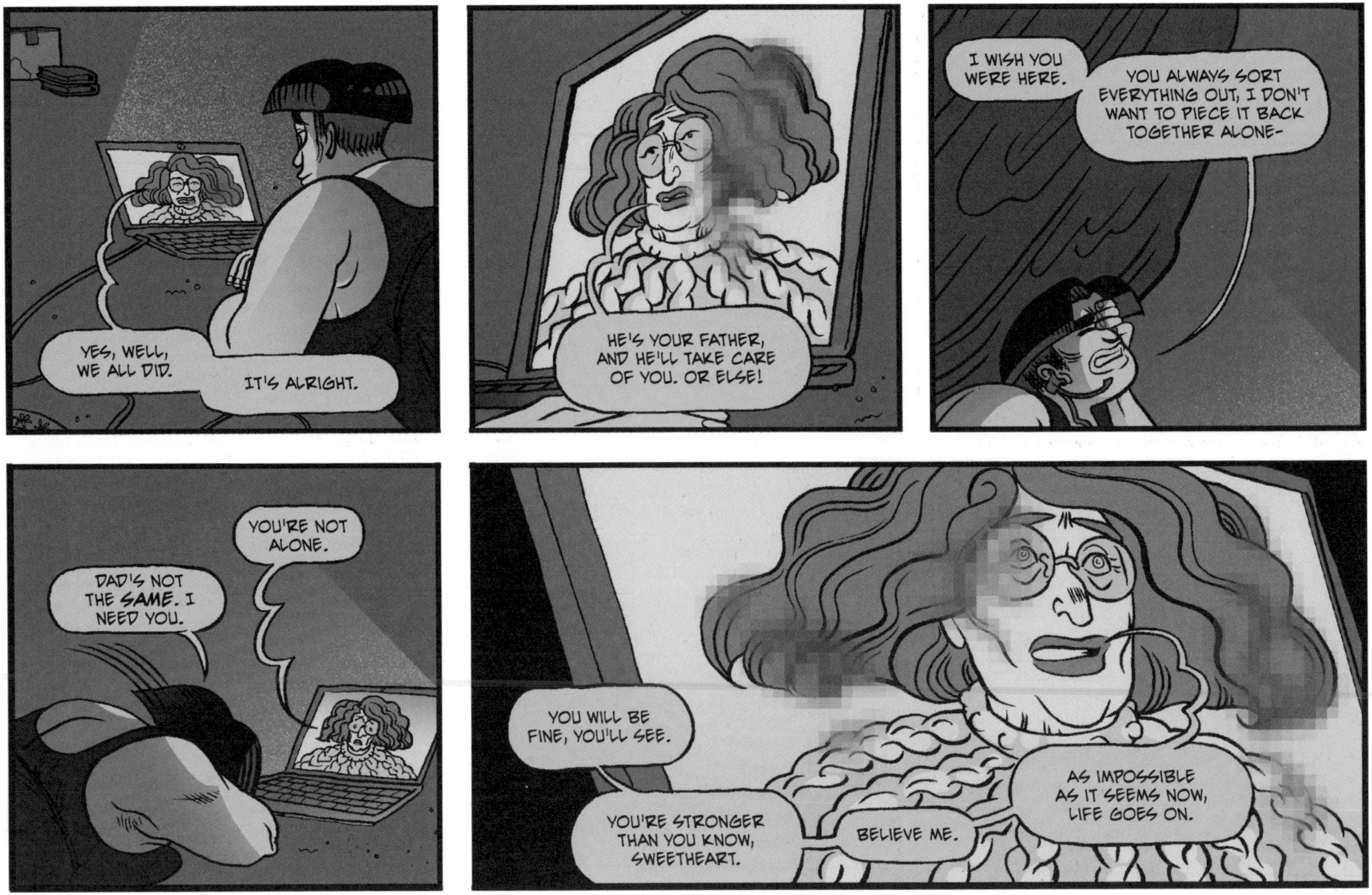
YES, WELL, WE ALL DID.
IT'S ALRIGHT.
HE'S YOUR FATHER, AND HE'LL TAKE CARE OF YOU. OR ELSE!
I WISH YOU WERE HERE.
YOU ALWAYS SORT EVERYTHING OUT, I DON'T WANT TO PIECE IT BACK TOGETHER ALONE-
DAD'S NOT THE **SAME**. I NEED YOU.
YOU'RE NOT ALONE.
YOU WILL BE FINE, YOU'LL SEE.
YOU'RE STRONGER THAN YOU KNOW, SWEETHEART.
BELIEVE ME.
AS IMPOSSIBLE AS IT SEEMS NOW, LIFE GOES ON.

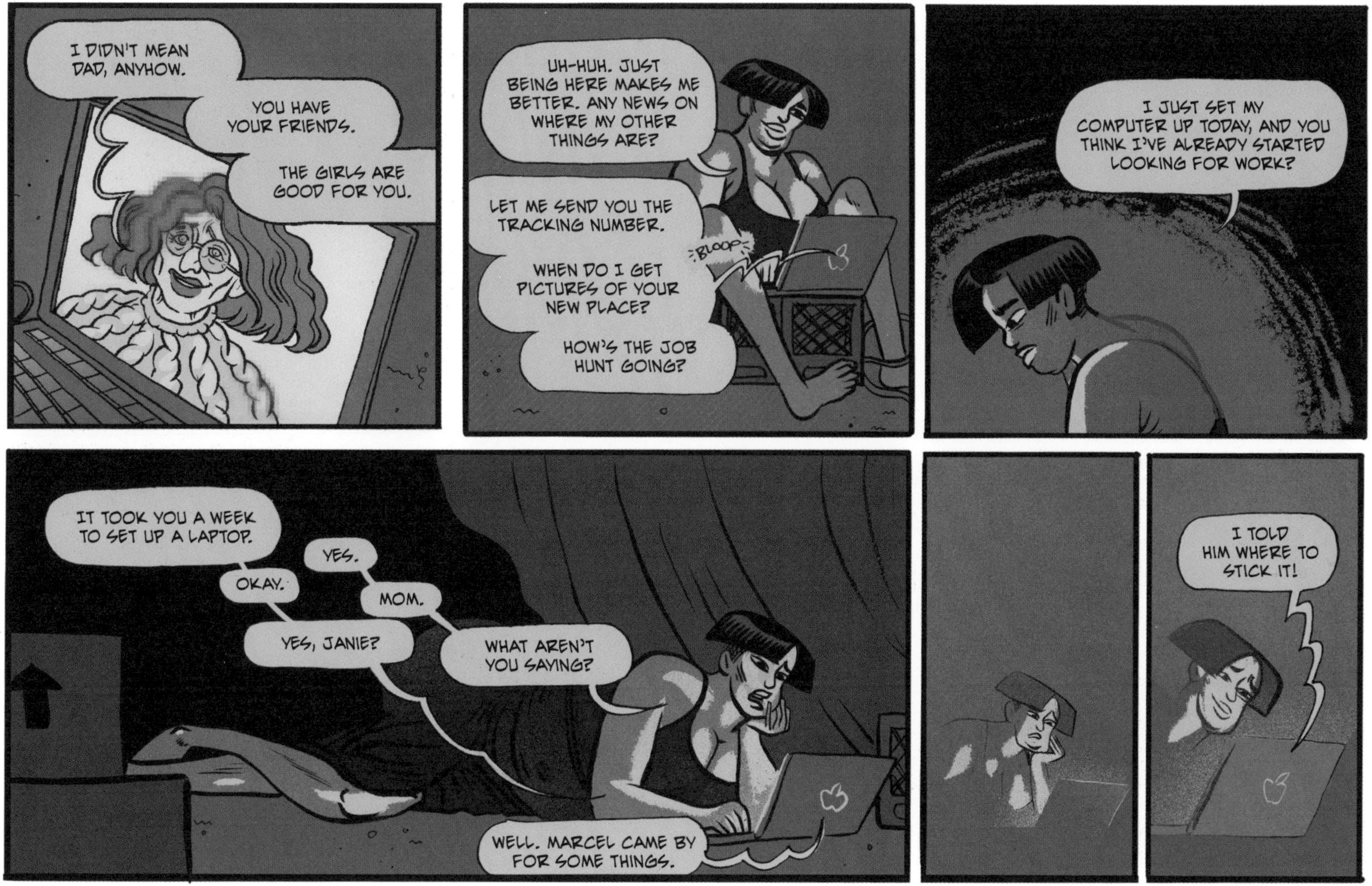
I DIDN'T MEAN DAD, ANYHOW.
YOU HAVE YOUR FRIENDS.
THE GIRLS ARE GOOD FOR YOU.
UH-HUH. JUST BEING HERE MAKES ME BETTER. ANY NEWS ON WHERE MY OTHER THINGS ARE?
LET ME SEND YOU THE TRACKING NUMBER.
BLOOP
WHEN DO I GET PICTURES OF YOUR NEW PLACE?
HOW'S THE JOB HUNT GOING?
I JUST SET MY COMPUTER UP TODAY, AND YOU THINK I'VE ALREADY STARTED LOOKING FOR WORK?
IT TOOK YOU A WEEK TO SET UP A LAPTOP.
OKAY.
YES.
MOM.
YES, JANIE?
WHAT AREN'T YOU SAYING?
WELL. MARCEL CAME BY FOR SOME THINGS.
I TOLD HIM WHERE TO STICK IT!

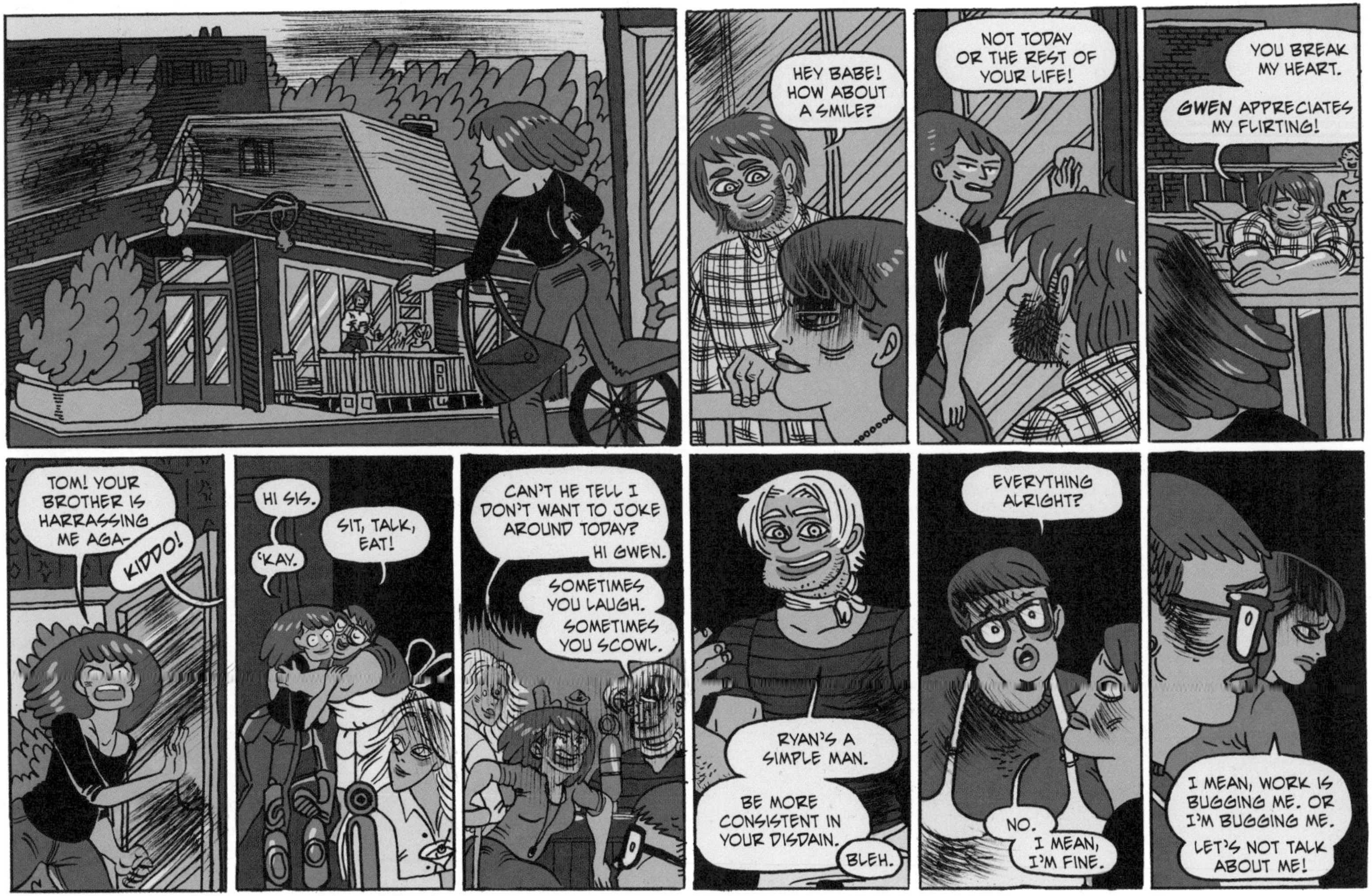
HEY BABE! HOW ABOUT A SMILE?
NOT TODAY OR THE REST OF YOUR LIFE!
YOU BREAK MY HEART.
GWEN APPRECIATES MY FLIRTING!
TOM! YOUR BROTHER IS HARRASSING ME AGA-
KIDDO!
HI SIS.
'KAY.
SIT, TALK, EAT!
CAN'T HE TELL I DON'T WANT TO JOKE AROUND TODAY?
HI GWEN.
SOMETIMES YOU LAUGH. SOMETIMES YOU SCOWL.
RYAN'S A SIMPLE MAN.
BE MORE CONSISTENT IN YOUR DISDAIN.
BLEH.
EVERYTHING ALRIGHT?
NO.
I MEAN, I'M FINE.
I MEAN, WORK IS BUGGING ME. OR I'M BUGGING ME.
LET'S NOT TALK ABOUT ME!

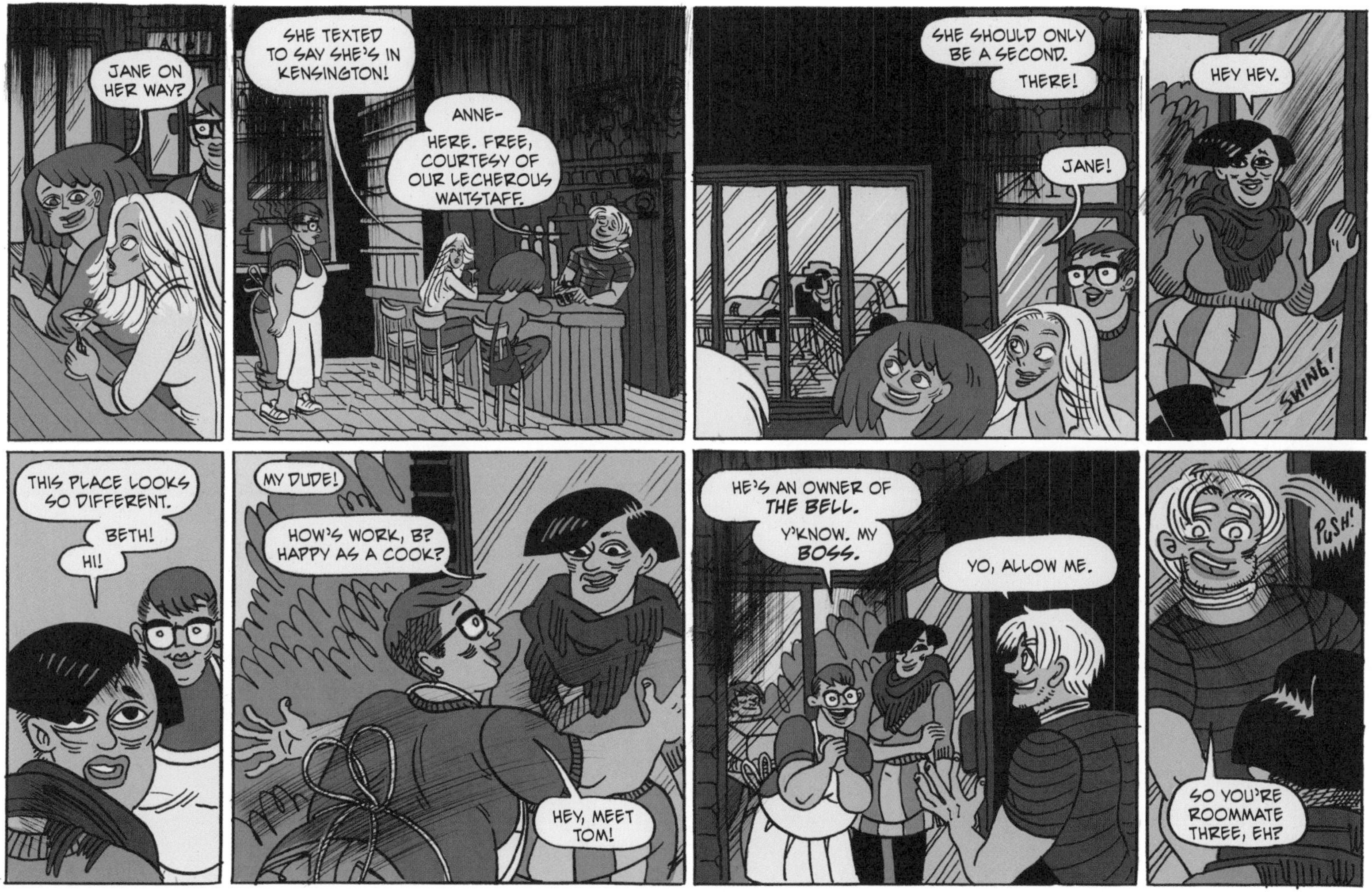
JANE ON HER WAY?
SHE TEXTED TO SAY SHE'S IN KENSINGTON!
ANNE-
HERE. FREE, COURTESY OF OUR LECHEROUS WAITSTAFF.
SHE SHOULD ONLY BE A SECOND.
THERE!
JANE!
HEY HEY.
SWING!
THIS PLACE LOOKS SO DIFFERENT.
BETH!
HI!
MY DUDE!
HOW'S WORK, B? HAPPY AS A COOK?
HEY, MEET TOM!
HE'S AN OWNER OF **THE BELL.**
Y'KNOW. MY **BOSS.**
YO, ALLOW ME.
PUSH!
SO YOU'RE ROOMMATE THREE, EH?

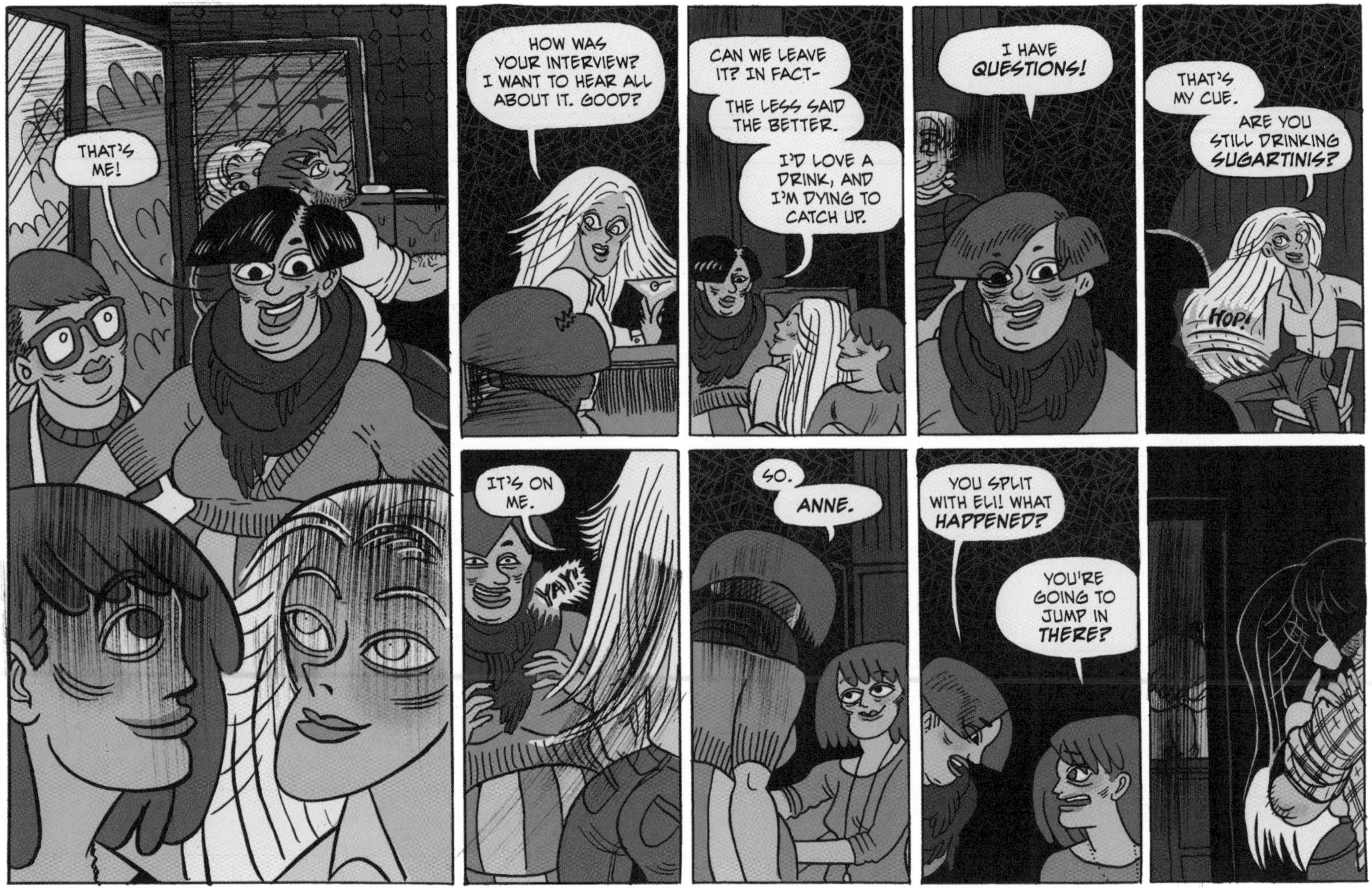
THAT'S ME!
HOW WAS YOUR INTERVIEW? I WANT TO HEAR ALL ABOUT IT. GOOD?
CAN WE LEAVE IT? IN FACT-
THE LESS SAID THE BETTER.
I'D LOVE A DRINK, AND I'M DYING TO CATCH UP.
I HAVE QUESTIONS!
THAT'S MY CUE.
ARE YOU STILL DRINKING SUGARTINIS?
HOP!
IT'S ON ME.
YAY!
SO.
ANNE.
YOU SPLIT WITH ELI! WHAT HAPPENED?
YOU'RE GOING TO JUMP IN THERE?

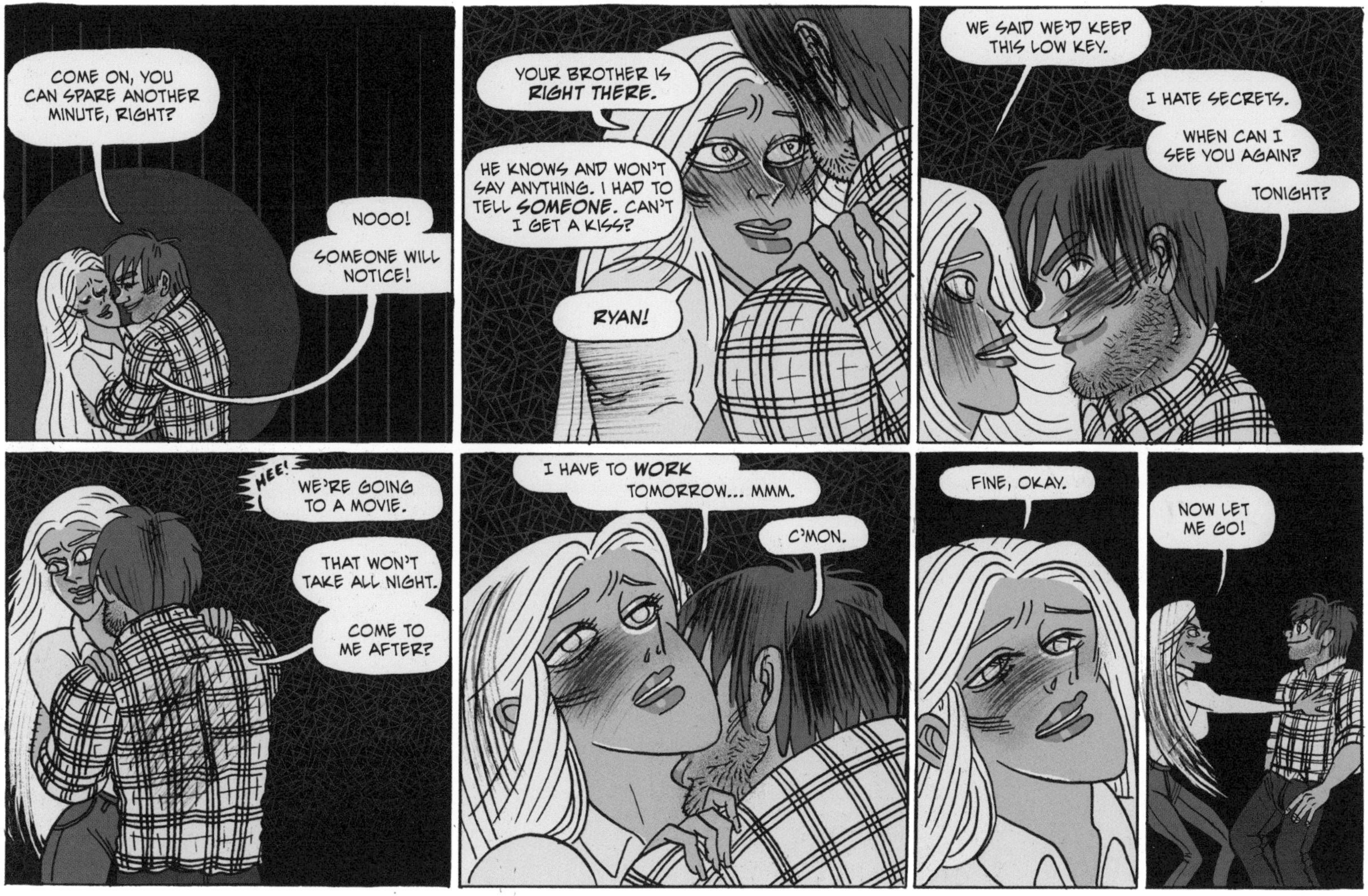
COME ON, YOU CAN SPARE ANOTHER MINUTE, RIGHT?
NOOO!
SOMEONE WILL NOTICE!
YOUR BROTHER IS RIGHT THERE.
HE KNOWS AND WON'T SAY ANYTHING. I HAD TO TELL SOMEONE. CAN'T I GET A KISS?
RYAN!
WE SAID WE'D KEEP THIS LOW KEY.
I HATE SECRETS.
WHEN CAN I SEE YOU AGAIN?
TONIGHT?
HEE!
WE'RE GOING TO A MOVIE.
THAT WON'T TAKE ALL NIGHT.
COME TO ME AFTER?
I HAVE TO WORK TOMORROW... MMM.
C'MON.
FINE, OKAY.
NOW LET ME GO!

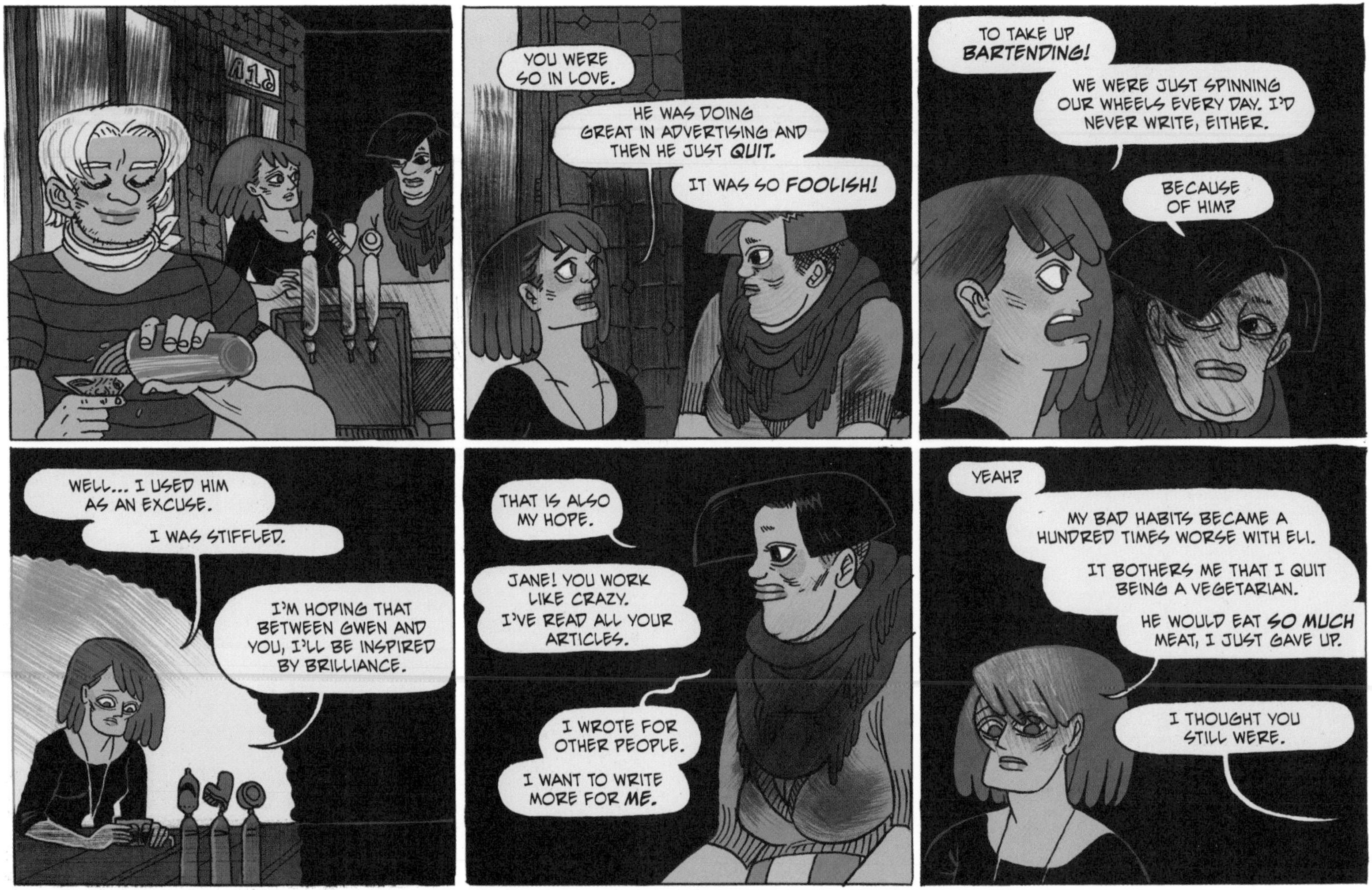
YOU WERE SO IN LOVE.
HE WAS DOING GREAT IN ADVERTISING AND THEN HE JUST QUIT.
IT WAS SO FOOLISH!
TO TAKE UP BARTENDING!
WE WERE JUST SPINNING OUR WHEELS EVERY DAY. I'D NEVER WRITE, EITHER.
BECAUSE OF HIM?
WELL... I USED HIM AS AN EXCUSE.
I WAS STIFFLED.
I'M HOPING THAT BETWEEN GWEN AND YOU, I'LL BE INSPIRED BY BRILLIANCE.
THAT IS ALSO MY HOPE.
JANE! YOU WORK LIKE CRAZY.
I'VE READ ALL YOUR ARTICLES.
I WROTE FOR OTHER PEOPLE.
I WANT TO WRITE MORE FOR ME.
YEAH?
MY BAD HABITS BECAME A HUNDRED TIMES WORSE WITH ELI.
IT BOTHERS ME THAT I QUIT BEING A VEGETARIAN.
HE WOULD EAT SO MUCH MEAT, I JUST GAVE UP.
I THOUGHT YOU STILL WERE.

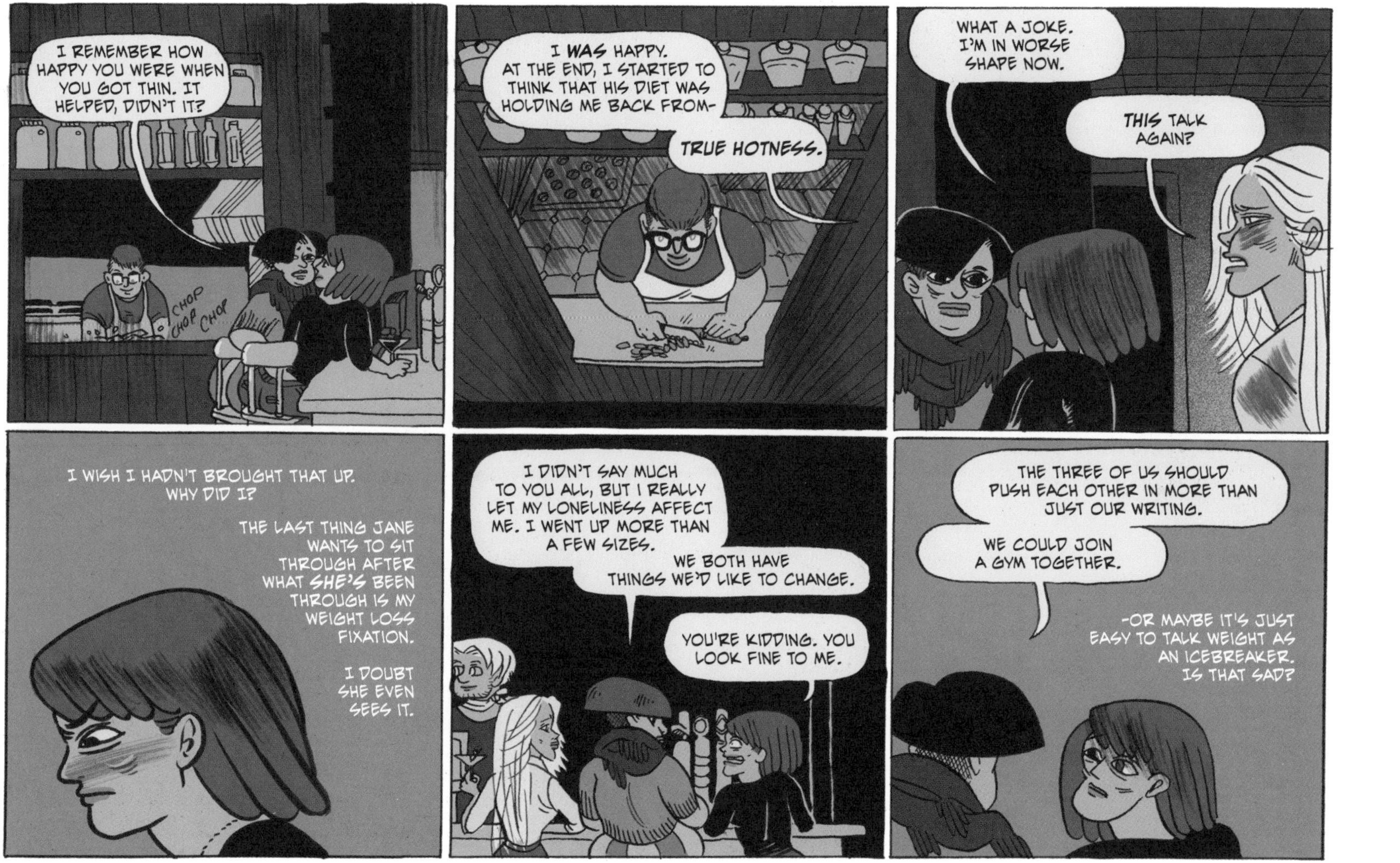
I REMEMBER HOW HAPPY YOU WERE WHEN YOU GOT THIN. IT HELPED, DIDN'T IT?
CHOP CHOP CHOP
I WAS HAPPY. AT THE END, I STARTED TO THINK THAT HIS DIET WAS HOLDING ME BACK FROM-
TRUE HOTNESS.
WHAT A JOKE. I'M IN WORSE SHAPE NOW.
THIS TALK AGAIN?
I WISH I HADN'T BROUGHT THAT UP. WHY DID I?
THE LAST THING JANE WANTS TO SIT THROUGH AFTER WHAT SHE'S BEEN THROUGH IS MY WEIGHT LOSS FIXATION.
I DOUBT SHE EVEN SEES IT.
I DIDN'T SAY MUCH TO YOU ALL, BUT I REALLY LET MY LONELINESS AFFECT ME. I WENT UP MORE THAN A FEW SIZES.
WE BOTH HAVE THINGS WE'D LIKE TO CHANGE.
YOU'RE KIDDING. YOU LOOK FINE TO ME.
THE THREE OF US SHOULD PUSH EACH OTHER IN MORE THAN JUST OUR WRITING.
WE COULD JOIN A GYM TOGETHER.
-OR MAYBE IT'S JUST EASY TO TALK WEIGHT AS AN ICEBREAKER. IS THAT SAD?

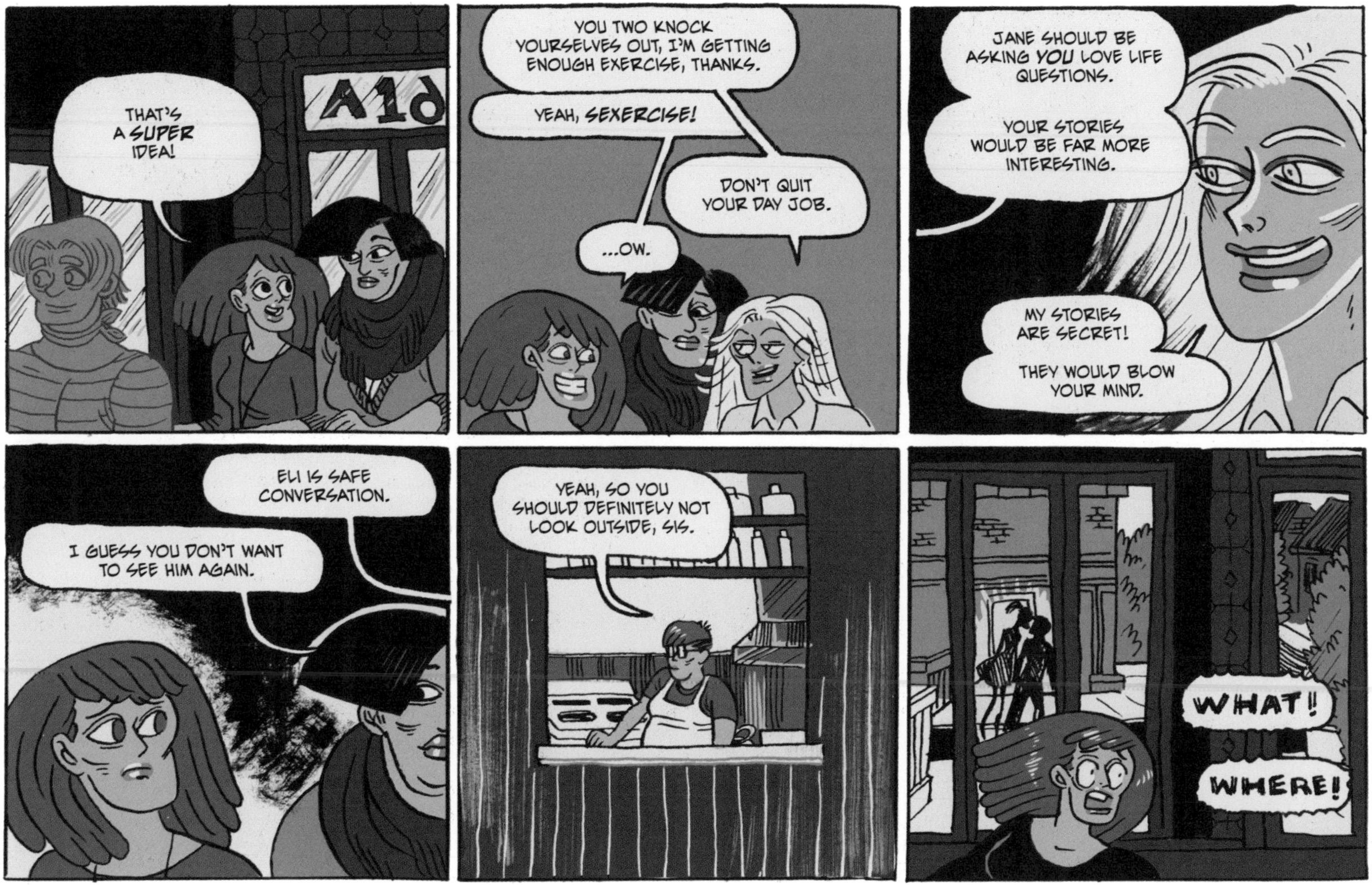
THAT'S A SUPER IDEA!
A1
YOU TWO KNOCK YOURSELVES OUT, I'M GETTING ENOUGH EXERCISE, THANKS.
YEAH, SEXERCISE!
DON'T QUIT YOUR DAY JOB.
...OW.
JANE SHOULD BE ASKING YOU LOVE LIFE QUESTIONS.
YOUR STORIES WOULD BE FAR MORE INTERESTING.
MY STORIES ARE SECRET!
THEY WOULD BLOW YOUR MIND.
ELI IS SAFE CONVERSATION.
I GUESS YOU DON'T WANT TO SEE HIM AGAIN.
YEAH, SO YOU SHOULD DEFINITELY NOT LOOK OUTSIDE, SIS.
WHAT!!
WHERE!

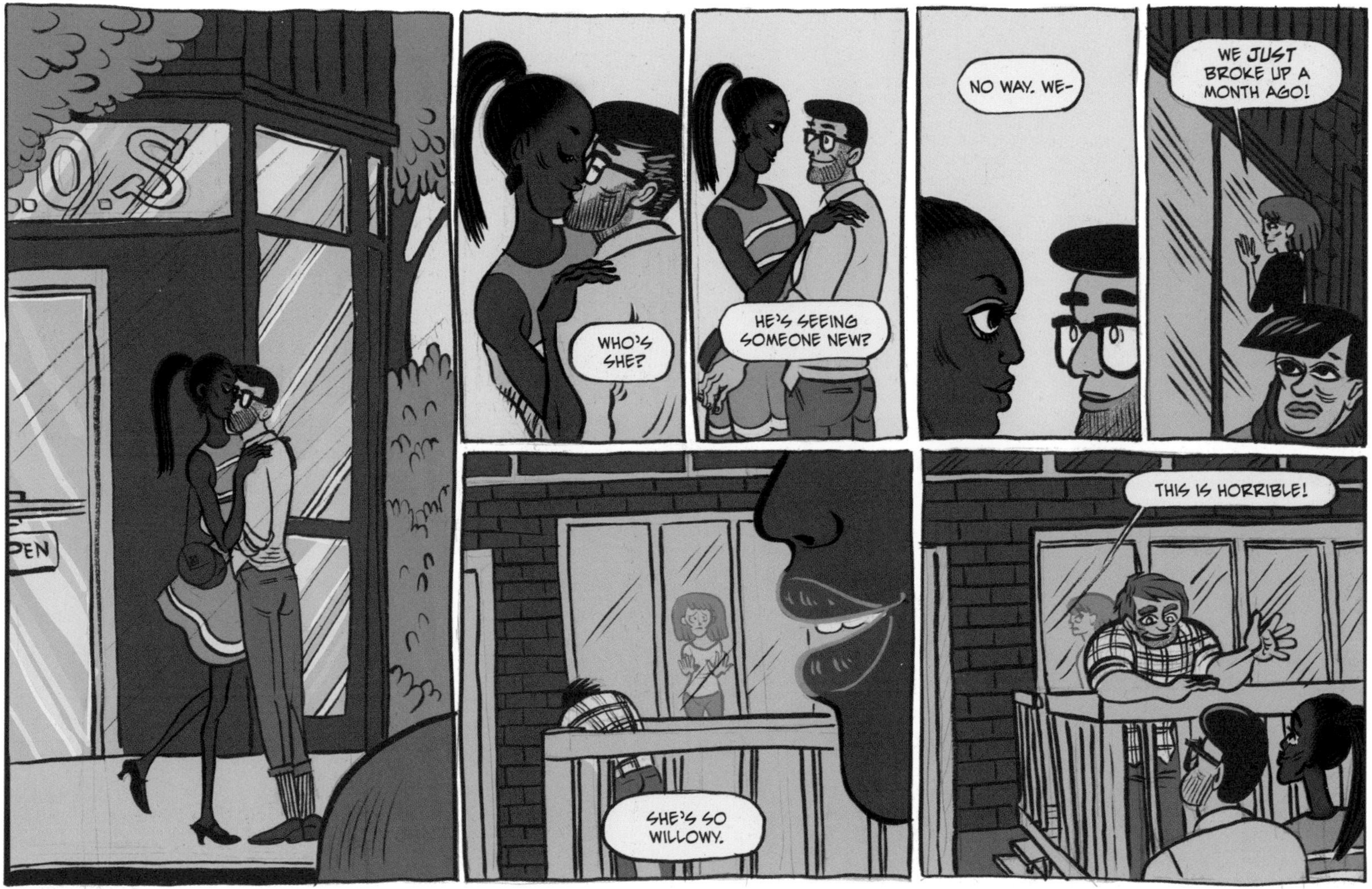
WHO'S SHE?
HE'S SEEING SOMEONE NEW?
NO WAY. WE-
WE JUST BROKE UP A MONTH AGO!
SHE'S SO WILLOWY.
THIS IS HORRIBLE!

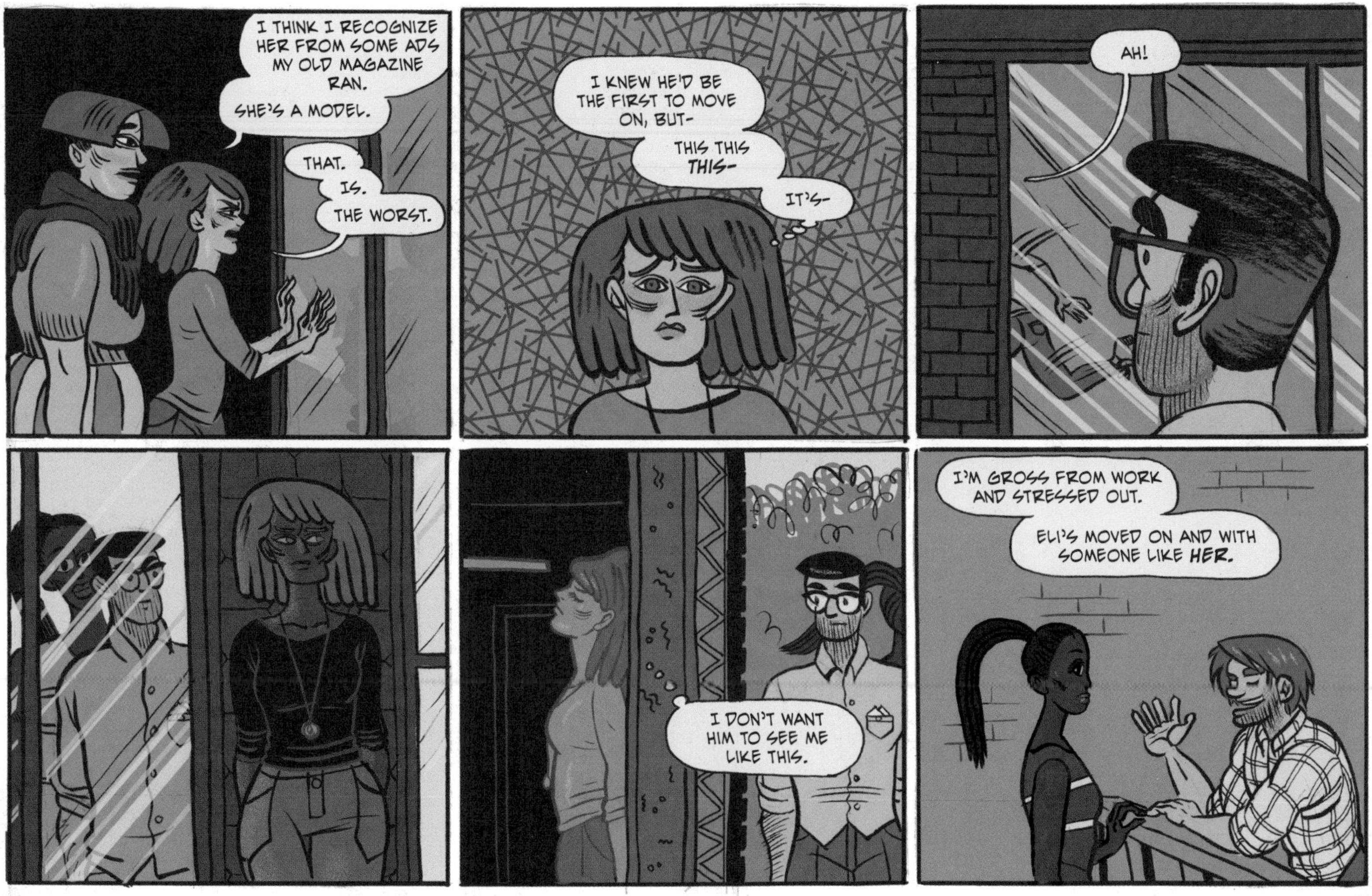
I THINK I RECOGNIZE HER FROM SOME ADS MY OLD MAGAZINE RAN.
SHE'S A MODEL.
THAT.
IS.
THE WORST.
I KNEW HE'D BE THE FIRST TO MOVE ON, BUT-
THIS THIS THIS-
IT'S-
AH!
I DON'T WANT HIM TO SEE ME LIKE THIS.
I'M GROSS FROM WORK AND STRESSED OUT.
ELI'S MOVED ON AND WITH SOMEONE LIKE HER.

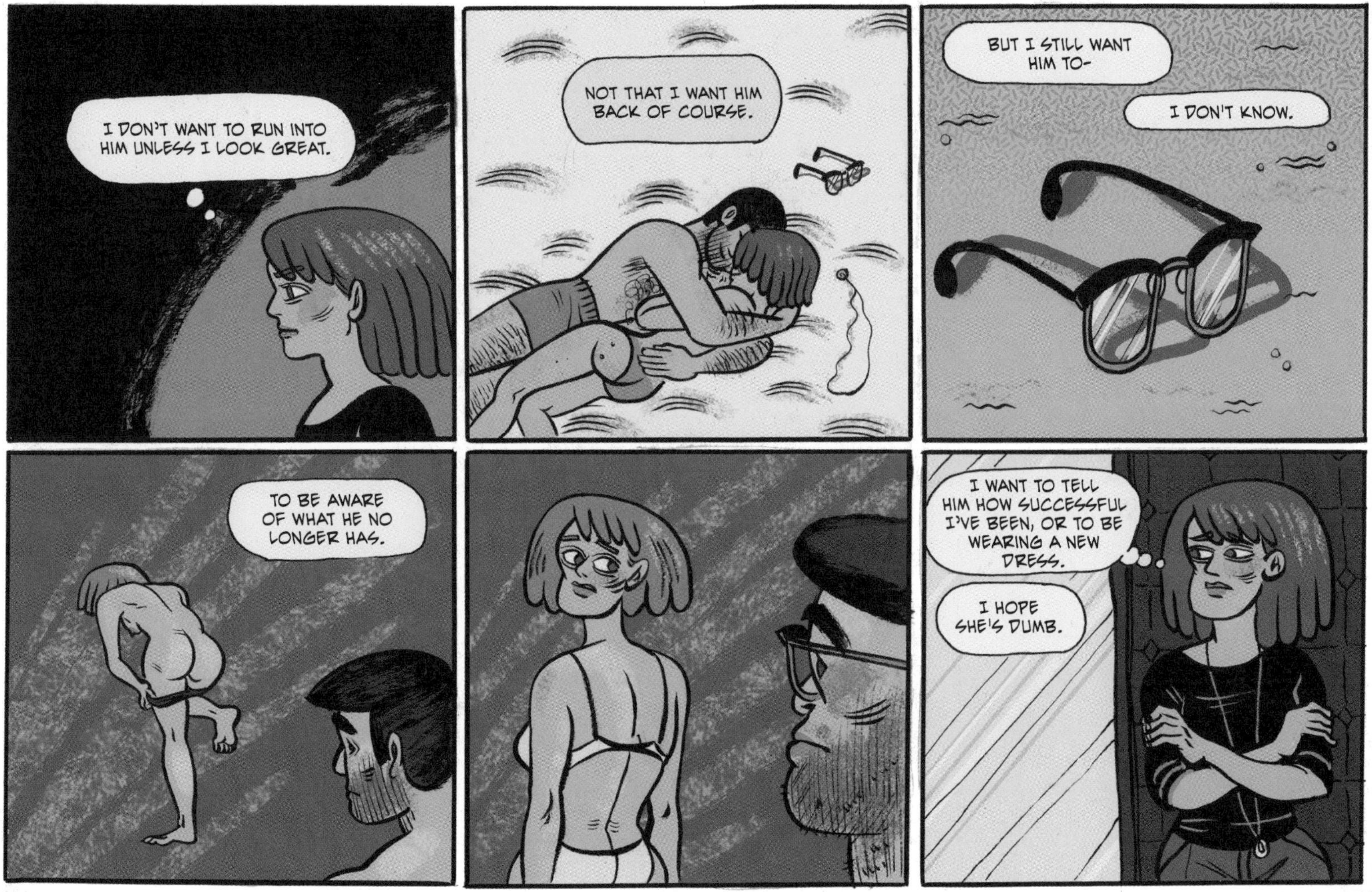
I DON'T WANT TO RUN INTO HIM UNLESS I LOOK GREAT.
NOT THAT I WANT HIM BACK OF COURSE.
BUT I STILL WANT HIM TO-
I DON'T KNOW.
TO BE AWARE OF WHAT HE NO LONGER HAS.
I WANT TO TELL HIM HOW SUCCESSFUL I'VE BEEN, OR TO BE WEARING A NEW DRESS.
I HOPE SHE'S DUMB.

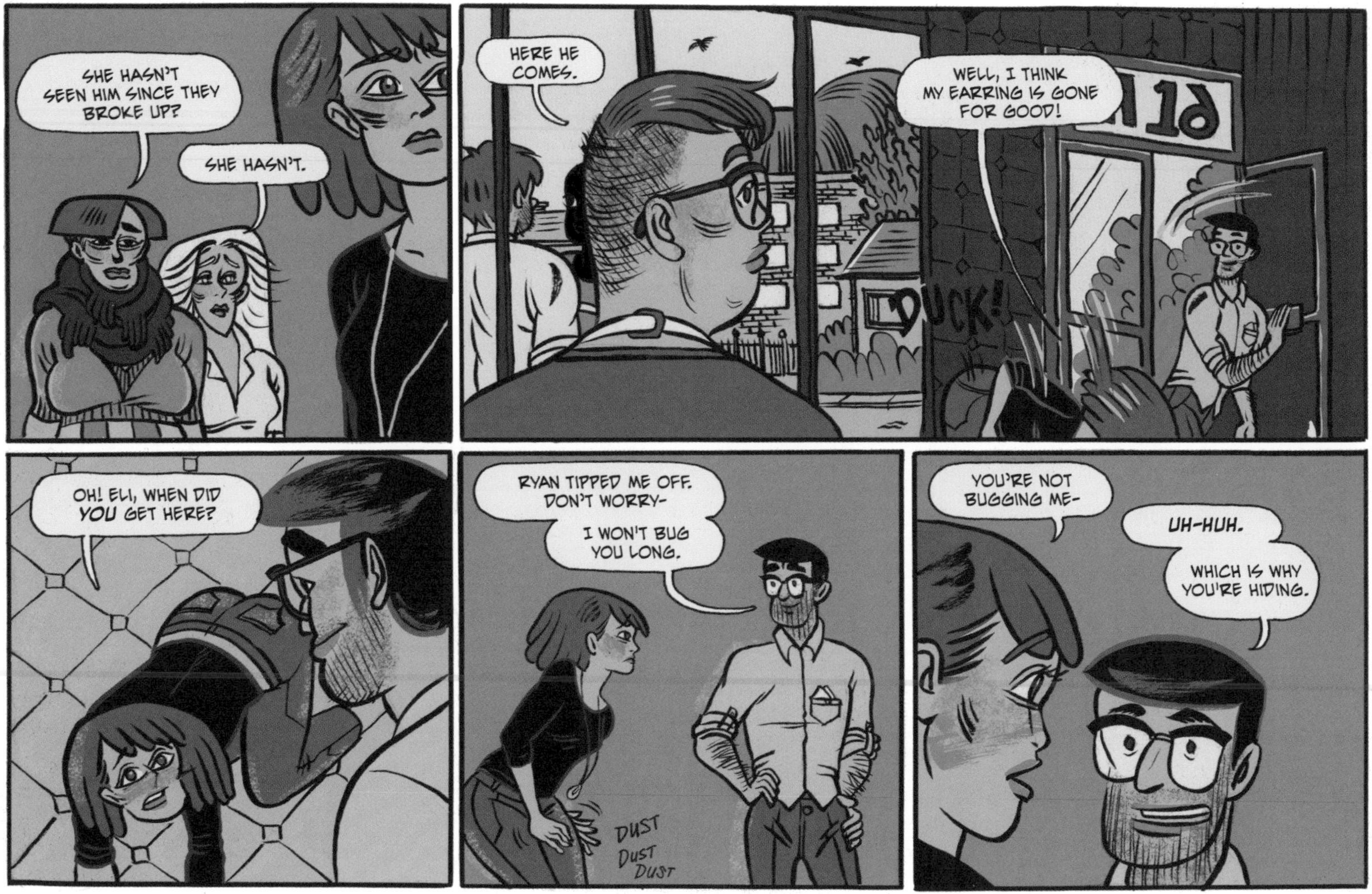
SHE HASN'T SEEN HIM SINCE THEY BROKE UP?
SHE HASN'T.
HERE HE COMES.
WELL, I THINK MY EARRING IS GONE FOR GOOD!
DUCK!
OH! ELI, WHEN DID YOU GET HERE?
RYAN TIPPED ME OFF. DON'T WORRY-
I WON'T BUG YOU LONG.
DUST DUST DUST
YOU'RE NOT BUGGING ME-
UH-HUH.
WHICH IS WHY YOU'RE HIDING.

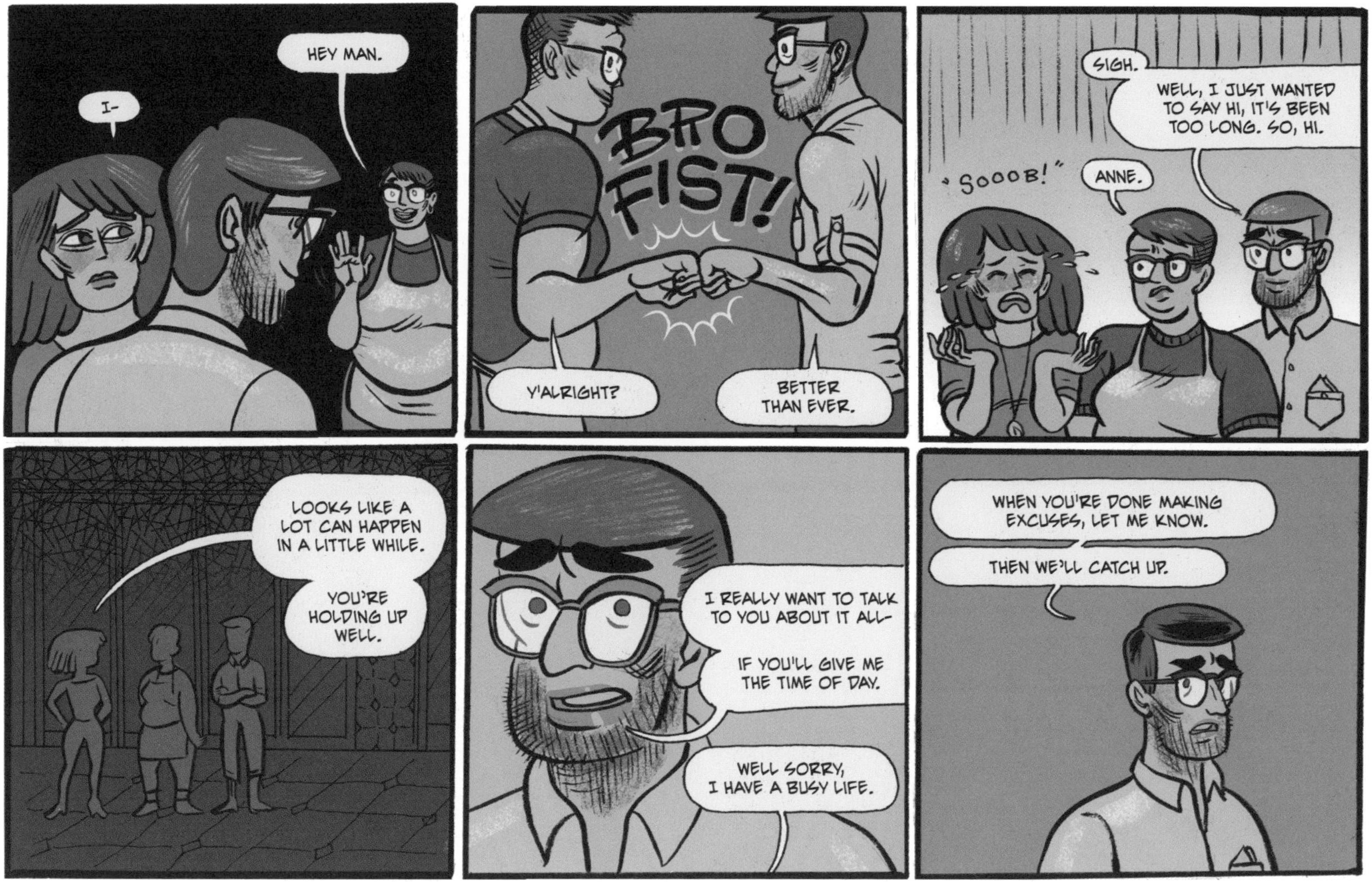
HEY MAN.
I-
BRO FIST!
Y'ALRIGHT?
BETTER THAN EVER.
SIGH.
WELL, I JUST WANTED TO SAY HI, IT'S BEEN TOO LONG. SO, HI.
"SOOOB!"
ANNE.
LOOKS LIKE A LOT CAN HAPPEN IN A LITTLE WHILE.
YOU'RE HOLDING UP WELL.
I REALLY WANT TO TALK TO YOU ABOUT IT ALL-
IF YOU'LL GIVE ME THE TIME OF DAY.
WELL SORRY, I HAVE A BUSY LIFE.
WHEN YOU'RE DONE MAKING EXCUSES, LET ME KNOW.
THEN WE'LL CATCH UP.

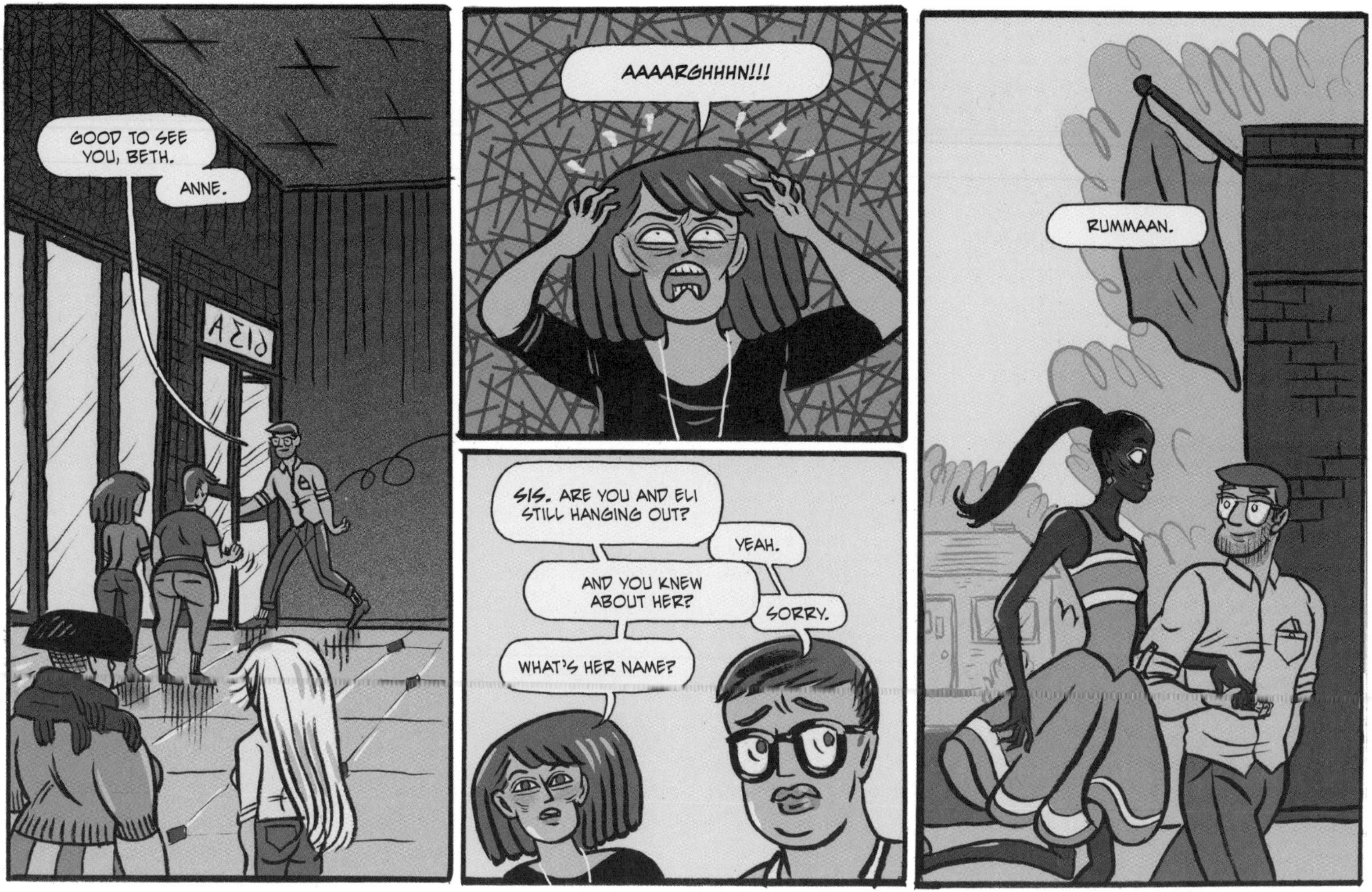
GOOD TO SEE YOU, BETH.
ANNE.
ΑΣΙΔ
AAAARGHHHN!!!
SIS. ARE YOU AND ELI STILL HANGING OUT?
YEAH.
AND YOU KNEW ABOUT HER?
SORRY.
WHAT'S HER NAME?
RUMMAAN.

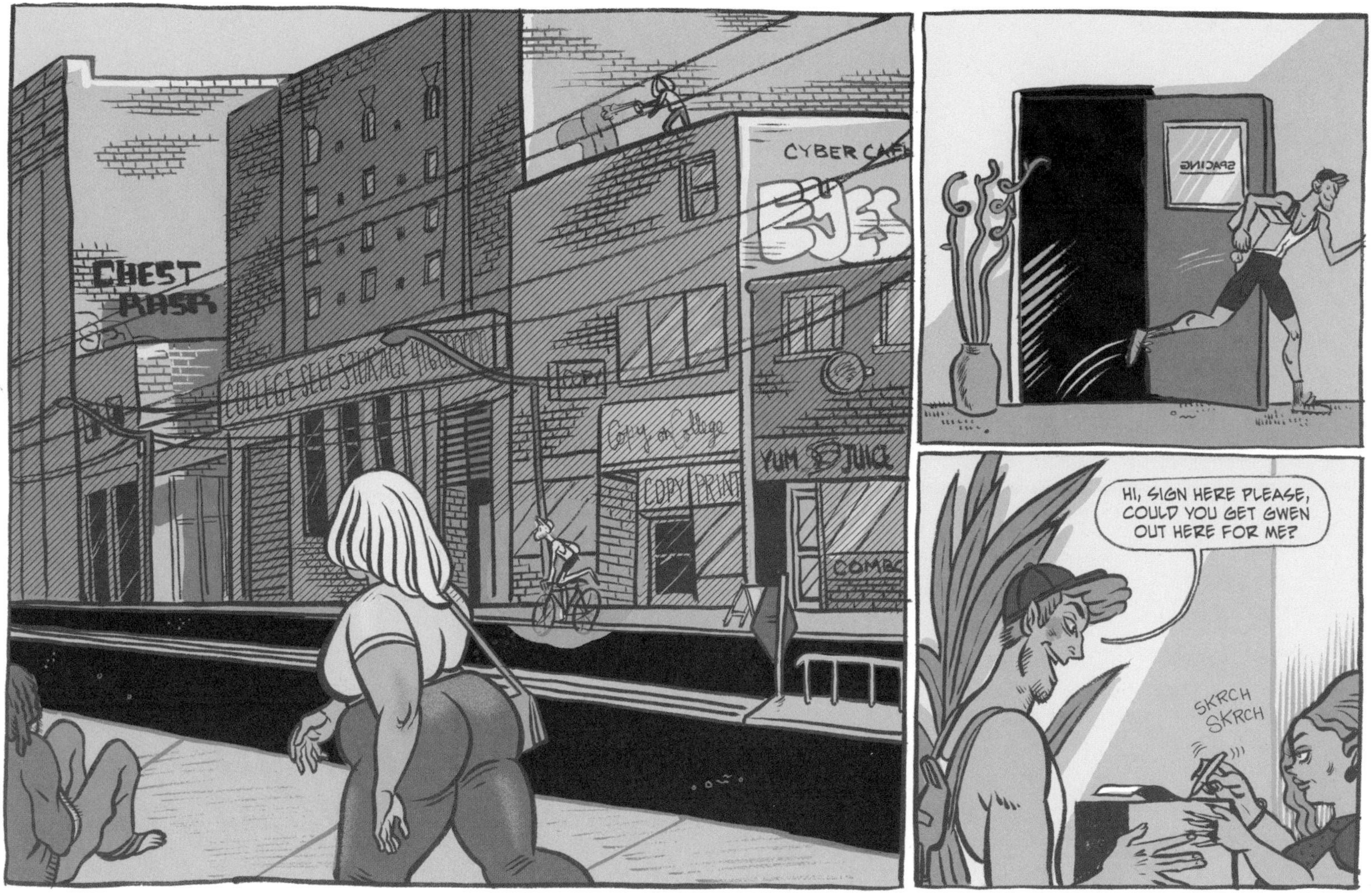
COLLEGE SELF STORAGE
Copy on College
COPY PRINT
YUM JUICE
HI, SIGN HERE PLEASE, COULD YOU GET GWEN OUT HERE FOR ME?
SKRCH SKRCH

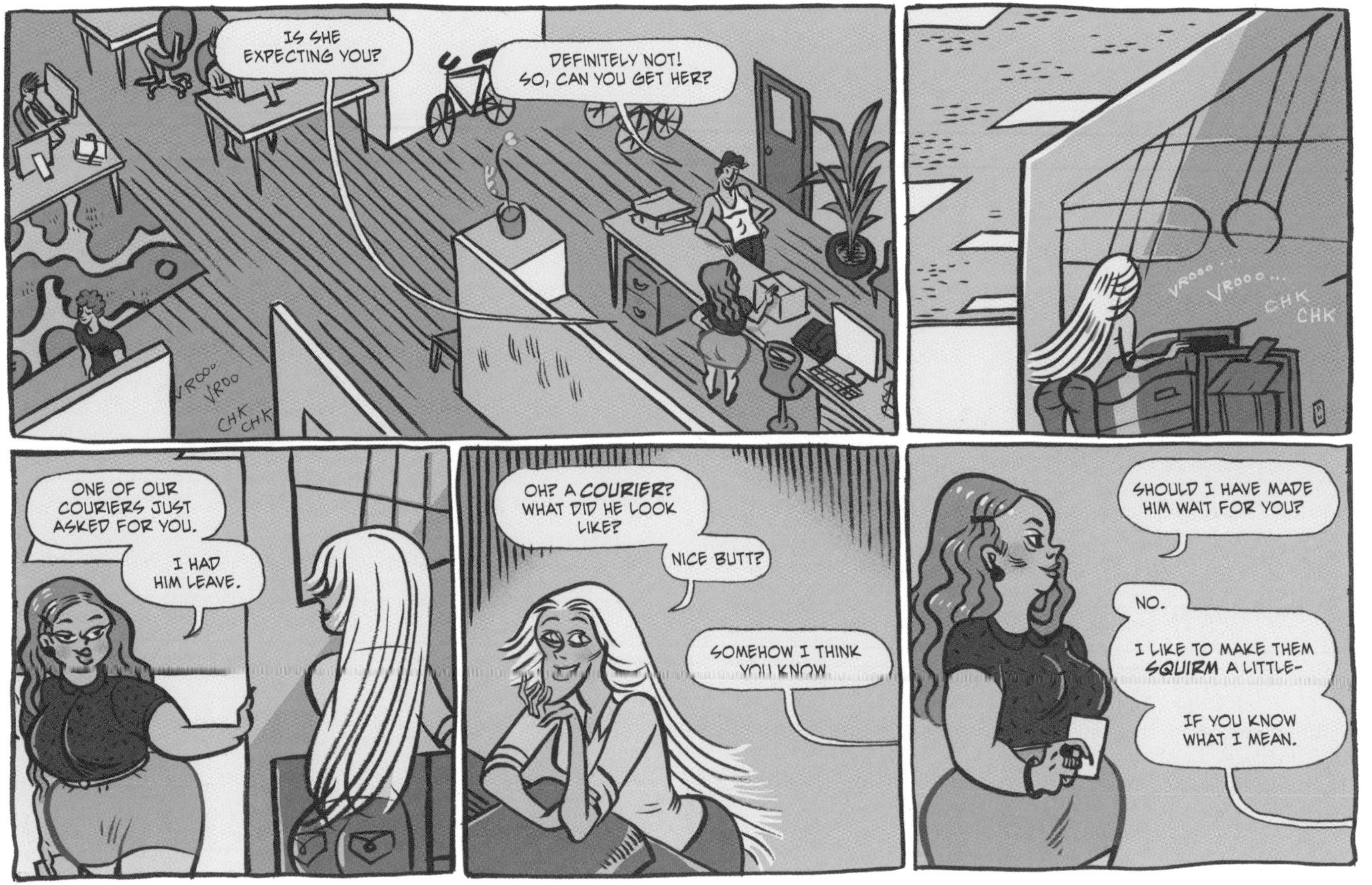
IS SHE EXPECTING YOU?
DEFINITELY NOT! SO, CAN YOU GET HER?
VROOO VROO
CHK CHK
VROOO.... VROOO...
CHK CHK
ONE OF OUR COURIERS JUST ASKED FOR YOU.
I HAD HIM LEAVE.
OH? A COURIER? WHAT DID HE LOOK LIKE?
NICE BUTT?
SOMEHOW I THINK YOU KNOW.
SHOULD I HAVE MADE HIM WAIT FOR YOU?
NO.
I LIKE TO MAKE THEM SQUIRM A LITTLE-
IF YOU KNOW WHAT I MEAN.

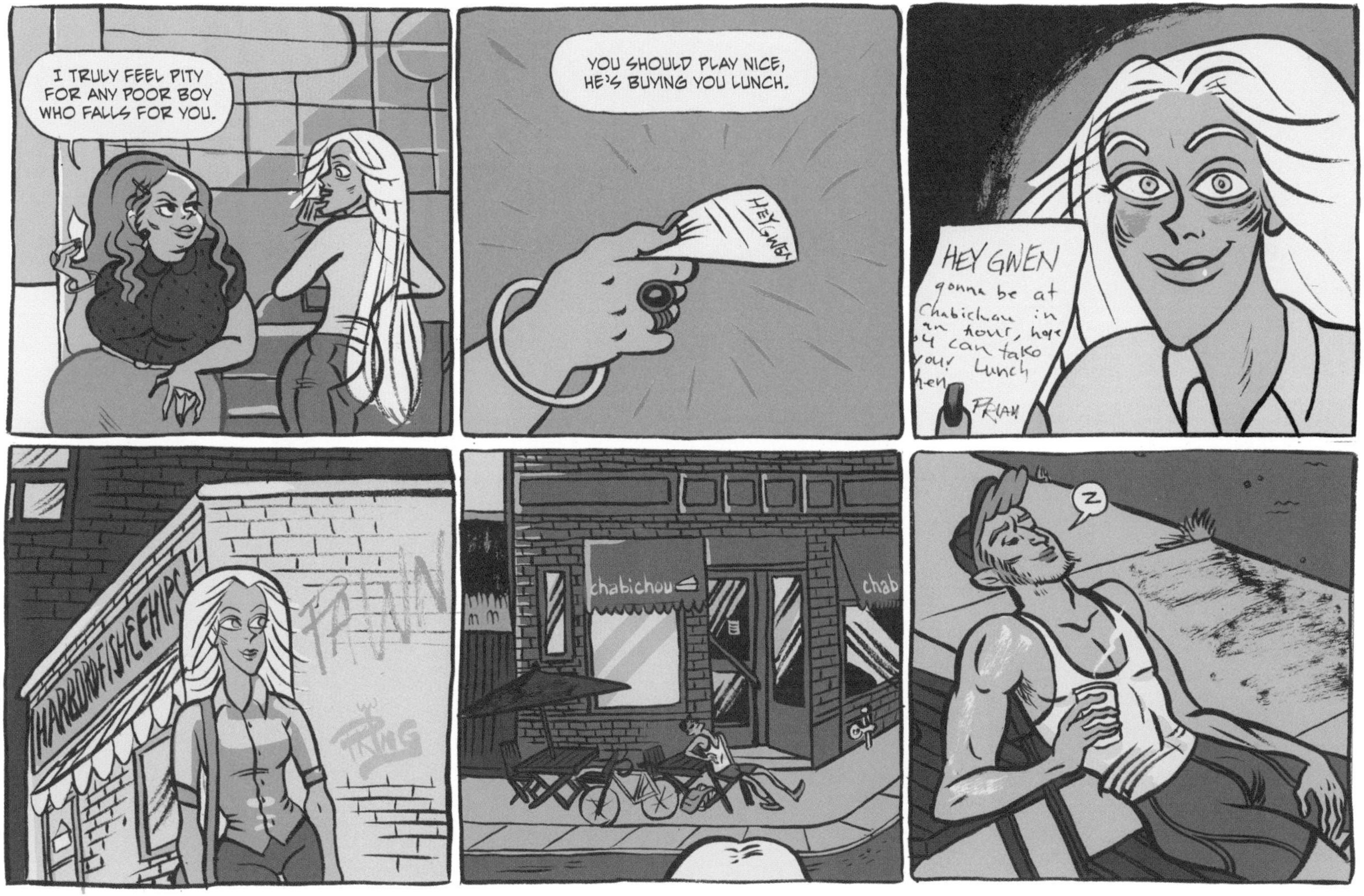
I TRULY FEEL PITY FOR ANY POOR BOY WHO FALLS FOR YOU.
YOU SHOULD PLAY NICE, HE'S BUYING YOU LUNCH.
HEY GWEN
HEY GWEN
gonna be at Chabichou in an hour, hope u can take your lunch hen.
Z
chabichou
chab

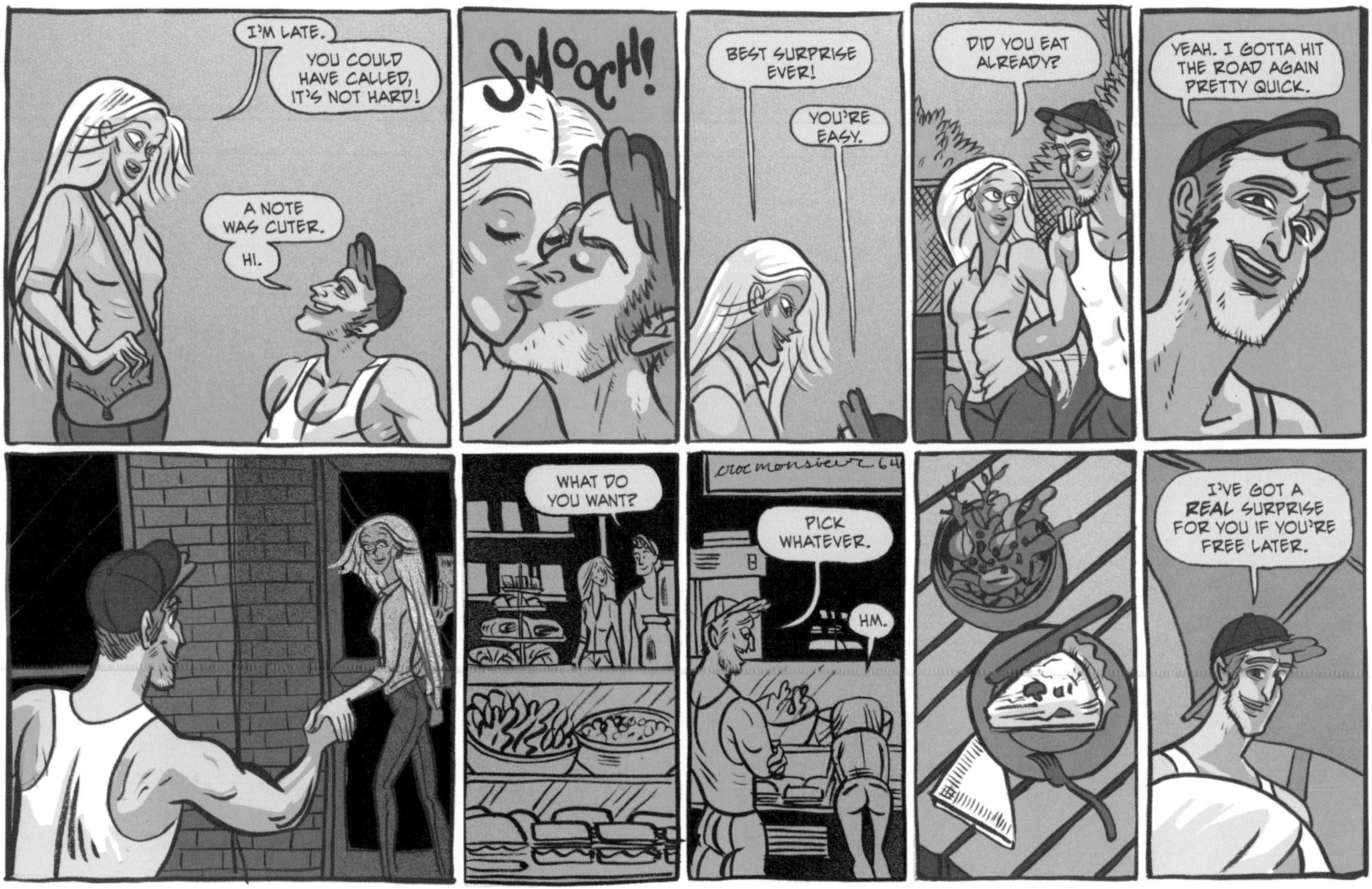
I'M LATE.
YOU COULD HAVE CALLED, IT'S NOT HARD!
A NOTE WAS CUTER.
HI.
SMOOCH!
BEST SURPRISE EVER!
YOU'RE EASY.
DID YOU EAT ALREADY?
YEAH. I GOTTA HIT THE ROAD AGAIN PRETTY QUICK.
WHAT DO YOU WANT?
croc monsieur 6.4
PICK WHATEVER.
HM.
I'VE GOT A REAL SURPRISE FOR YOU IF YOU'RE FREE LATER.

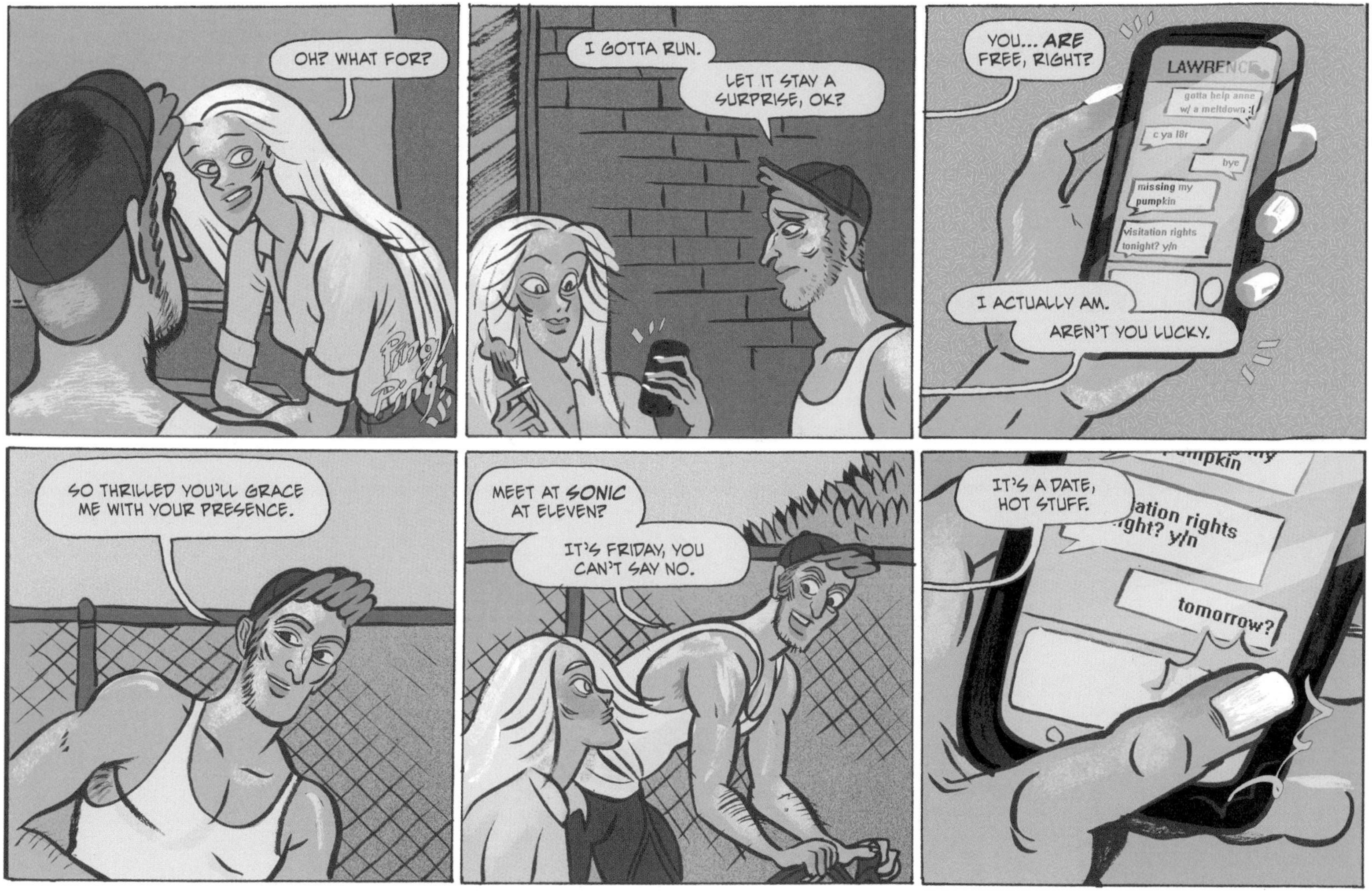
OH? WHAT FOR?
Ping! Ping!
I GOTTA RUN.
LET IT STAY A SURPRISE, OK?
YOU... ARE FREE, RIGHT?
gotta help anne w/ a meltdown :(
c ya l8r
bye
missing my pumpkin
visitation rights tonight? y/n
I ACTUALLY AM.
AREN'T YOU LUCKY.
SO THRILLED YOU'LL GRACE ME WITH YOUR PRESENCE.
MEET AT SONIC AT ELEVEN?
IT'S FRIDAY, YOU CAN'T SAY NO.
IT'S A DATE, HOT STUFF.
tomorrow?

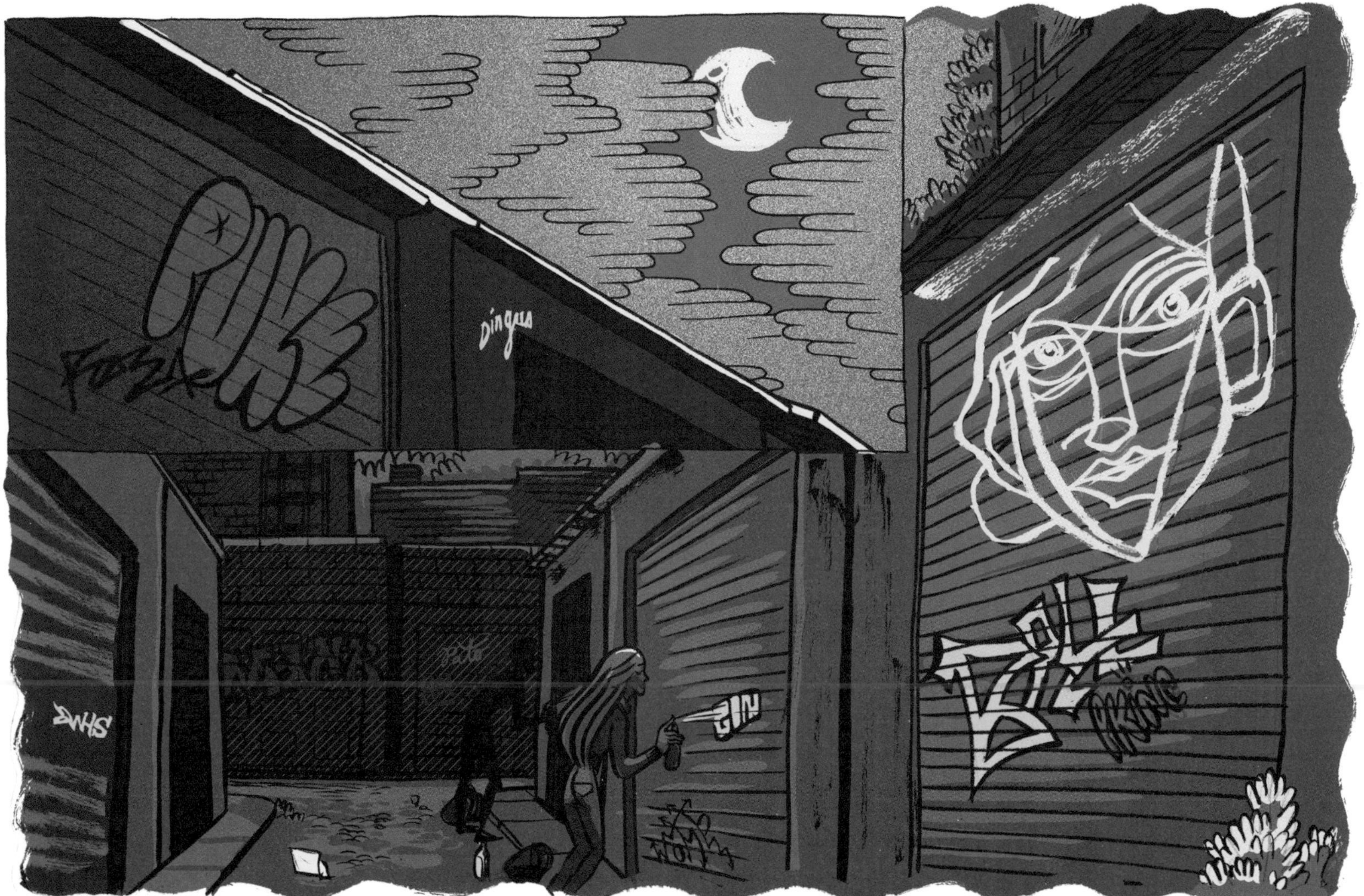
dingus

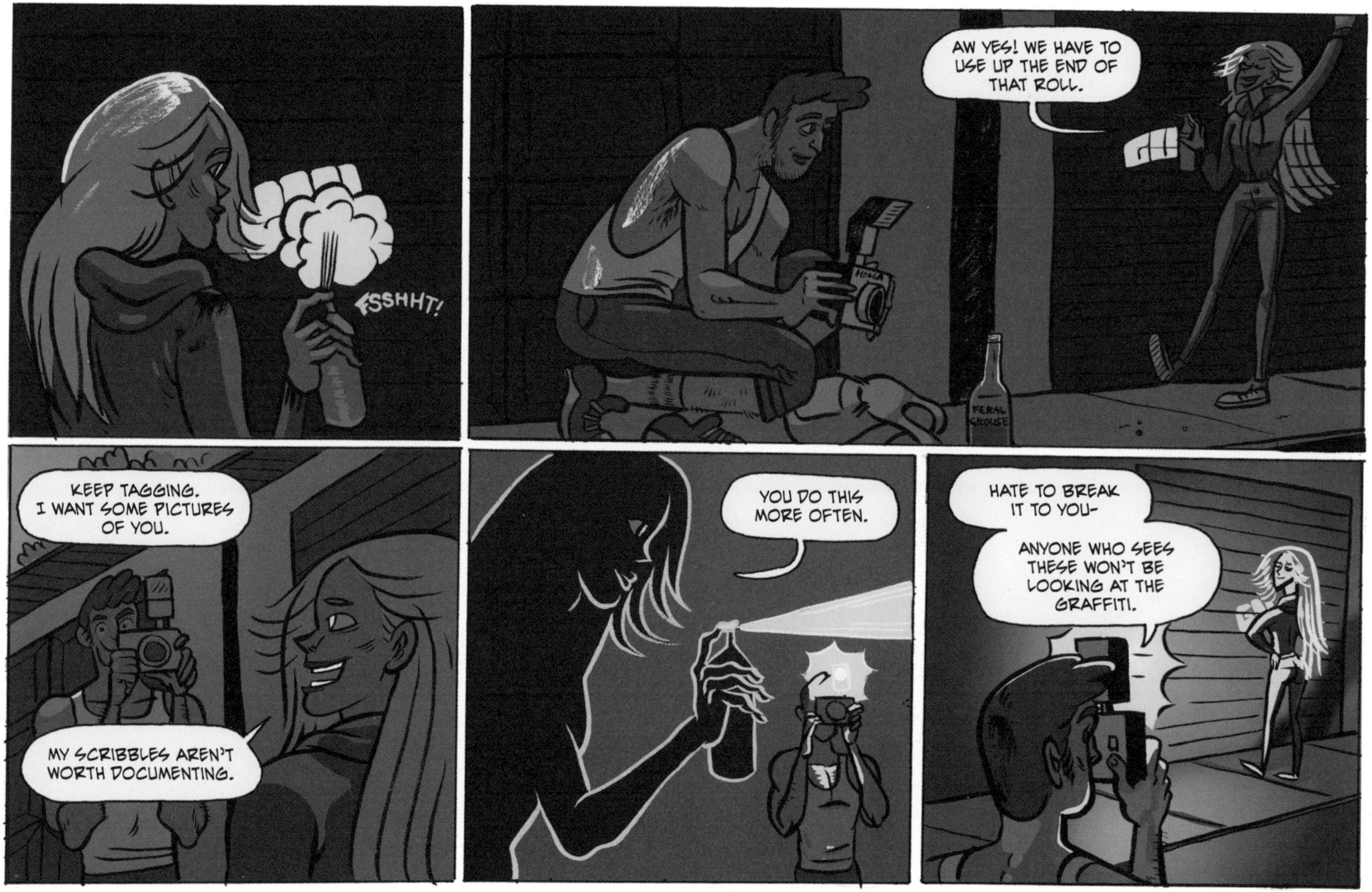
FSSHHT!
AW YES! WE HAVE TO USE UP THE END OF THAT ROLL.
FERAL GROUSE
KEEP TAGGING. I WANT SOME PICTURES OF YOU.
MY SCRIBBLES AREN'T WORTH DOCUMENTING.
YOU DO THIS MORE OFTEN.
HATE TO BREAK IT TO YOU-
ANYONE WHO SEES THESE WON'T BE LOOKING AT THE GRAFFITI.

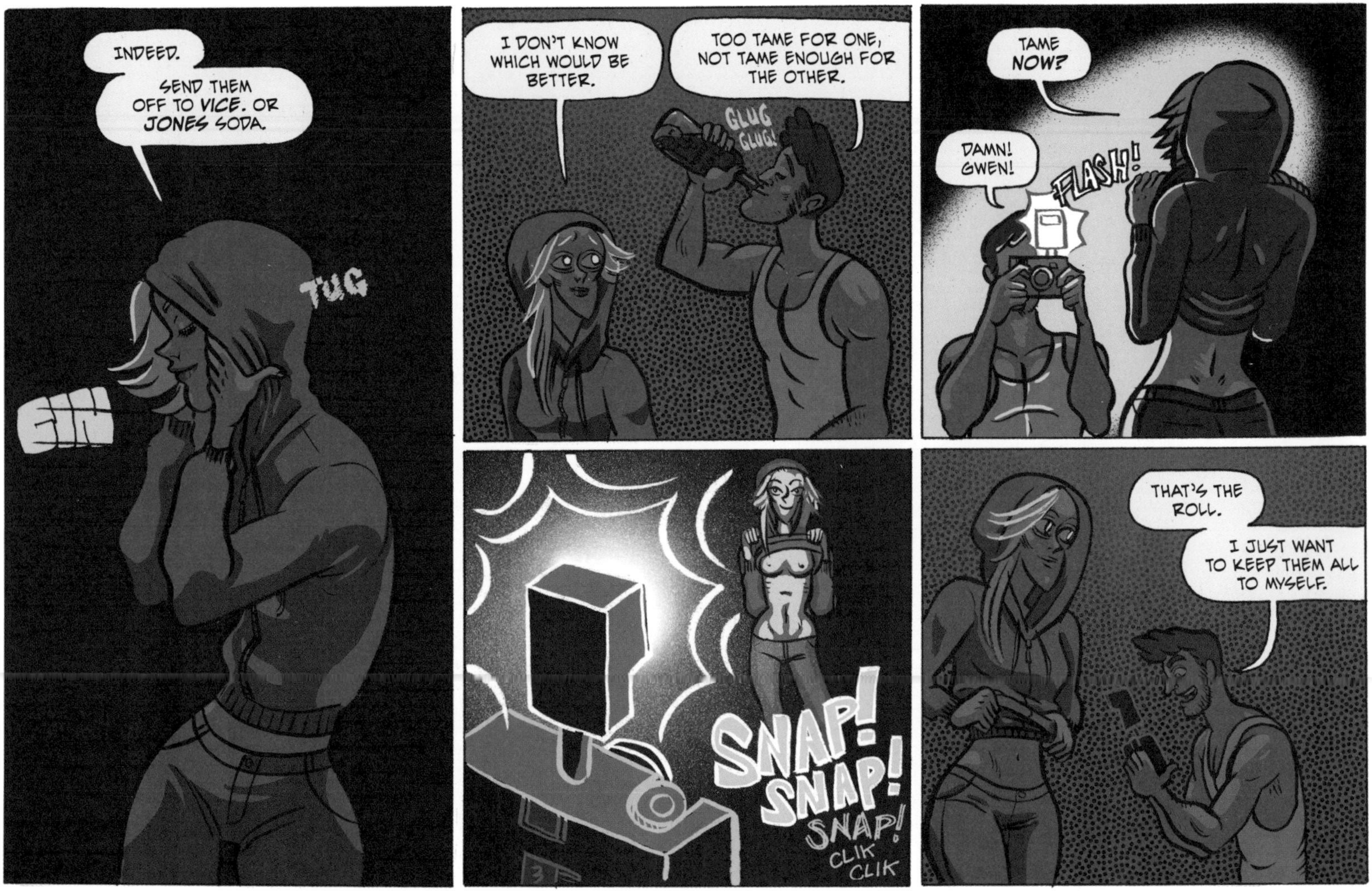
INDEED.
SEND THEM OFF TO VICE. OR JONES SODA.
TUG
I DON'T KNOW WHICH WOULD BE BETTER.
TOO TAME FOR ONE, NOT TAME ENOUGH FOR THE OTHER.
GLUG GLUG!
TAME NOW?
DAMN! GWEN!
FLASH!
SNAP! SNAP! SNAP!
CLIK CLIK
THAT'S THE ROLL.
I JUST WANT TO KEEP THEM ALL TO MYSELF.

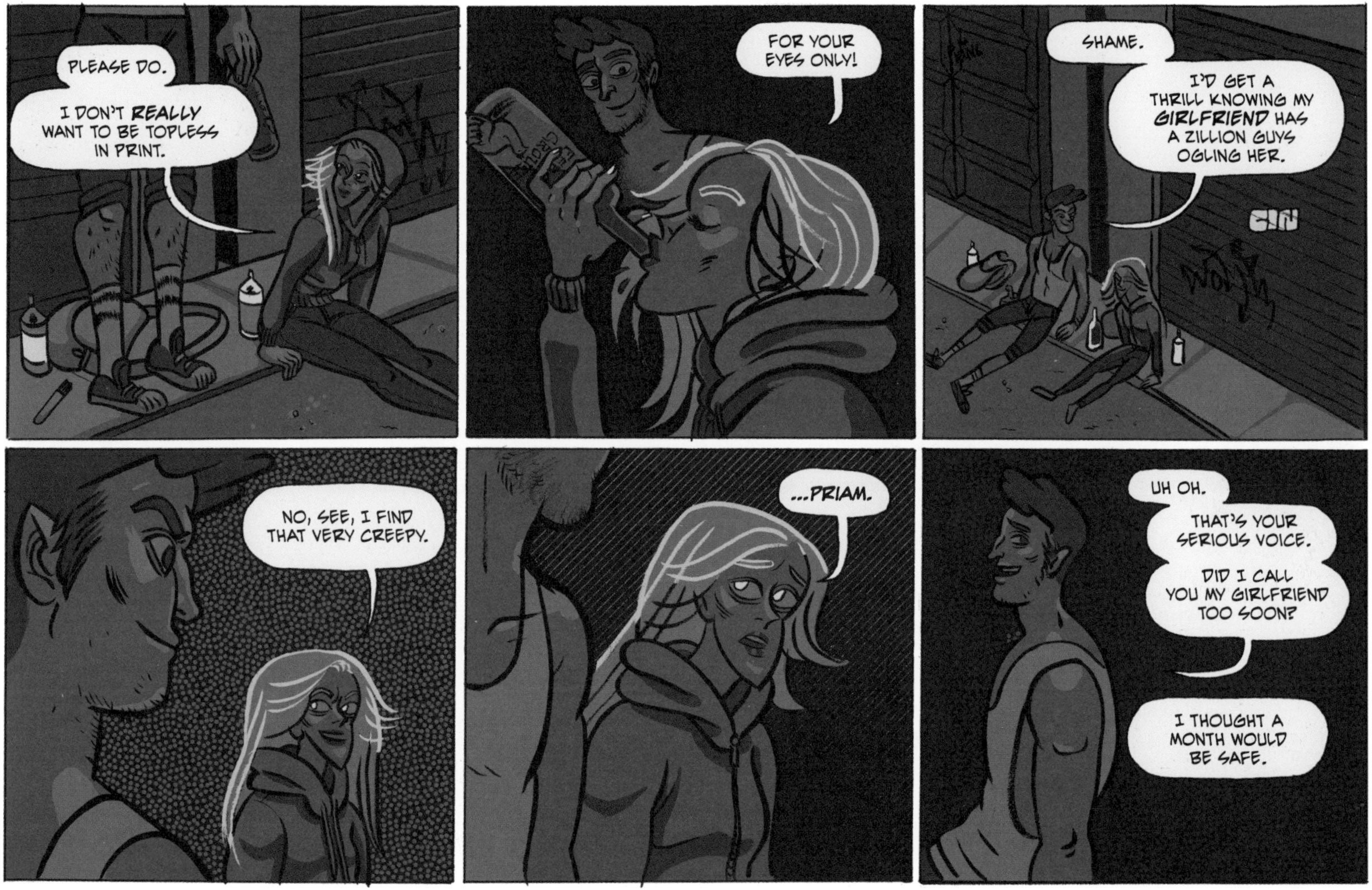
PLEASE DO.
I DON'T REALLY WANT TO BE TOPLESS IN PRINT.
FOR YOUR EYES ONLY!
SHAME.
I'D GET A THRILL KNOWING MY GIRLFRIEND HAS A ZILLION GUYS OGLING HER.
NO, SEE, I FIND THAT VERY CREEPY.
...PRIAM.
UH OH.
THAT'S YOUR SERIOUS VOICE.
DID I CALL YOU MY GIRLFRIEND TOO SOON?
I THOUGHT A MONTH WOULD BE SAFE.

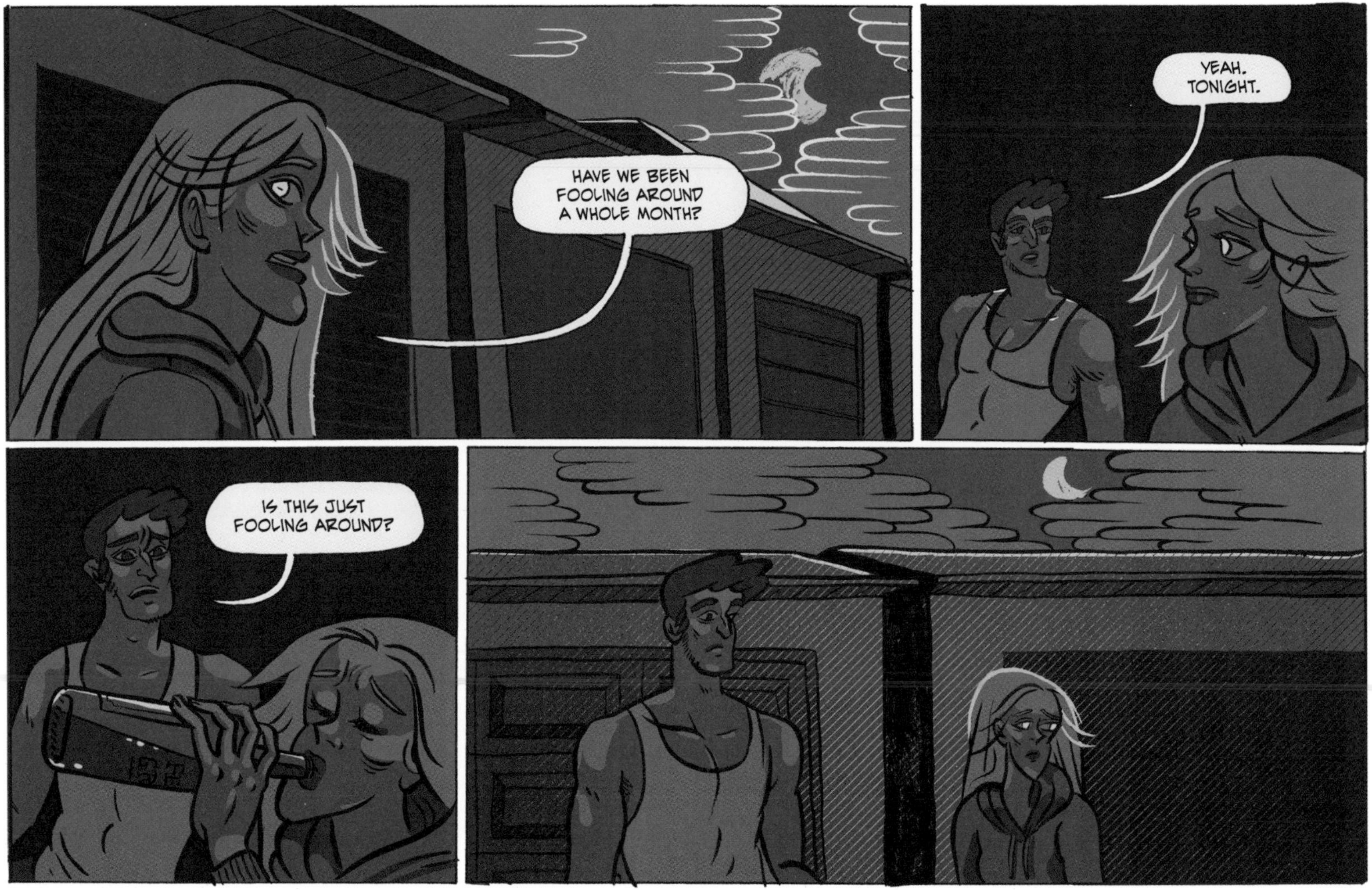
HAVE WE BEEN FOOLING AROUND A WHOLE MONTH?
YEAH. TONIGHT.
IS THIS JUST FOOLING AROUND?

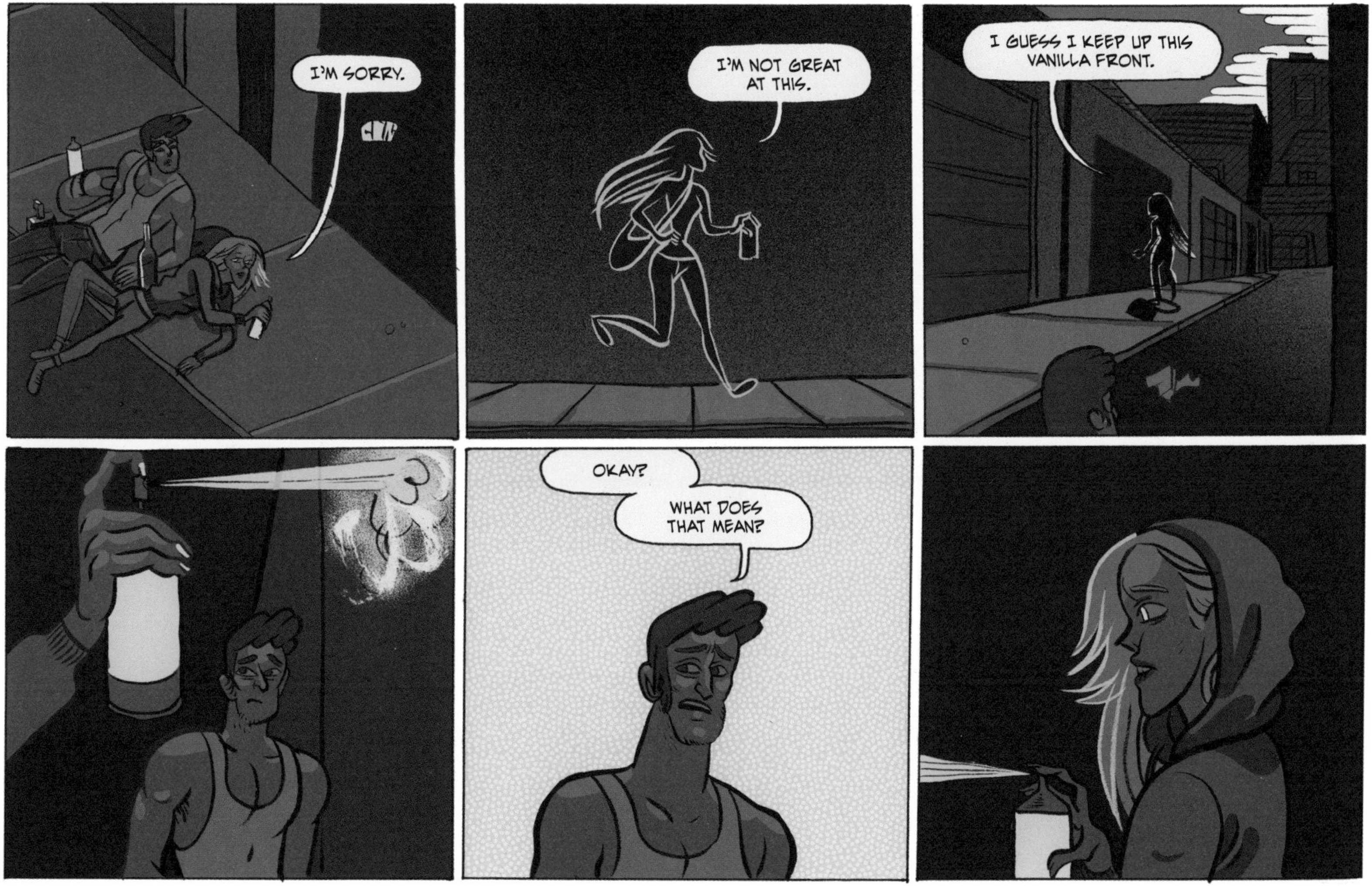

I'M SORRY.
I'M NOT GREAT AT THIS.
I GUESS I KEEP UP THIS VANILLA FRONT.
OKAY?
WHAT DOES THAT MEAN?

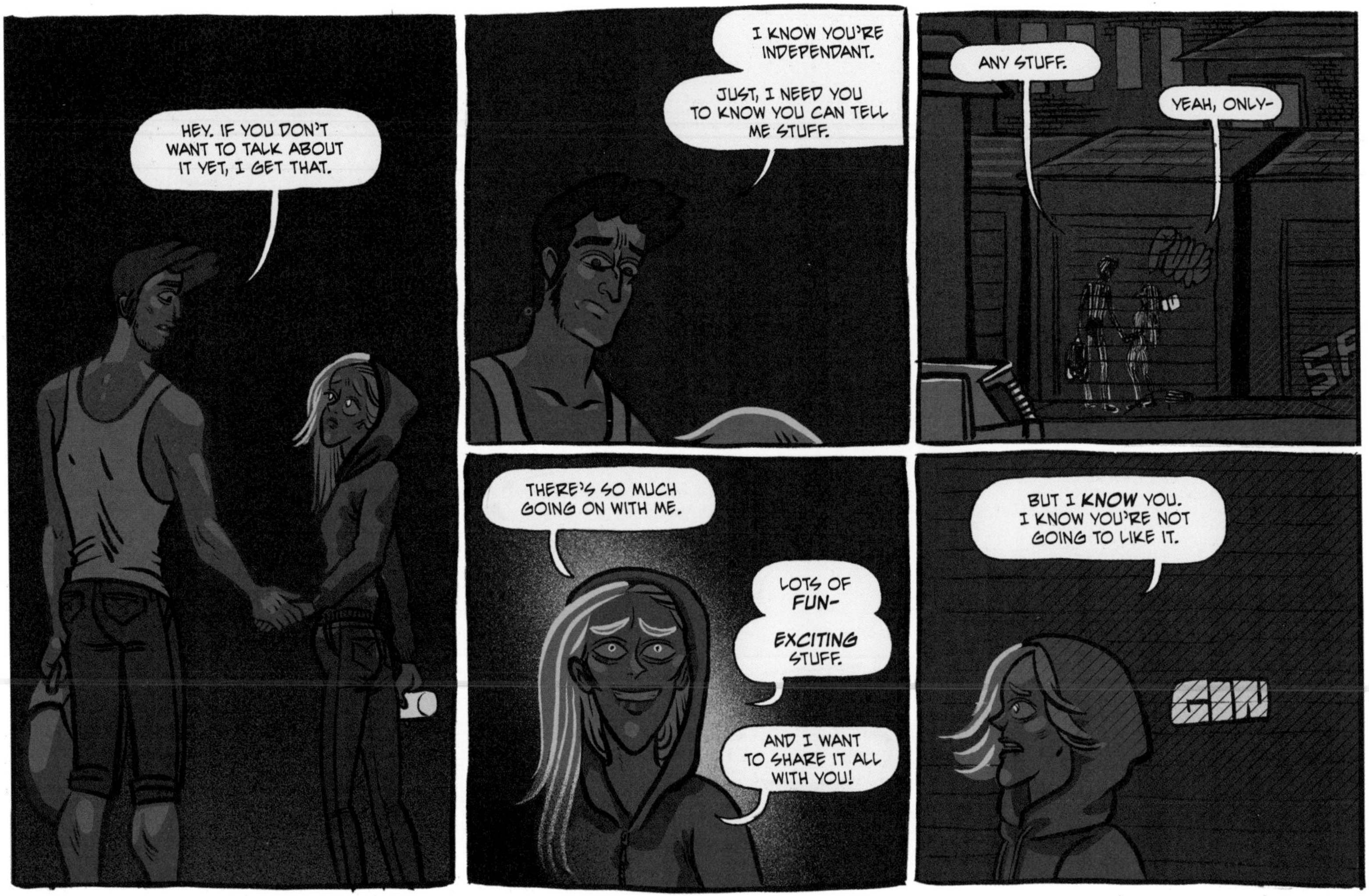
HEY. IF YOU DON'T WANT TO TALK ABOUT IT YET, I GET THAT.
I KNOW YOU'RE INDEPENDANT.
JUST, I NEED YOU TO KNOW YOU CAN TELL ME STUFF.
ANY STUFF.
YEAH, ONLY-
THERE'S SO MUCH GOING ON WITH ME.
LOTS OF FUN-
EXCITING STUFF.
AND I WANT TO SHARE IT ALL WITH YOU!
BUT I KNOW YOU. I KNOW YOU'RE NOT GOING TO LIKE IT.

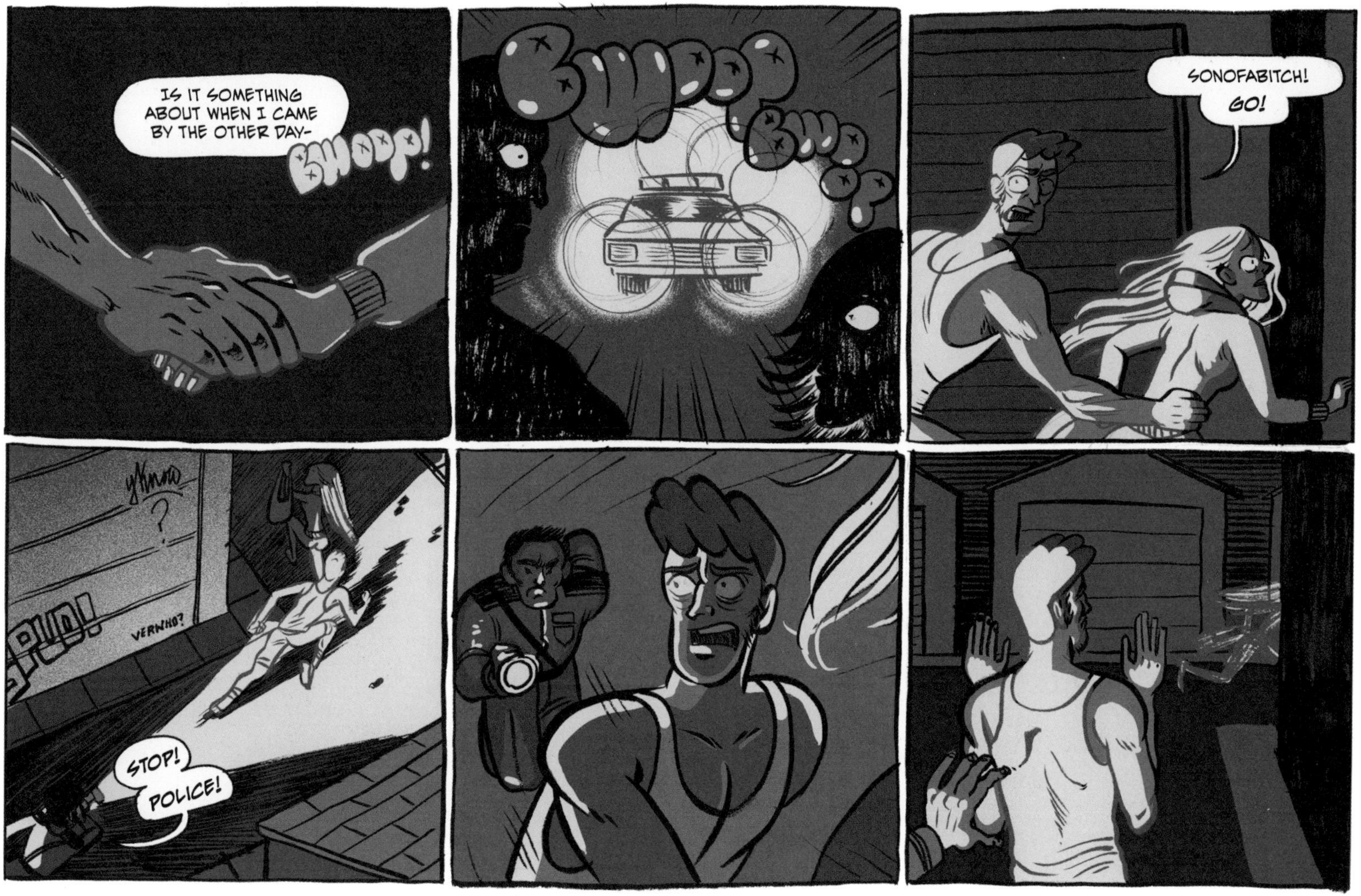
IS IT SOMETHING ABOUT WHEN I CAME BY THE OTHER DAY-
BWOOP!
BWOOP BWOOP
SONOFABITCH! GO!
STOP! POLICE!

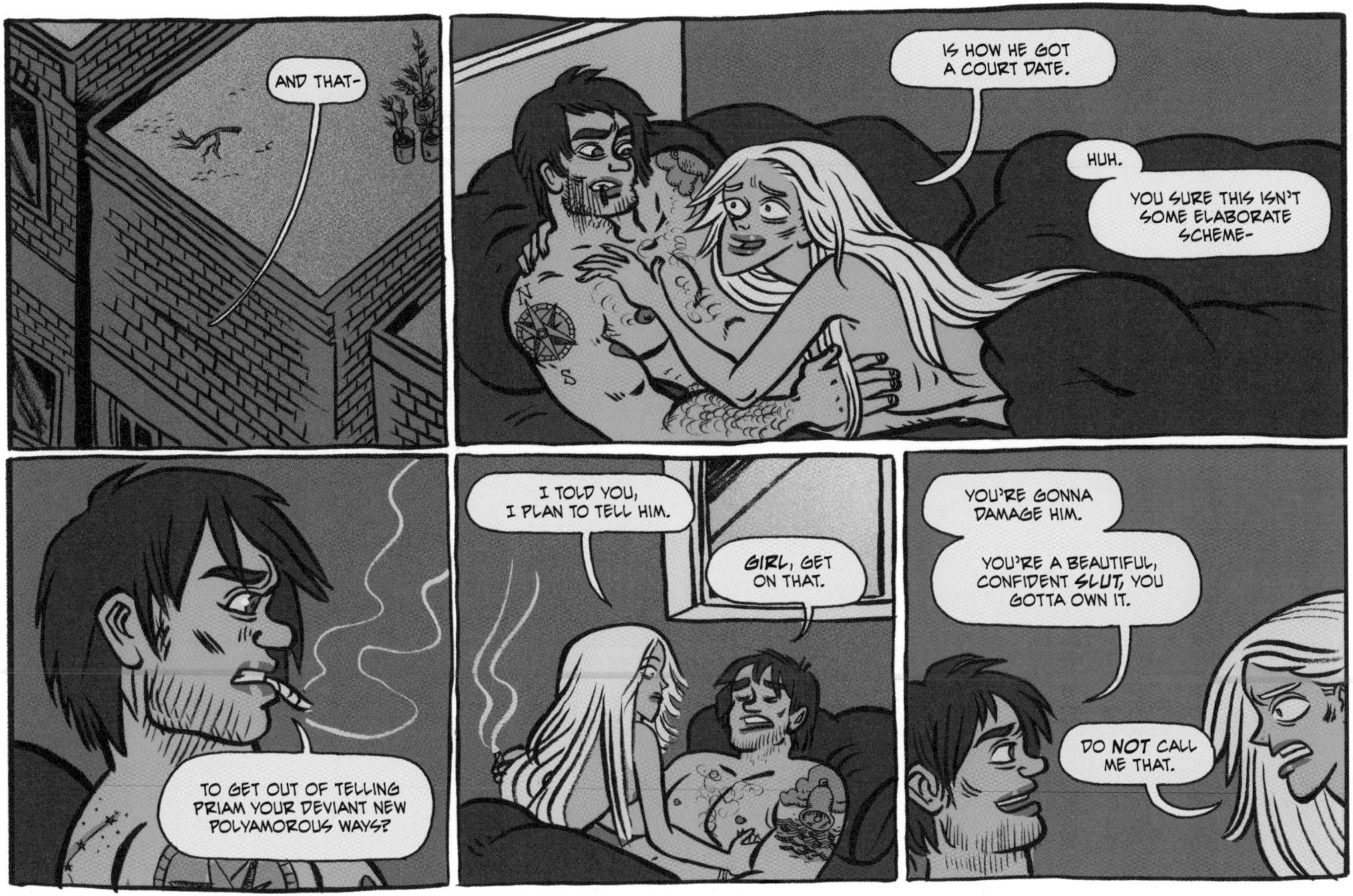
AND THAT-
IS HOW HE GOT A COURT DATE.
HUH.
YOU SURE THIS ISN'T SOME ELABORATE SCHEME-
TO GET OUT OF TELLING PRIAM YOUR DEVIANT NEW POLYAMOROUS WAYS?
I TOLD YOU, I PLAN TO TELL HIM.
GIRL, GET ON THAT.
YOU'RE GONNA DAMAGE HIM.
YOU'RE A BEAUTIFUL, CONFIDENT SLUT, YOU GOTTA OWN IT.
DO NOT CALL ME THAT.

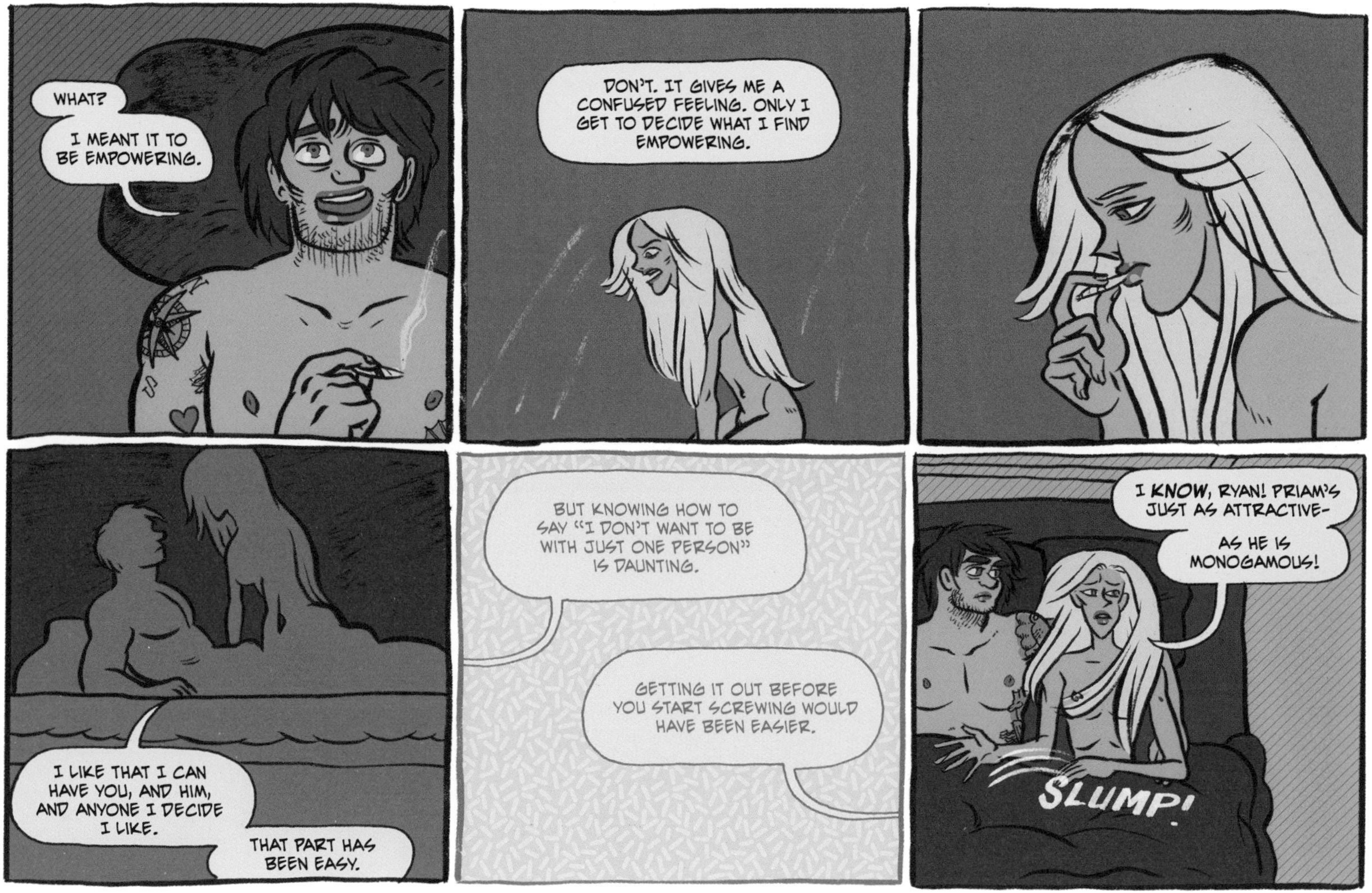
WHAT?
I MEANT IT TO BE EMPOWERING.
DON'T. IT GIVES ME A CONFUSED FEELING. ONLY I GET TO DECIDE WHAT I FIND EMPOWERING.
I LIKE THAT I CAN HAVE YOU, AND HIM, AND ANYONE I DECIDE I LIKE.
THAT PART HAS BEEN EASY.
BUT KNOWING HOW TO SAY "I DON'T WANT TO BE WITH JUST ONE PERSON" IS DAUNTING.
GETTING IT OUT BEFORE YOU START SCREWING WOULD HAVE BEEN EASIER.
I KNOW, RYAN! PRIAM'S JUST AS ATTRACTIVE-
AS HE IS MONOGAMOUS!
SLUMP!

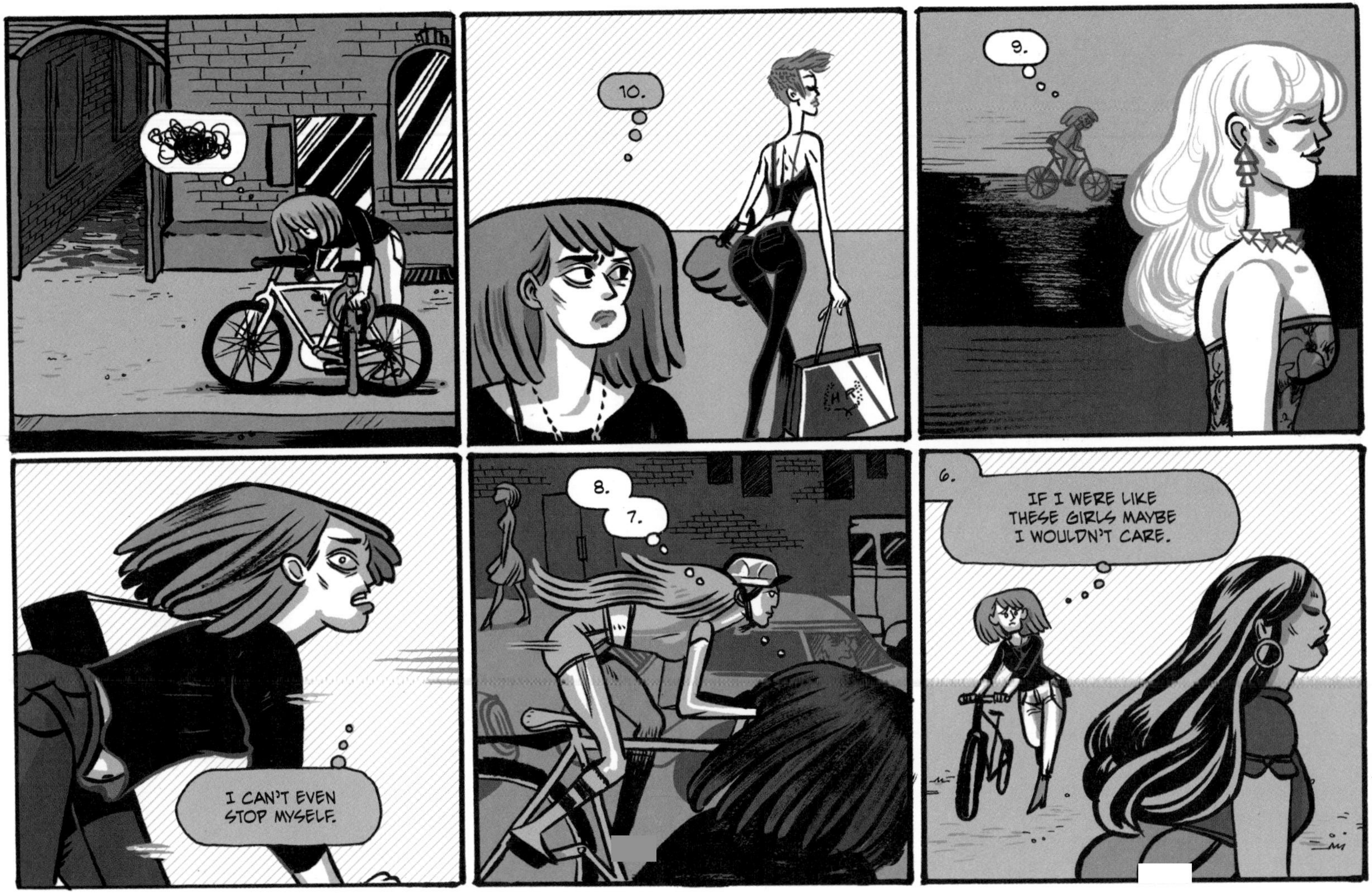
10.
9.
I CAN'T EVEN STOP MYSELF.
8.
7.
6.
IF I WERE LIKE THESE GIRLS MAYBE I WOULDN'T CARE.

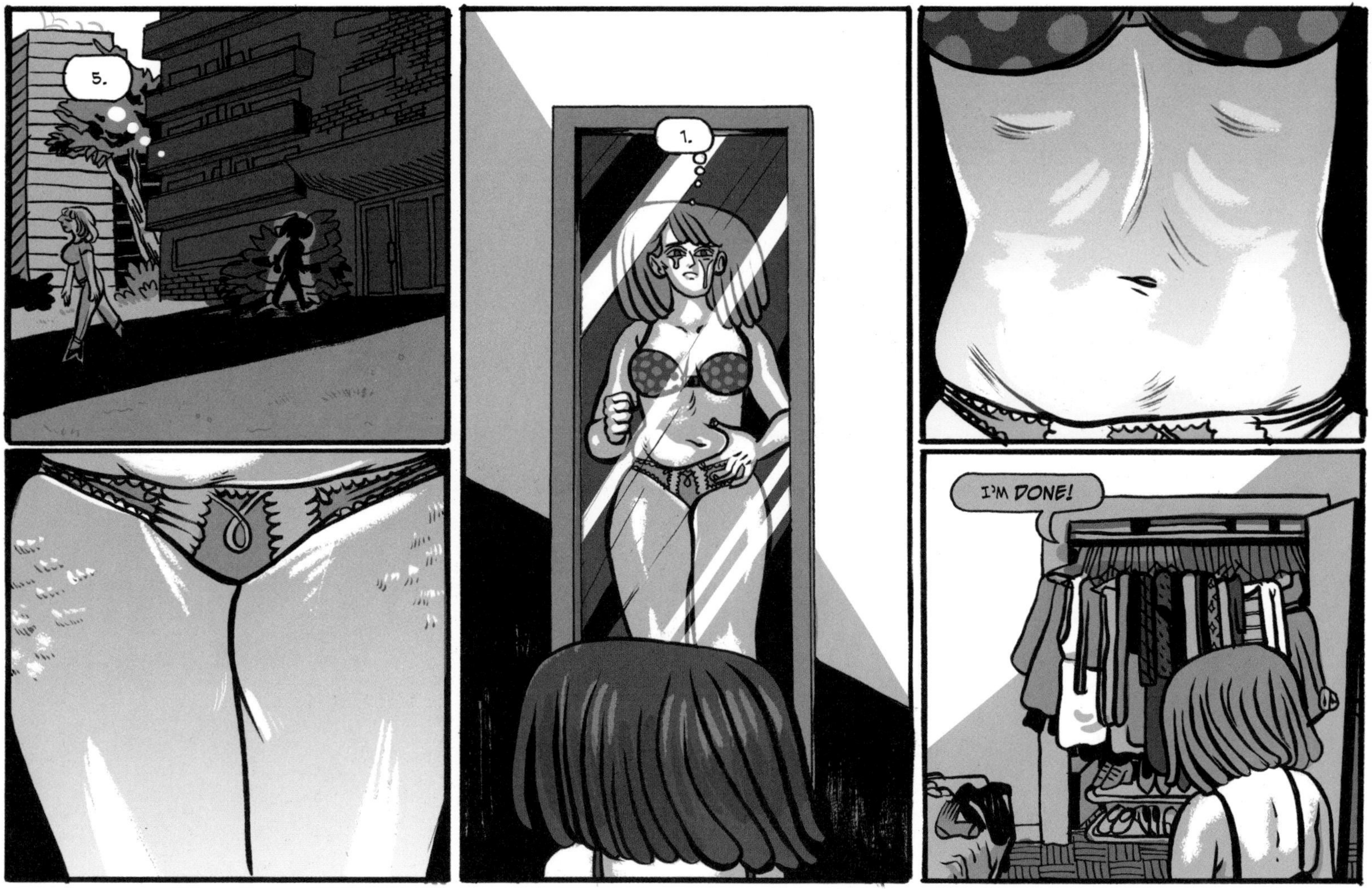
5.
1.
I'M DONE!

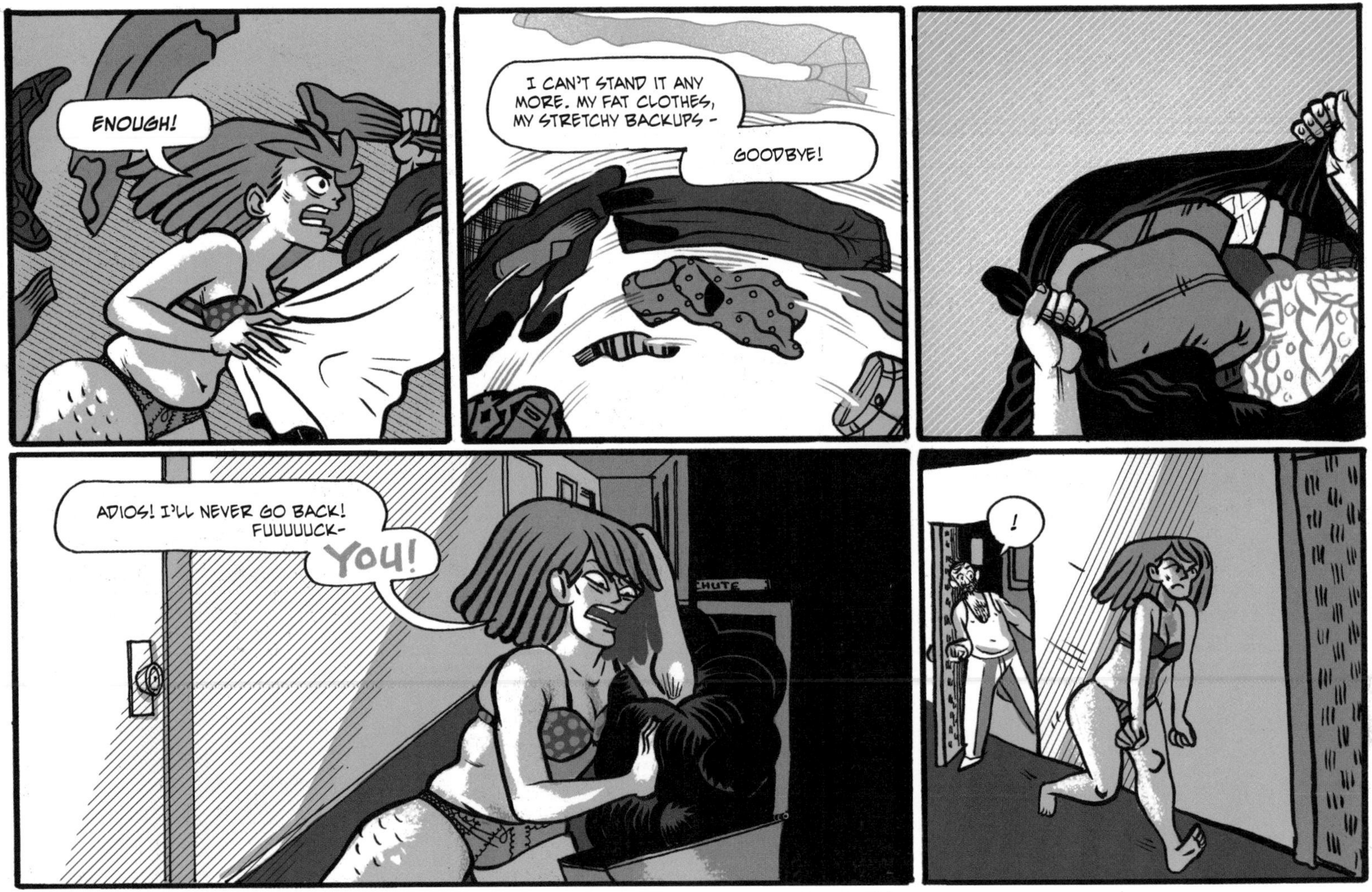
ENOUGH!
I CAN'T STAND IT ANY MORE. MY FAT CLOTHES, MY STRETCHY BACKUPS -
GOODBYE!
ADIOS! I'LL NEVER GO BACK! FUUUUUCK-
YOU!
CHUTE
!

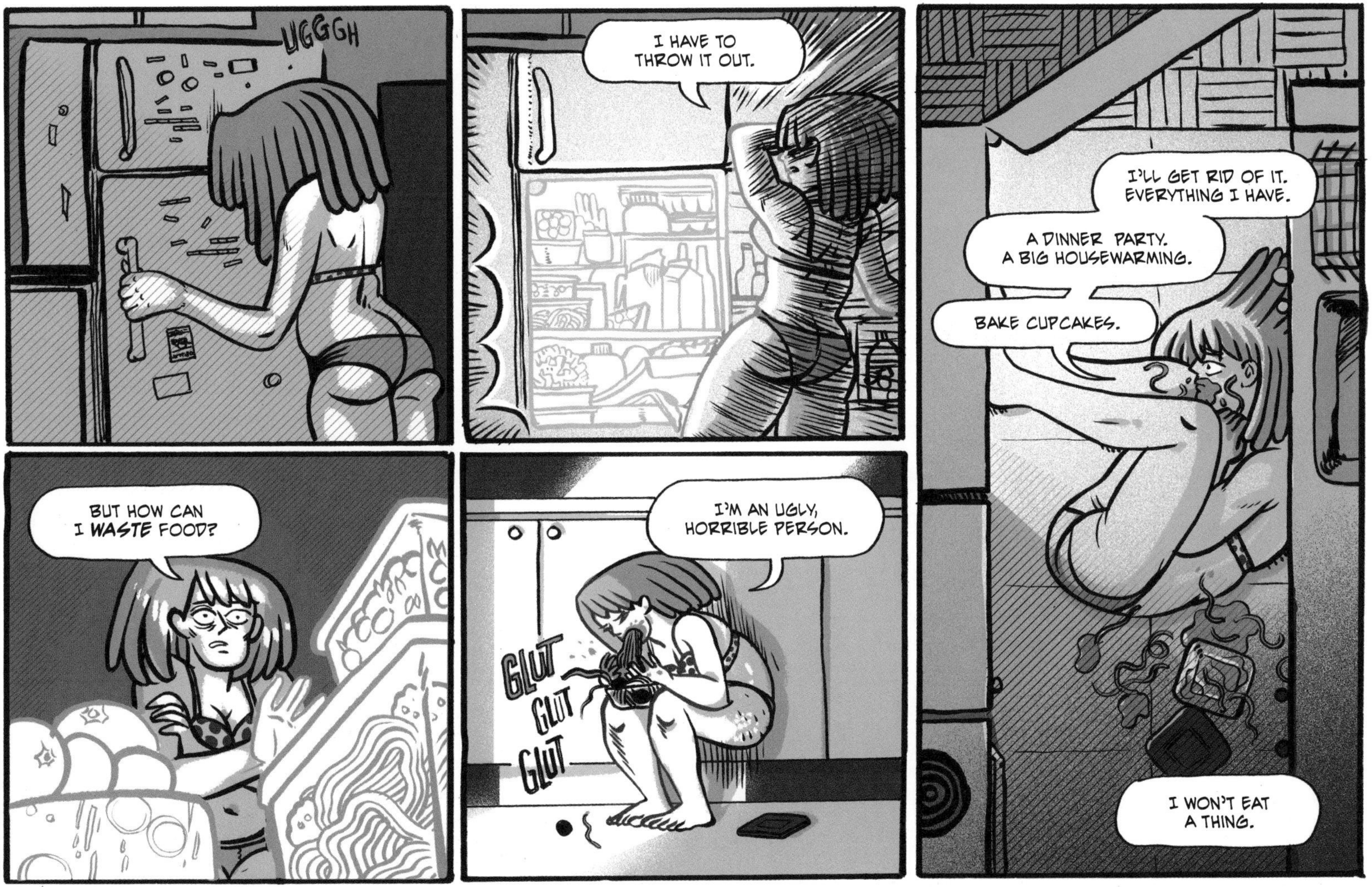
UGGGH
I HAVE TO THROW IT OUT.
I'LL GET RID OF IT. EVERYTHING I HAVE.
A DINNER PARTY. A BIG HOUSEWARMING.
BAKE CUPCAKES.
BUT HOW CAN I **WASTE** FOOD?
I'M AN UGLY, HORRIBLE PERSON.
GLUT GLUT GLUT
I WON'T EAT A THING.

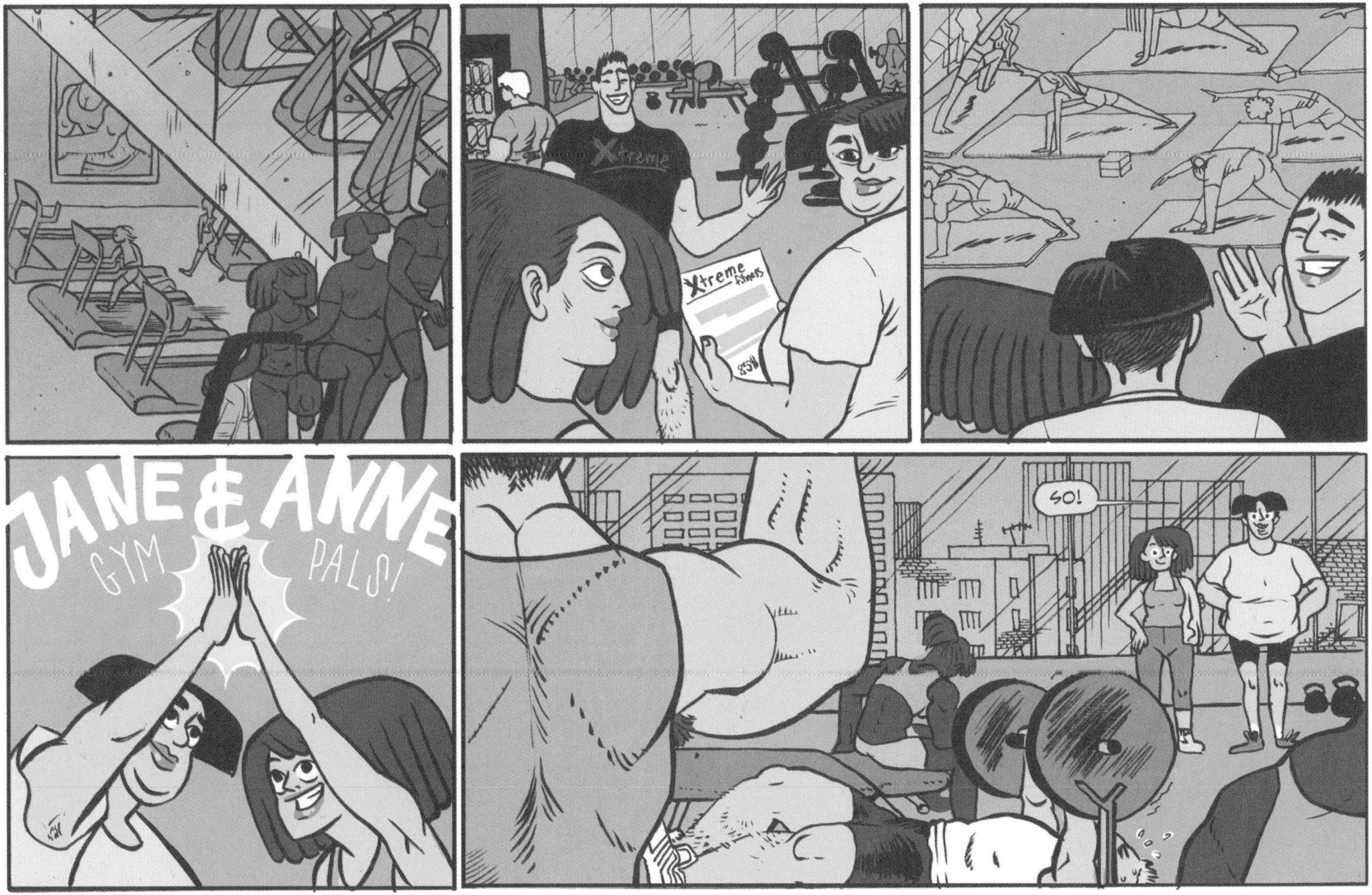

Xtreme fitness
JANE & ANNE
GYM PALS!
SO!

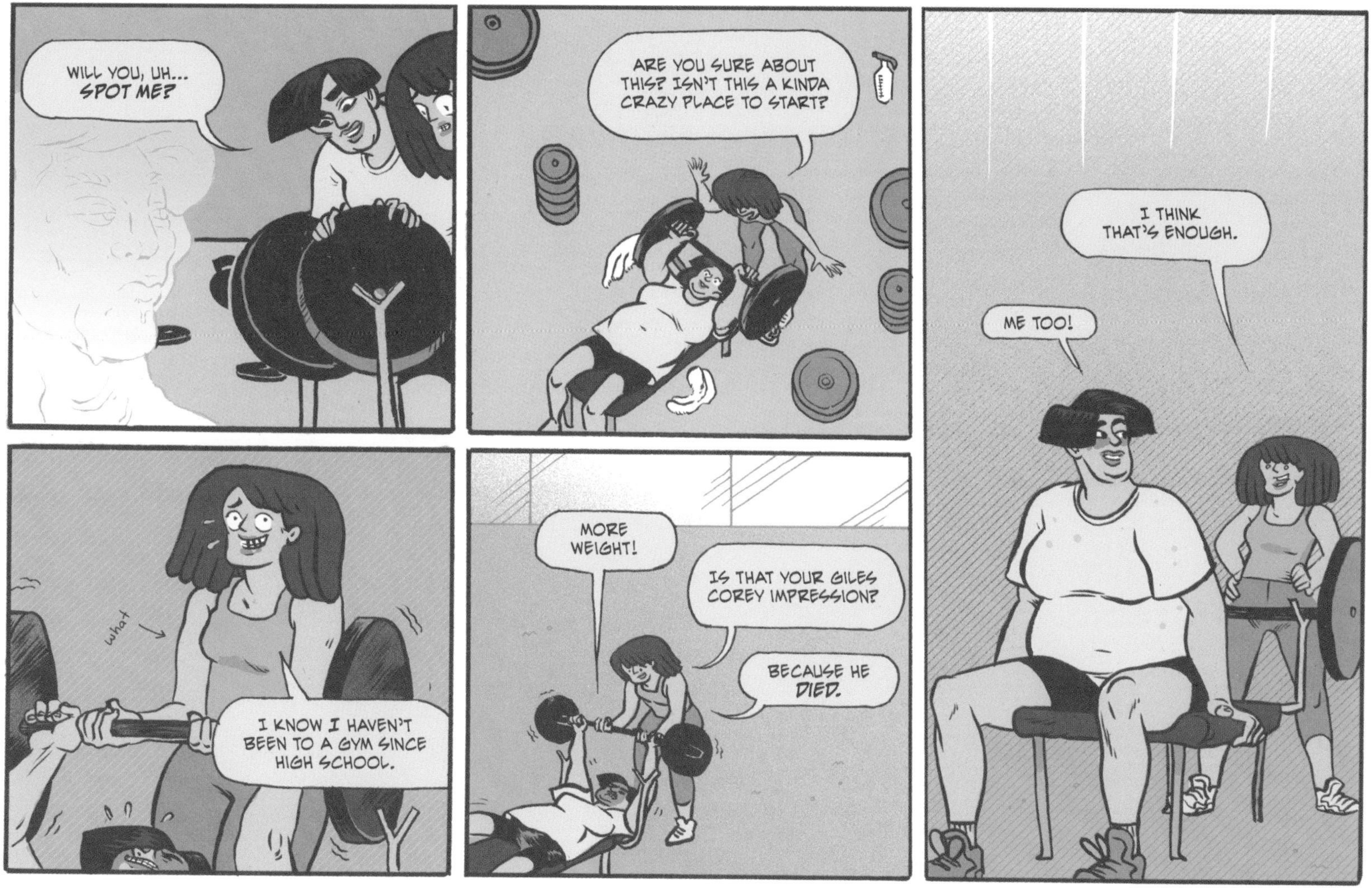
WILL YOU, UH... SPOT ME?
ARE YOU SURE ABOUT THIS? ISN'T THIS A KINDA CRAZY PLACE TO START?
what
I KNOW I HAVEN'T BEEN TO A GYM SINCE HIGH SCHOOL.
MORE WEIGHT!
IS THAT YOUR GILES COREY IMPRESSION?
BECAUSE HE DIED.
I THINK THAT'S ENOUGH.
ME TOO!

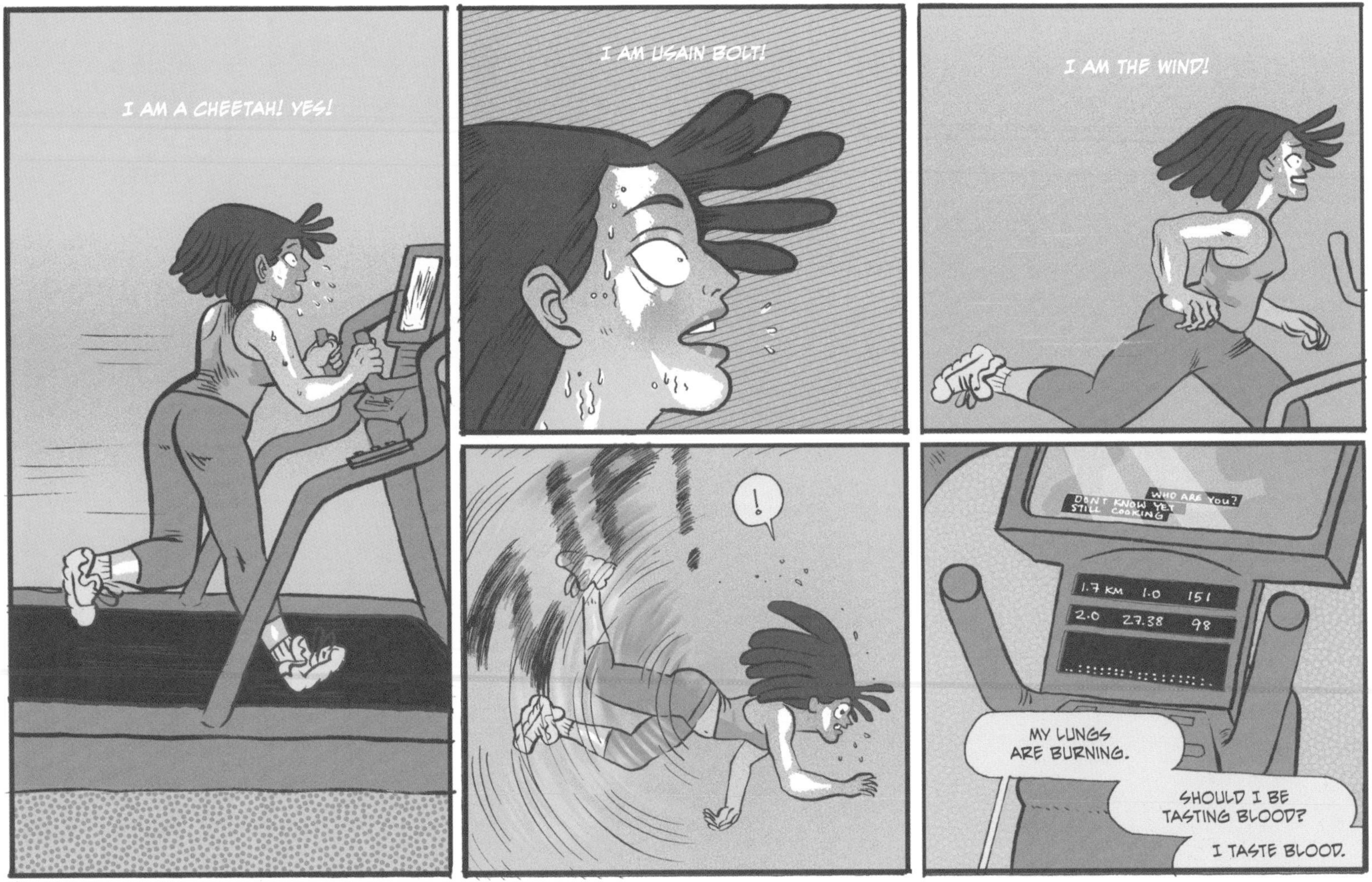
I AM A CHEETAH! YES!
I AM USAIN BOLT!
I AM THE WIND!
!
WHO ARE YOU?
DON'T KNOW YET
STILL COOKING
1.7 KM 1.0 151
2.0 27.38 98
MY LUNGS ARE BURNING.
SHOULD I BE TASTING BLOOD?
I TASTE BLOOD.

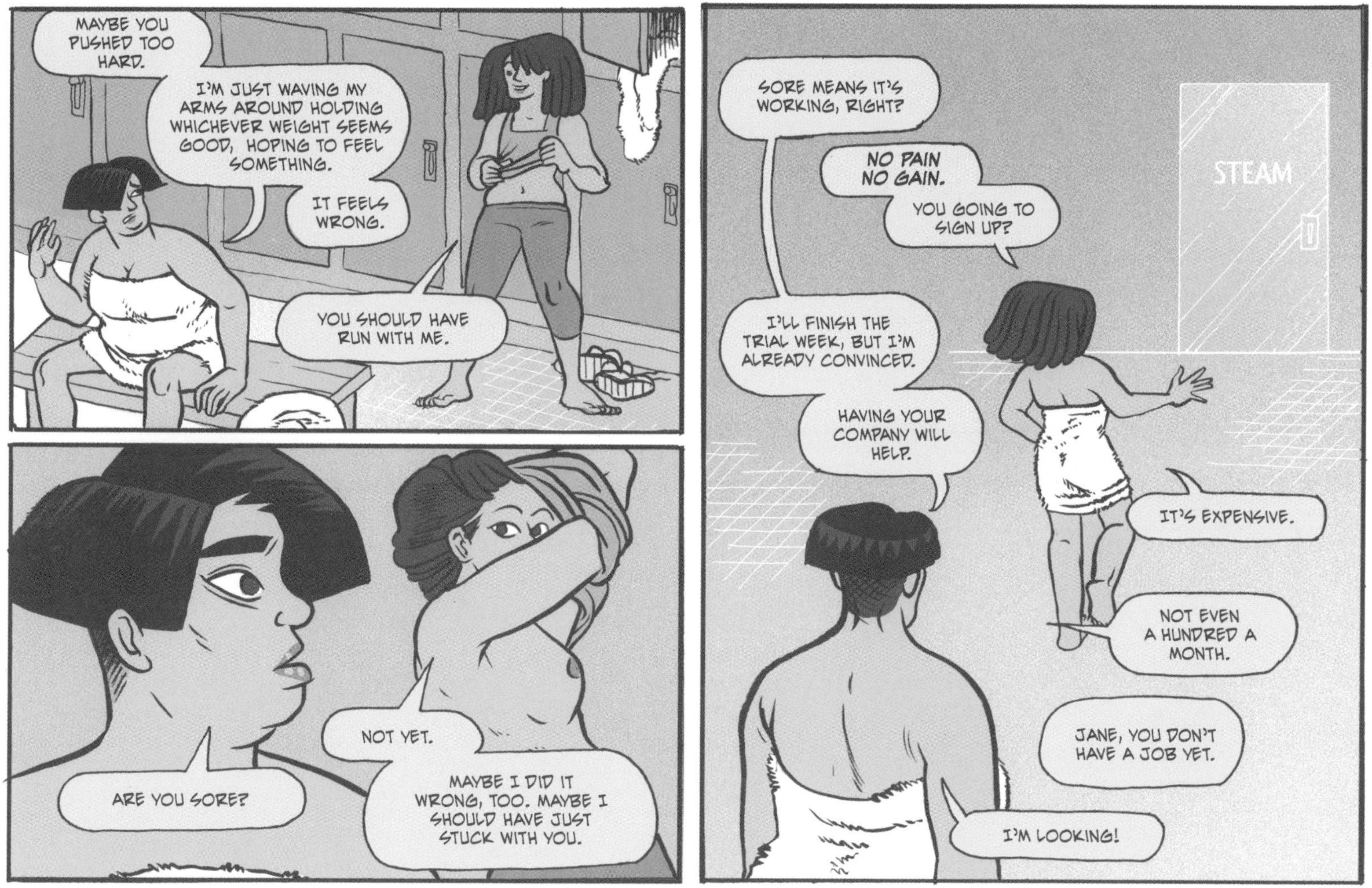
MAYBE YOU PUSHED TOO HARD.
I'M JUST WAVING MY ARMS AROUND HOLDING WHICHEVER WEIGHT SEEMS GOOD, HOPING TO FEEL SOMETHING.
IT FEELS WRONG.
YOU SHOULD HAVE RUN WITH ME.
ARE YOU SORE?
NOT YET.
MAYBE I DID IT WRONG, TOO. MAYBE I SHOULD HAVE JUST STUCK WITH YOU.
SORE MEANS IT'S WORKING, RIGHT?
NO PAIN NO GAIN.
YOU GOING TO SIGN UP?
STEAM
I'LL FINISH THE TRIAL WEEK, BUT I'M ALREADY CONVINCED.
HAVING YOUR COMPANY WILL HELP.
IT'S EXPENSIVE.
NOT EVEN A HUNDRED A MONTH.
JANE, YOU DON'T HAVE A JOB YET.
I'M LOOKING!

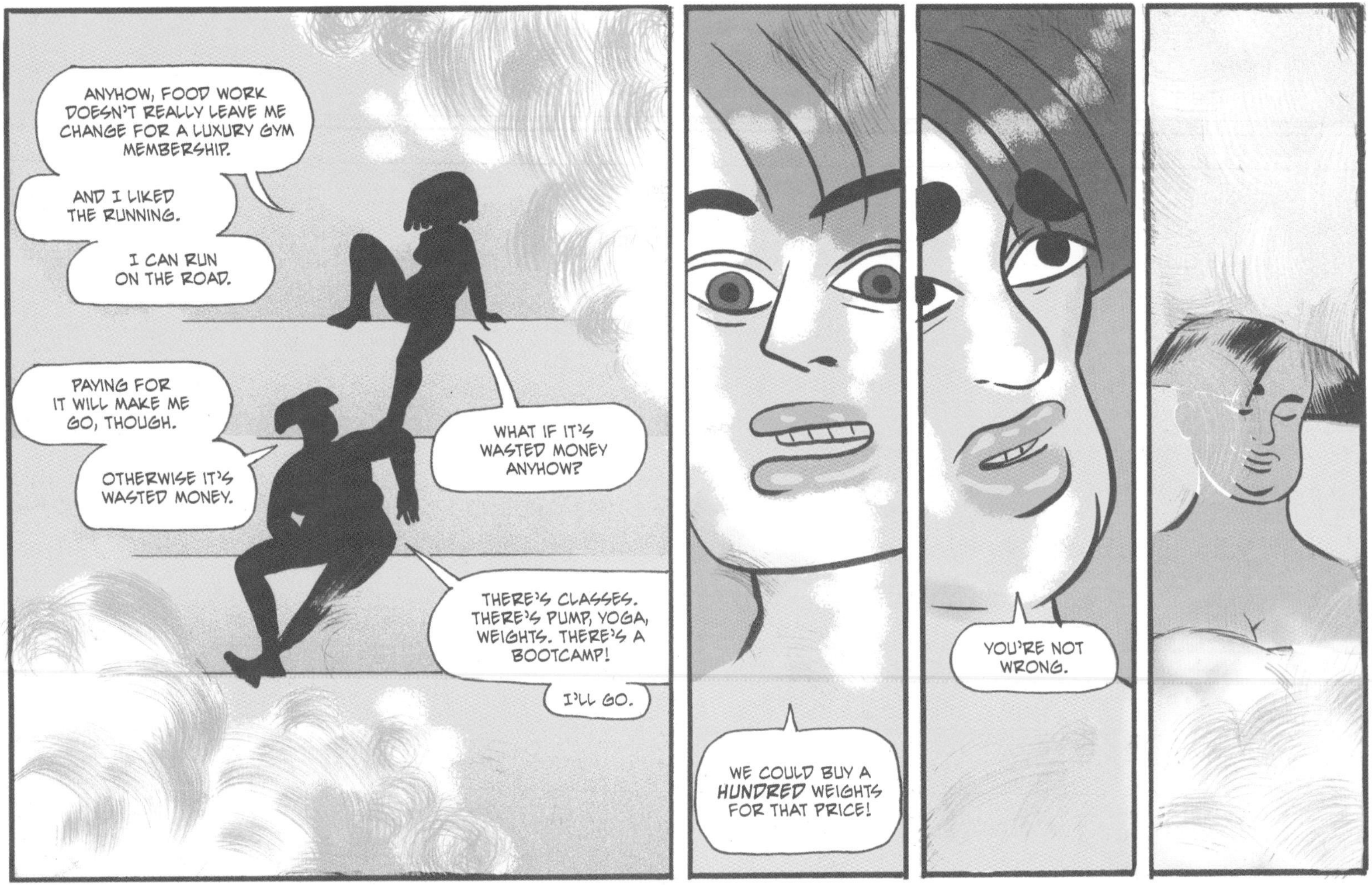
ANYHOW, FOOD WORK DOESN'T REALLY LEAVE ME CHANGE FOR A LUXURY GYM MEMBERSHIP.
AND I LIKED THE RUNNING.
I CAN RUN ON THE ROAD.
PAYING FOR IT WILL MAKE ME GO, THOUGH.
OTHERWISE IT'S WASTED MONEY.
WHAT IF IT'S WASTED MONEY ANYHOW?
THERE'S CLASSES. THERE'S PUMP, YOGA, WEIGHTS. THERE'S A BOOTCAMP!
I'LL GO.
WE COULD BUY A ***HUNDRED*** WEIGHTS FOR THAT PRICE!
YOU'RE NOT WRONG.

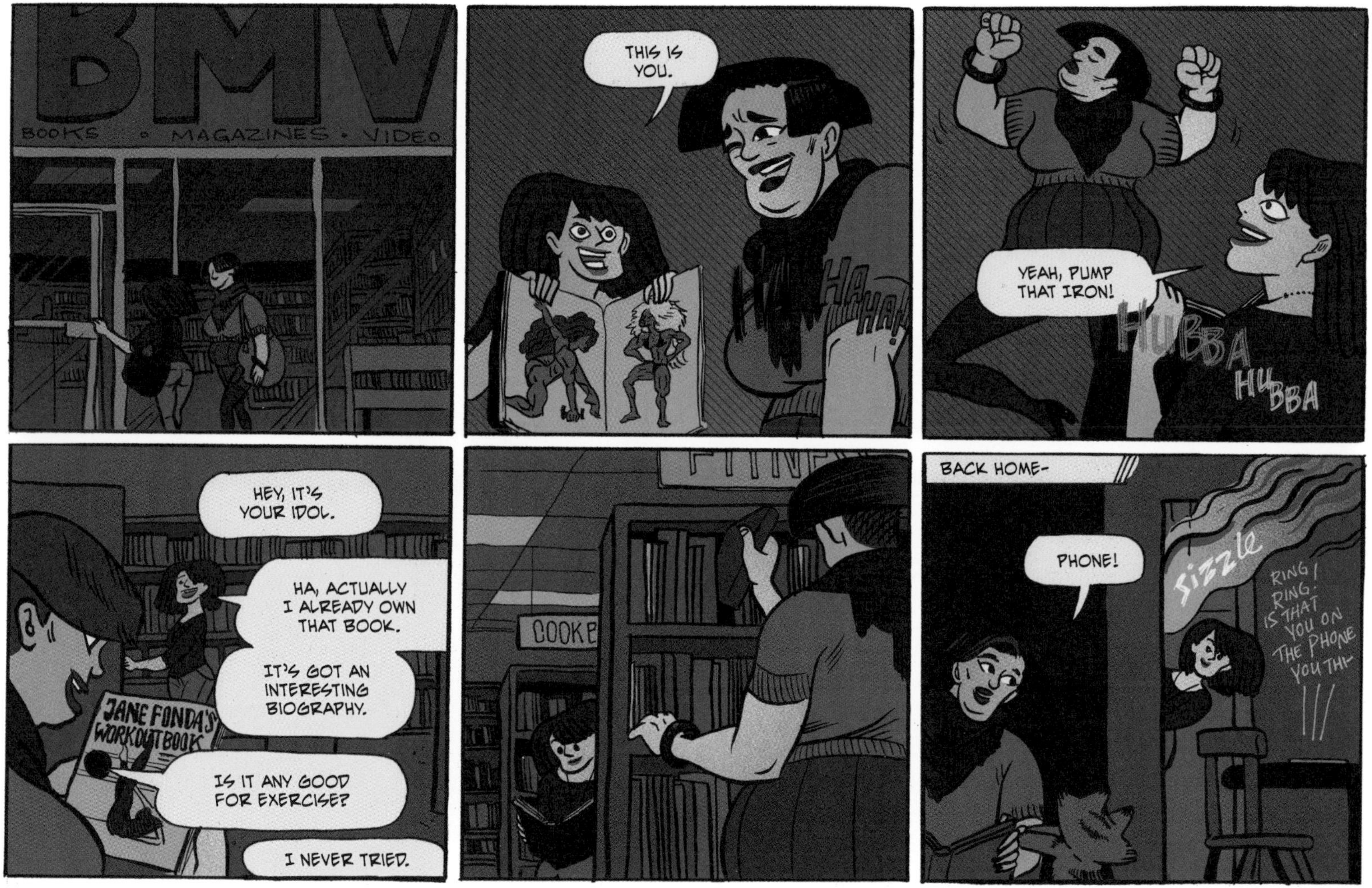
BMV
BOOKS • MAGAZINES • VIDEO
THIS IS YOU.
HA HA HA!
YEAH, PUMP THAT IRON!
HUBBA HUBBA
HEY, IT'S YOUR IDOL.
HA, ACTUALLY I ALREADY OWN THAT BOOK.
IT'S GOT AN INTERESTING BIOGRAPHY.
JANE FONDA'S WORKOUT BOOK
IS IT ANY GOOD FOR EXERCISE?
I NEVER TRIED.
COOKB
BACK HOME-
PHONE!
sizzle
RING! RING! IS THAT YOU ON THE PHONE YOU THI-

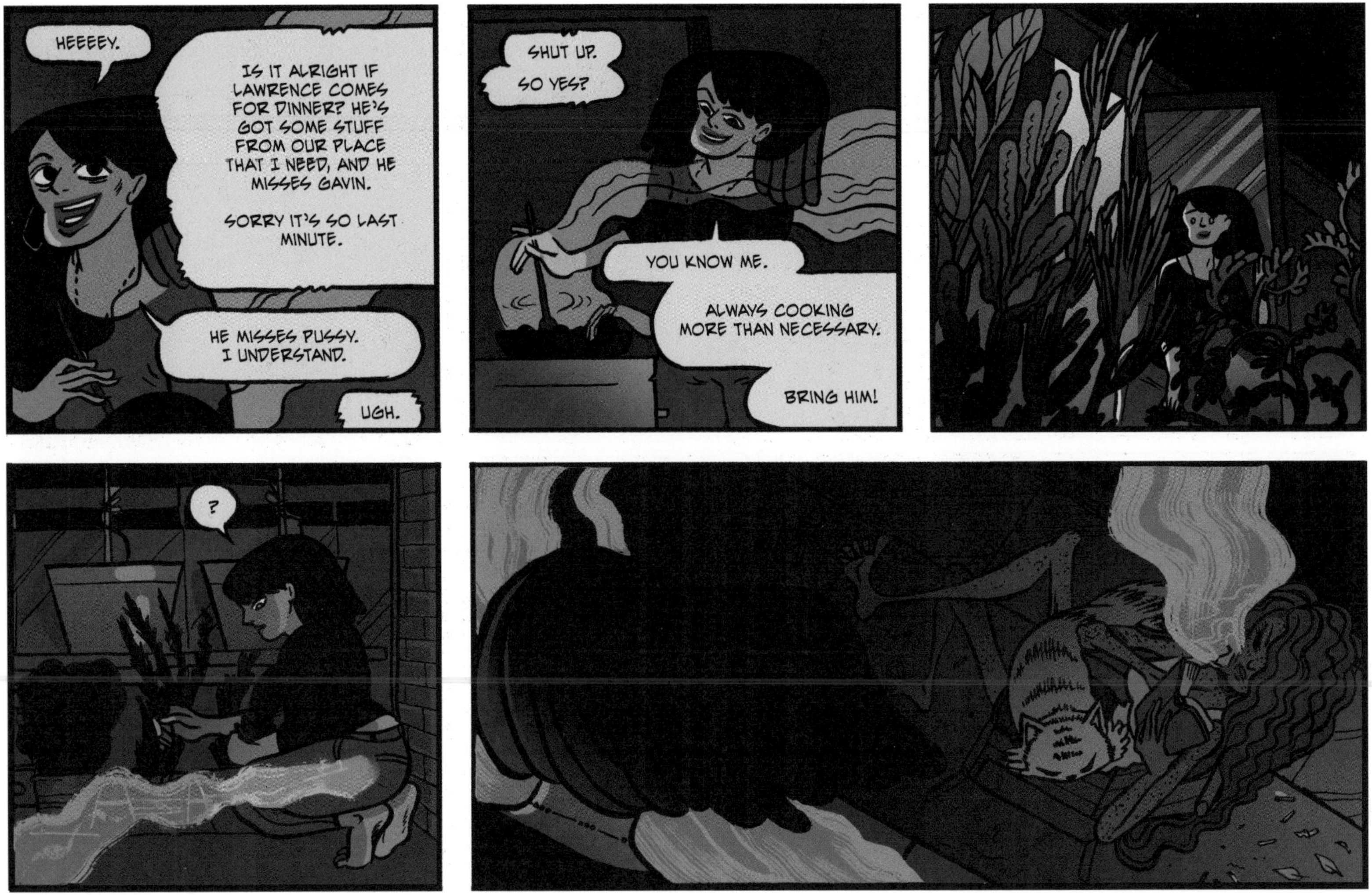
HEEEEY.
IS IT ALRIGHT IF LAWRENCE COMES FOR DINNER? HE'S GOT SOME STUFF FROM OUR PLACE THAT I NEED, AND HE MISSES GAVIN.
SORRY IT'S SO LAST MINUTE.
HE MISSES PUSSY. I UNDERSTAND.
UGH.
SHUT UP.
SO YES?
YOU KNOW ME.
ALWAYS COOKING MORE THAN NECESSARY.
BRING HIM!
?

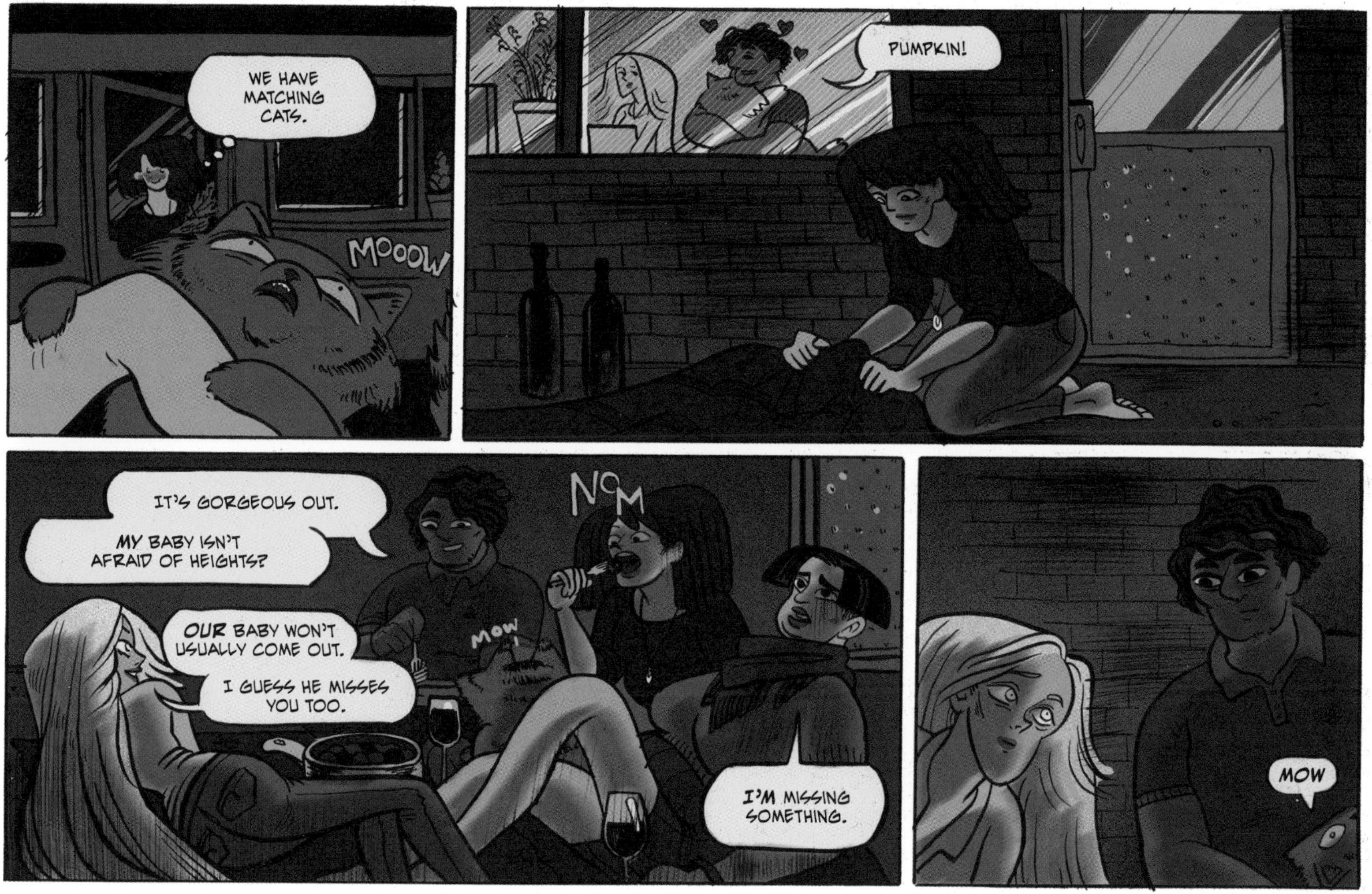
WE HAVE MATCHING CATS.
MOOOW
PUMPKIN!
IT'S GORGEOUS OUT.
MY BABY ISN'T AFRAID OF HEIGHTS?
NOM
MOW
OUR BABY WON'T USUALLY COME OUT.
I GUESS HE MISSES YOU TOO.
I'M MISSING SOMETHING.
MOW

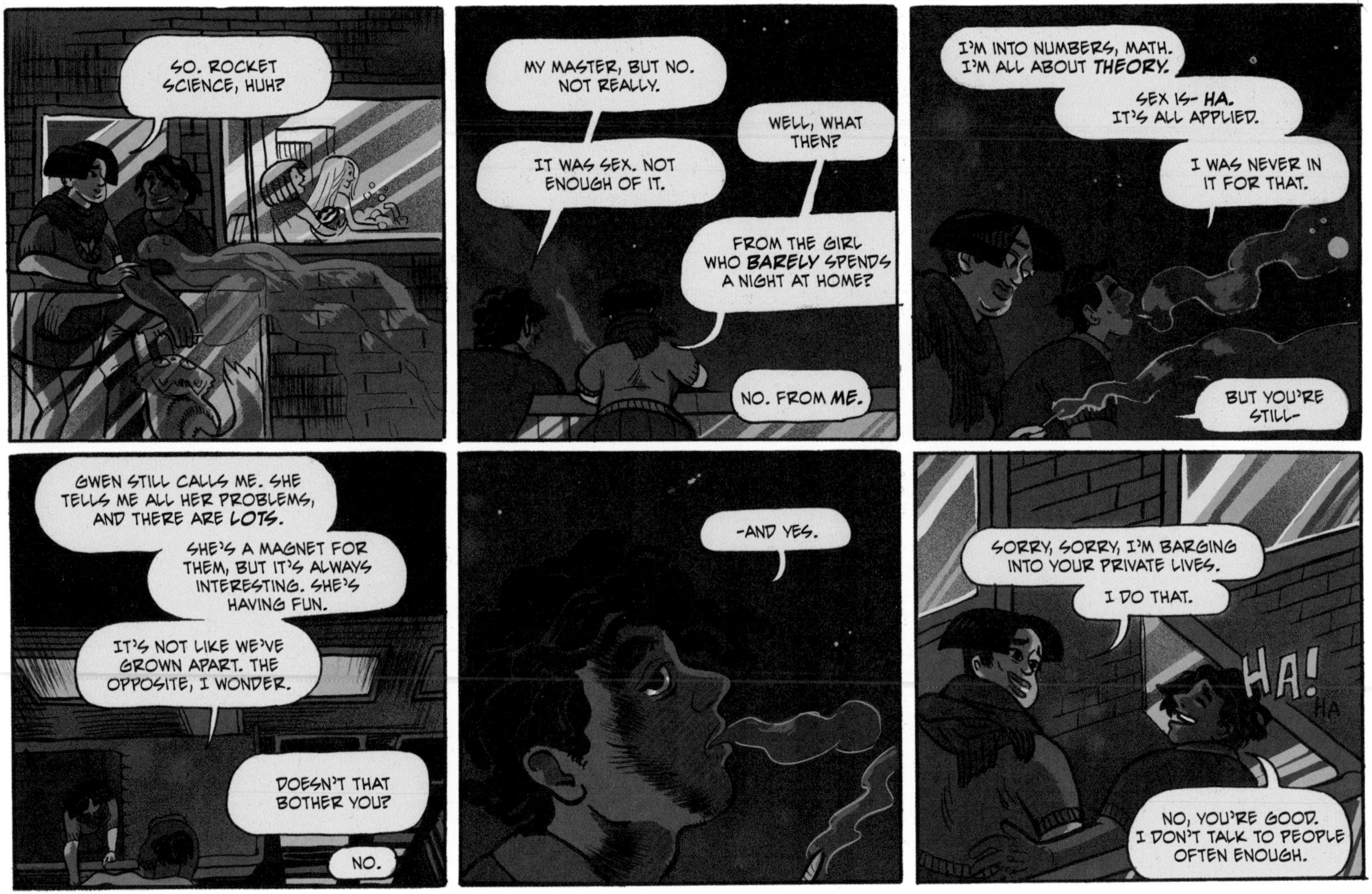
SO. ROCKET SCIENCE, HUH?
MY MASTER, BUT NO. NOT REALLY.
IT WAS SEX. NOT ENOUGH OF IT.
WELL, WHAT THEN?
FROM THE GIRL WHO BARELY SPENDS A NIGHT AT HOME?
NO. FROM ME.
I'M INTO NUMBERS, MATH. I'M ALL ABOUT THEORY.
SEX IS- HA. IT'S ALL APPLIED.
I WAS NEVER IN IT FOR THAT.
BUT YOU'RE STILL-
GWEN STILL CALLS ME. SHE TELLS ME ALL HER PROBLEMS, AND THERE ARE LOTS.
SHE'S A MAGNET FOR THEM, BUT IT'S ALWAYS INTERESTING. SHE'S HAVING FUN.
IT'S NOT LIKE WE'VE GROWN APART. THE OPPOSITE, I WONDER.
DOESN'T THAT BOTHER YOU?
NO.
-AND YES.
SORRY, SORRY, I'M BARGING INTO YOUR PRIVATE LIVES.
I DO THAT.
HA! HA
NO, YOU'RE GOOD. I DON'T TALK TO PEOPLE OFTEN ENOUGH.

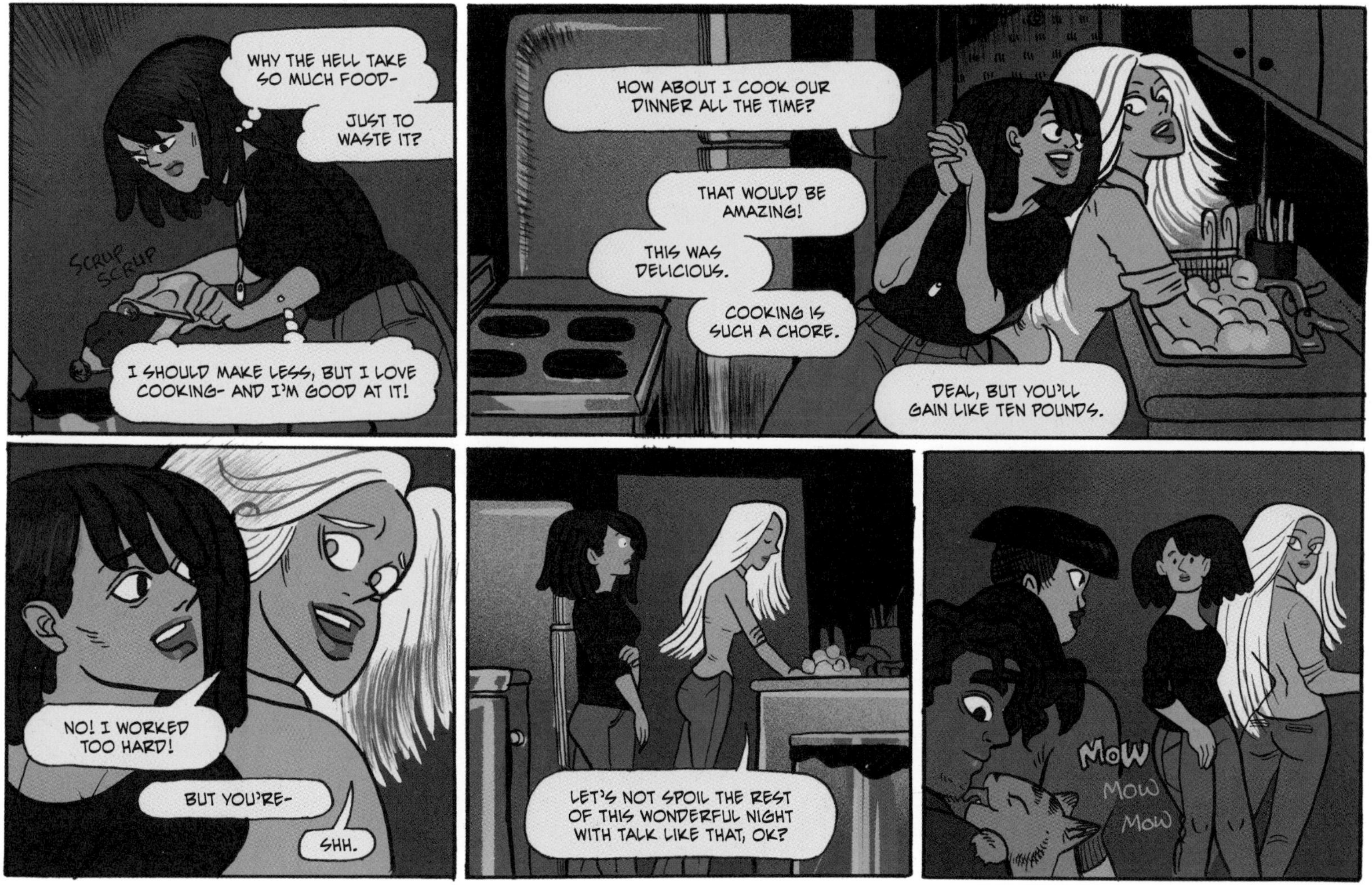
WHY THE HELL TAKE SO MUCH FOOD-
JUST TO WASTE IT?
SCRUP SCRUP
I SHOULD MAKE LESS, BUT I LOVE COOKING- AND I'M GOOD AT IT!
HOW ABOUT I COOK OUR DINNER ALL THE TIME?
THAT WOULD BE AMAZING!
THIS WAS DELICIOUS.
COOKING IS SUCH A CHORE.
DEAL, BUT YOU'LL GAIN LIKE TEN POUNDS.
NO! I WORKED TOO HARD!
BUT YOU'RE-
SHH.
LET'S NOT SPOIL THE REST OF THIS WONDERFUL NIGHT WITH TALK LIKE THAT, OK?
MOW
MOW
MOW

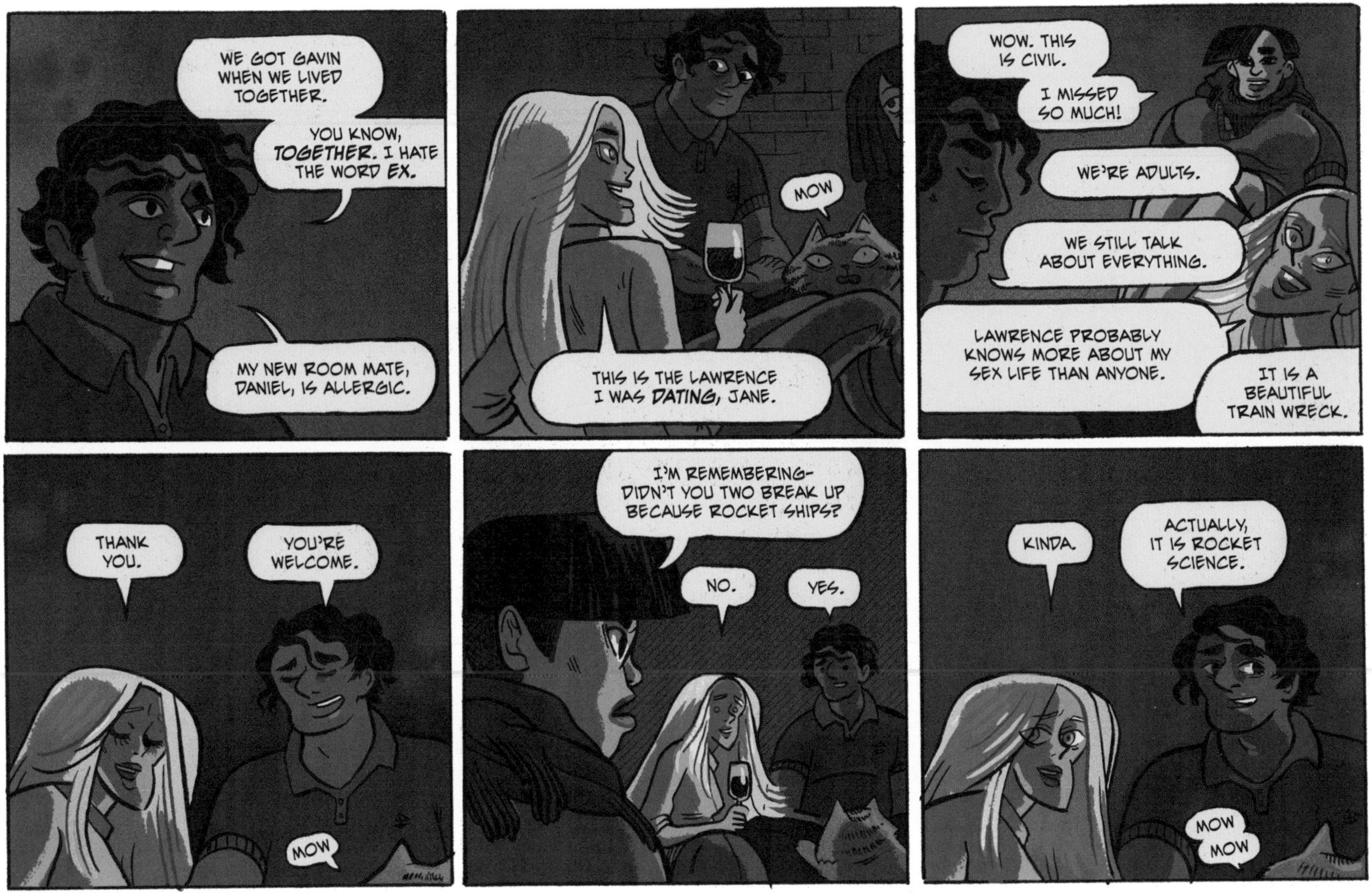
WE GOT GAVIN WHEN WE LIVED TOGETHER.
YOU KNOW, TOGETHER. I HATE THE WORD EX.
MY NEW ROOM MATE, DANIEL, IS ALLERGIC.
MOW
THIS IS THE LAWRENCE I WAS DATING, JANE.
WOW. THIS IS CIVIL.
I MISSED SO MUCH!
WE'RE ADULTS.
WE STILL TALK ABOUT EVERYTHING.
LAWRENCE PROBABLY KNOWS MORE ABOUT MY SEX LIFE THAN ANYONE.
IT IS A BEAUTIFUL TRAIN WRECK.
THANK YOU.
YOU'RE WELCOME.
MOW
I'M REMEMBERING- DIDN'T YOU TWO BREAK UP BECAUSE ROCKET SHIPS?
NO.
YES.
KINDA.
ACTUALLY, IT IS ROCKET SCIENCE.
MOW MOW

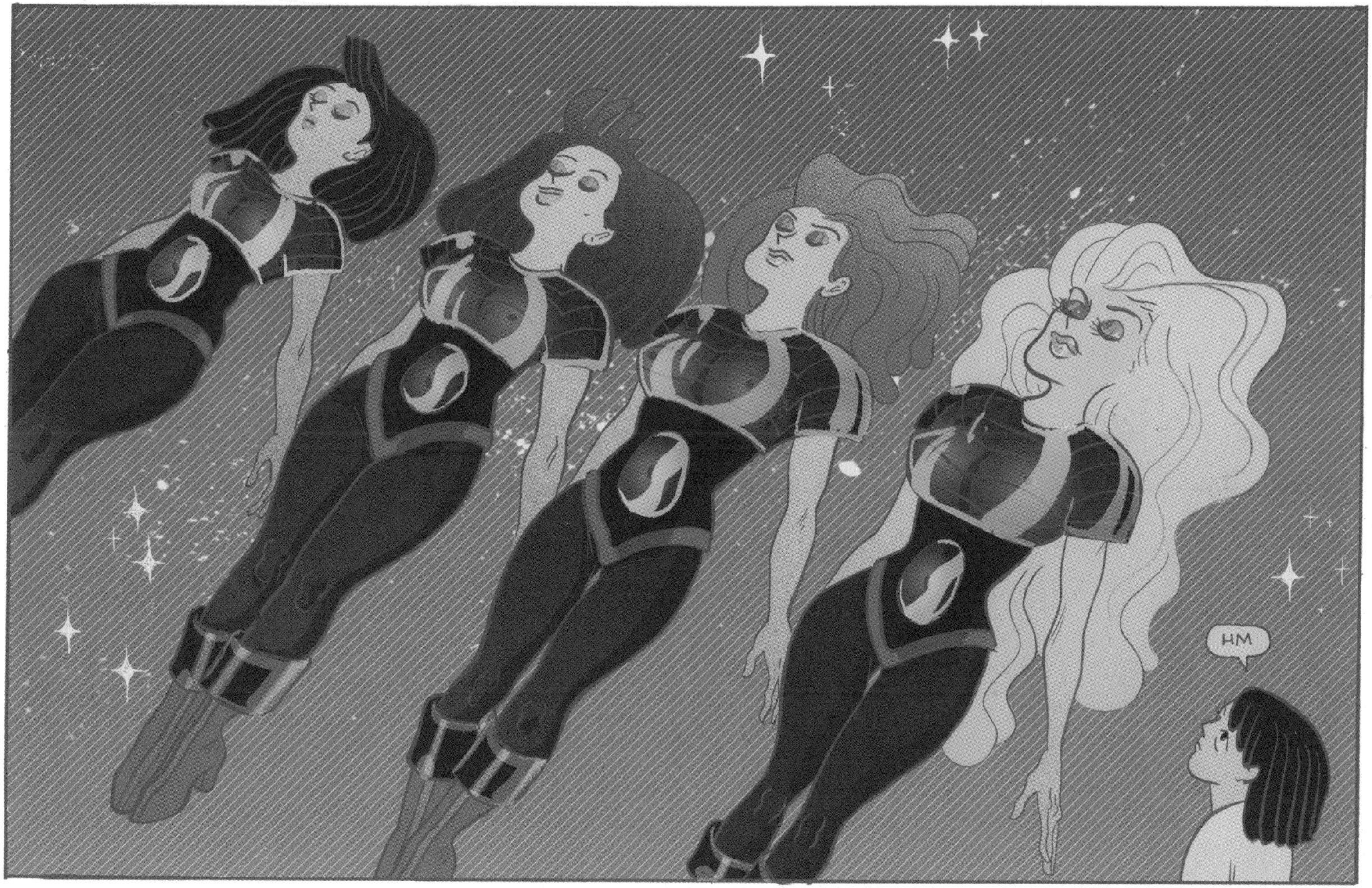
HM

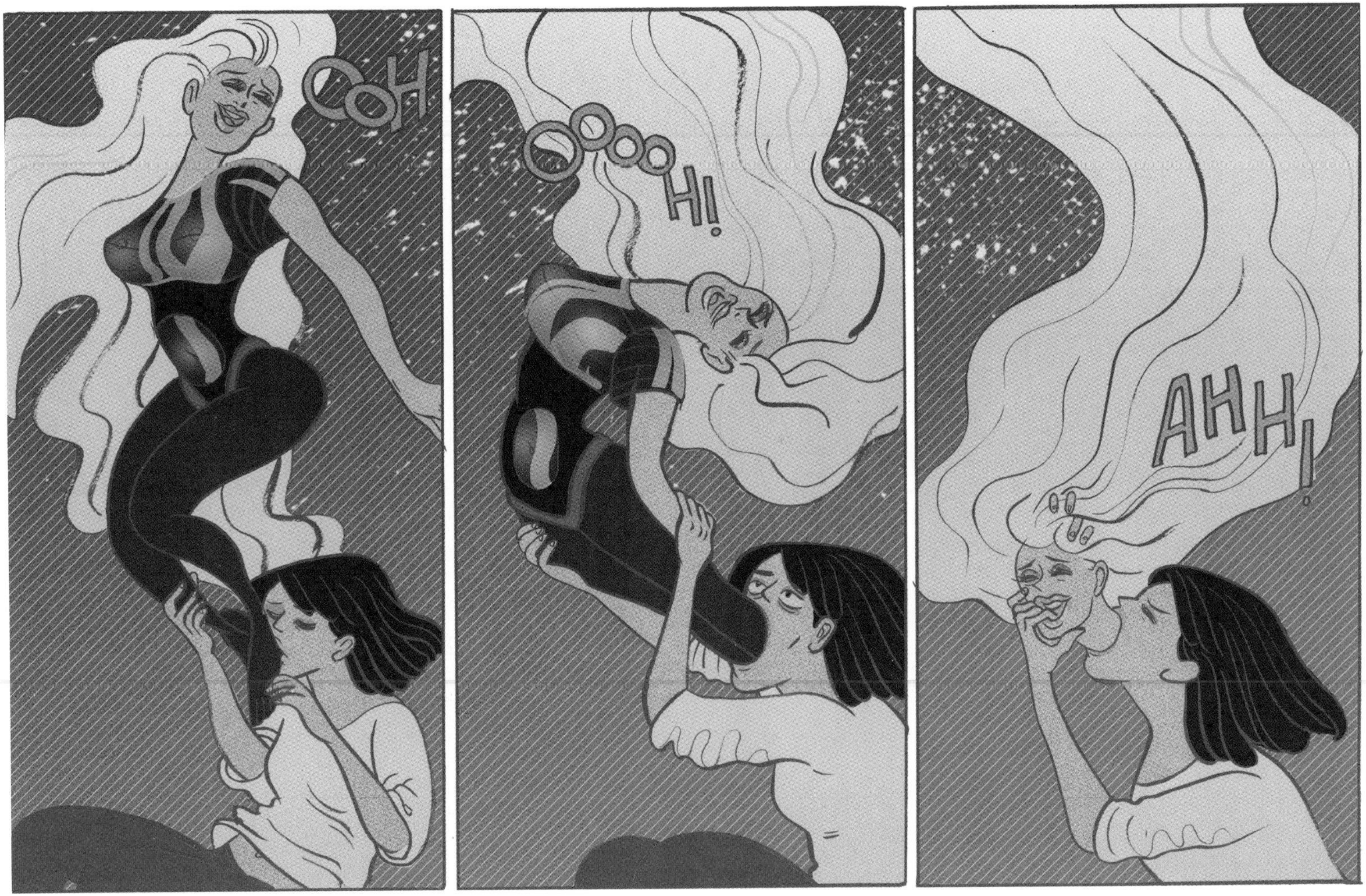
OOH
OOOOOH!
AHH!

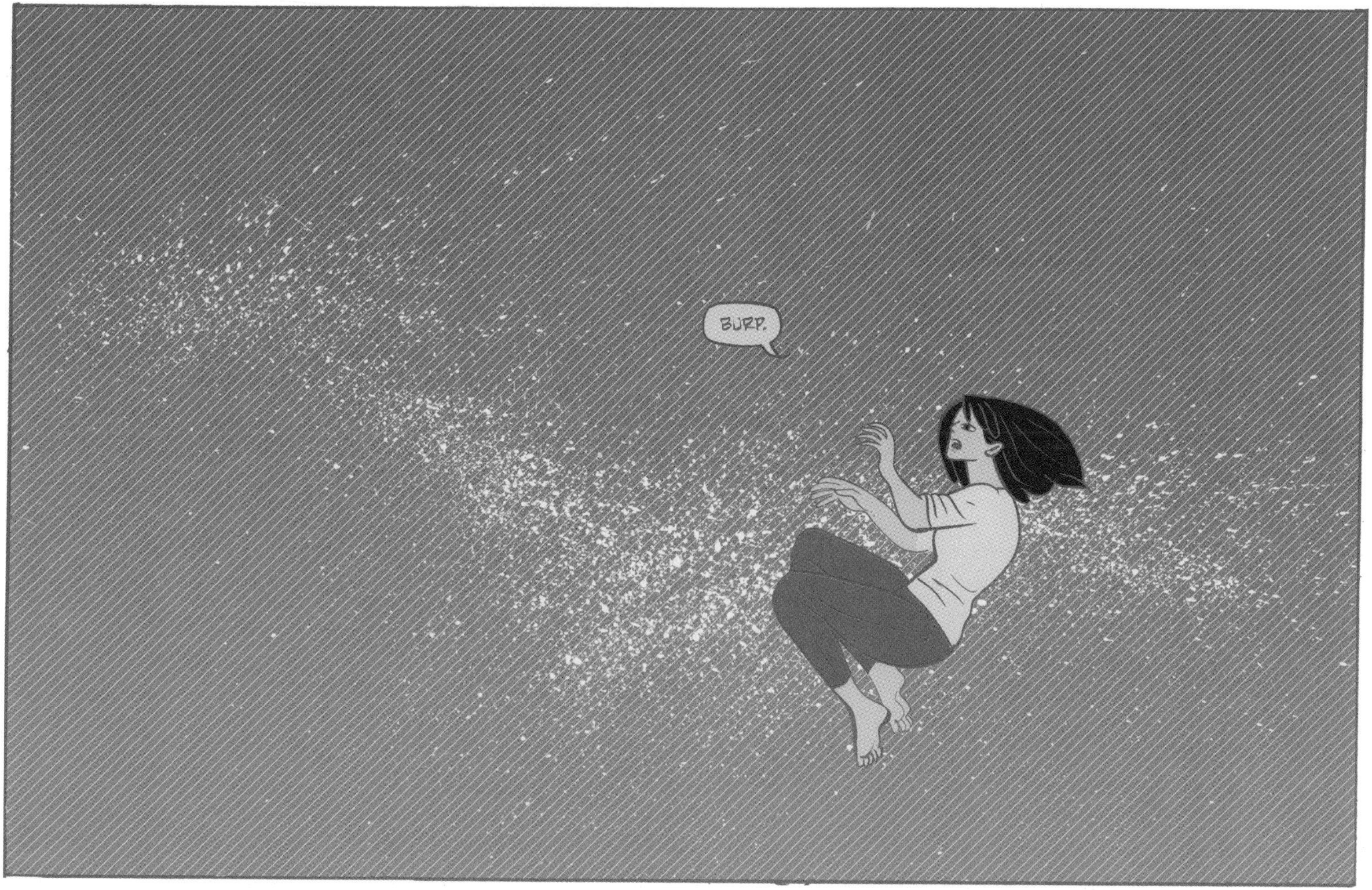
BURP.

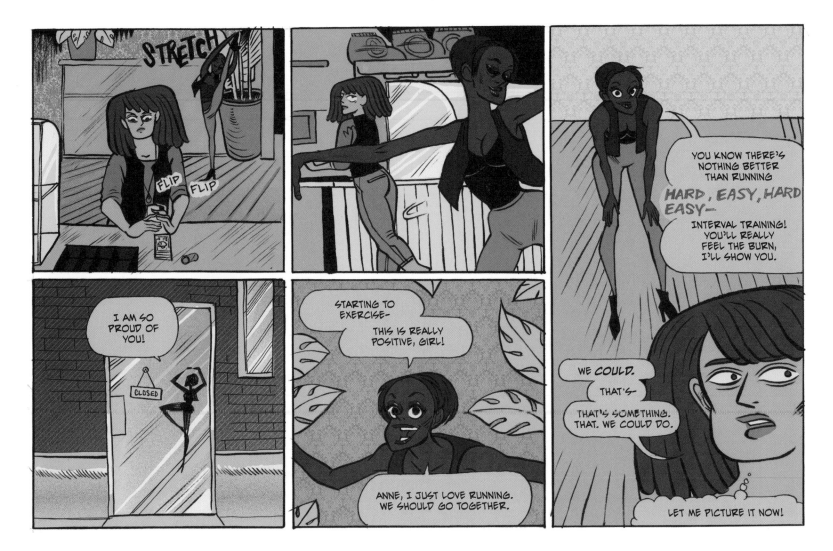

STRETCH

FLIP FLIP

I AM SO PROUD OF YOU!

CLOSED

STARTING TO EXERCISE—

THIS IS REALLY POSITIVE, GIRL!

ANNE, I JUST LOVE RUNNING. WE SHOULD GO TOGETHER.

YOU KNOW THERE'S NOTHING BETTER THAN RUNNING *HARD, EASY, HARD EASY—*

INTERVAL TRAINING! YOU'LL REALLY FEEL THE BURN, I'LL SHOW YOU.

WE *COULD.*

THAT'S—

THAT'S SOMETHING. THAT. WE COULD DO.

LET ME PICTURE IT NOW!

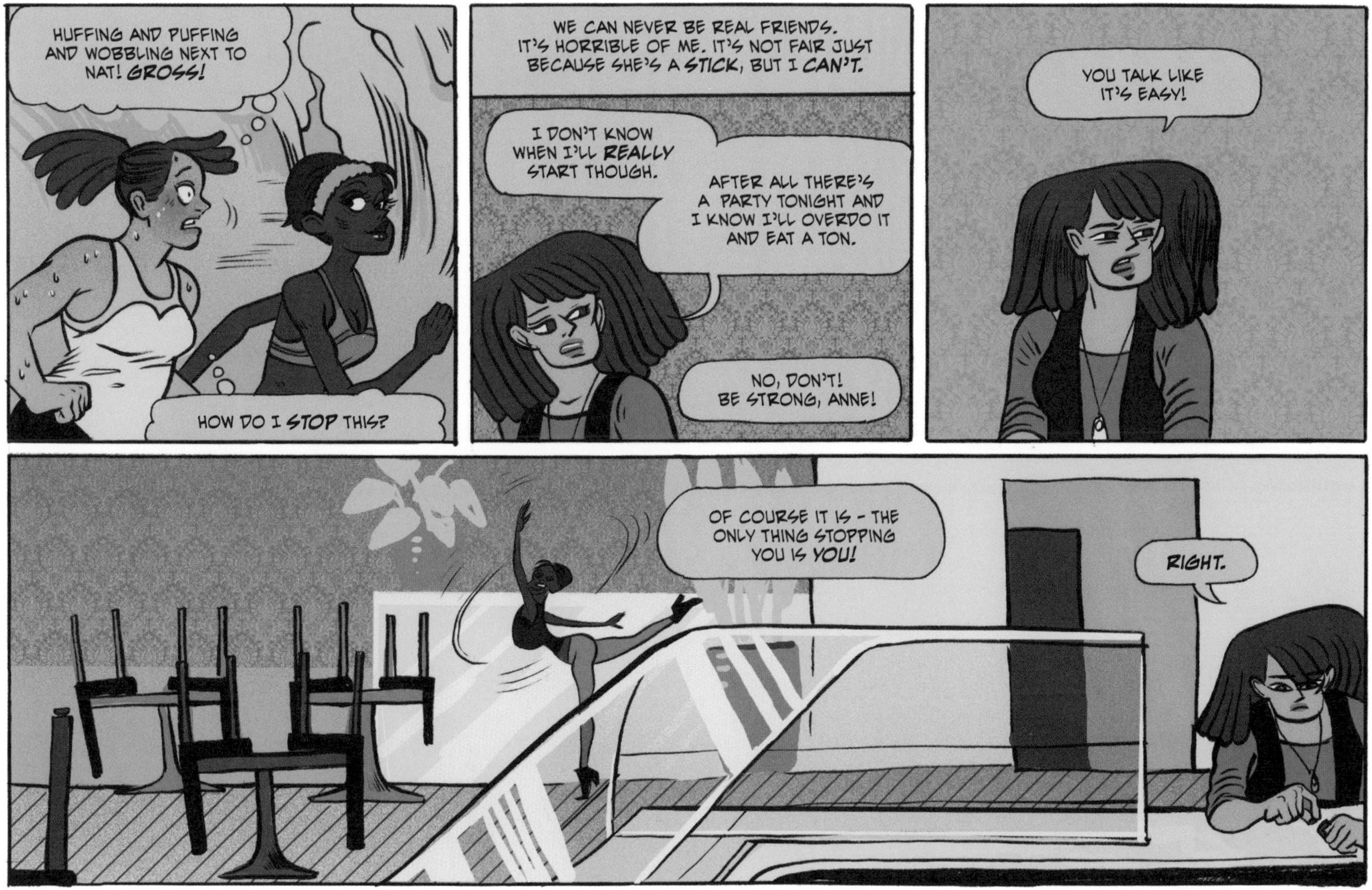
HUFFING AND PUFFING AND WOBBLING NEXT TO NAT! GROSS!
HOW DO I STOP THIS?
WE CAN NEVER BE REAL FRIENDS. IT'S HORRIBLE OF ME. IT'S NOT FAIR JUST BECAUSE SHE'S A STICK, BUT I CAN'T.
I DON'T KNOW WHEN I'LL REALLY START THOUGH.
AFTER ALL THERE'S A PARTY TONIGHT AND I KNOW I'LL OVERDO IT AND EAT A TON.
NO, DON'T! BE STRONG, ANNE!
YOU TALK LIKE IT'S EASY!
OF COURSE IT IS - THE ONLY THING STOPPING YOU IS YOU!
RIGHT.

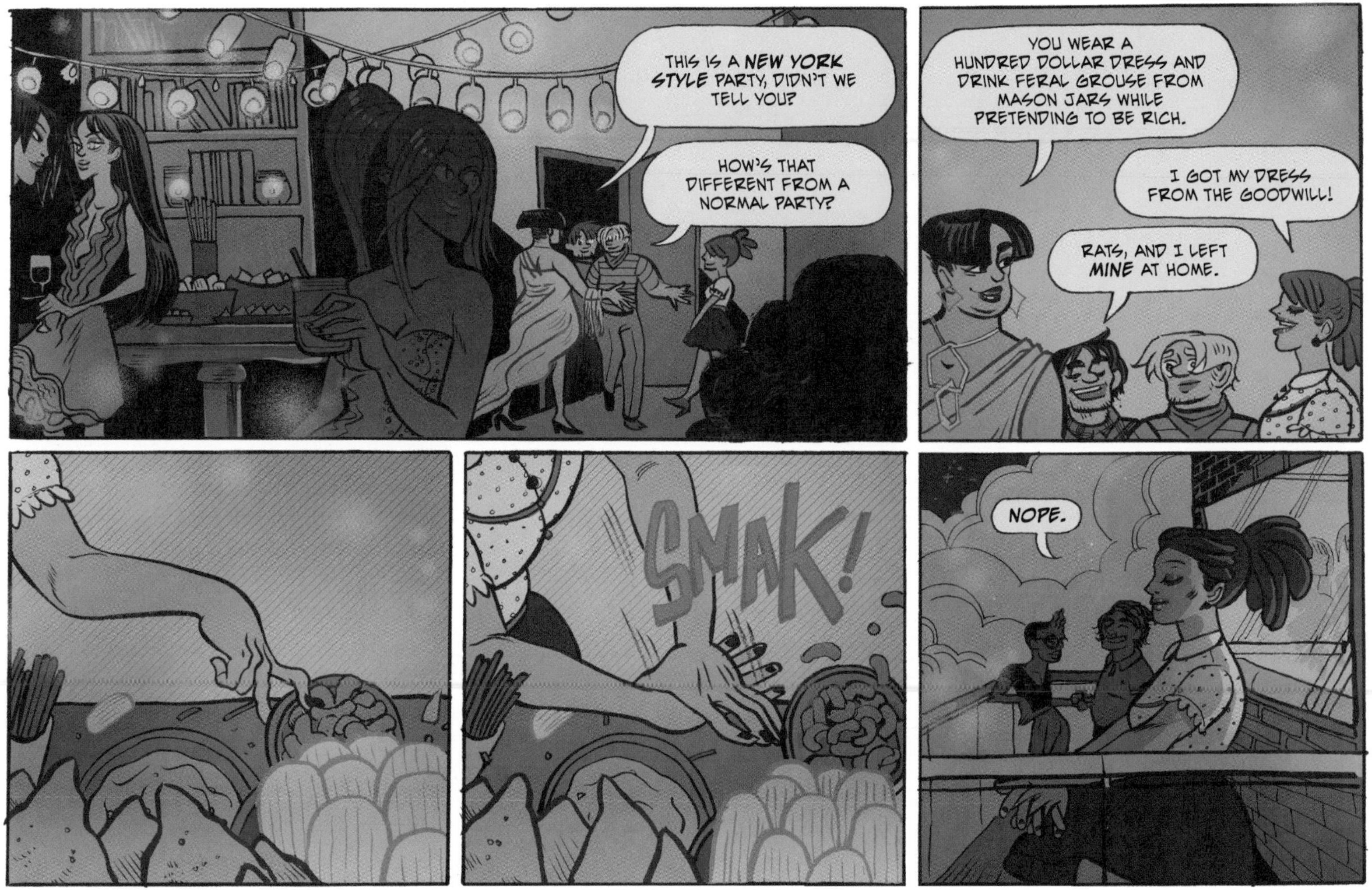
THIS IS A NEW YORK STYLE PARTY, DIDN'T WE TELL YOU?
HOW'S THAT DIFFERENT FROM A NORMAL PARTY?
YOU WEAR A HUNDRED DOLLAR DRESS AND DRINK FERAL GROUSE FROM MASON JARS WHILE PRETENDING TO BE RICH.
I GOT MY DRESS FROM THE GOODWILL!
RATS, AND I LEFT MINE AT HOME.
SMAK!
NOPE.

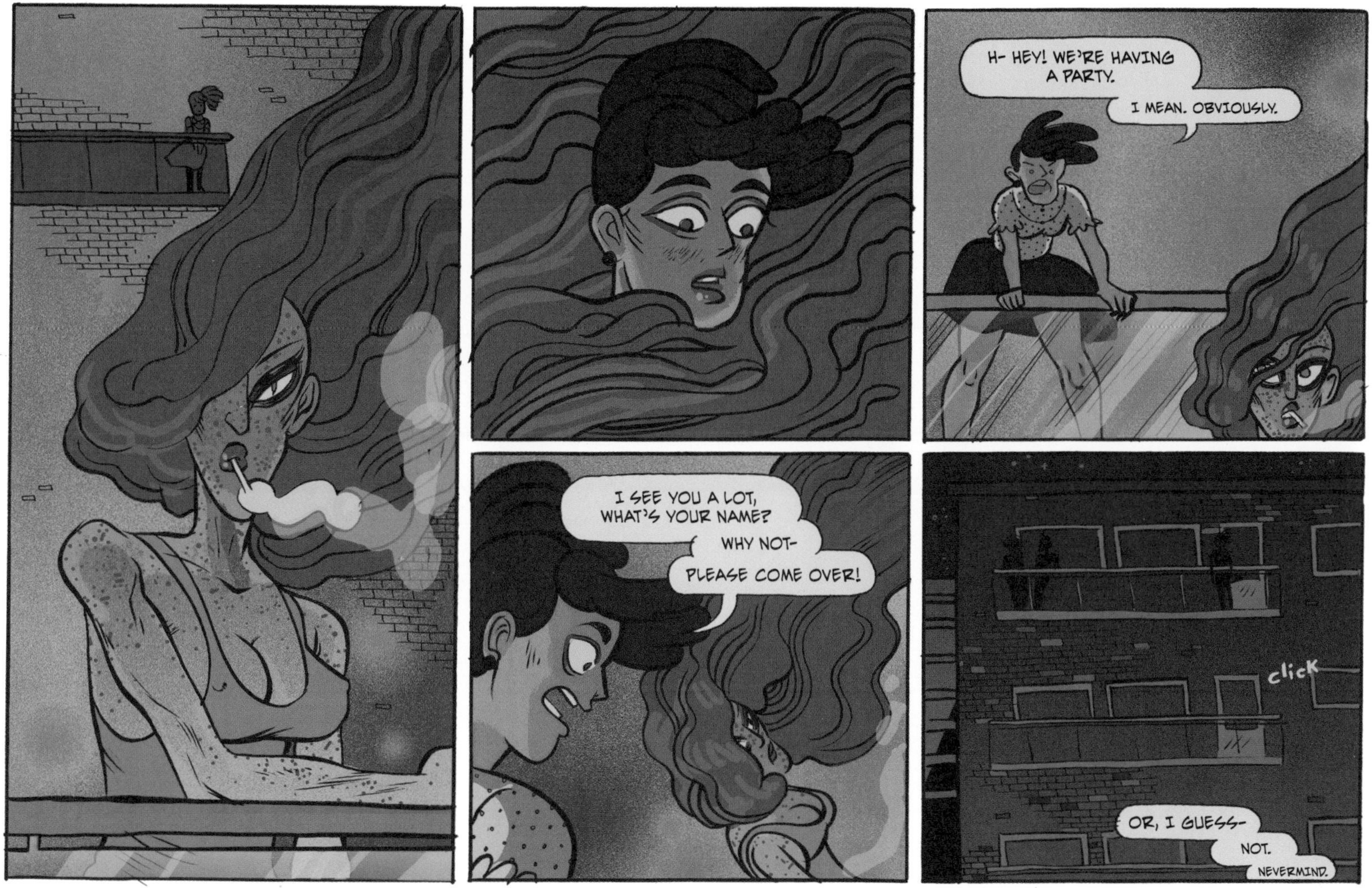
H- HEY! WE'RE HAVING A PARTY.
I MEAN. OBVIOUSLY.
I SEE YOU A LOT, WHAT'S YOUR NAME?
WHY NOT-
PLEASE COME OVER!
click
OR, I GUESS-
NOT.
NEVERMIND.

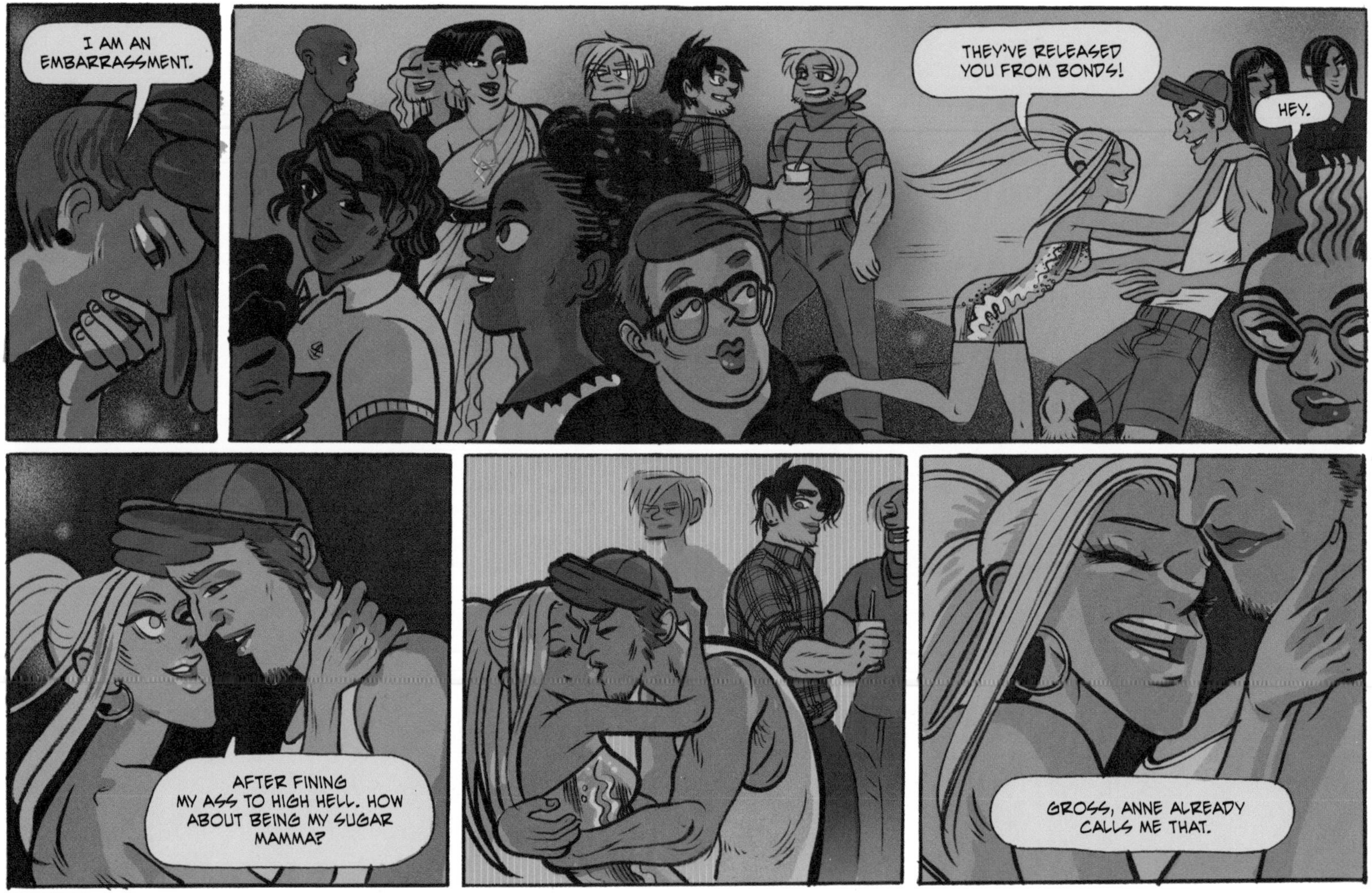
I AM AN EMBARRASSMENT.
THEY'VE RELEASED YOU FROM BONDS!
HEY.
AFTER FINING MY ASS TO HIGH HELL. HOW ABOUT BEING MY SUGAR MAMMA?
GROSS, ANNE ALREADY CALLS ME THAT.

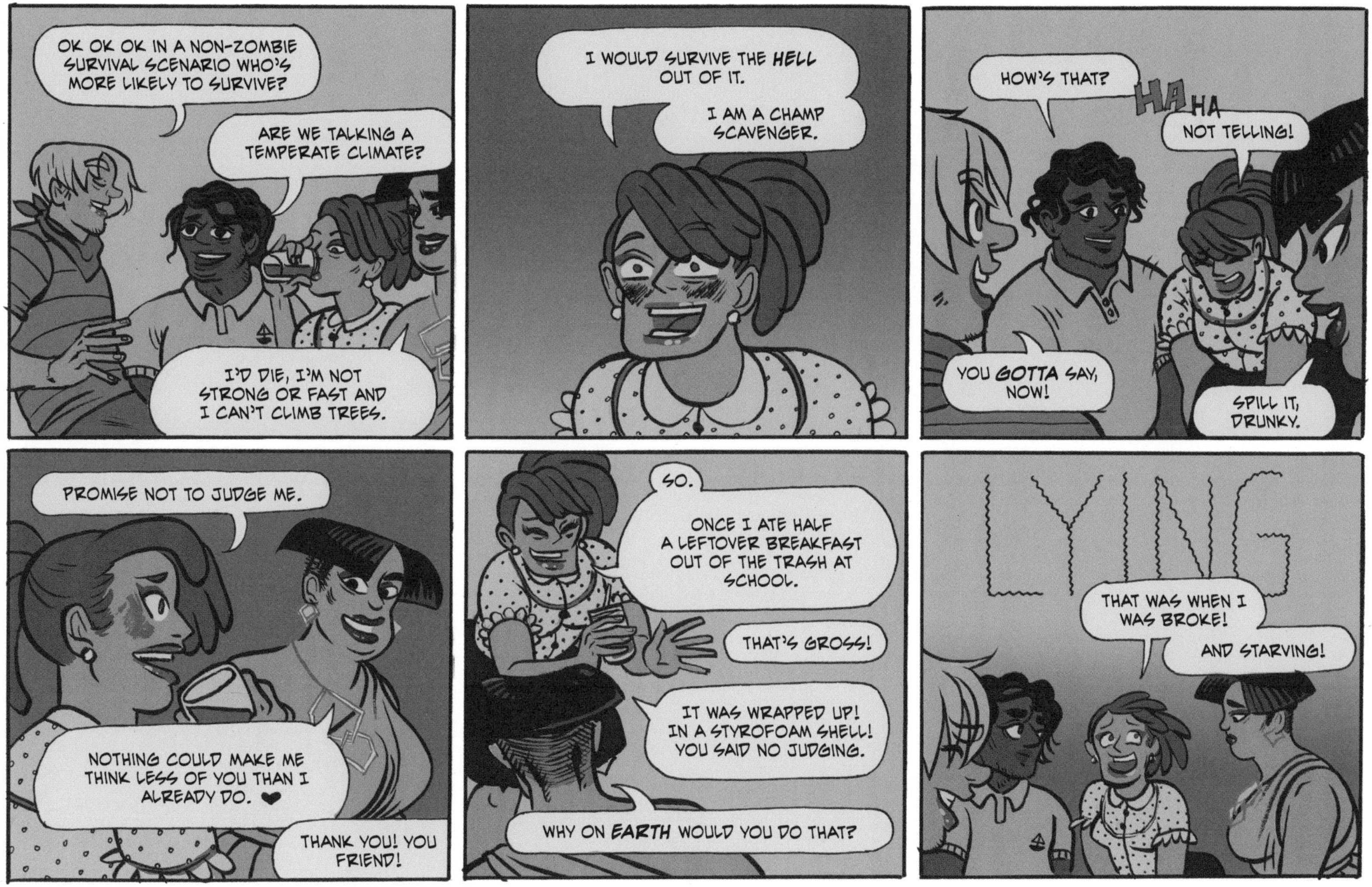

OK OK OK IN A NON-ZOMBIE SURVIVAL SCENARIO WHO'S MORE LIKELY TO SURVIVE?
ARE WE TALKING A TEMPERATE CLIMATE?
I'D DIE, I'M NOT STRONG OR FAST AND I CAN'T CLIMB TREES.
I WOULD SURVIVE THE **HELL** OUT OF IT.
I AM A CHAMP SCAVENGER.
HOW'S THAT?
HA HA
NOT TELLING!
YOU **GOTTA** SAY, NOW!
SPILL IT, DRUNKY.
PROMISE NOT TO JUDGE ME.
NOTHING COULD MAKE ME THINK LESS OF YOU THAN I ALREADY DO. ❤
THANK YOU! YOU FRIEND!
SO.
ONCE I ATE HALF A LEFTOVER BREAKFAST OUT OF THE TRASH AT SCHOOL.
THAT'S GROSS!
IT WAS WRAPPED UP! IN A STYROFOAM SHELL! YOU SAID NO JUDGING.
WHY ON **EARTH** WOULD YOU DO THAT?
LYING
THAT WAS WHEN I WAS BROKE!
AND STARVING!

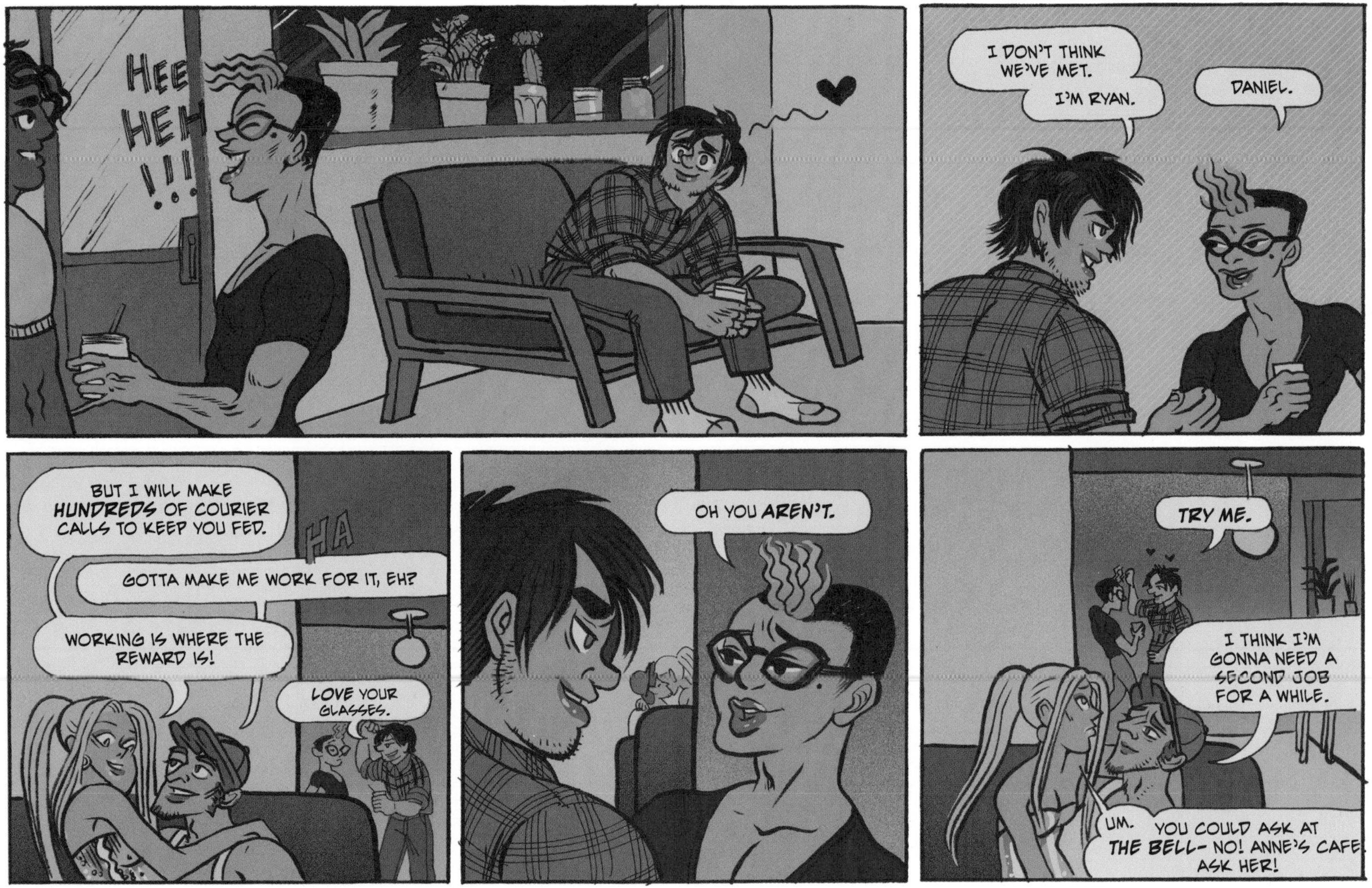
HEE HEH !!!
I DON'T THINK WE'VE MET.
I'M RYAN.
DANIEL.
BUT I WILL MAKE HUNDREDS OF COURIER CALLS TO KEEP YOU FED.
HA
GOTTA MAKE ME WORK FOR IT, EH?
WORKING IS WHERE THE REWARD IS!
LOVE YOUR GLASSES.
OH YOU AREN'T.
TRY ME.
I THINK I'M GONNA NEED A SECOND JOB FOR A WHILE.
UM.
YOU COULD ASK AT THE BELL- NO! ANNE'S CAFE. ASK HER!

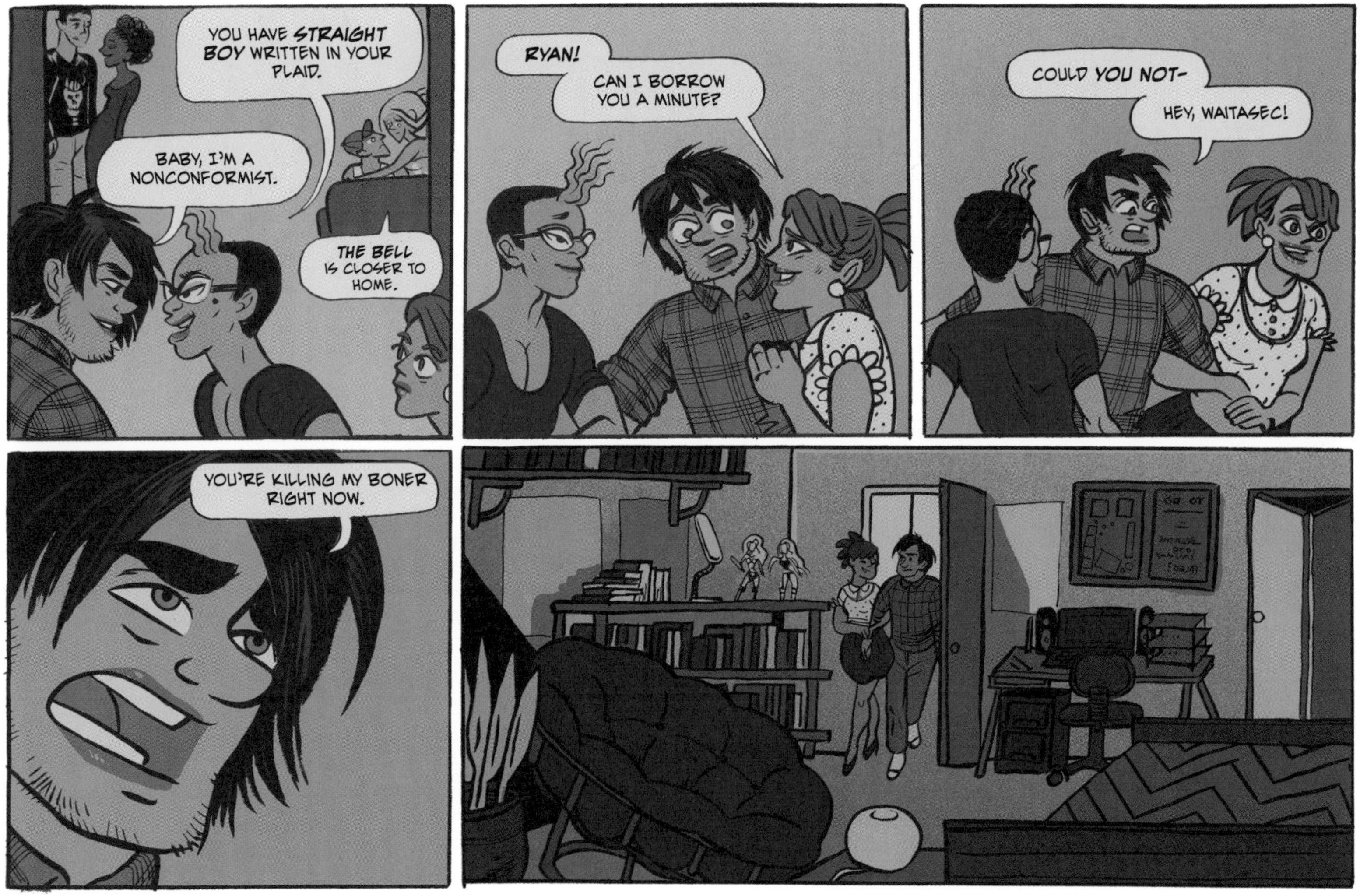
YOU HAVE STRAIGHT BOY WRITTEN IN YOUR PLAID.
BABY, I'M A NONCONFORMIST.
THE BELL IS CLOSER TO HOME.
RYAN!
CAN I BORROW YOU A MINUTE?
COULD YOU NOT-
HEY, WAITASEC!
YOU'RE KILLING MY BONER RIGHT NOW.

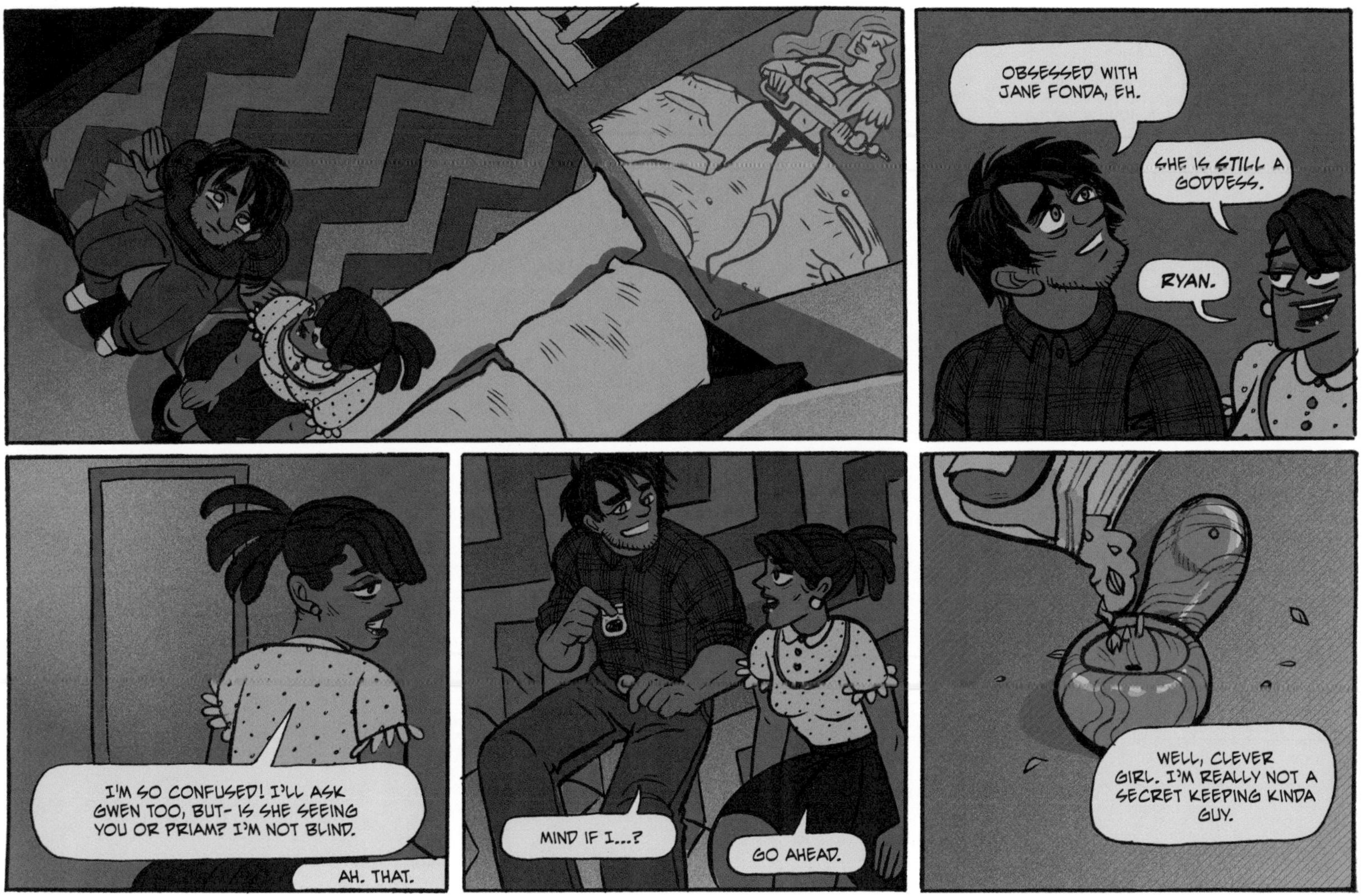
OBSESSED WITH JANE FONDA, EH.
SHE IS STILL A GODDESS.
RYAN.
I'M SO CONFUSED! I'LL ASK GWEN TOO, BUT- IS SHE SEEING YOU OR PRIAM? I'M NOT BLIND.
AH. THAT.
MIND IF I...?
GO AHEAD.
WELL, CLEVER GIRL. I'M REALLY NOT A SECRET KEEPING KINDA GUY.

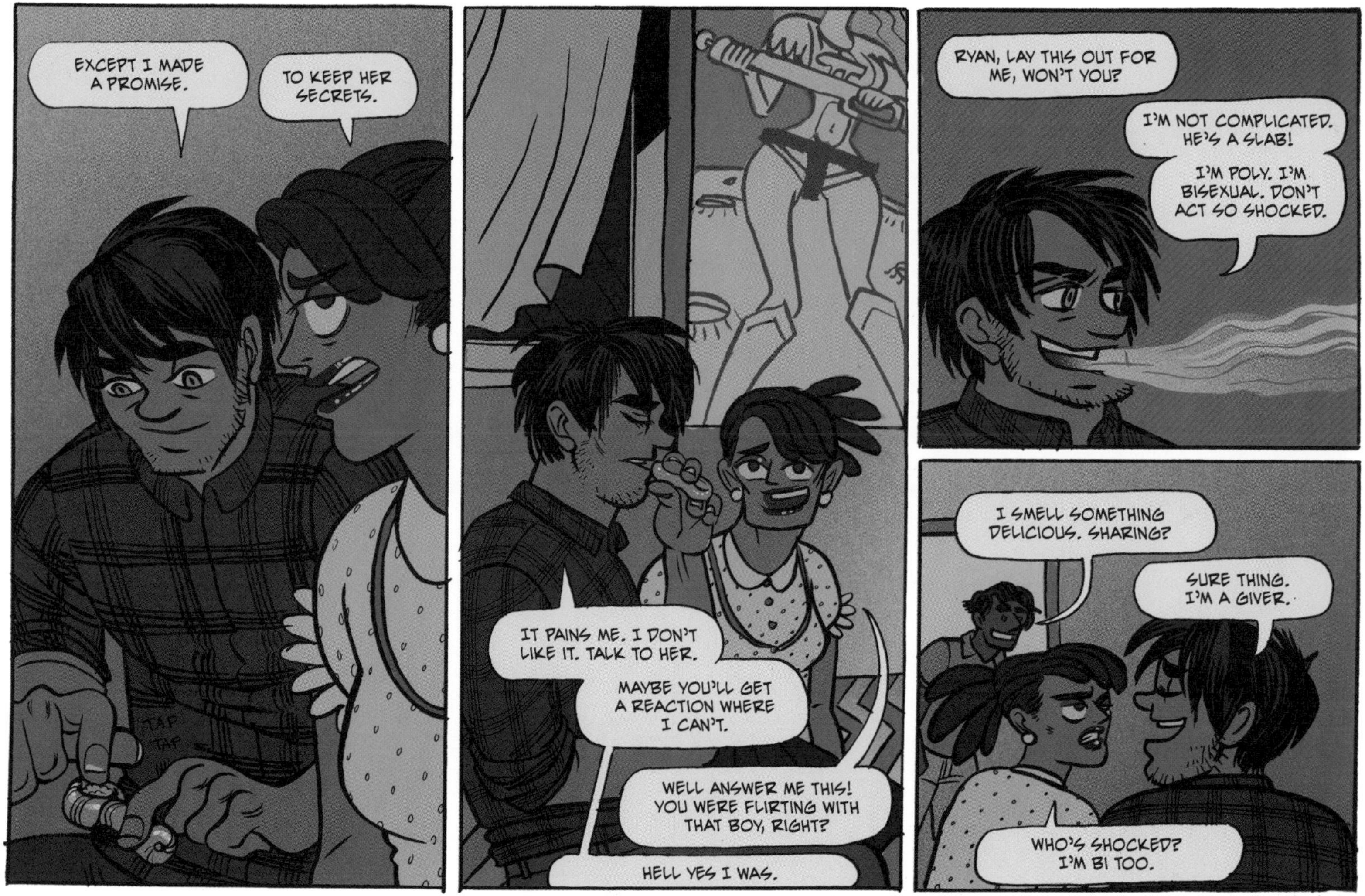
EXCEPT I MADE A PROMISE.
TO KEEP HER SECRETS.
TAP TAP
IT PAINS ME. I DON'T LIKE IT. TALK TO HER.
MAYBE YOU'LL GET A REACTION WHERE I CAN'T.
WELL ANSWER ME THIS! YOU WERE FLIRTING WITH THAT BOY, RIGHT?
HELL YES I WAS.
RYAN, LAY THIS OUT FOR ME, WON'T YOU?
I'M NOT COMPLICATED. HE'S A SLAB!
I'M POLY. I'M BISEXUAL. DON'T ACT SO SHOCKED.
I SMELL SOMETHING DELICIOUS. SHARING?
SURE THING. I'M A GIVER.
WHO'S SHOCKED? I'M BI TOO.

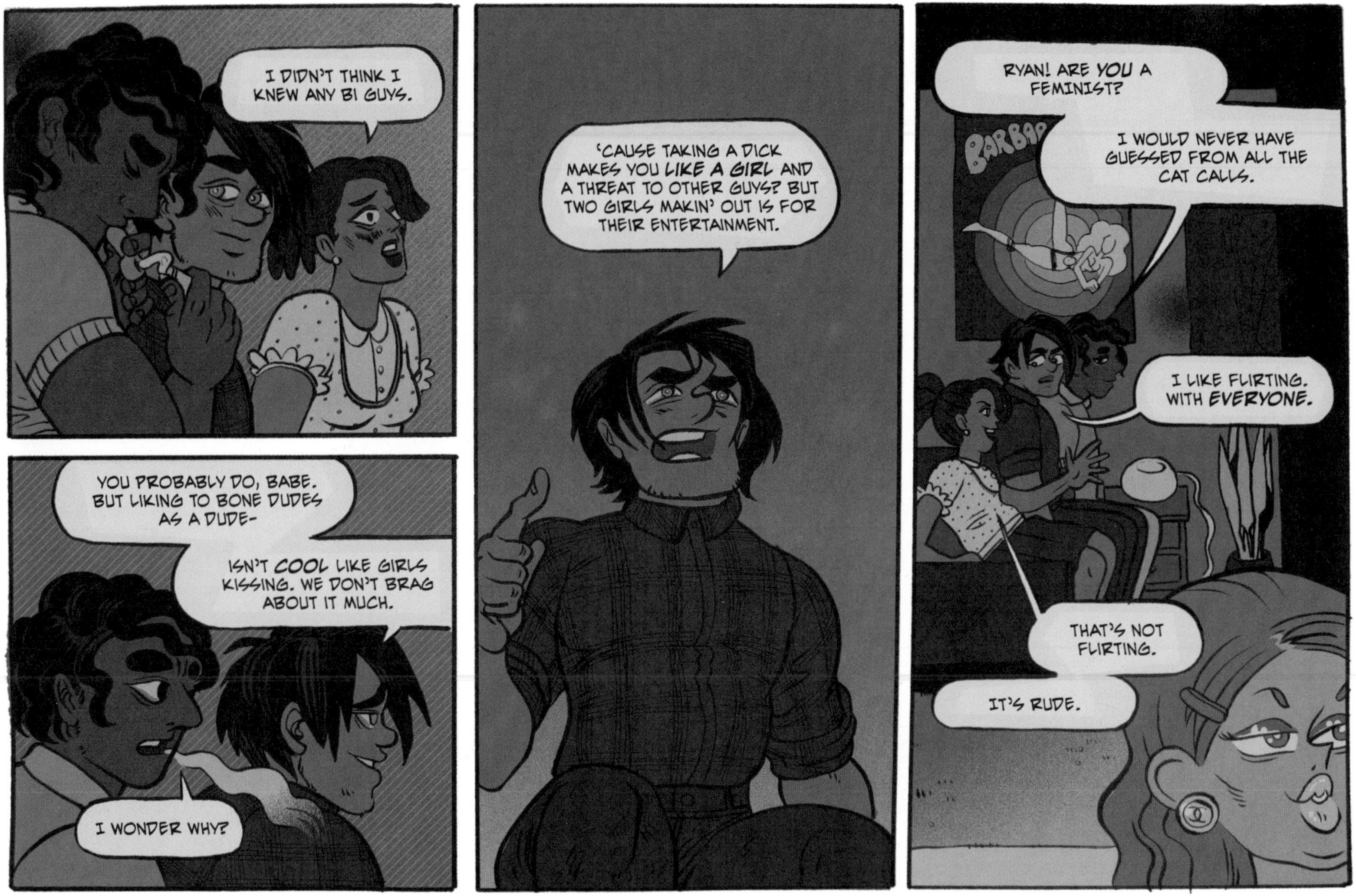
I DIDN'T THINK I KNEW ANY BI GUYS.
YOU PROBABLY DO, BABE. BUT LIKING TO BONE DUDES AS A DUDE-
ISN'T COOL LIKE GIRLS KISSING. WE DON'T BRAG ABOUT IT MUCH.
I WONDER WHY?
'CAUSE TAKING A DICK MAKES YOU LIKE A GIRL AND A THREAT TO OTHER GUYS? BUT TWO GIRLS MAKIN' OUT IS FOR THEIR ENTERTAINMENT.
RYAN! ARE YOU A FEMINIST?
I WOULD NEVER HAVE GUESSED FROM ALL THE CAT CALLS.
I LIKE FLIRTING. WITH EVERYONE.
THAT'S NOT FLIRTING.
IT'S RUDE.

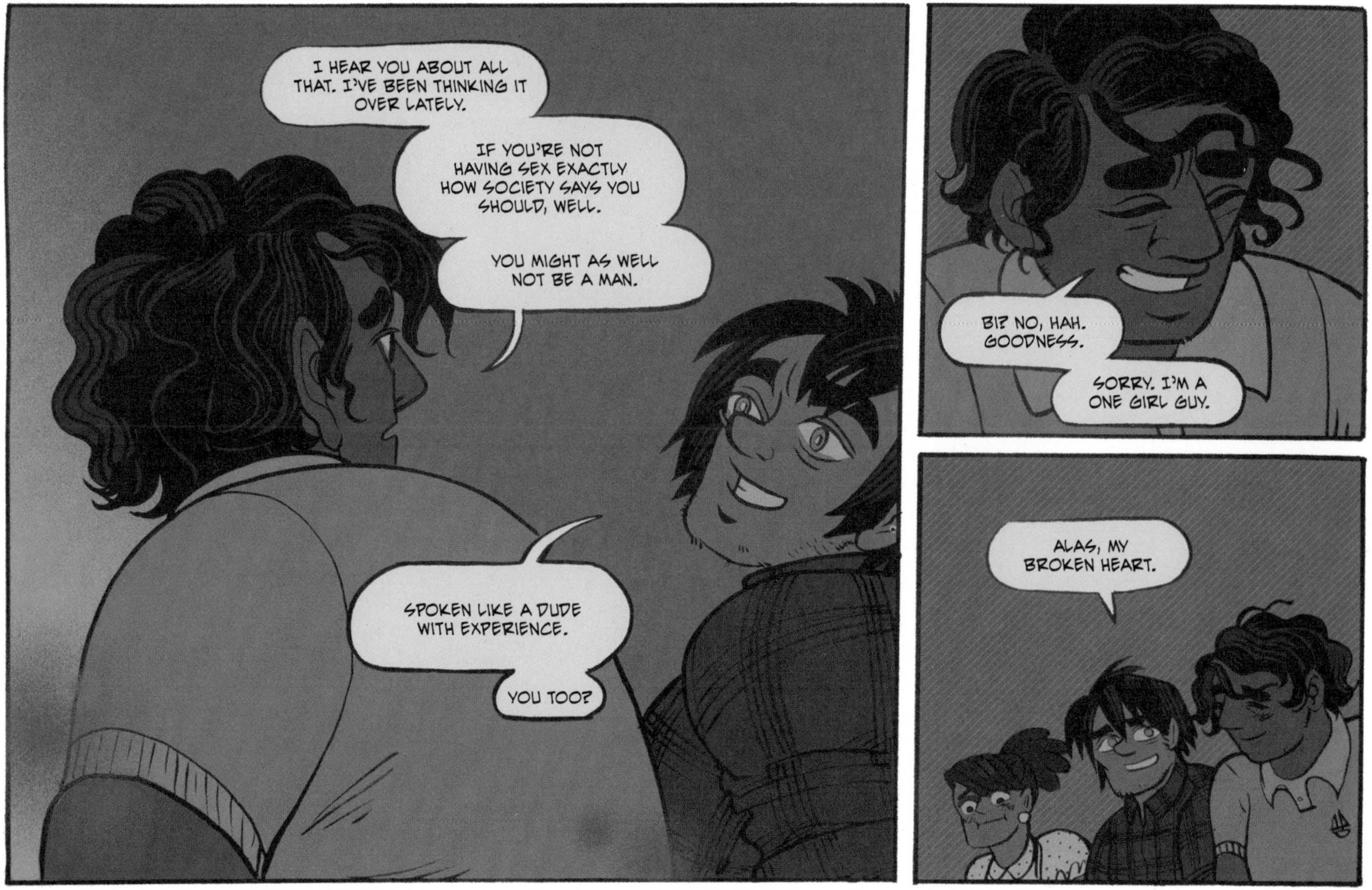
I HEAR YOU ABOUT ALL THAT. I'VE BEEN THINKING IT OVER LATELY.
IF YOU'RE NOT HAVING SEX EXACTLY HOW SOCIETY SAYS YOU SHOULD, WELL.
YOU MIGHT AS WELL NOT BE A MAN.
SPOKEN LIKE A DUDE WITH EXPERIENCE.
YOU TOO?
BI? NO, HAH. GOODNESS.
SORRY. I'M A ONE GIRL GUY.
ALAS, MY BROKEN HEART.

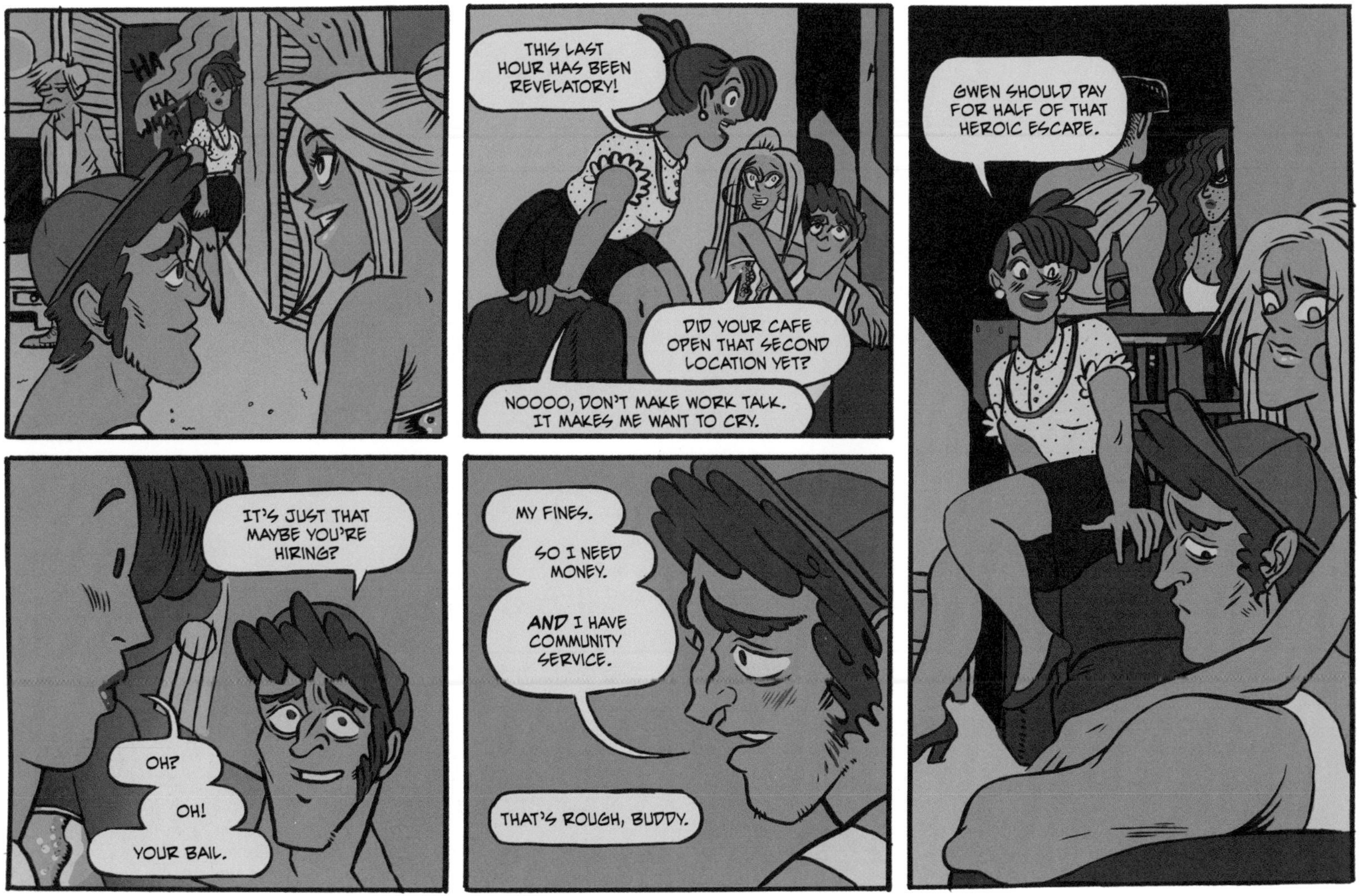
HA HA HA
THIS LAST HOUR HAS BEEN REVELATORY!
DID YOUR CAFE OPEN THAT SECOND LOCATION YET?
NOOOO, DON'T MAKE WORK TALK. IT MAKES ME WANT TO CRY.
GWEN SHOULD PAY FOR HALF OF THAT HEROIC ESCAPE.
IT'S JUST THAT MAYBE YOU'RE HIRING?
OH?
OH!
YOUR BAIL.
MY FINES.
SO I NEED MONEY.
AND I HAVE COMMUNITY SERVICE.
THAT'S ROUGH, BUDDY.

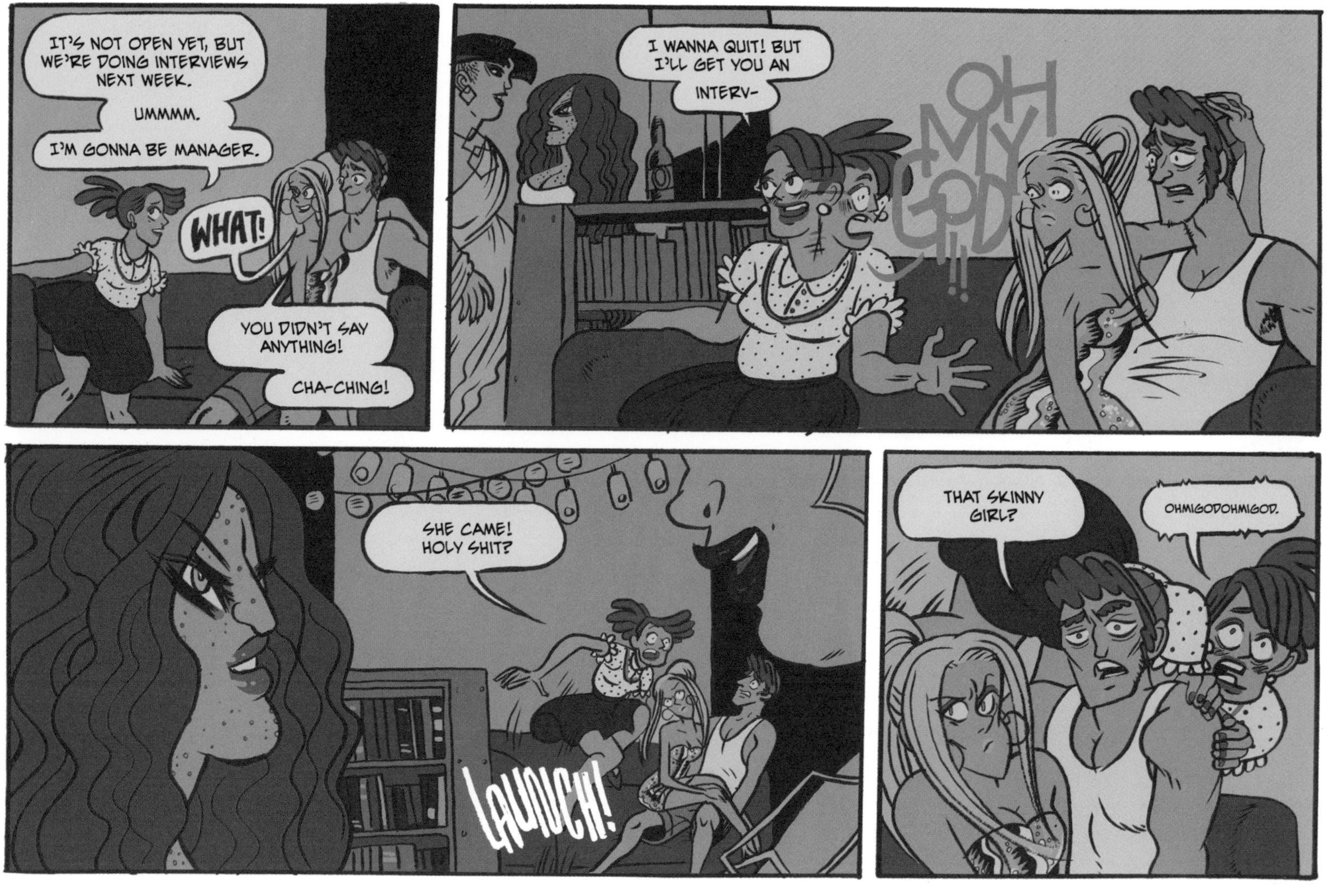
IT'S NOT OPEN YET, BUT WE'RE DOING INTERVIEWS NEXT WEEK.
UMMMM.
I'M GONNA BE MANAGER.
WHAT!
YOU DIDN'T SAY ANYTHING!
CHA-CHING!
I WANNA QUIT! BUT I'LL GET YOU AN
INTERV-
OH MY GOD!!!
SHE CAME! HOLY SHIT?
LAUNCH!
THAT SKINNY GIRL?
OHMIGODOHMIGOD.

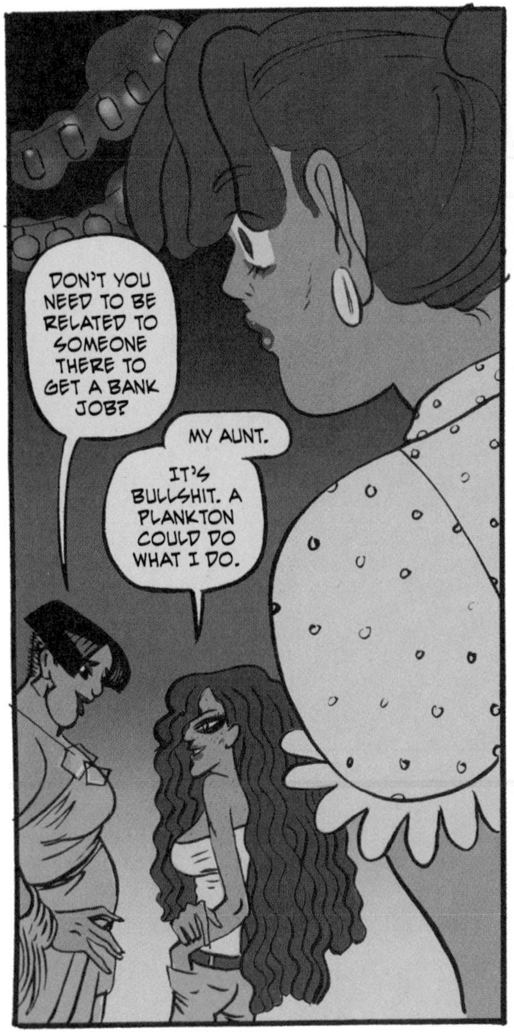
DON'T YOU NEED TO BE RELATED TO SOMEONE THERE TO GET A BANK JOB?
MY AUNT.
IT'S BULLSHIT. A PLANKTON COULD DO WHAT I DO.

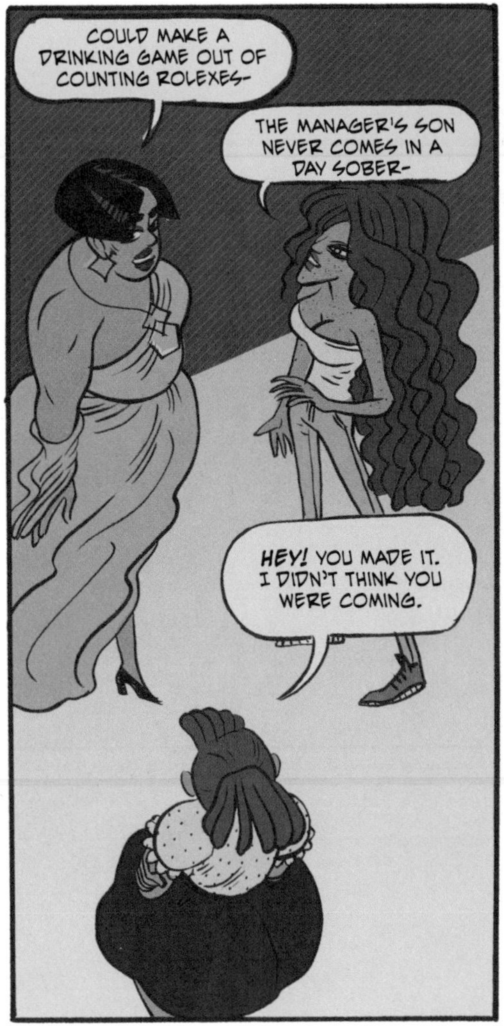
COULD MAKE A DRINKING GAME OUT OF COUNTING ROLEXES-
THE MANAGER'S SON NEVER COMES IN A DAY SOBER-
HEY! YOU MADE IT. I DIDN'T THINK YOU WERE COMING.

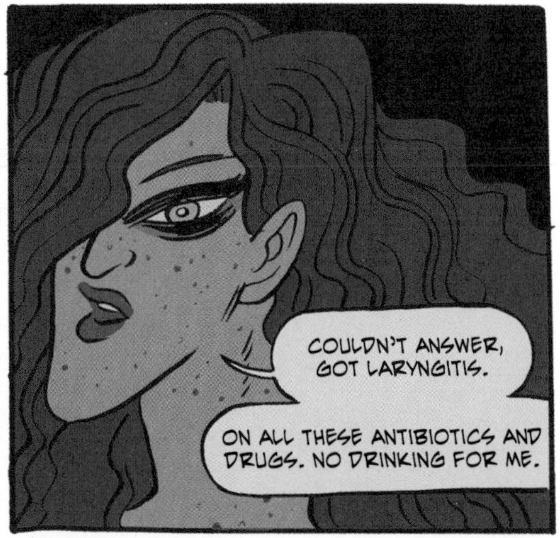
COULDN'T ANSWER, GOT LARYNGITIS.
ON ALL THESE ANTIBIOTICS AND DRUGS. NO DRINKING FOR ME.

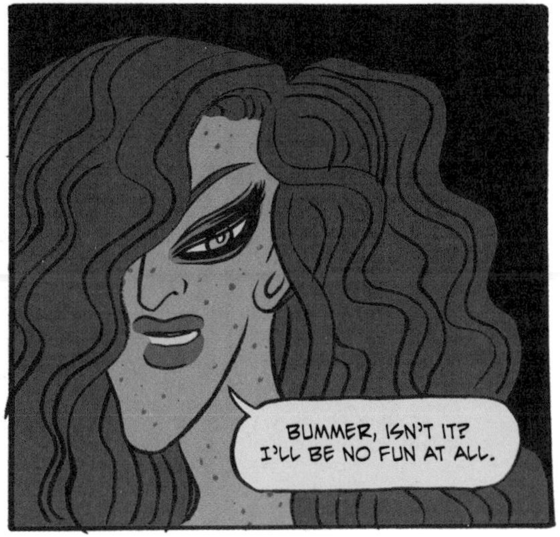
BUMMER, ISN'T IT? I'LL BE NO FUN AT ALL.

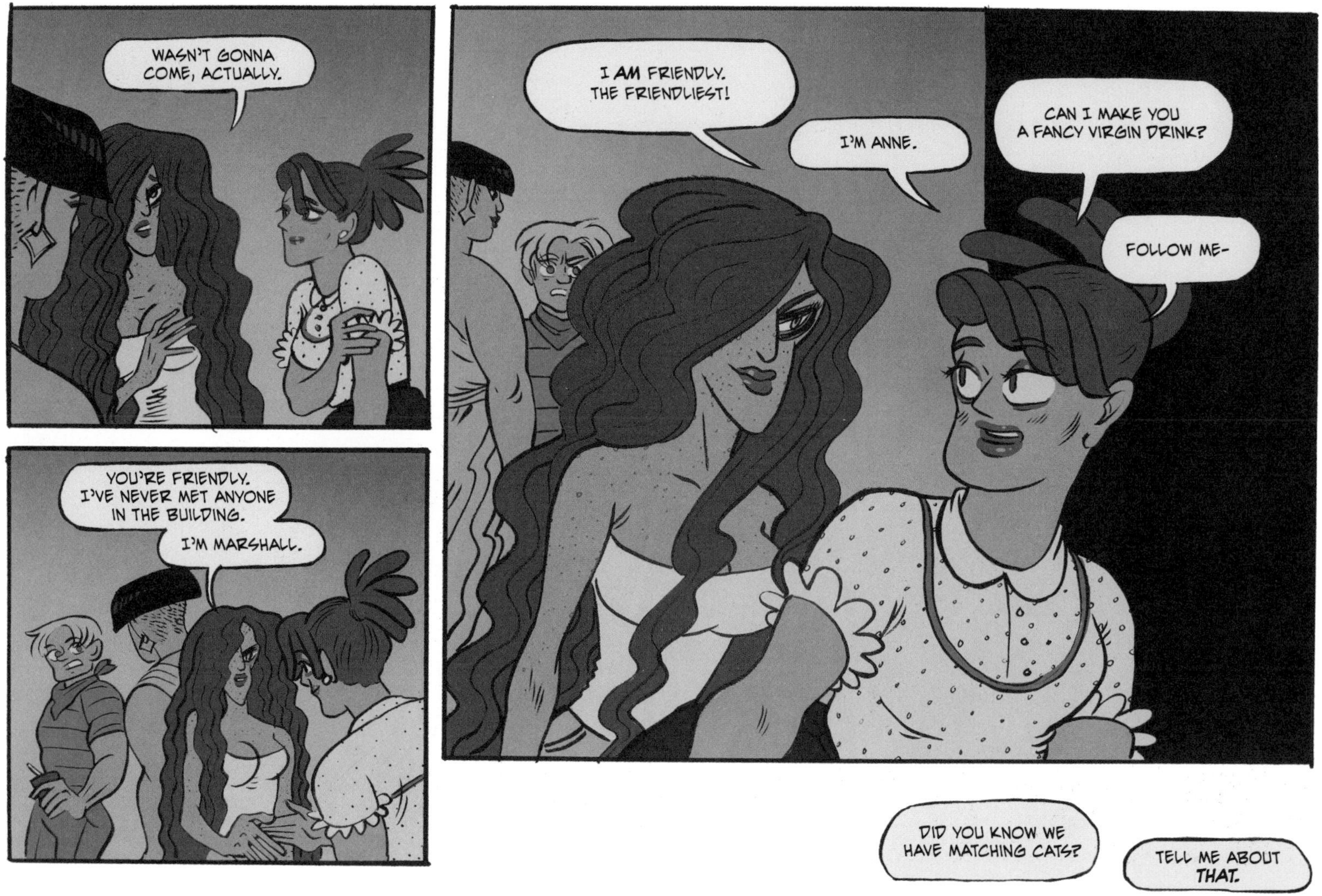
WASN'T GONNA COME, ACTUALLY.
YOU'RE FRIENDLY. I'VE NEVER MET ANYONE IN THE BUILDING.
I'M MARSHALL.
I **AM** FRIENDLY. THE FRIENDLIEST!
I'M ANNE.
CAN I MAKE YOU A FANCY VIRGIN DRINK?
FOLLOW ME-
DID YOU KNOW WE HAVE MATCHING CATS?
TELL ME ABOUT ***THAT.***

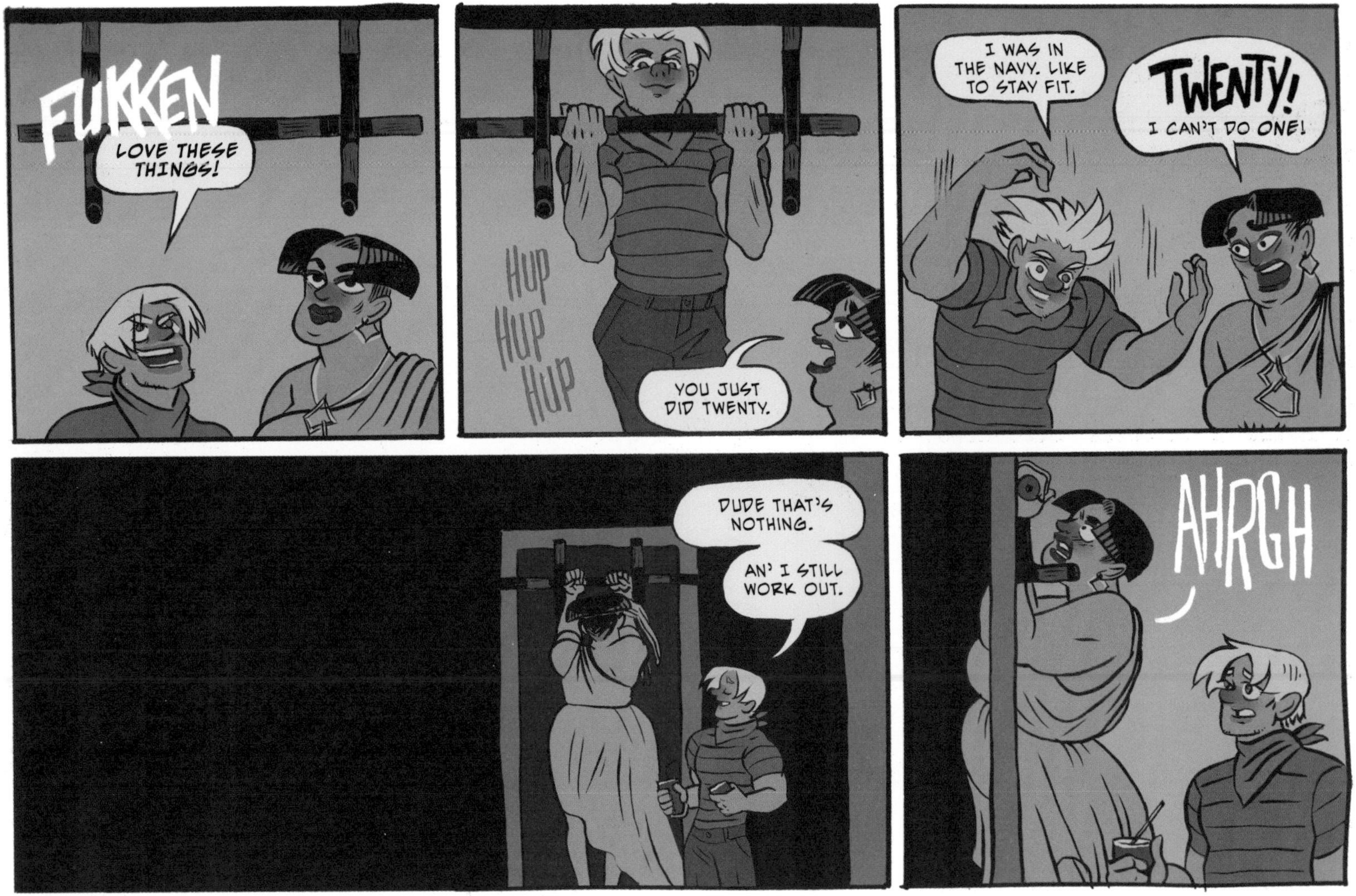
FUKKEN
LOVE THESE THINGS!
HUP HUP HUP
YOU JUST DID TWENTY.
I WAS IN THE NAVY. LIKE TO STAY FIT.
TWENTY! I CAN'T DO ONE!
DUDE THAT'S NOTHING.
AN' I STILL WORK OUT.
AHRGH

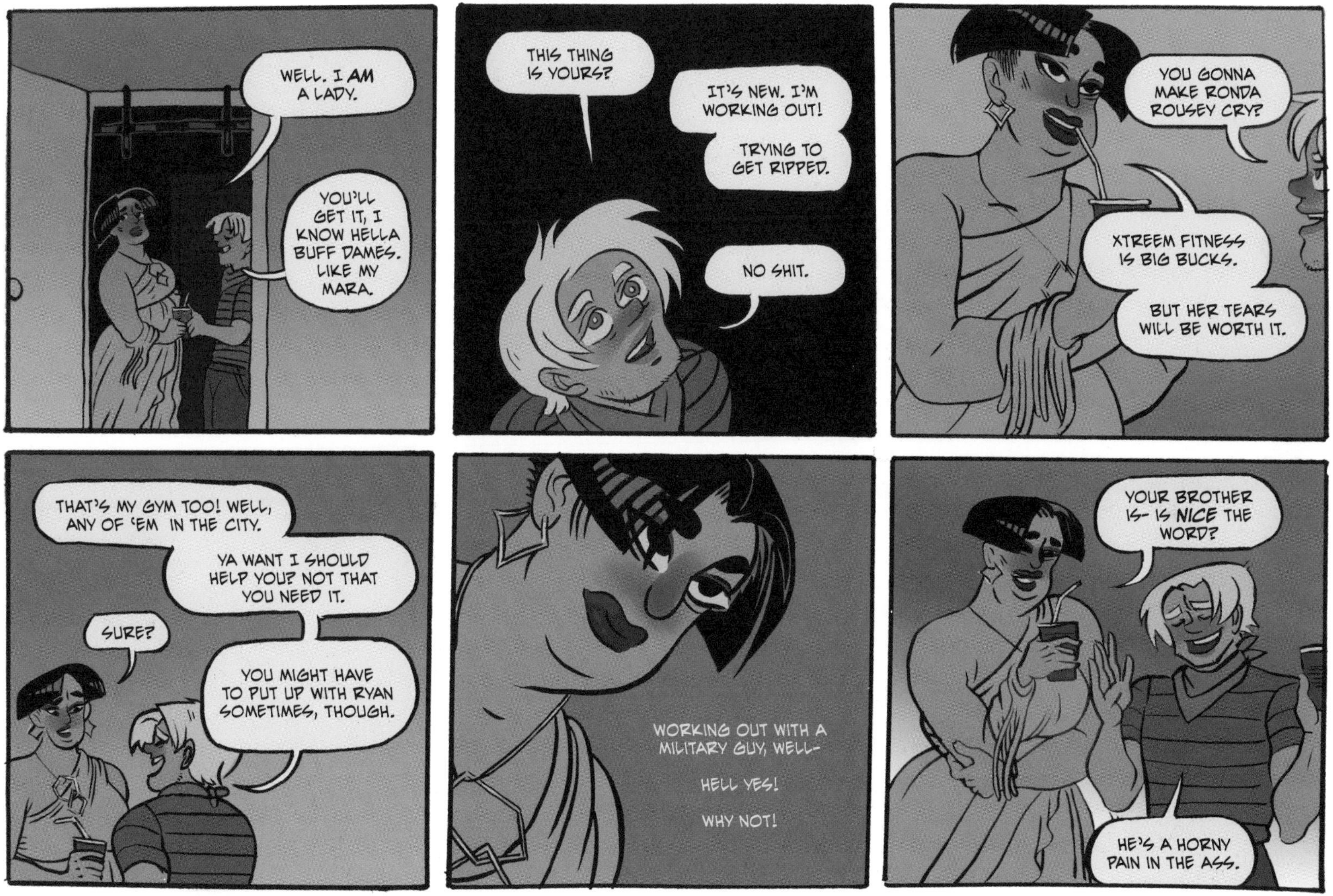

WELL. I AM A LADY.
YOU'LL GET IT, I KNOW HELLA BUFF DAMES. LIKE MY MARA.
THIS THING IS YOURS?
IT'S NEW. I'M WORKING OUT!
TRYING TO GET RIPPED.
NO SHIT.
YOU GONNA MAKE RONDA ROUSEY CRY?
XTREEM FITNESS IS BIG BUCKS.
BUT HER TEARS WILL BE WORTH IT.
THAT'S MY GYM TOO! WELL, ANY OF 'EM IN THE CITY.
YA WANT I SHOULD HELP YOU? NOT THAT YOU NEED IT.
SURE?
YOU MIGHT HAVE TO PUT UP WITH RYAN SOMETIMES, THOUGH.
WORKING OUT WITH A MILITARY GUY, WELL-
HELL YES!
WHY NOT!
YOUR BROTHER IS- IS NICE THE WORD?
HE'S A HORNY PAIN IN THE ASS.

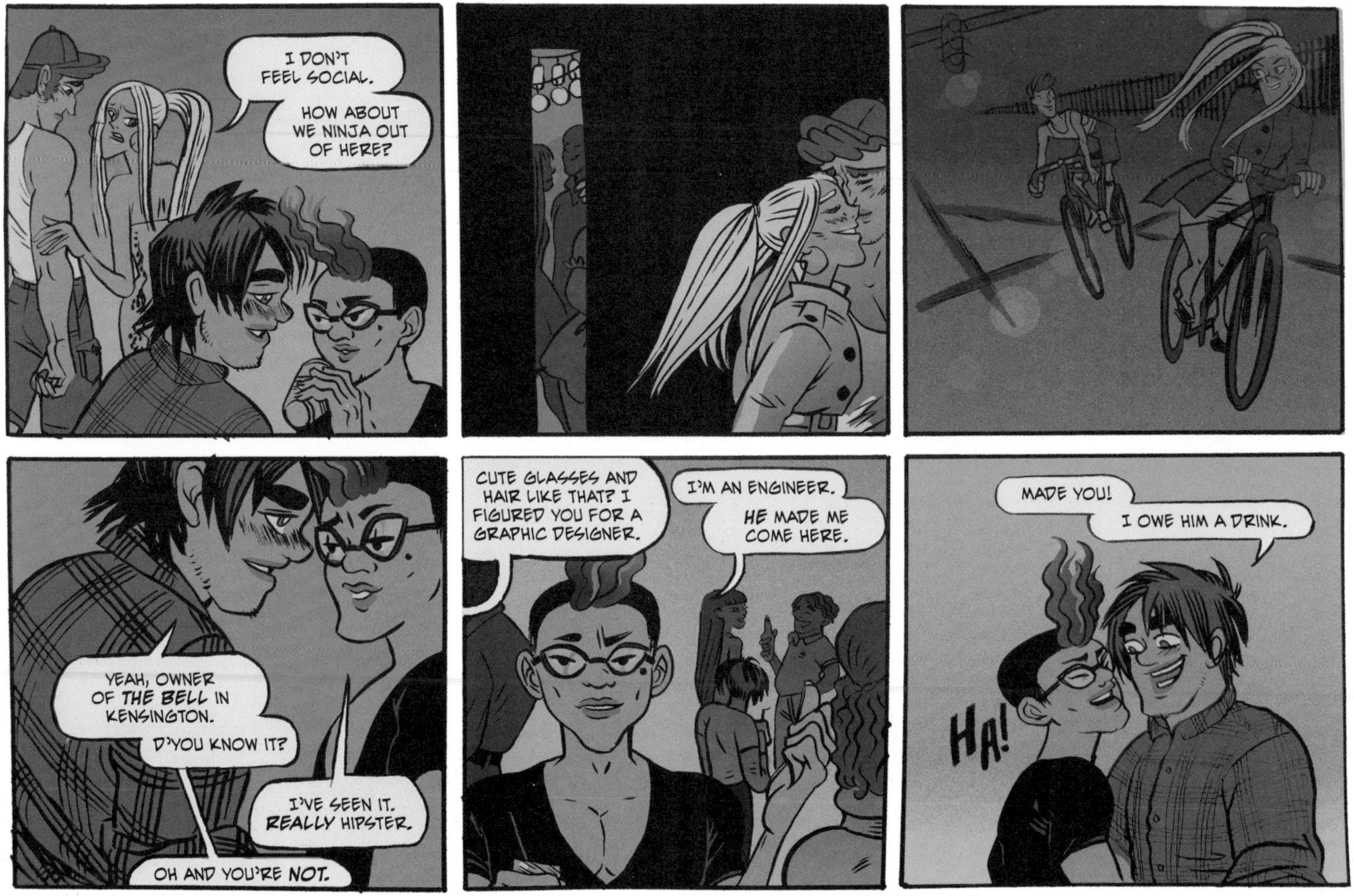
I DON'T FEEL SOCIAL.
HOW ABOUT WE NINJA OUT OF HERE?
YEAH, OWNER OF THE BELL IN KENSINGTON.
D'YOU KNOW IT?
I'VE SEEN IT. REALLY HIPSTER.
OH AND YOU'RE NOT.
CUTE GLASSES AND HAIR LIKE THAT? I FIGURED YOU FOR A GRAPHIC DESIGNER.
I'M AN ENGINEER.
HE MADE ME COME HERE.
MADE YOU!
I OWE HIM A DRINK.
HA!

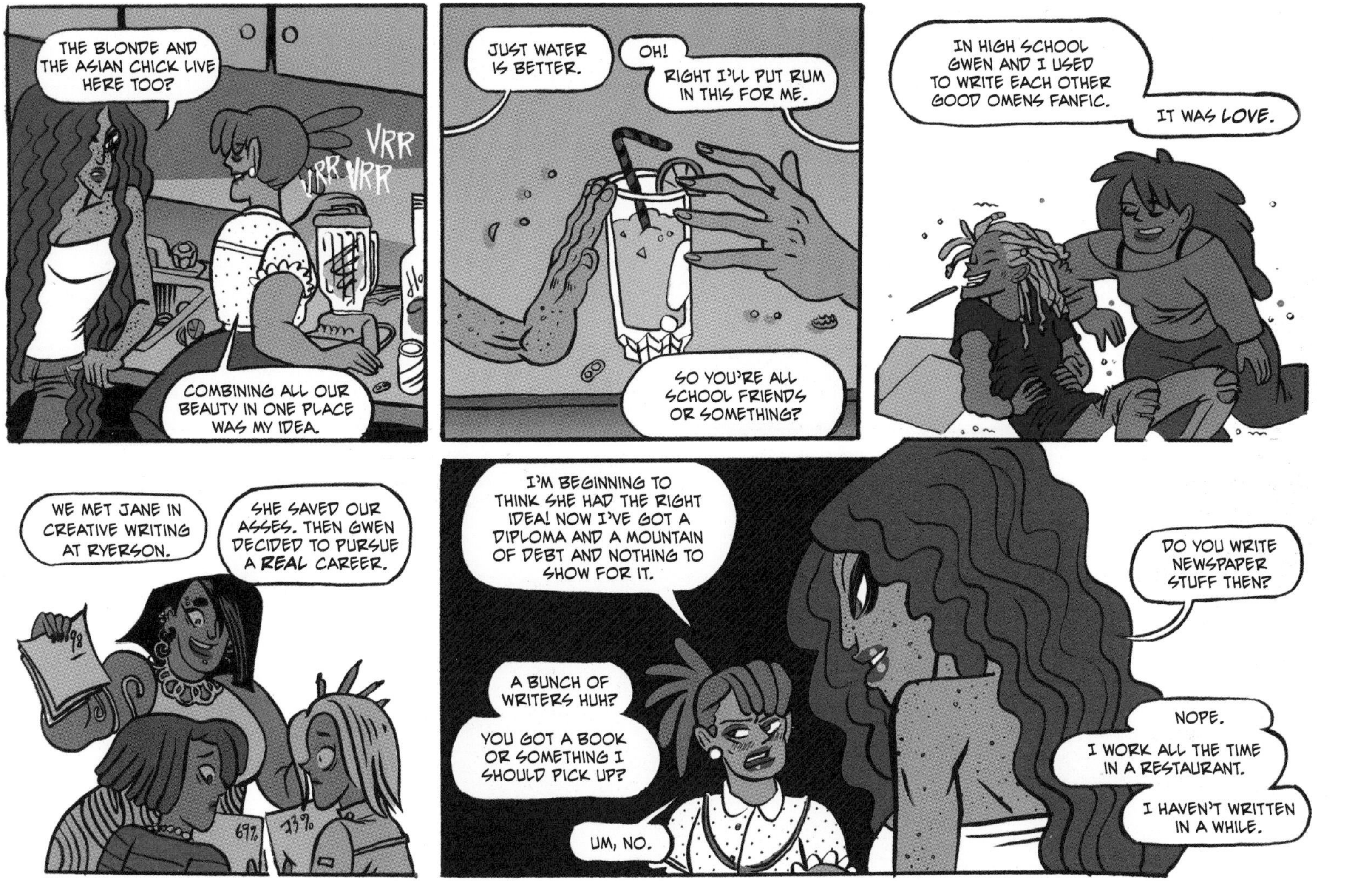
THE BLONDE AND THE ASIAN CHICK LIVE HERE TOO?
VRR
VRR VRR
COMBINING ALL OUR BEAUTY IN ONE PLACE WAS MY IDEA.
JUST WATER IS BETTER.
OH!
RIGHT I'LL PUT RUM IN THIS FOR ME.
SO YOU'RE ALL SCHOOL FRIENDS OR SOMETHING?
IN HIGH SCHOOL GWEN AND I USED TO WRITE EACH OTHER GOOD OMENS FANFIC.
IT WAS LOVE.
WE MET JANE IN CREATIVE WRITING AT RYERSON.
SHE SAVED OUR ASSES. THEN GWEN DECIDED TO PURSUE A REAL CAREER.
I'M BEGINNING TO THINK SHE HAD THE RIGHT IDEA! NOW I'VE GOT A DIPLOMA AND A MOUNTAIN OF DEBT AND NOTHING TO SHOW FOR IT.
DO YOU WRITE NEWSPAPER STUFF THEN?
A BUNCH OF WRITERS HUH?
YOU GOT A BOOK OR SOMETHING I SHOULD PICK UP?
UM, NO.
NOPE.
I WORK ALL THE TIME IN A RESTAURANT.
I HAVEN'T WRITTEN IN A WHILE.

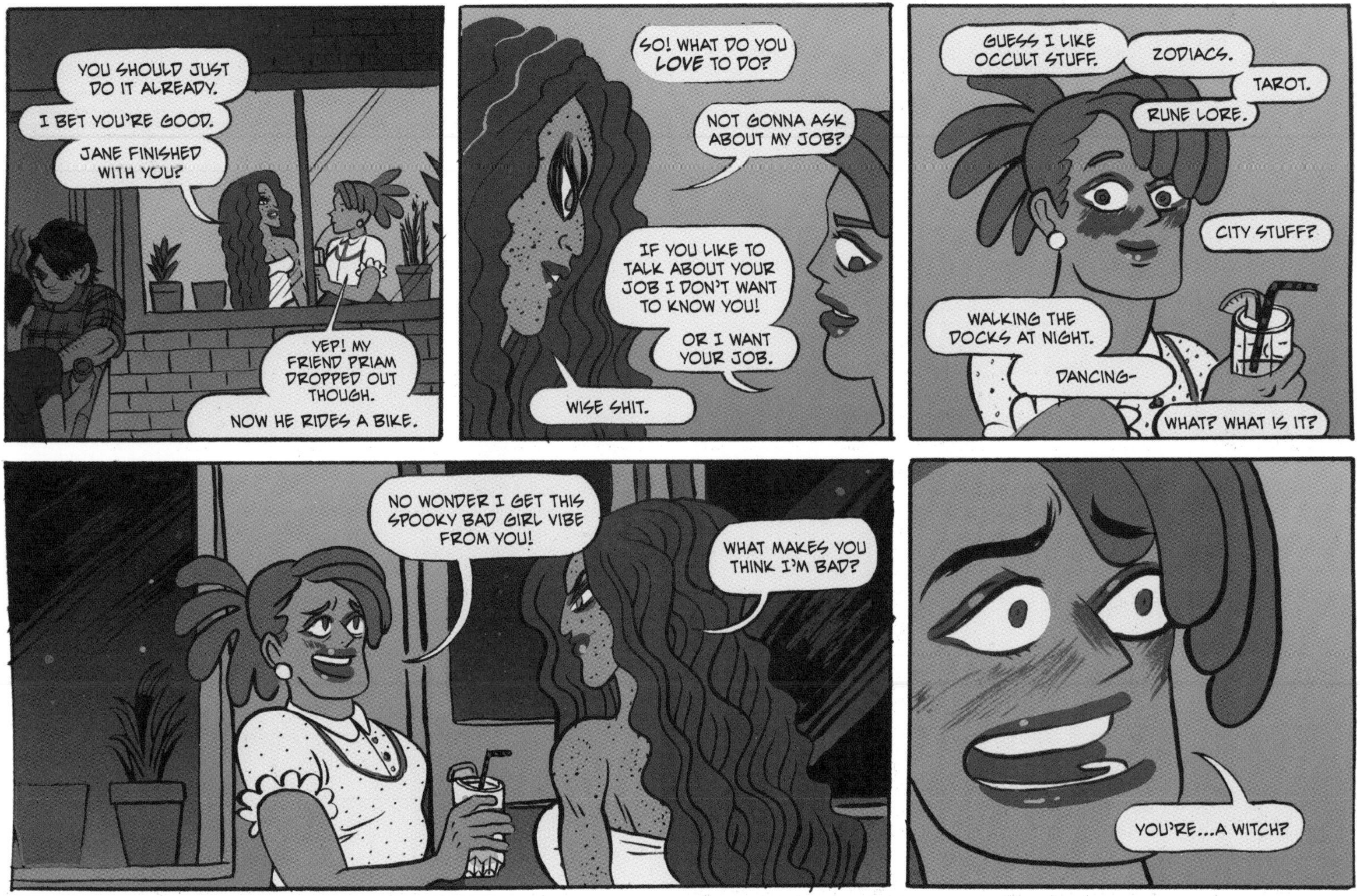

YOU SHOULD JUST DO IT ALREADY.
I BET YOU'RE GOOD.
JANE FINISHED WITH YOU?
YEP! MY FRIEND PRIAM DROPPED OUT THOUGH.
NOW HE RIDES A BIKE.
SO! WHAT DO YOU *LOVE* TO DO?
NOT GONNA ASK ABOUT MY JOB?
IF YOU LIKE TO TALK ABOUT YOUR JOB I DON'T WANT TO KNOW YOU!
OR I WANT YOUR JOB.
WISE SHIT.
GUESS I LIKE OCCULT STUFF.
ZODIACS.
TAROT.
RUNE LORE.
CITY STUFF?
WALKING THE DOCKS AT NIGHT.
DANCING-
WHAT? WHAT IS IT?
NO WONDER I GET THIS SPOOKY BAD GIRL VIBE FROM YOU!
WHAT MAKES YOU THINK I'M BAD?
YOU'RE...A WITCH?

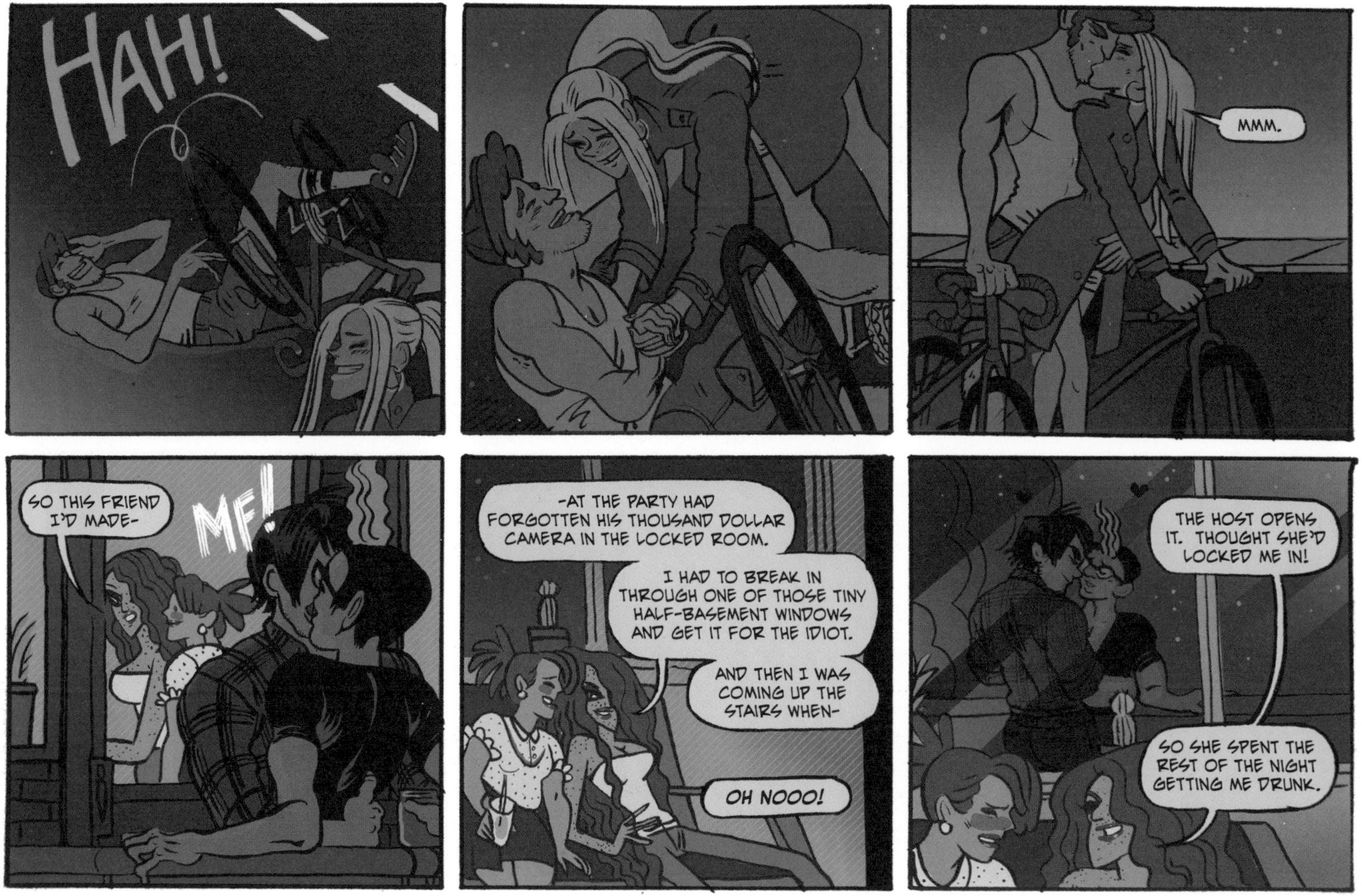
HAH!
MMM.
SO THIS FRIEND I'D MADE-
MF!
-AT THE PARTY HAD FORGOTTEN HIS THOUSAND DOLLAR CAMERA IN THE LOCKED ROOM.
I HAD TO BREAK IN THROUGH ONE OF THOSE TINY HALF-BASEMENT WINDOWS AND GET IT FOR THE IDIOT.
AND THEN I WAS COMING UP THE STAIRS WHEN-
OH NOOO!
THE HOST OPENS IT. THOUGHT SHE'D LOCKED ME IN!
SO SHE SPENT THE REST OF THE NIGHT GETTING ME DRUNK.

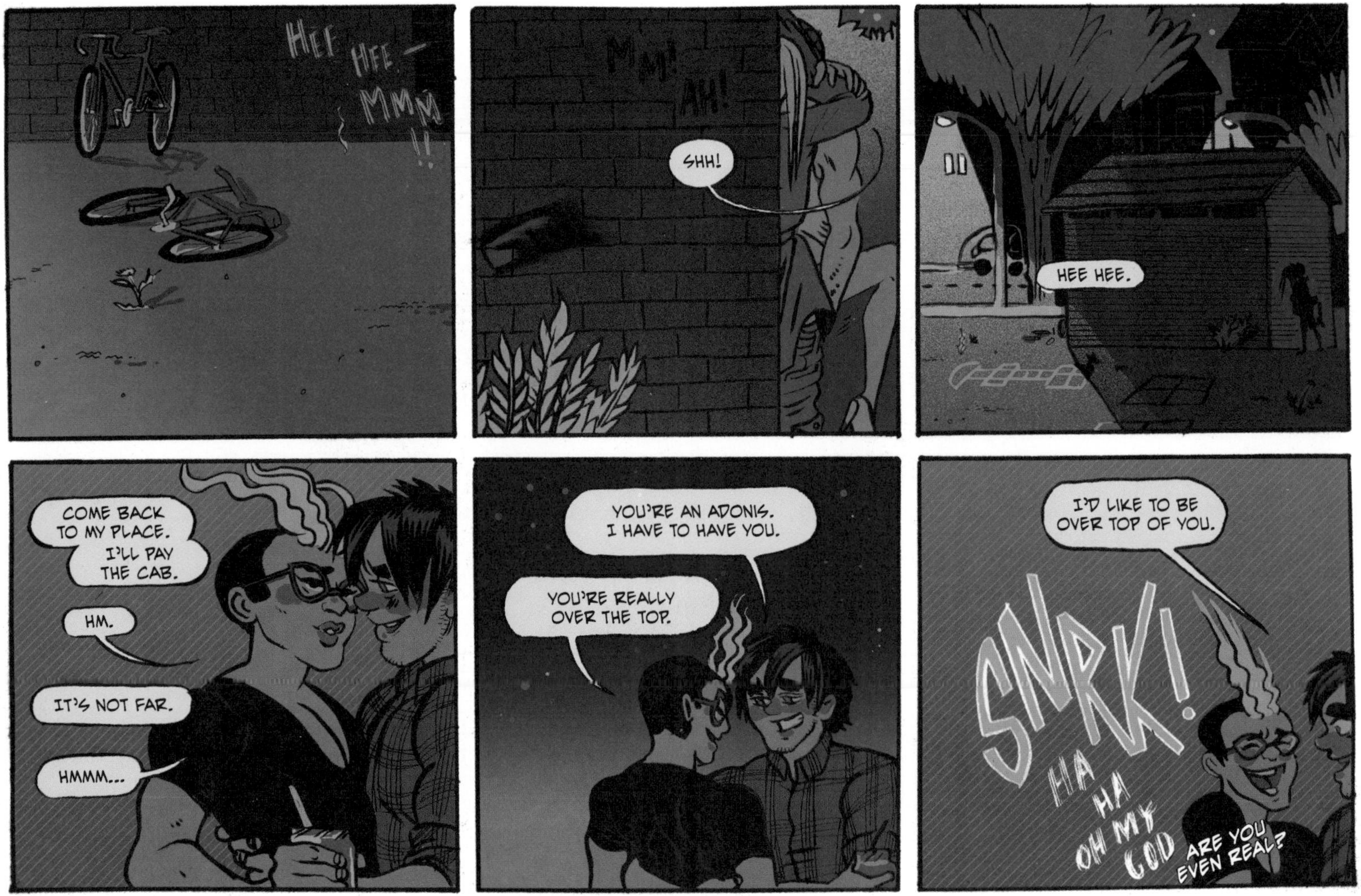
HEE
HEE—
MMM
!!
MM!
AH!
SHH!
HEE HEE.
COME BACK TO MY PLACE.
I'LL PAY THE CAB.
HM.
IT'S NOT FAR.
HMMM...
YOU'RE AN ADONIS. I HAVE TO HAVE YOU.
YOU'RE REALLY OVER THE TOP.
I'D LIKE TO BE OVER TOP OF YOU.
SNRK!
HA
HA
OH MY GOD
ARE YOU EVEN REAL?

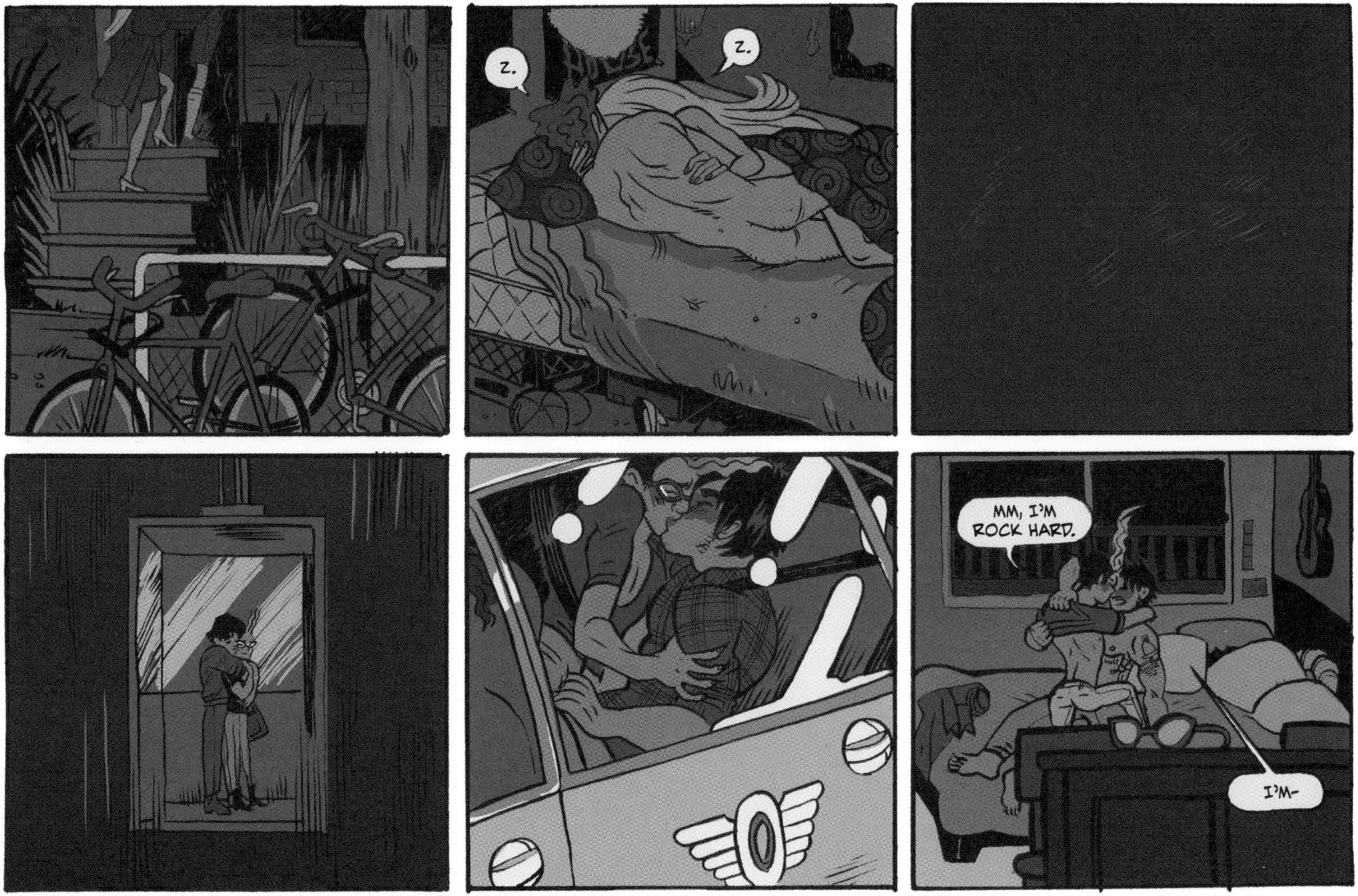
Z.
Z.
MM, I'M ROCK HARD.
I'M-

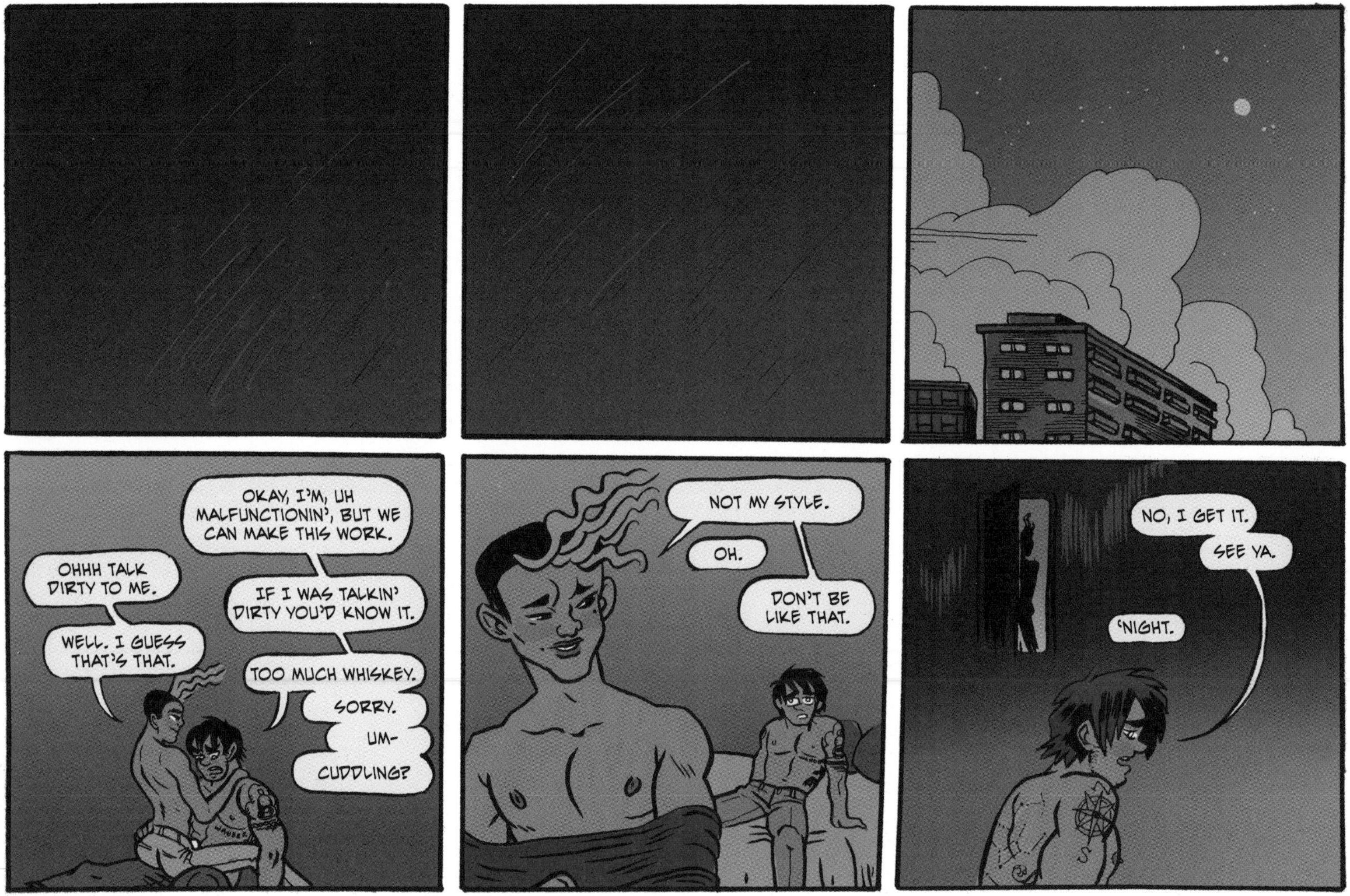
OKAY, I'M, UH MALFUNCTIONIN', BUT WE CAN MAKE THIS WORK.
OHHH TALK DIRTY TO ME.
IF I WAS TALKIN' DIRTY YOU'D KNOW IT.
WELL. I GUESS THAT'S THAT.
TOO MUCH WHISKEY.
SORRY.
UM-
CUDDLING?
NOT MY STYLE.
OH.
DON'T BE LIKE THAT.
NO, I GET IT.
SEE YA.
'NIGHT.

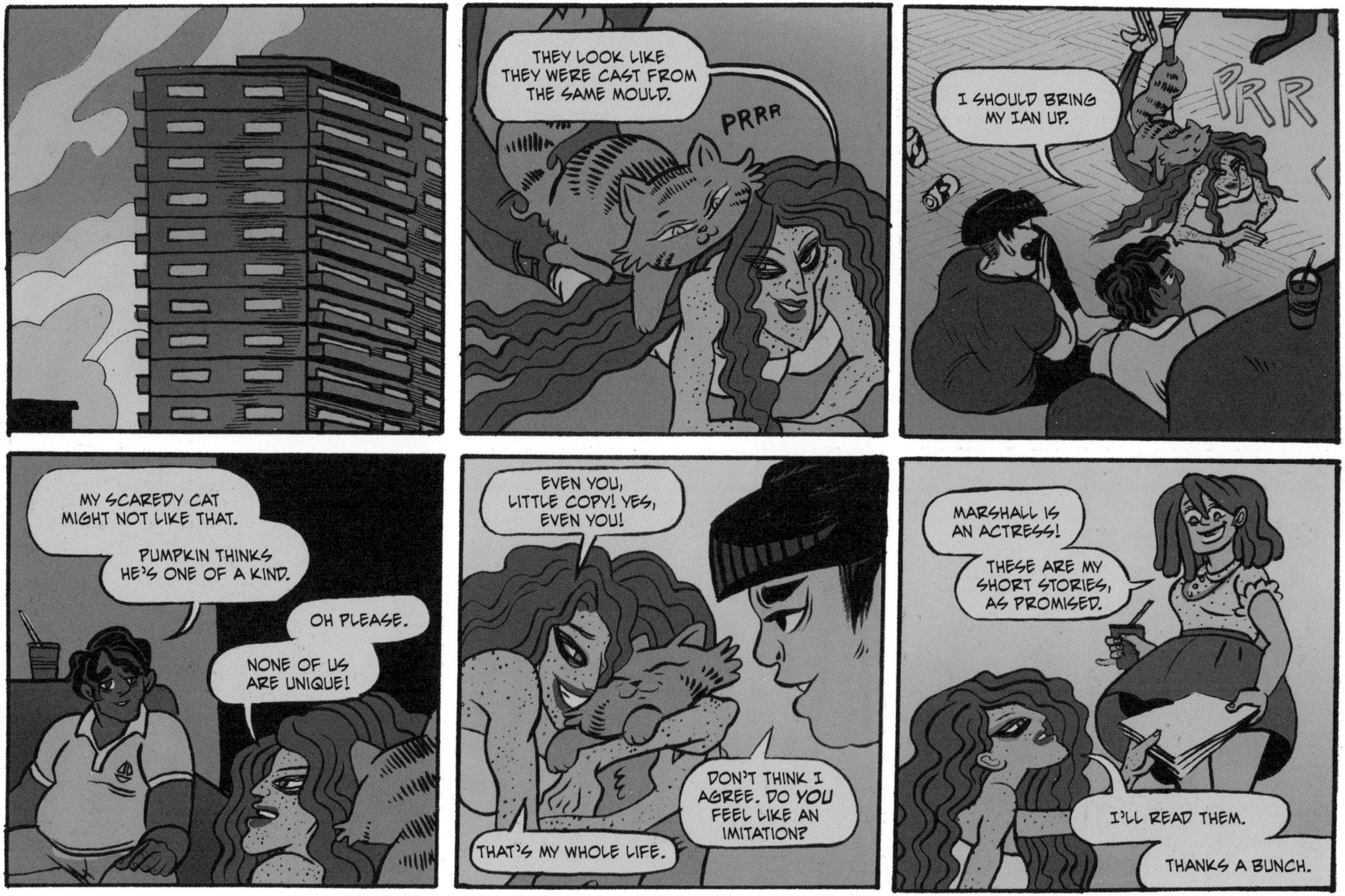
THEY LOOK LIKE THEY WERE CAST FROM THE SAME MOULD.
PRRR
I SHOULD BRING MY IAN UP.
PRR
MY SCAREDY CAT MIGHT NOT LIKE THAT.
PUMPKIN THINKS HE'S ONE OF A KIND.
OH PLEASE.
NONE OF US ARE UNIQUE!
EVEN YOU, LITTLE COPY! YES, EVEN YOU!
DON'T THINK I AGREE. DO YOU FEEL LIKE AN IMITATION?
THAT'S MY WHOLE LIFE.
MARSHALL IS AN ACTRESS!
THESE ARE MY SHORT STORIES, AS PROMISED.
I'LL READ THEM.
THANKS A BUNCH.

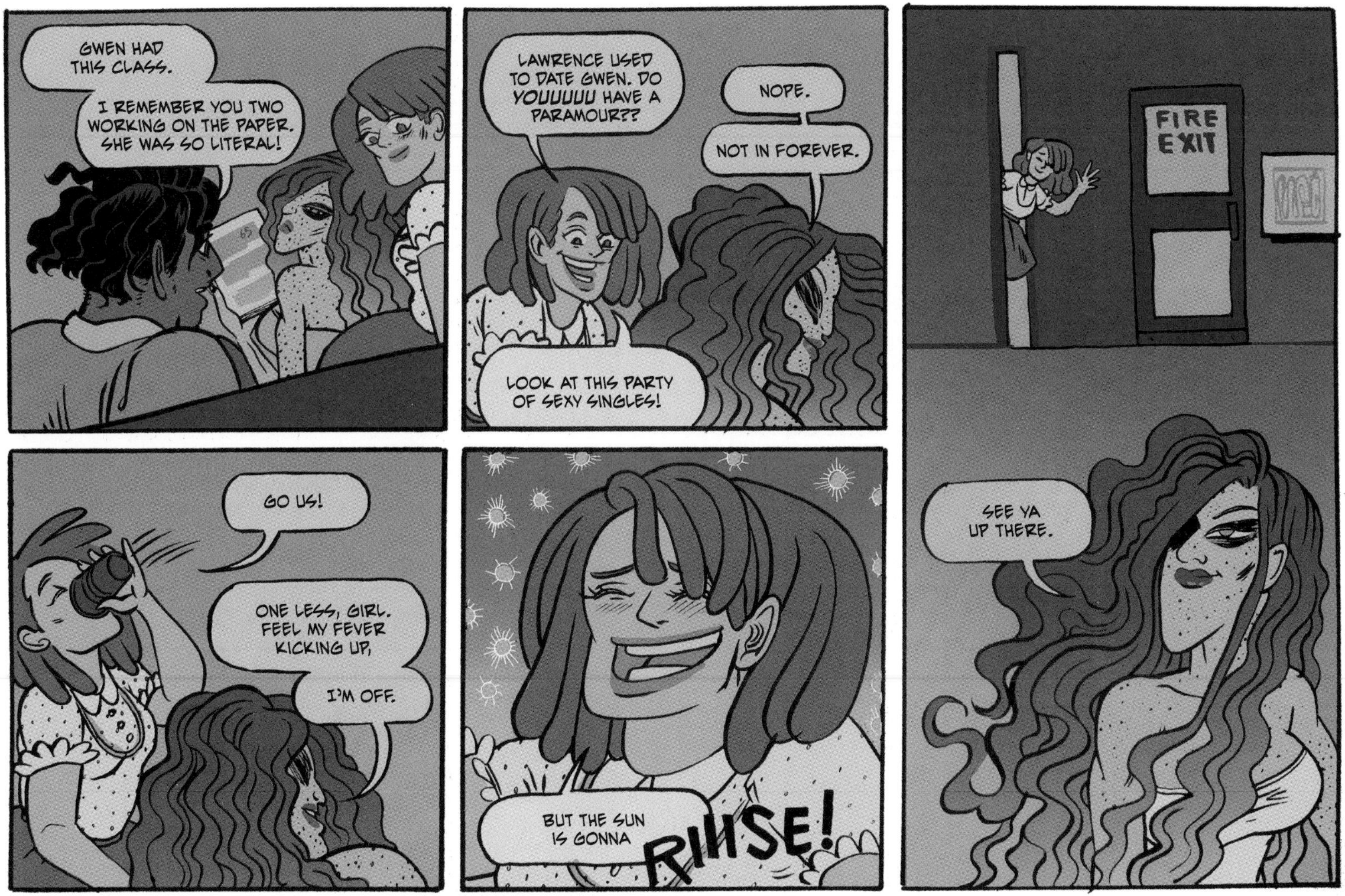
GWEN HAD THIS CLASS.
I REMEMBER YOU TWO WORKING ON THE PAPER. SHE WAS SO LITERAL!
LAWRENCE USED TO DATE GWEN. DO YOUUUUU HAVE A PARAMOUR??
NOPE.
NOT IN FOREVER.
LOOK AT THIS PARTY OF SEXY SINGLES!
FIRE EXIT
GO US!
ONE LESS, GIRL. FEEL MY FEVER KICKING UP,
I'M OFF.
BUT THE SUN IS GONNA
RIIISE!
SEE YA UP THERE.

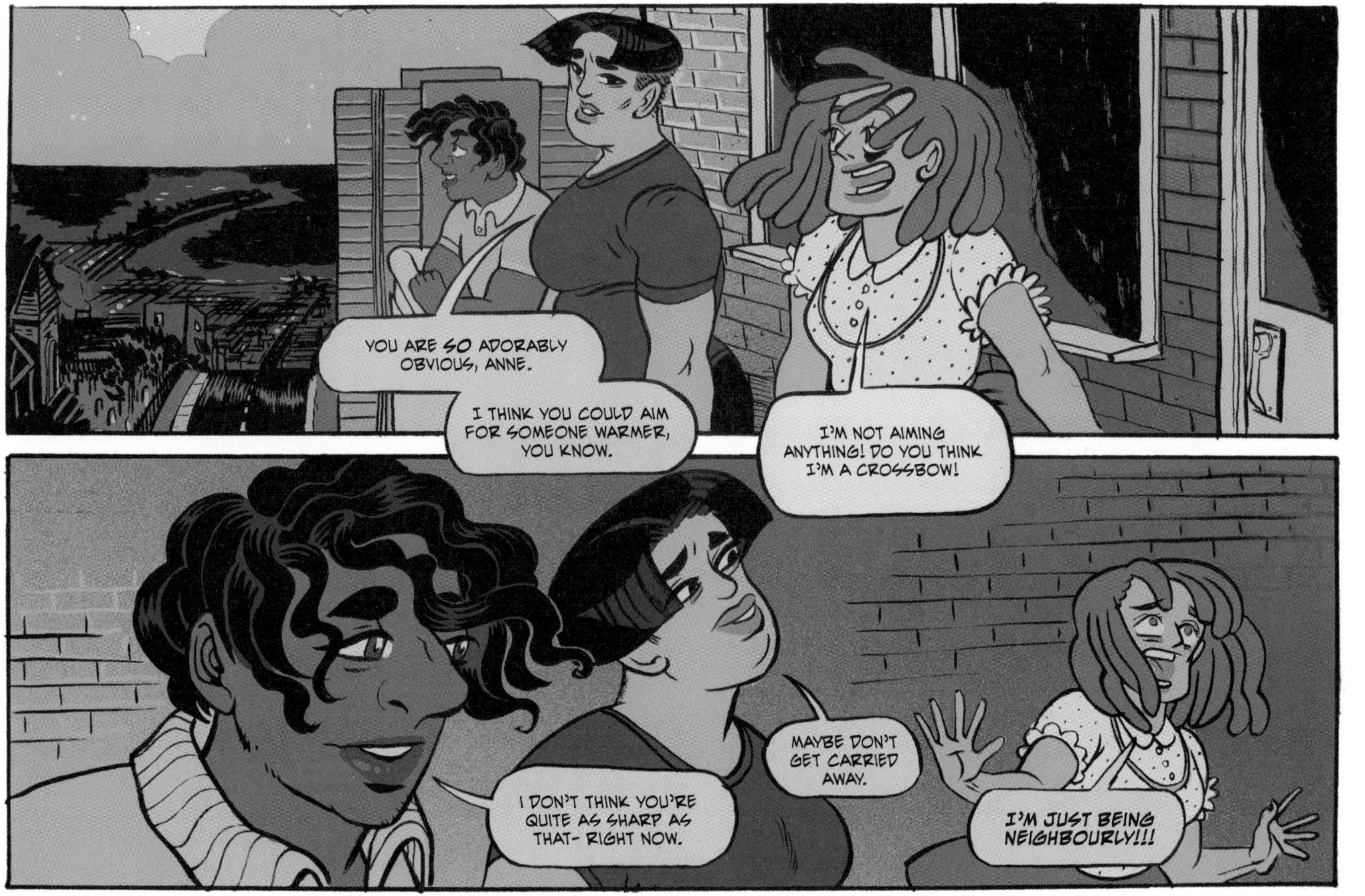
YOU ARE SO ADORABLY OBVIOUS, ANNE.
I THINK YOU COULD AIM FOR SOMEONE WARMER, YOU KNOW.
I'M NOT AIMING ANYTHING! DO YOU THINK I'M A CROSSBOW!
I DON'T THINK YOU'RE QUITE AS SHARP AS THAT- RIGHT NOW.
MAYBE DON'T GET CARRIED AWAY.
I'M JUST BEING NEIGHBOURLY!!!

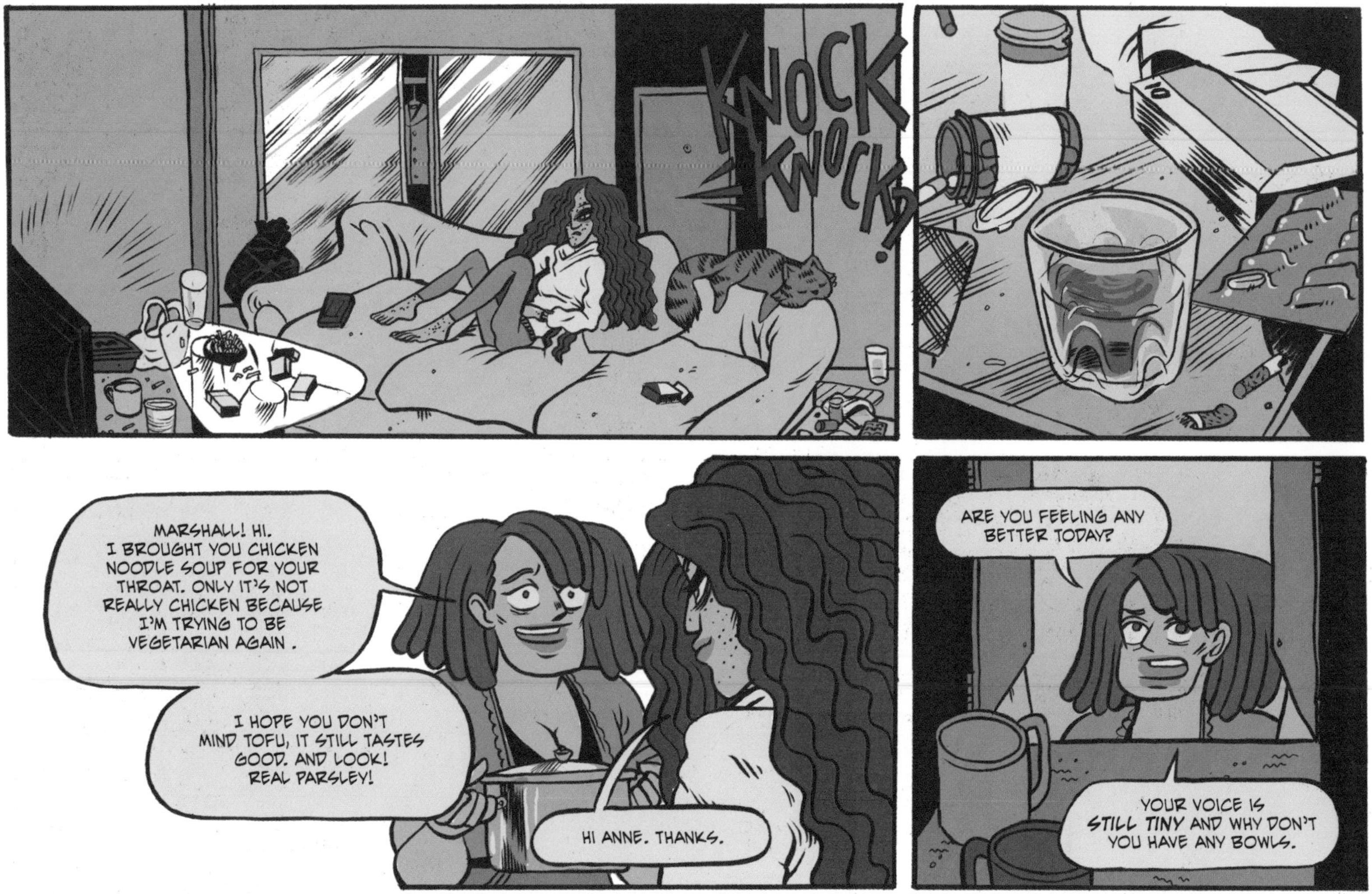
KNOCK KNOCK!
MARSHALL! HI. I BROUGHT YOU CHICKEN NOODLE SOUP FOR YOUR THROAT. ONLY IT'S NOT REALLY CHICKEN BECAUSE I'M TRYING TO BE VEGETARIAN AGAIN .
I HOPE YOU DON'T MIND TOFU, IT STILL TASTES GOOD. AND LOOK! REAL PARSLEY!
HI ANNE. THANKS.
ARE YOU FEELING ANY BETTER TODAY?
YOUR VOICE IS STILL TINY AND WHY DON'T YOU HAVE ANY BOWLS.

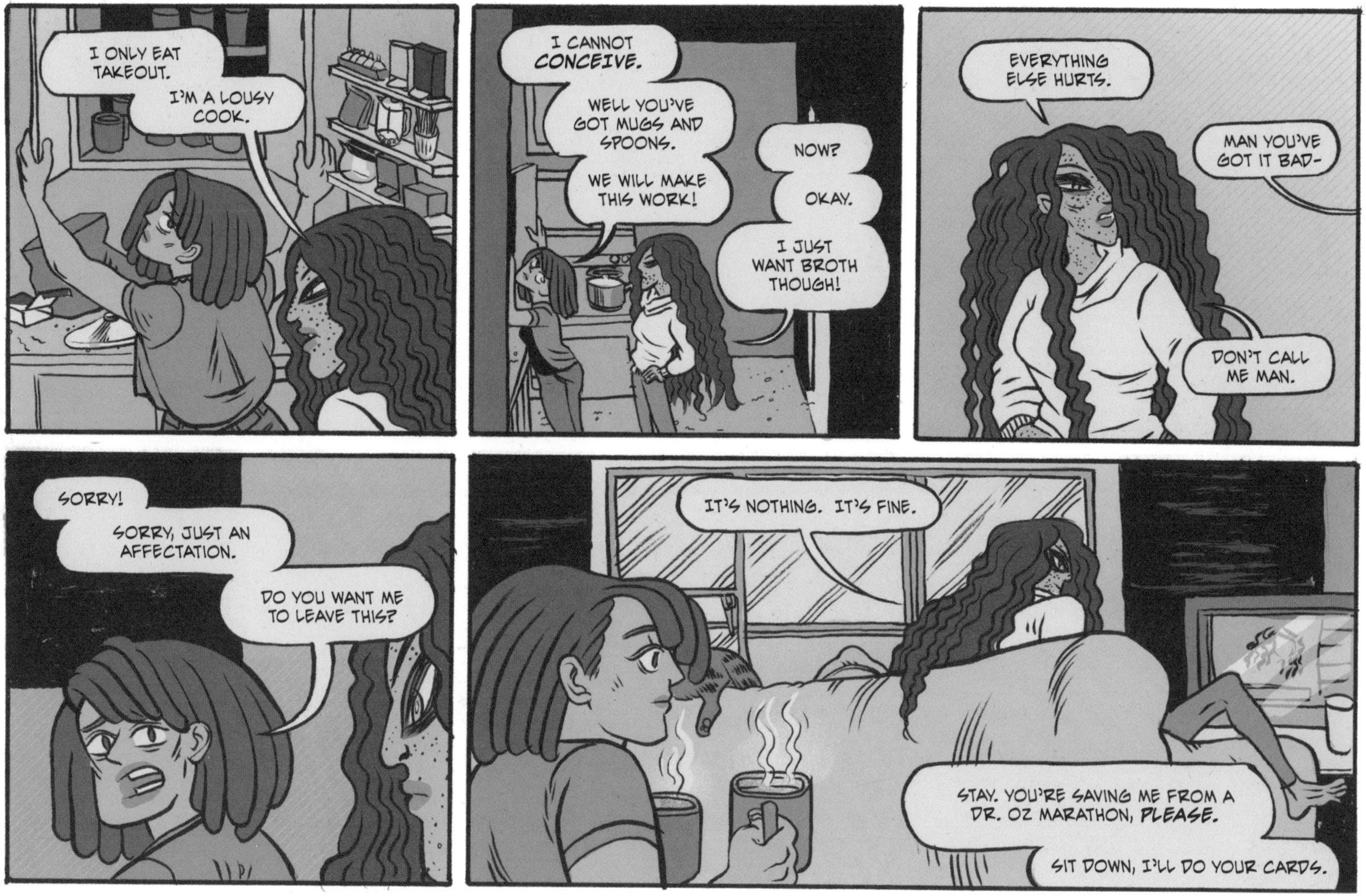
I ONLY EAT TAKEOUT.
I'M A LOUSY COOK.
I CANNOT CONCEIVE.
WELL YOU'VE GOT MUGS AND SPOONS.
WE WILL MAKE THIS WORK!
NOW?
OKAY.
I JUST WANT BROTH THOUGH!
EVERYTHING ELSE HURTS.
MAN YOU'VE GOT IT BAD-
DON'T CALL ME MAN.
SORRY!
SORRY, JUST AN AFFECTATION.
DO YOU WANT ME TO LEAVE THIS?
IT'S NOTHING. IT'S FINE.
STAY. YOU'RE SAVING ME FROM A DR. OZ MARATHON, PLEASE.
SIT DOWN, I'LL DO YOUR CARDS.

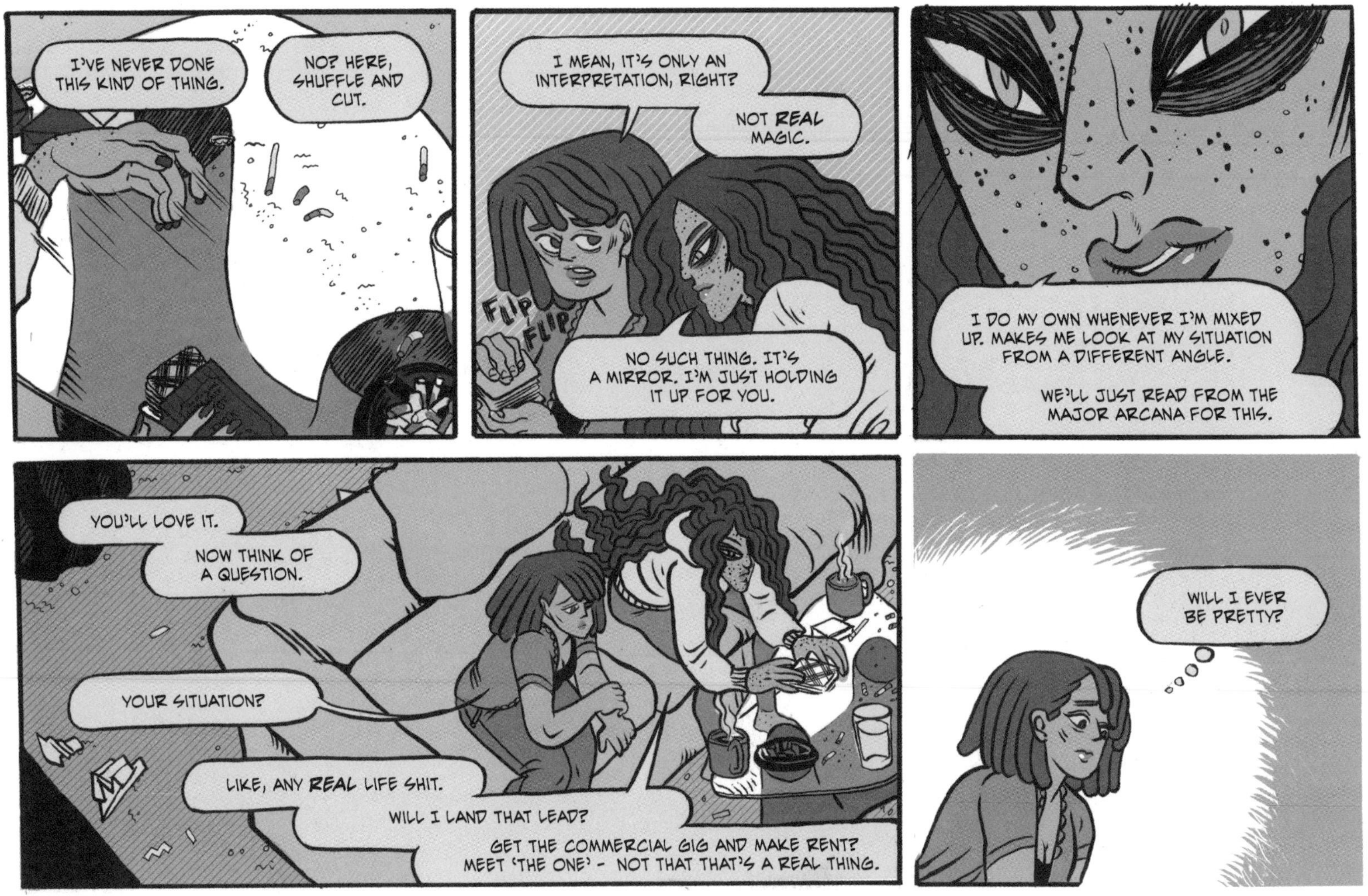
I'VE NEVER DONE THIS KIND OF THING.
NO? HERE, SHUFFLE AND CUT.
I MEAN, IT'S ONLY AN INTERPRETATION, RIGHT?
NOT REAL MAGIC.
FLIP FLIP
NO SUCH THING. IT'S A MIRROR. I'M JUST HOLDING IT UP FOR YOU.
I DO MY OWN WHENEVER I'M MIXED UP. MAKES ME LOOK AT MY SITUATION FROM A DIFFERENT ANGLE.
WE'LL JUST READ FROM THE MAJOR ARCANA FOR THIS.
YOU'LL LOVE IT.
NOW THINK OF A QUESTION.
YOUR SITUATION?
LIKE, ANY REAL LIFE SHIT.
WILL I LAND THAT LEAD?
GET THE COMMERCIAL GIG AND MAKE RENT?
MEET 'THE ONE' - NOT THAT THAT'S A REAL THING.
WILL I EVER BE PRETTY?

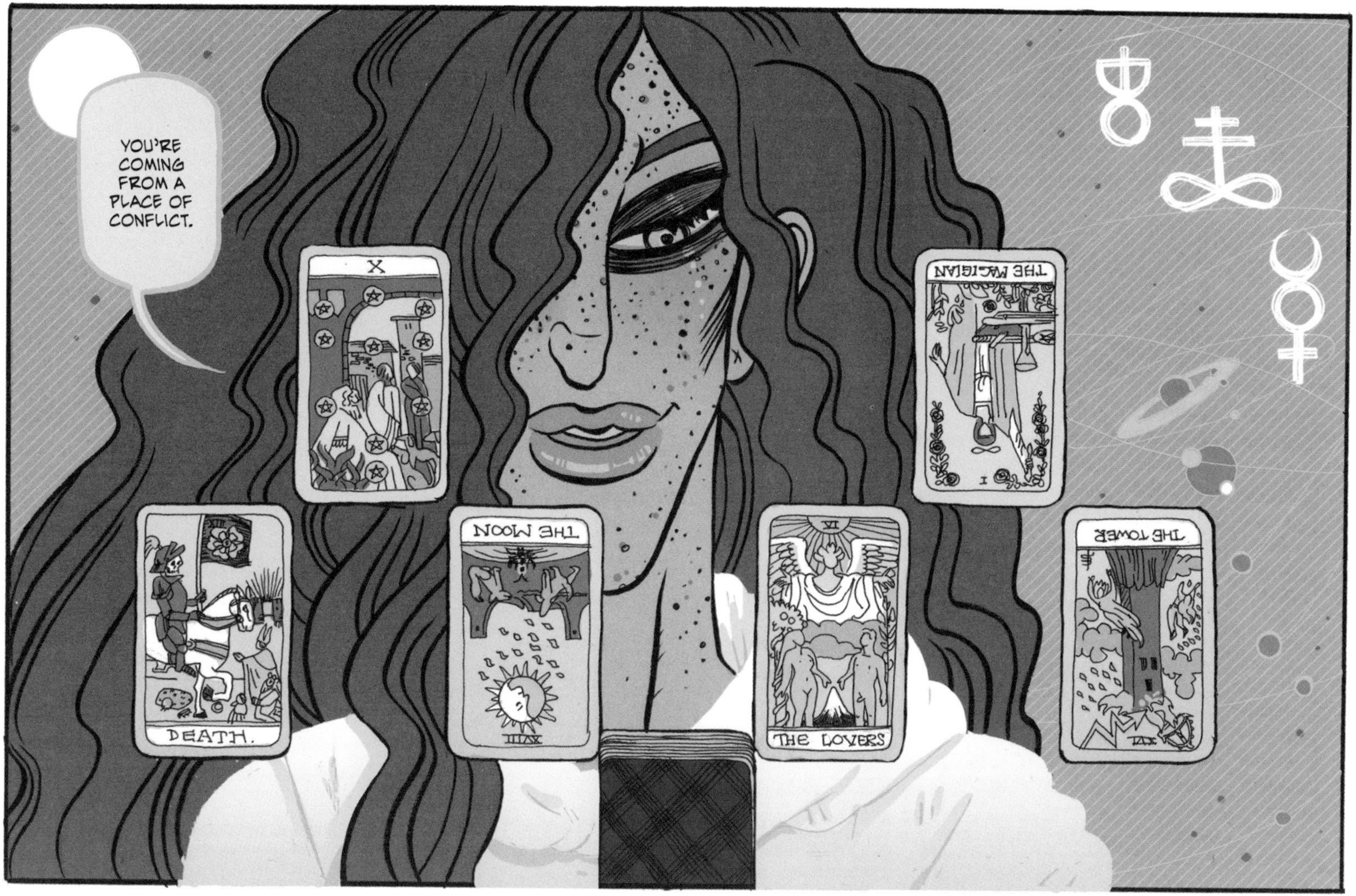
YOU'RE COMING FROM A PLACE OF CONFLICT.
X
THE MAGICIAN
I
DEATH.
THE MOON
XVIII
VI
THE LOVERS
THE TOWER

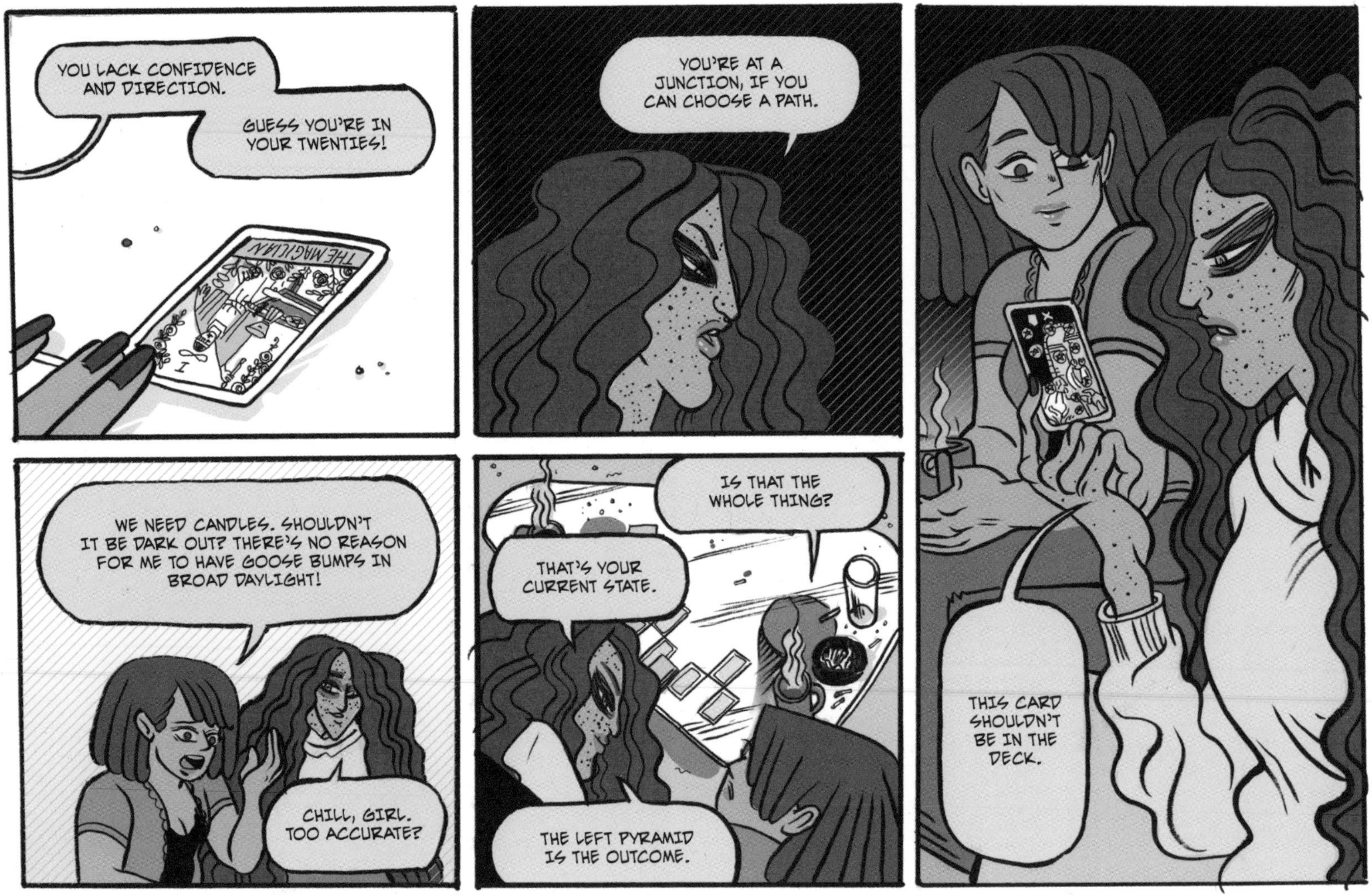
YOU LACK CONFIDENCE AND DIRECTION.
GUESS YOU'RE IN YOUR TWENTIES!
THE MAGICIAN
YOU'RE AT A JUNCTION, IF YOU CAN CHOOSE A PATH.
THIS CARD SHOULDN'T BE IN THE DECK.
WE NEED CANDLES. SHOULDN'T IT BE DARK OUT? THERE'S NO REASON FOR ME TO HAVE GOOSE BUMPS IN BROAD DAYLIGHT!
CHILL, GIRL. TOO ACCURATE?
IS THAT THE WHOLE THING?
THAT'S YOUR CURRENT STATE.
THE LEFT PYRAMID IS THE OUTCOME.

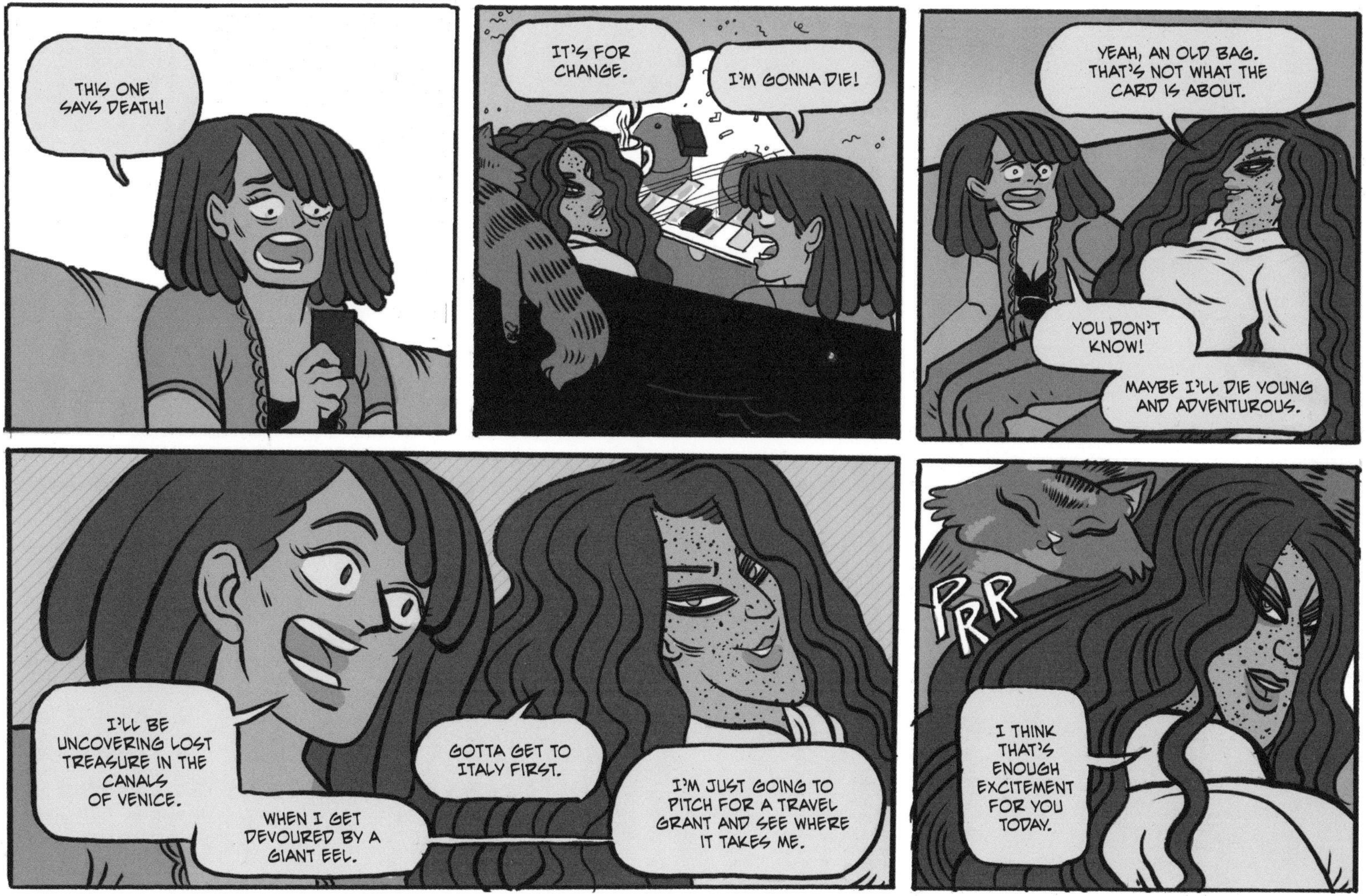
THIS ONE SAYS DEATH!
IT'S FOR CHANGE.
I'M GONNA DIE!
YEAH, AN OLD BAG. THAT'S NOT WHAT THE CARD IS ABOUT.
YOU DON'T KNOW!
MAYBE I'LL DIE YOUNG AND ADVENTUROUS.
I'LL BE UNCOVERING LOST TREASURE IN THE CANALS OF VENICE.
WHEN I GET DEVOURED BY A GIANT EEL.
GOTTA GET TO ITALY FIRST.
I'M JUST GOING TO PITCH FOR A TRAVEL GRANT AND SEE WHERE IT TAKES ME.
PRR
I THINK THAT'S ENOUGH EXCITEMENT FOR YOU TODAY.

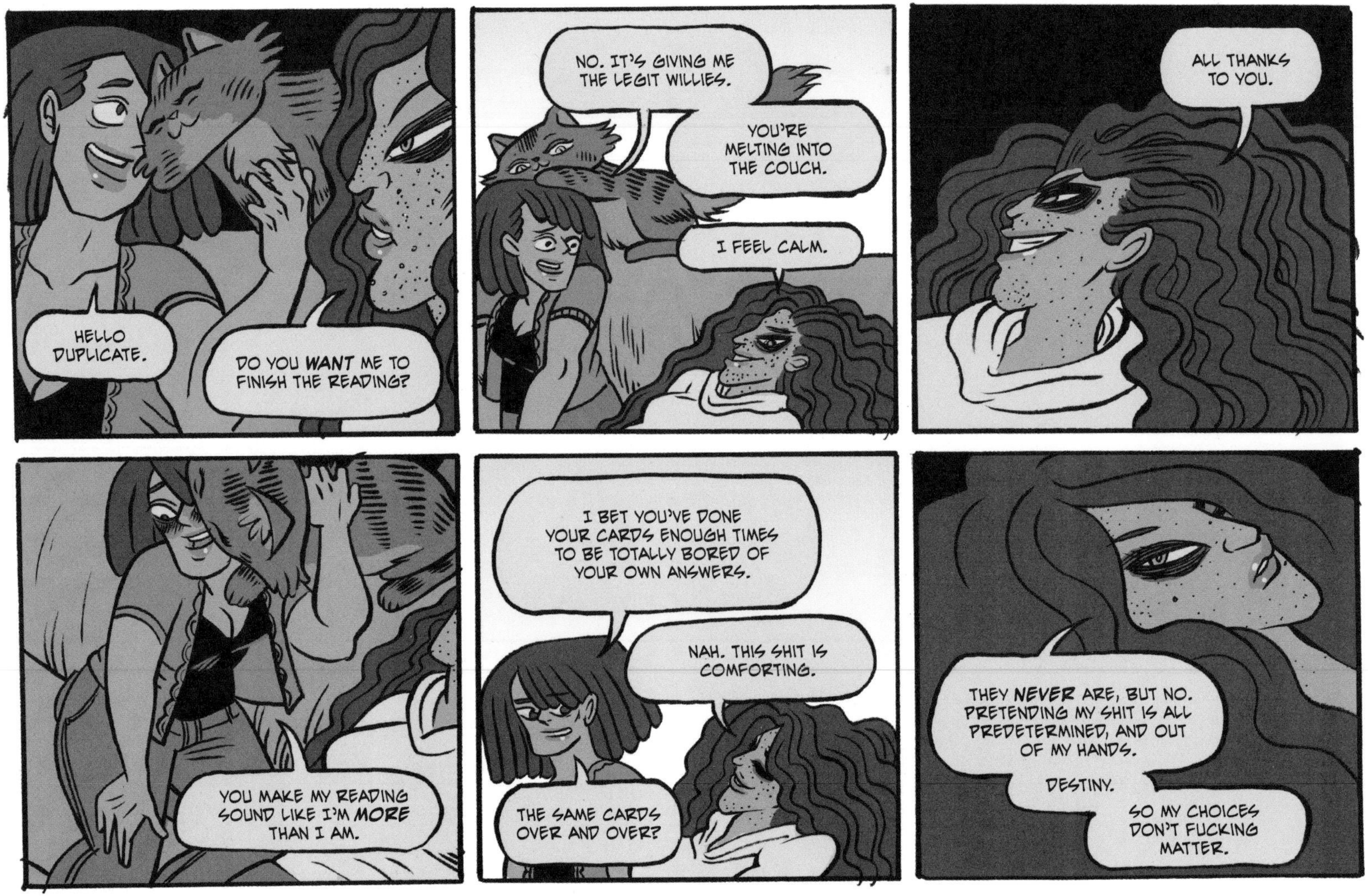
HELLO DUPLICATE.
DO YOU WANT ME TO FINISH THE READING?
NO. IT'S GIVING ME THE LEGIT WILLIES.
YOU'RE MELTING INTO THE COUCH.
I FEEL CALM.
ALL THANKS TO YOU.
YOU MAKE MY READING SOUND LIKE I'M MORE THAN I AM.
I BET YOU'VE DONE YOUR CARDS ENOUGH TIMES TO BE TOTALLY BORED OF YOUR OWN ANSWERS.
NAH. THIS SHIT IS COMFORTING.
THE SAME CARDS OVER AND OVER?
THEY NEVER ARE, BUT NO. PRETENDING MY SHIT IS ALL PREDETERMINED, AND OUT OF MY HANDS.
DESTINY.
SO MY CHOICES DON'T FUCKING MATTER.

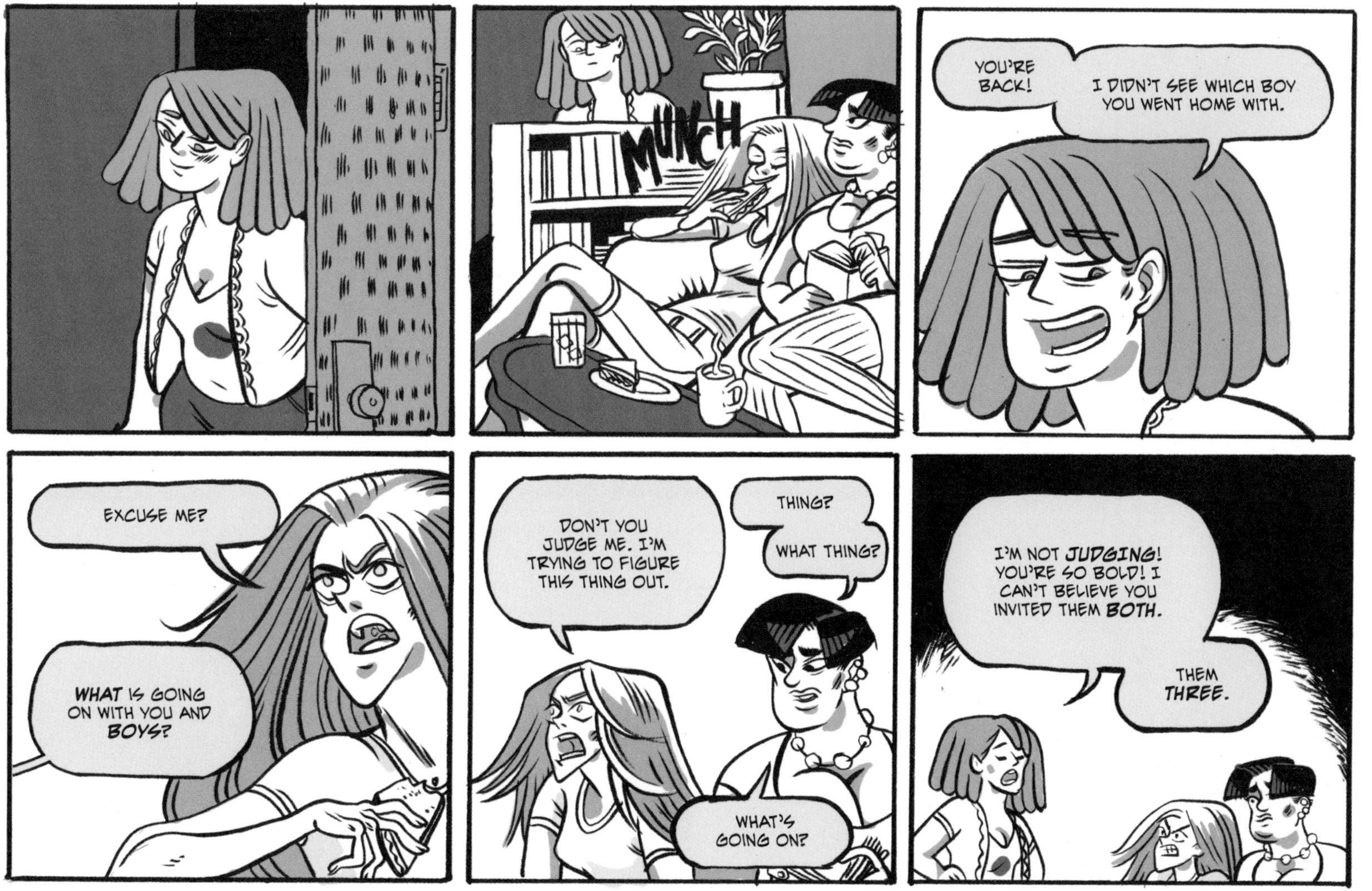
MUNCH
YOU'RE BACK!
I DIDN'T SEE WHICH BOY YOU WENT HOME WITH.
EXCUSE ME?
WHAT IS GOING ON WITH YOU AND BOYS?
DON'T YOU JUDGE ME. I'M TRYING TO FIGURE THIS THING OUT.
THING?
WHAT THING?
WHAT'S GOING ON?
I'M NOT JUDGING! YOU'RE SO BOLD! I CAN'T BELIEVE YOU INVITED THEM BOTH.
THEM THREE.

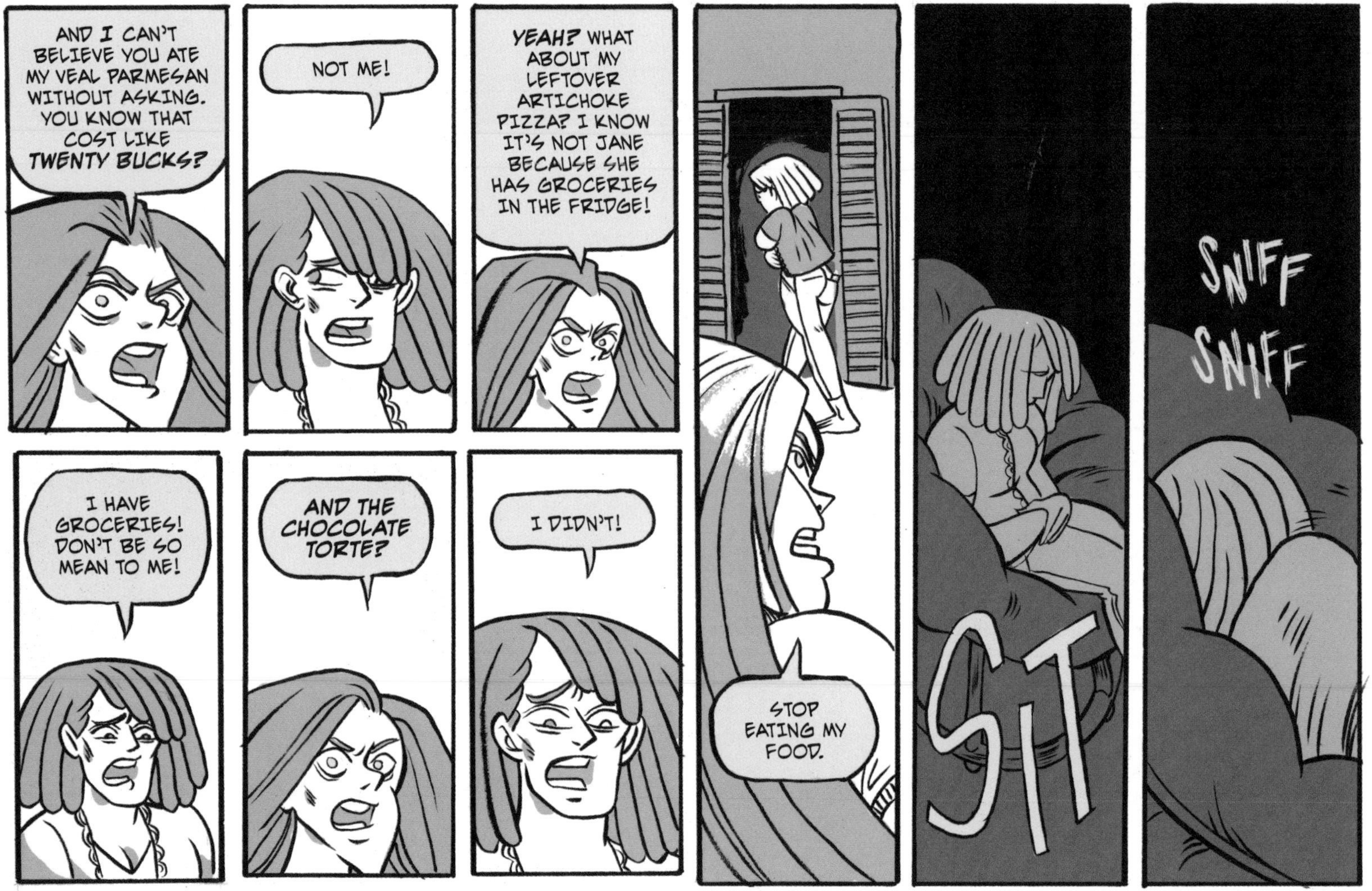
AND I CAN'T BELIEVE YOU ATE MY VEAL PARMESAN WITHOUT ASKING. YOU KNOW THAT COST LIKE TWENTY BUCKS?
NOT ME!
YEAH? WHAT ABOUT MY LEFTOVER ARTICHOKE PIZZA? I KNOW IT'S NOT JANE BECAUSE SHE HAS GROCERIES IN THE FRIDGE!
I HAVE GROCERIES! DON'T BE SO MEAN TO ME!
AND THE CHOCOLATE TORTE?
I DIDN'T!
STOP EATING MY FOOD.
SIT
SNIFF
SNIFF

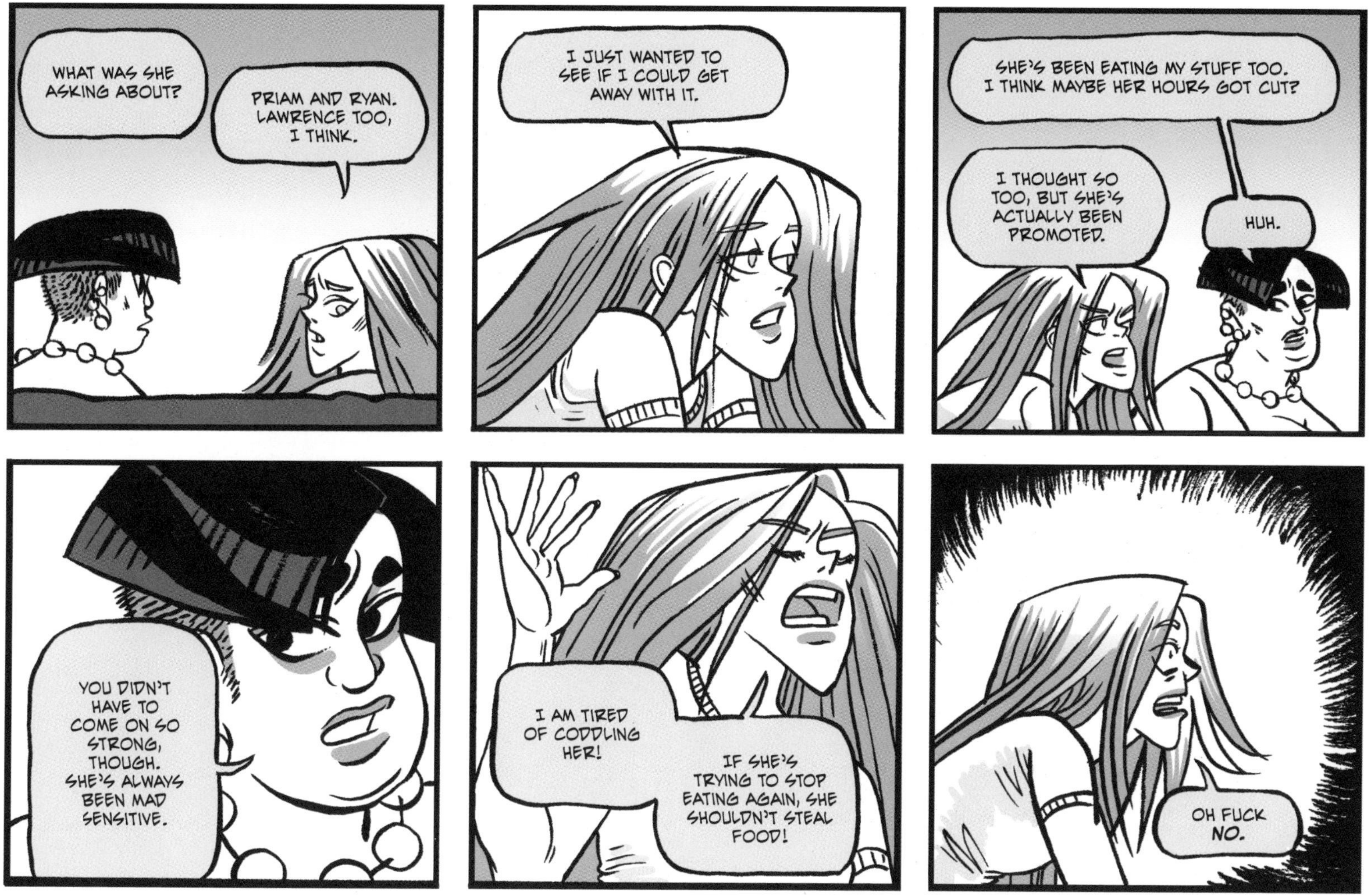
WHAT WAS SHE ASKING ABOUT?
PRIAM AND RYAN. LAWRENCE TOO, I THINK.
I JUST WANTED TO SEE IF I COULD GET AWAY WITH IT.
SHE'S BEEN EATING MY STUFF TOO. I THINK MAYBE HER HOURS GOT CUT?
I THOUGHT SO TOO, BUT SHE'S ACTUALLY BEEN PROMOTED.
HUH.
YOU DIDN'T HAVE TO COME ON SO STRONG, THOUGH. SHE'S ALWAYS BEEN MAD SENSITIVE.
I AM TIRED OF CODDLING HER!
IF SHE'S TRYING TO STOP EATING AGAIN, SHE SHOULDN'T STEAL FOOD!
OH FUCK NO.

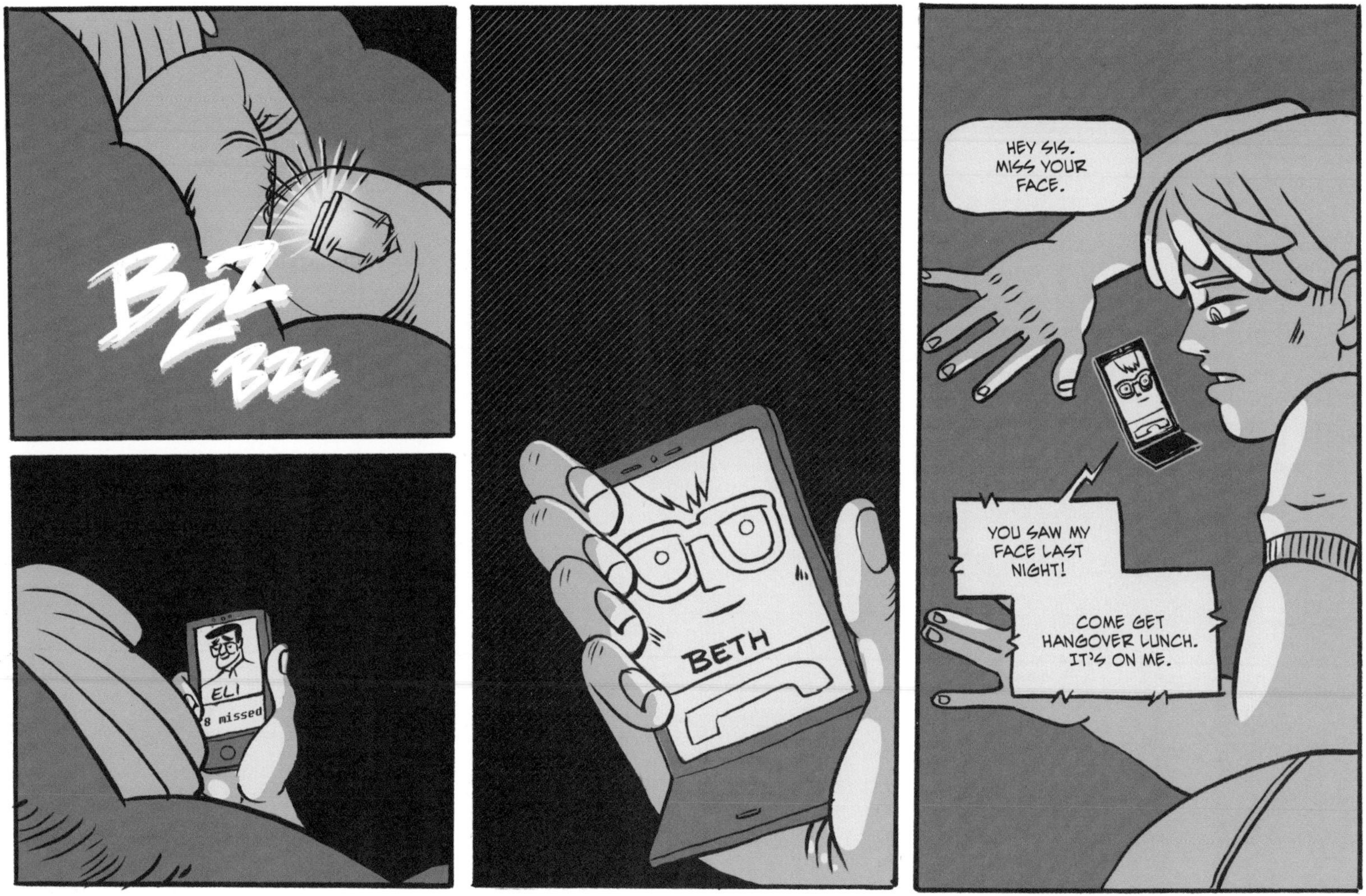
BZZ BZZ
ELI
8 missed
BETH
HEY SIS. MISS YOUR FACE.
YOU SAW MY FACE LAST NIGHT!
COME GET HANGOVER LUNCH. IT'S ON ME.

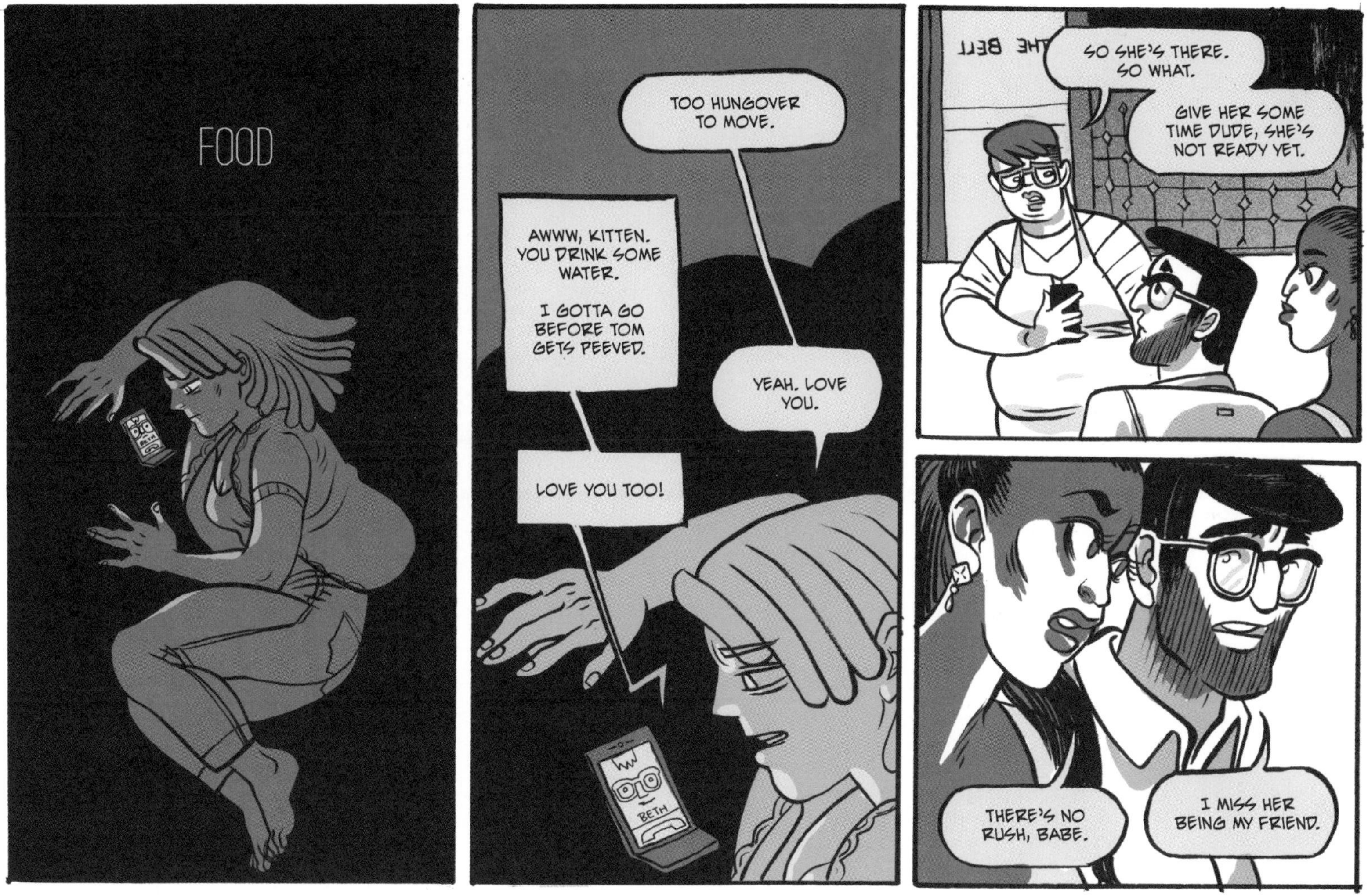
FOOD
TOO HUNGOVER TO MOVE.
AWWW, KITTEN. YOU DRINK SOME WATER.
I GOTTA GO BEFORE TOM GETS PEEVED.
YEAH. LOVE YOU.
LOVE YOU TOO!
BETH
SO SHE'S THERE. SO WHAT.
GIVE HER SOME TIME DUDE, SHE'S NOT READY YET.
THERE'S NO RUSH, BABE.
I MISS HER BEING MY FRIEND.

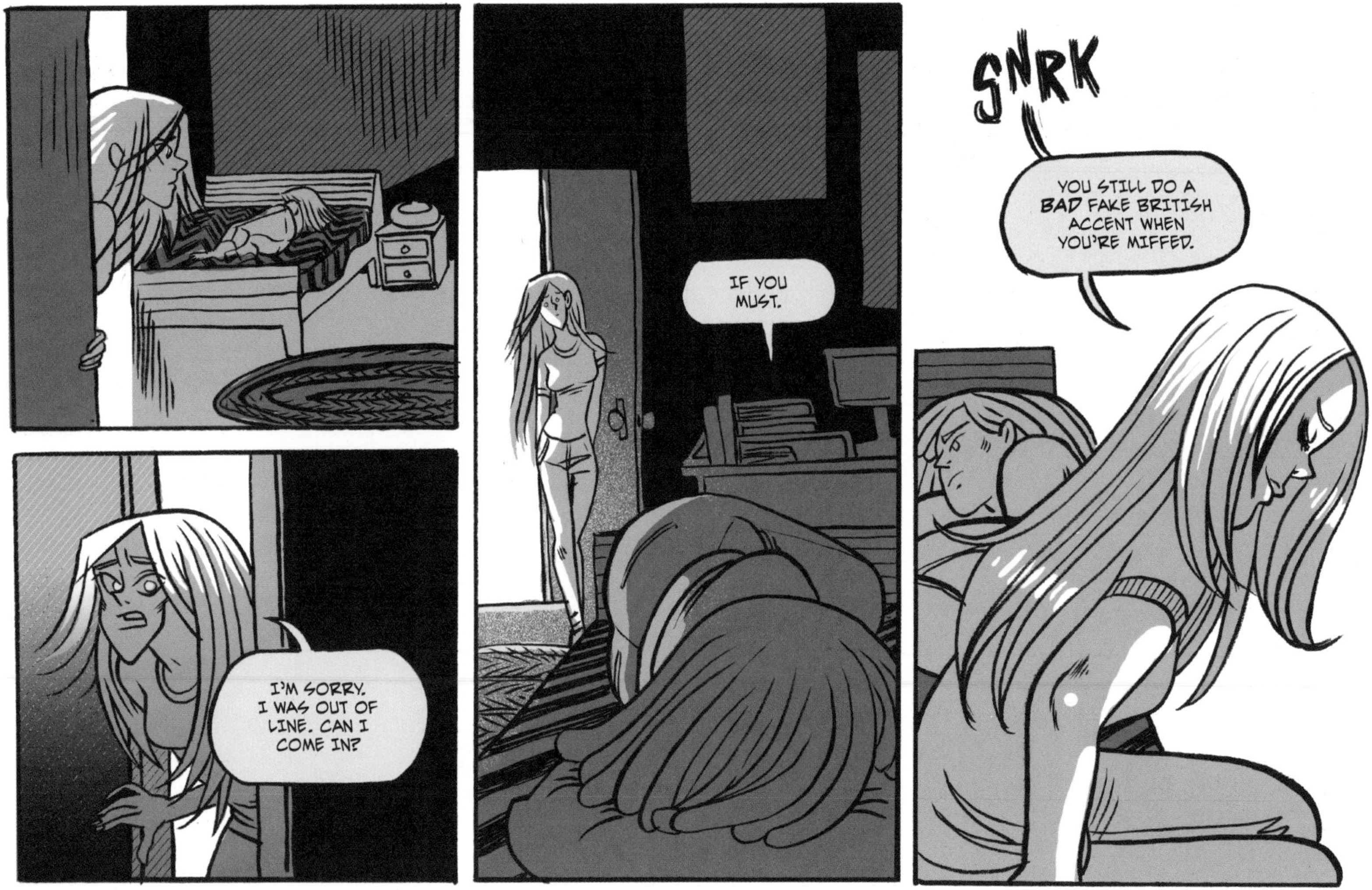
I'M SORRY. I WAS OUT OF LINE. CAN I COME IN?
IF YOU MUST.
SNRK
YOU STILL DO A BAD FAKE BRITISH ACCENT WHEN YOU'RE MIFFED.

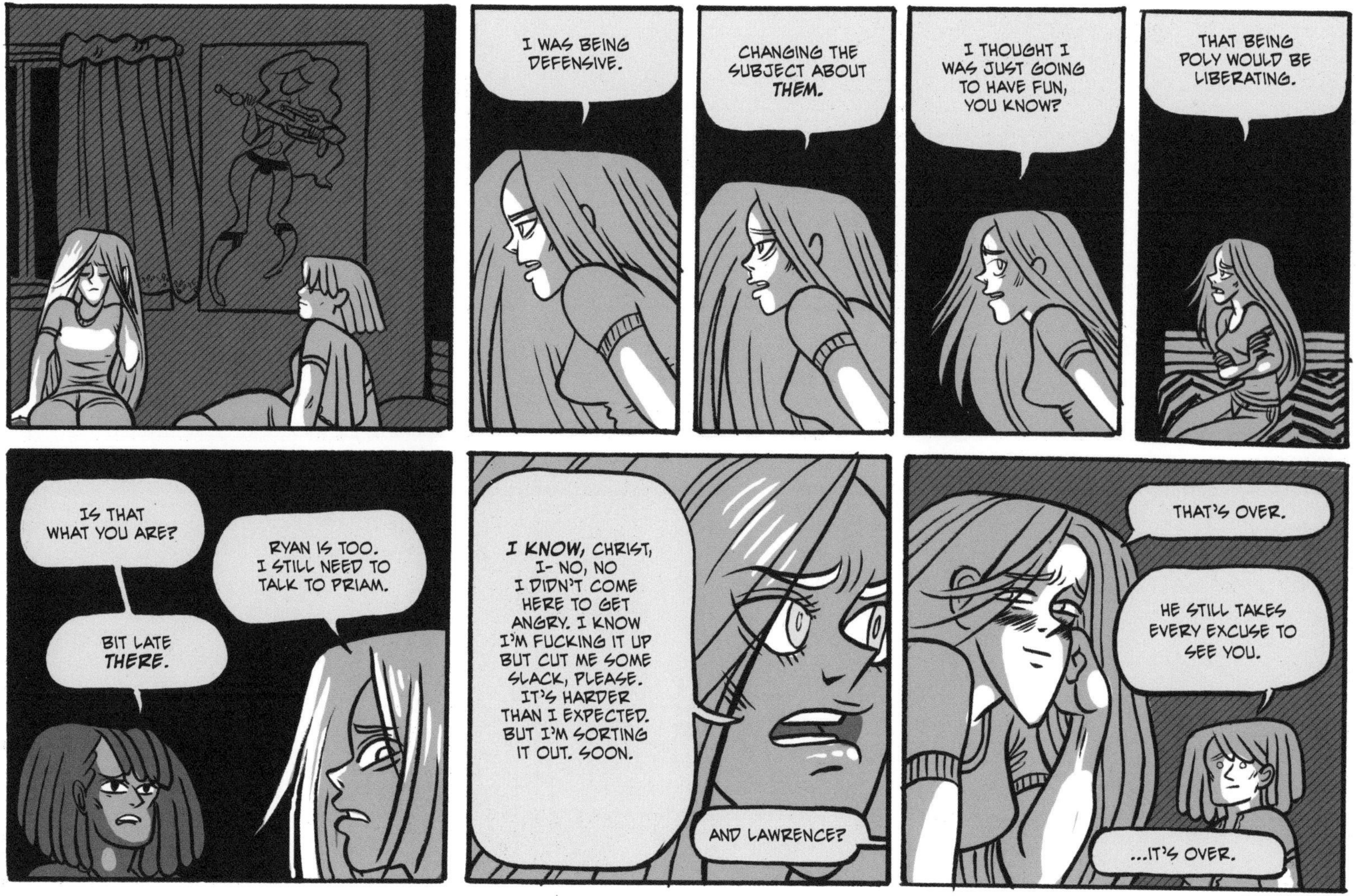
I WAS BEING DEFENSIVE.
CHANGING THE SUBJECT ABOUT *THEM.*
I THOUGHT I WAS JUST GOING TO HAVE FUN, YOU KNOW?
THAT BEING POLY WOULD BE LIBERATING.
IS THAT WHAT YOU ARE?
BIT LATE *THERE.*
RYAN IS TOO. I STILL NEED TO TALK TO PRIAM.
I KNOW, CHRIST, I- NO, NO I DIDN'T COME HERE TO GET ANGRY. I KNOW I'M FUCKING IT UP BUT CUT ME SOME SLACK, PLEASE. IT'S HARDER THAN I EXPECTED. BUT I'M SORTING IT OUT. SOON.
AND LAWRENCE?
THAT'S OVER.
HE STILL TAKES EVERY EXCUSE TO SEE YOU.
...IT'S OVER.

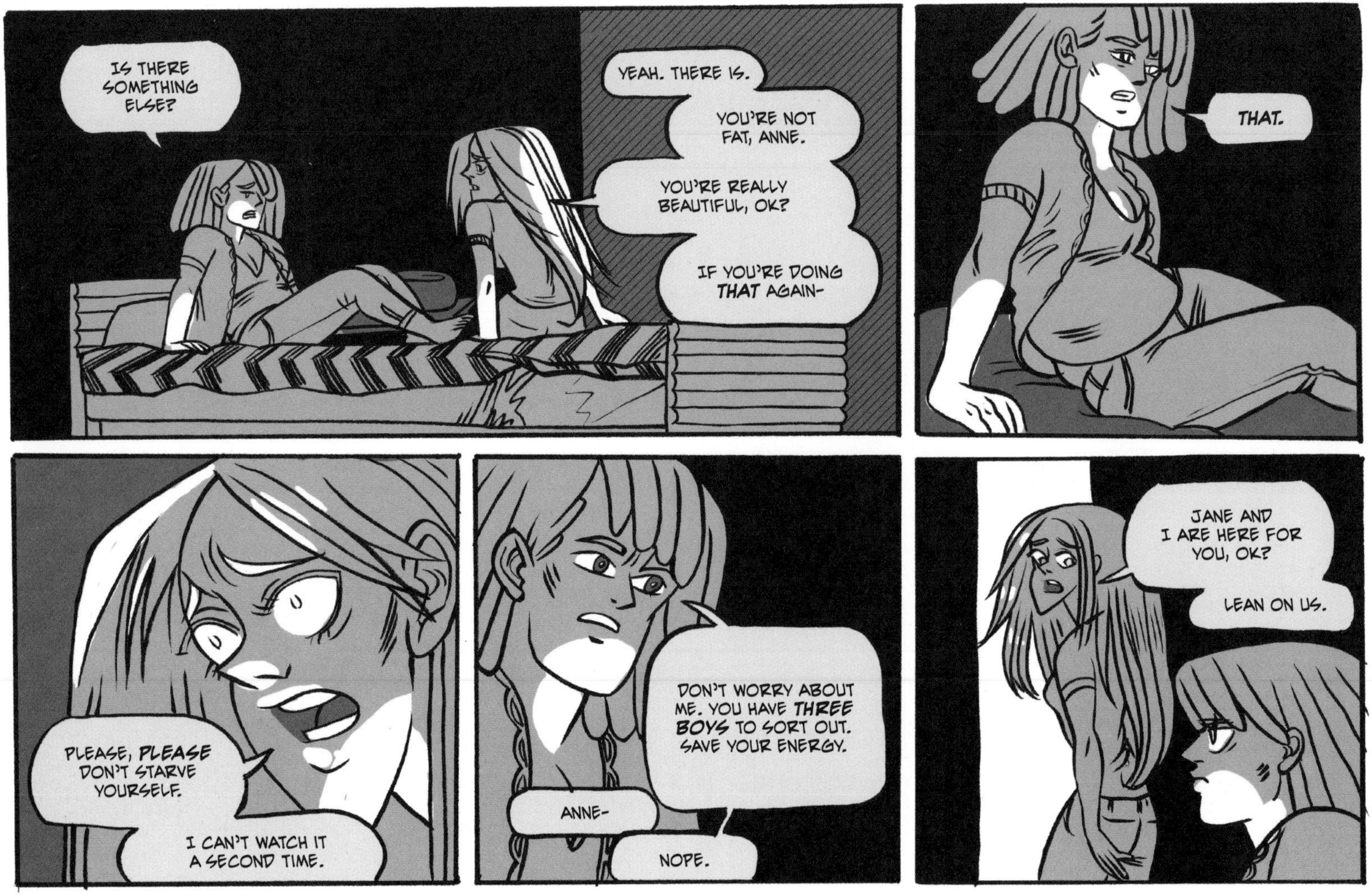
IS THERE SOMETHING ELSE?
YEAH. THERE IS.
YOU'RE NOT FAT, ANNE.
YOU'RE REALLY BEAUTIFUL, OK?
IF YOU'RE DOING **THAT** AGAIN-
THAT.
PLEASE, **PLEASE** DON'T STARVE YOURSELF.
I CAN'T WATCH IT A SECOND TIME.
DON'T WORRY ABOUT ME. YOU HAVE **THREE BOYS** TO SORT OUT. SAVE YOUR ENERGY.
ANNE-
NOPE.
JANE AND I ARE HERE FOR YOU, OK?
LEAN ON US.

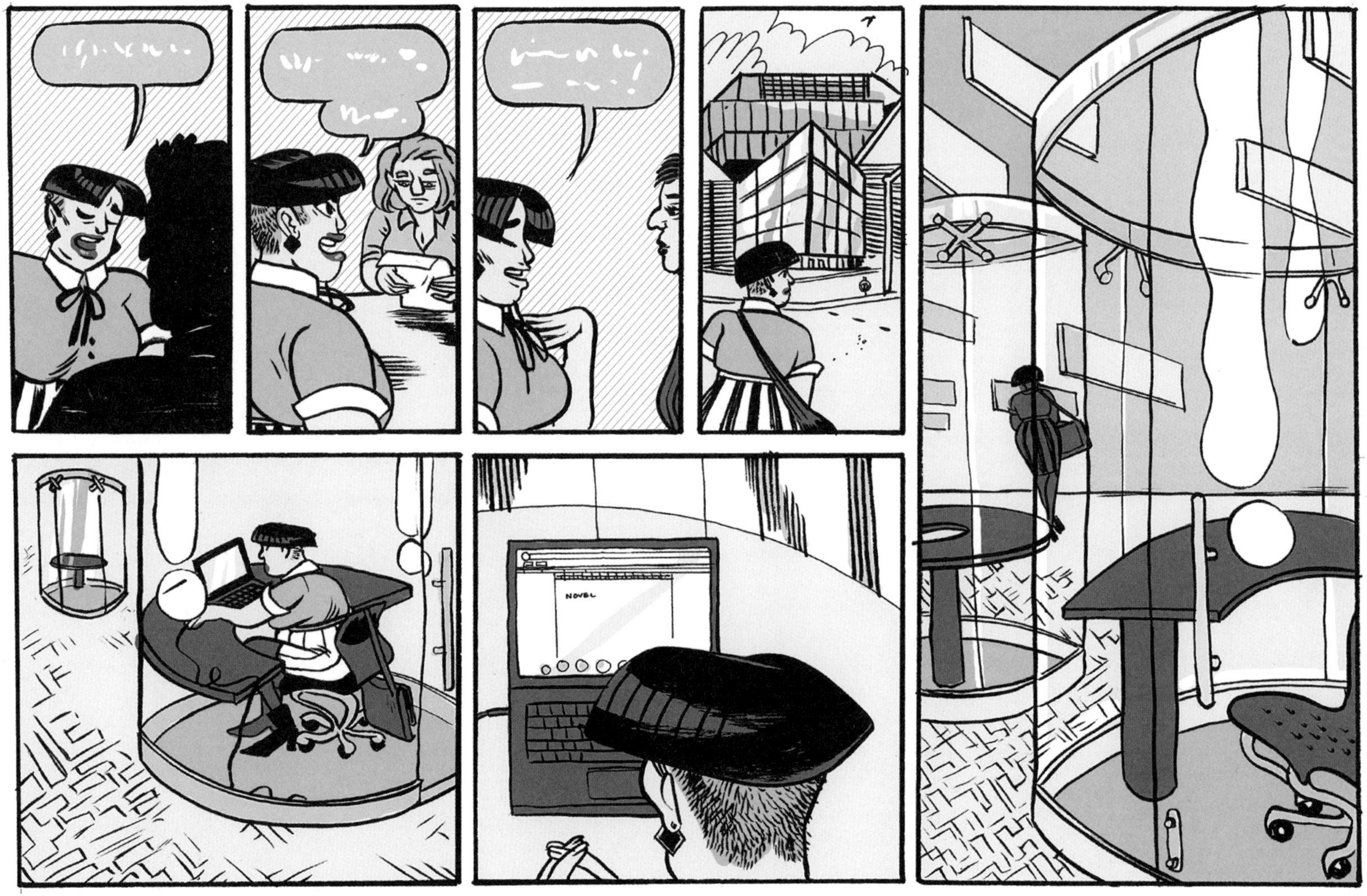
NOVEL

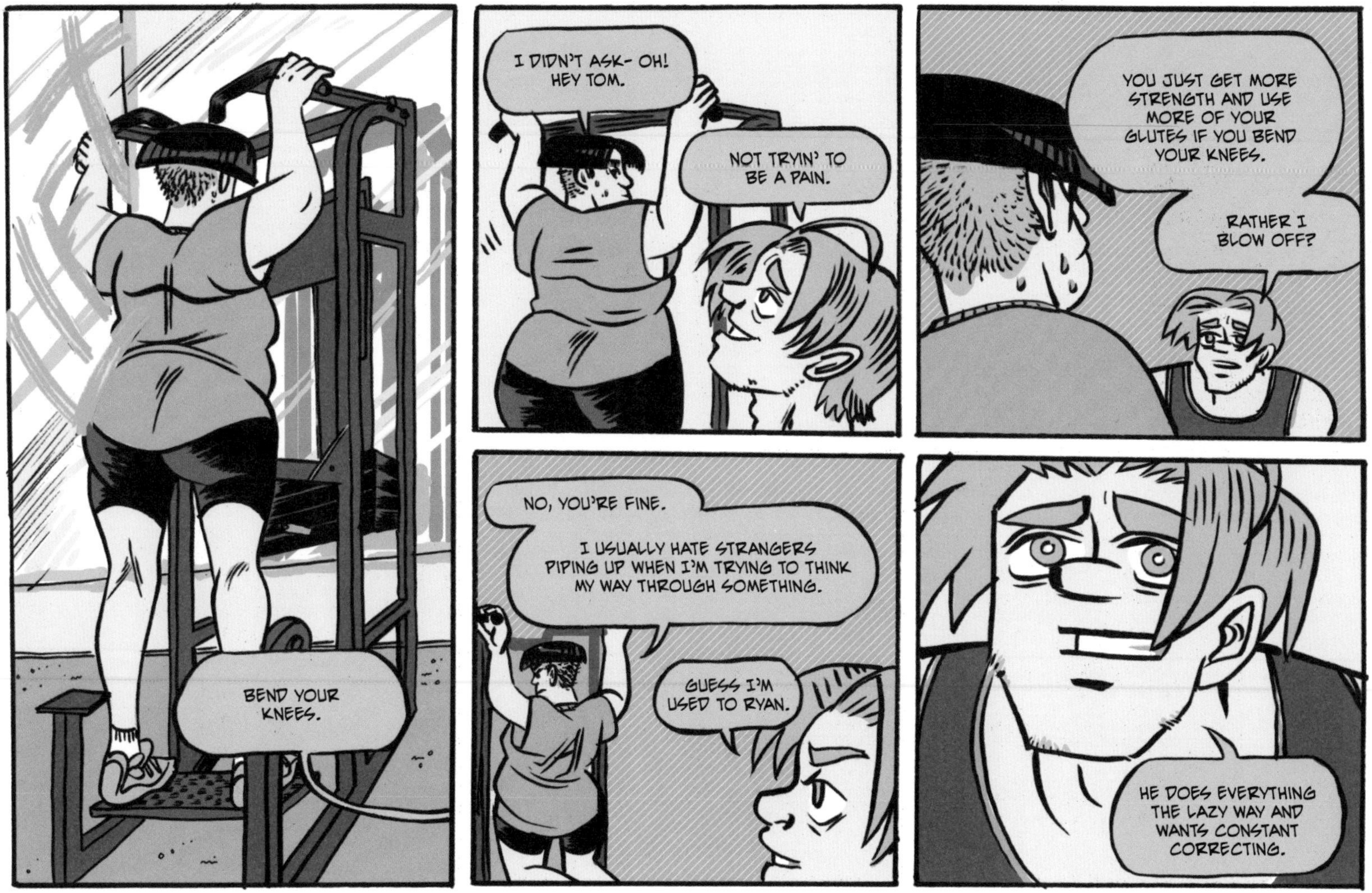
BEND YOUR KNEES.
I DIDN'T ASK- OH! HEY TOM.
NOT TRYIN' TO BE A PAIN.
YOU JUST GET MORE STRENGTH AND USE MORE OF YOUR GLUTES IF YOU BEND YOUR KNEES.
RATHER I BLOW OFF?
NO, YOU'RE FINE.
I USUALLY HATE STRANGERS PIPING UP WHEN I'M TRYING TO THINK MY WAY THROUGH SOMETHING.
GUESS I'M USED TO RYAN.
HE DOES EVERYTHING THE LAZY WAY AND WANTS CONSTANT CORRECTING.

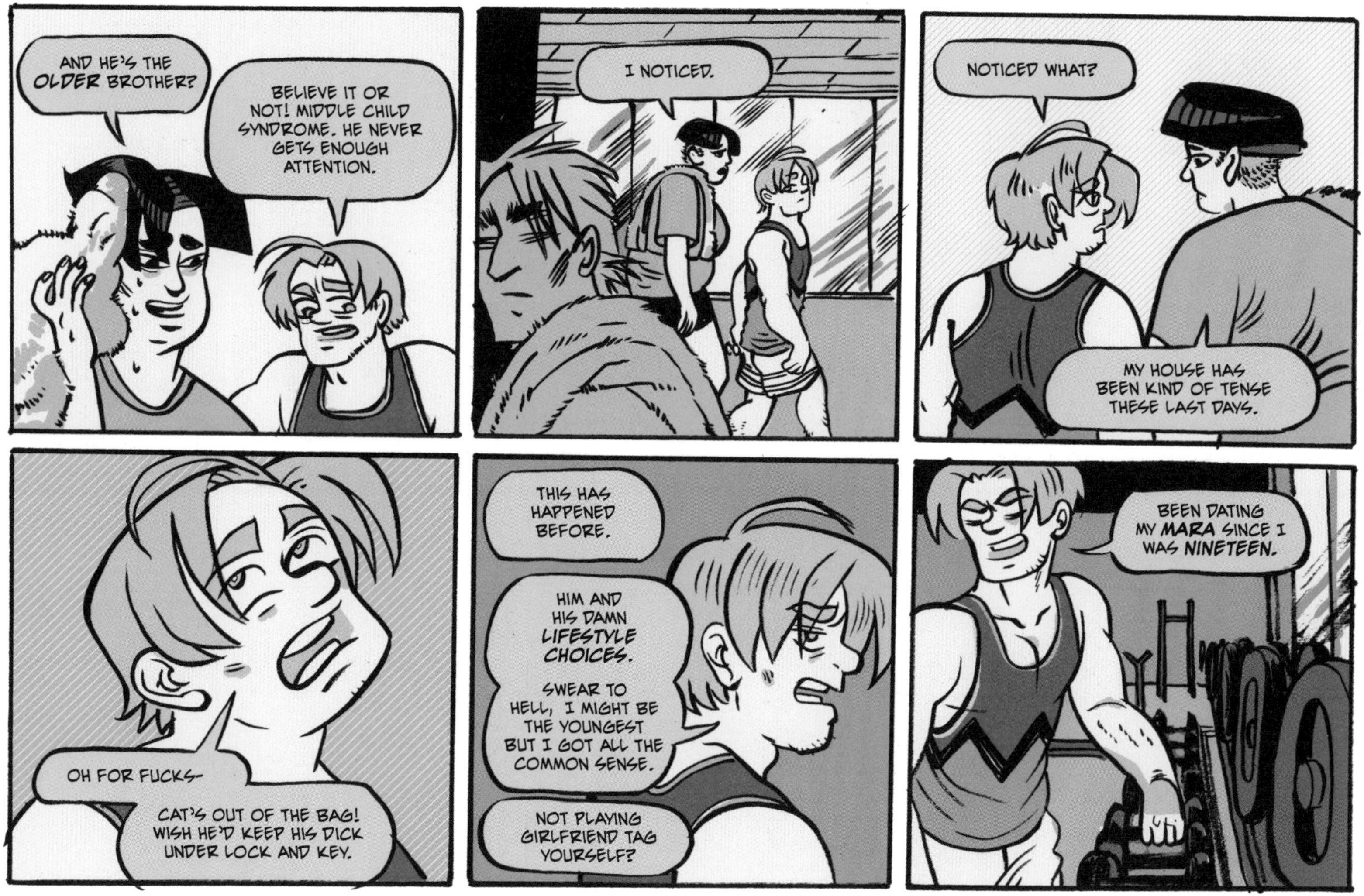
AND HE'S THE OLDER BROTHER?
BELIEVE IT OR NOT! MIDDLE CHILD SYNDROME. HE NEVER GETS ENOUGH ATTENTION.
I NOTICED.
NOTICED WHAT?
MY HOUSE HAS BEEN KIND OF TENSE THESE LAST DAYS.
OH FOR FUCKS-
CAT'S OUT OF THE BAG! WISH HE'D KEEP HIS DICK UNDER LOCK AND KEY.
THIS HAS HAPPENED BEFORE.
HIM AND HIS DAMN LIFESTYLE CHOICES.
SWEAR TO HELL, I MIGHT BE THE YOUNGEST BUT I GOT ALL THE COMMON SENSE.
NOT PLAYING GIRLFRIEND TAG YOURSELF?
BEEN DATING MY MARA SINCE I WAS NINETEEN.

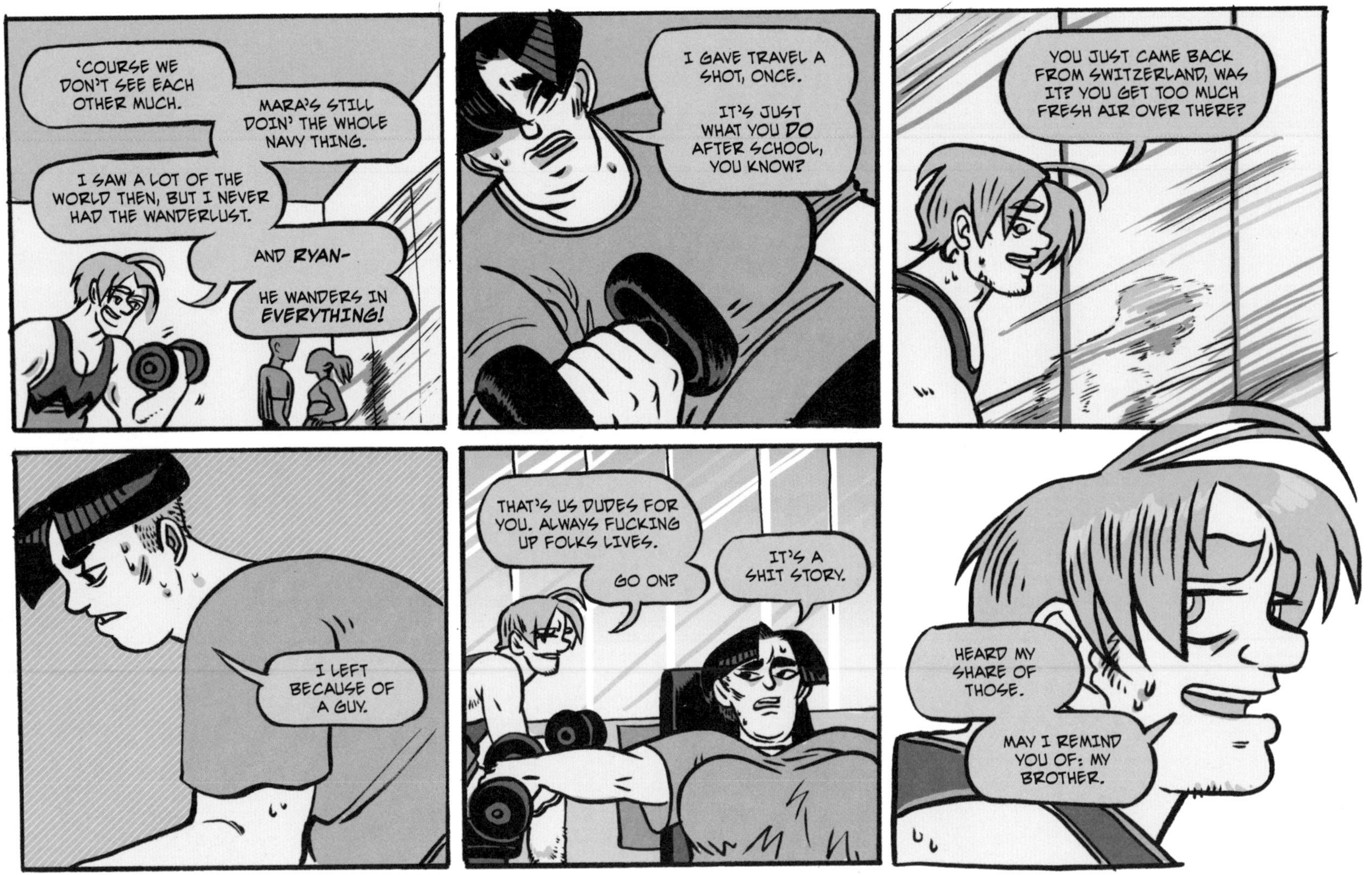
'COURSE WE DON'T SEE EACH OTHER MUCH.
MARA'S STILL DOIN' THE WHOLE NAVY THING.
I SAW A LOT OF THE WORLD THEN, BUT I NEVER HAD THE WANDERLUST.
AND RYAN-
HE WANDERS IN EVERYTHING!
I GAVE TRAVEL A SHOT, ONCE.
IT'S JUST WHAT YOU DO AFTER SCHOOL, YOU KNOW?
YOU JUST CAME BACK FROM SWITZERLAND, WAS IT? YOU GET TOO MUCH FRESH AIR OVER THERE?
I LEFT BECAUSE OF A GUY.
THAT'S US DUDES FOR YOU. ALWAYS FUCKING UP FOLKS LIVES.
GO ON?
IT'S A SHIT STORY.
HEARD MY SHARE OF THOSE.
MAY I REMIND YOU OF: MY BROTHER.

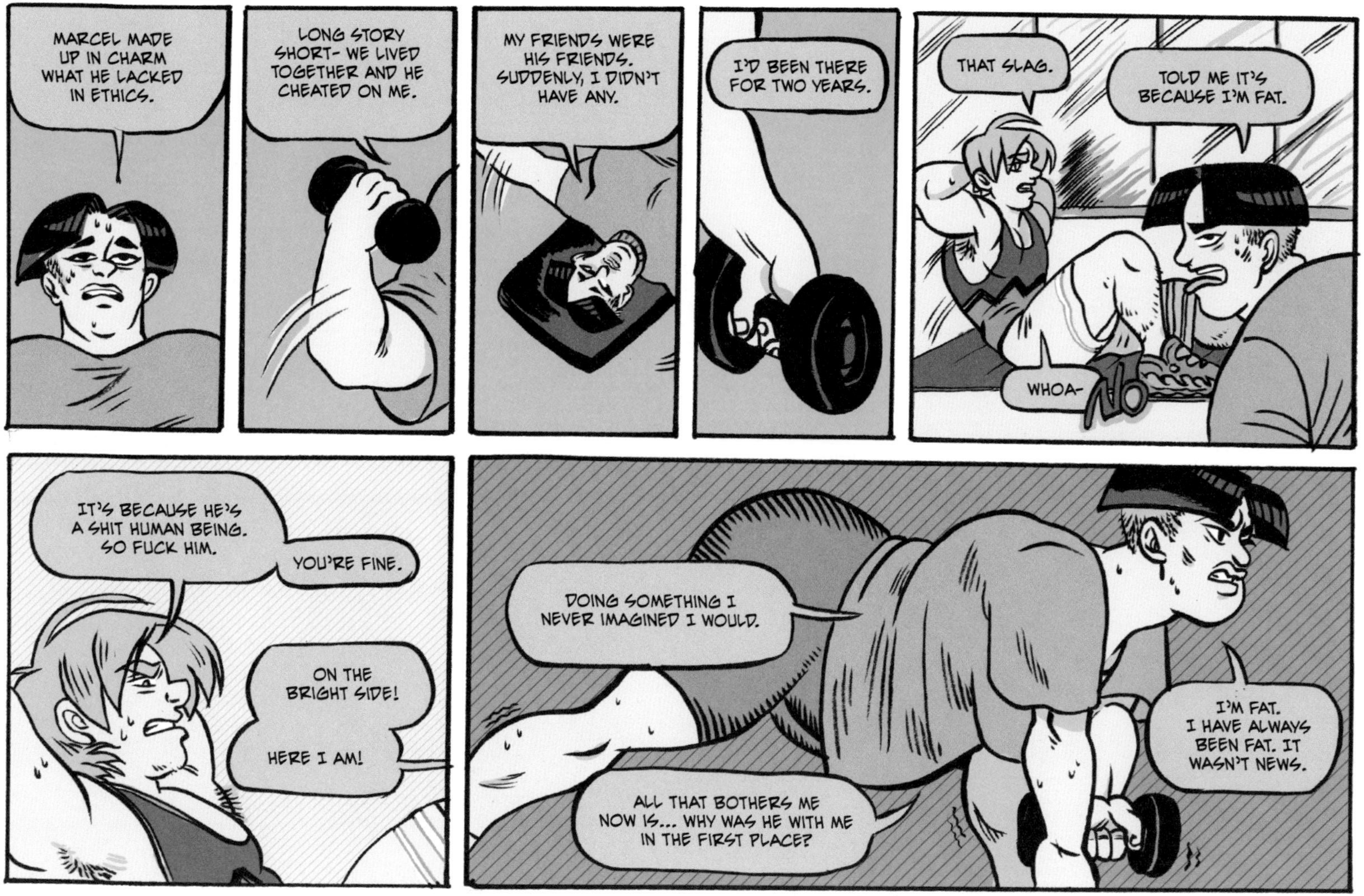
MARCEL MADE UP IN CHARM WHAT HE LACKED IN ETHICS.
LONG STORY SHORT- WE LIVED TOGETHER AND HE CHEATED ON ME.
MY FRIENDS WERE HIS FRIENDS. SUDDENLY, I DIDN'T HAVE ANY.
I'D BEEN THERE FOR TWO YEARS.
THAT SLAG.
TOLD ME IT'S BECAUSE I'M FAT.
WHOA-
IT'S BECAUSE HE'S A SHIT HUMAN BEING. SO FUCK HIM.
YOU'RE FINE.
ON THE BRIGHT SIDE!
HERE I AM!
DOING SOMETHING I NEVER IMAGINED I WOULD.
I'M FAT. I HAVE ALWAYS BEEN FAT. IT WASN'T NEWS.
ALL THAT BOTHERS ME NOW IS... WHY WAS HE WITH ME IN THE FIRST PLACE?

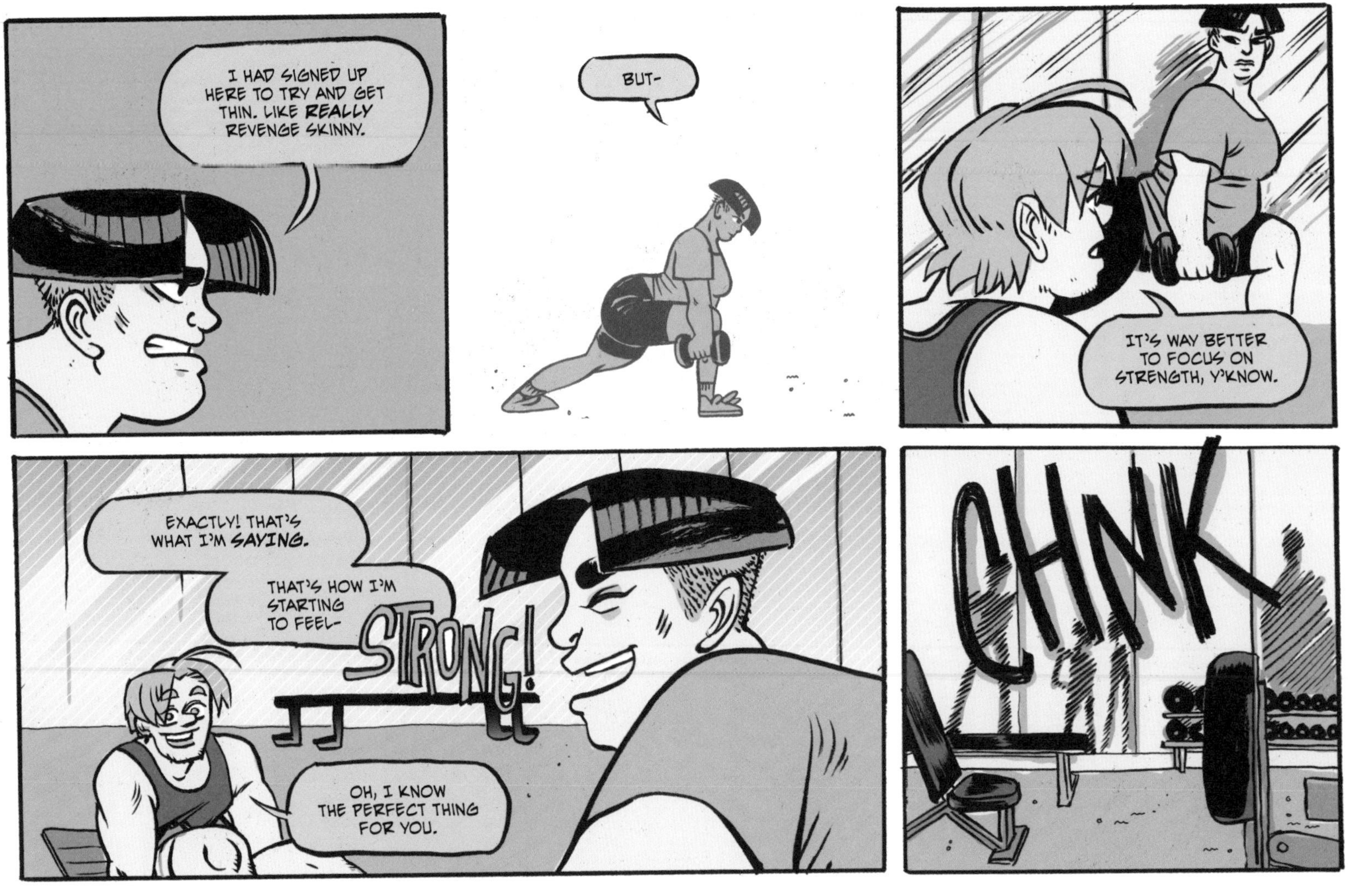
I HAD SIGNED UP HERE TO TRY AND GET THIN. LIKE **REALLY** REVENGE SKINNY.
BUT-
IT'S WAY BETTER TO FOCUS ON STRENGTH, Y'KNOW.
EXACTLY! THAT'S WHAT I'M **SAYING.**
THAT'S HOW I'M STARTING TO FEEL-
STRONG!
OH, I KNOW THE PERFECT THING FOR YOU.
CHNK

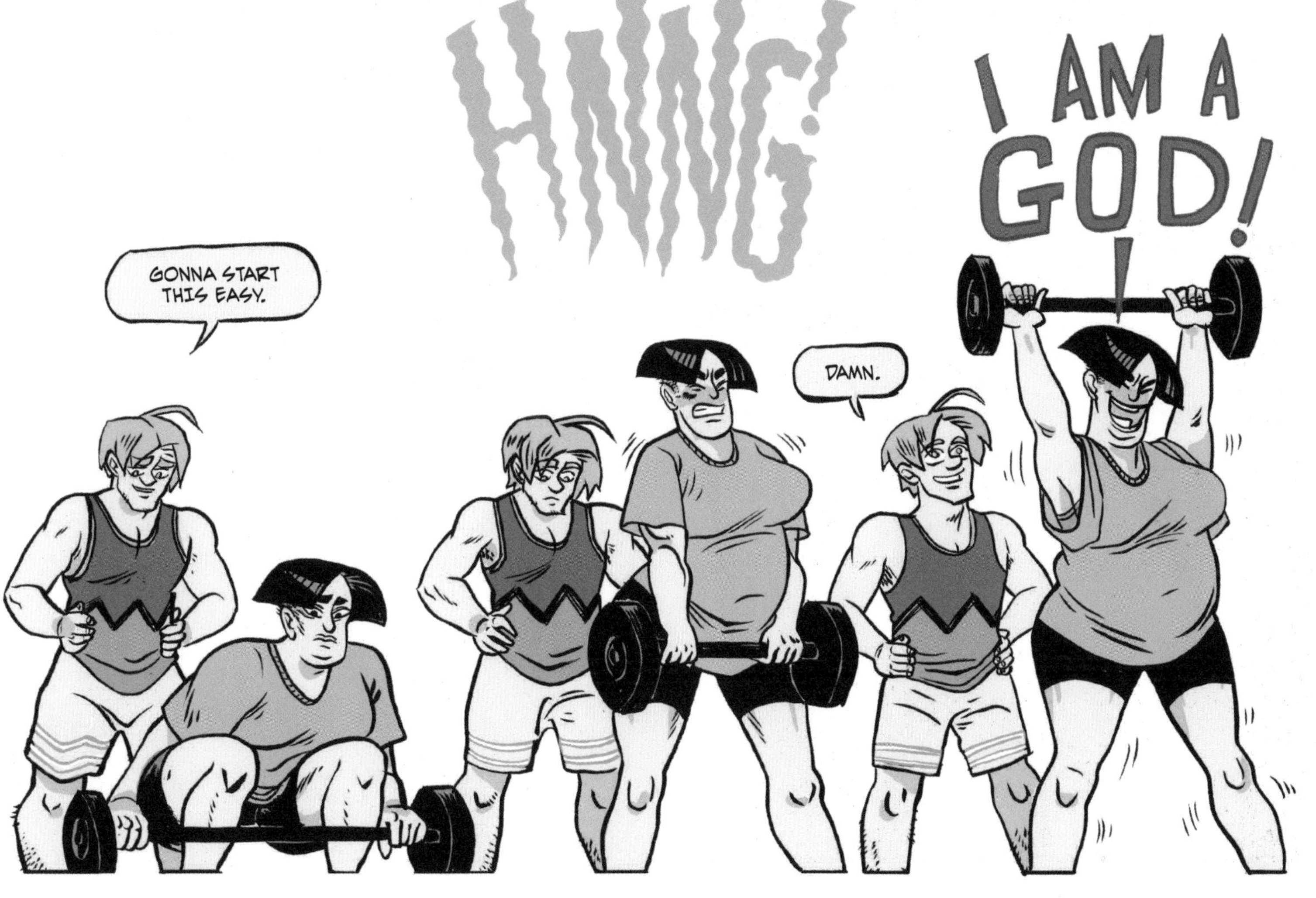
GONNA START THIS EASY.
HNNG!
DAMN.
I AM A GOD!

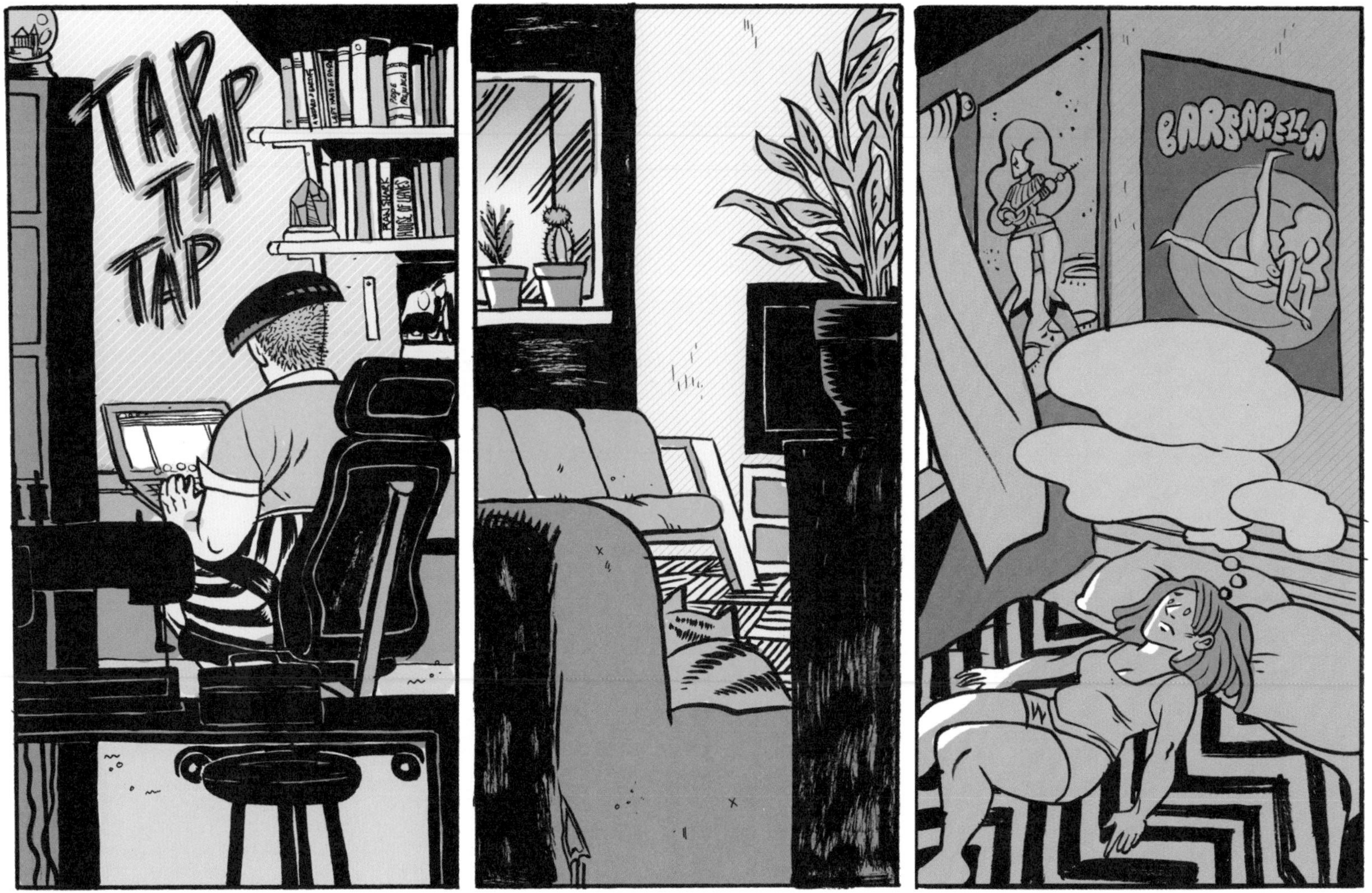
TAP TAP TAP TAP
HOUSE OF LEAVES
BARBARELLA

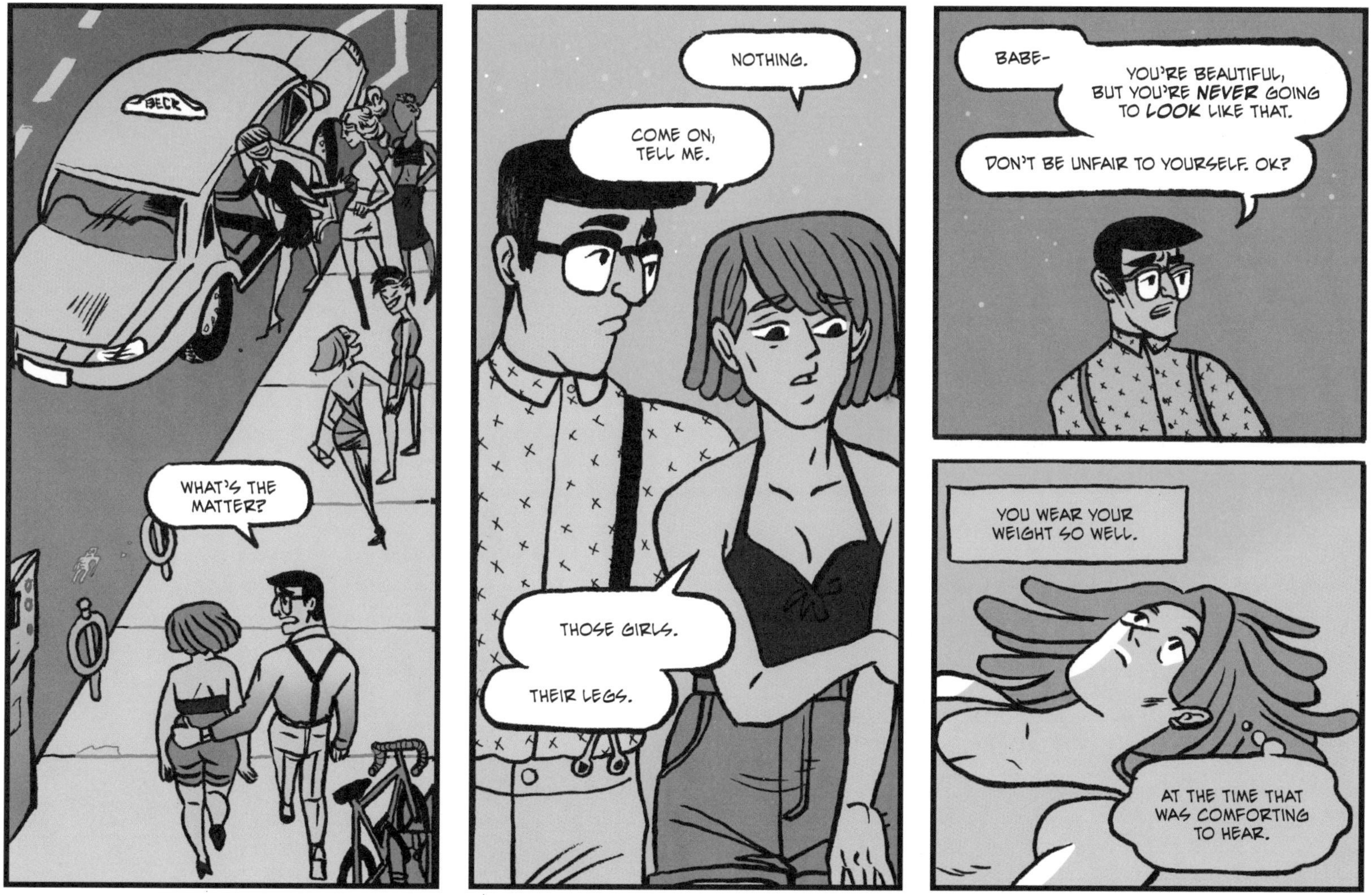
BECK
WHAT'S THE MATTER?
NOTHING.
COME ON, TELL ME.
THOSE GIRLS.
THEIR LEGS.
BABE-
YOU'RE BEAUTIFUL, BUT YOU'RE NEVER GOING TO LOOK LIKE THAT.
DON'T BE UNFAIR TO YOURSELF. OK?
YOU WEAR YOUR WEIGHT SO WELL.
AT THE TIME THAT WAS COMFORTING TO HEAR.

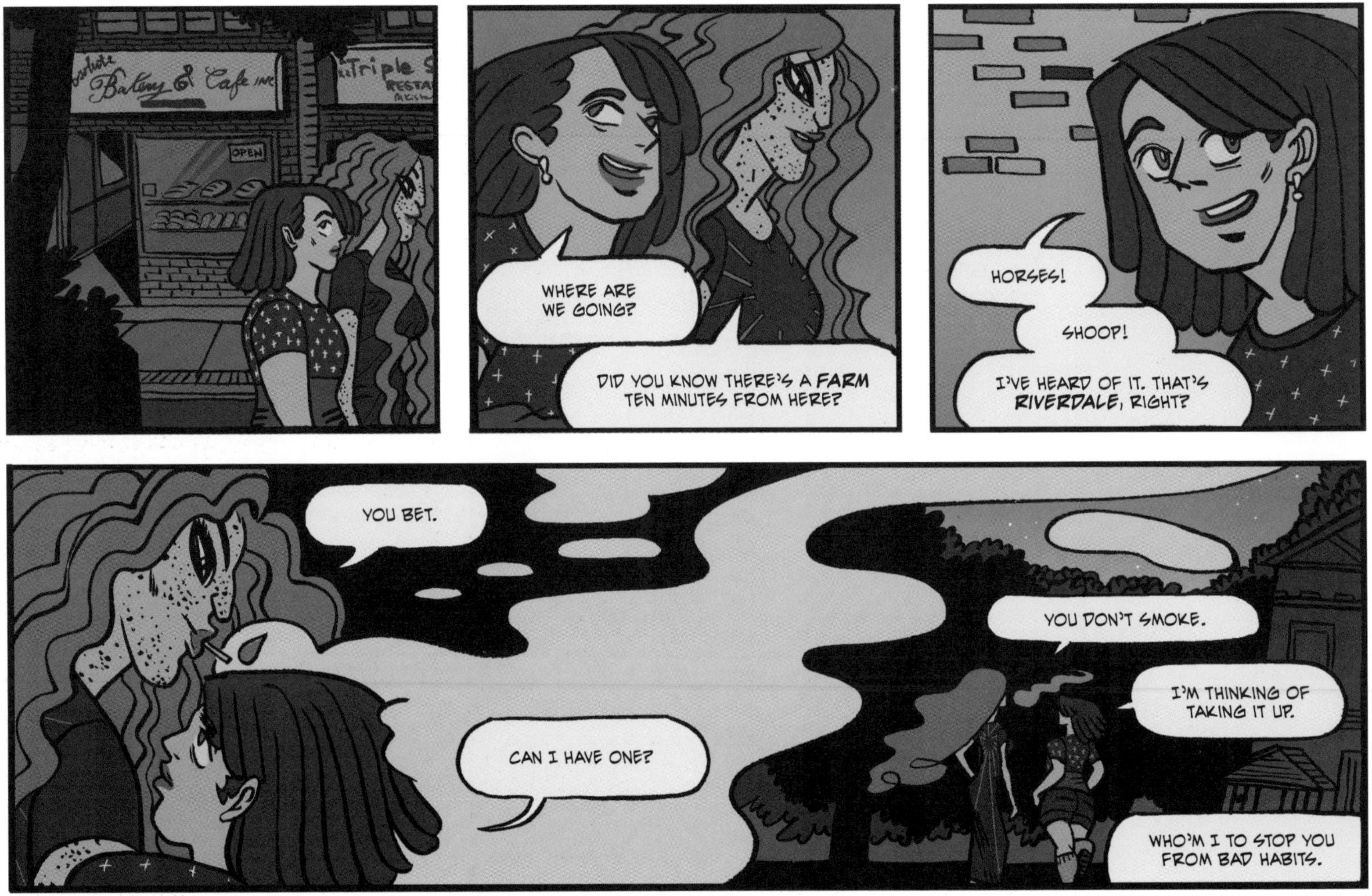
Bakery & Cafe inc
OPEN
WHERE ARE WE GOING?
DID YOU KNOW THERE'S A **FARM** TEN MINUTES FROM HERE?
HORSES!
SHOOP!
I'VE HEARD OF IT. THAT'S **RIVERDALE**, RIGHT?
YOU BET.
CAN I HAVE ONE?
YOU DON'T SMOKE.
I'M THINKING OF TAKING IT UP.
WHO'M I TO STOP YOU FROM BAD HABITS.

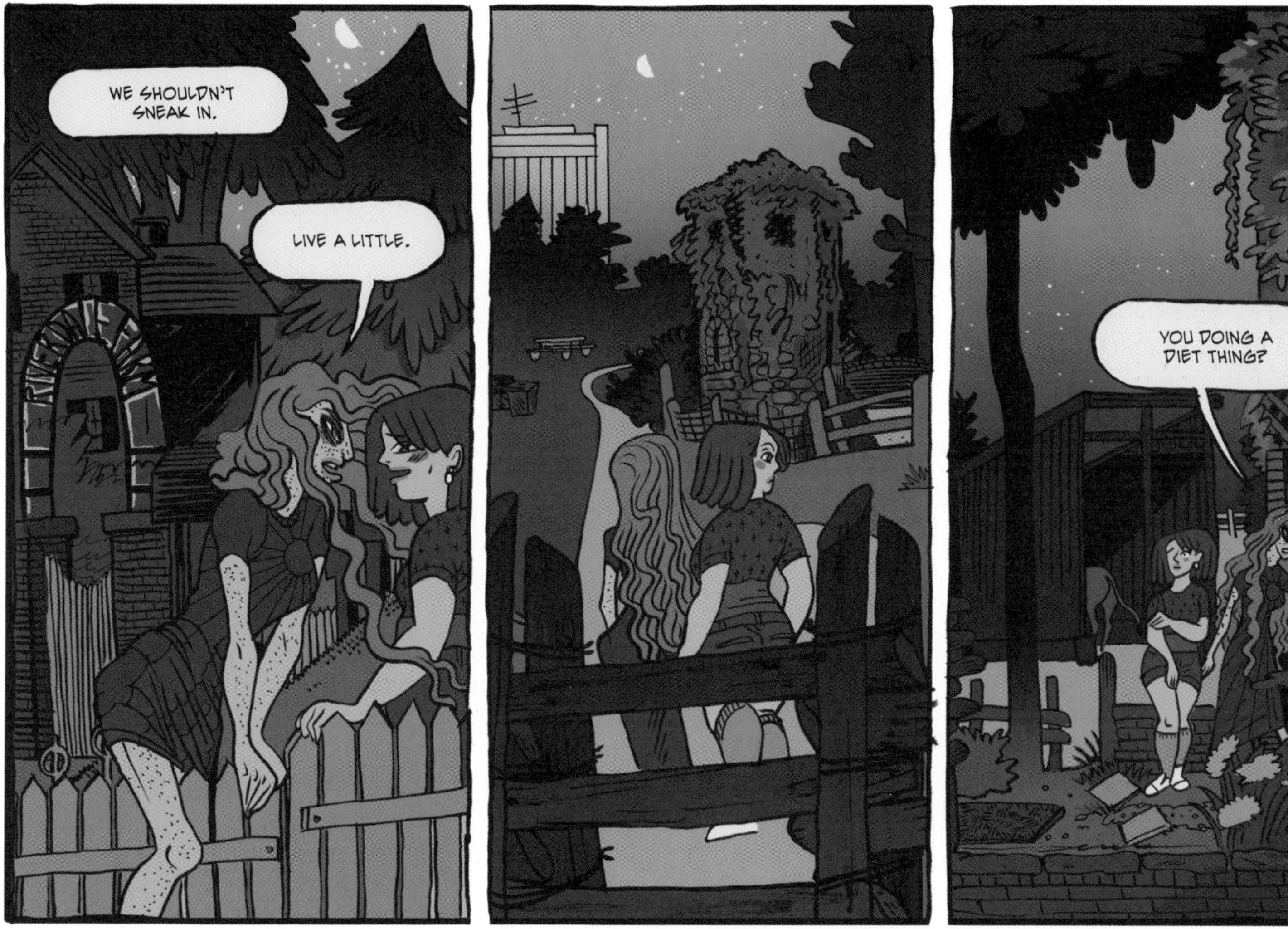
WE SHOULDN'T SNEAK IN.
LIVE A LITTLE.
YOU DOING A DIET THING?

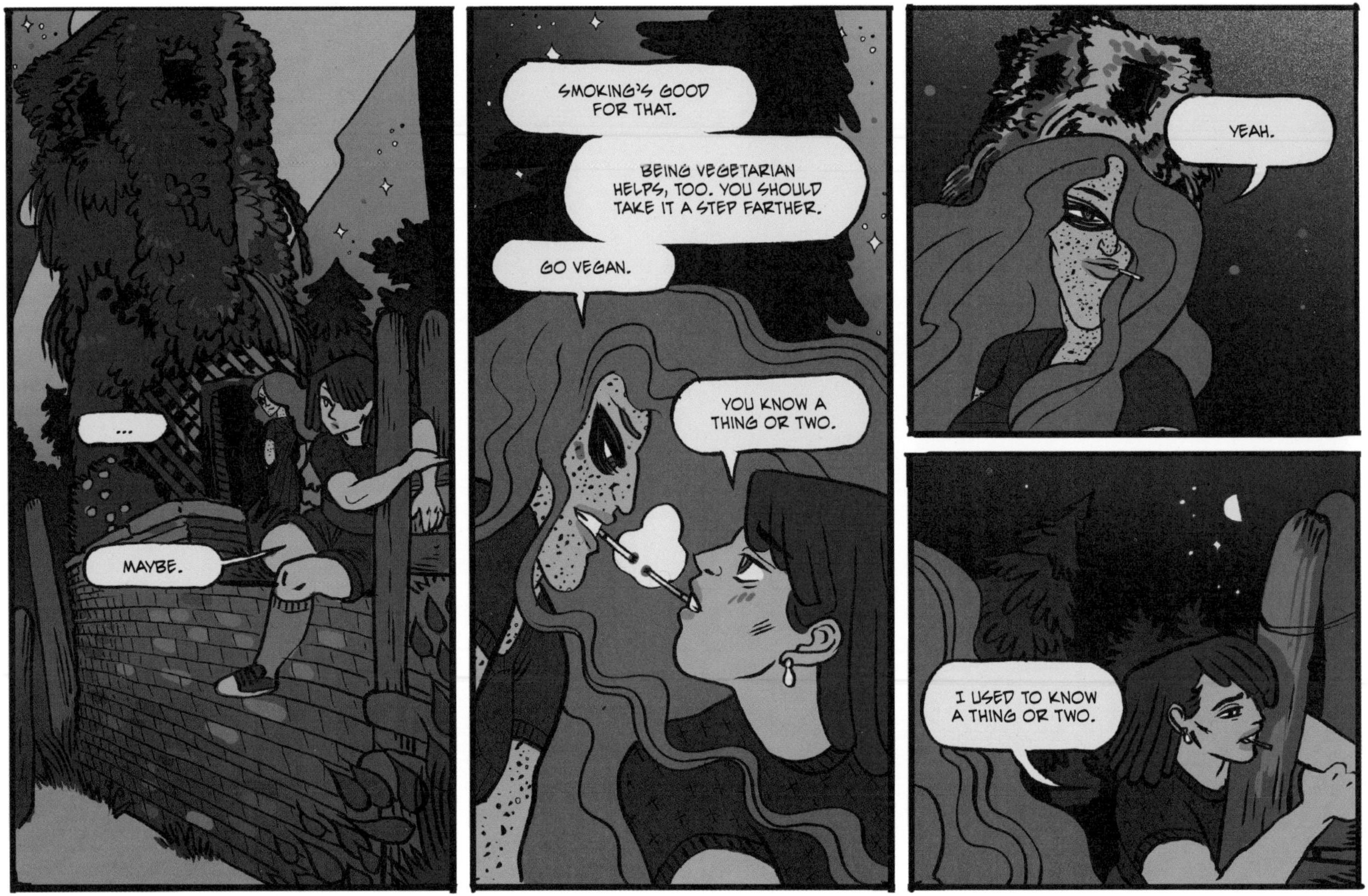
...
MAYBE.
SMOKING'S GOOD FOR THAT.
BEING VEGETARIAN HELPS, TOO. YOU SHOULD TAKE IT A STEP FARTHER.
GO VEGAN.
YOU KNOW A THING OR TWO.
YEAH.
I USED TO KNOW A THING OR TWO.

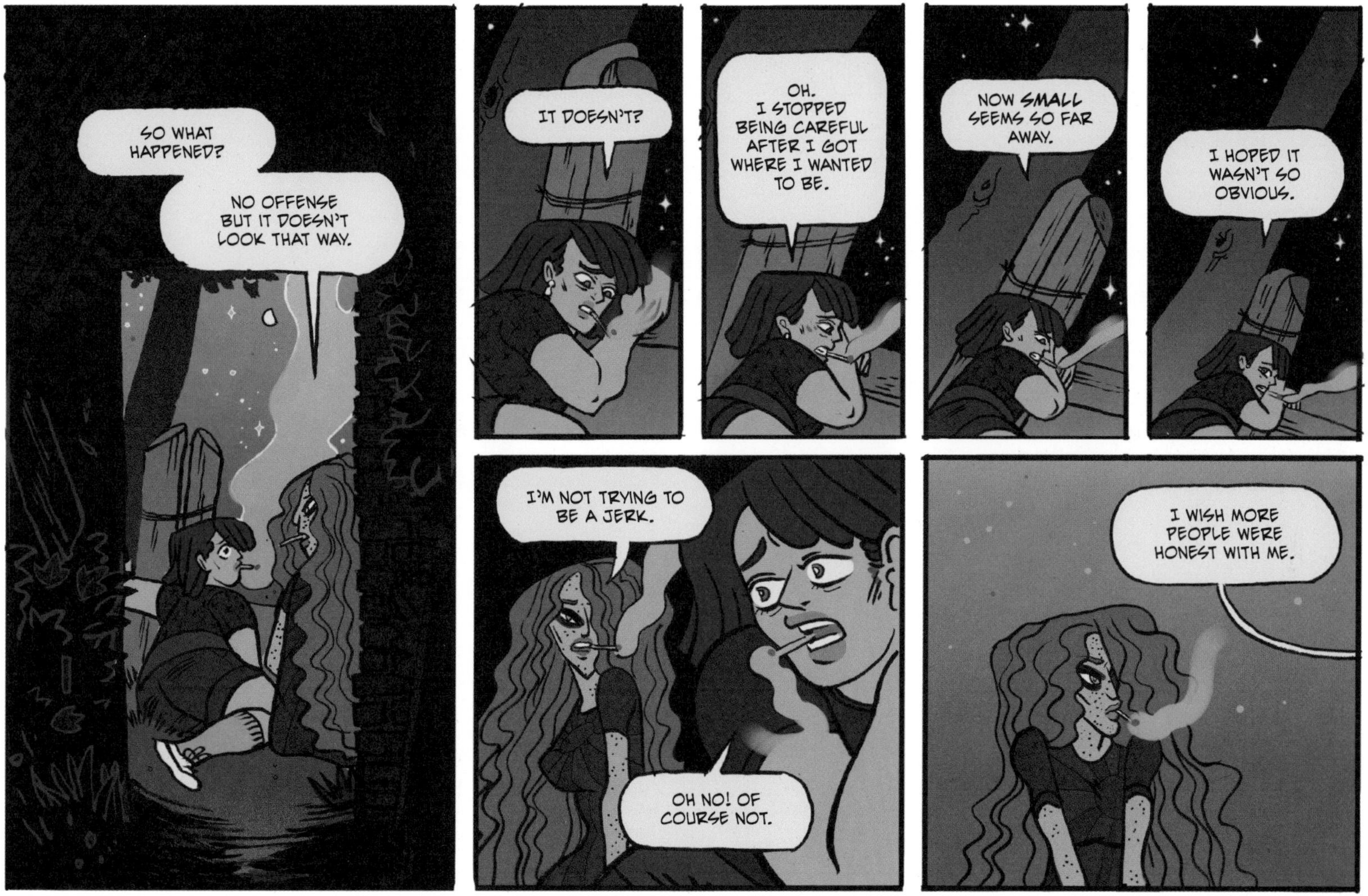

SO WHAT HAPPENED?
NO OFFENSE BUT IT DOESN'T LOOK THAT WAY.
IT DOESN'T?
OH. I STOPPED BEING CAREFUL AFTER I GOT WHERE I WANTED TO BE.
NOW SMALL SEEMS SO FAR AWAY.
I HOPED IT WASN'T SO OBVIOUS.
I'M NOT TRYING TO BE A JERK.
OH NO! OF COURSE NOT.
I WISH MORE PEOPLE WERE HONEST WITH ME.

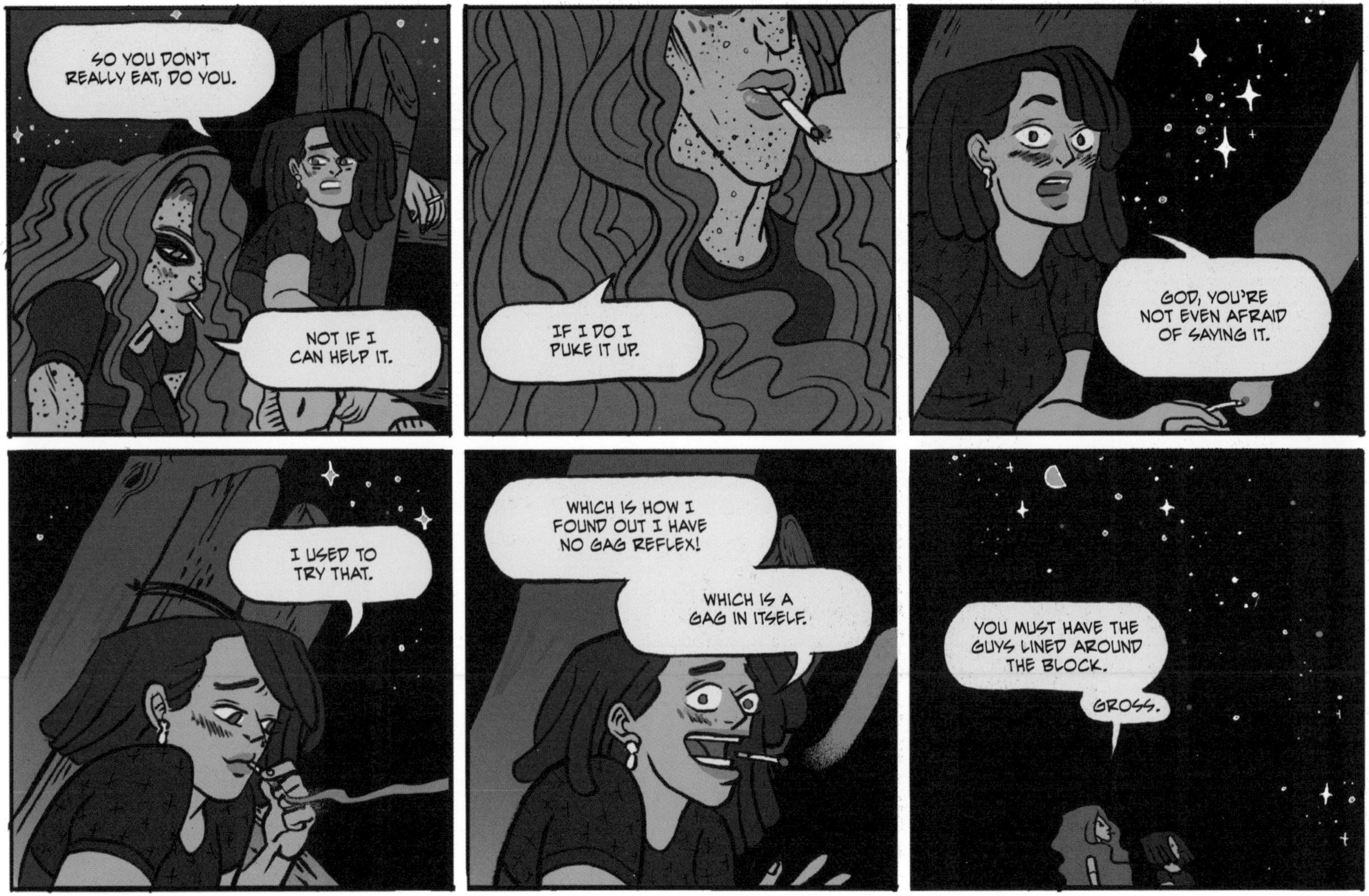
SO YOU DON'T REALLY EAT, DO YOU.
NOT IF I CAN HELP IT.
IF I DO I PUKE IT UP.
GOD, YOU'RE NOT EVEN AFRAID OF SAYING IT.
I USED TO TRY THAT.
WHICH IS HOW I FOUND OUT I HAVE NO GAG REFLEX!
WHICH IS A GAG IN ITSELF.
YOU MUST HAVE THE GUYS LINED AROUND THE BLOCK.
GROSS.

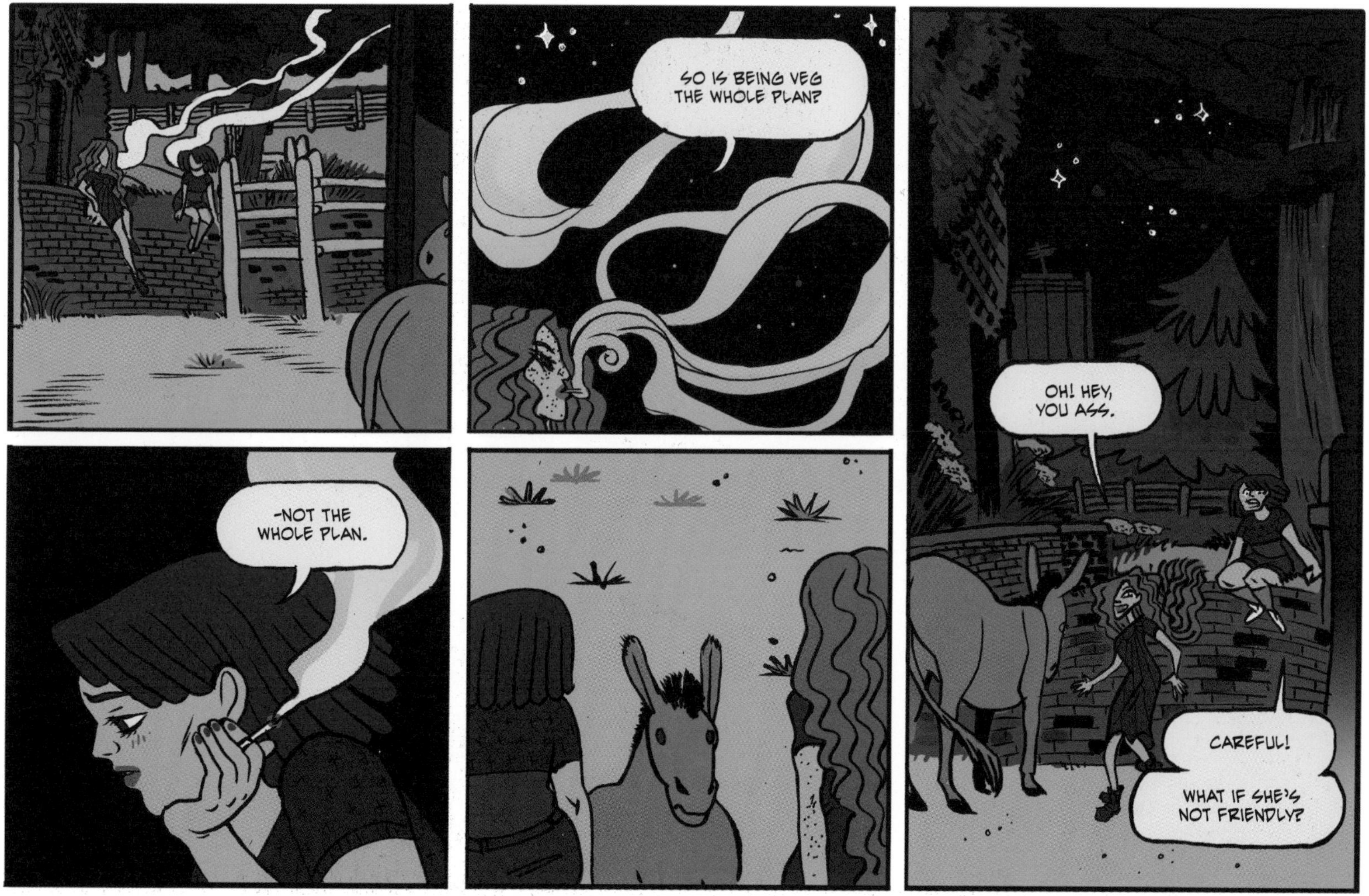
SO IS BEING VEG THE WHOLE PLAN?
-NOT THE WHOLE PLAN.
OH! HEY, YOU ASS.
CAREFUL!
WHAT IF SHE'S NOT FRIENDLY?

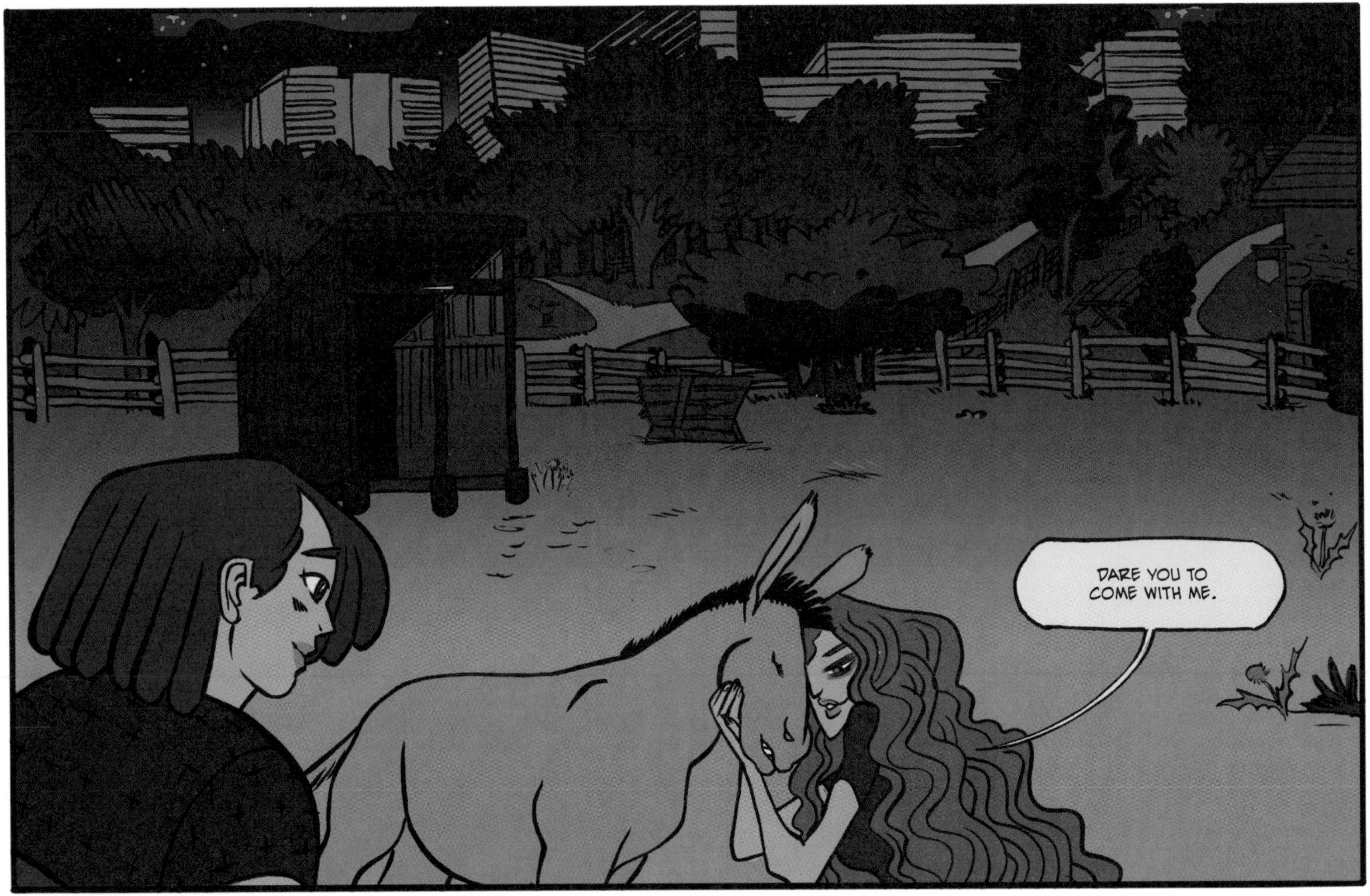
DARE YOU TO COME WITH ME.

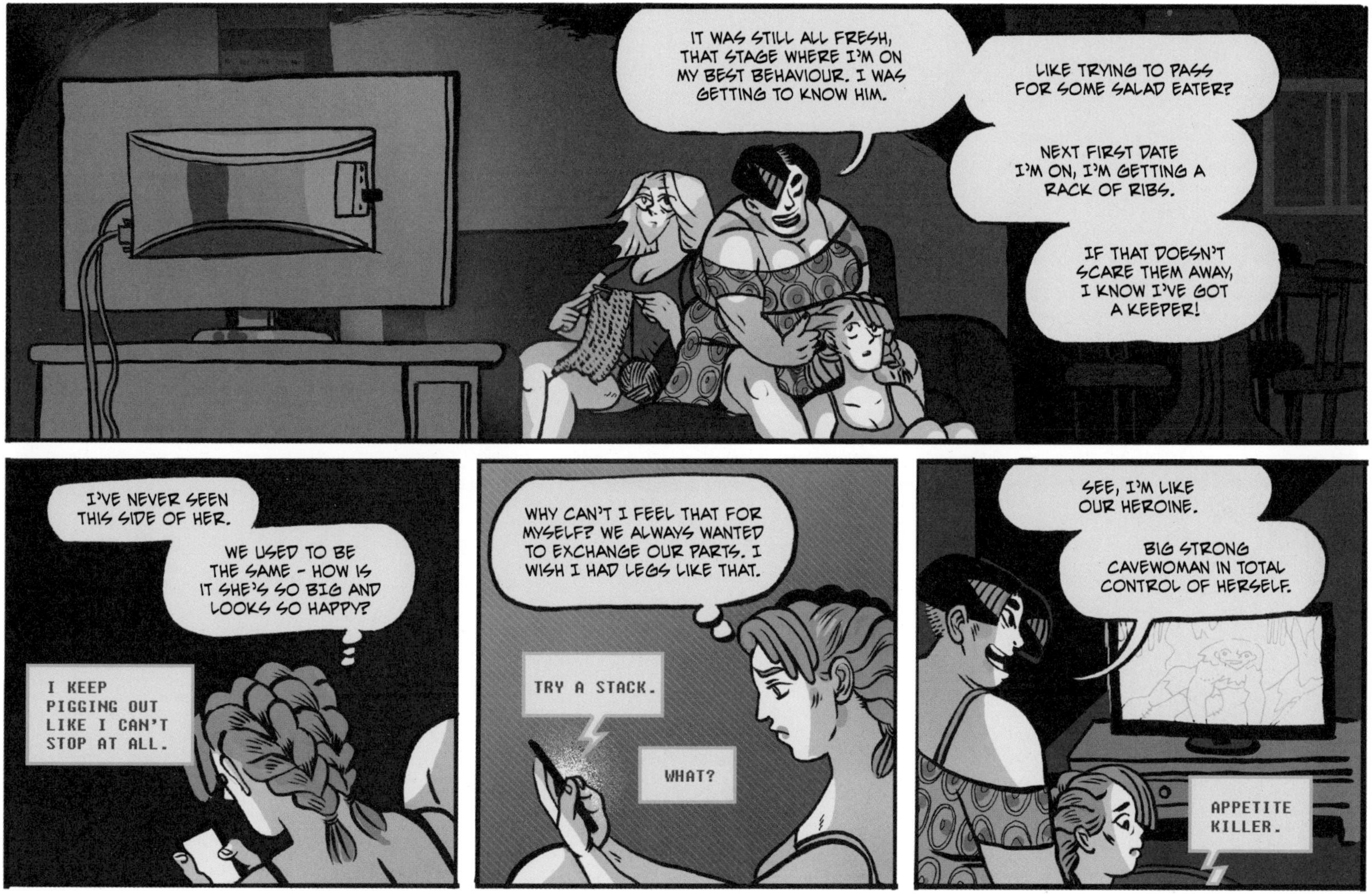
IT WAS STILL ALL FRESH, THAT STAGE WHERE I'M ON MY BEST BEHAVIOUR. I WAS GETTING TO KNOW HIM.
LIKE TRYING TO PASS FOR SOME SALAD EATER?
NEXT FIRST DATE I'M ON, I'M GETTING A RACK OF RIBS.
IF THAT DOESN'T SCARE THEM AWAY, I KNOW I'VE GOT A KEEPER!
I'VE NEVER SEEN THIS SIDE OF HER.
WE USED TO BE THE SAME - HOW IS IT SHE'S SO BIG AND LOOKS SO HAPPY?
I KEEP PIGGING OUT LIKE I CAN'T STOP AT ALL.
WHY CAN'T I FEEL THAT FOR MYSELF? WE ALWAYS WANTED TO EXCHANGE OUR PARTS. I WISH I HAD LEGS LIKE THAT.
TRY A STACK.
WHAT?
SEE, I'M LIKE OUR HEROINE.
BIG STRONG CAVEWOMAN IN TOTAL CONTROL OF HERSELF.
APPETITE KILLER.

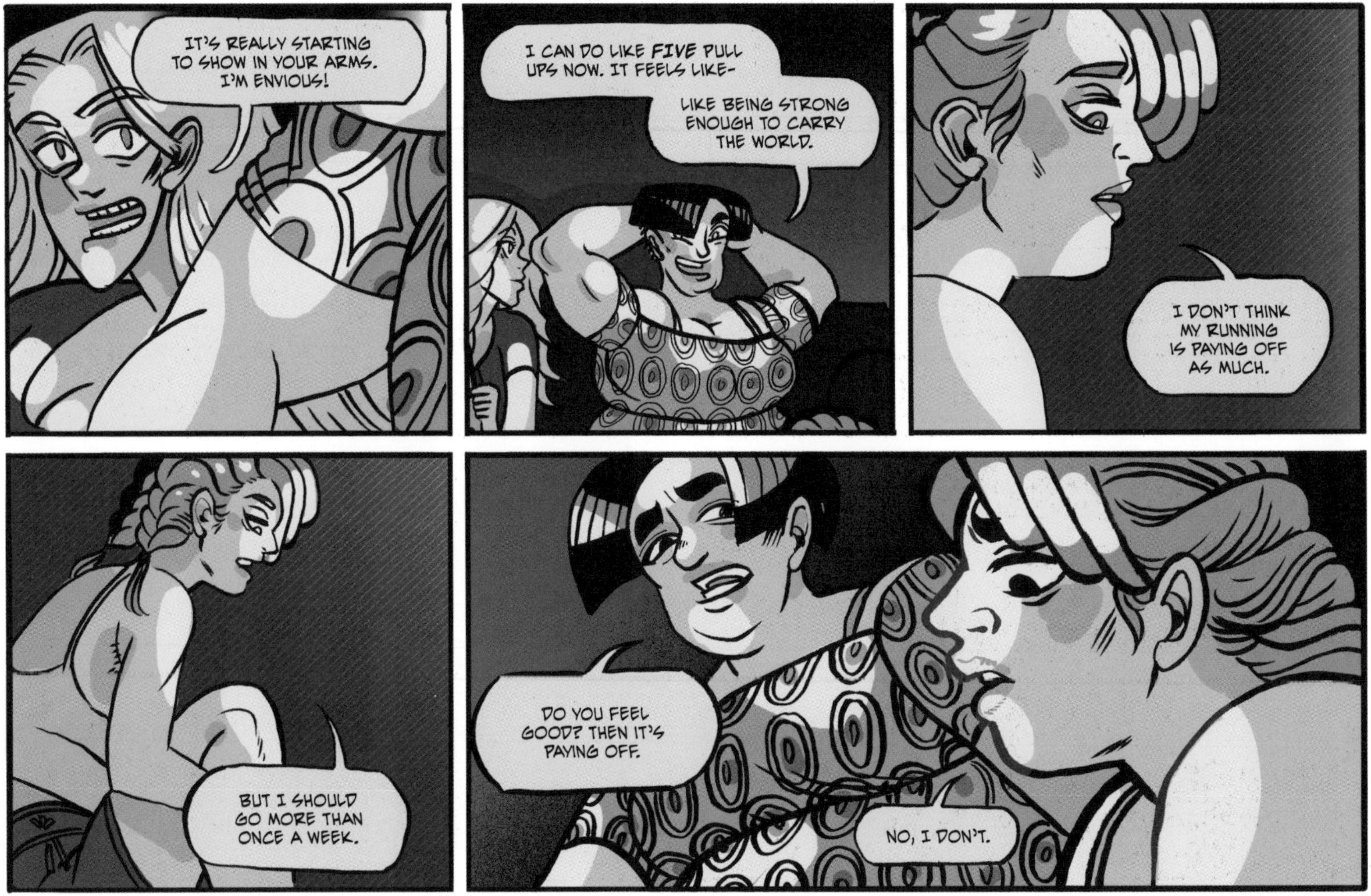
IT'S REALLY STARTING TO SHOW IN YOUR ARMS. I'M ENVIOUS!
I CAN DO LIKE **FIVE** PULL UPS NOW. IT FEELS LIKE-
LIKE BEING STRONG ENOUGH TO CARRY THE WORLD.
I DON'T THINK MY RUNNING IS PAYING OFF AS MUCH.
BUT I SHOULD GO MORE THAN ONCE A WEEK.
DO YOU FEEL GOOD? THEN IT'S PAYING OFF.
NO, I DON'T.

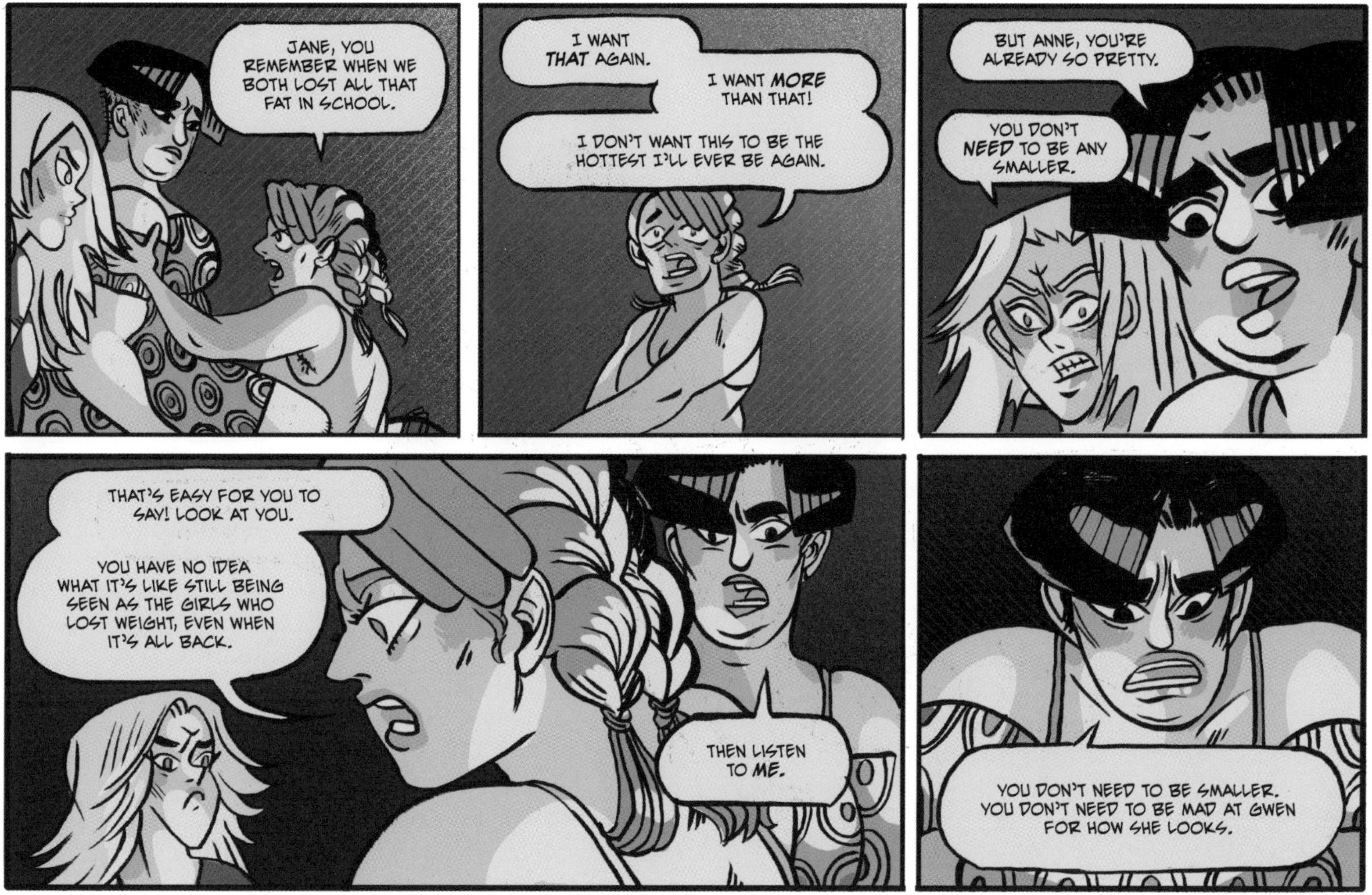
JANE, YOU REMEMBER WHEN WE BOTH LOST ALL THAT FAT IN SCHOOL.
I WANT THAT AGAIN.
I WANT MORE THAN THAT!
I DON'T WANT THIS TO BE THE HOTTEST I'LL EVER BE AGAIN.
BUT ANNE, YOU'RE ALREADY SO PRETTY.
YOU DON'T NEED TO BE ANY SMALLER.
THAT'S EASY FOR YOU TO SAY! LOOK AT YOU.
YOU HAVE NO IDEA WHAT IT'S LIKE STILL BEING SEEN AS THE GIRLS WHO LOST WEIGHT, EVEN WHEN IT'S ALL BACK.
THEN LISTEN TO ME.
YOU DON'T NEED TO BE SMALLER. YOU DON'T NEED TO BE MAD AT GWEN FOR HOW SHE LOOKS.

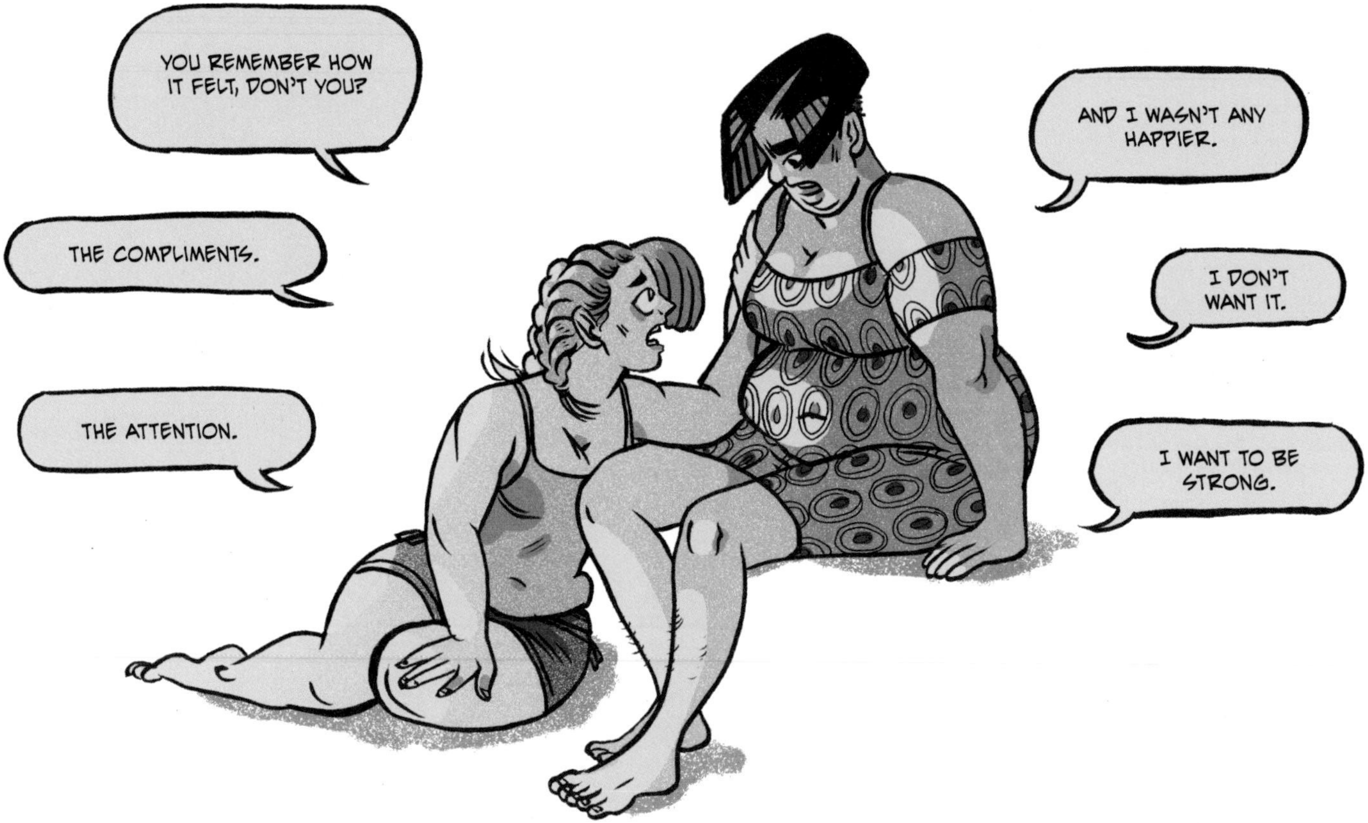
YOU REMEMBER HOW IT FELT, DON'T YOU?
THE COMPLIMENTS.
THE ATTENTION.
AND I WASN'T ANY HAPPIER.
I DON'T WANT IT.
I WANT TO BE STRONG.

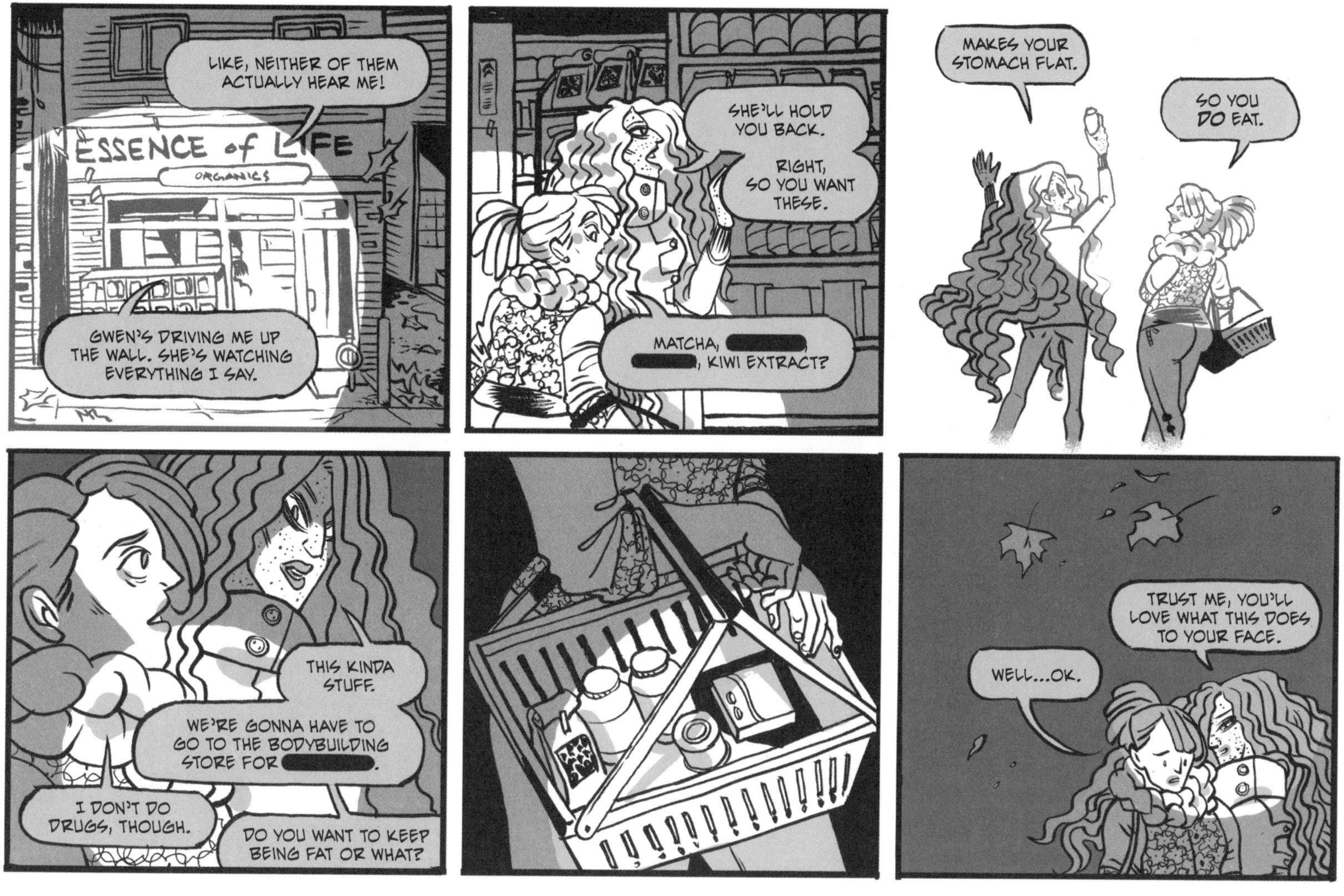
LIKE, NEITHER OF THEM ACTUALLY HEAR ME!
ESSENCE of LIFE
ORGANICS
GWEN'S DRIVING ME UP THE WALL. SHE'S WATCHING EVERYTHING I SAY.
SHE'LL HOLD YOU BACK.
RIGHT, SO YOU WANT THESE.
MATCHA, [redacted], [redacted], KIWI EXTRACT?
MAKES YOUR STOMACH FLAT.
SO YOU DO EAT.
THIS KINDA STUFF.
WE'RE GONNA HAVE TO GO TO THE BODYBUILDING STORE FOR [redacted].
I DON'T DO DRUGS, THOUGH.
DO YOU WANT TO KEEP BEING FAT OR WHAT?
TRUST ME, YOU'LL LOVE WHAT THIS DOES TO YOUR FACE.
WELL...OK.

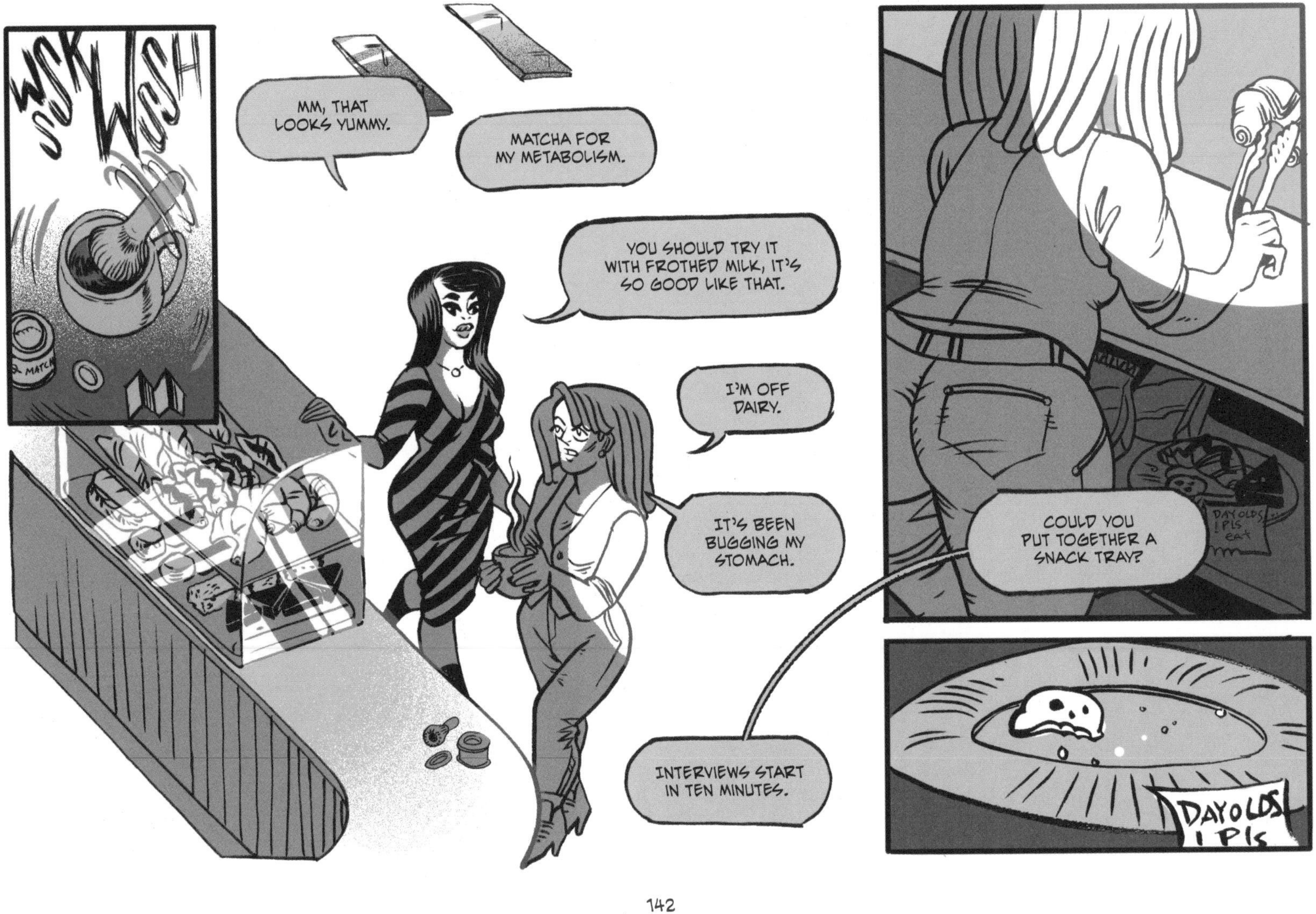
MM, THAT LOOKS YUMMY.
MATCHA FOR MY METABOLISM.
YOU SHOULD TRY IT WITH FROTHED MILK, IT'S SO GOOD LIKE THAT.
I'M OFF DAIRY.
IT'S BEEN BUGGING MY STOMACH.
INTERVIEWS START IN TEN MINUTES.
COULD YOU PUT TOGETHER A SNACK TRAY?

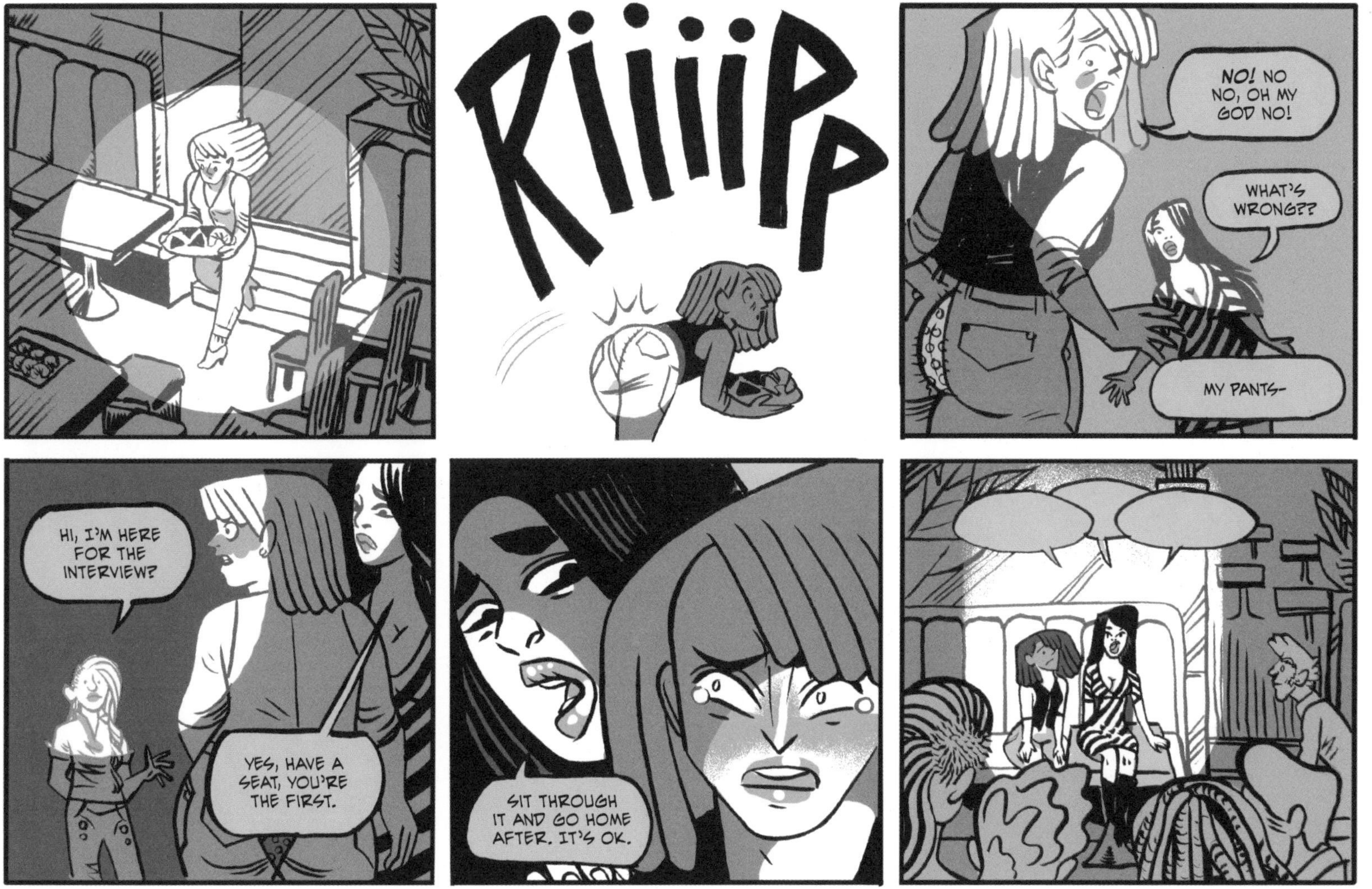
RiiiiPP
NO! NO NO, OH MY GOD NO!
WHAT'S WRONG??
MY PANTS-
HI, I'M HERE FOR THE INTERVIEW?
YES, HAVE A SEAT, YOU'RE THE FIRST.
SIT THROUGH IT AND GO HOME AFTER. IT'S OK.

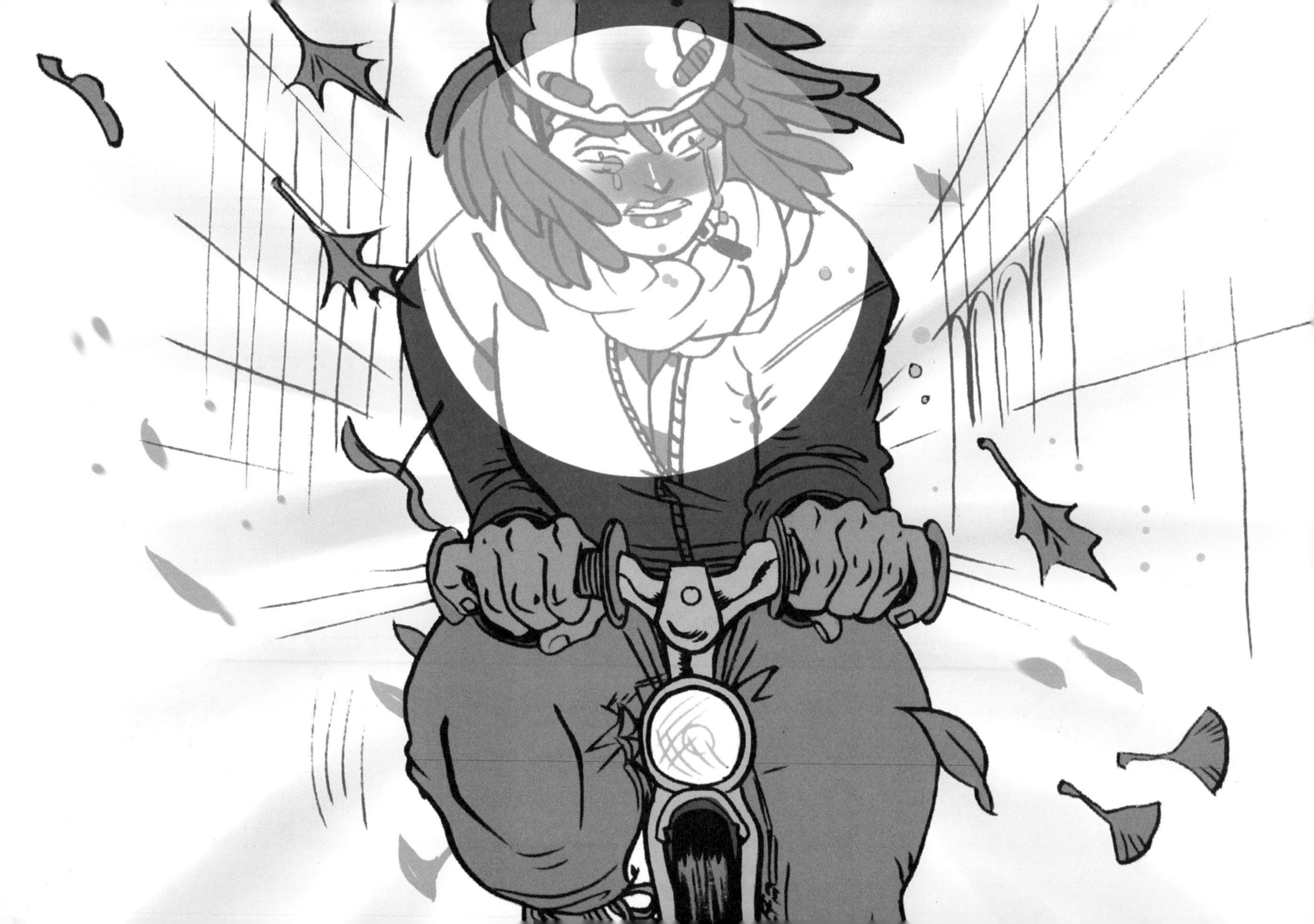

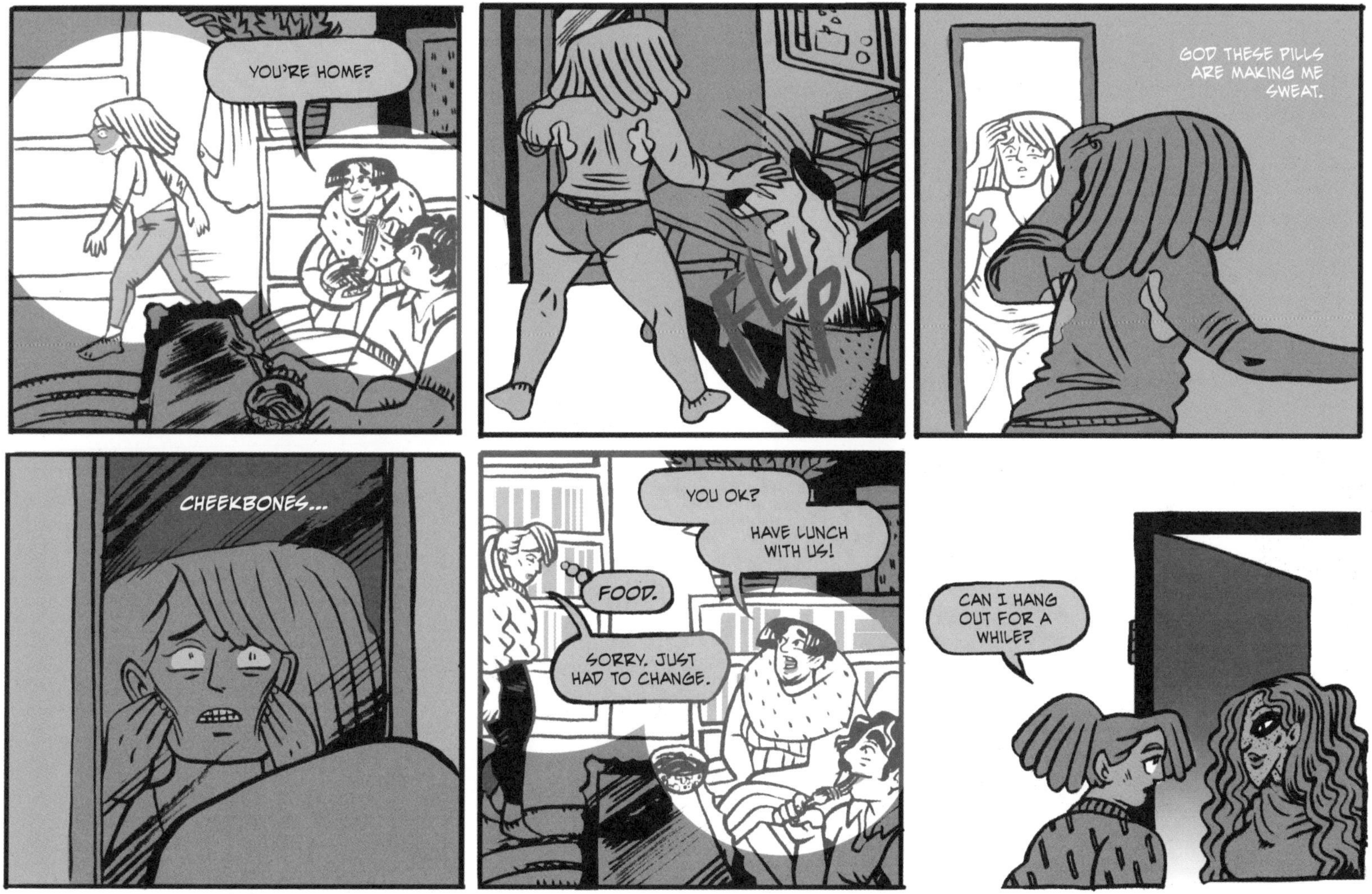
YOU'RE HOME?
FLUP
GOD THESE PILLS ARE MAKING ME SWEAT.
CHEEKBONES...
YOU OK?
HAVE LUNCH WITH US!
FOOD.
SORRY. JUST HAD TO CHANGE.
CAN I HANG OUT FOR A WHILE?

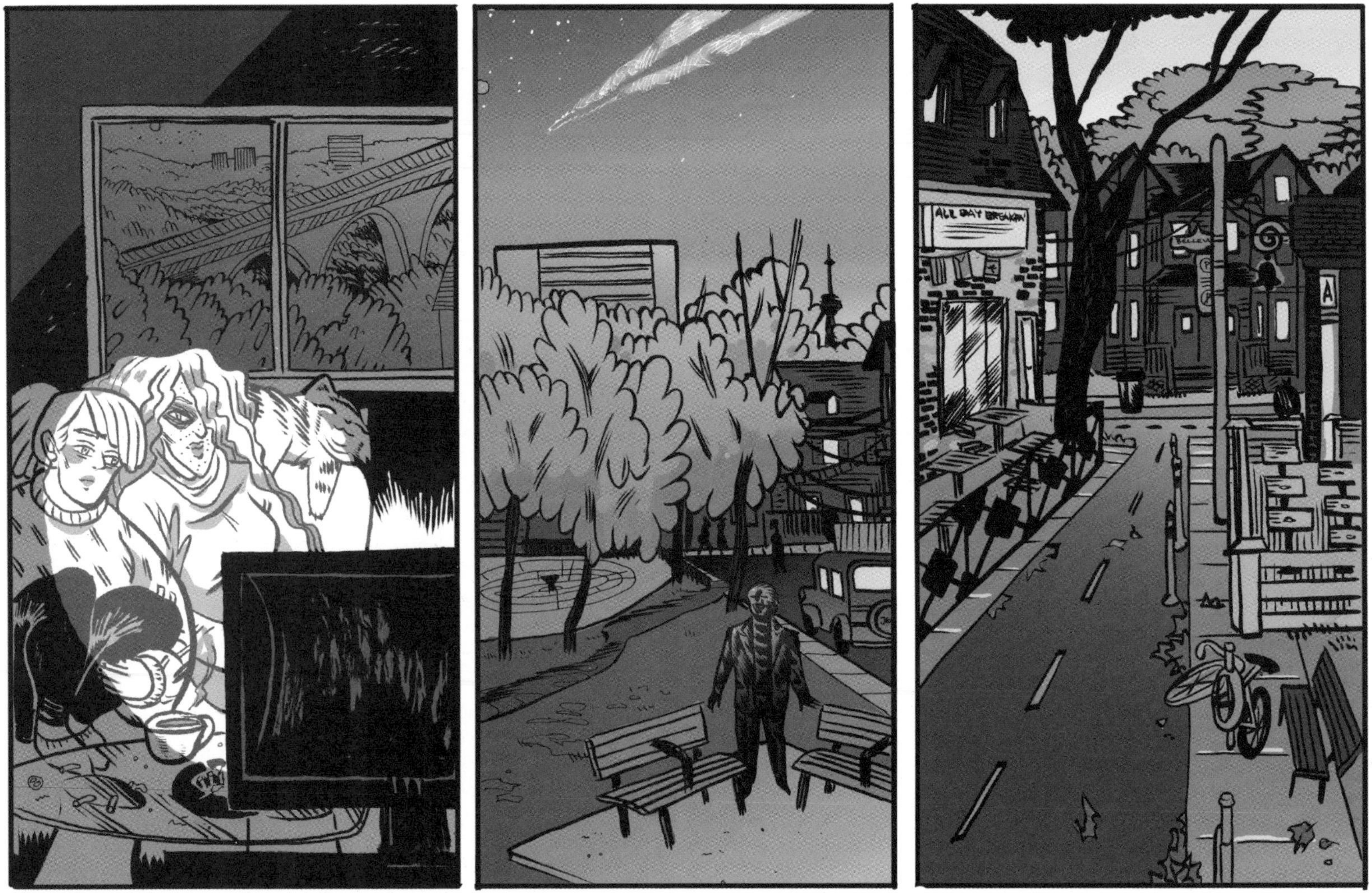
ALL DAY
A

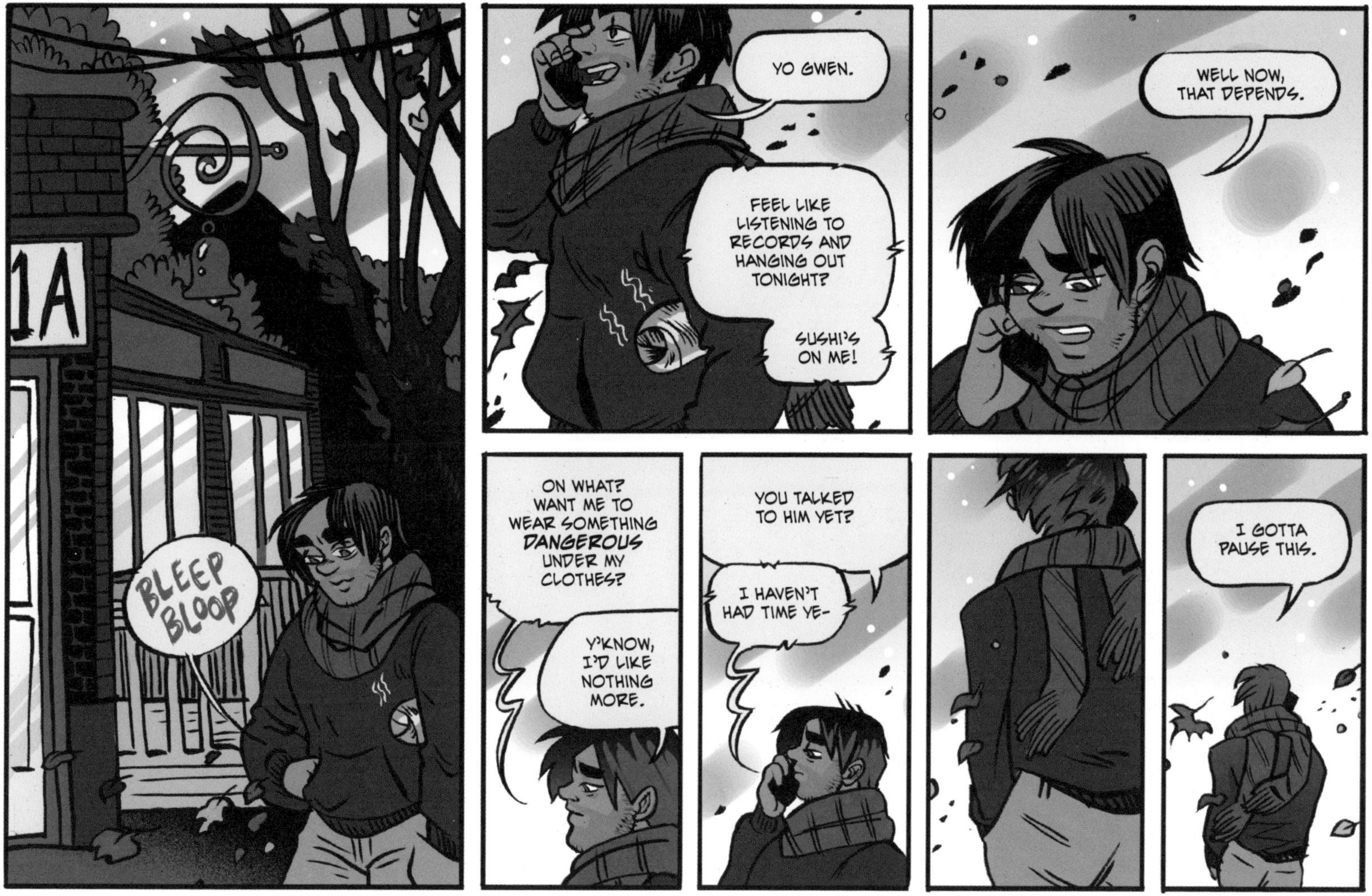

1A
BLEEP BLOOP
YO GWEN.
FEEL LIKE LISTENING TO RECORDS AND HANGING OUT TONIGHT?
SUSHI'S ON ME!
WELL NOW, THAT DEPENDS.
ON WHAT? WANT ME TO WEAR SOMETHING **DANGEROUS** UNDER MY CLOTHES?
Y'KNOW, I'D LIKE NOTHING MORE.
YOU TALKED TO HIM YET?
I HAVEN'T HAD TIME YE-
I GOTTA PAUSE THIS.

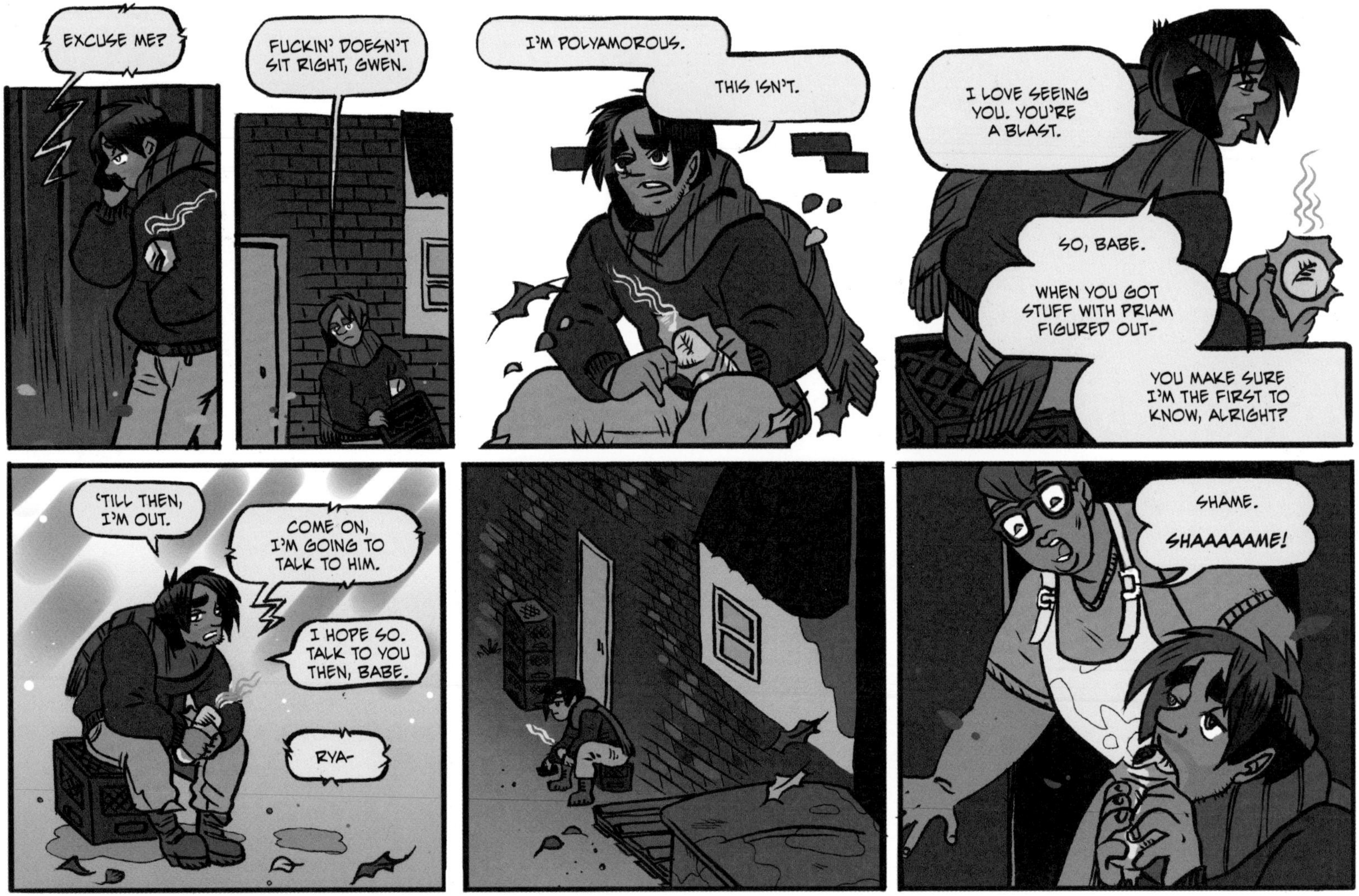
EXCUSE ME?
FUCKIN' DOESN'T SIT RIGHT, GWEN.
I'M POLYAMOROUS.
THIS ISN'T.
I LOVE SEEING YOU. YOU'RE A BLAST.
SO, BABE.
WHEN YOU GOT STUFF WITH PRIAM FIGURED OUT-
YOU MAKE SURE I'M THE FIRST TO KNOW, ALRIGHT?
'TILL THEN, I'M OUT.
COME ON, I'M GOING TO TALK TO HIM.
I HOPE SO. TALK TO YOU THEN, BABE.
RYA-
SHAME.
SHAAAAAME!

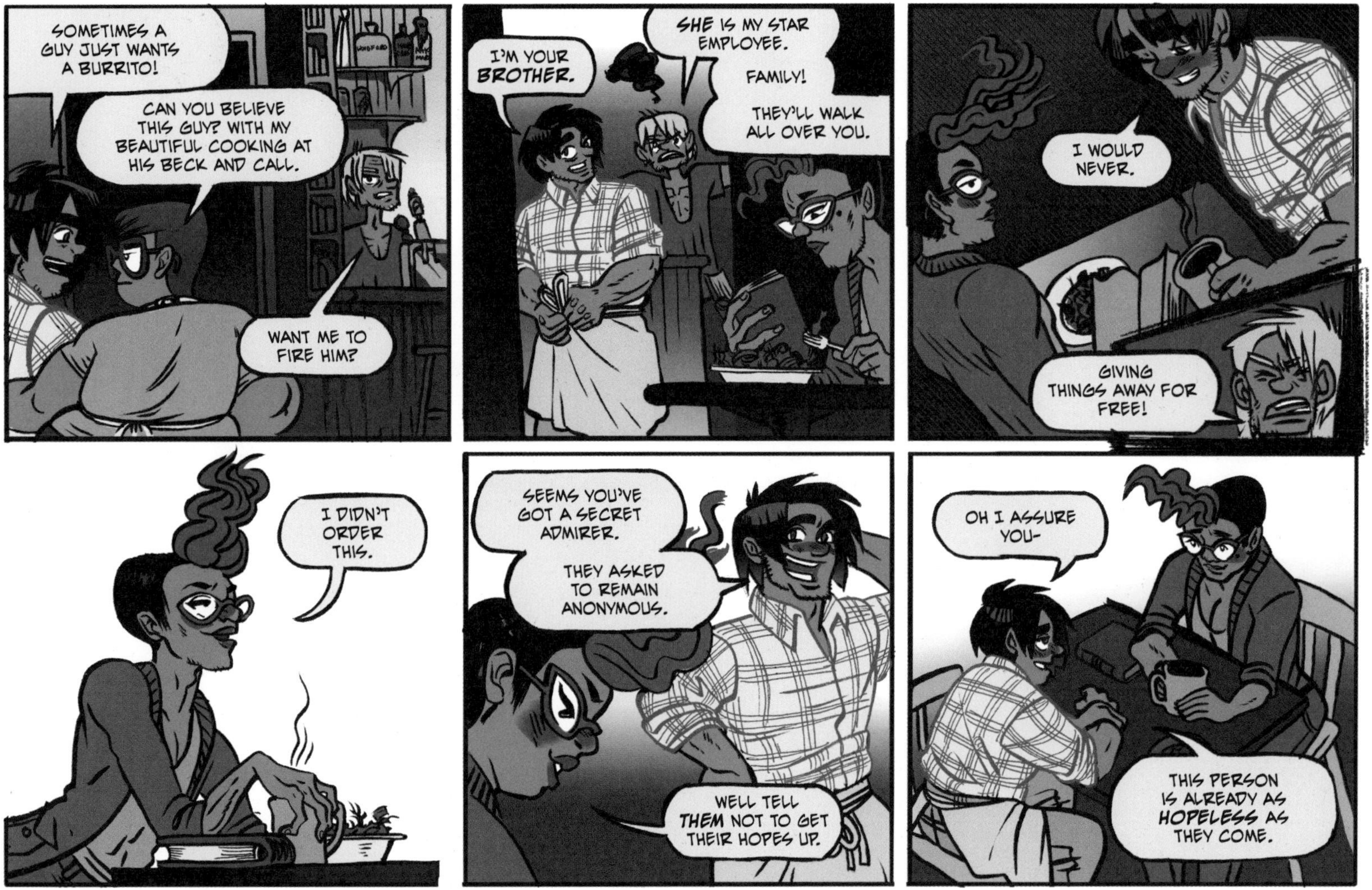
SOMETIMES A GUY JUST WANTS A BURRITO!
CAN YOU BELIEVE THIS GUY? WITH MY BEAUTIFUL COOKING AT HIS BECK AND CALL.
WANT ME TO FIRE HIM?
I'M YOUR **BROTHER.**
SHE IS MY STAR EMPLOYEE.
FAMILY!
THEY'LL WALK ALL OVER YOU.
I WOULD NEVER.
GIVING THINGS AWAY FOR FREE!
I DIDN'T ORDER THIS.
SEEMS YOU'VE GOT A SECRET ADMIRER.
THEY ASKED TO REMAIN ANONYMOUS.
WELL TELL **THEM** NOT TO GET THEIR HOPES UP.
OH I ASSURE YOU-
THIS PERSON IS ALREADY AS **HOPELESS** AS THEY COME.

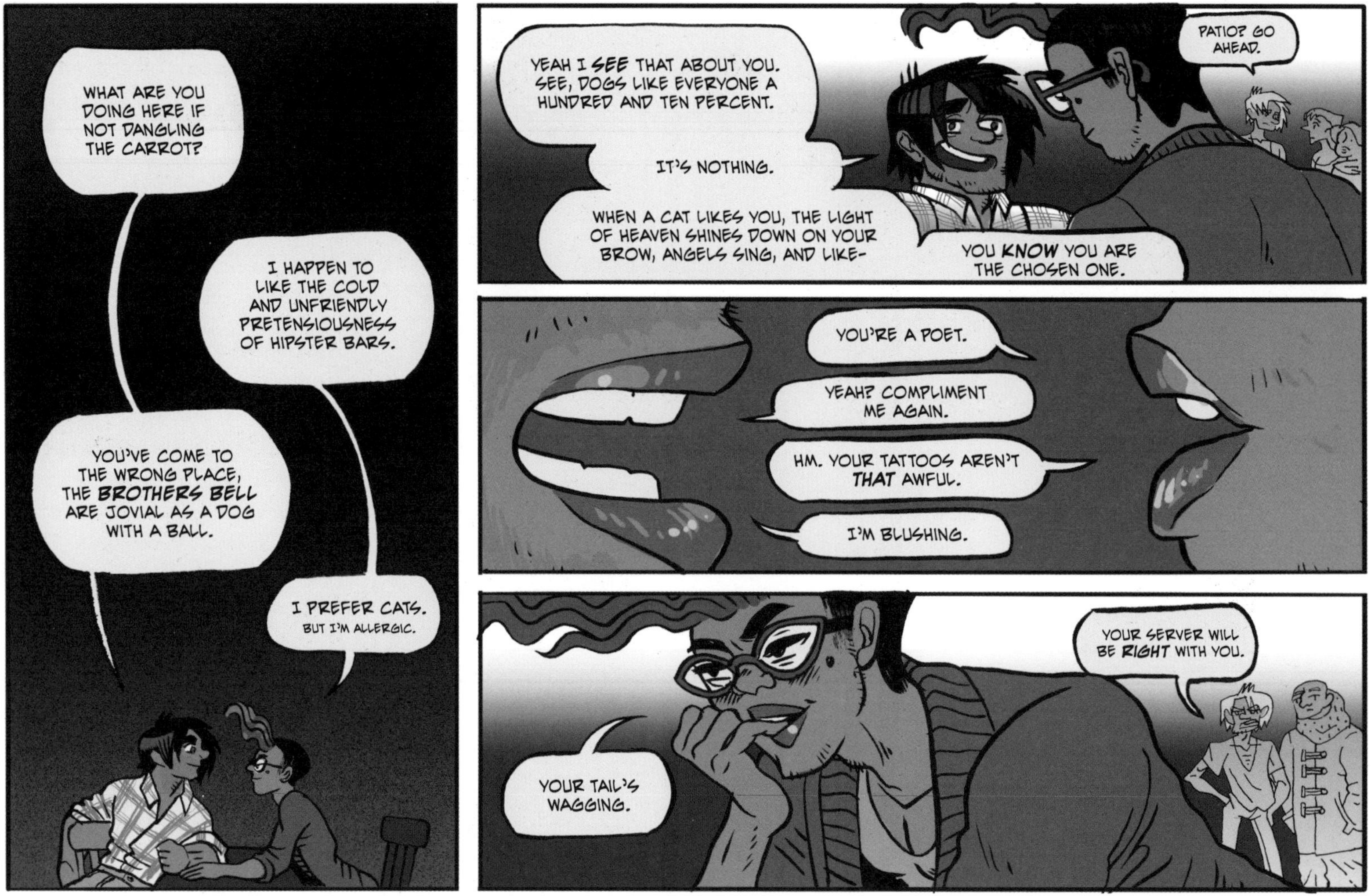
WHAT ARE YOU DOING HERE IF NOT DANGLING THE CARROT?
I HAPPEN TO LIKE THE COLD AND UNFRIENDLY PRETENSIOUSNESS OF HIPSTER BARS.
YOU'VE COME TO THE WRONG PLACE, THE **BROTHERS BELL** ARE JOVIAL AS A DOG WITH A BALL.
I PREFER CATS.
BUT I'M ALLERGIC.
YEAH I ***SEE*** THAT ABOUT YOU. SEE, DOGS LIKE EVERYONE A HUNDRED AND TEN PERCENT.
IT'S NOTHING.
WHEN A CAT LIKES YOU, THE LIGHT OF HEAVEN SHINES DOWN ON YOUR BROW, ANGELS SING, AND LIKE-
YOU ***KNOW*** YOU ARE THE CHOSEN ONE.
PATIO? GO AHEAD.
YOU'RE A POET.
YEAH? COMPLIMENT ME AGAIN.
HM. YOUR TATTOOS AREN'T ***THAT*** AWFUL.
I'M BLUSHING.
YOUR TAIL'S WAGGING.
YOUR SERVER WILL BE ***RIGHT*** WITH YOU.

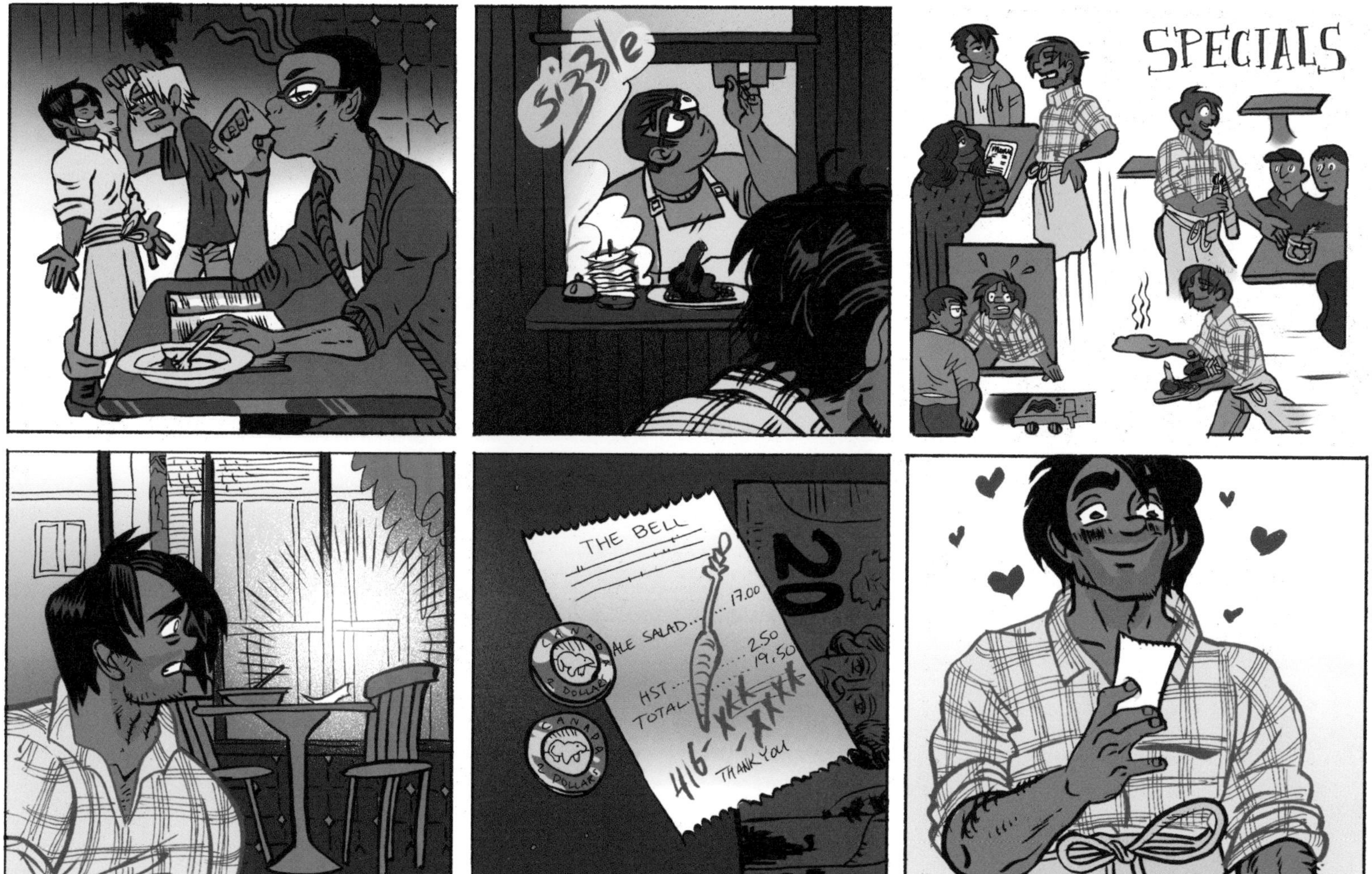
sizzle
SPECIALS
THE BELL
ALE SALAD 17.00
HST 2.50
TOTAL 19.50
416-XXX-XXXX
THANK YOU
CANADA
2 DOLLARS
CANADA
2 DOLLARS
20

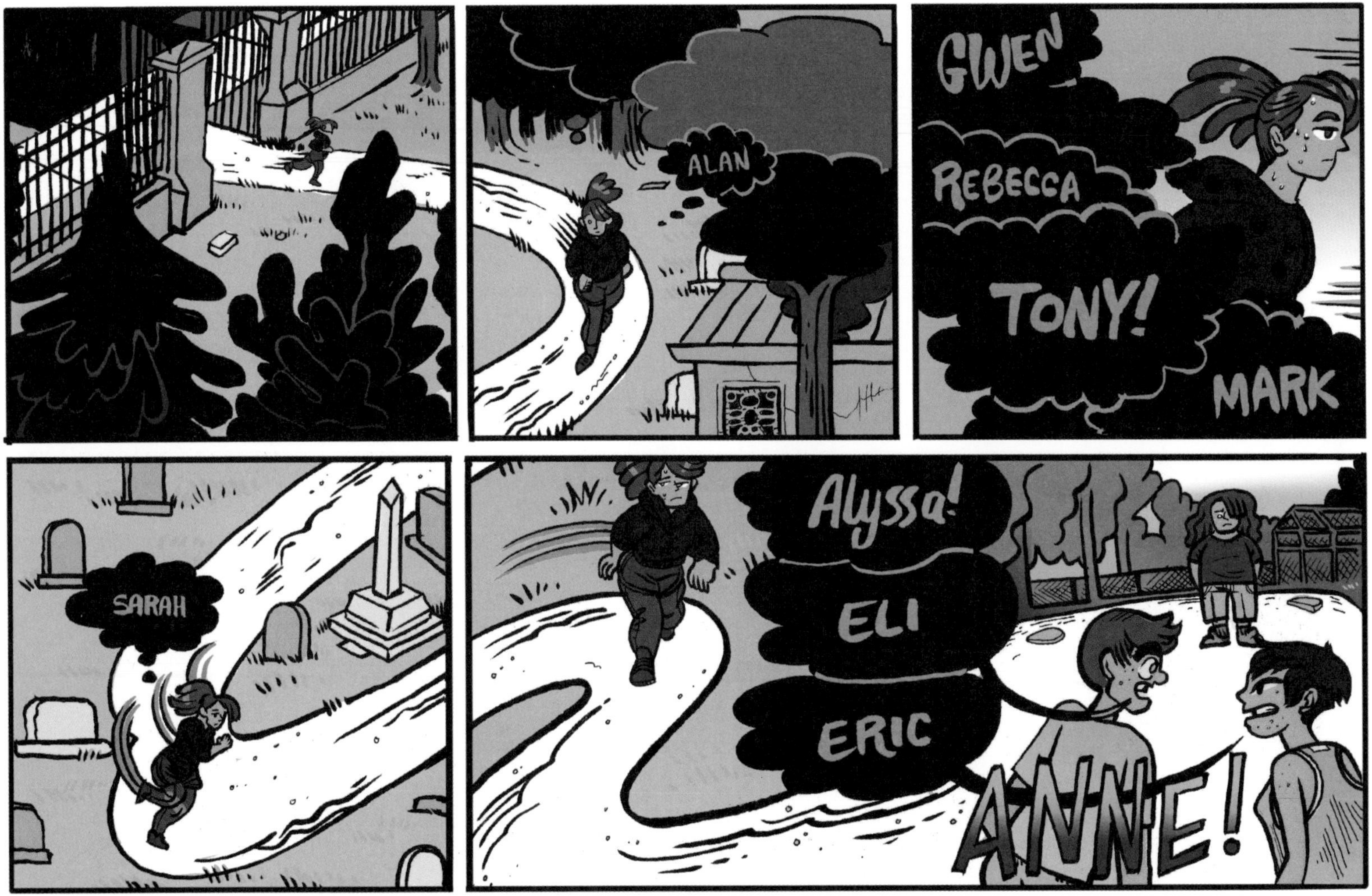
ALAN
GWEN
REBECCA
TONY!
MARK
SARAH
Alyssa!
ELI
ERIC
ANNE!

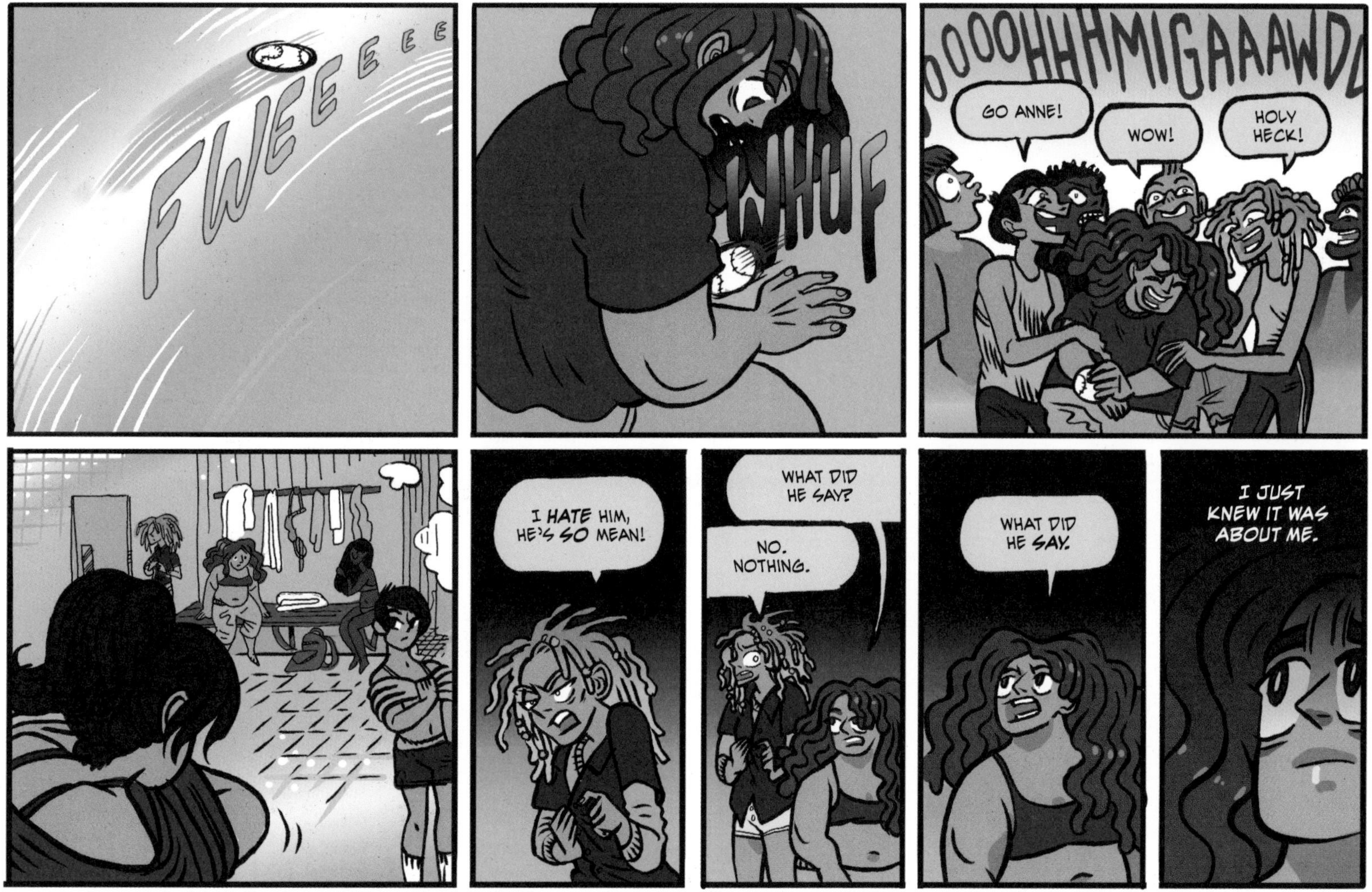

FWEEEEEE
WHUF
OOOOHHHMIGAAAWD
GO ANNE!
WOW!
HOLY HECK!
I HATE HIM, HE'S SO MEAN!
WHAT DID HE SAY?
NO. NOTHING.
WHAT DID HE SAY.
I JUST KNEW IT WAS ABOUT ME.

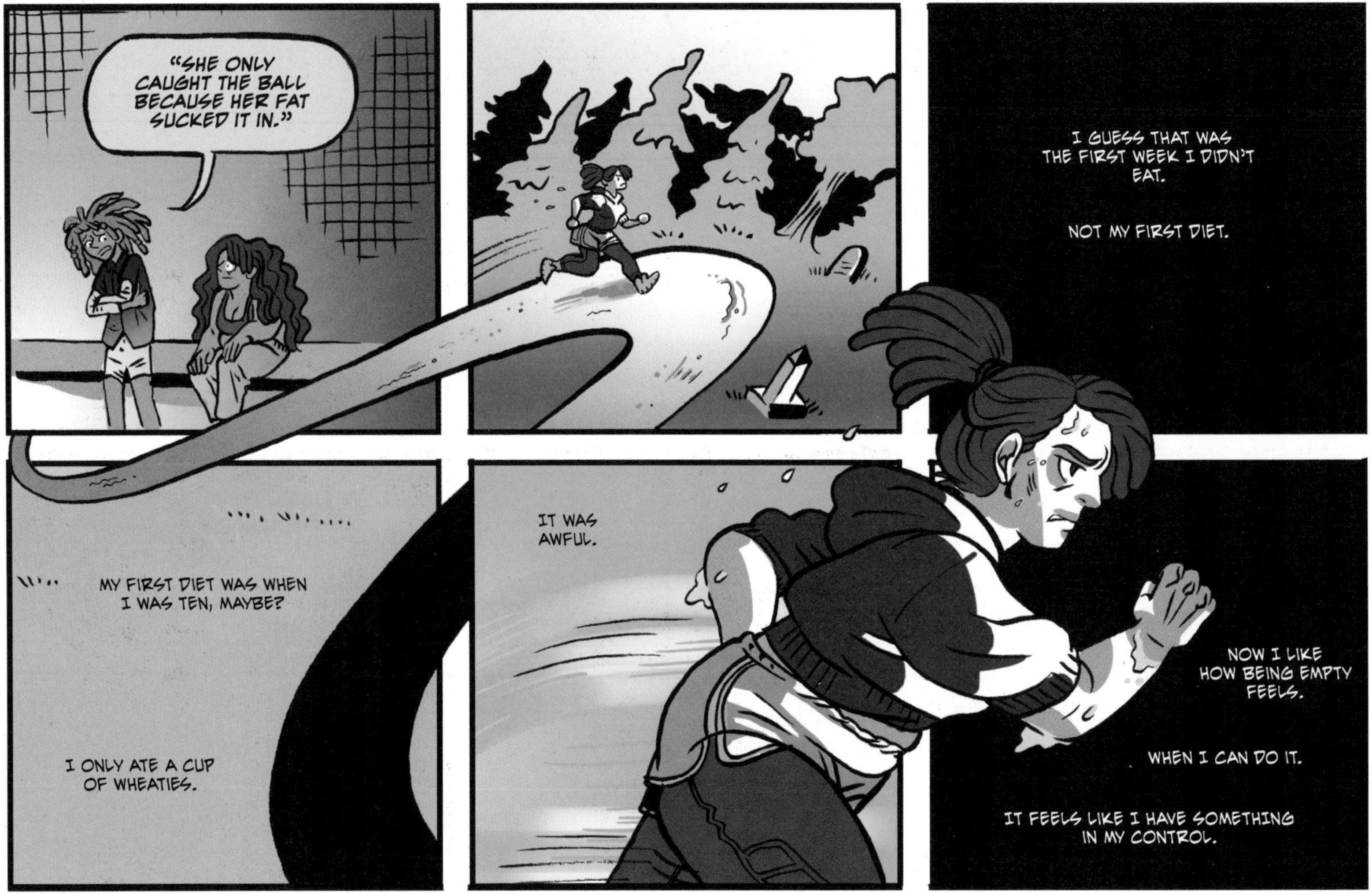
"SHE ONLY CAUGHT THE BALL BECAUSE HER FAT SUCKED IT IN."
I GUESS THAT WAS THE FIRST WEEK I DIDN'T EAT.
NOT MY FIRST DIET.
"'. '"....
"'..
MY FIRST DIET WAS WHEN I WAS TEN, MAYBE?
I ONLY ATE A CUP OF WHEATIES.
IT WAS AWFUL.
NOW I LIKE HOW BEING EMPTY FEELS.
WHEN I CAN DO IT.
IT FEELS LIKE I HAVE SOMETHING IN MY CONTROL.

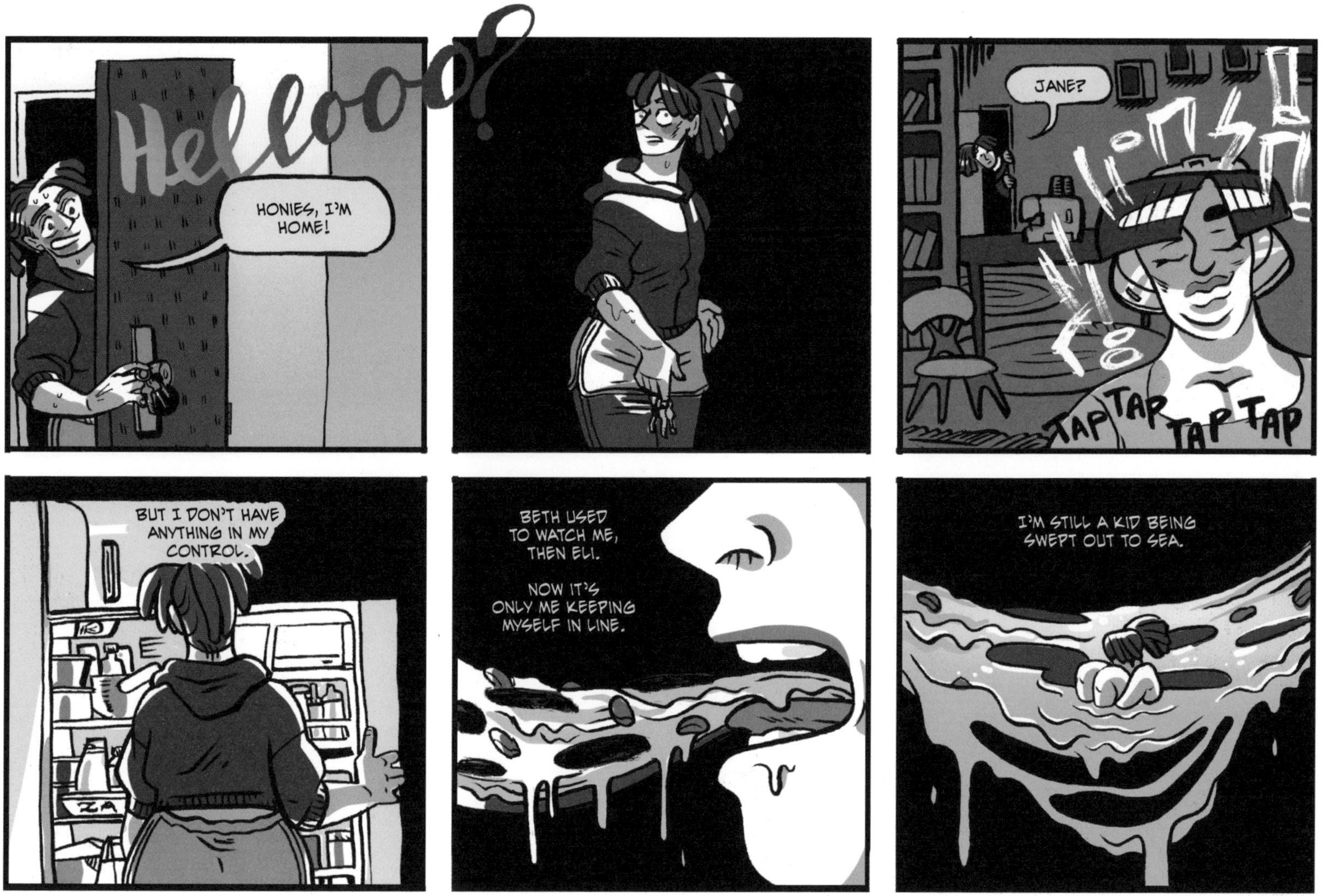
Hellooo?
HONIES, I'M HOME!
JANE?
TAP TAP TAP TAP
BUT I DON'T HAVE ANYTHING IN MY CONTROL.
ZA
BETH USED TO WATCH ME, THEN ELI.
NOW IT'S ONLY ME KEEPING MYSELF IN LINE.
I'M STILL A KID BEING SWEPT OUT TO SEA.

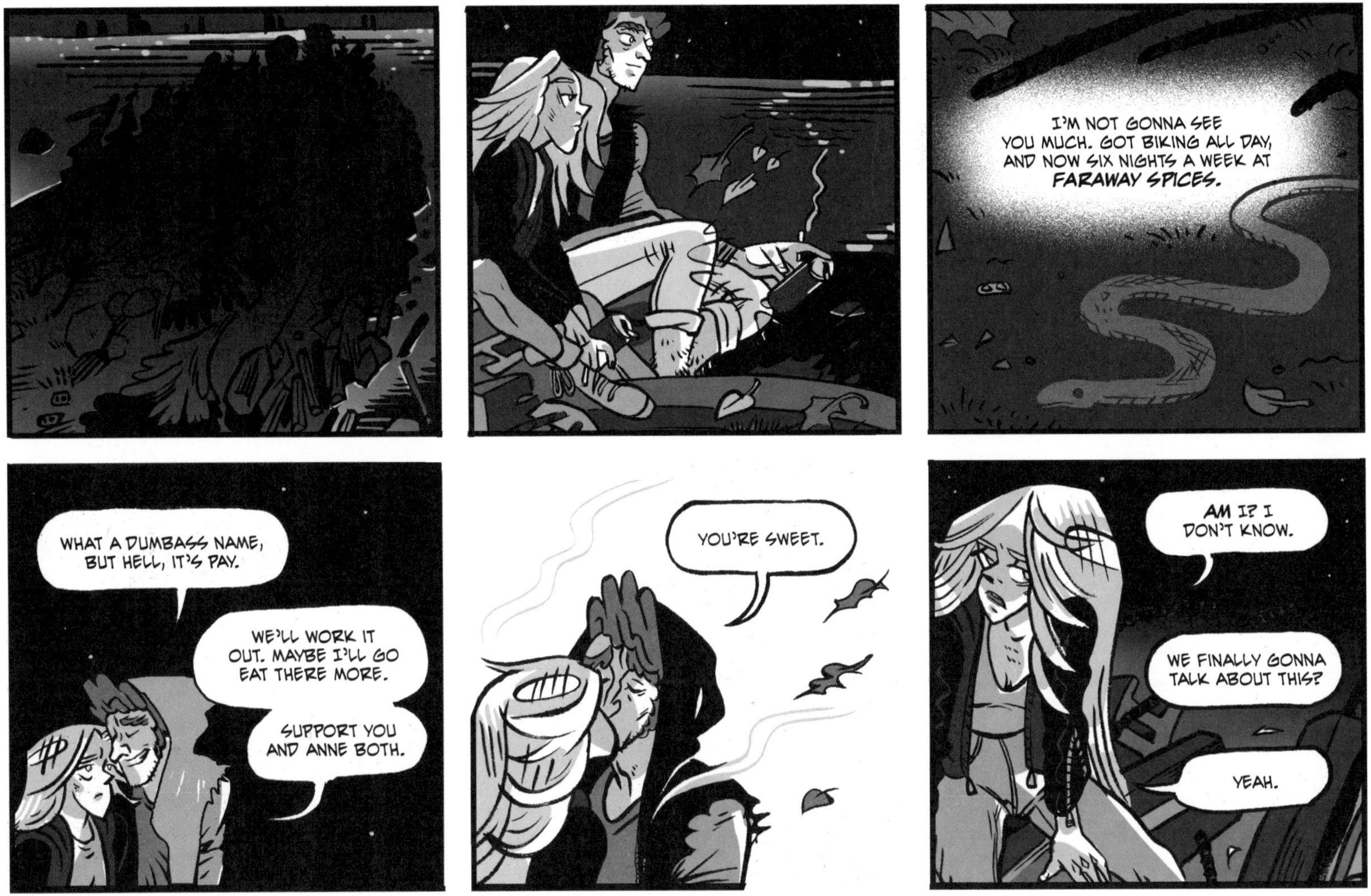
I'M NOT GONNA SEE YOU MUCH. GOT BIKING ALL DAY, AND NOW SIX NIGHTS A WEEK AT **FARAWAY SPICES.**
WHAT A DUMBASS NAME, BUT HELL, IT'S PAY.
WE'LL WORK IT OUT. MAYBE I'LL GO EAT THERE MORE.
SUPPORT YOU AND ANNE BOTH.
YOU'RE SWEET.
AM I? I DON'T KNOW.
WE FINALLY GONNA TALK ABOUT THIS?
YEAH.

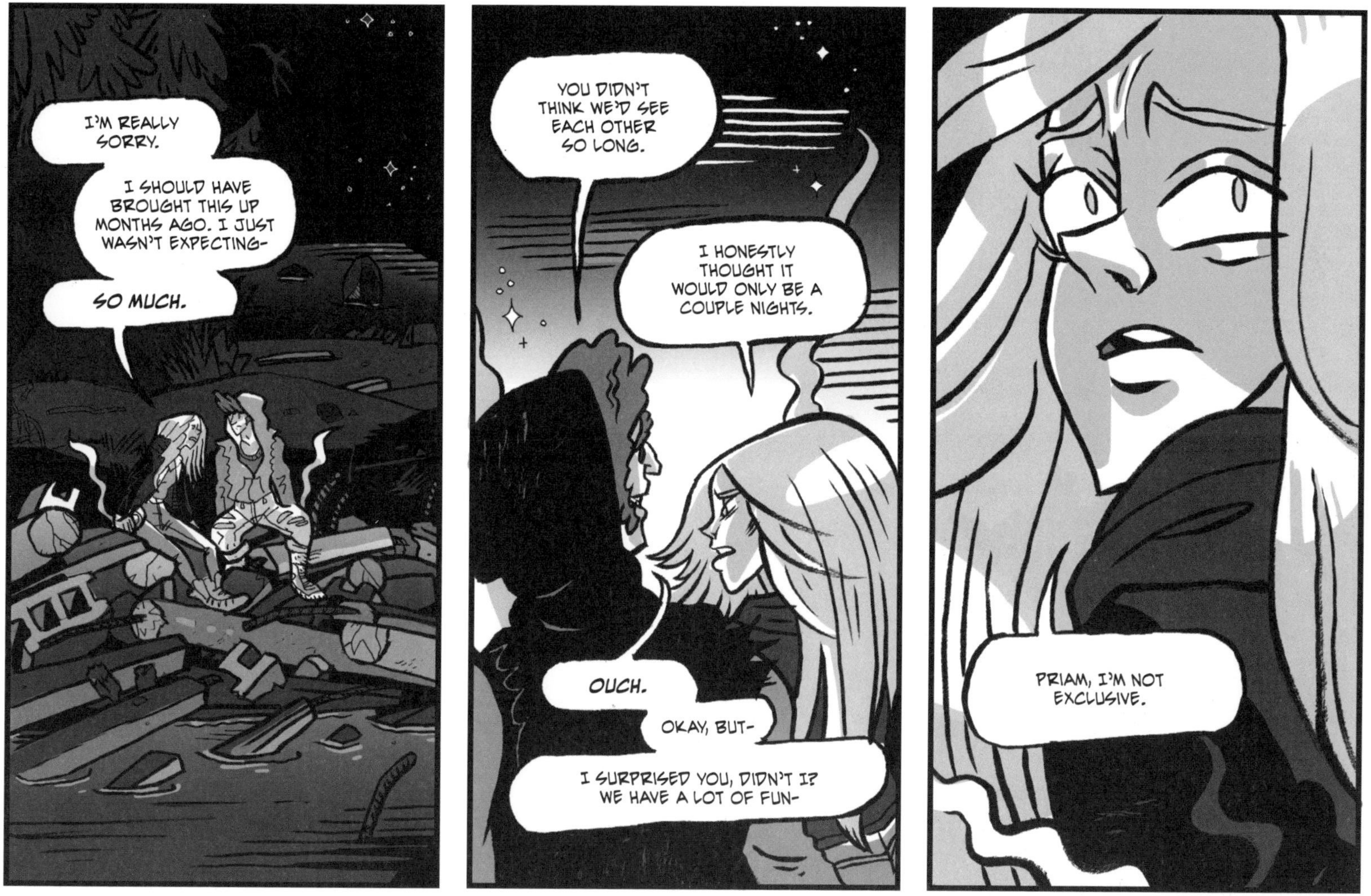
I'M REALLY SORRY.
I SHOULD HAVE BROUGHT THIS UP MONTHS AGO. I JUST WASN'T EXPECTING-
SO MUCH.
YOU DIDN'T THINK WE'D SEE EACH OTHER SO LONG.
I HONESTLY THOUGHT IT WOULD ONLY BE A COUPLE NIGHTS.
OUCH.
OKAY, BUT-
I SURPRISED YOU, DIDN'T I? WE HAVE A LOT OF FUN-
PRIAM, I'M NOT EXCLUSIVE.

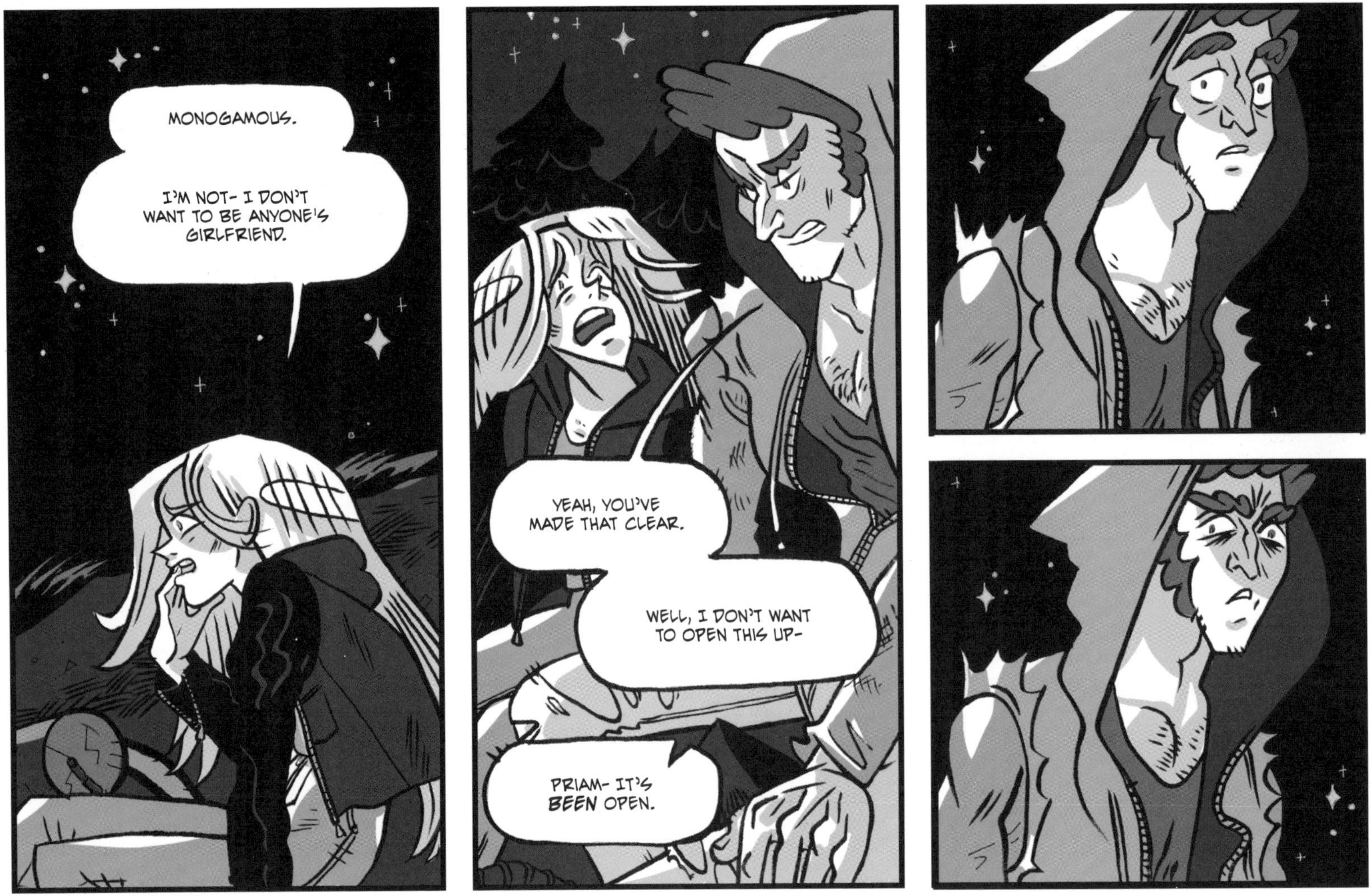
MONOGAMOUS.
I'M NOT- I DON'T WANT TO BE ANYONE'S GIRLFRIEND.
YEAH, YOU'VE MADE THAT CLEAR.
WELL, I DON'T WANT TO OPEN THIS UP-
PRIAM- IT'S **BEEN** OPEN.

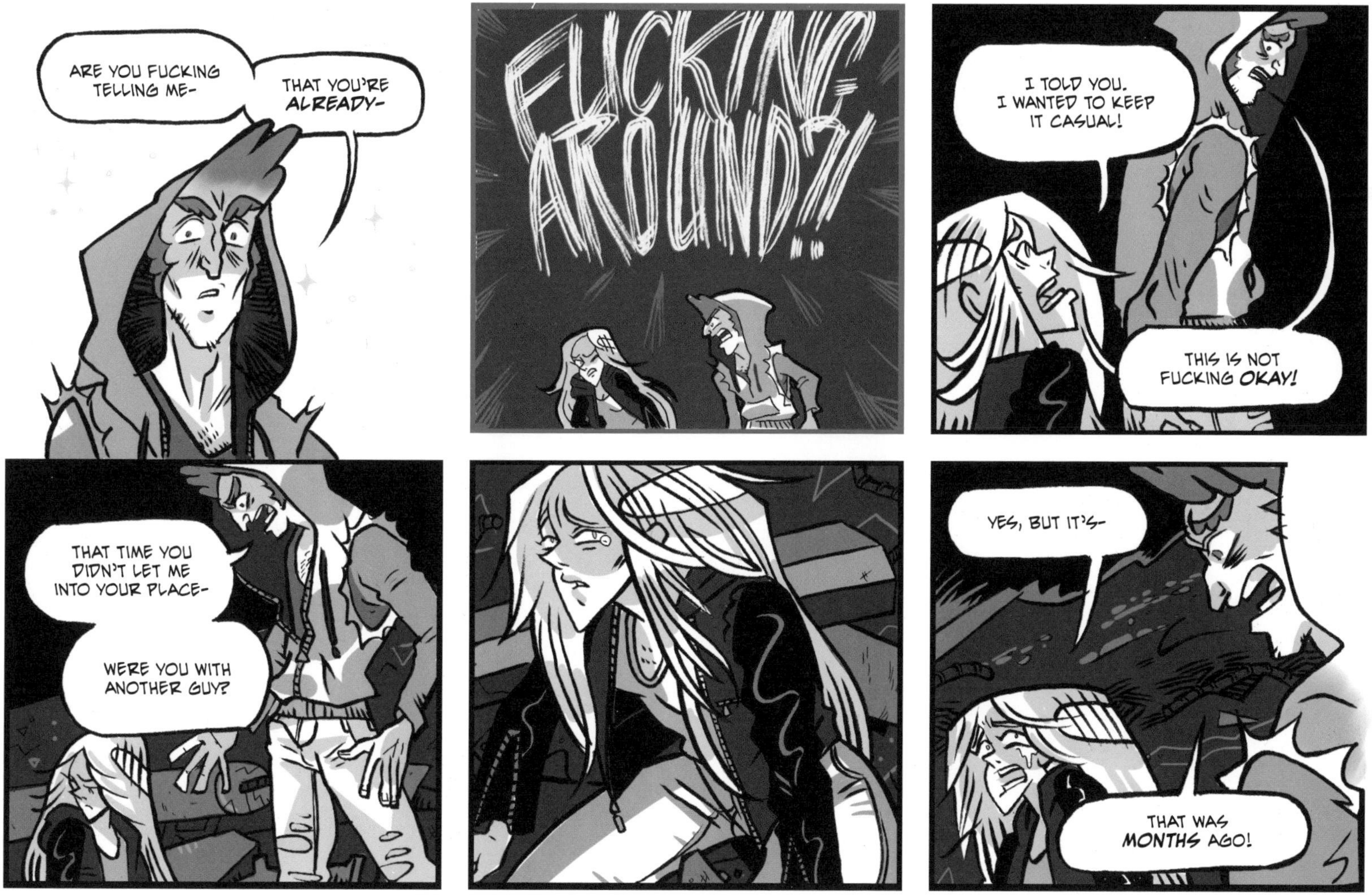
ARE YOU FUCKING TELLING ME-
THAT YOU'RE ALREADY-
FUCKING AROUND?!
I TOLD YOU. I WANTED TO KEEP IT CASUAL!
THIS IS NOT FUCKING OKAY!
THAT TIME YOU DIDN'T LET ME INTO YOUR PLACE-
WERE YOU WITH ANOTHER GUY?
YES, BUT IT'S-
THAT WAS MONTHS AGO!

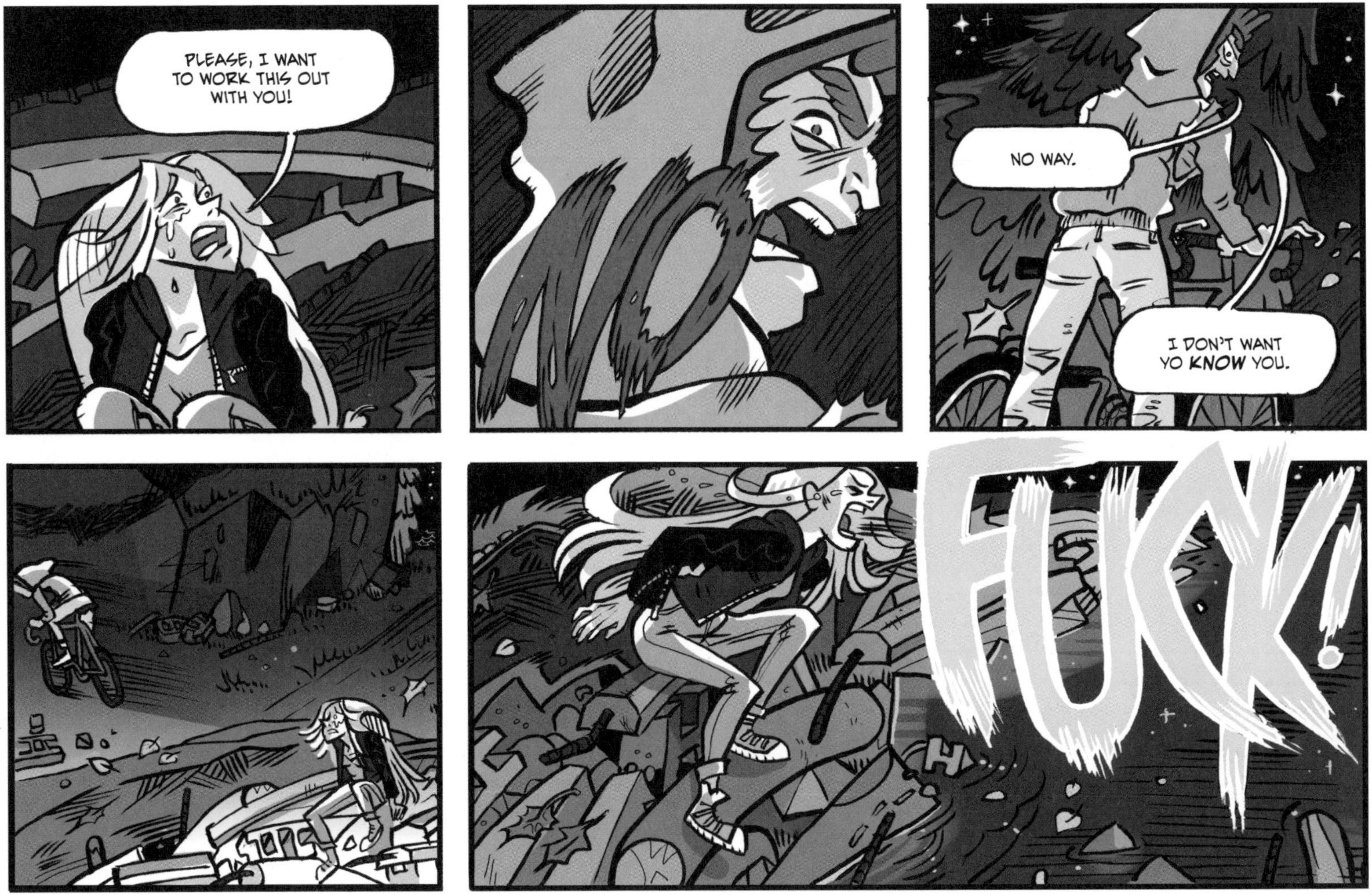
PLEASE, I WANT TO WORK THIS OUT WITH YOU!
NO
NO WAY.
I DON'T WANT YO **KNOW** YOU.
FUCK!
H

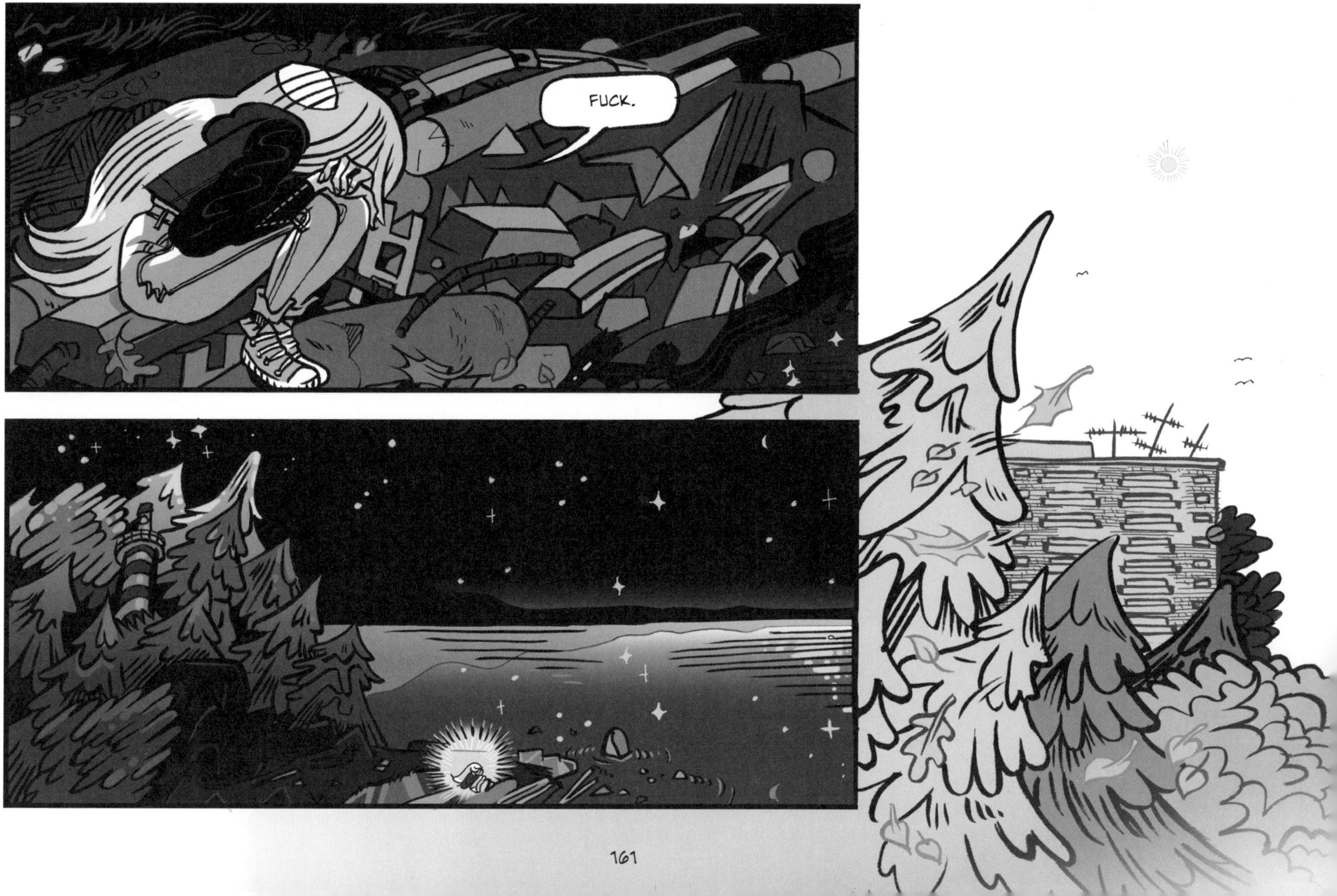
FUCK.

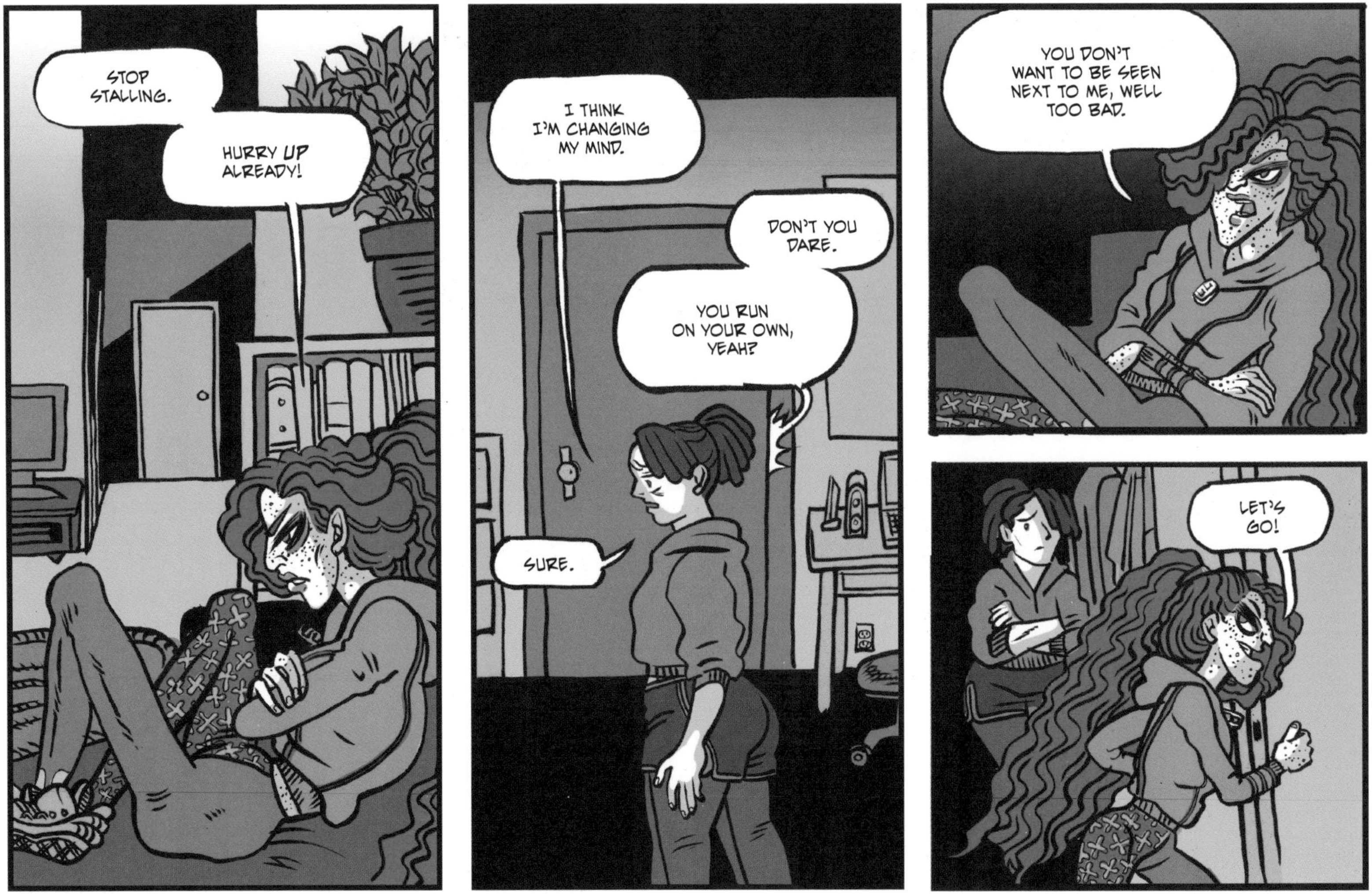
STOP STALLING.
HURRY UP ALREADY!
I THINK I'M CHANGING MY MIND.
DON'T YOU DARE.
YOU RUN ON YOUR OWN, YEAH?
SURE.
YOU DON'T WANT TO BE SEEN NEXT TO ME, WELL TOO BAD.
LET'S GO!

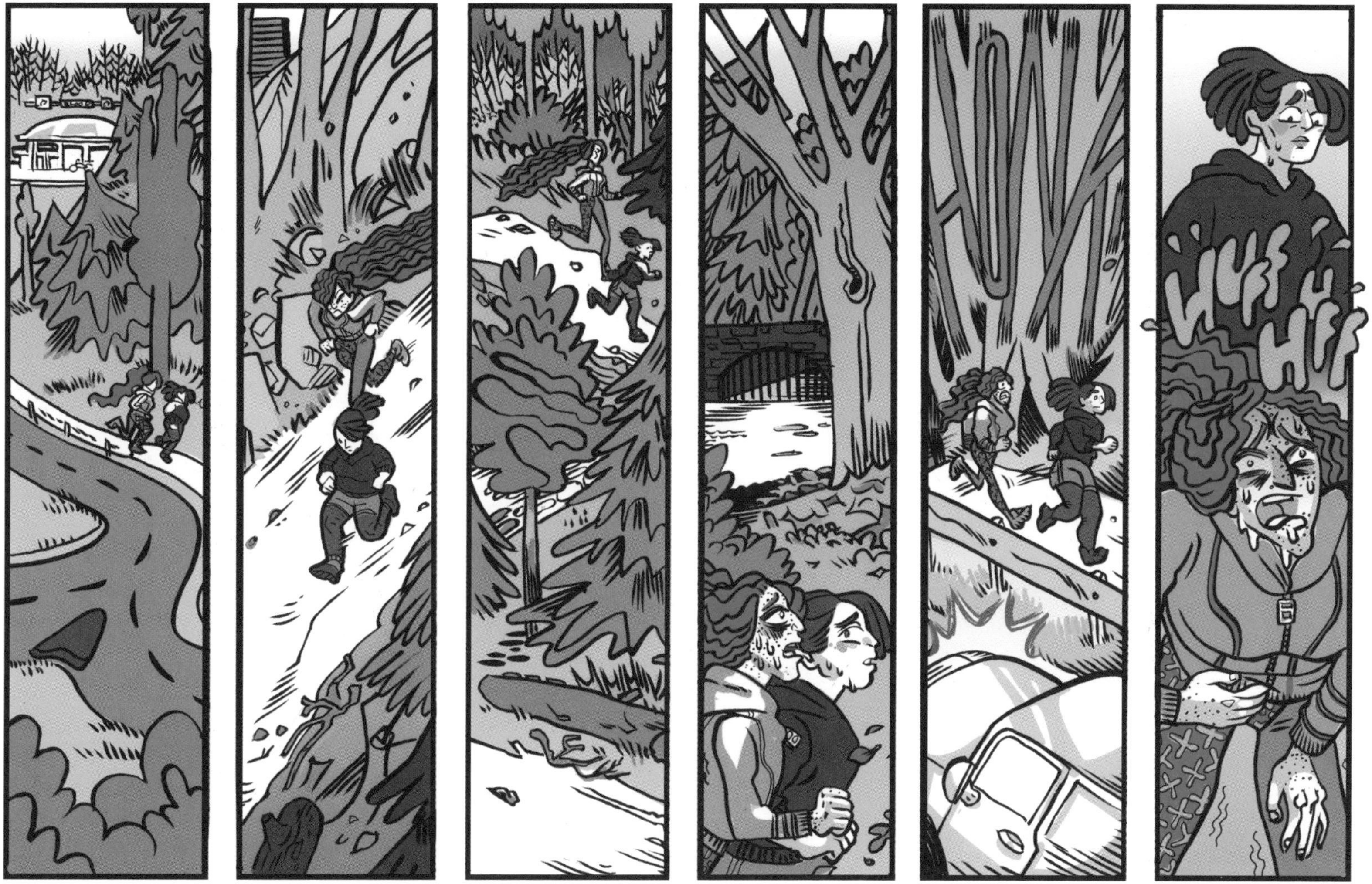
HONK
HUFF
HUFF

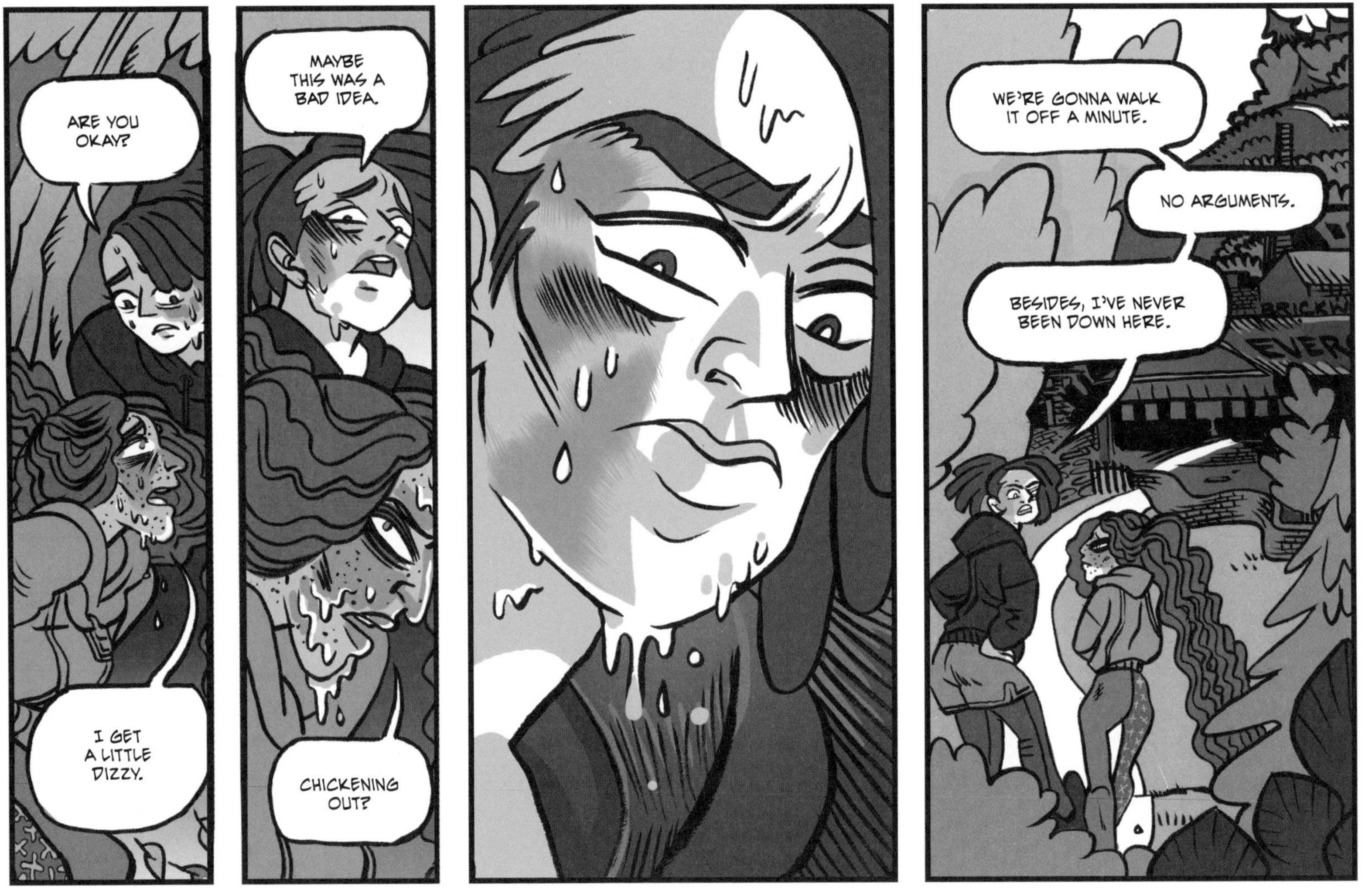
ARE YOU OKAY?
I GET A LITTLE DIZZY.
MAYBE THIS WAS A BAD IDEA.
CHICKENING OUT?
WE'RE GONNA WALK IT OFF A MINUTE.
NO ARGUMENTS.
BESIDES, I'VE NEVER BEEN DOWN HERE.

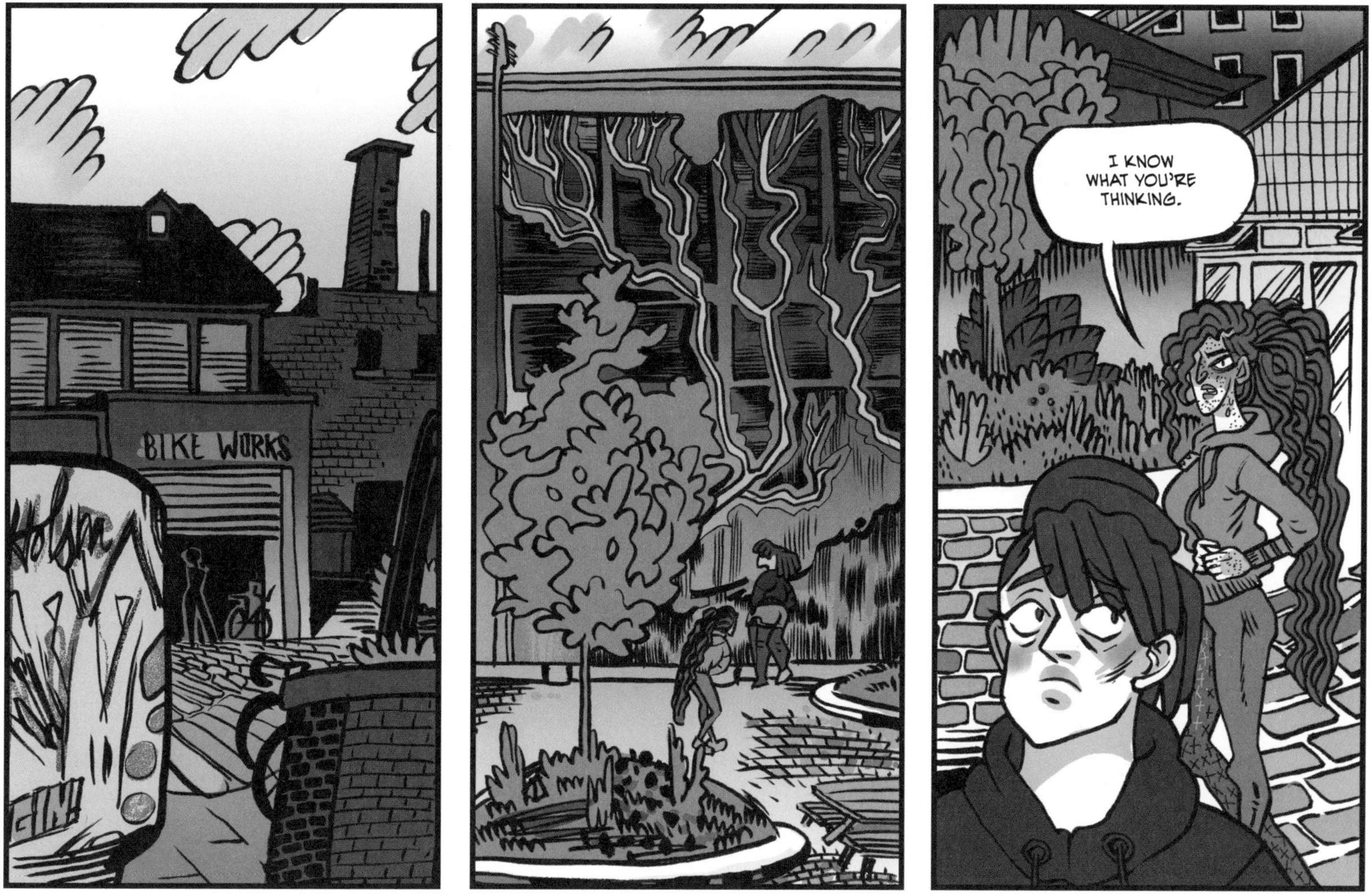
BIKE WORKS
I KNOW WHAT YOU'RE THINKING.

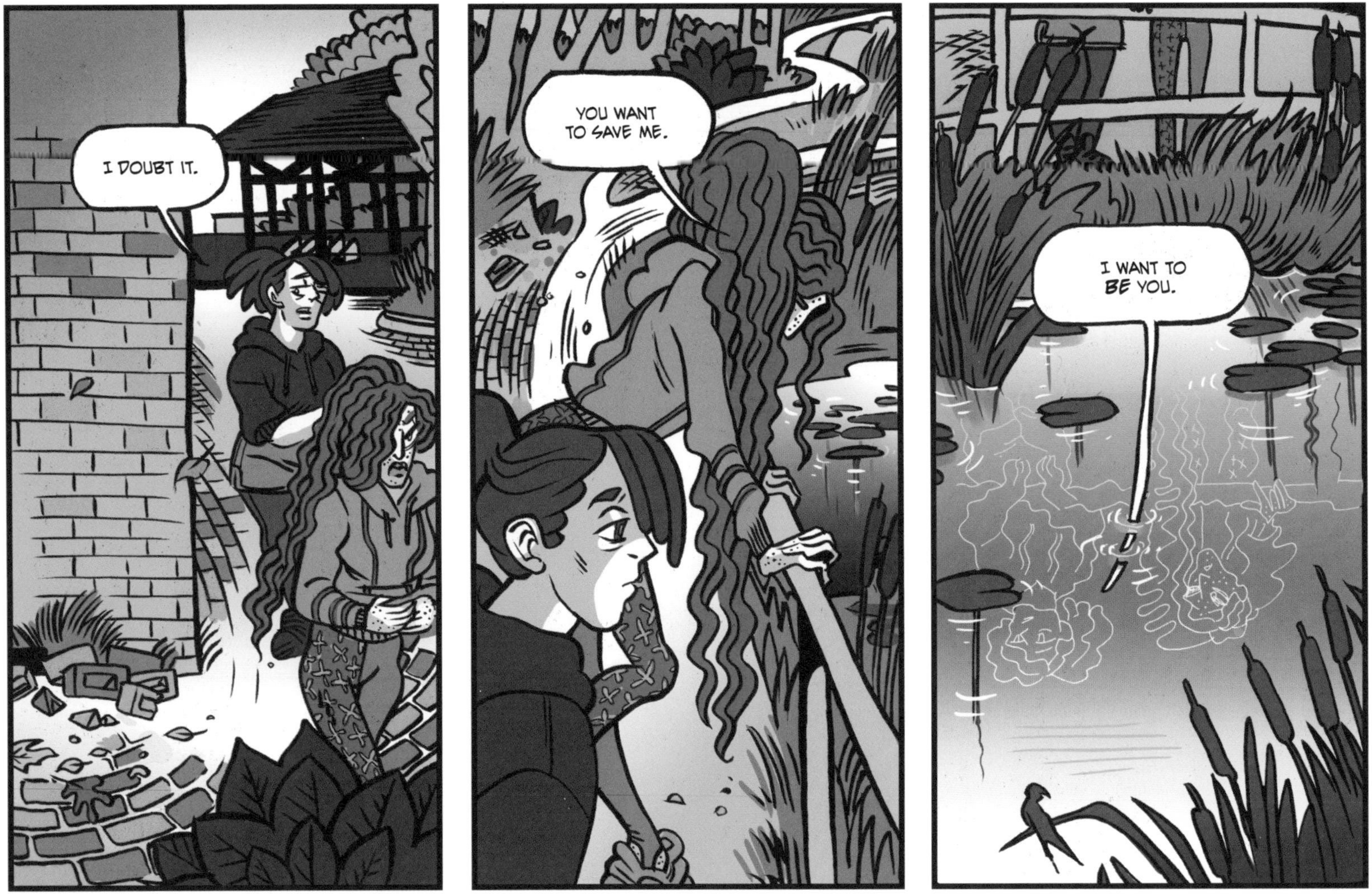
I DOUBT IT.
YOU WANT TO SAVE ME.
I WANT TO BE YOU.

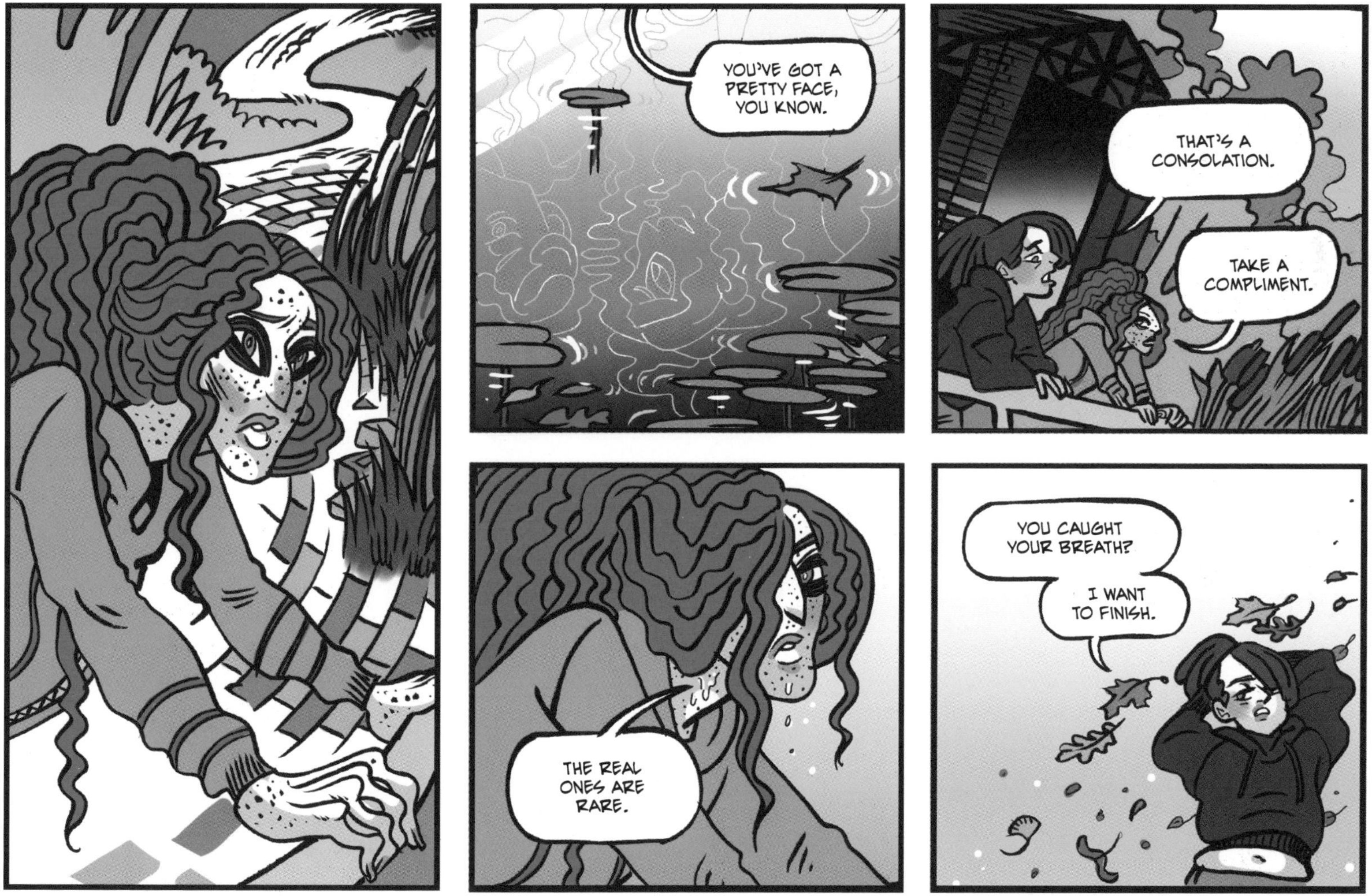
YOU'VE GOT A PRETTY FACE, YOU KNOW.
THAT'S A CONSOLATION.
TAKE A COMPLIMENT.
THE REAL ONES ARE RARE.
YOU CAUGHT YOUR BREATH?
I WANT TO FINISH.

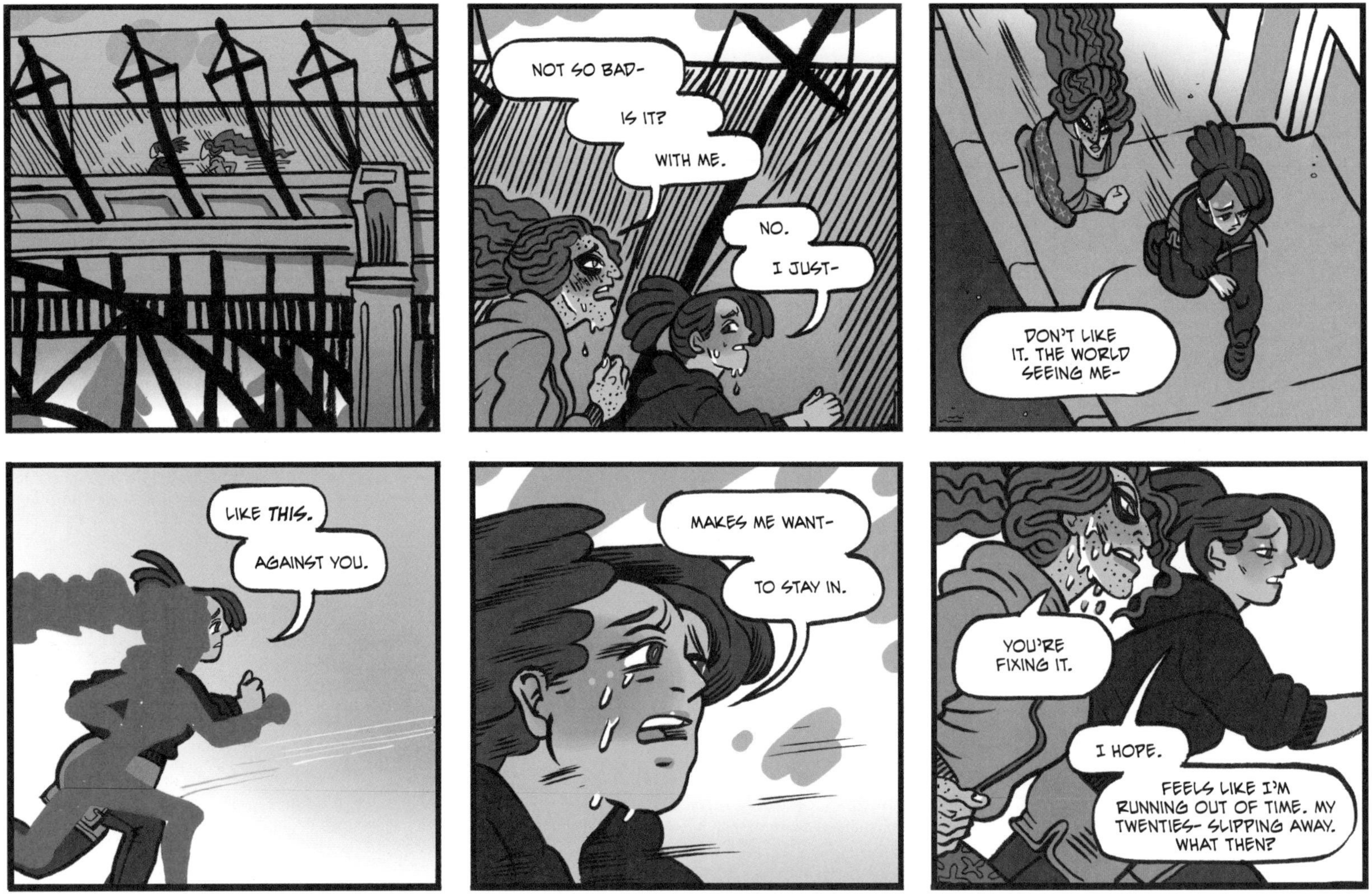
NOT SO BAD-
IS IT?
WITH ME.
NO.
I JUST-
DON'T LIKE IT. THE WORLD SEEING ME-
LIKE THIS.
AGAINST YOU.
MAKES ME WANT-
TO STAY IN.
YOU'RE FIXING IT.
I HOPE.
FEELS LIKE I'M RUNNING OUT OF TIME. MY TWENTIES- SLIPPING AWAY. WHAT THEN?

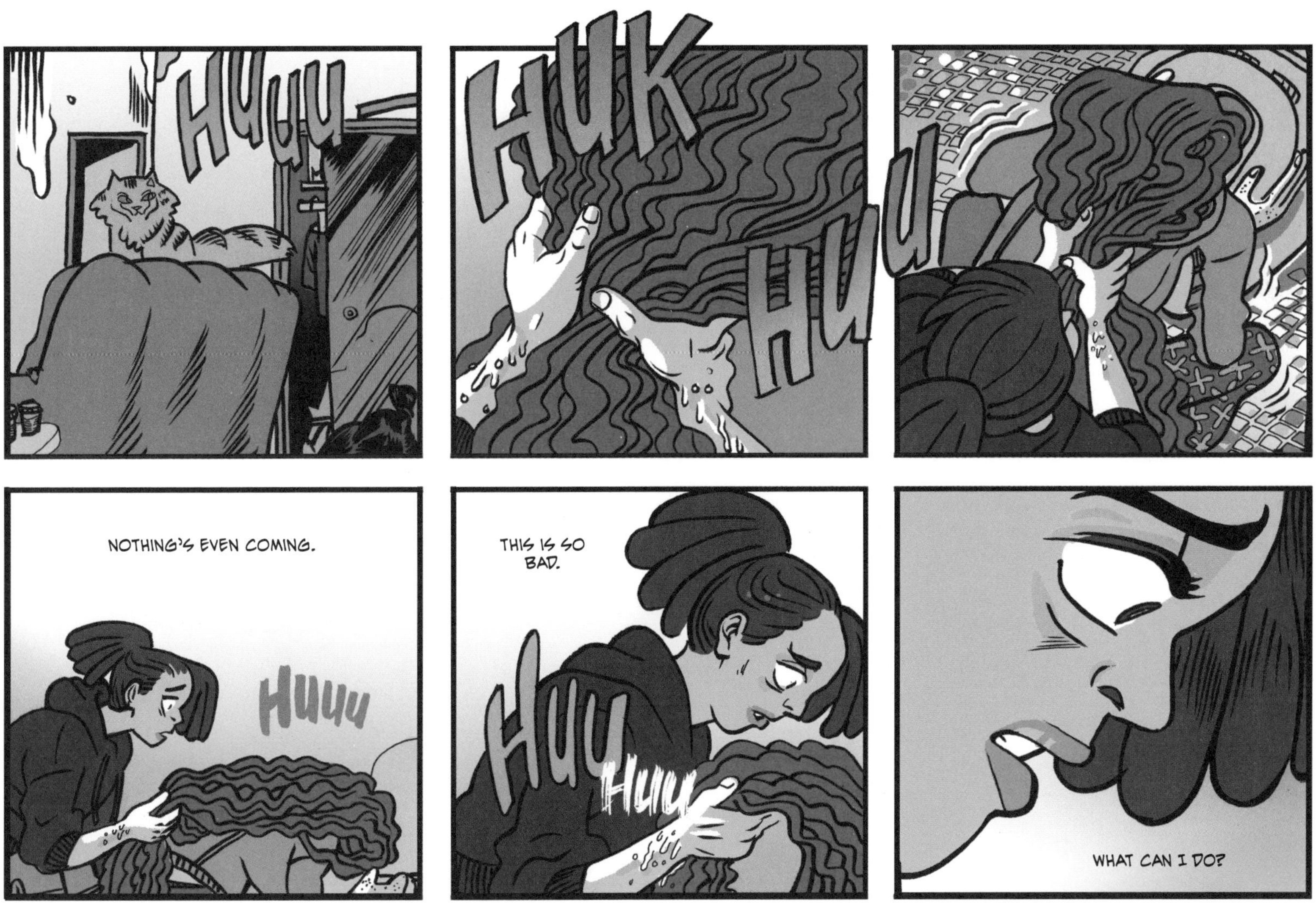
HUUU
HUK
HUU
NOTHING'S EVEN COMING.
HUUU
THIS IS SO BAD.
HUU
HUU
WHAT CAN I DO?

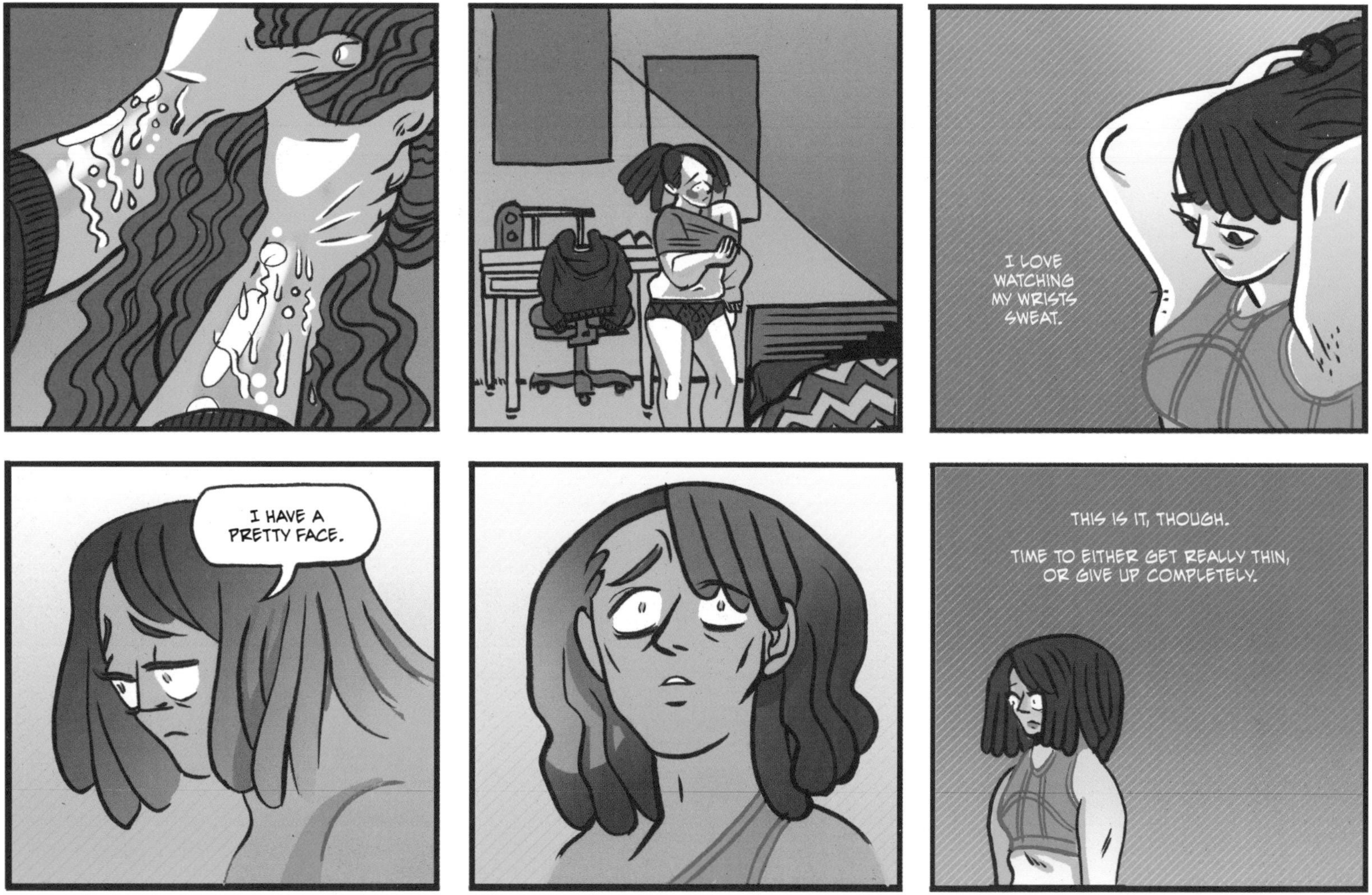
I LOVE WATCHING MY WRISTS SWEAT.
I HAVE A PRETTY FACE.
THIS IS IT, THOUGH.
TIME TO EITHER GET REALLY THIN, OR GIVE UP COMPLETELY.

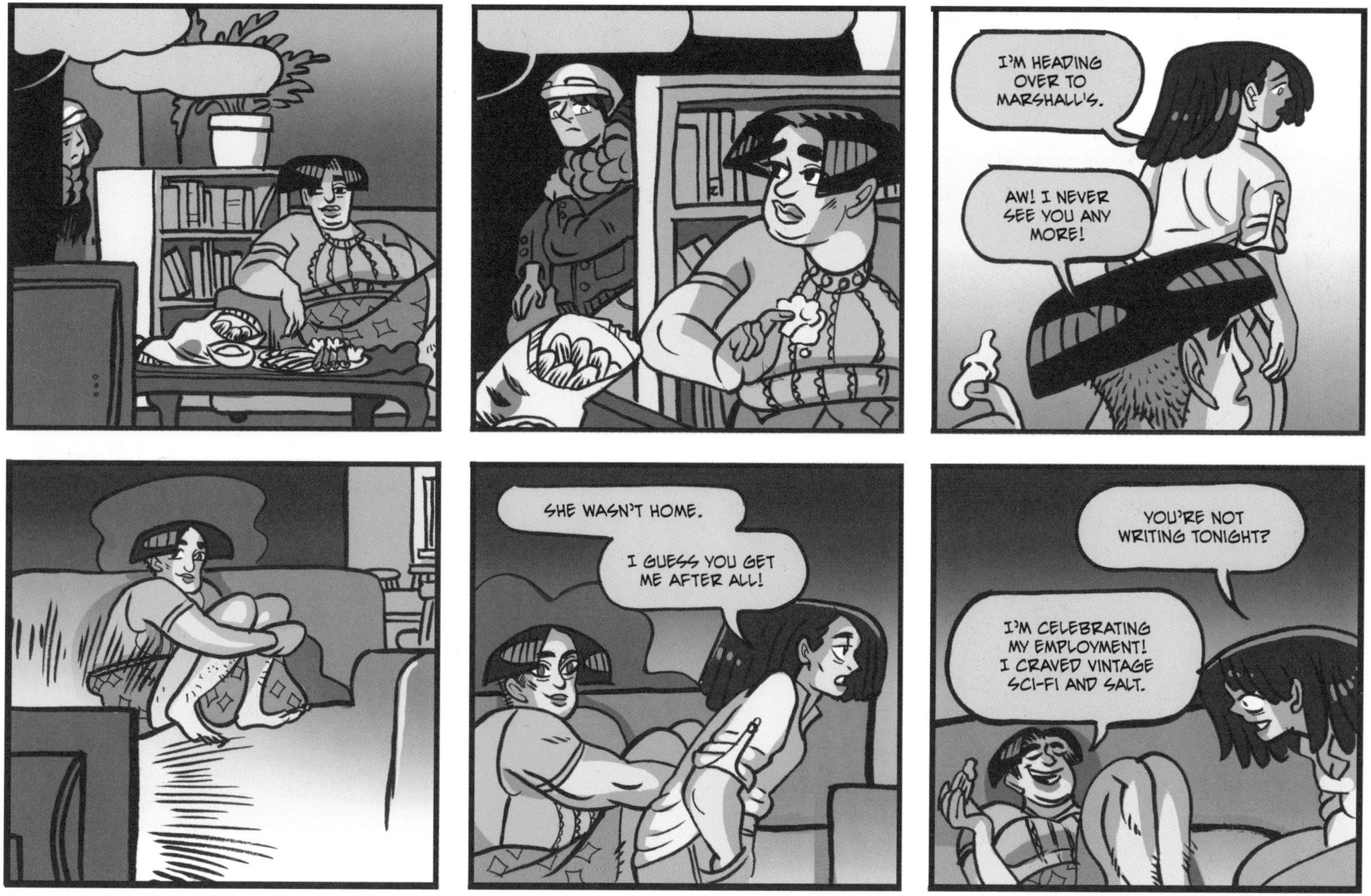
I'M HEADING OVER TO MARSHALL'S.
AW! I NEVER SEE YOU ANY MORE!
SHE WASN'T HOME.
I GUESS YOU GET ME AFTER ALL!
YOU'RE NOT WRITING TONIGHT?
I'M CELEBRATING MY EMPLOYMENT! I CRAVED VINTAGE SCI-FI AND SALT.

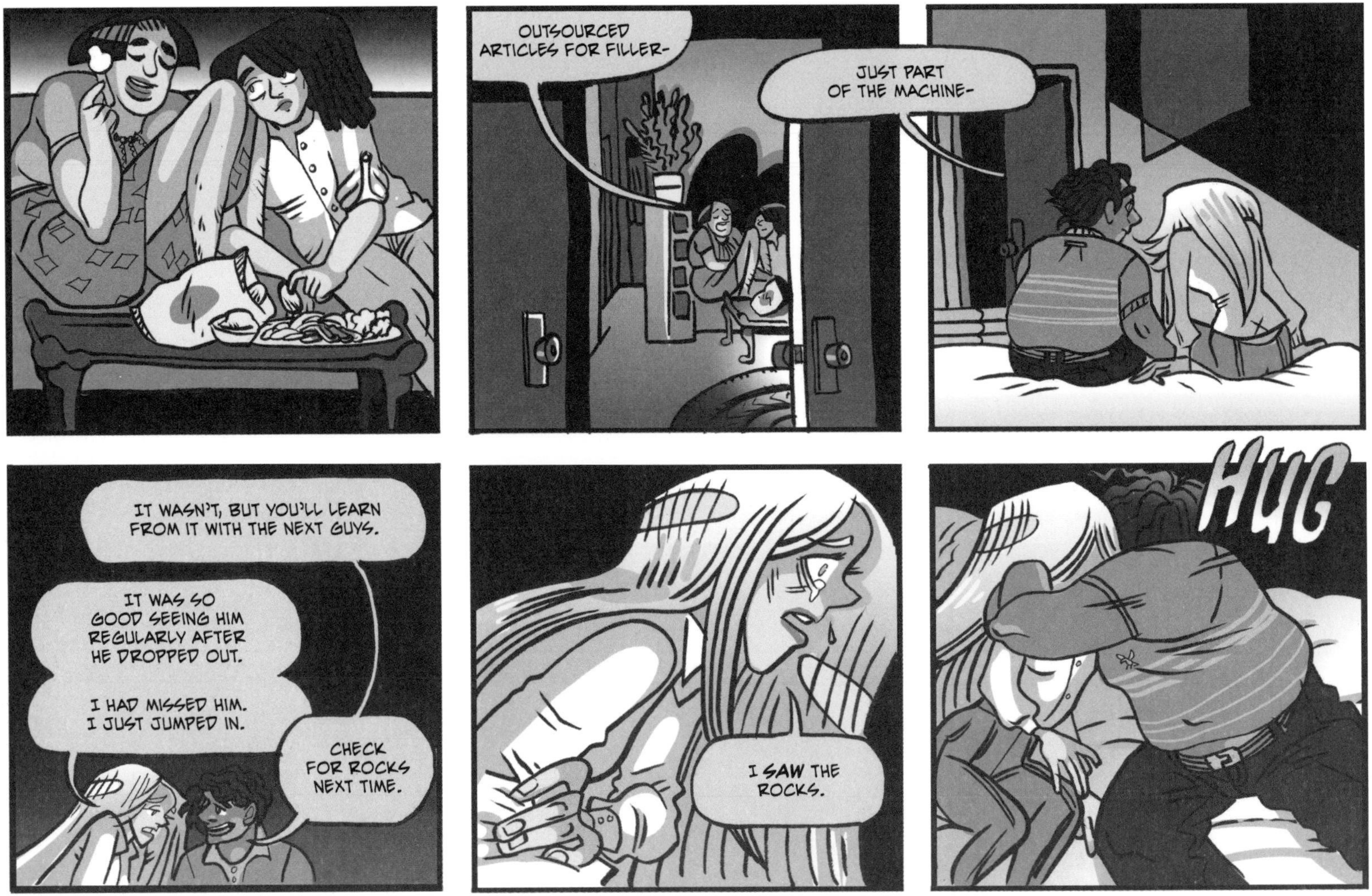

OUTSOURCED ARTICLES FOR FILLER-
JUST PART OF THE MACHINE-
IT WASN'T, BUT YOU'LL LEARN FROM IT WITH THE NEXT GUYS.
IT WAS SO GOOD SEEING HIM REGULARLY AFTER HE DROPPED OUT.
I HAD MISSED HIM. I JUST JUMPED IN.
CHECK FOR ROCKS NEXT TIME.
I SAW THE ROCKS.
HUG

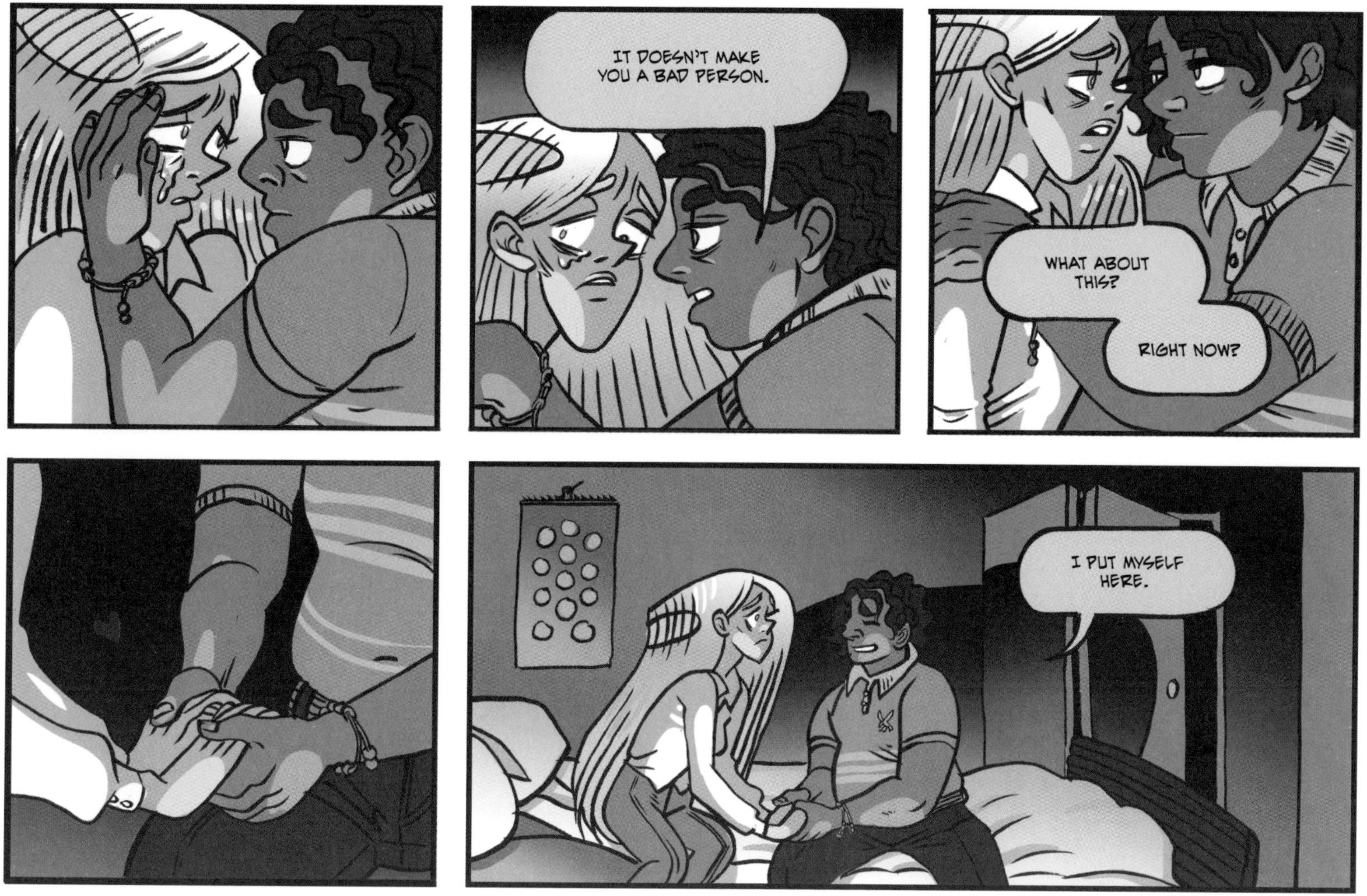
IT DOESN'T MAKE YOU A BAD PERSON.
WHAT ABOUT THIS?
RIGHT NOW?
I PUT MYSELF HERE.

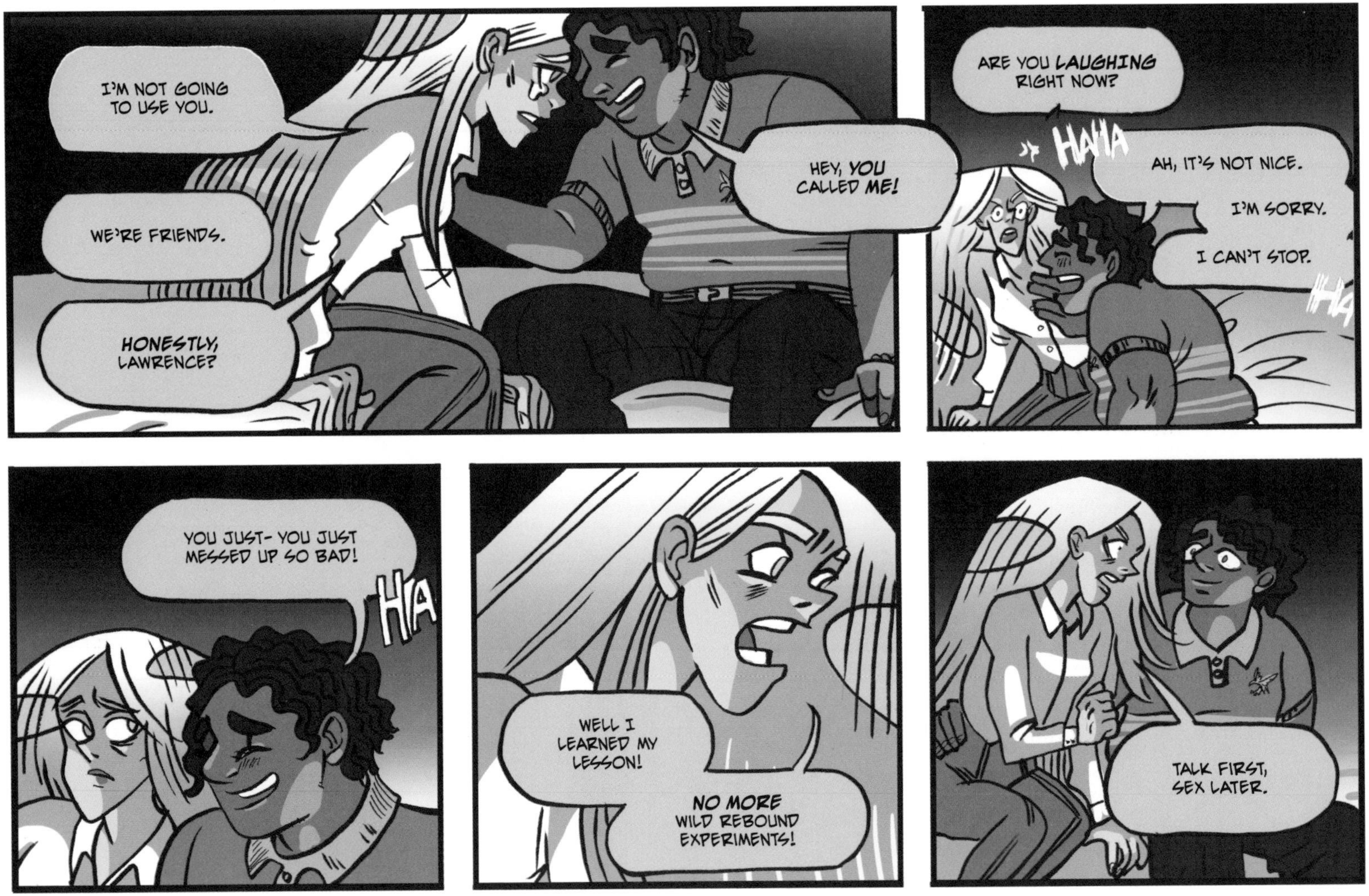
I'M NOT GOING TO USE YOU.
WE'RE FRIENDS.
HONESTLY, LAWRENCE?
HEY, YOU CALLED ME!
ARE YOU LAUGHING RIGHT NOW?
HAHA
AH, IT'S NOT NICE.
I'M SORRY.
I CAN'T STOP.
HA
YOU JUST- YOU JUST MESSED UP SO BAD!
HA
WELL I LEARNED MY LESSON!
NO MORE WILD REBOUND EXPERIMENTS!
TALK FIRST, SEX LATER.

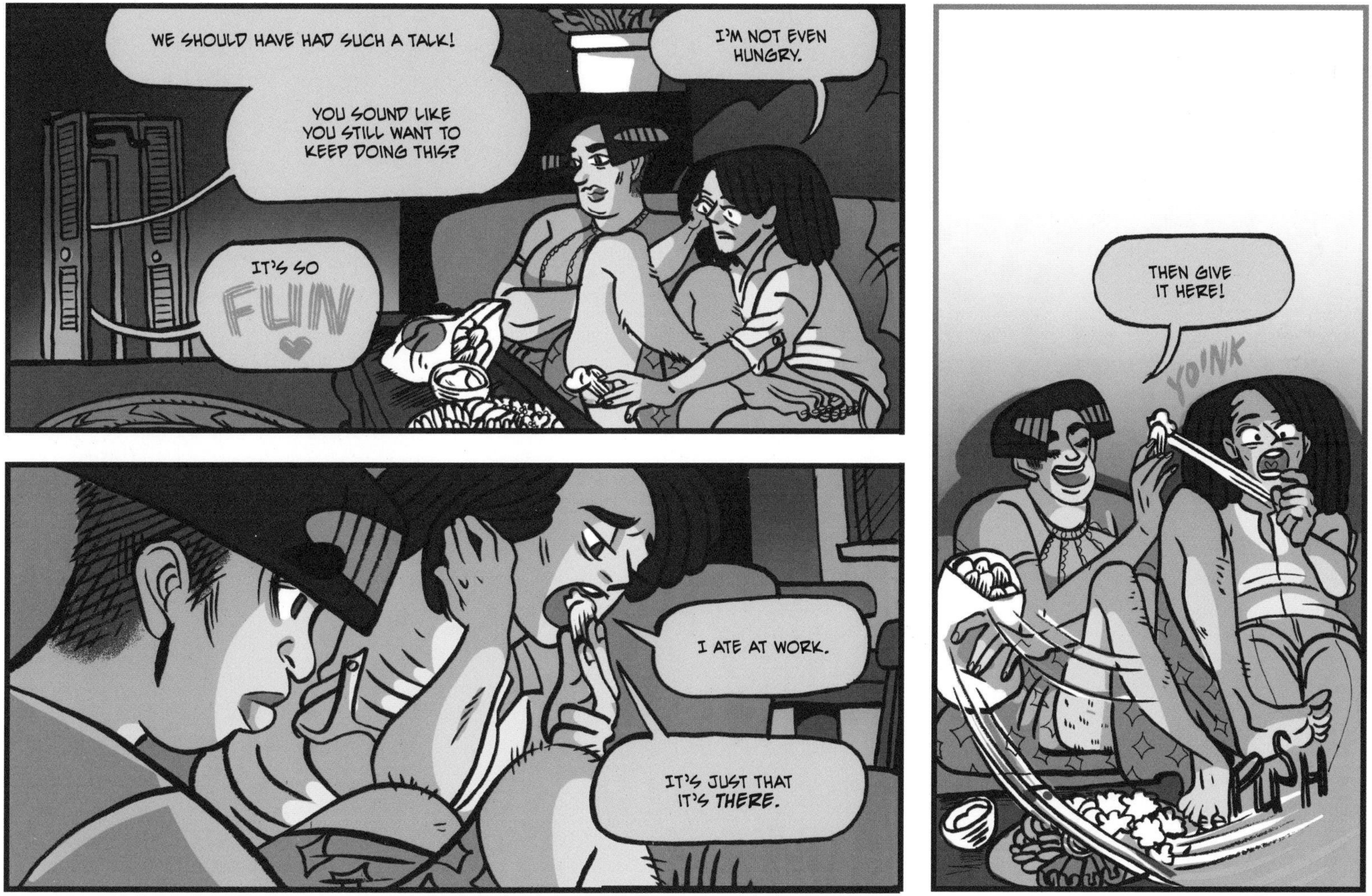
WE SHOULD HAVE HAD SUCH A TALK!
YOU SOUND LIKE YOU STILL WANT TO KEEP DOING THIS?
IT'S SO FUN
I'M NOT EVEN HUNGRY.
I ATE AT WORK.
IT'S JUST THAT IT'S THERE.
THEN GIVE IT HERE!
YO'INK
FLNH

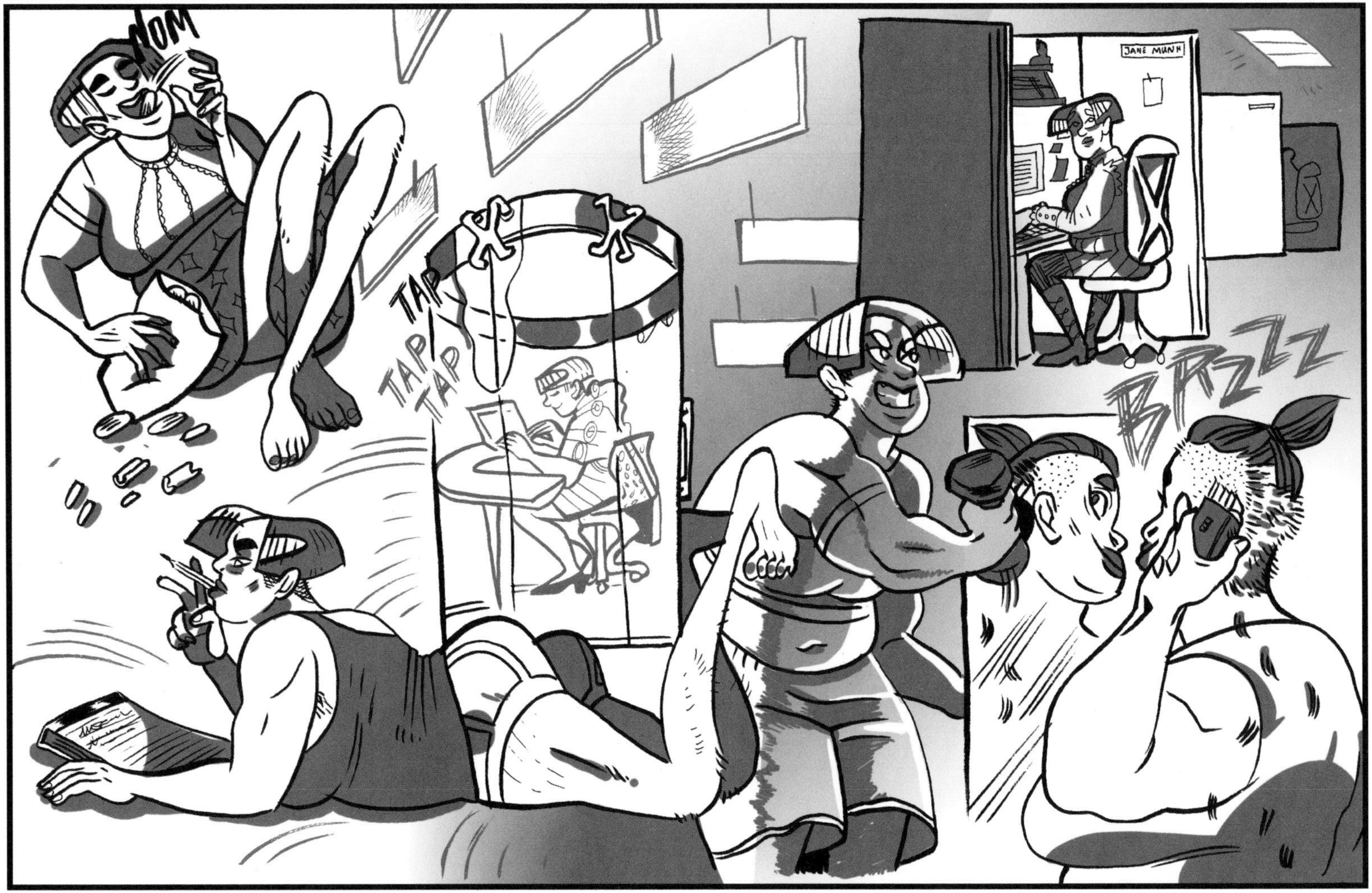
NOM
JANE MUNH
TAP
TAP
TAP
BRZZZ

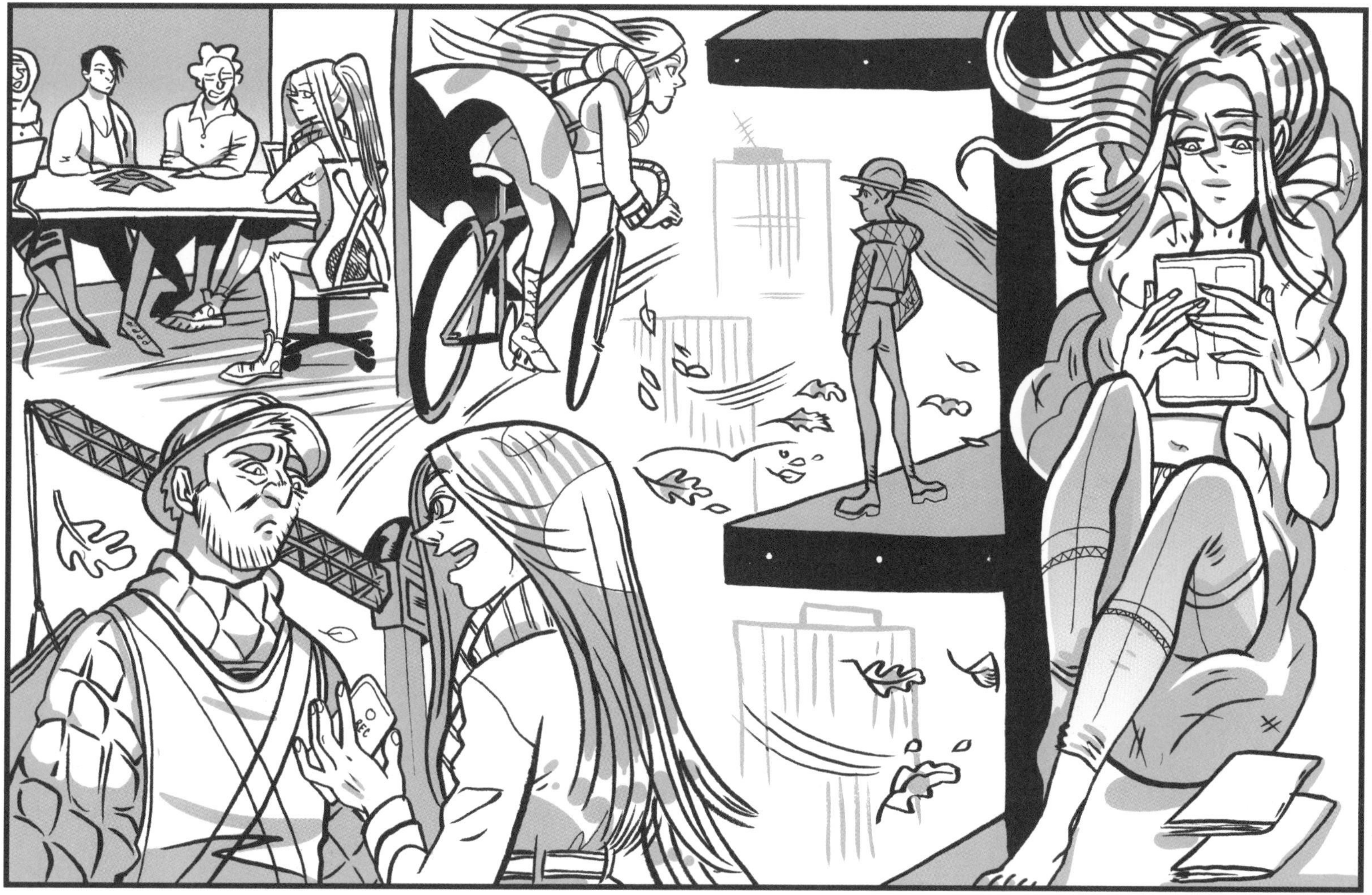
REC

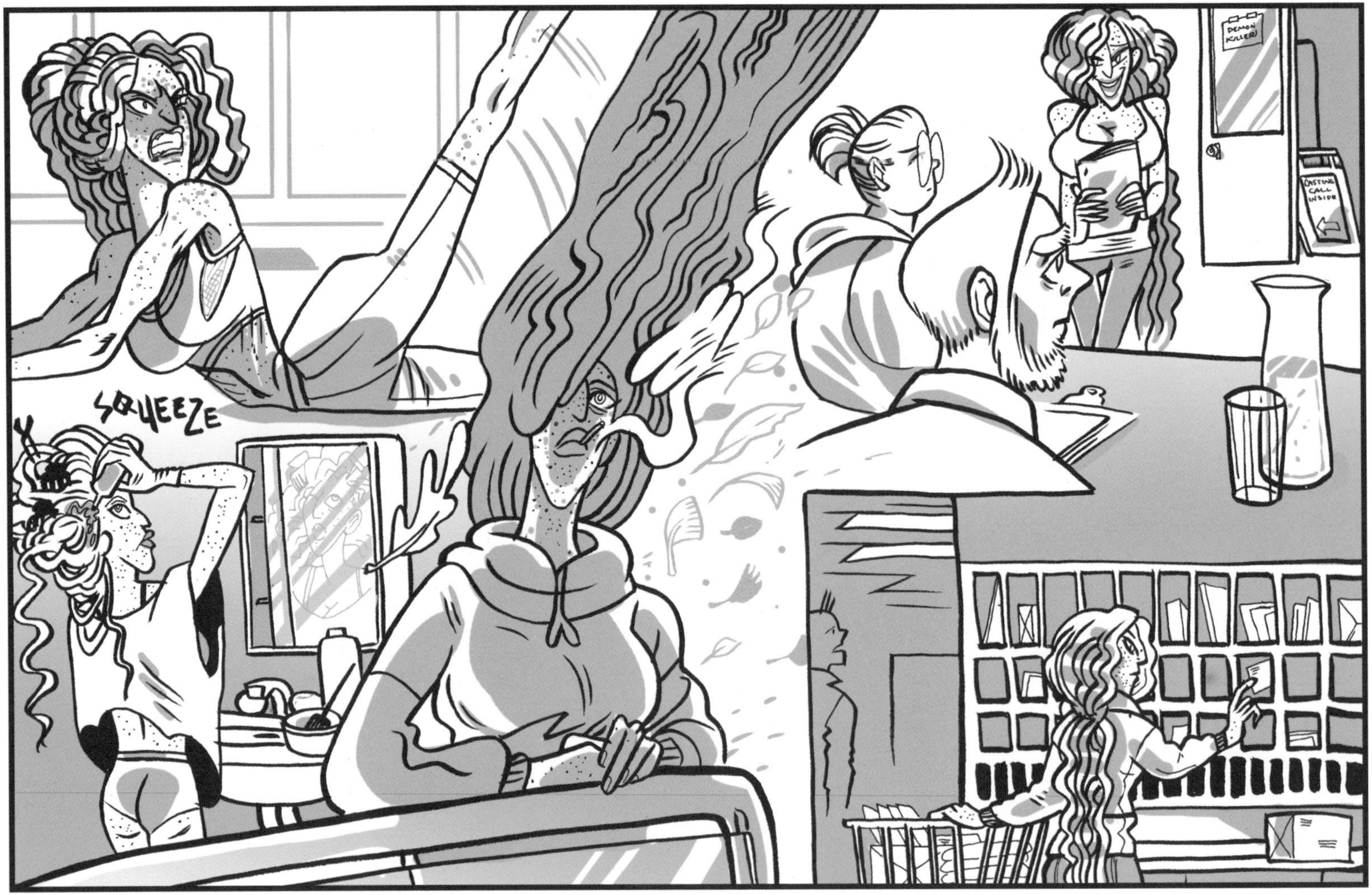
SQUEEZE
DEMON KILLER!
CASTING CALL INSIDE

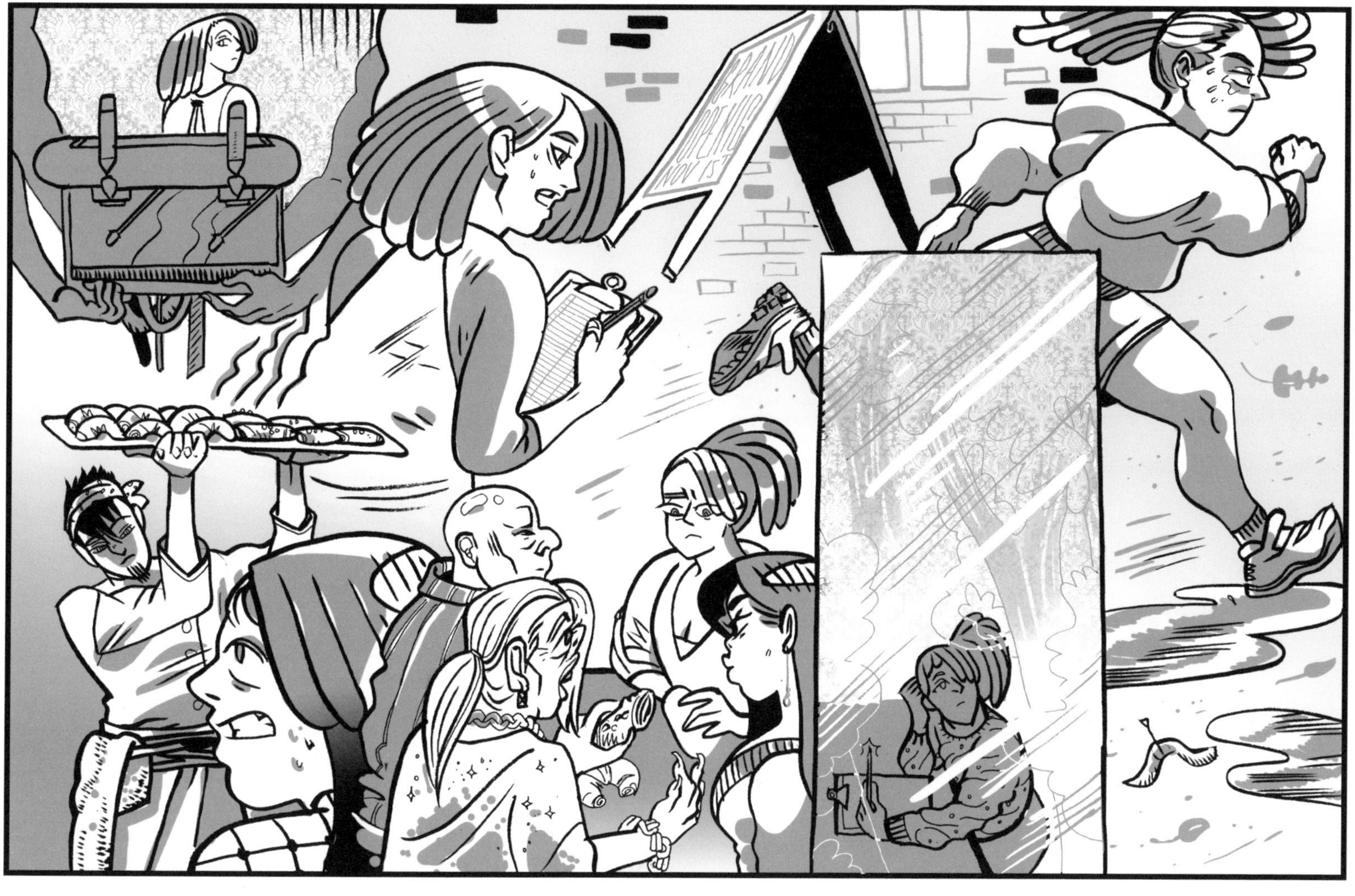
GRAND OPENING
NOV 1ST

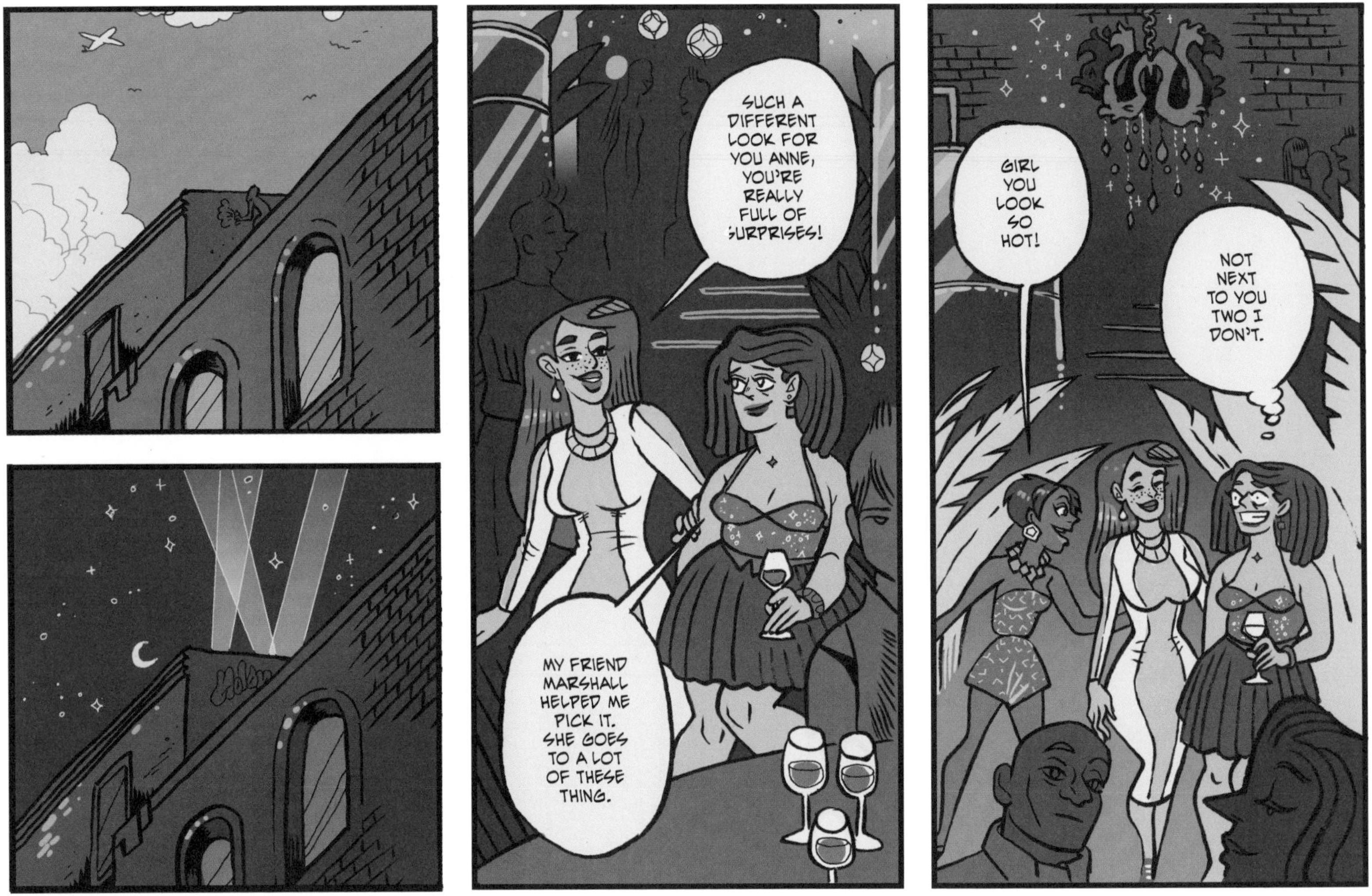
SUCH A DIFFERENT LOOK FOR YOU ANNE, YOU'RE REALLY FULL OF SURPRISES!
MY FRIEND MARSHALL HELPED ME PICK IT. SHE GOES TO A LOT OF THESE THING.
GIRL YOU LOOK SO HOT!
NOT NEXT TO YOU TWO I DON'T.

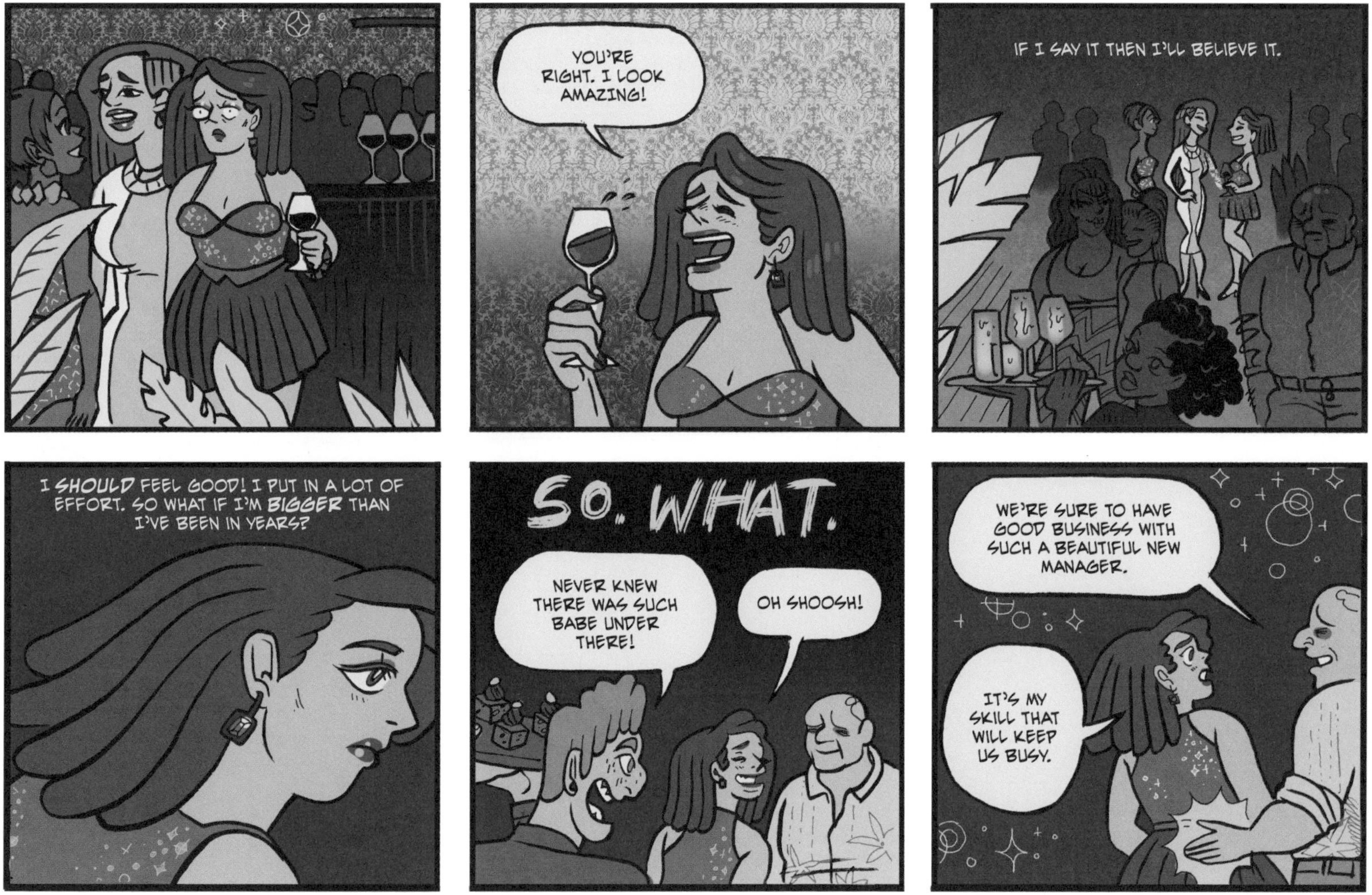
YOU'RE RIGHT. I LOOK AMAZING!
IF I SAY IT THEN I'LL BELIEVE IT.
I SHOULD FEEL GOOD! I PUT IN A LOT OF EFFORT. SO WHAT IF I'M BIGGER THAN I'VE BEEN IN YEARS?
SO. WHAT.
NEVER KNEW THERE WAS SUCH BABE UNDER THERE!
OH SHOOSH!
WE'RE SURE TO HAVE GOOD BUSINESS WITH SUCH A BEAUTIFUL NEW MANAGER.
IT'S MY SKILL THAT WILL KEEP US BUSY.

NICE.

YOU THINK?

YOUR WAIST LOOKS GREAT. YOU CINCHED?

NOPE. DOES IT?

YOINK

2 HOURS EARLIER.

I'VE NEVER BEEN IN SUCH EXPLOSIVE PAIN.

OH MY GOD I WANT TO DIE.

I'M SWEATING.

8 HOURS BEFORE *THAT*.

I'M SURE THIS IS A PERFECTLY GOOD IDEA.

Rx

LAX

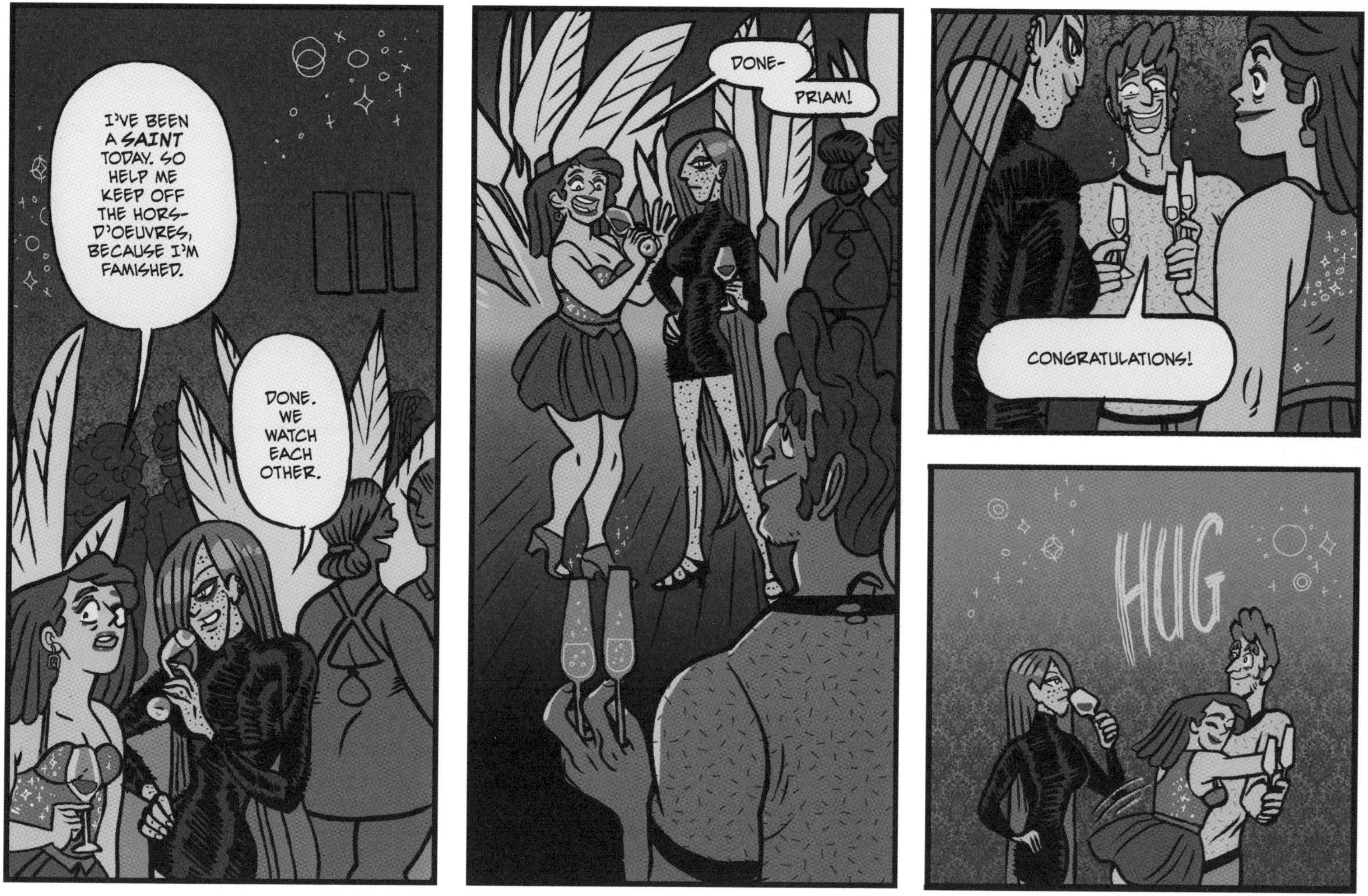
I'VE BEEN A SAINT TODAY. SO HELP ME KEEP OFF THE HORS-D'OEUVRES, BECAUSE I'M FAMISHED.
DONE. WE WATCH EACH OTHER.
DONE-
PRIAM!
CONGRATULATIONS!
HUG

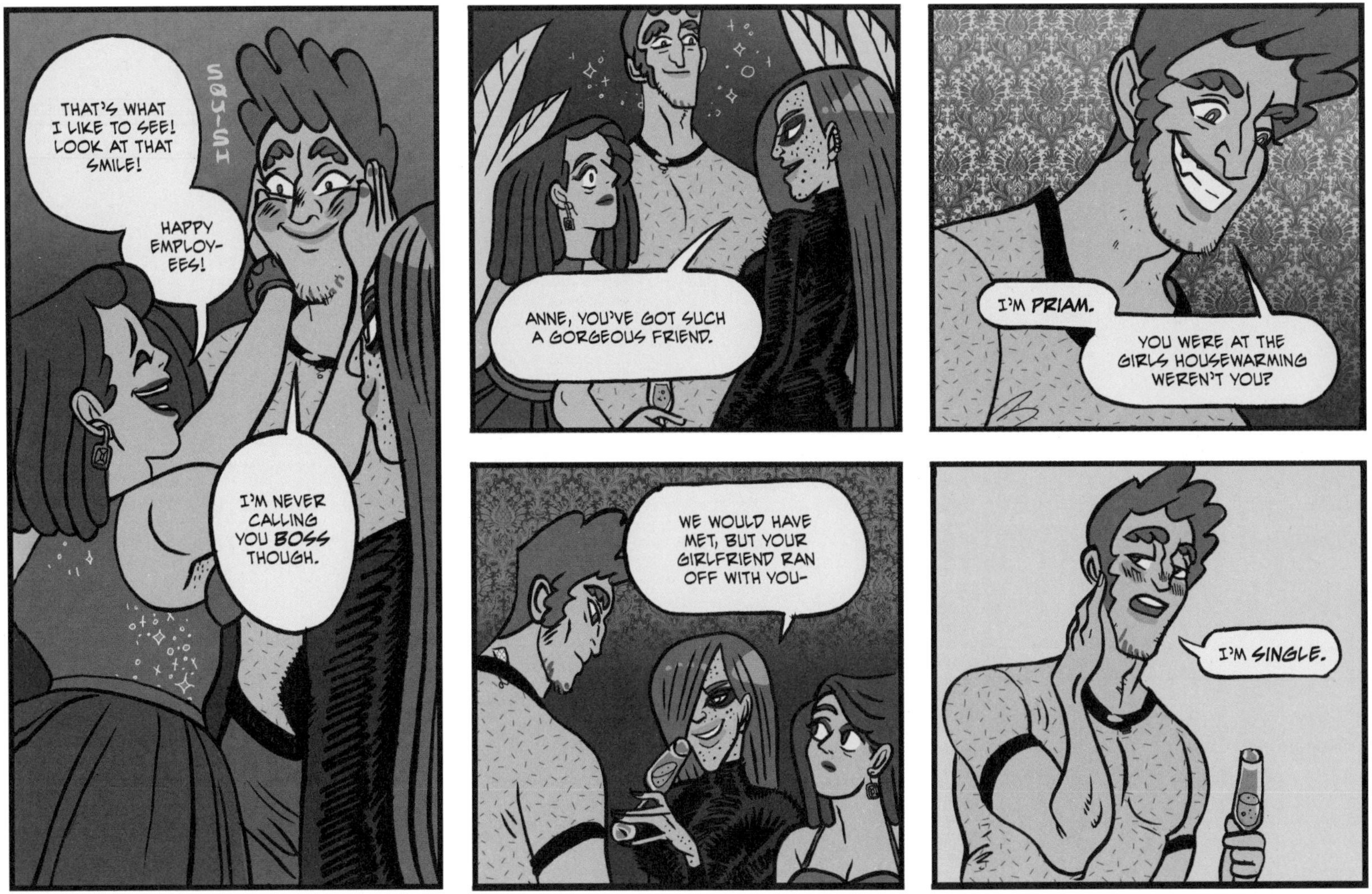
THAT'S WHAT I LIKE TO SEE! LOOK AT THAT SMILE!
SQUISH
HAPPY EMPLOY-EES!
I'M NEVER CALLING YOU BOSS THOUGH.
ANNE, YOU'VE GOT SUCH A GORGEOUS FRIEND.
I'M PRIAM.
YOU WERE AT THE GIRLS HOUSEWARMING WEREN'T YOU?
WE WOULD HAVE MET, BUT YOUR GIRLFRIEND RAN OFF WITH YOU-
I'M SINGLE.

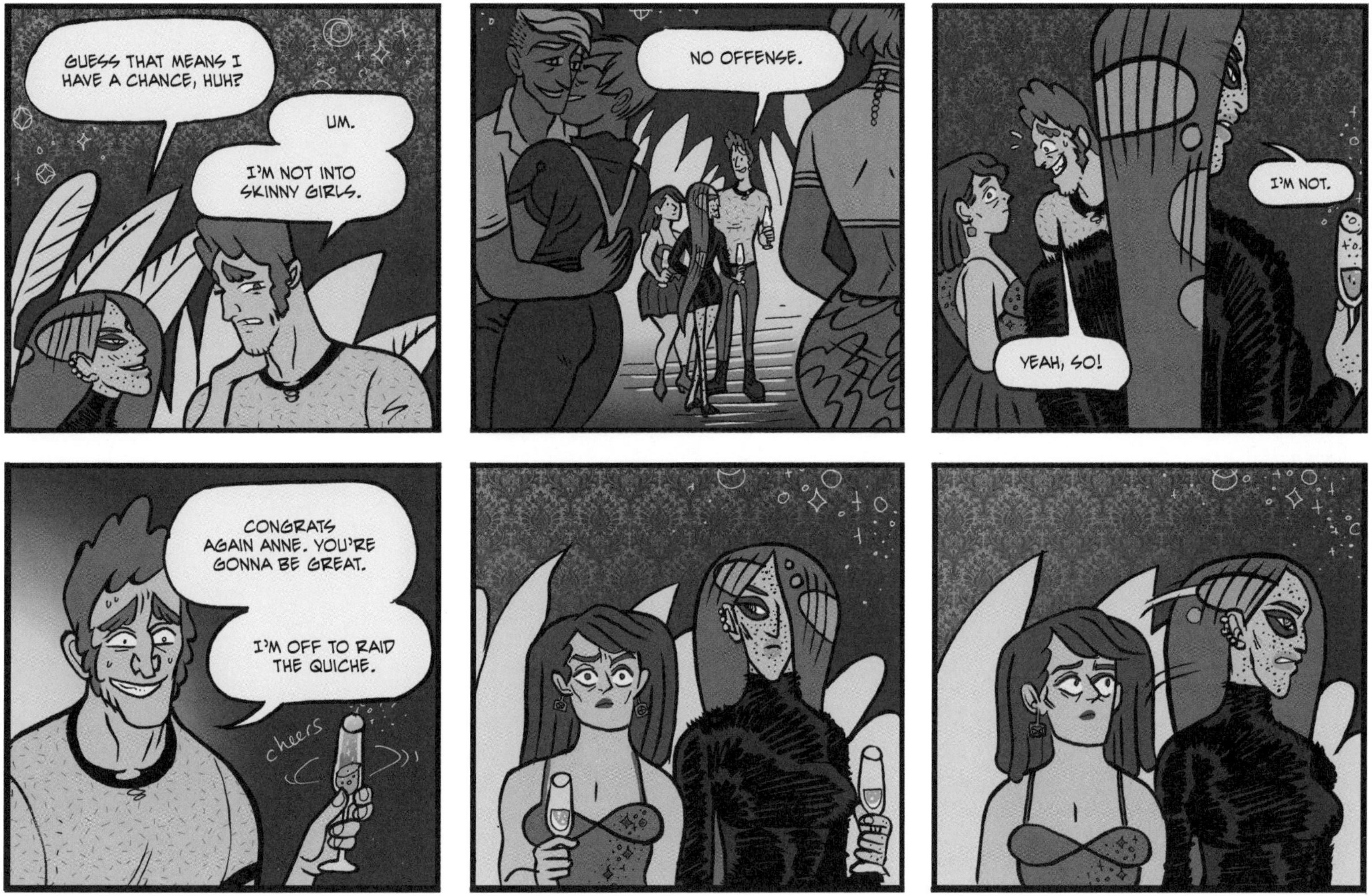
GUESS THAT MEANS I HAVE A CHANCE, HUH?
UM.
I'M NOT INTO SKINNY GIRLS.
NO OFFENSE.
I'M NOT.
YEAH, SO!
CONGRATS AGAIN ANNE. YOU'RE GONNA BE GREAT.
I'M OFF TO RAID THE QUICHE.
cheers

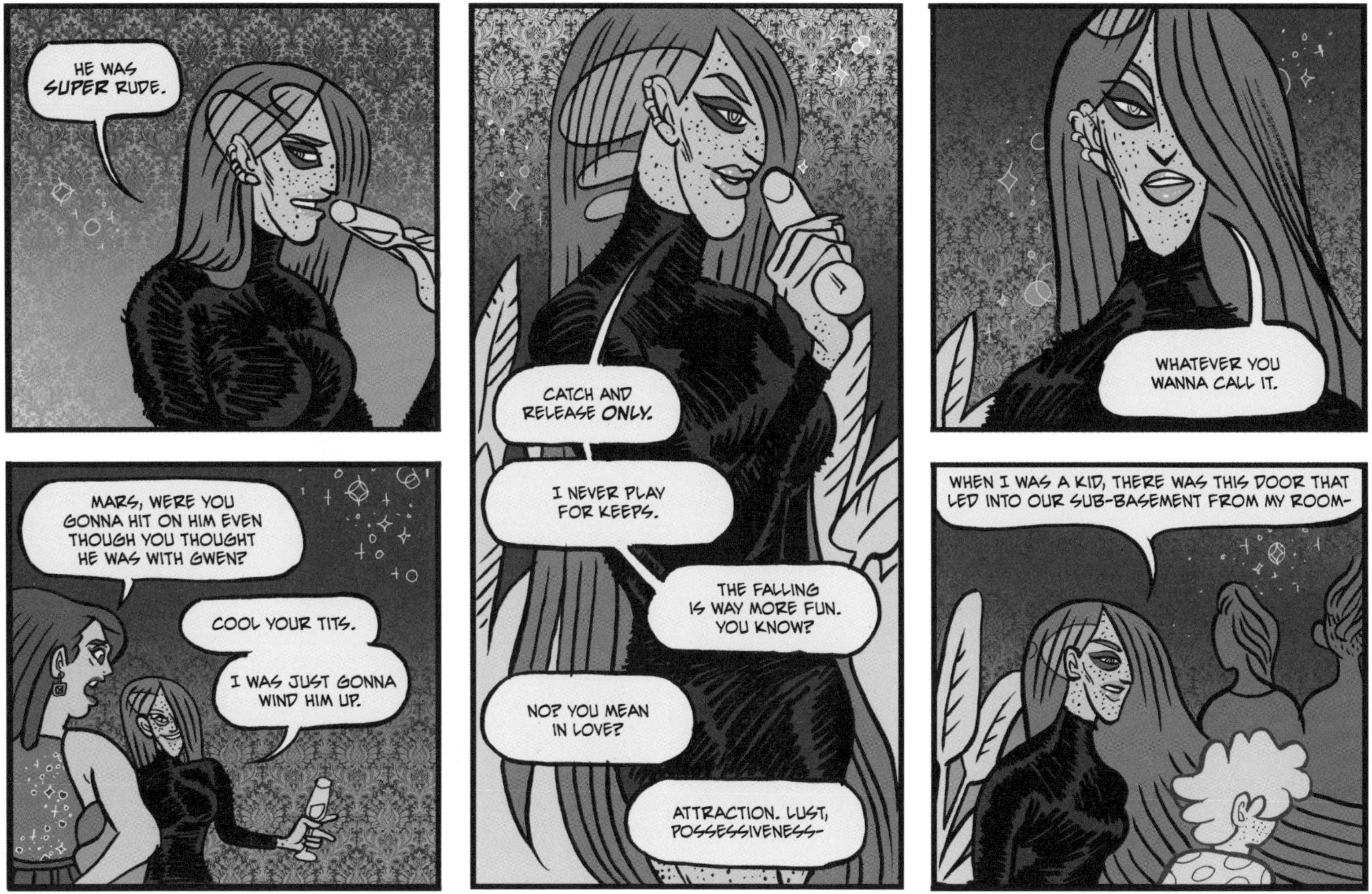
HE WAS SUPER RUDE.
MARS, WERE YOU GONNA HIT ON HIM EVEN THOUGH YOU THOUGHT HE WAS WITH GWEN?
COOL YOUR TITS.
I WAS JUST GONNA WIND HIM UP.
CATCH AND RELEASE ONLY.
I NEVER PLAY FOR KEEPS.
THE FALLING IS WAY MORE FUN. YOU KNOW?
NO? YOU MEAN IN LOVE?
ATTRACTION. LUST, POSSESSIVENESS-
WHATEVER YOU WANNA CALL IT.
WHEN I WAS A KID, THERE WAS THIS DOOR THAT LED INTO OUR SUB-BASEMENT FROM MY ROOM-

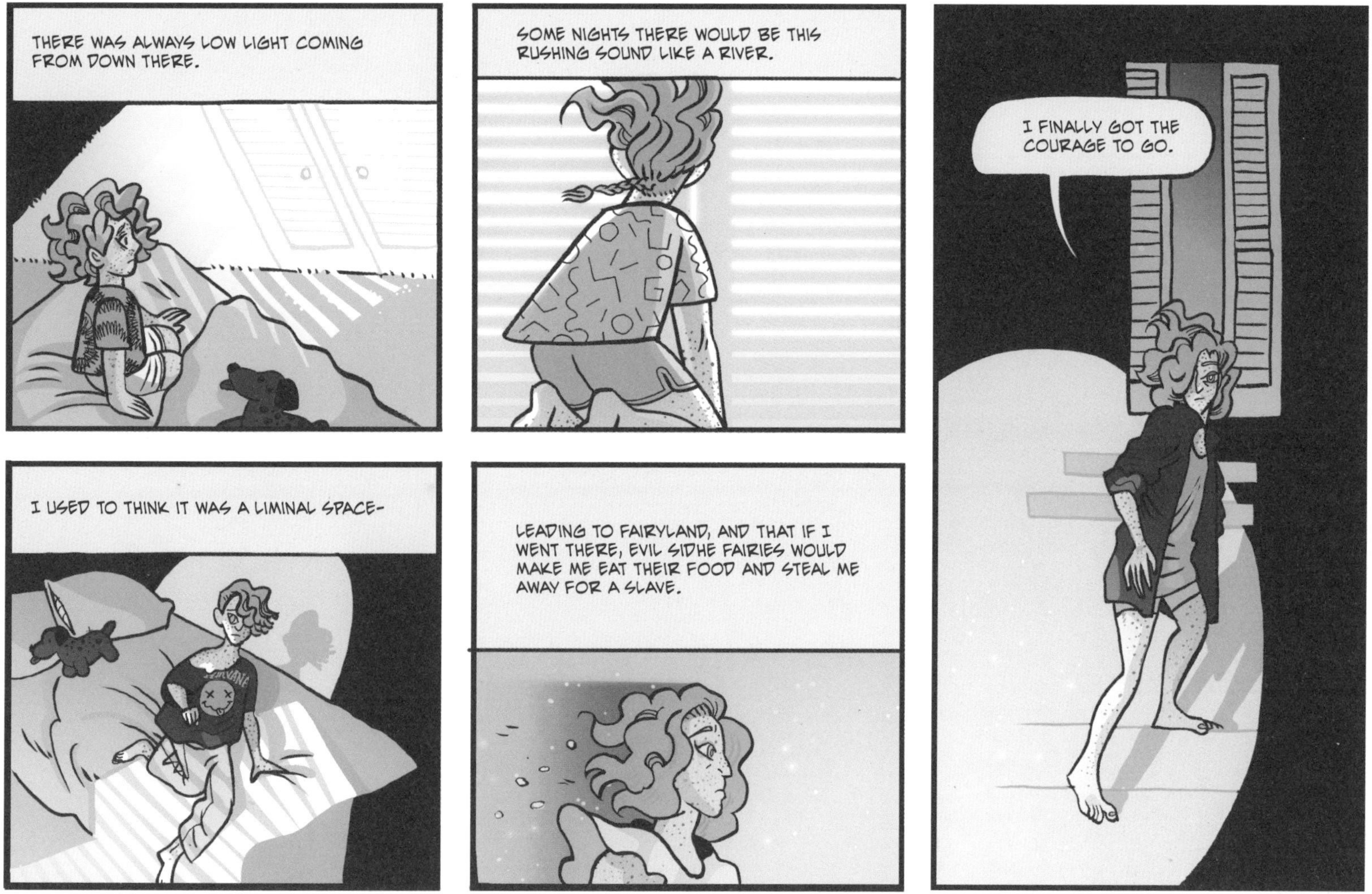
THERE WAS ALWAYS LOW LIGHT COMING FROM DOWN THERE.
SOME NIGHTS THERE WOULD BE THIS RUSHING SOUND LIKE A RIVER.
I USED TO THINK IT WAS A LIMINAL SPACE-
LEADING TO FAIRYLAND, AND THAT IF I WENT THERE, EVIL SIDHE FAIRIES WOULD MAKE ME EAT THEIR FOOD AND STEAL ME AWAY FOR A SLAVE.
I FINALLY GOT THE COURAGE TO GO.

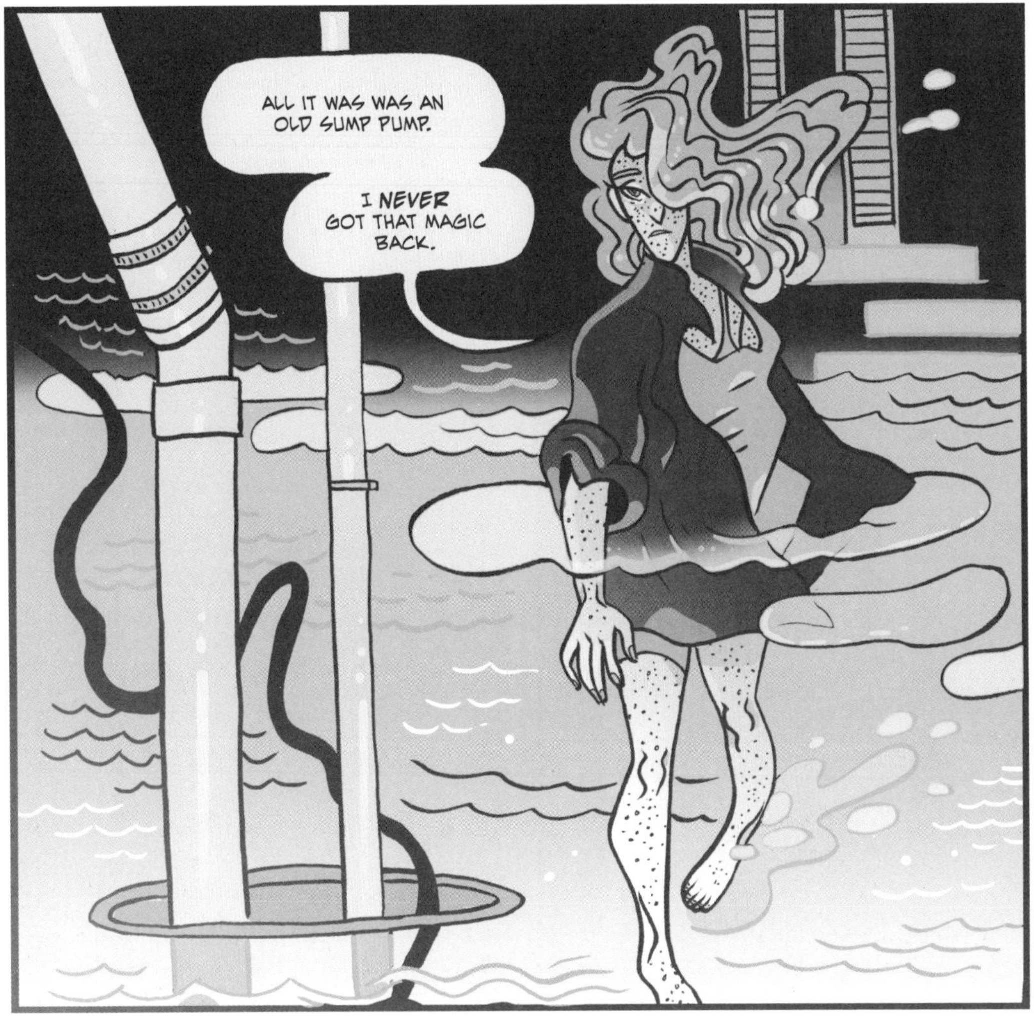
ALL IT WAS WAS AN OLD SUMP PUMP.
I NEVER GOT THAT MAGIC BACK.

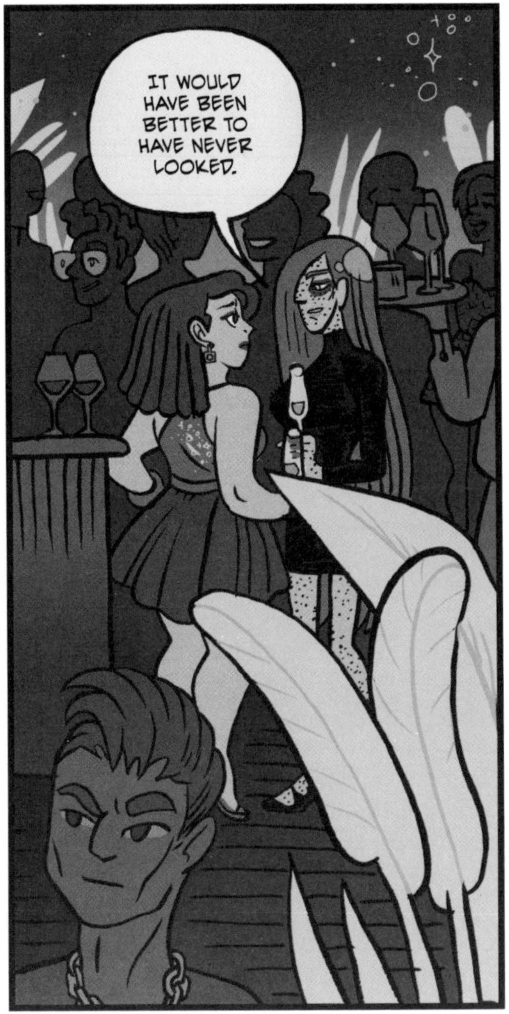
IT WOULD HAVE BEEN BETTER TO HAVE NEVER LOOKED.

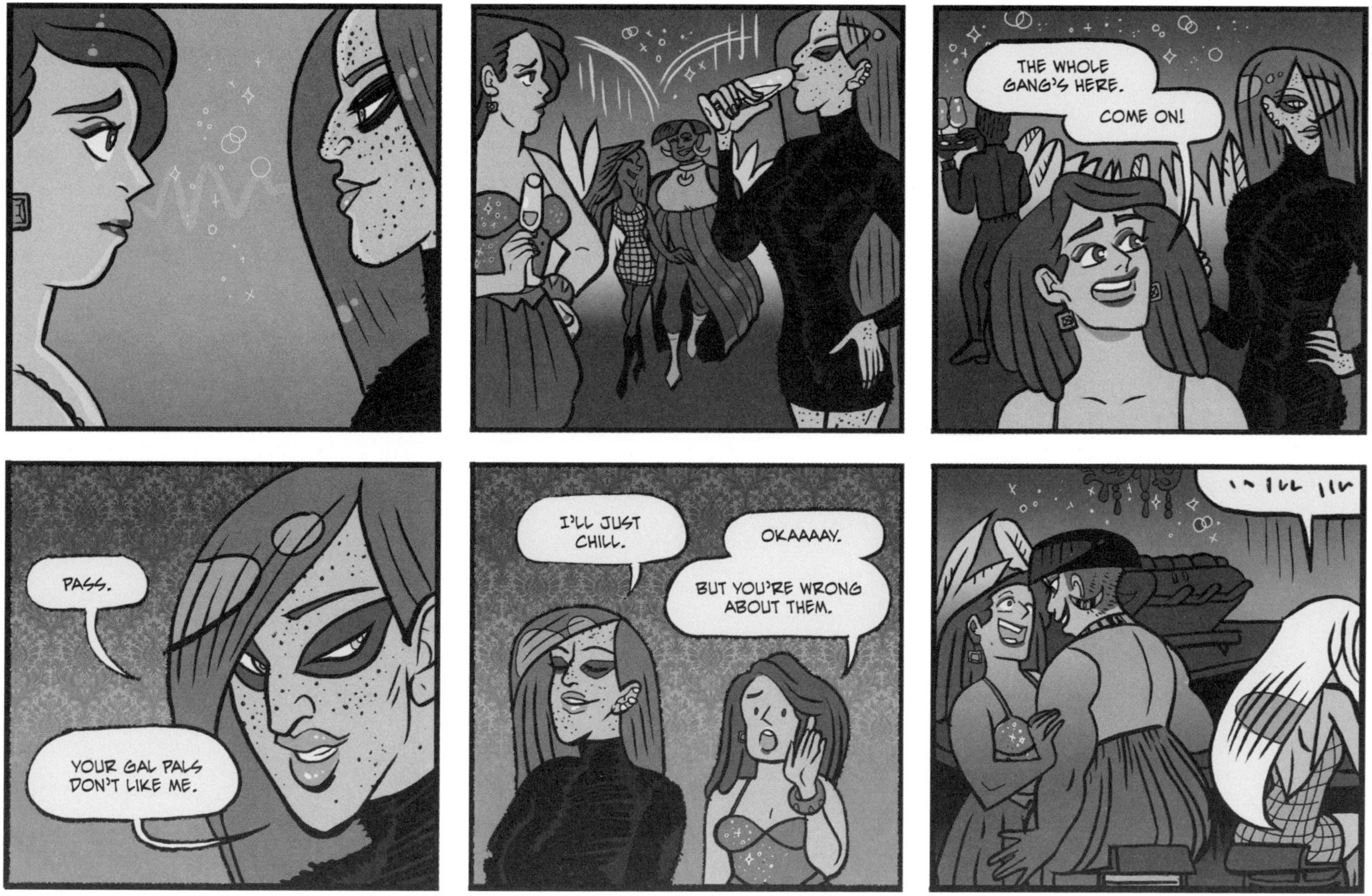
THE WHOLE GANG'S HERE.
COME ON!
PASS.
YOUR GAL PALS DON'T LIKE ME.
I'LL JUST CHILL.
OKAAAAY.
BUT YOU'RE WRONG ABOUT THEM.

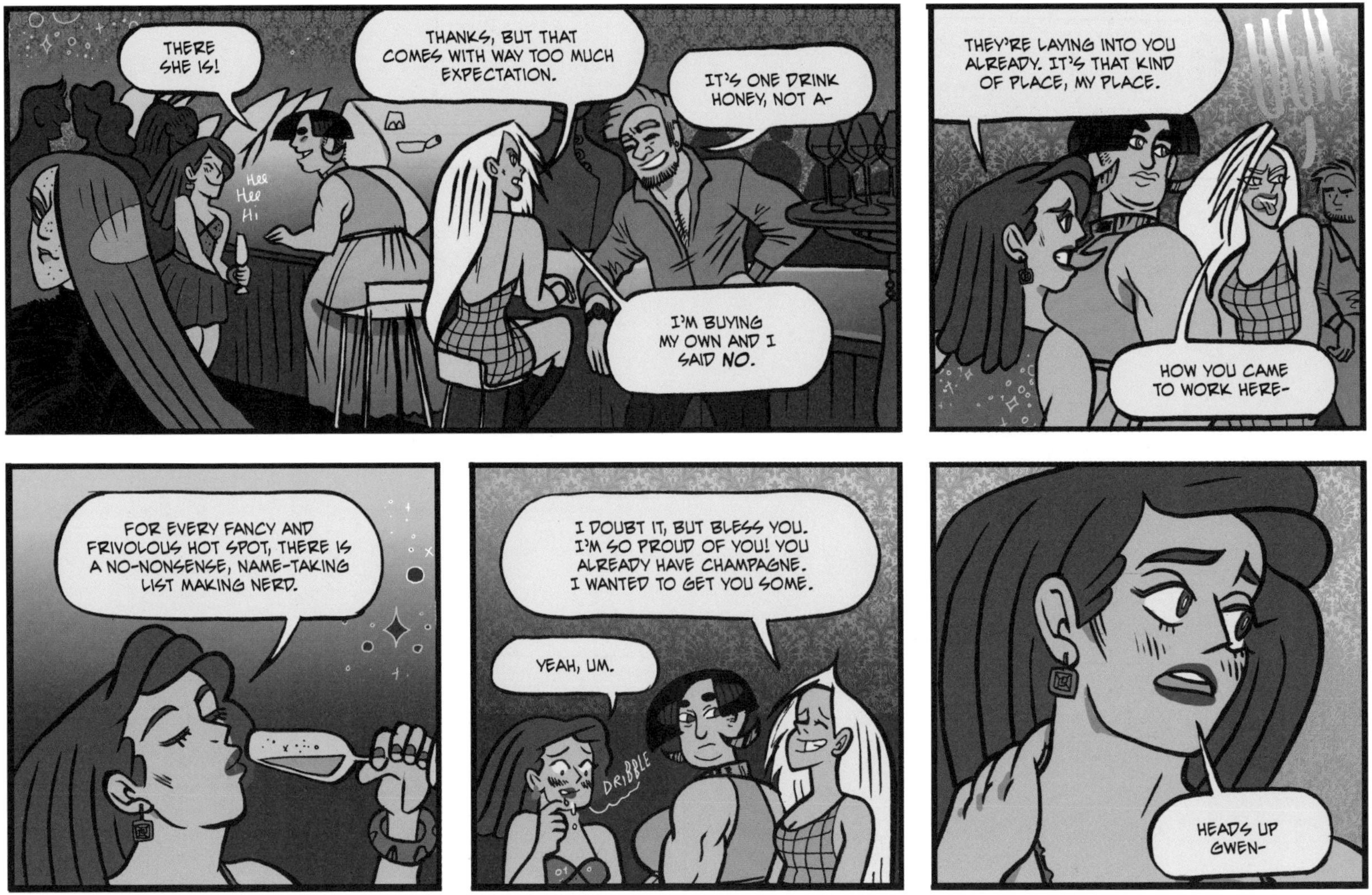

THERE SHE IS!
THANKS, BUT THAT COMES WITH WAY TOO MUCH EXPECTATION.
Hee Hee Hi
IT'S ONE DRINK HONEY, NOT A-
I'M BUYING MY OWN AND I SAID NO.
THEY'RE LAYING INTO YOU ALREADY. IT'S THAT KIND OF PLACE, MY PLACE.
UGH
HOW YOU CAME TO WORK HERE-
FOR EVERY FANCY AND FRIVOLOUS HOT SPOT, THERE IS A NO-NONSENSE, NAME-TAKING LIST MAKING NERD.
I DOUBT IT, BUT BLESS YOU. I'M SO PROUD OF YOU! YOU ALREADY HAVE CHAMPAGNE. I WANTED TO GET YOU SOME.
YEAH, UM.
DRIBBLE
HEADS UP GWEN-

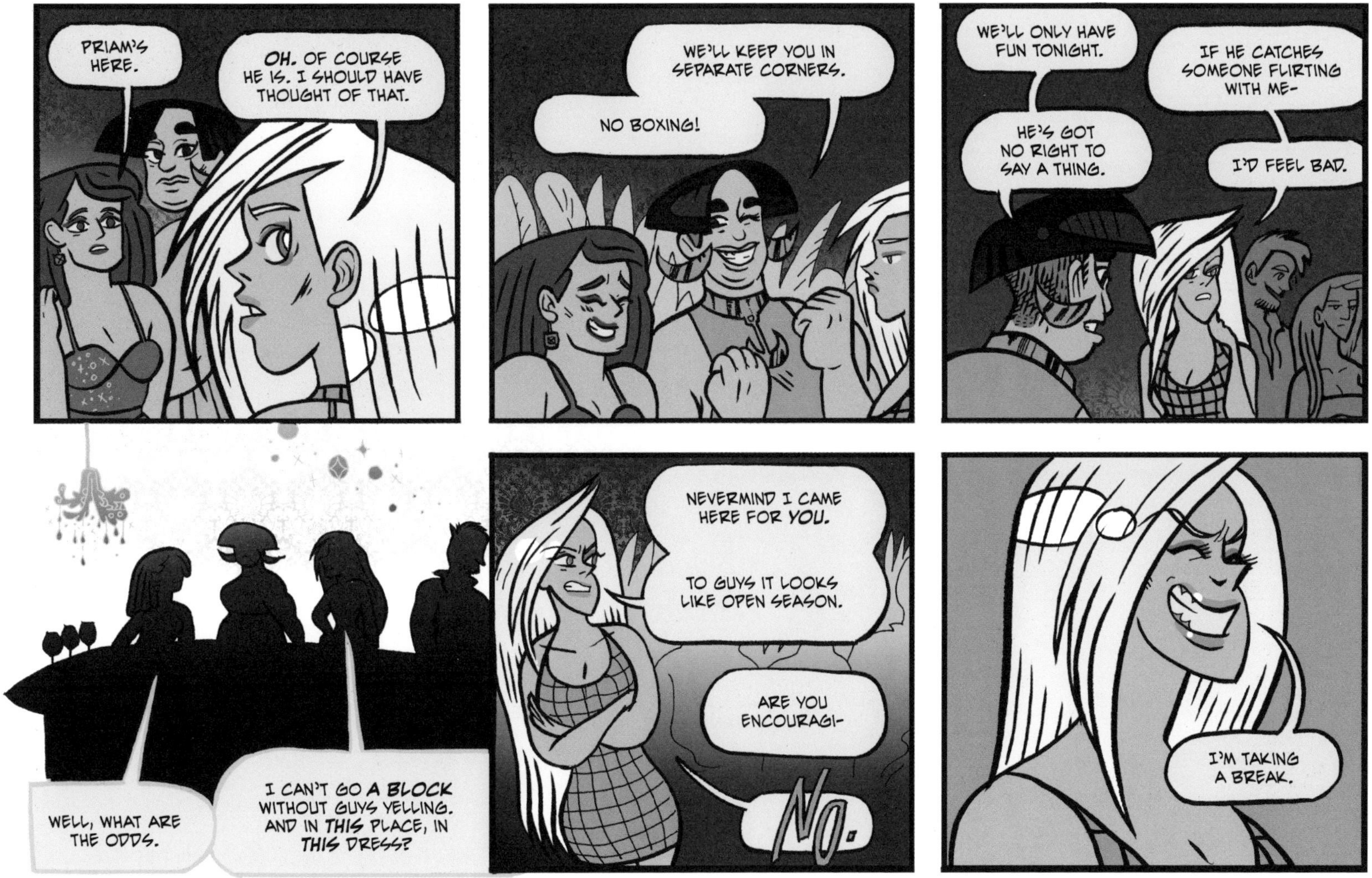
PRIAM'S HERE.
OH. OF COURSE HE IS. I SHOULD HAVE THOUGHT OF THAT.
WE'LL KEEP YOU IN SEPARATE CORNERS.
NO BOXING!
WE'LL ONLY HAVE FUN TONIGHT.
HE'S GOT NO RIGHT TO SAY A THING.
IF HE CATCHES SOMEONE FLIRTING WITH ME-
I'D FEEL BAD.
WELL, WHAT ARE THE ODDS.
I CAN'T GO A BLOCK WITHOUT GUYS YELLING. AND IN THIS PLACE, IN THIS DRESS?
NEVERMIND I CAME HERE FOR YOU.
TO GUYS IT LOOKS LIKE OPEN SEASON.
ARE YOU ENCOURAGI-
NO.
I'M TAKING A BREAK.

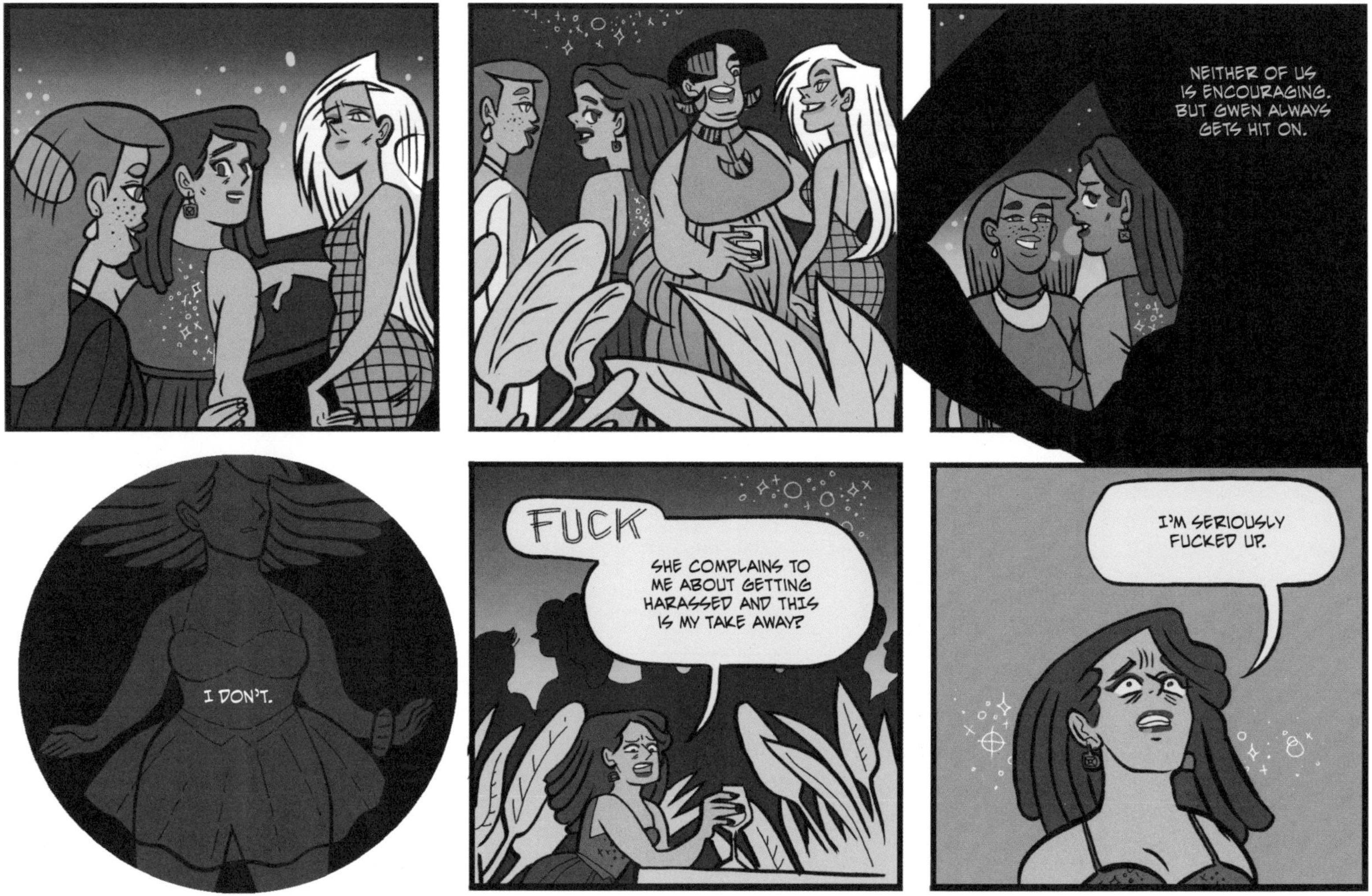
NEITHER OF US IS ENCOURAGING. BUT GWEN ALWAYS GETS HIT ON.
I DON'T.
FUCK
SHE COMPLAINS TO ME ABOUT GETTING HARASSED AND THIS IS MY TAKE AWAY?
I'M SERIOUSLY FUCKED UP.

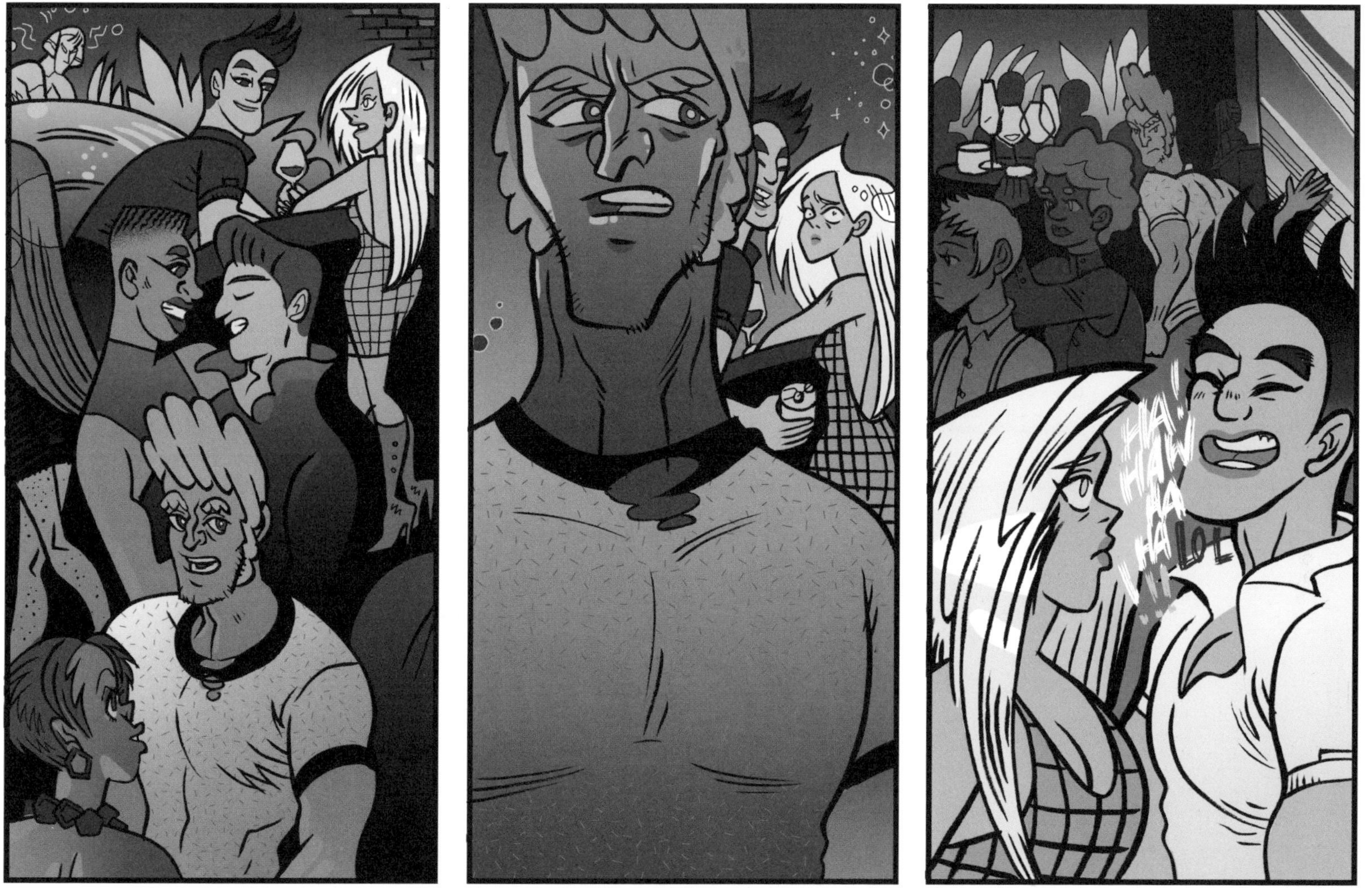
HA! HAW HAW HA HA
LOL

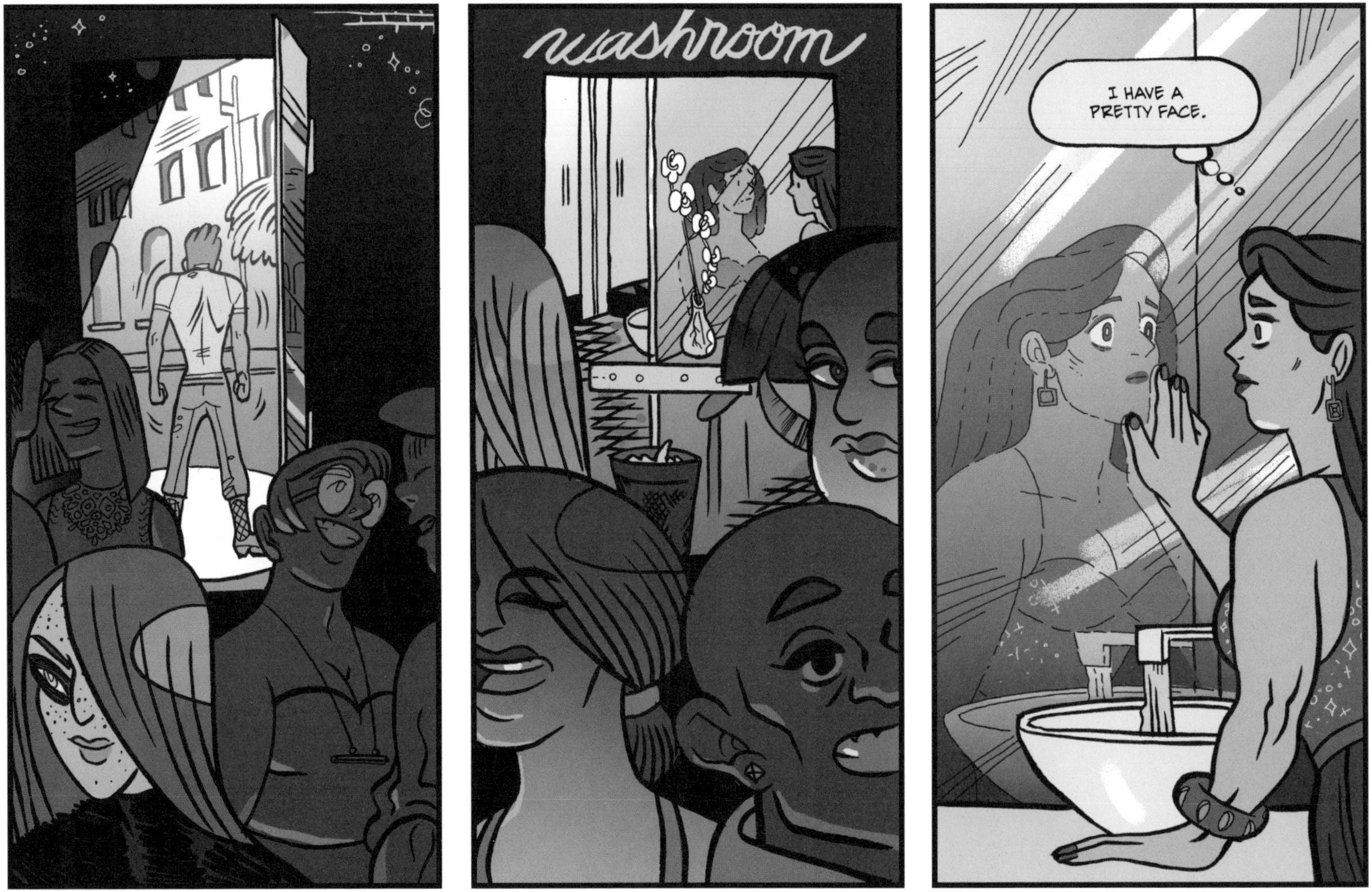
washroom
I HAVE A PRETTY FACE.

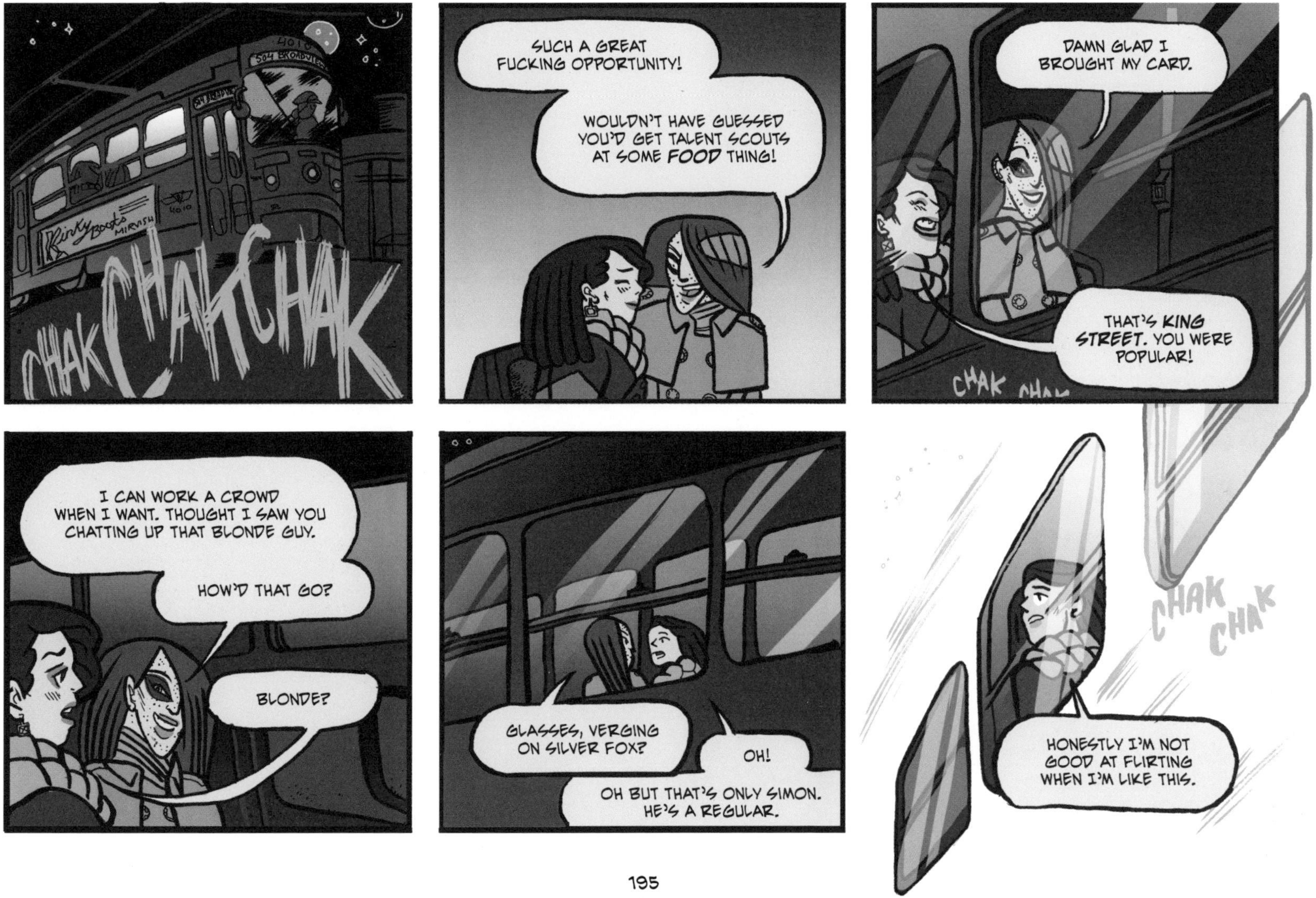
Kinky Boots
MIRVISH
CHAK CHAK CHAK
SUCH A GREAT FUCKING OPPORTUNITY!
WOULDN'T HAVE GUESSED YOU'D GET TALENT SCOUTS AT SOME **FOOD** THING!
DAMN GLAD I BROUGHT MY CARD.
THAT'S **KING STREET**. YOU WERE POPULAR!
CHAK CHAK
I CAN WORK A CROWD WHEN I WANT. THOUGHT I SAW YOU CHATTING UP THAT BLONDE GUY.
HOW'D THAT GO?
BLONDE?
GLASSES, VERGING ON SILVER FOX?
OH!
OH BUT THAT'S ONLY SIMON. HE'S A REGULAR.
CHAK CHAK
HONESTLY I'M NOT GOOD AT FLIRTING WHEN I'M LIKE THIS.

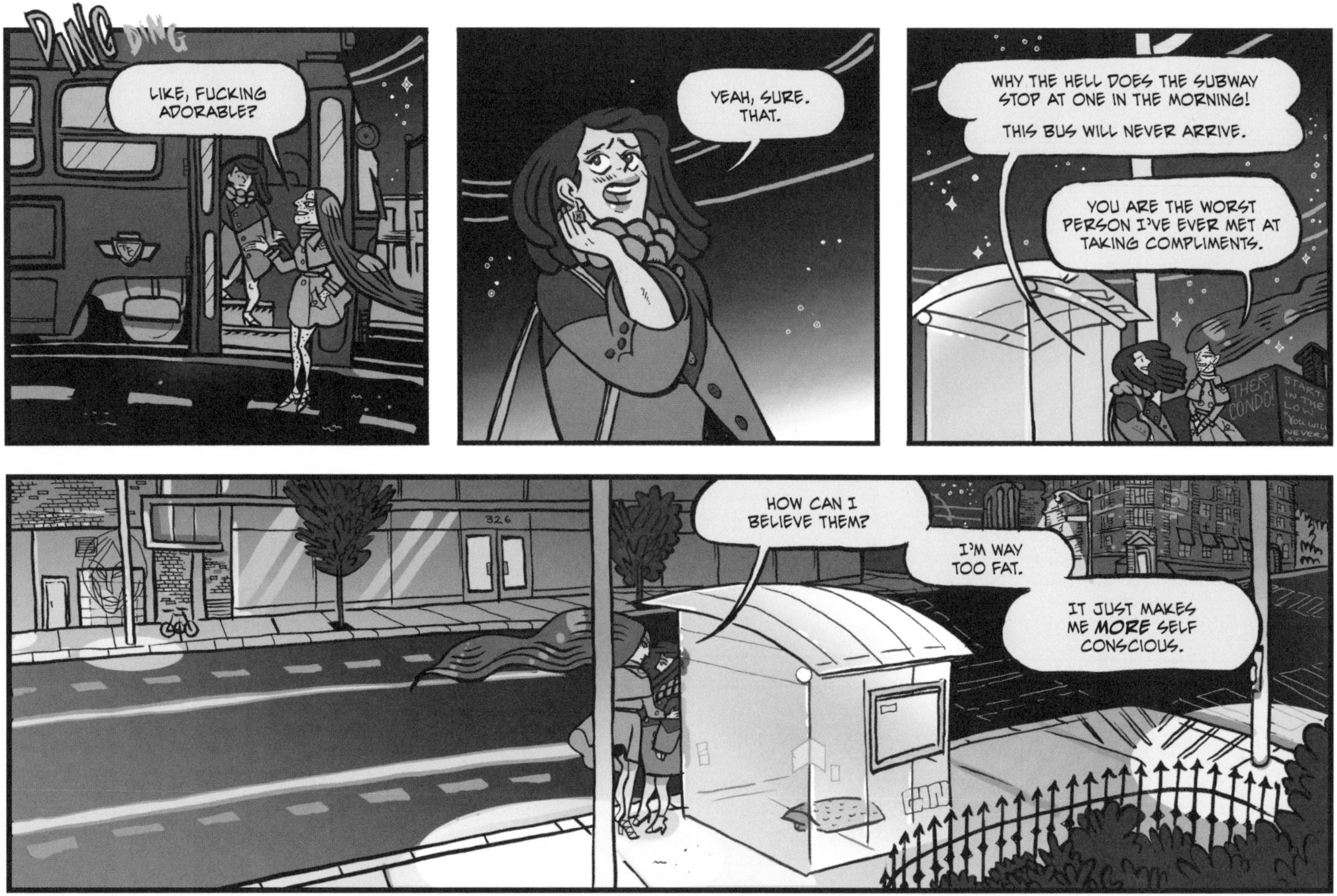
DING DING
LIKE, FUCKING ADORABLE?
YEAH, SURE. THAT.
WHY THE HELL DOES THE SUBWAY STOP AT ONE IN THE MORNING!
THIS BUS WILL NEVER ARRIVE.
YOU ARE THE WORST PERSON I'VE EVER MET AT TAKING COMPLIMENTS.
326
HOW CAN I BELIEVE THEM?
I'M WAY TOO FAT.
IT JUST MAKES ME **MORE** SELF CONSCIOUS.

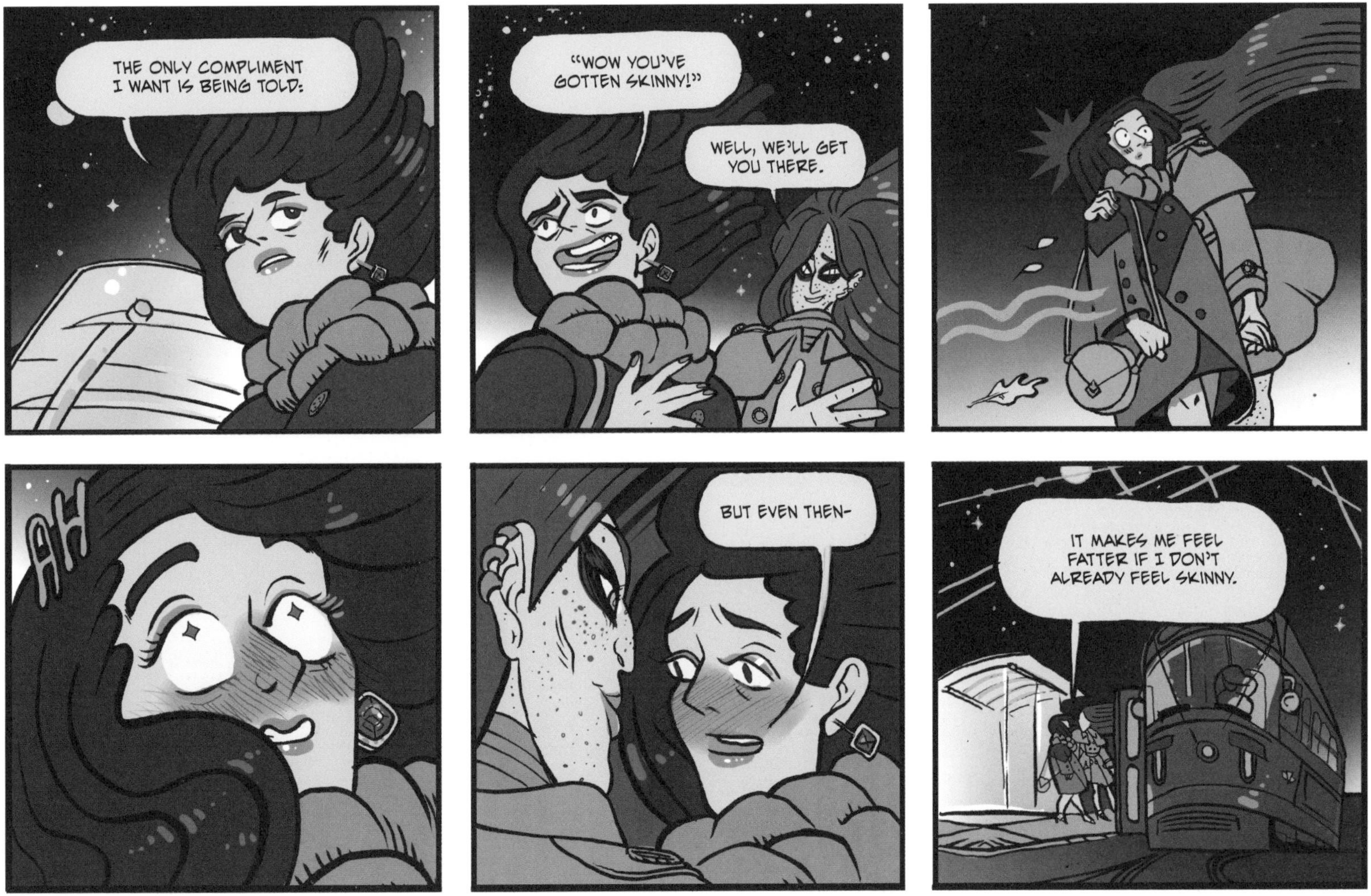
THE ONLY COMPLIMENT I WANT IS BEING TOLD:
“WOW YOU'VE GOTTEN SKINNY!”
WELL, WE'LL GET YOU THERE.
AH
BUT EVEN THEN-
IT MAKES ME FEEL FATTER IF I DON'T ALREADY FEEL SKINNY.

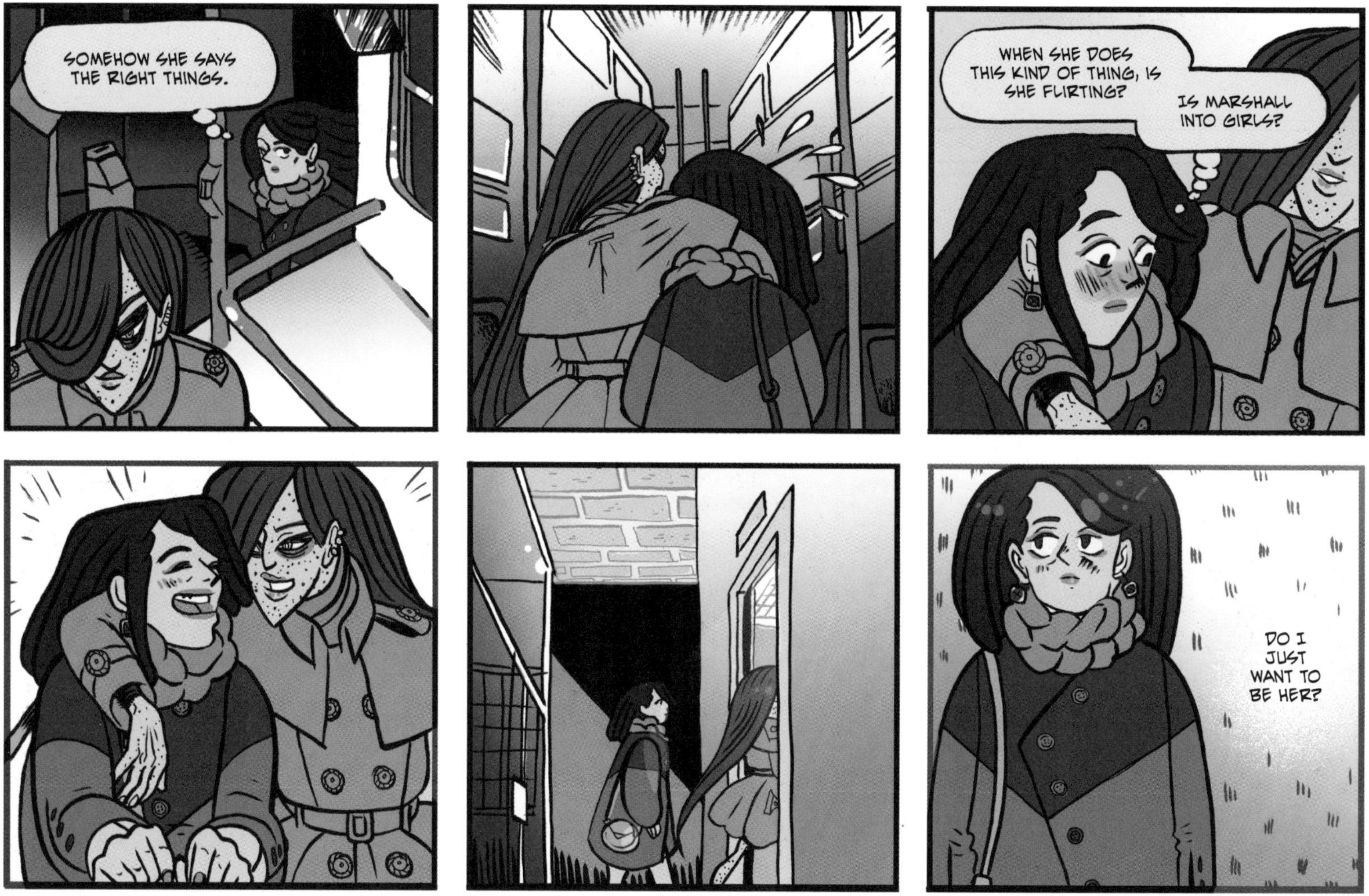
SOMEHOW SHE SAYS THE RIGHT THINGS.
WHEN SHE DOES THIS KIND OF THING, IS SHE FLIRTING?
IS MARSHALL INTO GIRLS?
DO I JUST WANT TO BE HER?

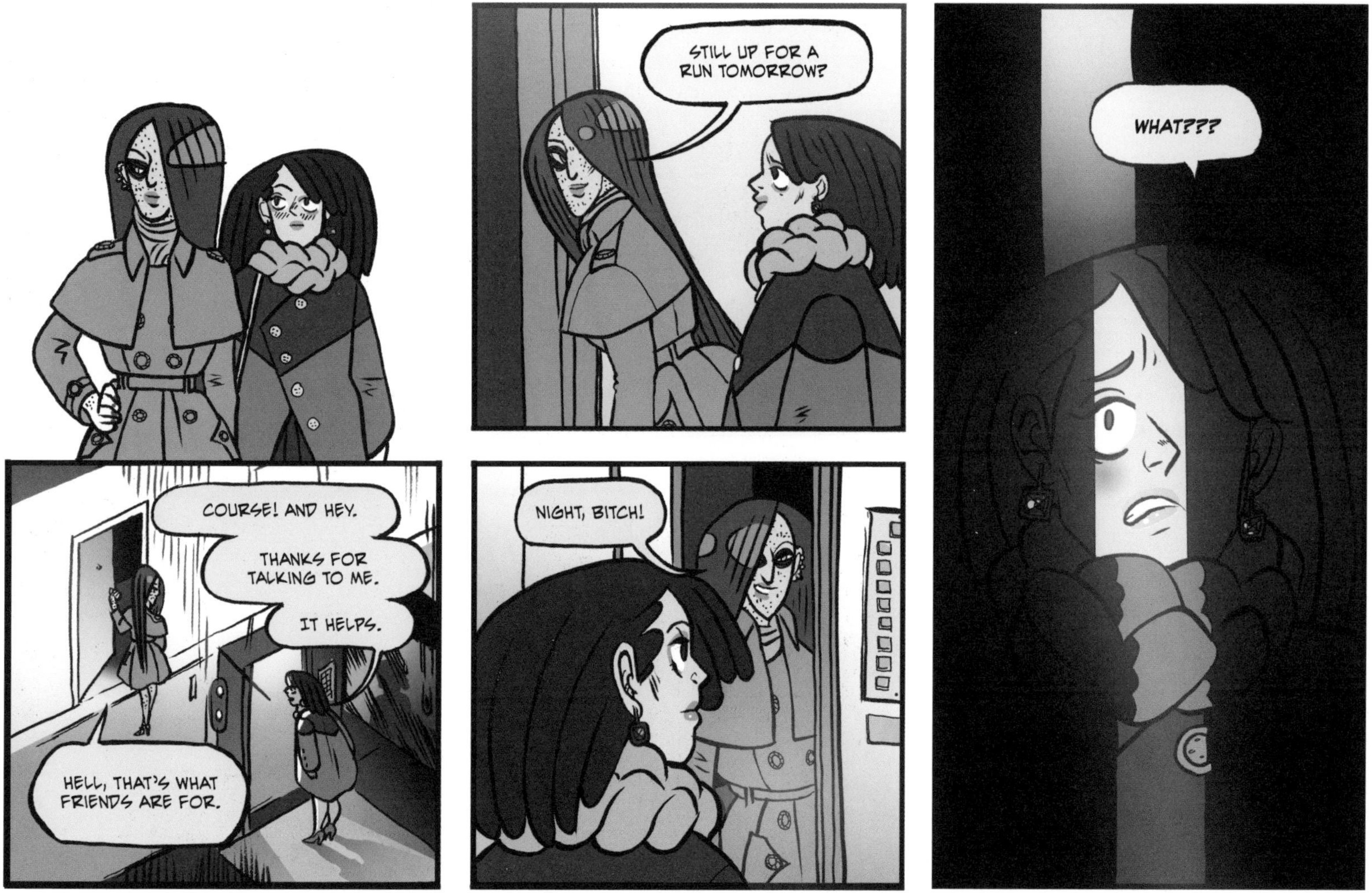
STILL UP FOR A RUN TOMORROW?
COURSE! AND HEY.
THANKS FOR TALKING TO ME.
IT HELPS.
HELL, THAT'S WHAT FRIENDS ARE FOR.
NIGHT, BITCH!
WHAT???

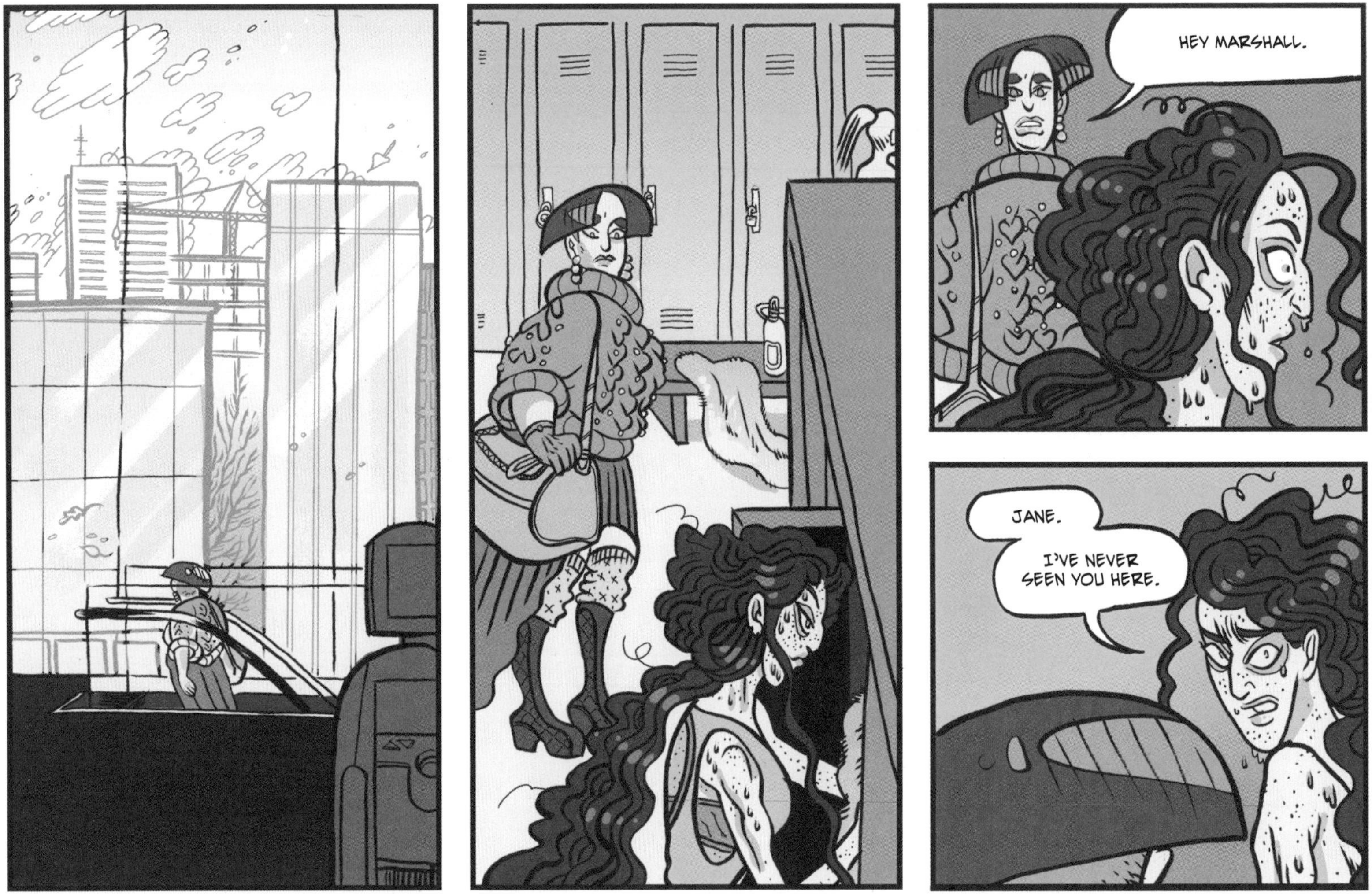
HEY MARSHALL.
JANE.
I'VE NEVER SEEN YOU HERE.

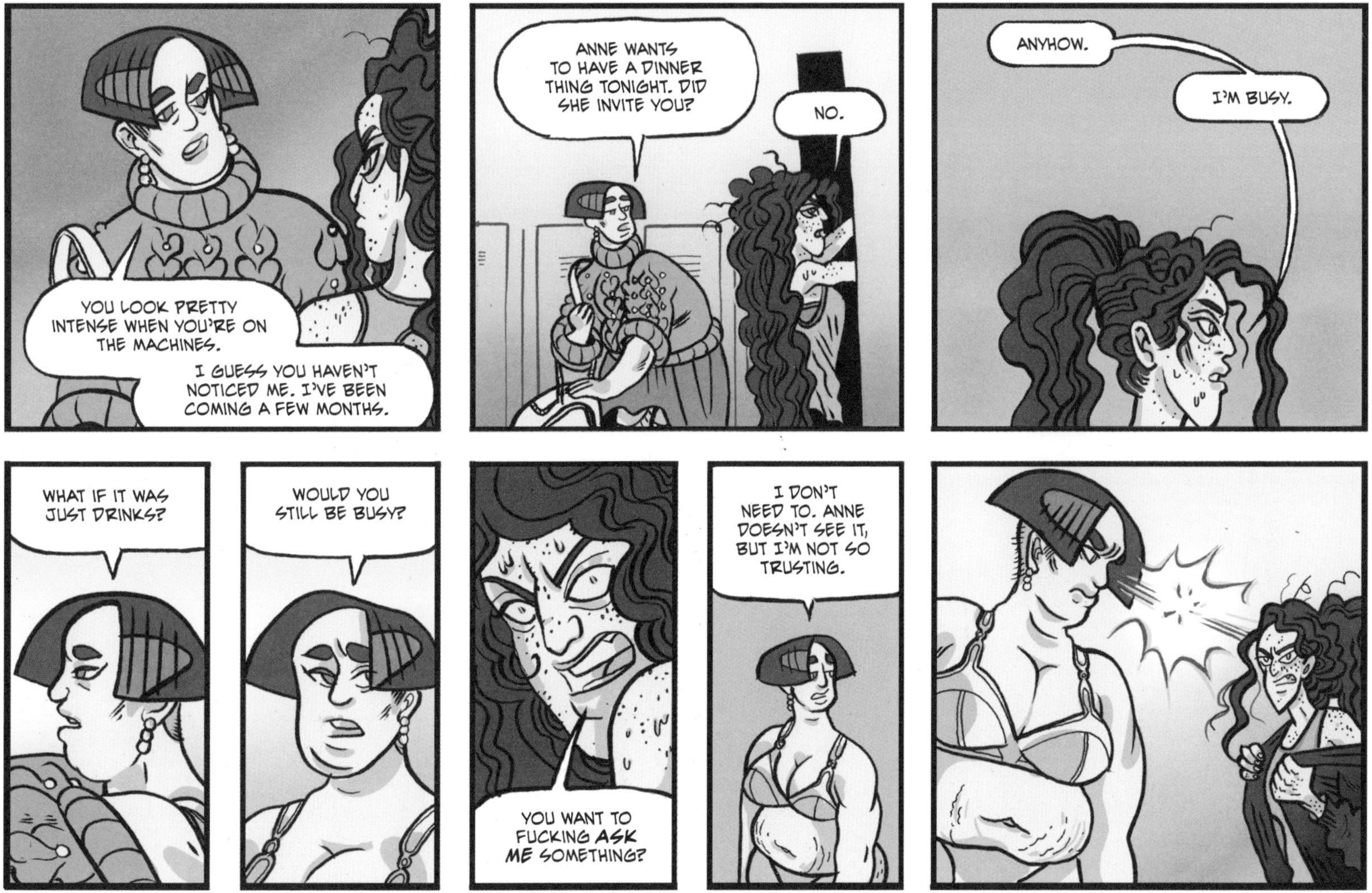
YOU LOOK PRETTY INTENSE WHEN YOU'RE ON THE MACHINES.
I GUESS YOU HAVEN'T NOTICED ME. I'VE BEEN COMING A FEW MONTHS.
ANNE WANTS TO HAVE A DINNER THING TONIGHT. DID SHE INVITE YOU?
NO.
ANYHOW.
I'M BUSY.
WHAT IF IT WAS JUST DRINKS?
WOULD YOU STILL BE BUSY?
YOU WANT TO FUCKING ASK ME SOMETHING?
I DON'T NEED TO. ANNE DOESN'T SEE IT, BUT I'M NOT SO TRUSTING.

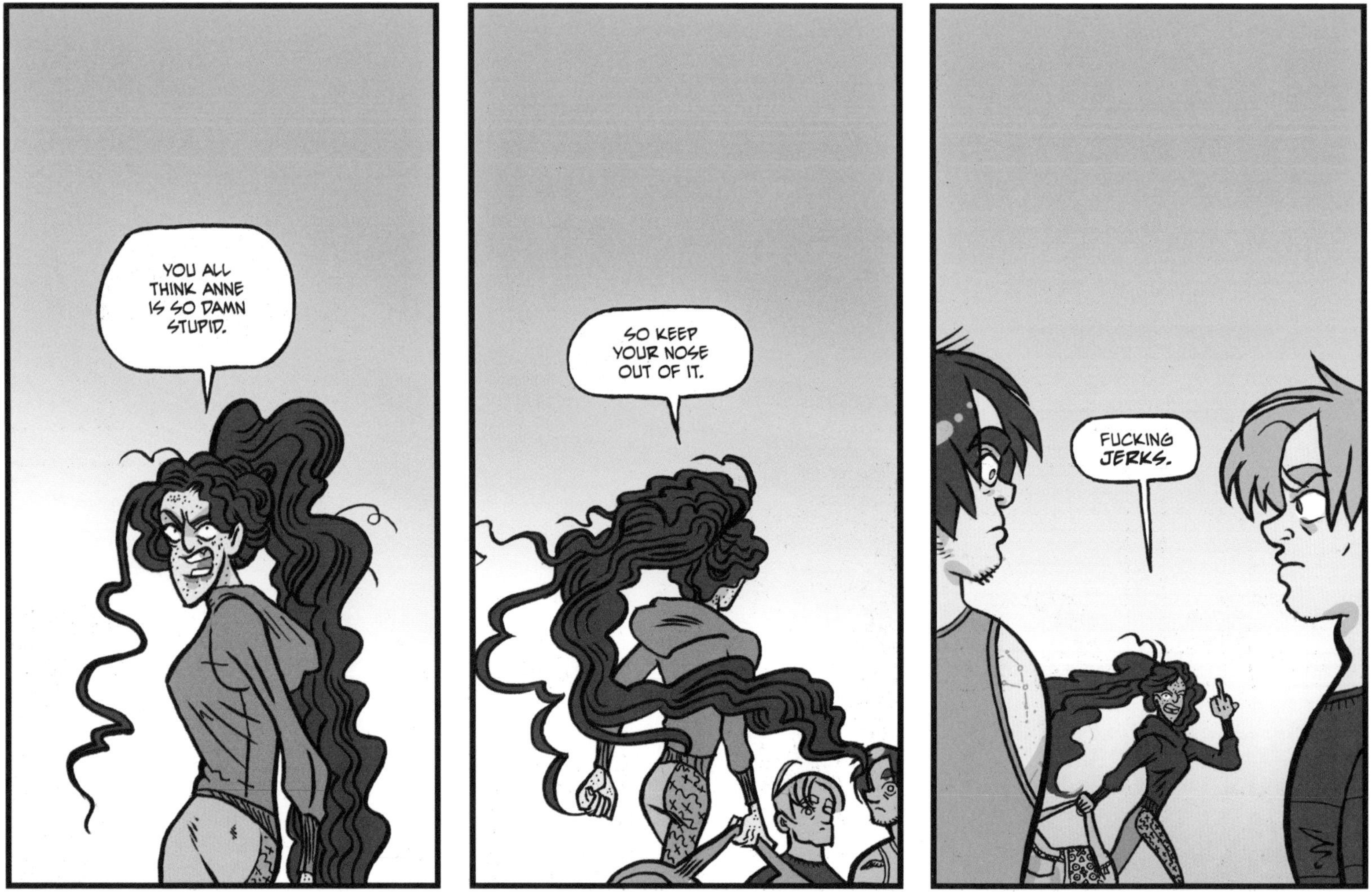
YOU ALL THINK ANNE IS SO DAMN STUPID.
SO KEEP YOUR NOSE OUT OF IT.
FUCKING JERKS.

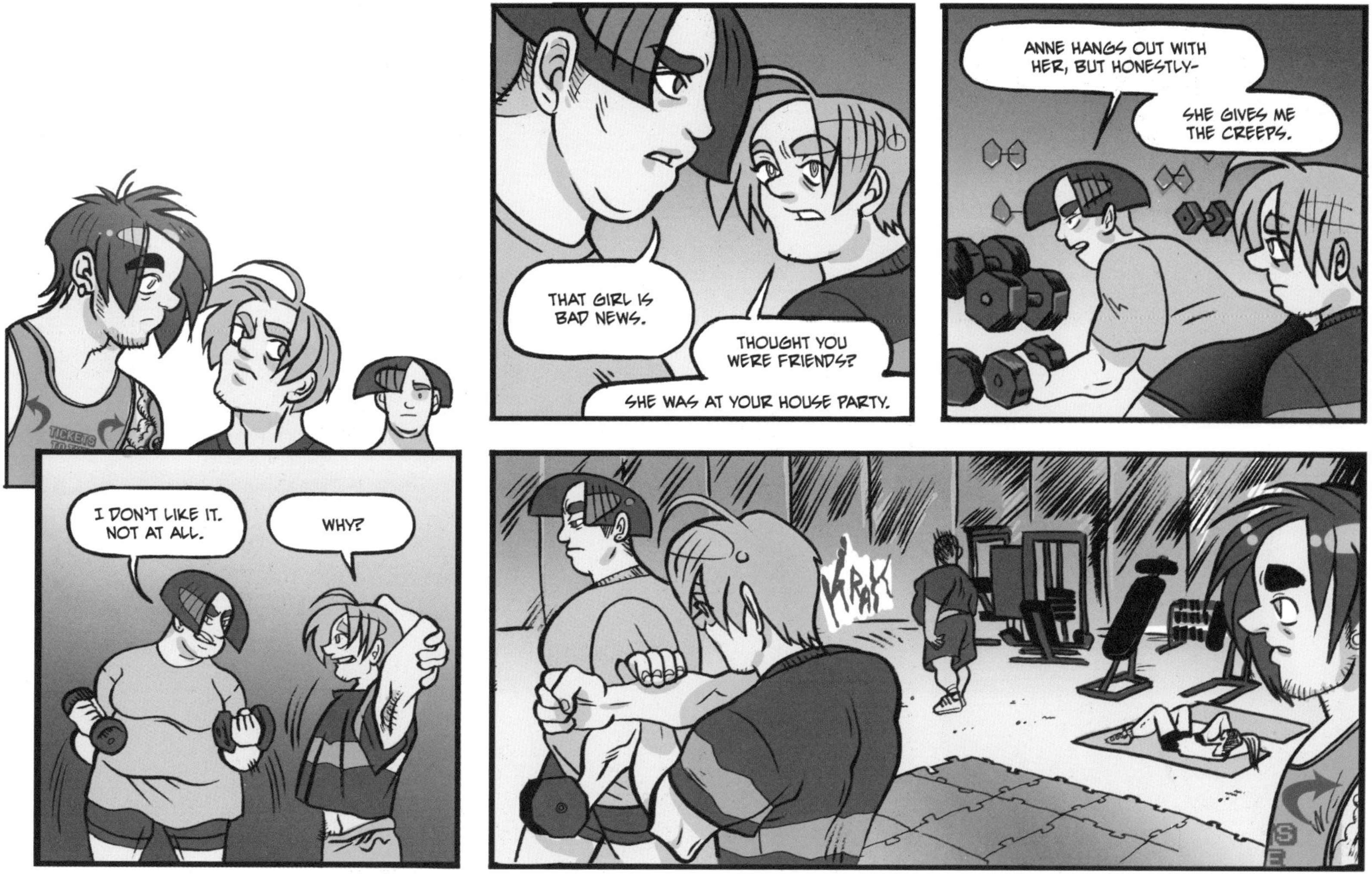
THAT GIRL IS BAD NEWS.
THOUGHT YOU WERE FRIENDS?
SHE WAS AT YOUR HOUSE PARTY.
ANNE HANGS OUT WITH HER, BUT HONESTLY-
SHE GIVES ME THE CREEPS.
I DON'T LIKE IT. NOT AT ALL.
WHY?
KRAK

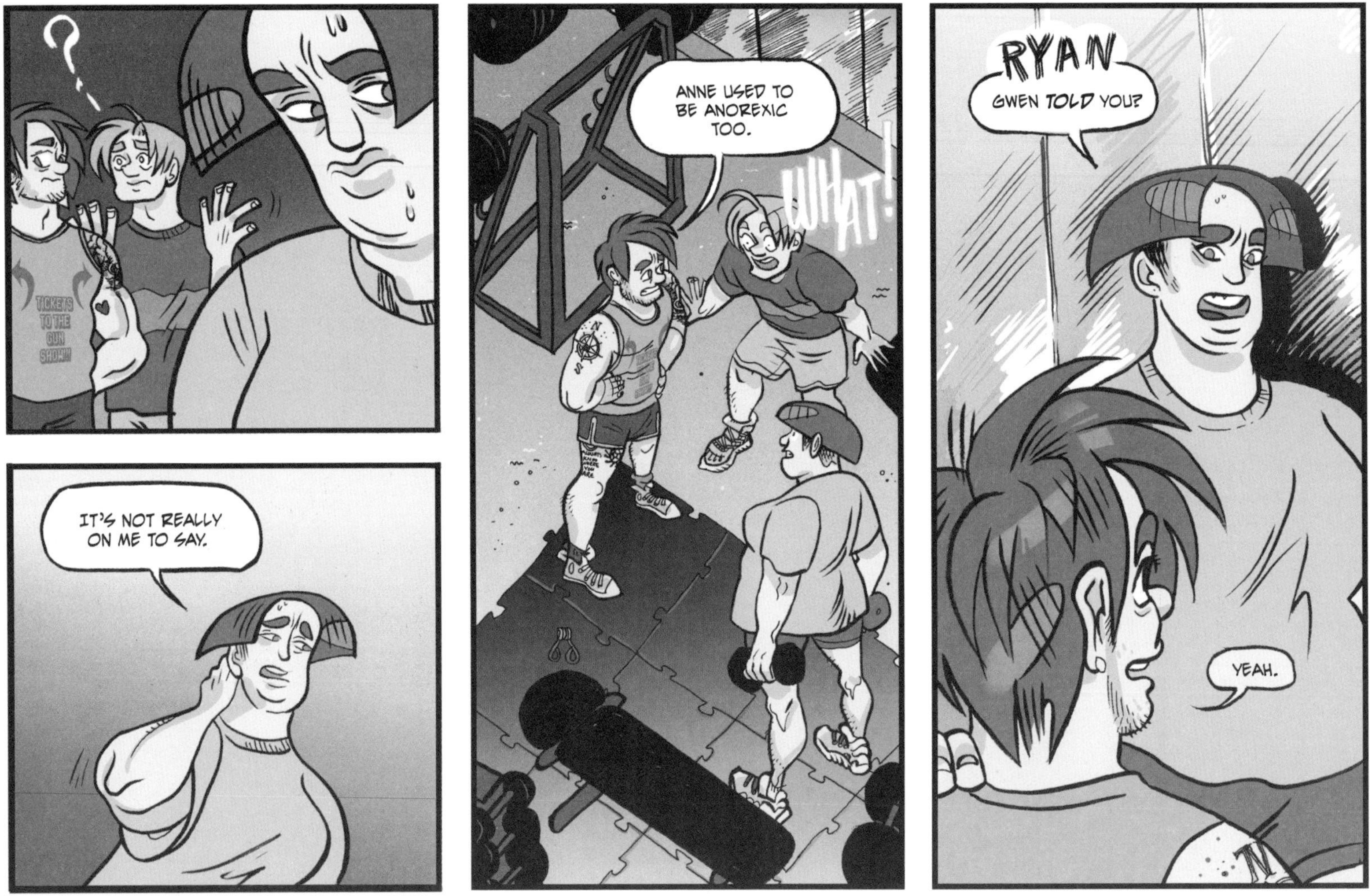
TICKETS TO THE GUN SHOW!!!
IT'S NOT REALLY ON ME TO SAY.
ANNE USED TO BE ANOREXIC TOO.
WHAT!
RYAN
GWEN **TOLD** YOU?
YEAH.

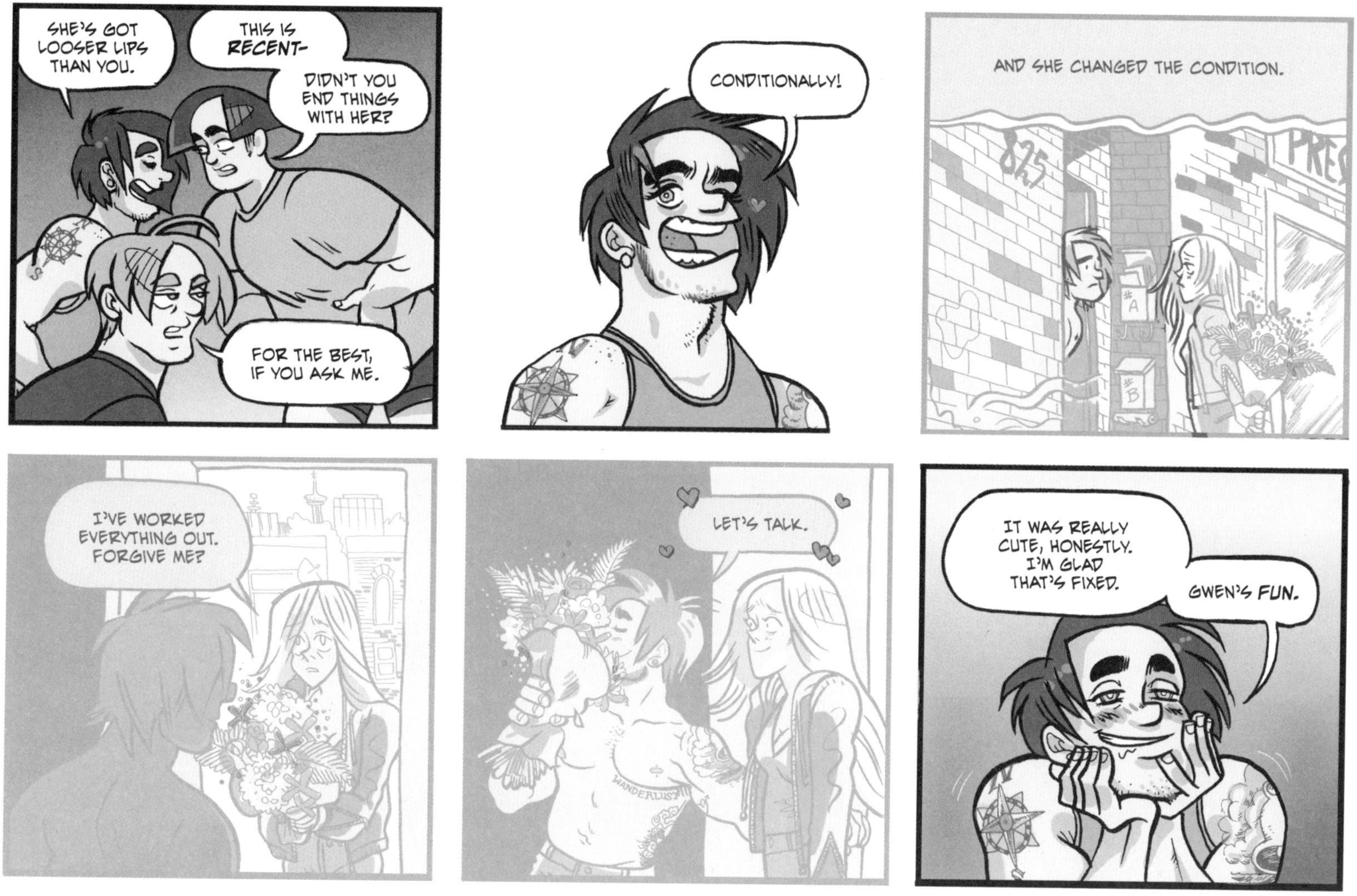
SHE'S GOT LOOSER LIPS THAN YOU.
THIS IS **RECENT**-
DIDN'T YOU END THINGS WITH HER?
FOR THE BEST, IF YOU ASK ME.
CONDITIONALLY!
AND SHE CHANGED THE CONDITION.
825
#A
#B
I'VE WORKED EVERYTHING OUT. FORGIVE ME?
LET'S TALK.
WANDERLUST
IT WAS REALLY CUTE, HONESTLY. I'M GLAD THAT'S FIXED.
GWEN'S **FUN**.

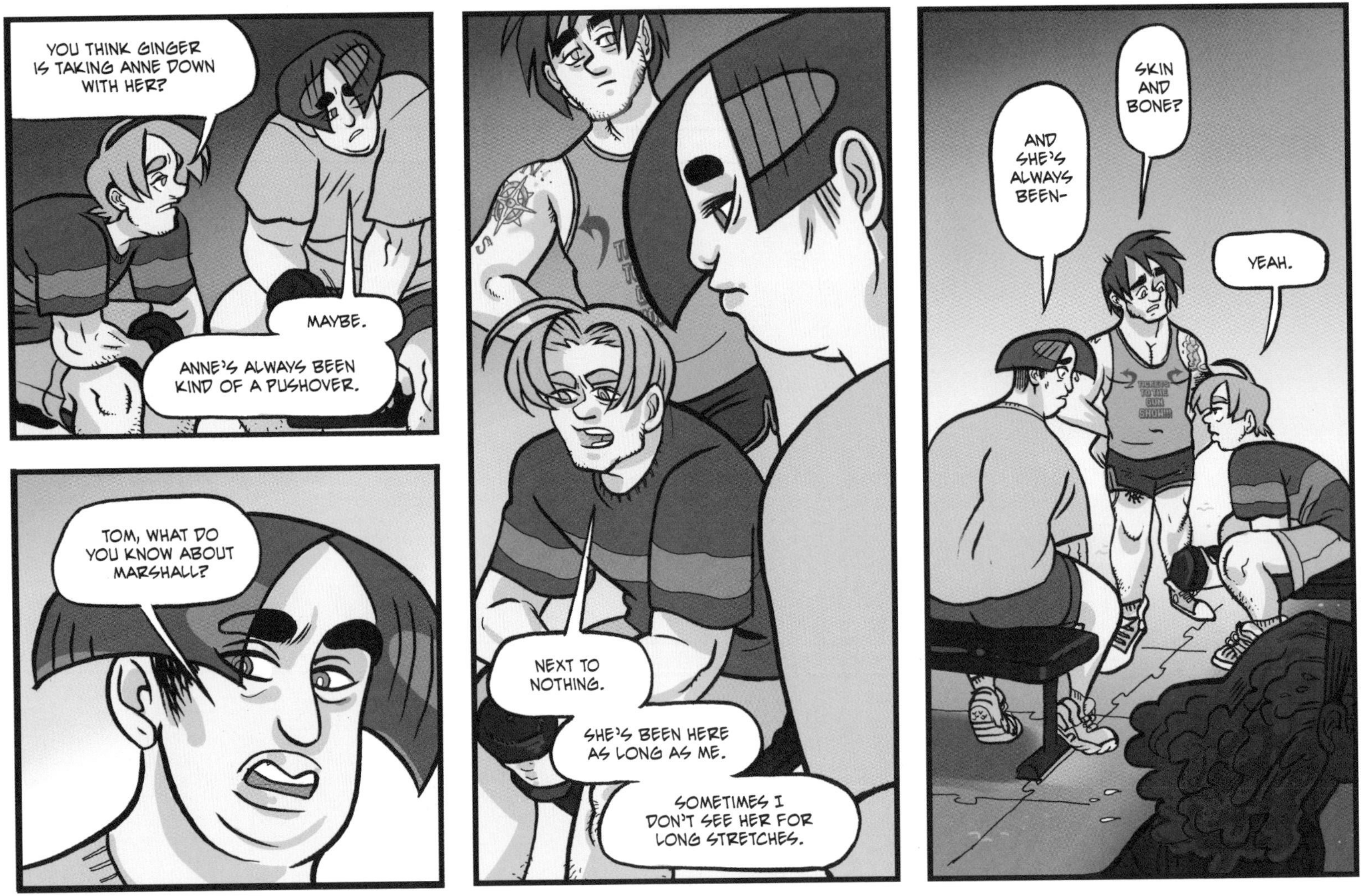
YOU THINK GINGER IS TAKING ANNE DOWN WITH HER?
MAYBE.
ANNE'S ALWAYS BEEN KIND OF A PUSHOVER.
TOM, WHAT DO YOU KNOW ABOUT MARSHALL?
NEXT TO NOTHING.
SHE'S BEEN HERE AS LONG AS ME.
SOMETIMES I DON'T SEE HER FOR LONG STRETCHES.
AND SHE'S ALWAYS BEEN-
SKIN AND BONE?
TICKETS TO THE GUN SHOW!!!
YEAH.

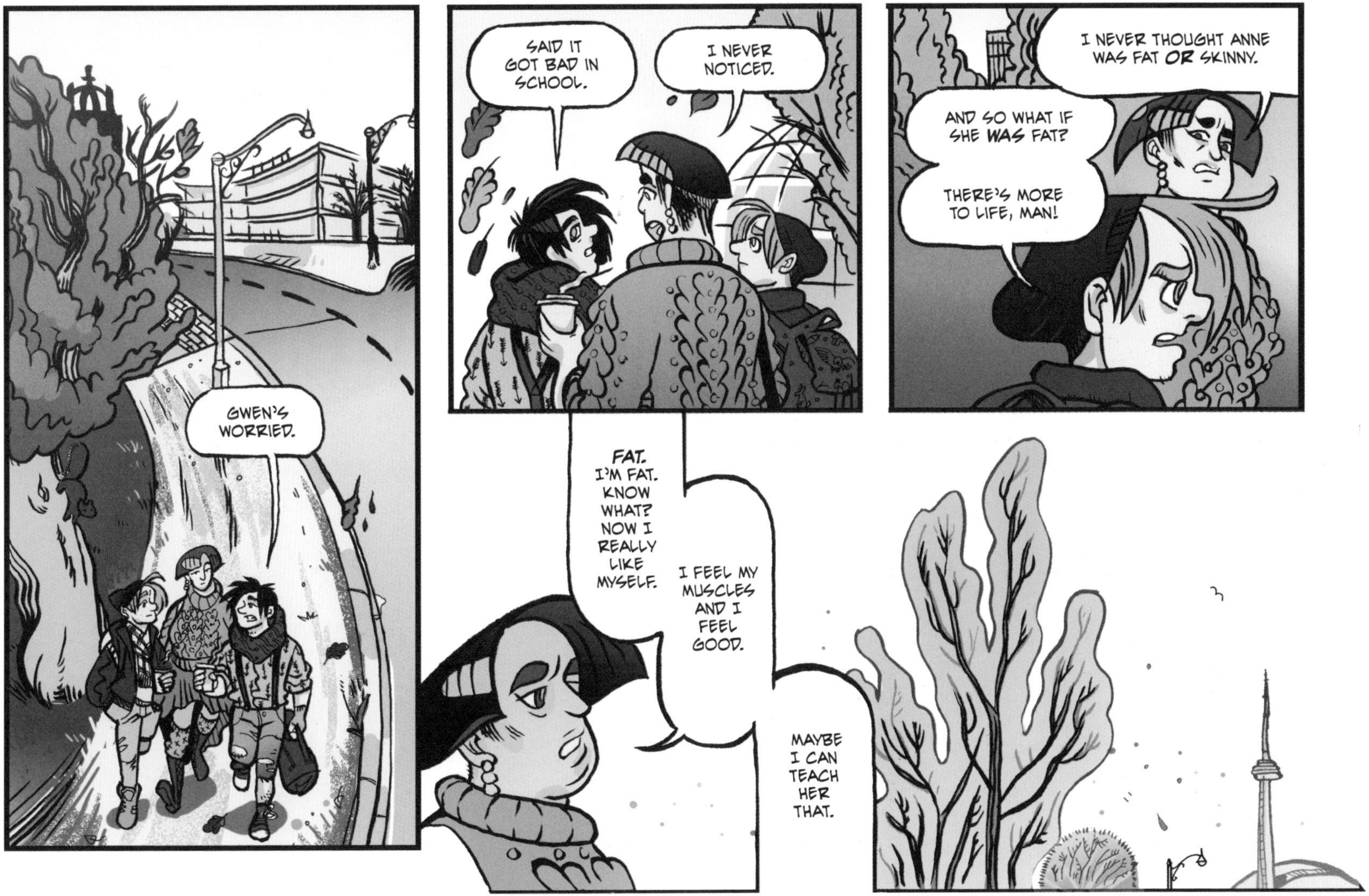
GWEN'S WORRIED.
SAID IT GOT BAD IN SCHOOL.
I NEVER NOTICED.
I NEVER THOUGHT ANNE WAS FAT **OR** SKINNY.
AND SO WHAT IF SHE **WAS** FAT?
THERE'S MORE TO LIFE, MAN!
FAT. I'M FAT. KNOW WHAT? NOW I REALLY LIKE MYSELF.
I FEEL MY MUSCLES AND I FEEL GOOD.
MAYBE I CAN TEACH HER THAT.

MARSHALL AND NAT TALK ABOUT ALL THESE SUPPLEMENTS.

SO MANY TRICKS FOR A FAST METABOLISM.

LEANNESS WITHOUT BULK.

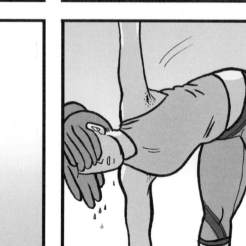

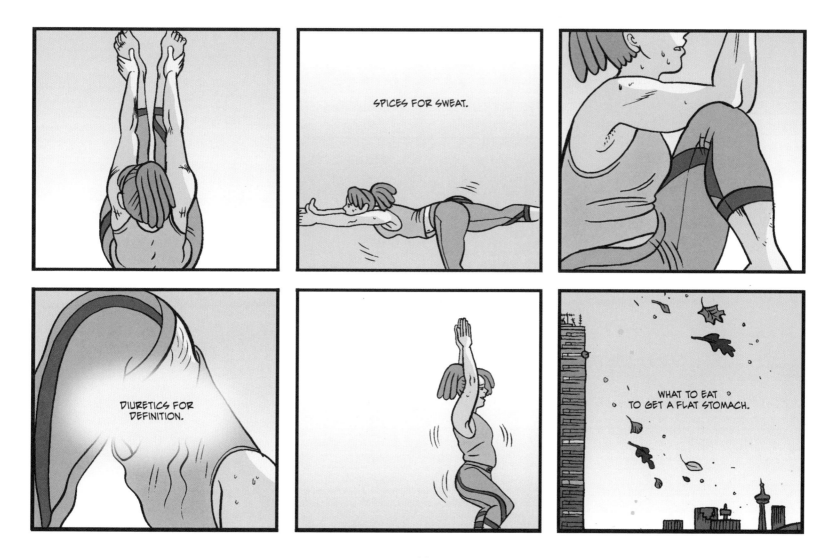

SPICES FOR SWEAT.

DIURETICS FOR
DEFINITION.

WHAT TO EAT
TO GET A FLAT STOMACH.

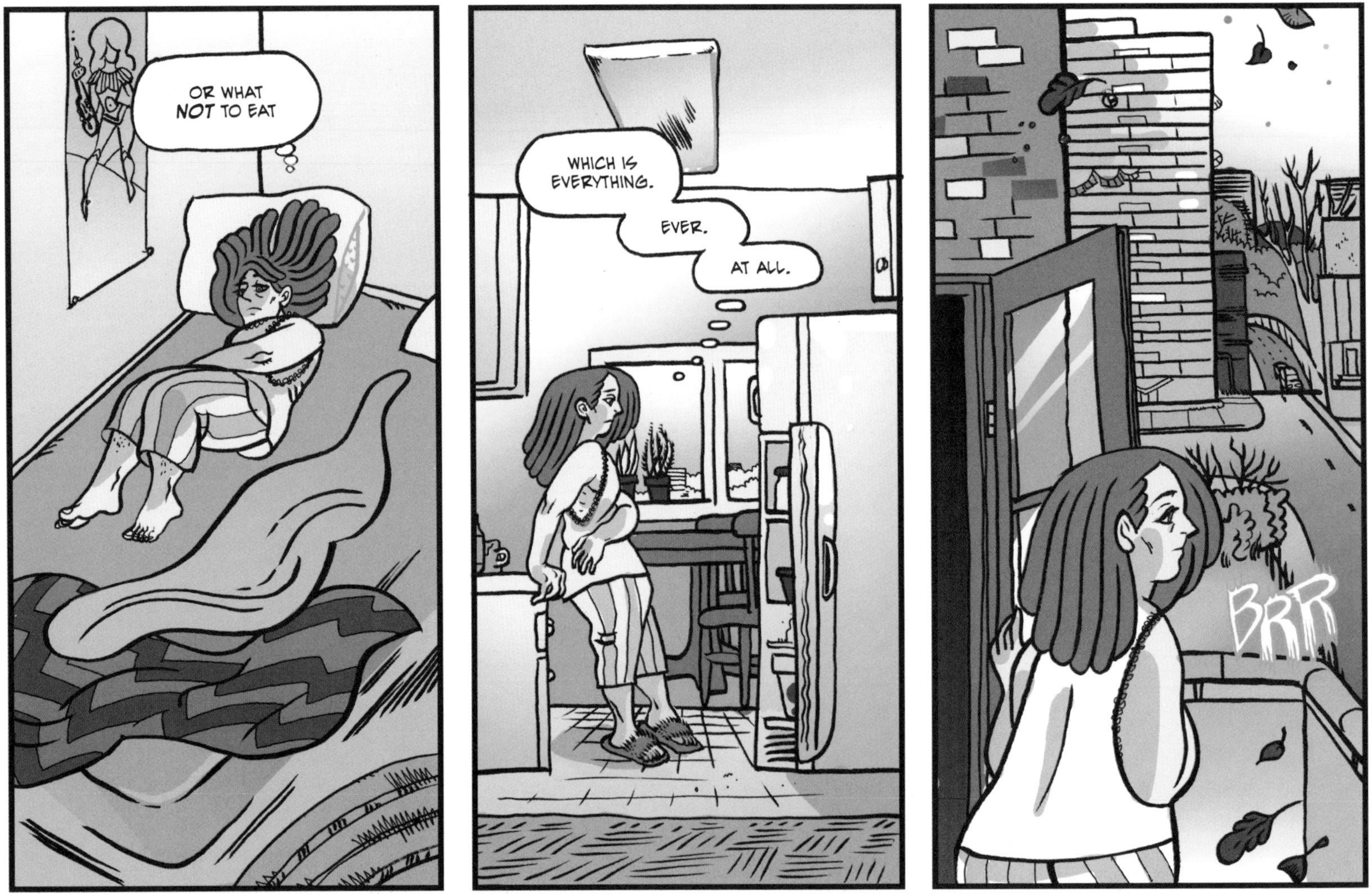
OR WHAT NOT TO EAT
WHICH IS EVERYTHING.
EVER.
AT ALL.
BRR

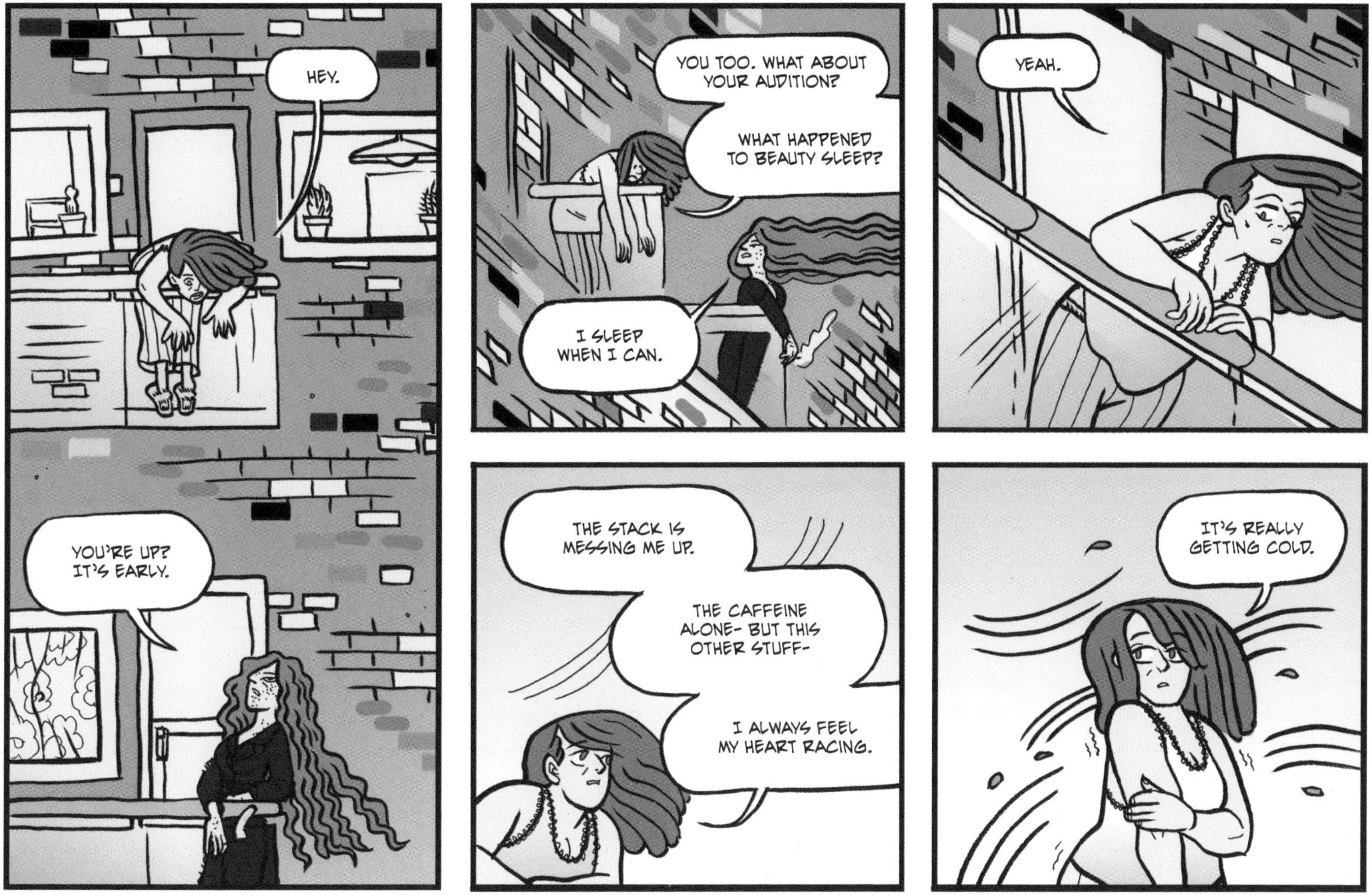
HEY.
YOU'RE UP? IT'S EARLY.
YOU TOO. WHAT ABOUT YOUR AUDITION?
WHAT HAPPENED TO BEAUTY SLEEP?
I SLEEP WHEN I CAN.
YEAH.
THE STACK IS MESSING ME UP.
THE CAFFEINE ALONE- BUT THIS OTHER STUFF-
I ALWAYS FEEL MY HEART RACING.
IT'S REALLY GETTING COLD.

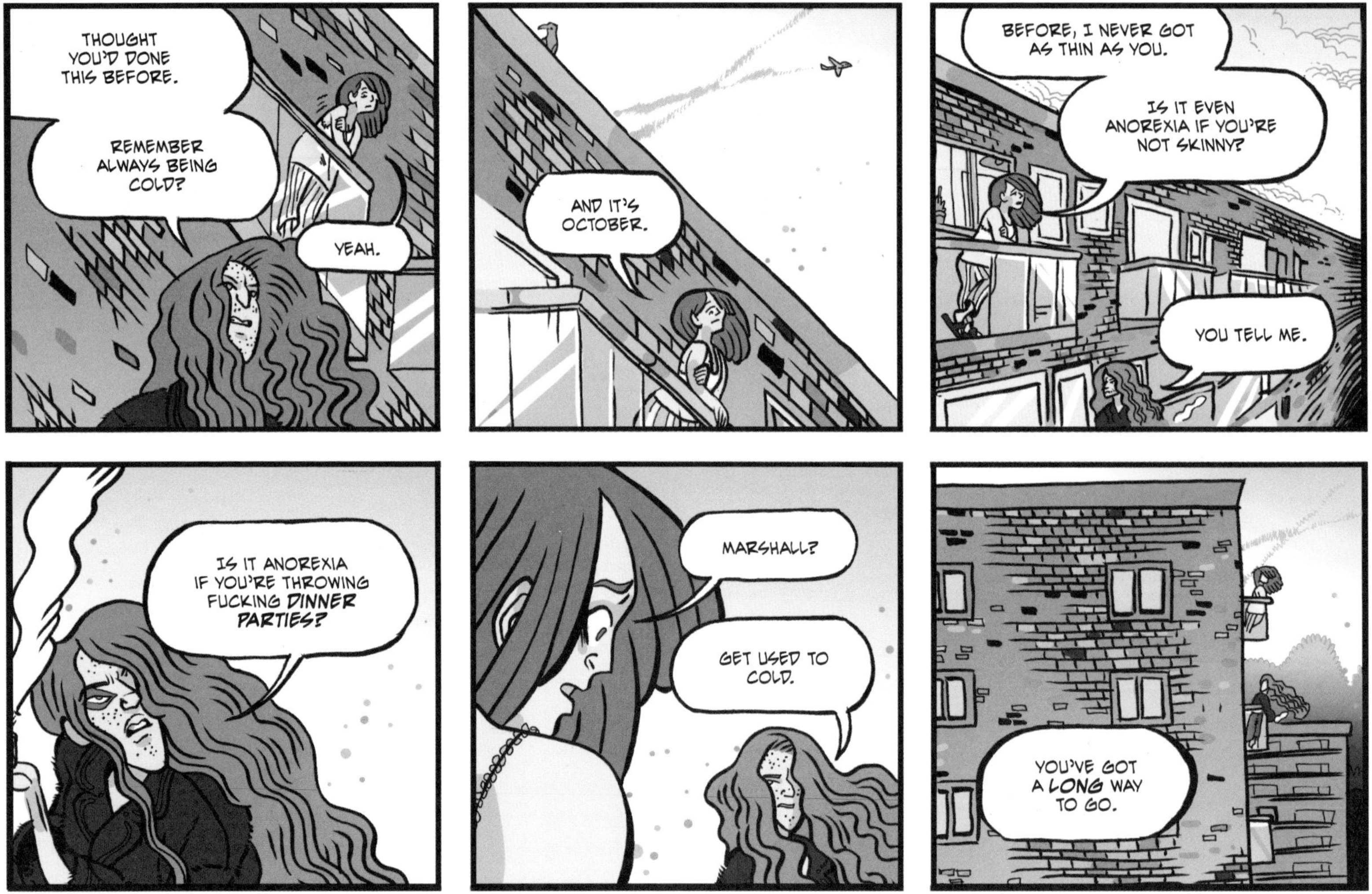
THOUGHT YOU'D DONE THIS BEFORE.
REMEMBER ALWAYS BEING COLD?
YEAH.
AND IT'S OCTOBER.
BEFORE, I NEVER GOT AS THIN AS YOU.
IS IT EVEN ANOREXIA IF YOU'RE NOT SKINNY?
YOU TELL ME.
IS IT ANOREXIA IF YOU'RE THROWING FUCKING DINNER PARTIES?
MARSHALL?
GET USED TO COLD.
YOU'VE GOT A LONG WAY TO GO.

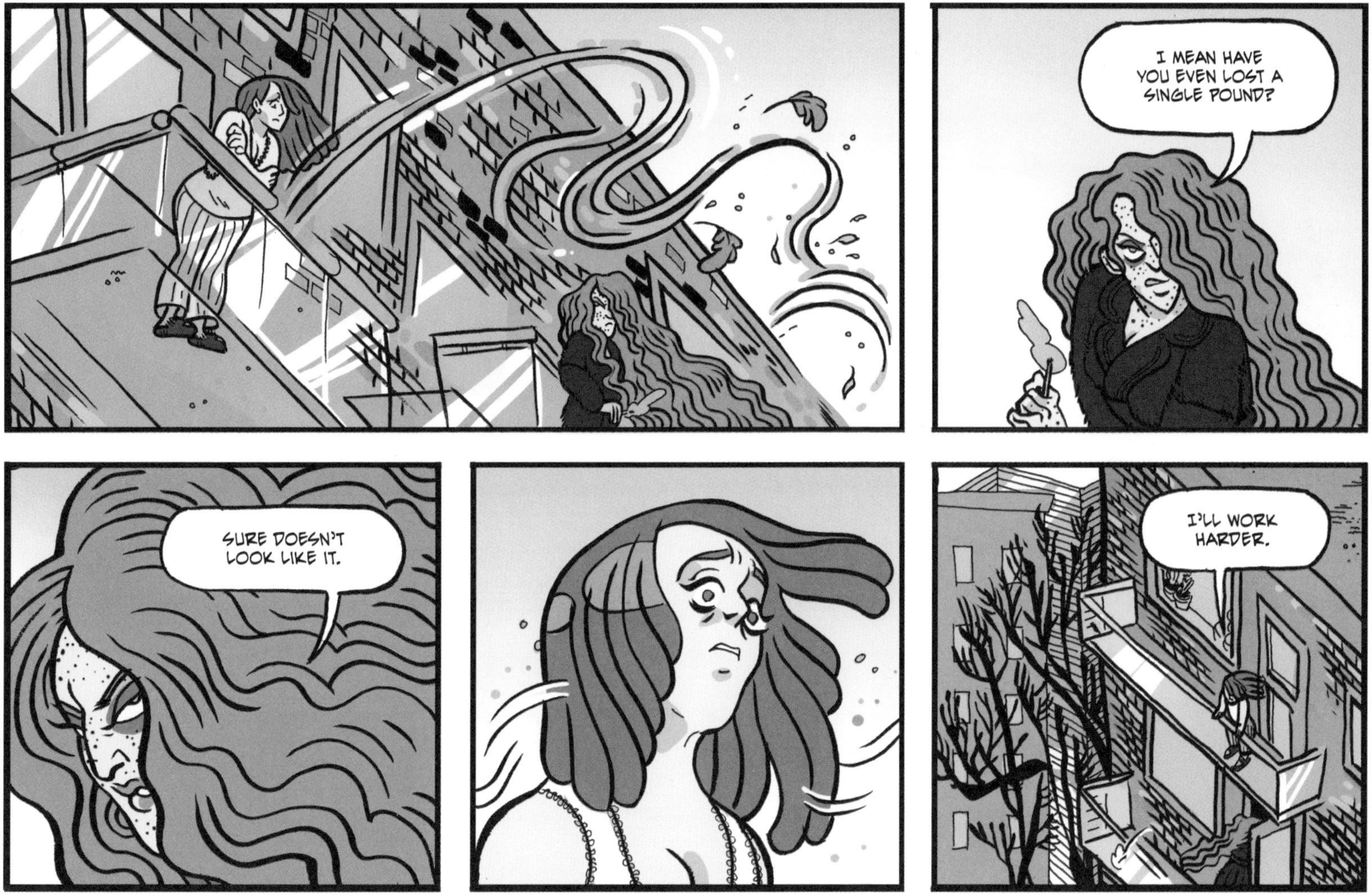
I MEAN HAVE YOU EVEN LOST A SINGLE POUND?
SURE DOESN'T LOOK LIKE IT.
I'LL WORK HARDER.

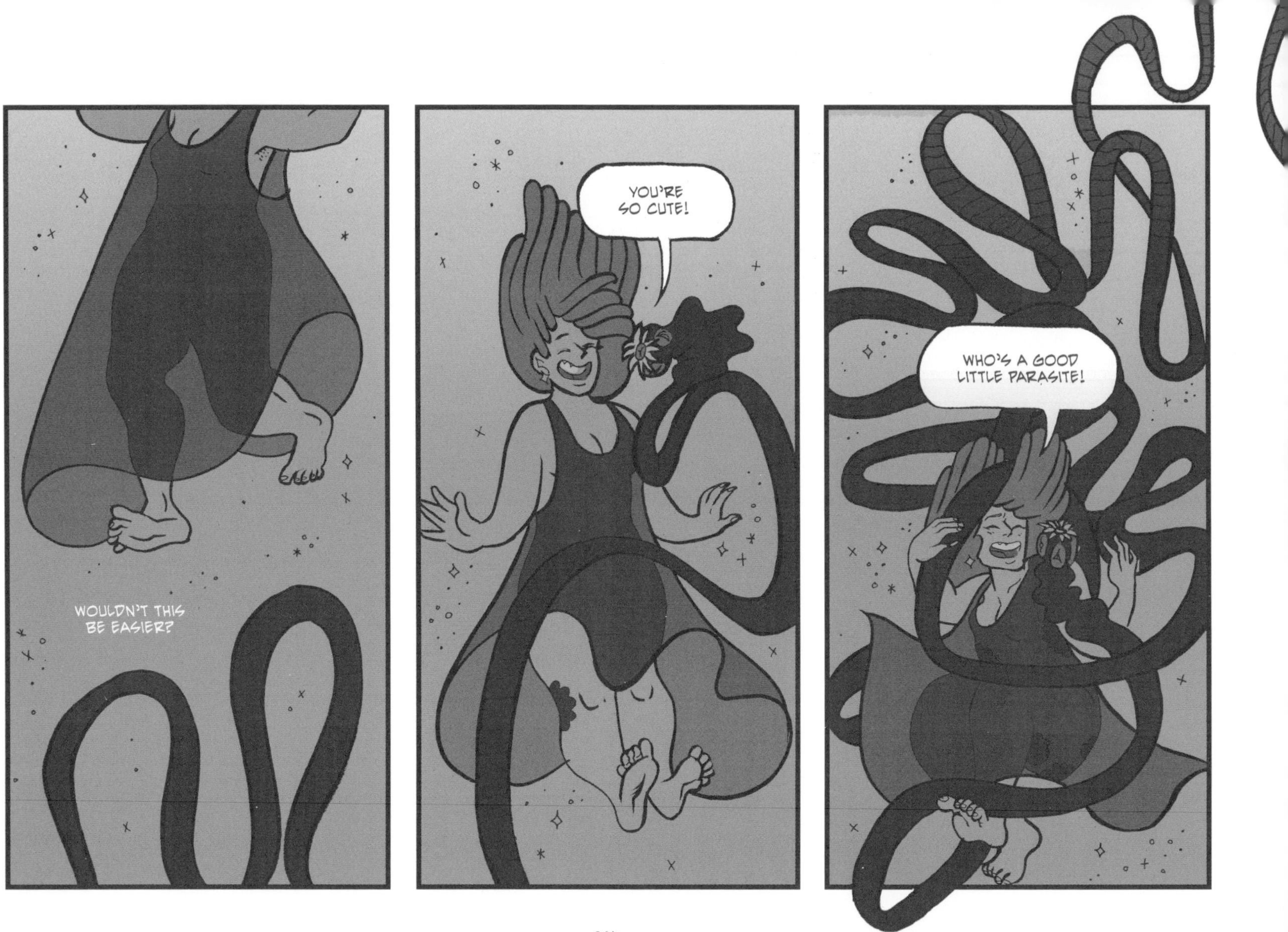
WOULDN'T THIS BE EASIER?
YOU'RE SO CUTE!
WHO'S A GOOD LITTLE PARASITE!

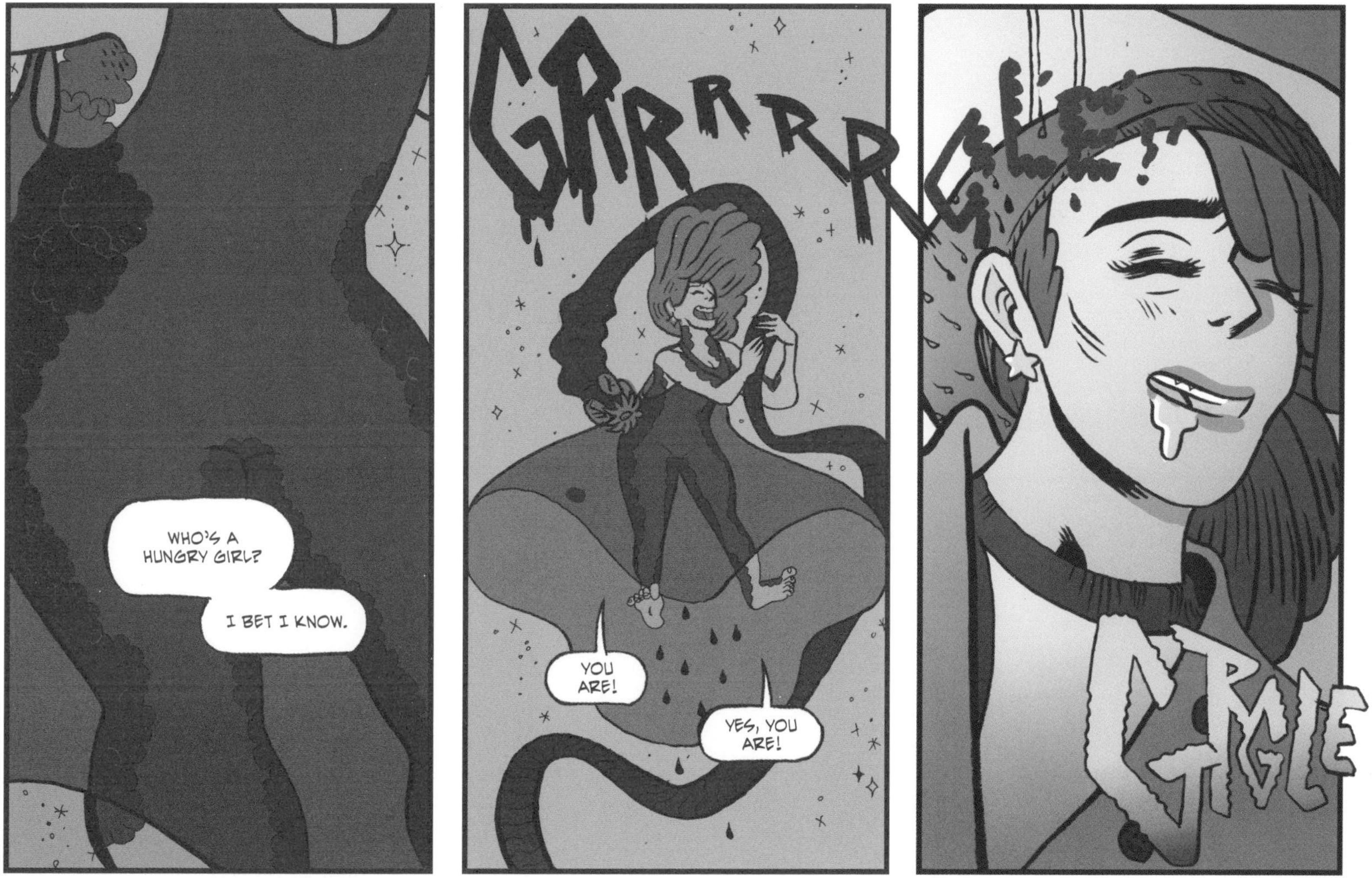
WHO'S A HUNGRY GIRL?
I BET I KNOW.
GRRRRRGLE
YOU ARE!
YES, YOU ARE!
GRGLE

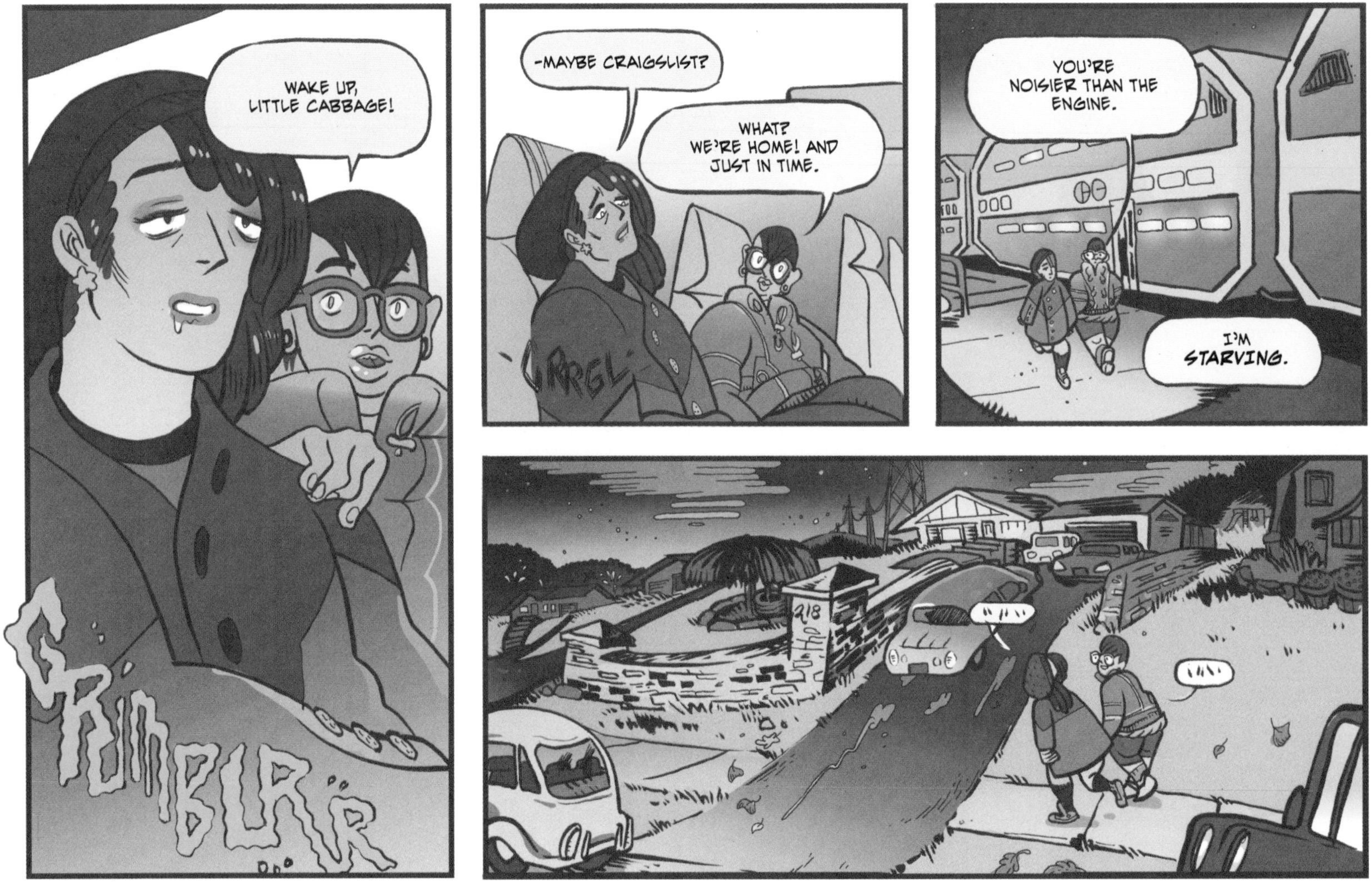
WAKE UP, LITTLE CABBAGE!
GRUMBLR'R
-MAYBE CRAIGSLIST?
WHAT? WE'RE HOME! AND JUST IN TIME.
GRRGL
YOU'RE NOISIER THAN THE ENGINE.
I'M STARVING.
218

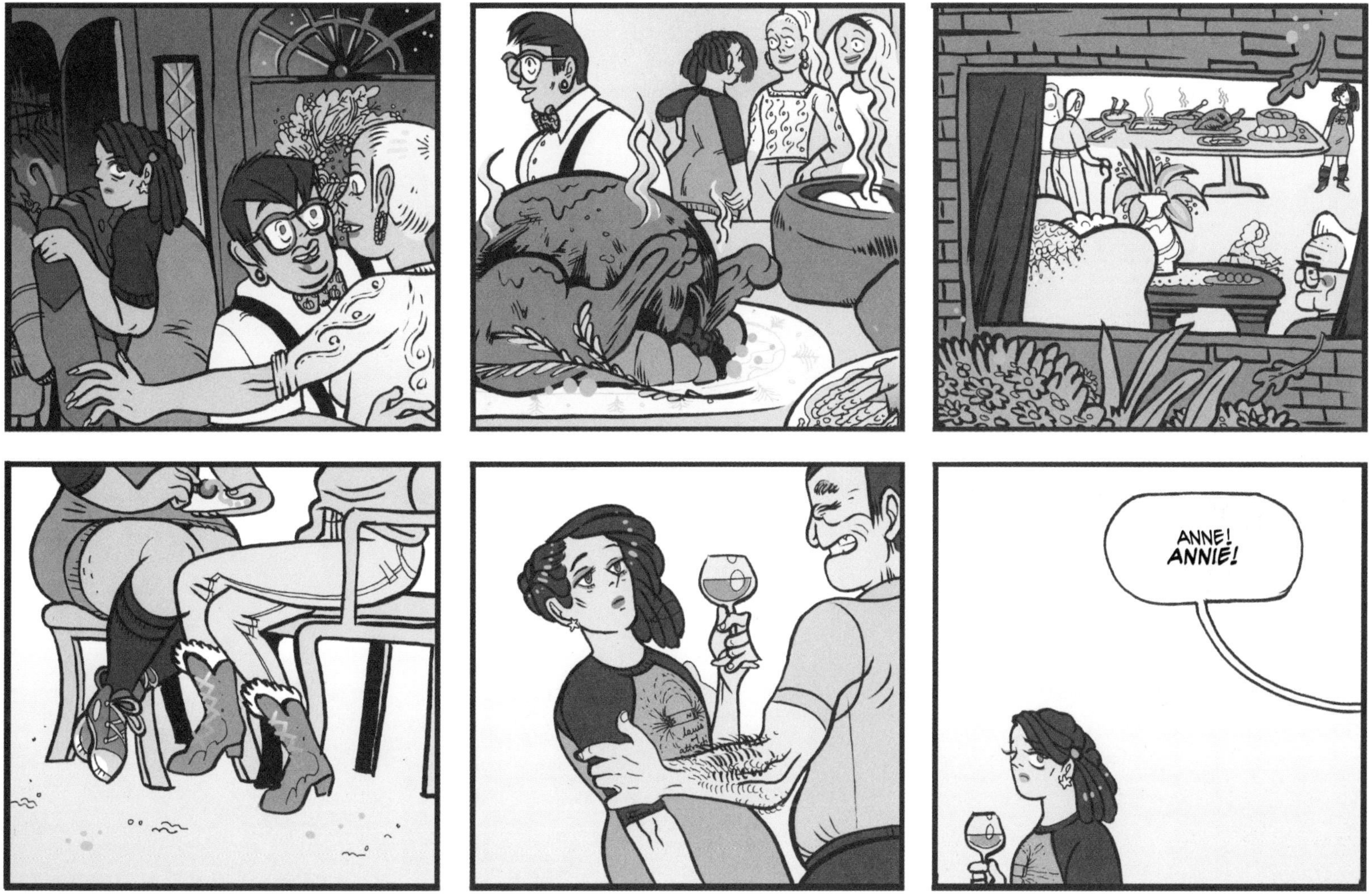
ANNE!
ANNIE!

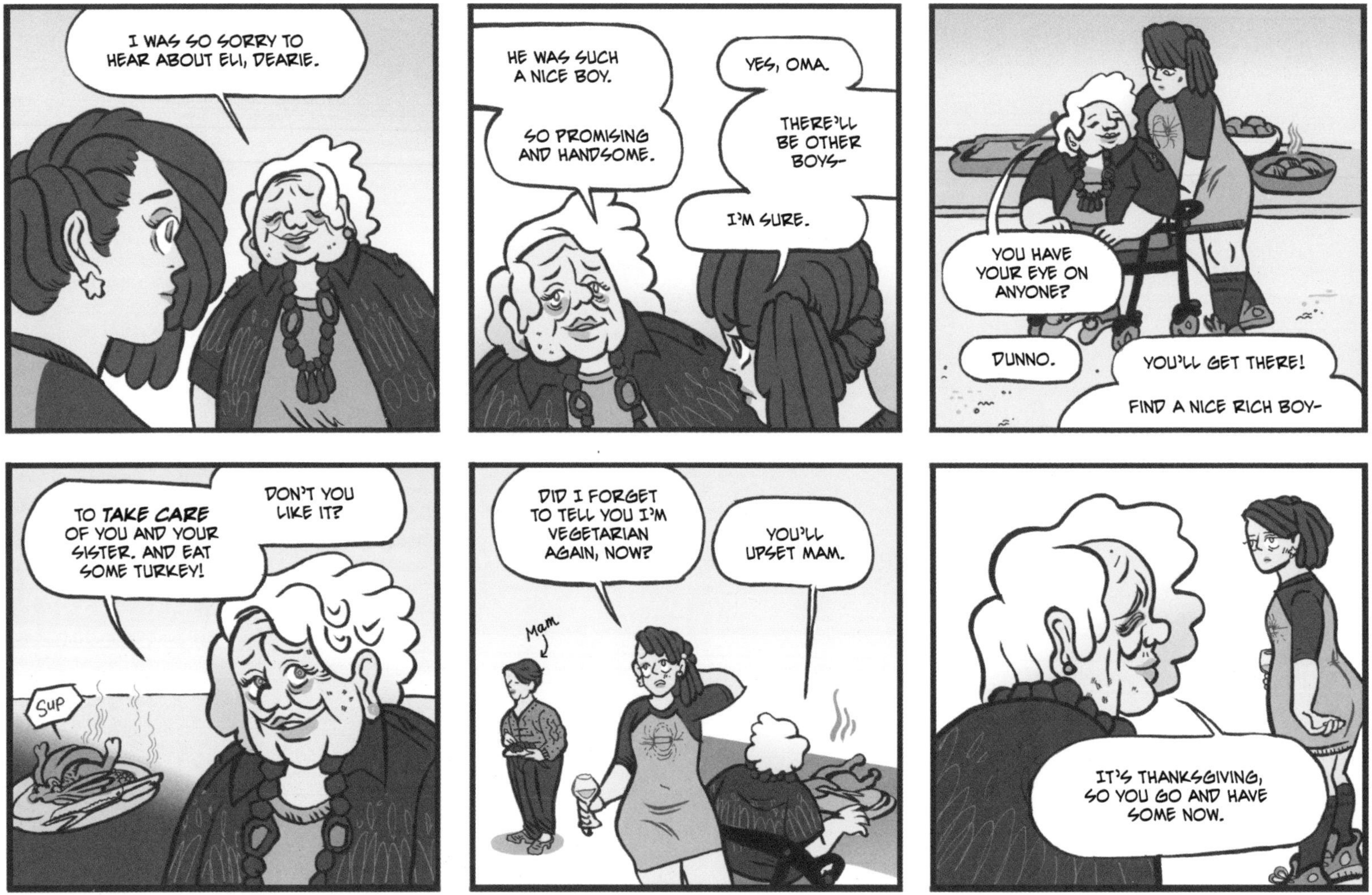
I WAS SO SORRY TO HEAR ABOUT ELI, DEARIE.
HE WAS SUCH A NICE BOY.
SO PROMISING AND HANDSOME.
YES, OMA.
THERE'LL BE OTHER BOYS-
I'M SURE.
YOU HAVE YOUR EYE ON ANYONE?
DUNNO.
YOU'LL GET THERE!
FIND A NICE RICH BOY-
TO ***TAKE CARE*** OF YOU AND YOUR SISTER. AND EAT SOME TURKEY!
DON'T YOU LIKE IT?
Sup
DID I FORGET TO TELL YOU I'M VEGETARIAN AGAIN, NOW?
YOU'LL UPSET MAM.
Mam
IT'S THANKSGIVING, SO YOU GO AND HAVE SOME NOW.

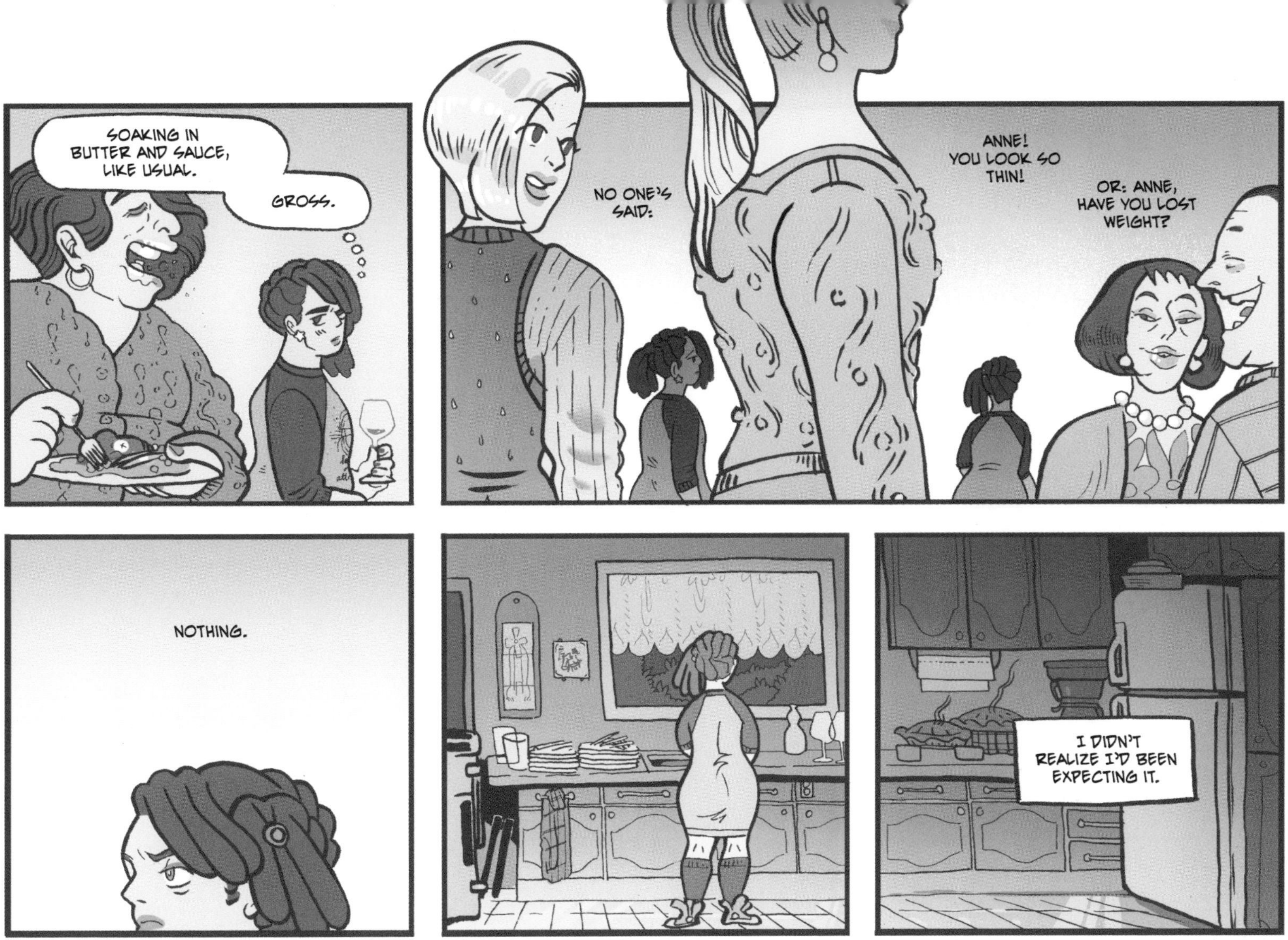
SOAKING IN BUTTER AND SAUCE, LIKE USUAL.
GROSS.
NO ONE'S SAID:
ANNE! YOU LOOK SO THIN!
OR: ANNE, HAVE YOU LOST WEIGHT?
NOTHING.
I DIDN'T REALIZE I'D BEEN EXPECTING IT.

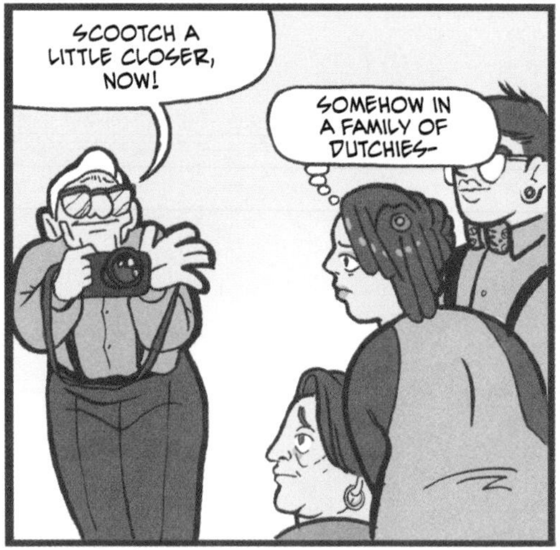
SCOOTCH A LITTLE CLOSER, NOW!
SOMEHOW IN A FAMILY OF DUTCHIES-

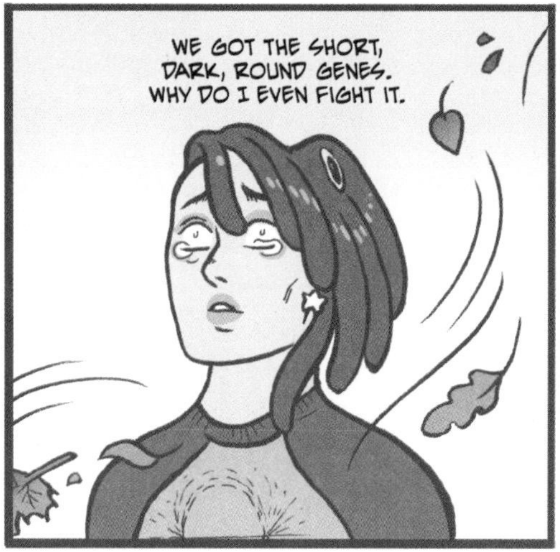
WE GOT THE SHORT, DARK, ROUND GENES. WHY DO I EVEN FIGHT IT.

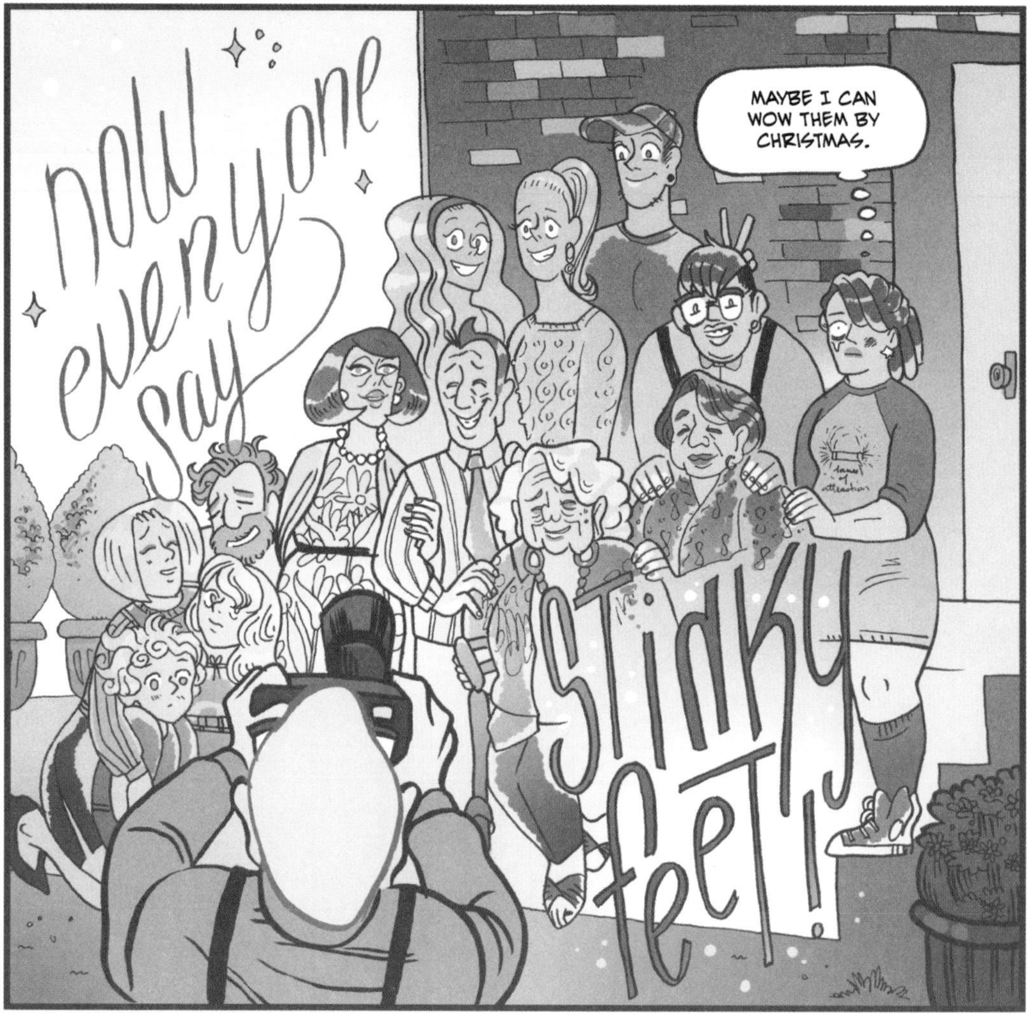
now every one say
MAYBE I CAN WOW THEM BY CHRISTMAS.
Stinky feet!

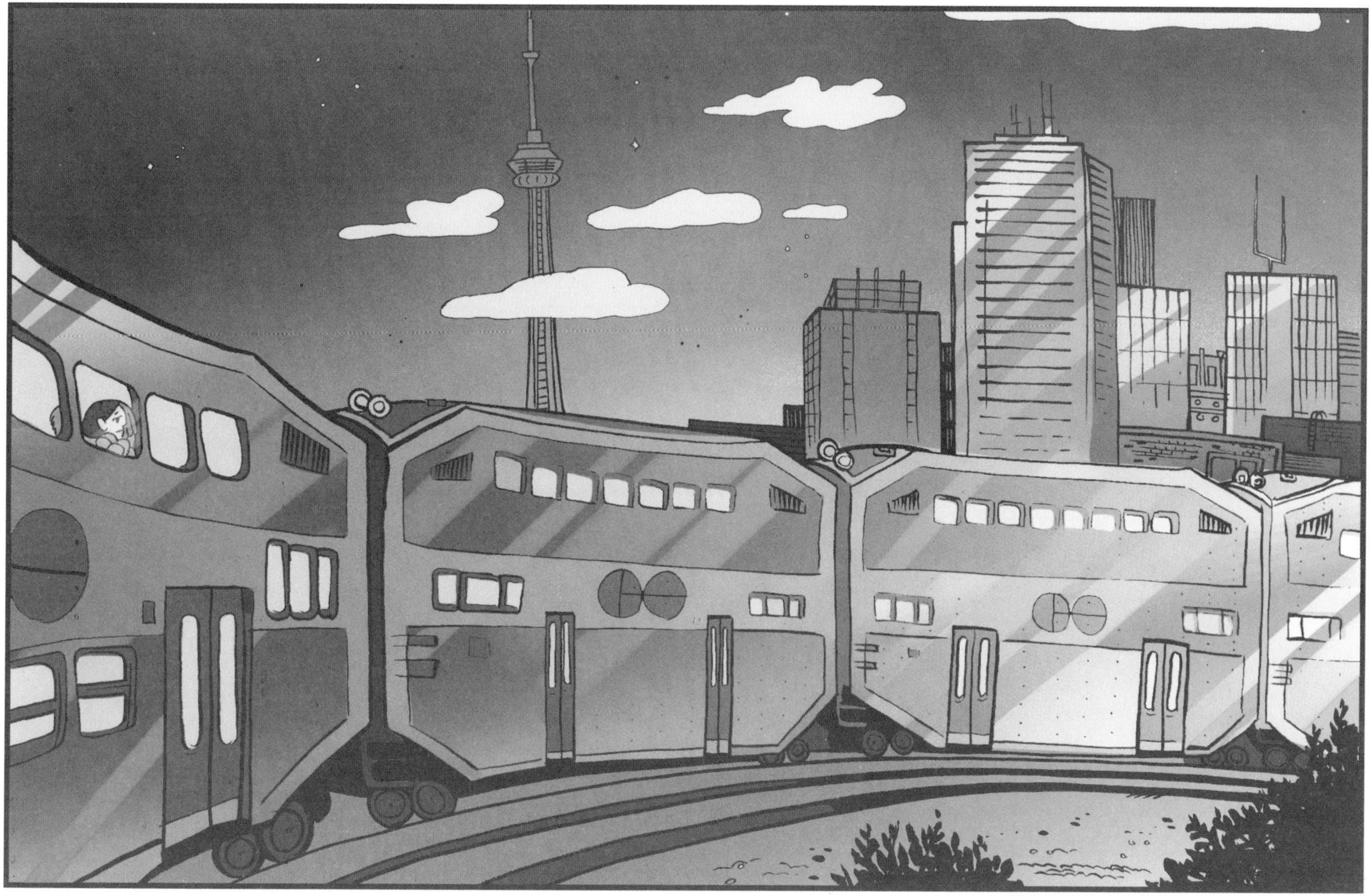

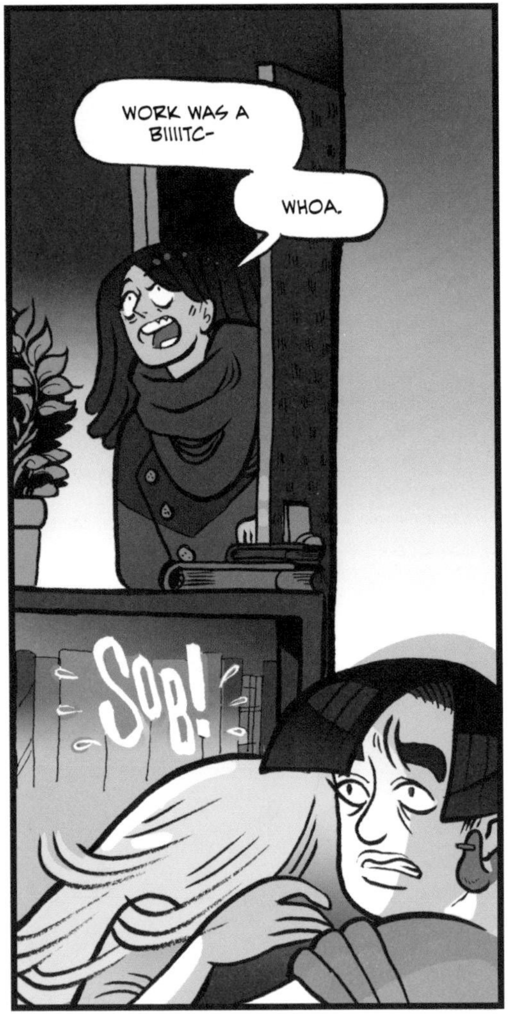
WORK WAS A BIIIITC-
WHOA.
SOB!

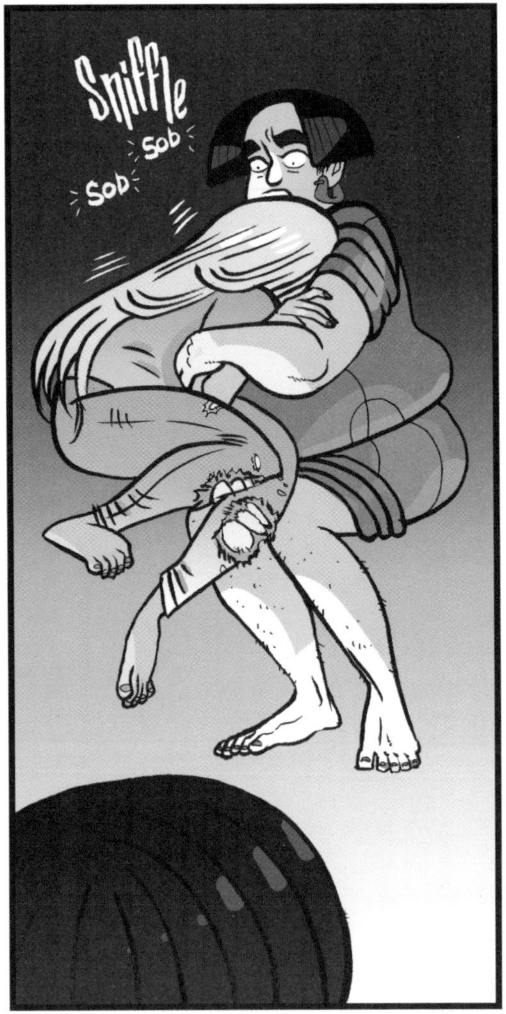
Sniffle
Sob
Sob

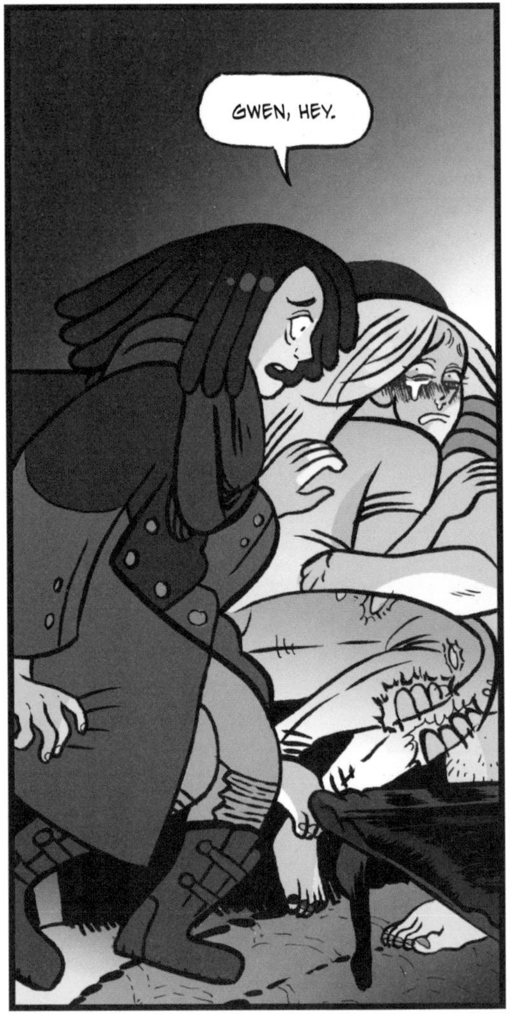
GWEN, HEY.

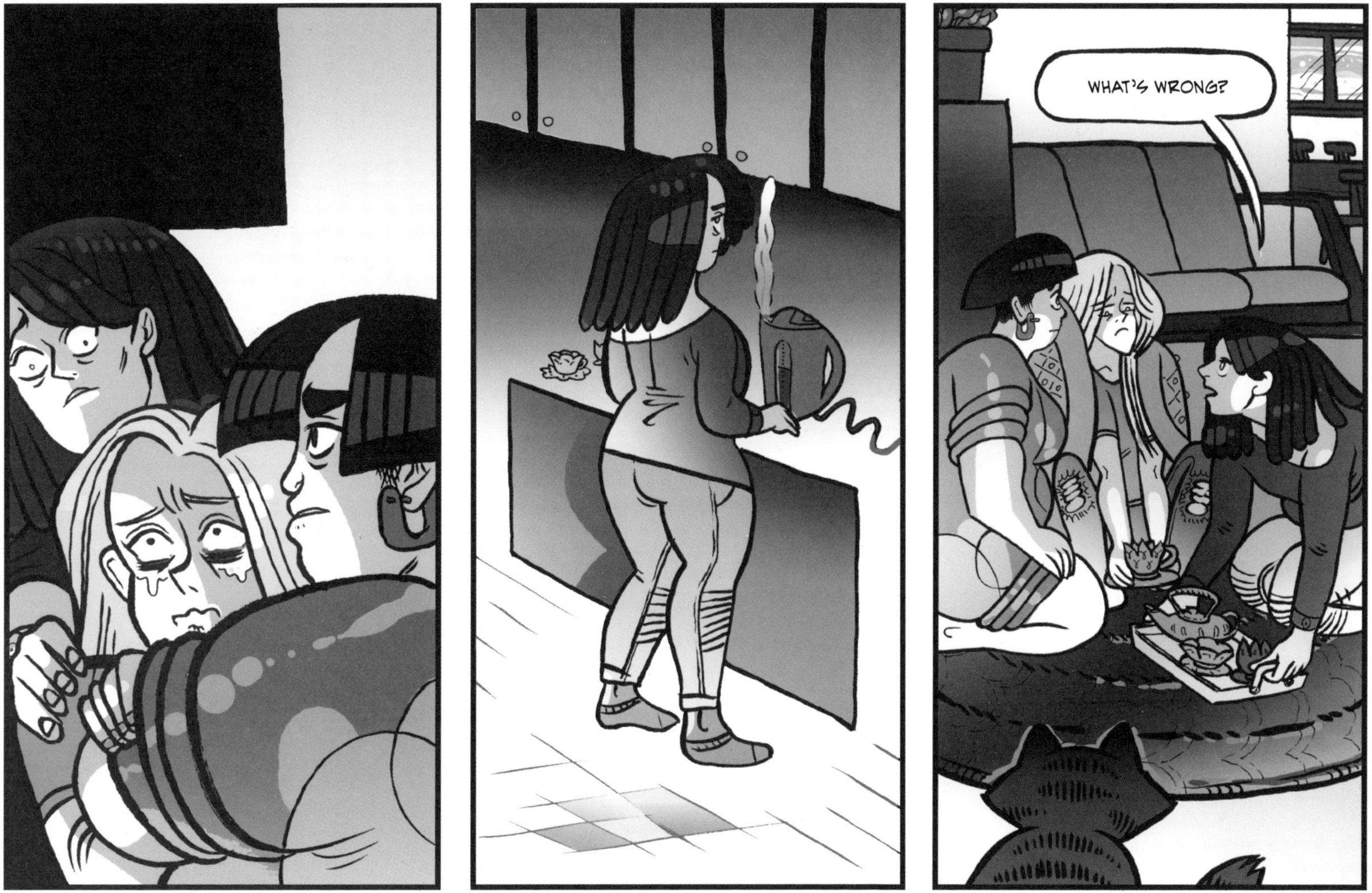
WHAT'S WRONG?

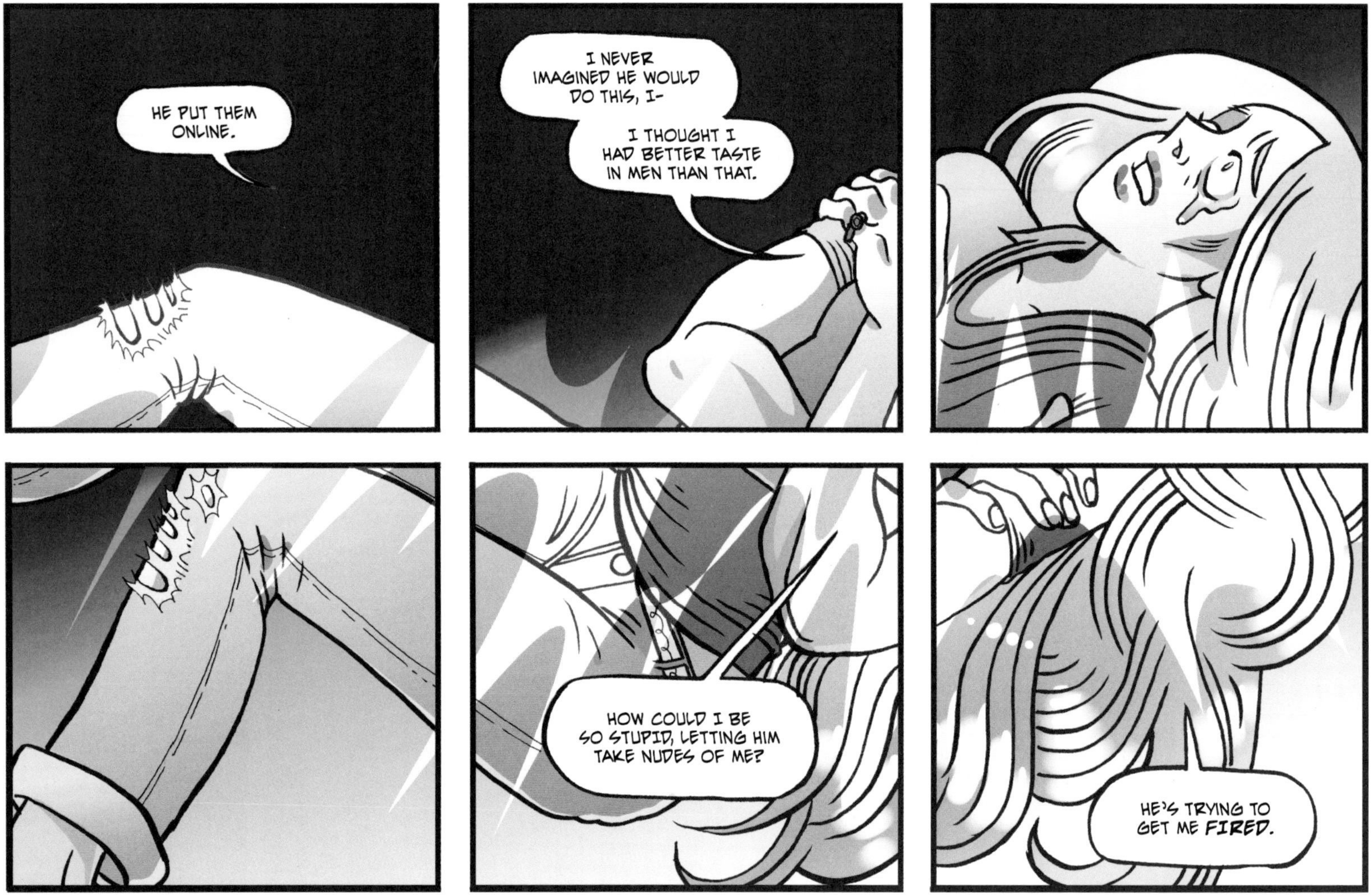
HE PUT THEM ONLINE.
I NEVER IMAGINED HE WOULD DO THIS, I-
I THOUGHT I HAD BETTER TASTE IN MEN THAN THAT.
HOW COULD I BE SO STUPID, LETTING HIM TAKE NUDES OF ME?
HE'S TRYING TO GET ME FIRED.

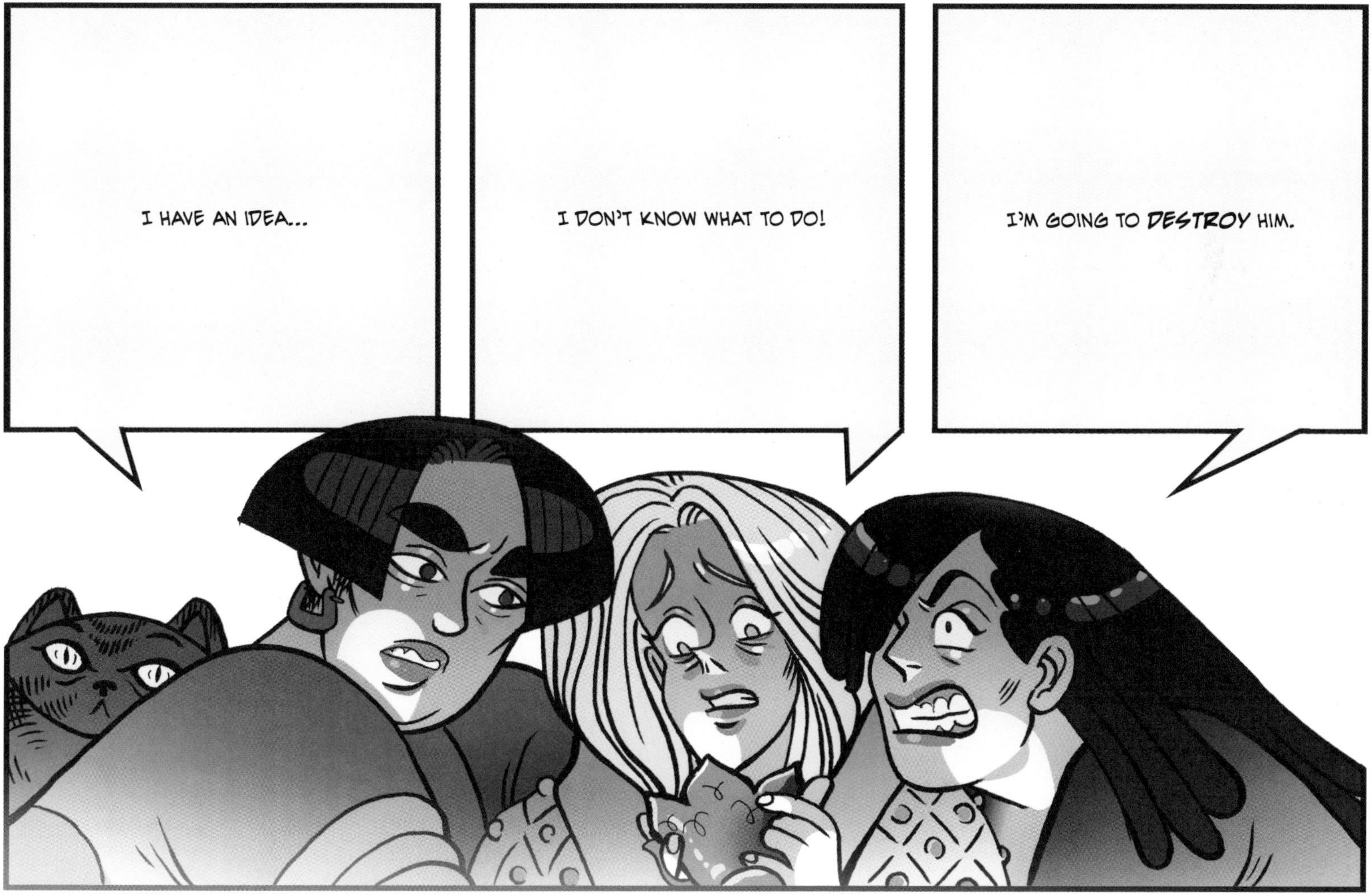
I HAVE AN IDEA...
I DON'T KNOW WHAT TO DO!
I'M GOING TO DESTROY HIM.

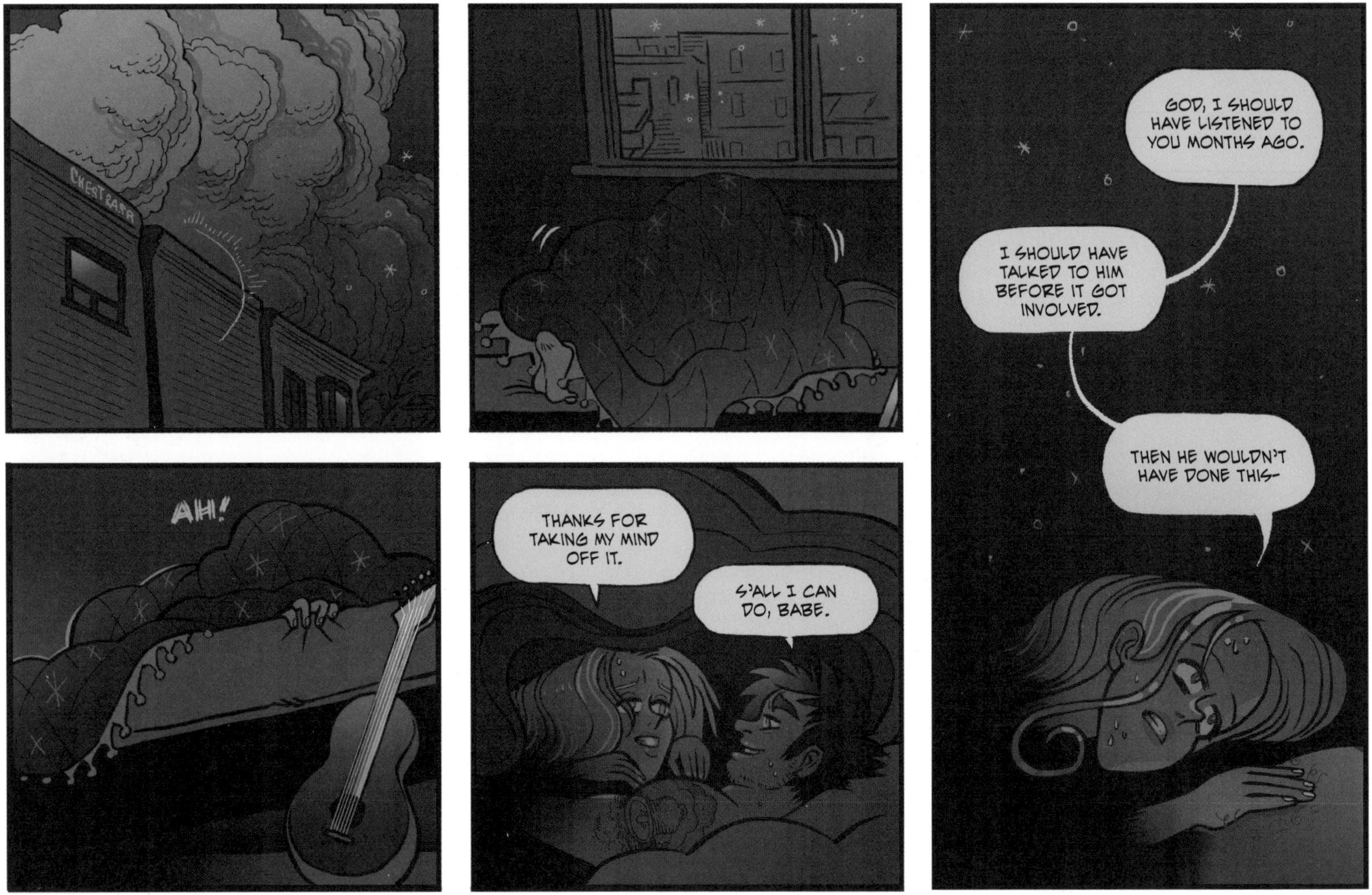
AH!
THANKS FOR TAKING MY MIND OFF IT.
S'ALL I CAN DO, BABE.
GOD, I SHOULD HAVE LISTENED TO YOU MONTHS AGO.
I SHOULD HAVE TALKED TO HIM BEFORE IT GOT INVOLVED.
THEN HE WOULDN'T HAVE DONE THIS-

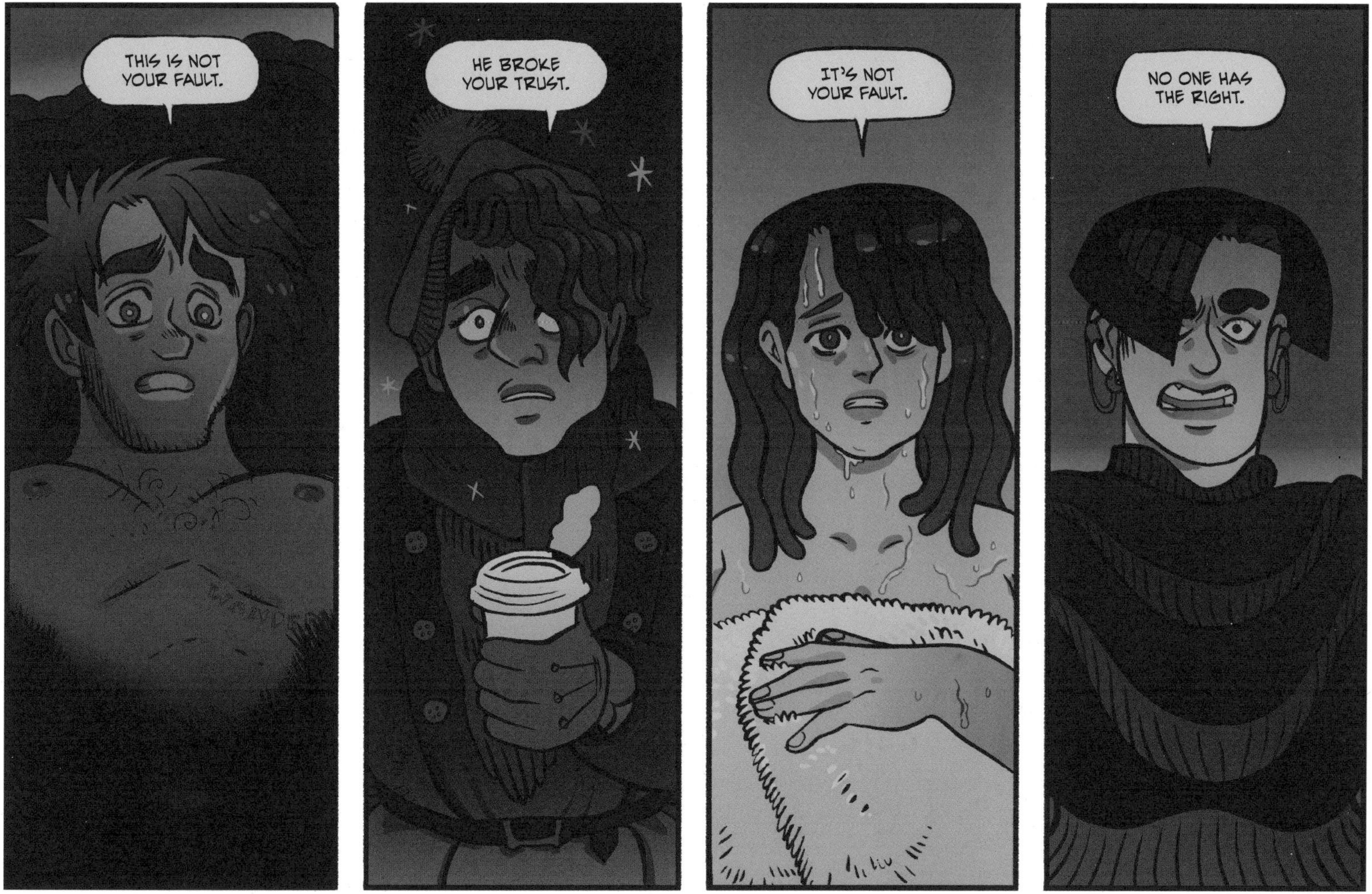
THIS IS NOT YOUR FAULT.
HE BROKE YOUR TRUST.
IT'S NOT YOUR FAULT.
NO ONE HAS THE RIGHT.

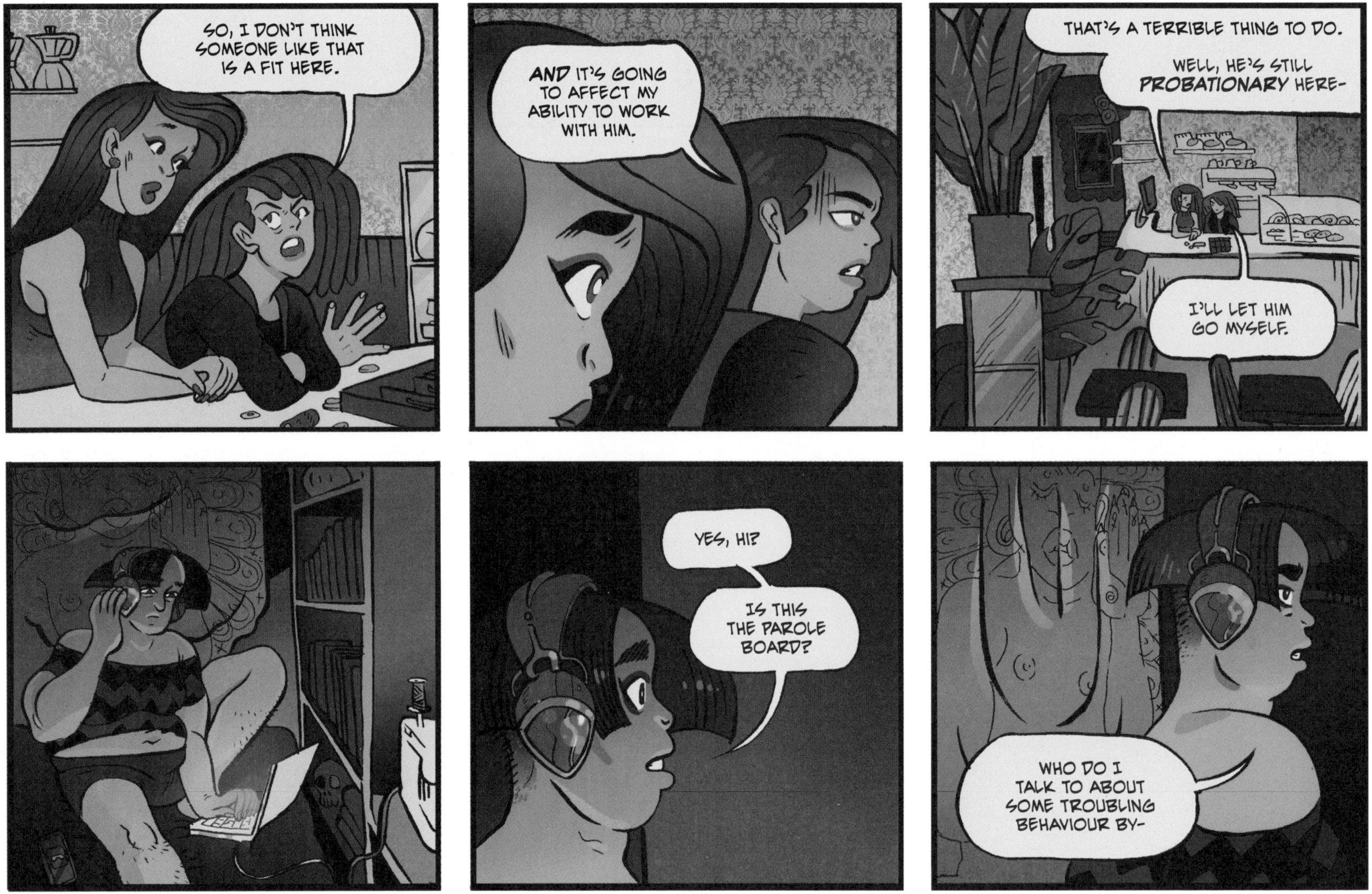
SO, I DON'T THINK SOMEONE LIKE THAT IS A FIT HERE.
AND IT'S GOING TO AFFECT MY ABILITY TO WORK WITH HIM.
THAT'S A TERRIBLE THING TO DO.
WELL, HE'S STILL PROBATIONARY HERE-
I'LL LET HIM GO MYSELF.
YES, HI?
IS THIS THE PAROLE BOARD?
WHO DO I TALK TO ABOUT SOME TROUBLING BEHAVIOUR BY-

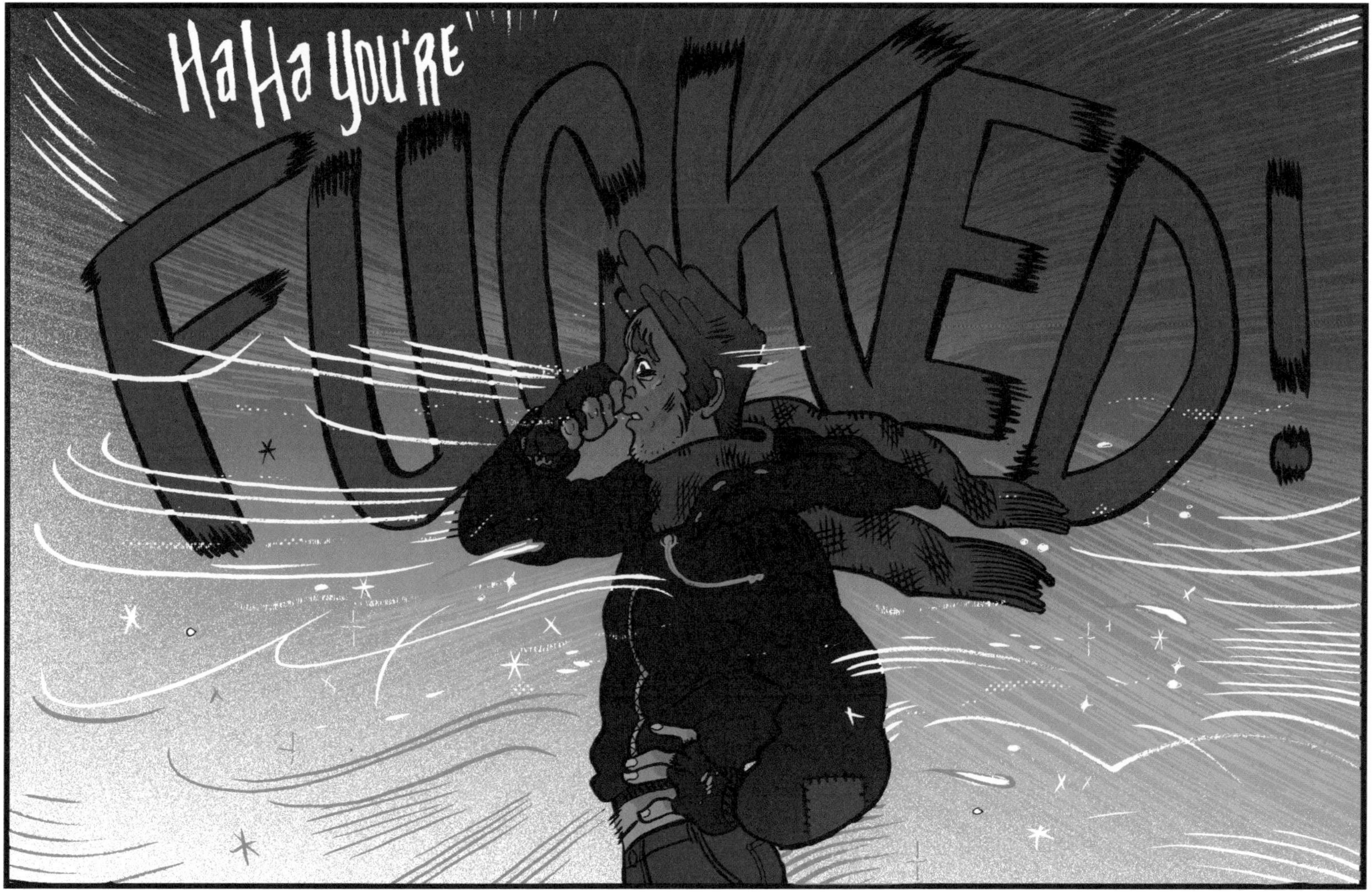
HaHa you're
FUCKED!

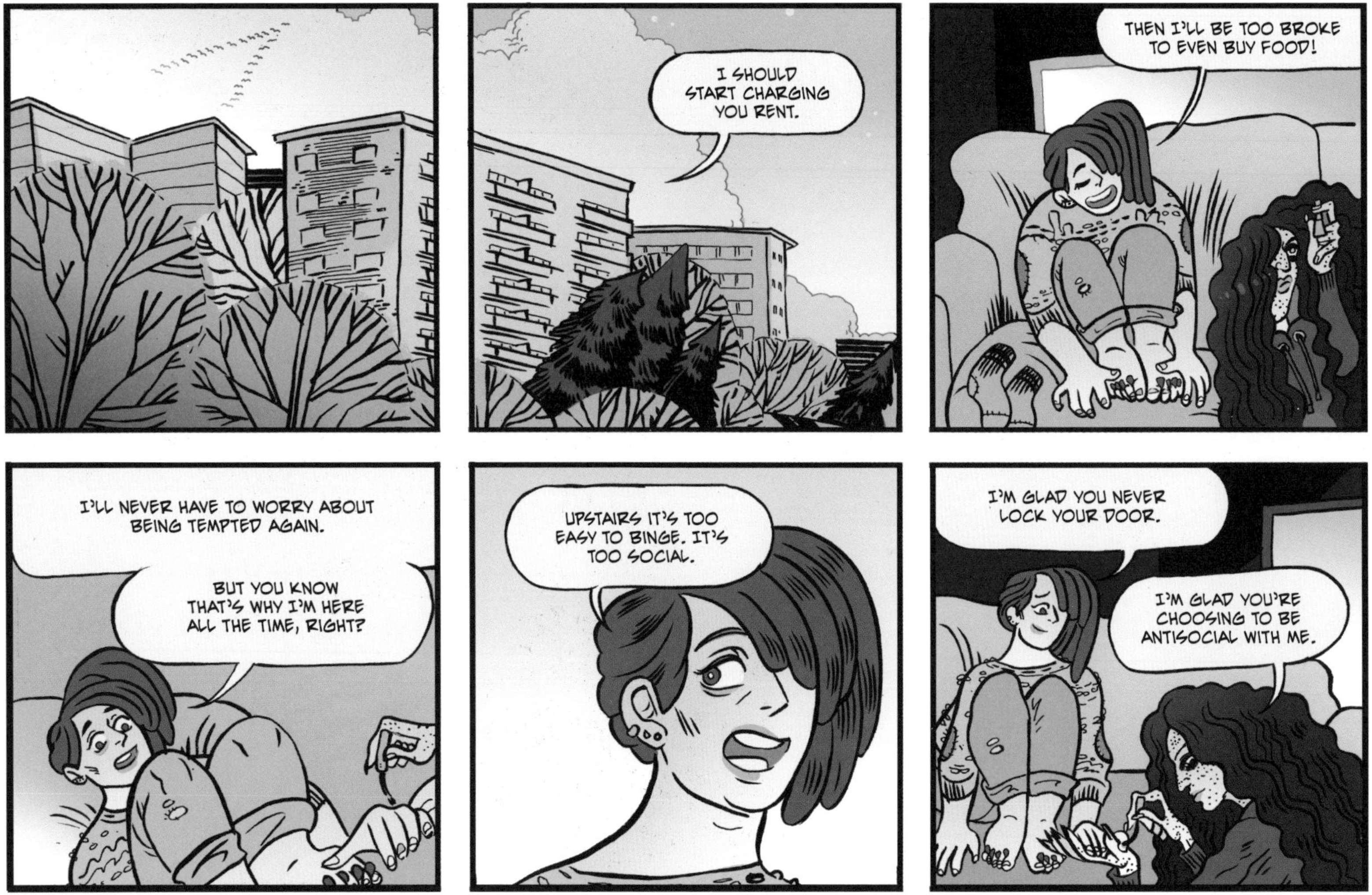
I SHOULD START CHARGING YOU RENT.
THEN I'LL BE TOO BROKE TO EVEN BUY FOOD!
I'LL NEVER HAVE TO WORRY ABOUT BEING TEMPTED AGAIN.
BUT YOU KNOW THAT'S WHY I'M HERE ALL THE TIME, RIGHT?
UPSTAIRS IT'S TOO EASY TO BINGE. IT'S TOO SOCIAL.
I'M GLAD YOU NEVER LOCK YOUR DOOR.
I'M GLAD YOU'RE CHOOSING TO BE ANTISOCIAL WITH ME.

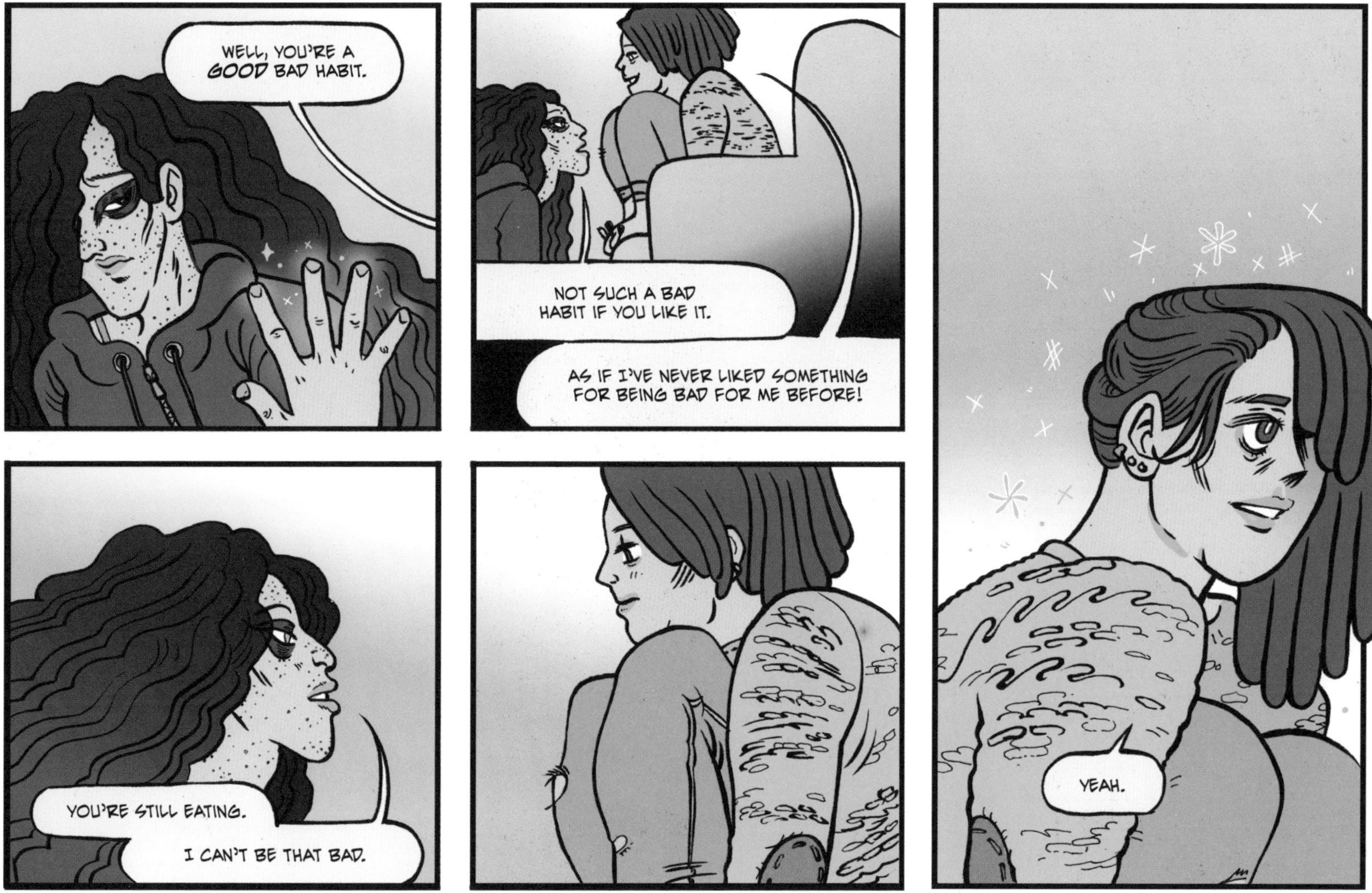
WELL, YOU'RE A GOOD BAD HABIT.
NOT SUCH A BAD HABIT IF YOU LIKE IT.
AS IF I'VE NEVER LIKED SOMETHING FOR BEING BAD FOR ME BEFORE!
YOU'RE STILL EATING.
I CAN'T BE THAT BAD.
YEAH.

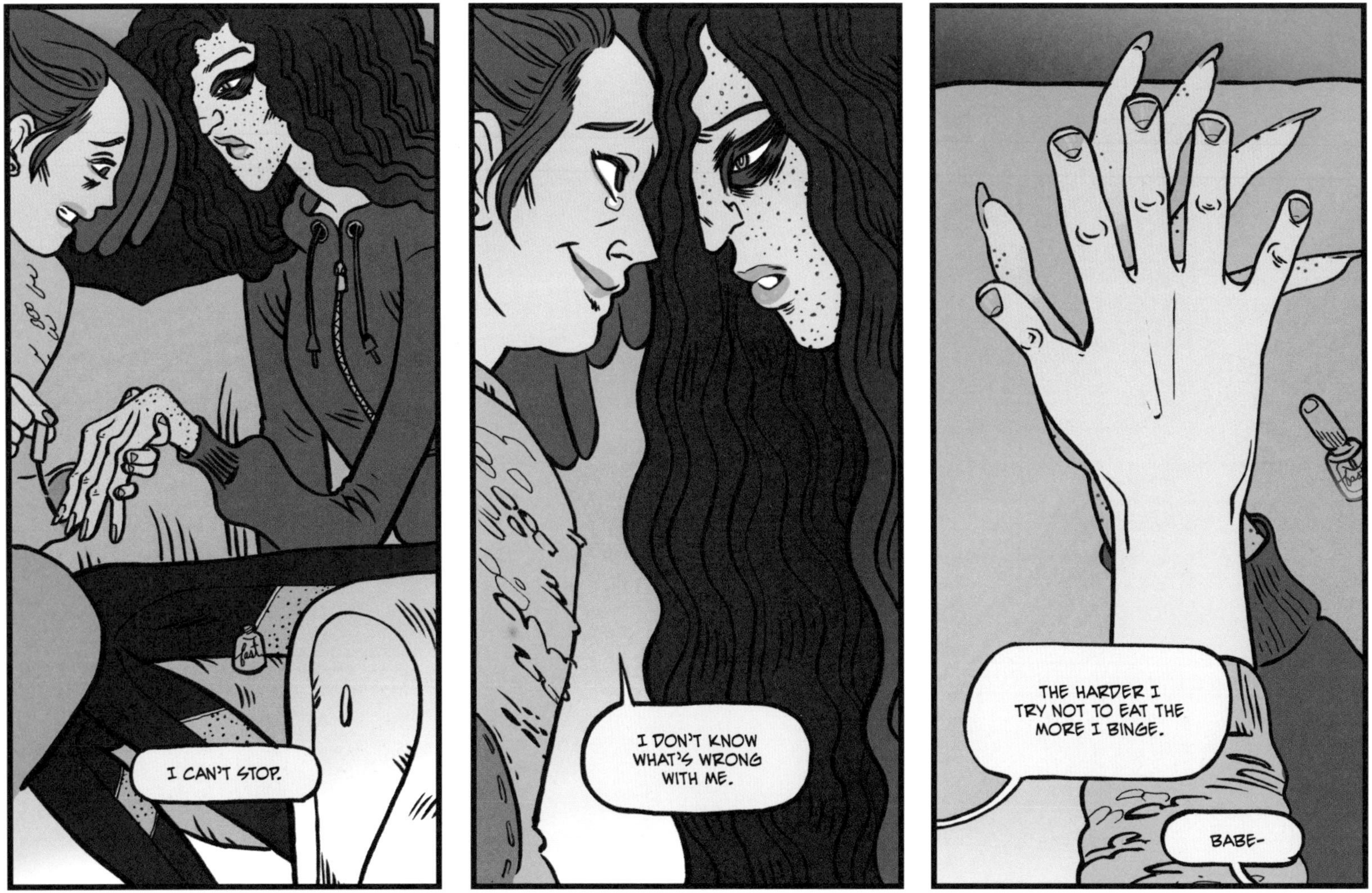
I CAN'T STOP.
I DON'T KNOW WHAT'S WRONG WITH ME.
THE HARDER I TRY NOT TO EAT THE MORE I BINGE.
BABE-

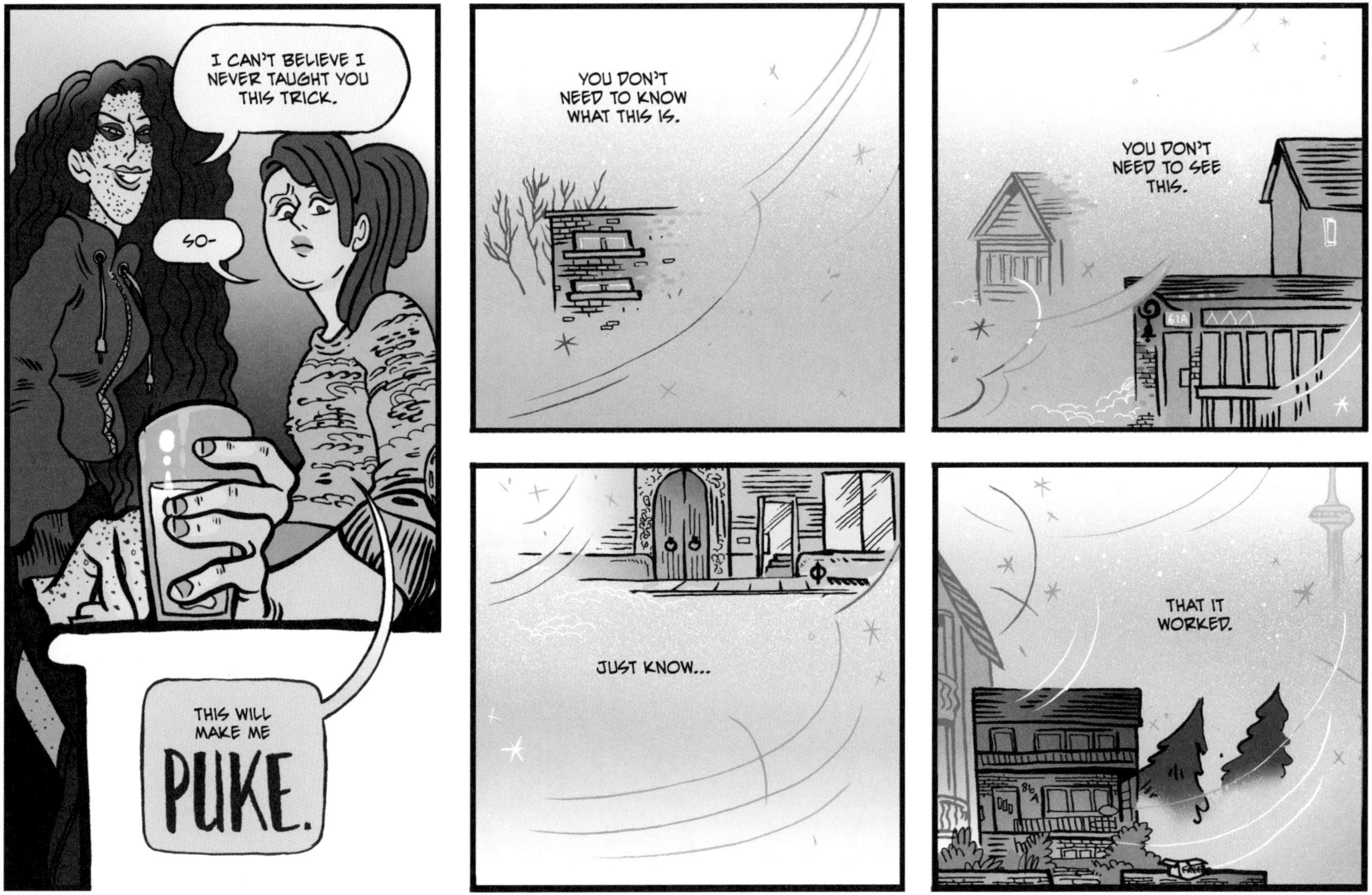
I CAN'T BELIEVE I NEVER TAUGHT YOU THIS TRICK.
SO-
THIS WILL MAKE ME PUKE.
YOU DON'T NEED TO KNOW WHAT THIS IS.
YOU DON'T NEED TO SEE THIS.
JUST KNOW...
THAT IT WORKED.

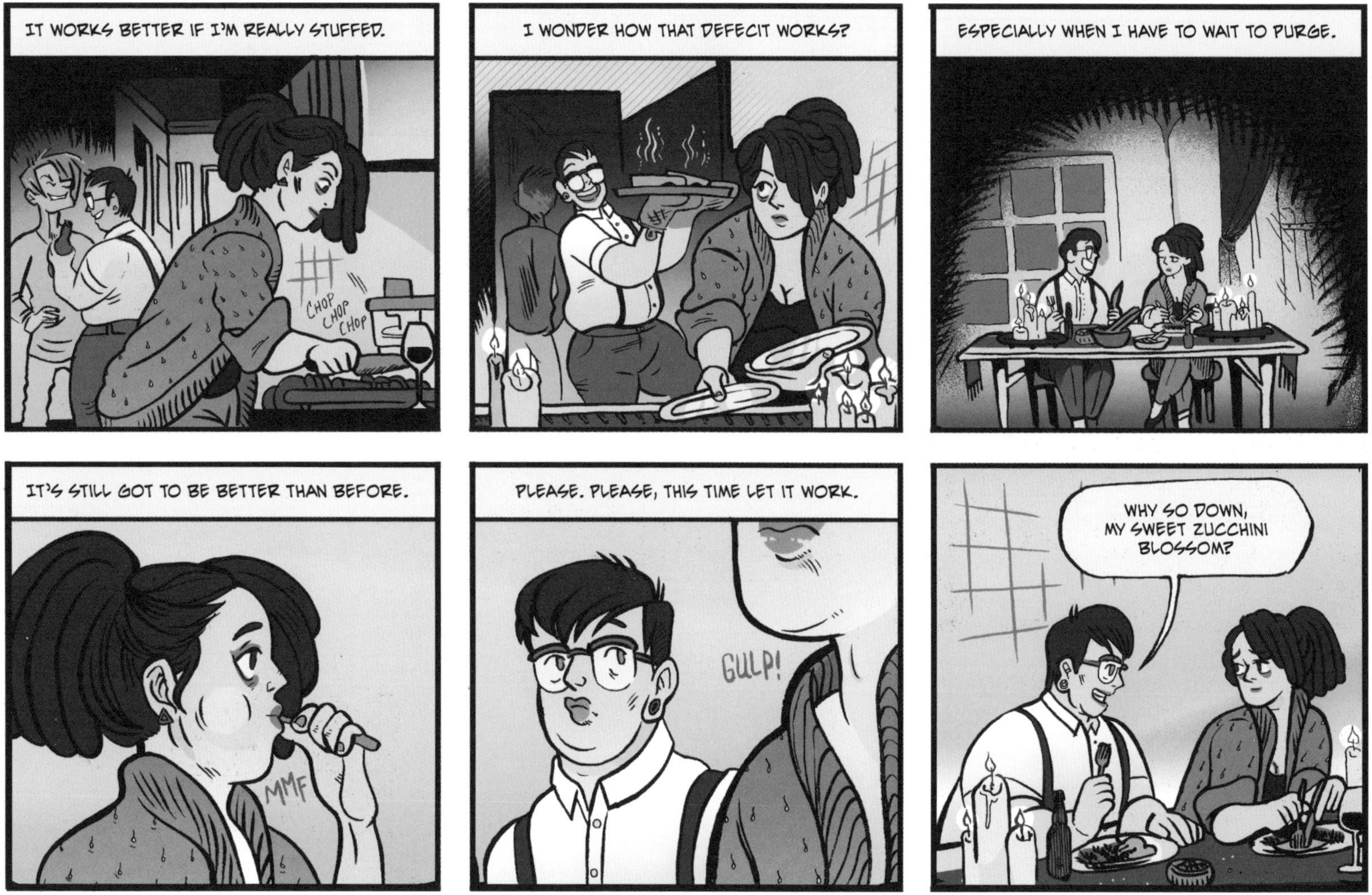
IT WORKS BETTER IF I'M REALLY STUFFED.
CHOP CHOP CHOP
I WONDER HOW THAT DEFECIT WORKS?
ESPECIALLY WHEN I HAVE TO WAIT TO PURGE.
IT'S STILL GOT TO BE BETTER THAN BEFORE.
MMF
PLEASE. PLEASE, THIS TIME LET IT WORK.
GULP!
WHY SO DOWN, MY SWEET ZUCCHINI BLOSSOM?

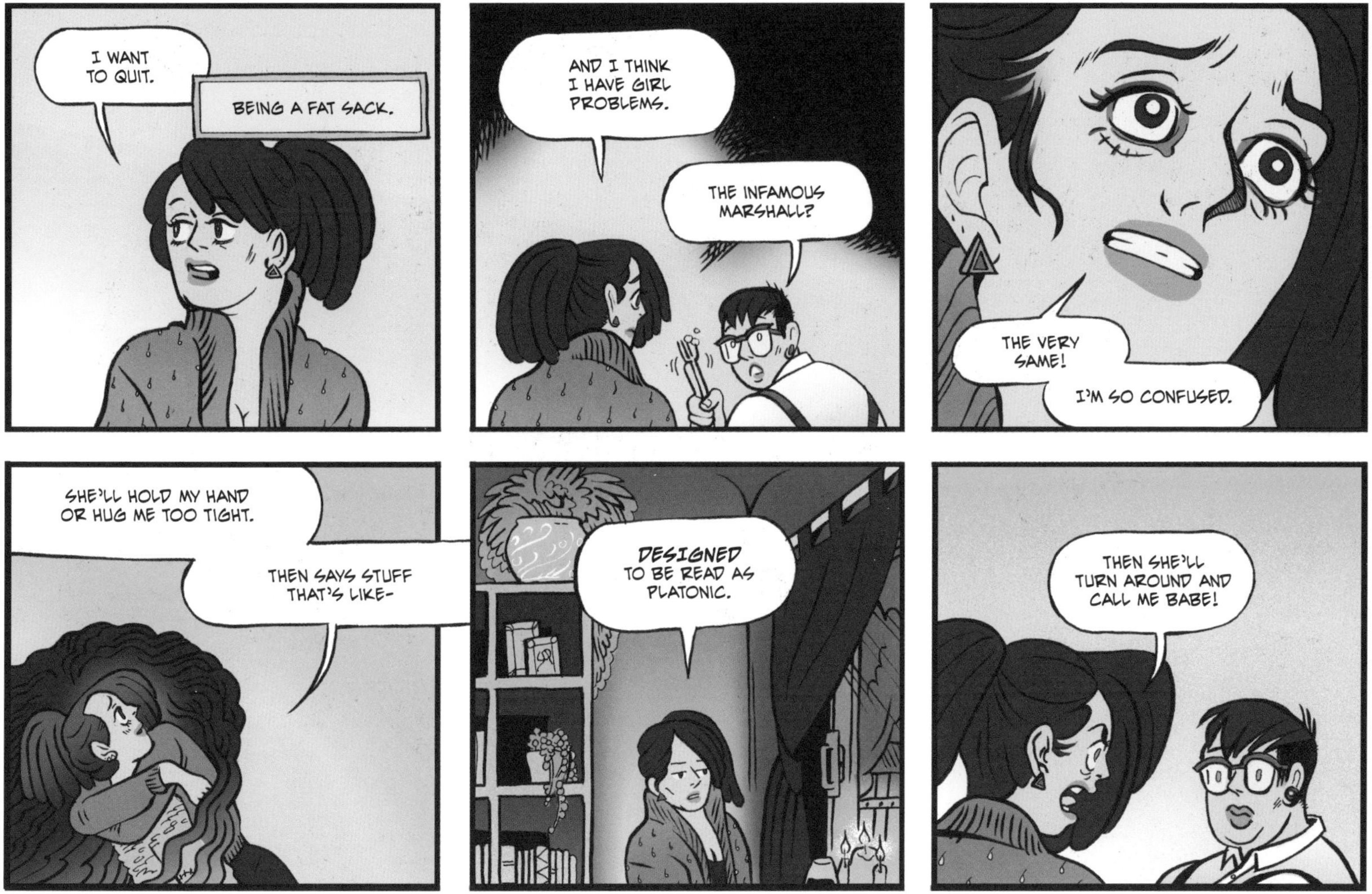
I WANT TO QUIT.
BEING A FAT SACK.
AND I THINK I HAVE GIRL PROBLEMS.
THE INFAMOUS MARSHALL?
THE VERY SAME!
I'M SO CONFUSED.
SHE'LL HOLD MY HAND OR HUG ME TOO TIGHT.
THEN SAYS STUFF THAT'S LIKE-
DESIGNED TO BE READ AS PLATONIC.
THEN SHE'LL TURN AROUND AND CALL ME BABE!

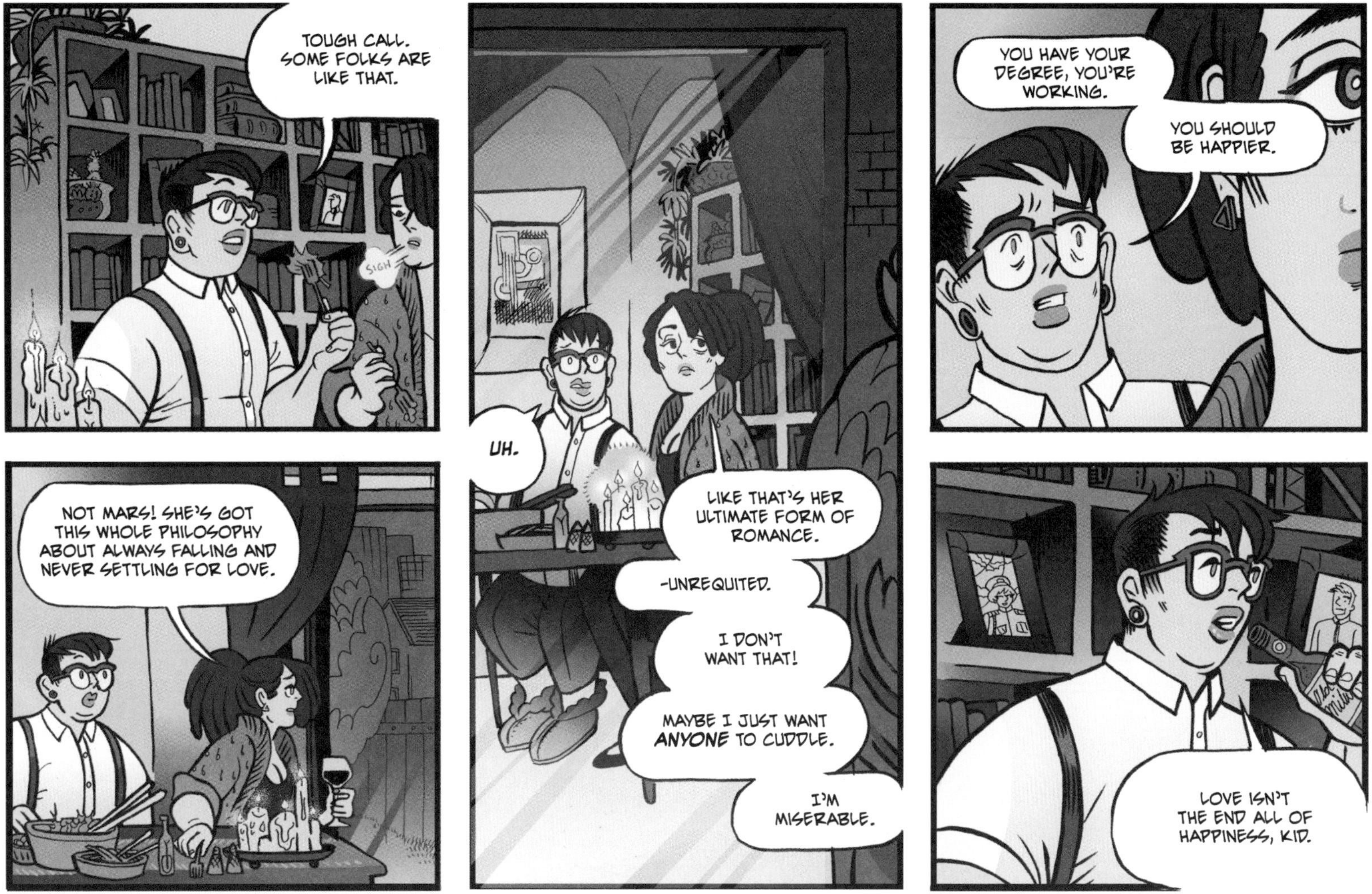
TOUGH CALL. SOME FOLKS ARE LIKE THAT.
SIGH
NOT MARS! SHE'S GOT THIS WHOLE PHILOSOPHY ABOUT ALWAYS FALLING AND NEVER SETTLING FOR LOVE.
UH.
LIKE THAT'S HER ULTIMATE FORM OF ROMANCE.
-UNREQUITED.
I DON'T WANT THAT!
MAYBE I JUST WANT **ANYONE** TO CUDDLE.
I'M MISERABLE.
YOU HAVE YOUR DEGREE, YOU'RE WORKING.
YOU SHOULD BE HAPPIER.
LOVE ISN'T THE END ALL OF HAPPINESS, KID.

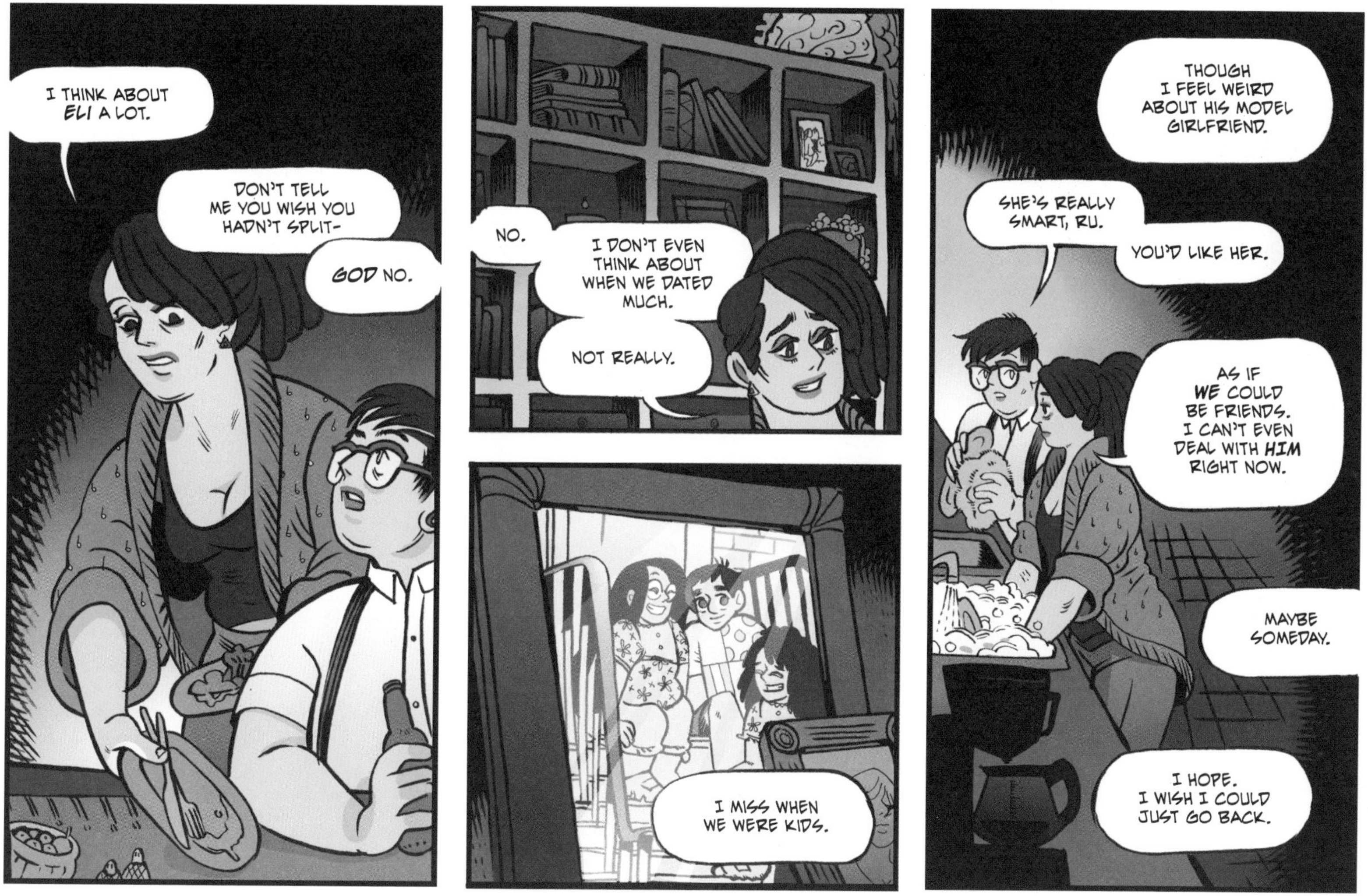
I THINK ABOUT ELI A LOT.
DON'T TELL ME YOU WISH YOU HADN'T SPLIT-
GOD NO.
NO.
I DON'T EVEN THINK ABOUT WHEN WE DATED MUCH.
NOT REALLY.
I MISS WHEN WE WERE KIDS.
THOUGH I FEEL WEIRD ABOUT HIS MODEL GIRLFRIEND.
SHE'S REALLY SMART, RU.
YOU'D LIKE HER.
AS IF WE COULD BE FRIENDS. I CAN'T EVEN DEAL WITH HIM RIGHT NOW.
MAYBE SOMEDAY.
I HOPE. I WISH I COULD JUST GO BACK.

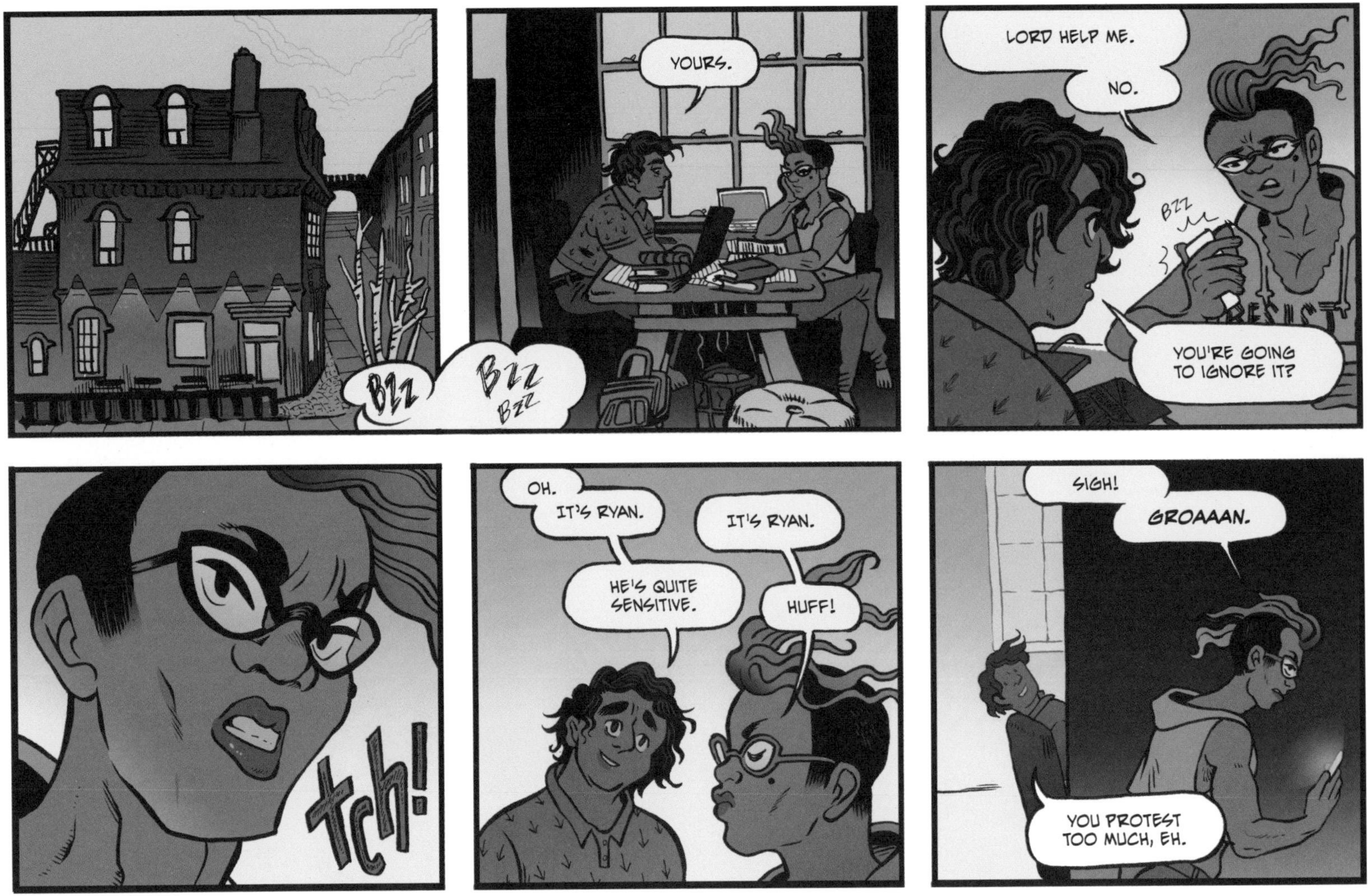
BZZ
BZZ
BZZ
YOURS.
LORD HELP ME.
NO.
BZZ
YOU'RE GOING TO IGNORE IT?
tch!
OH.
IT'S RYAN.
IT'S RYAN.
HE'S QUITE SENSITIVE.
HUFF!
SIGH!
GROAAAN.
YOU PROTEST TOO MUCH, EH.

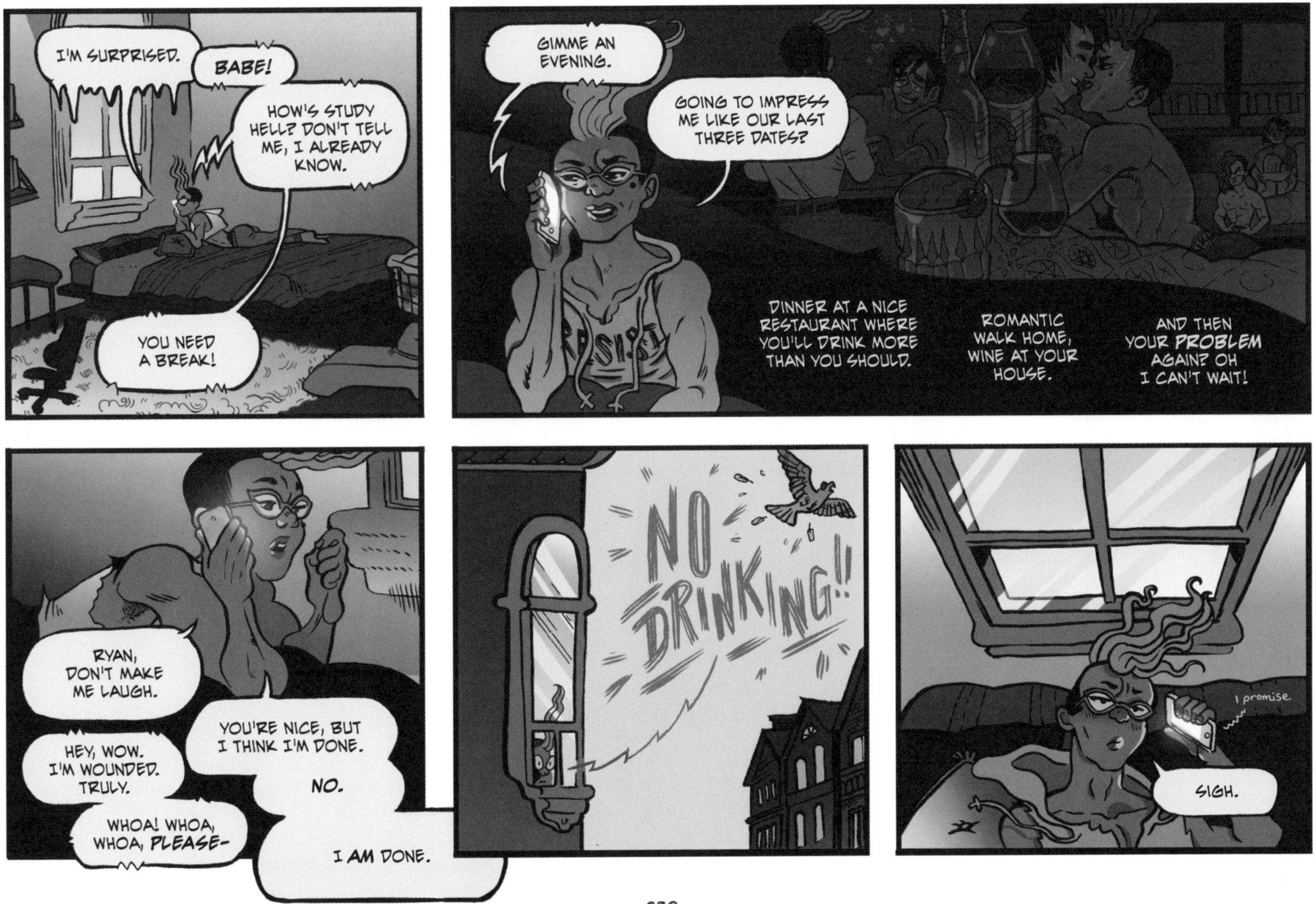
I'M SURPRISED.
BABE!
HOW'S STUDY HELL? DON'T TELL ME, I ALREADY KNOW.
YOU NEED A BREAK!
GIMME AN EVENING.
GOING TO IMPRESS ME LIKE OUR LAST THREE DATES?
DINNER AT A NICE RESTAURANT WHERE YOU'LL DRINK MORE THAN YOU SHOULD.
ROMANTIC WALK HOME, WINE AT YOUR HOUSE.
AND THEN YOUR **PROBLEM** AGAIN? OH I CAN'T WAIT!
RYAN, DON'T MAKE ME LAUGH.
HEY, WOW. I'M WOUNDED. TRULY.
YOU'RE NICE, BUT I THINK I'M DONE.
WHOA! WHOA, WHOA, **PLEASE-**
NO.
I **AM** DONE.
NO DRINKING!!
I promise
SIGH.

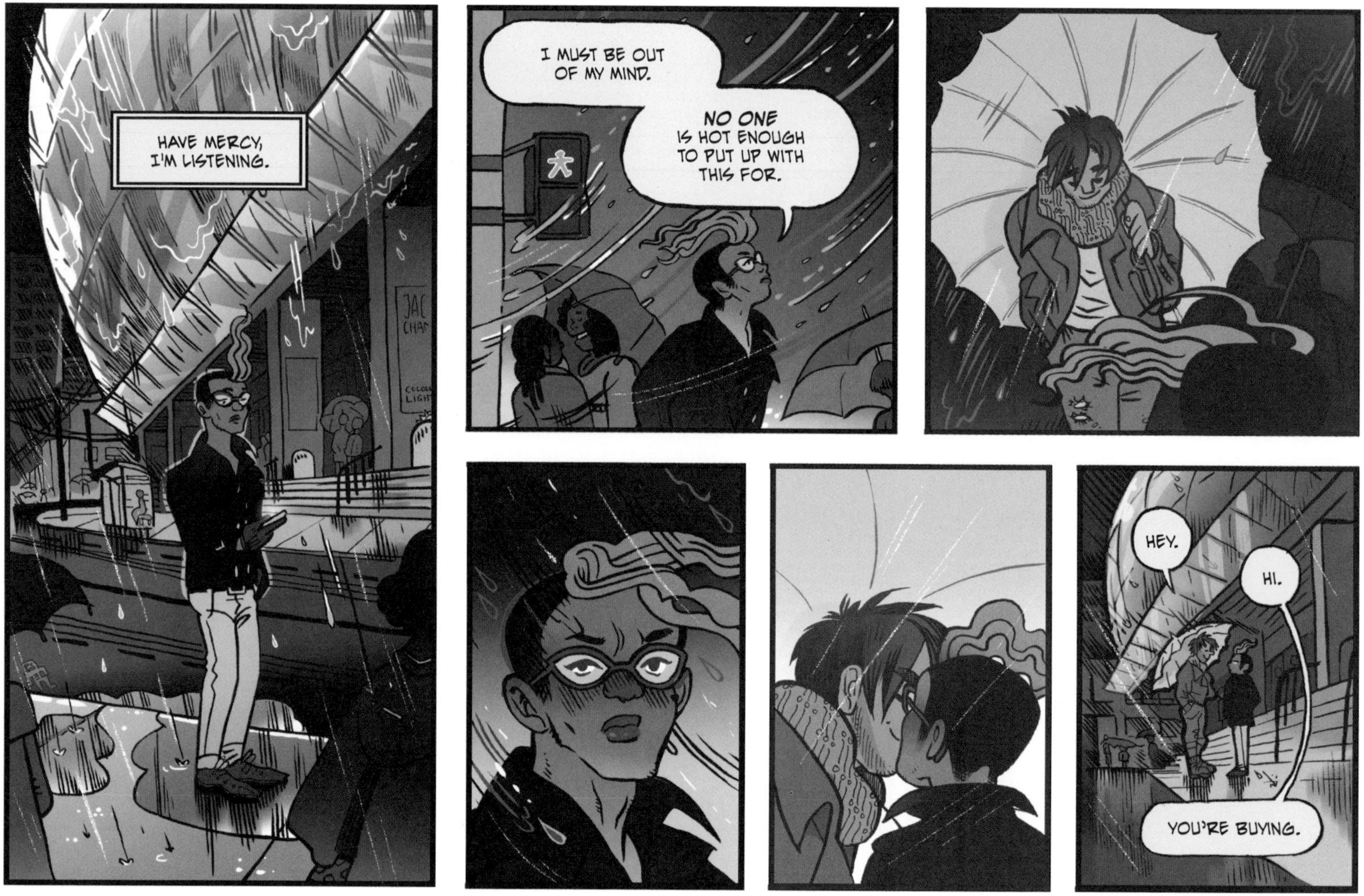
HAVE MERCY, I'M LISTENING.
I MUST BE OUT OF MY MIND.
NO ONE IS HOT ENOUGH TO PUT UP WITH THIS FOR.
HEY.
HI.
YOU'RE BUYING.

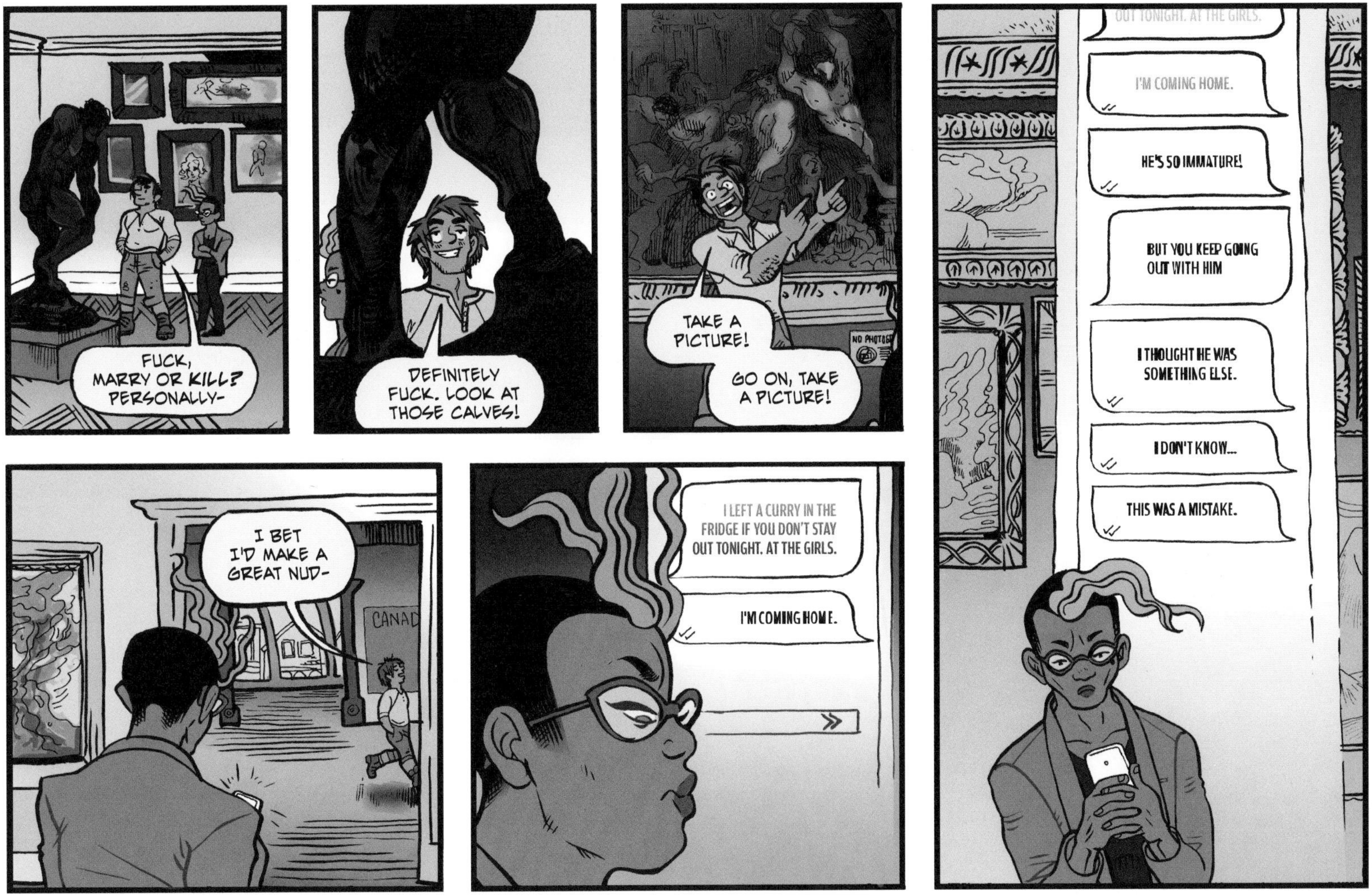
FUCK, MARRY OR KILL? PERSONALLY-
DEFINITELY FUCK. LOOK AT THOSE CALVES!
TAKE A PICTURE!
NO PHOTOG
GO ON, TAKE A PICTURE!
I BET I'D MAKE A GREAT NUD-
CANAD
I LEFT A CURRY IN THE FRIDGE IF YOU DON'T STAY OUT TONIGHT. AT THE GIRLS.
I'M COMING HOME.
OUT TONIGHT. AT THE GIRLS.
I'M COMING HOME.
HE'S SO IMMATURE!
BUT YOU KEEP GOING OUT WITH HIM
I THOUGHT HE WAS SOMETHING ELSE.
I DON'T KNOW...
THIS WAS A MISTAKE.

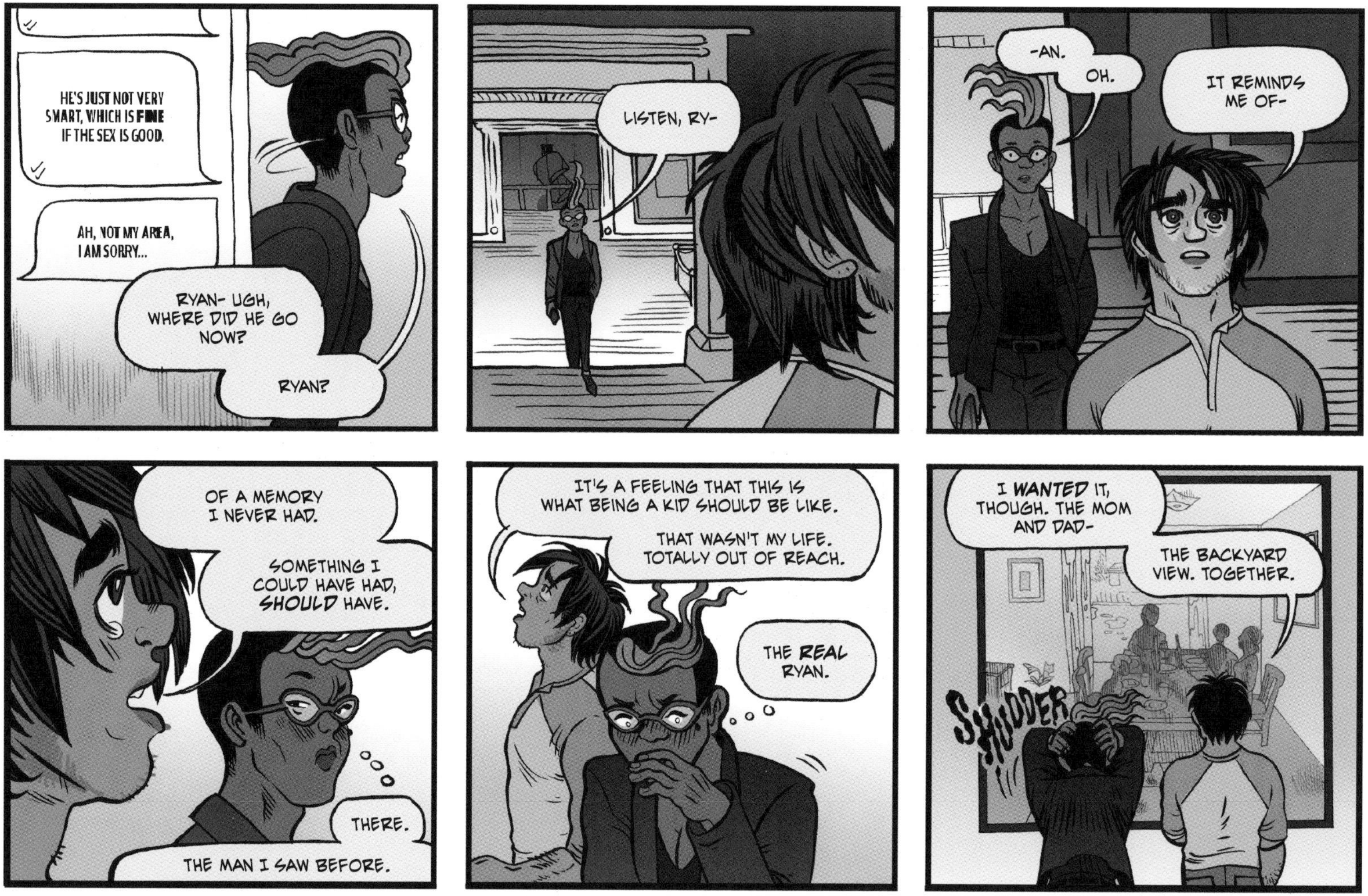
HE'S JUST NOT VERY SMART, WHICH IS FINE IF THE SEX IS GOOD.
AH, NOT MY AREA, I AM SORRY...
RYAN- UGH, WHERE DID HE GO NOW?
RYAN?
LISTEN, RY-
-AN.
OH.
IT REMINDS ME OF-
OF A MEMORY I NEVER HAD.
SOMETHING I COULD HAVE HAD, SHOULD HAVE.
THERE.
THE MAN I SAW BEFORE.
IT'S A FEELING THAT THIS IS WHAT BEING A KID SHOULD BE LIKE.
THAT WASN'T MY LIFE. TOTALLY OUT OF REACH.
THE REAL RYAN.
I WANTED IT, THOUGH. THE MOM AND DAD-
THE BACKYARD VIEW. TOGETHER.
SHUDDER

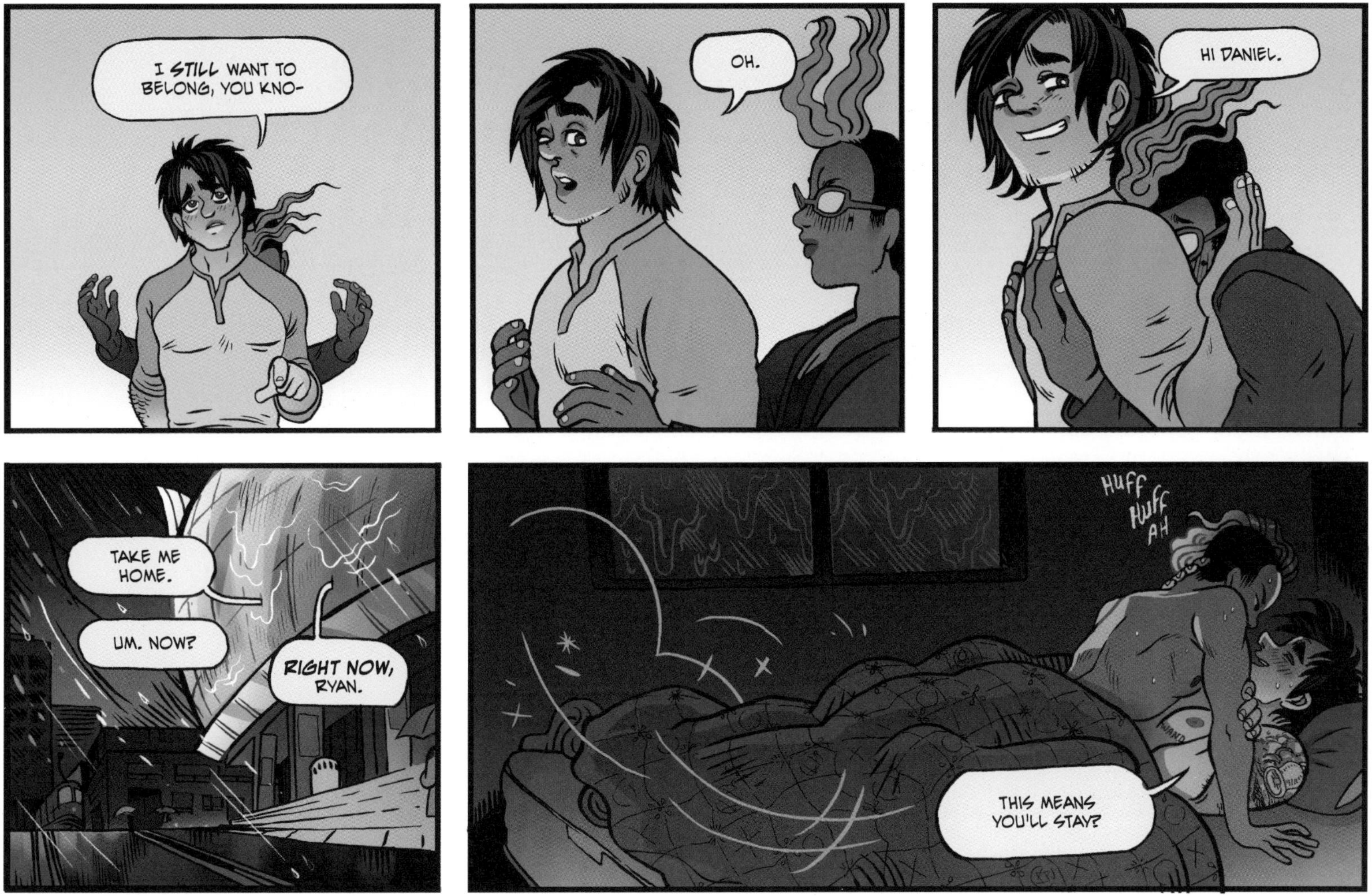
I STILL WANT TO BELONG, YOU KNO-
OH.
HI DANIEL.
TAKE ME HOME.
UM. NOW?
RIGHT NOW, RYAN.
HUFF HUFF AH
THIS MEANS YOU'LL STAY?

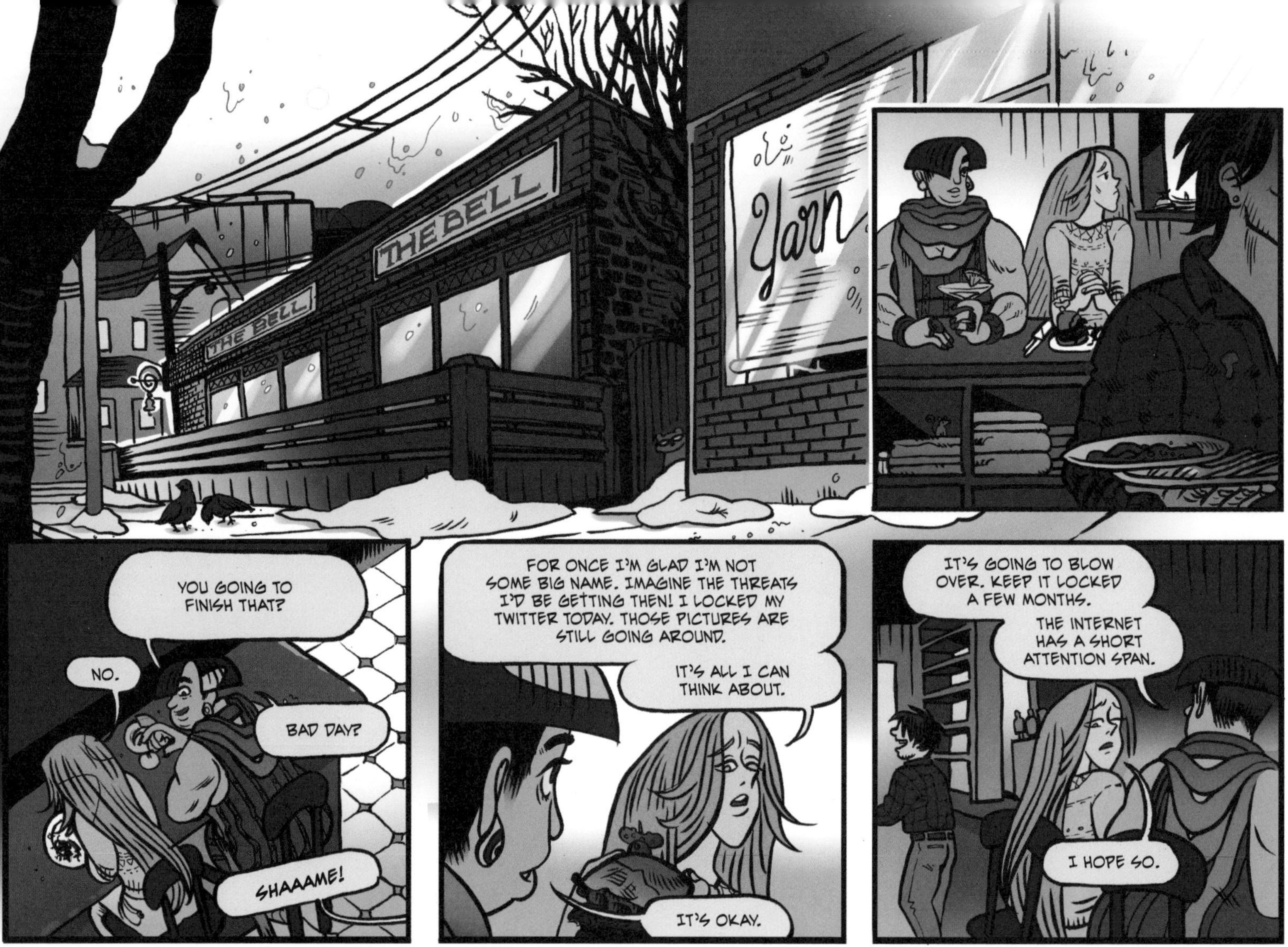
THE BELL
THE BELL
Yarn
YOU GOING TO FINISH THAT?
NO.
BAD DAY?
SHAAAME!
FOR ONCE I'M GLAD I'M NOT SOME BIG NAME. IMAGINE THE THREATS I'D BE GETTING THEN! I LOCKED MY TWITTER TODAY. THOSE PICTURES ARE STILL GOING AROUND.
IT'S ALL I CAN THINK ABOUT.
IT'S OKAY.
IT'S GOING TO BLOW OVER. KEEP IT LOCKED A FEW MONTHS.
THE INTERNET HAS A SHORT ATTENTION SPAN.
I HOPE SO.

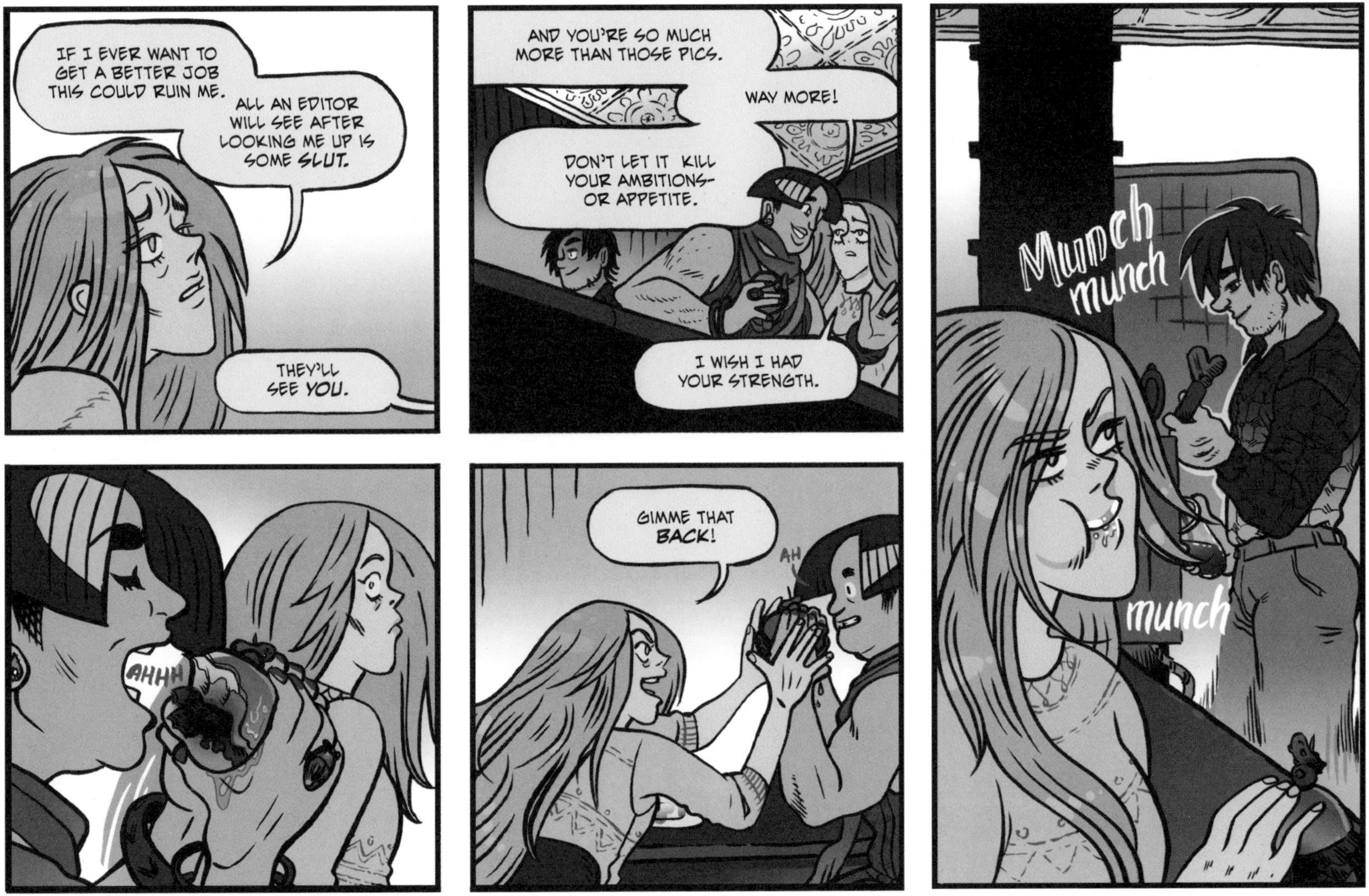
IF I EVER WANT TO GET A BETTER JOB THIS COULD RUIN ME.
ALL AN EDITOR WILL SEE AFTER LOOKING ME UP IS SOME SLUT.
THEY'LL SEE YOU.
AND YOU'RE SO MUCH MORE THAN THOSE PICS.
WAY MORE!
DON'T LET IT KILL YOUR AMBITIONS- OR APPETITE.
I WISH I HAD YOUR STRENGTH.
Munch munch
munch
AHHH
GIMME THAT BACK!
AH

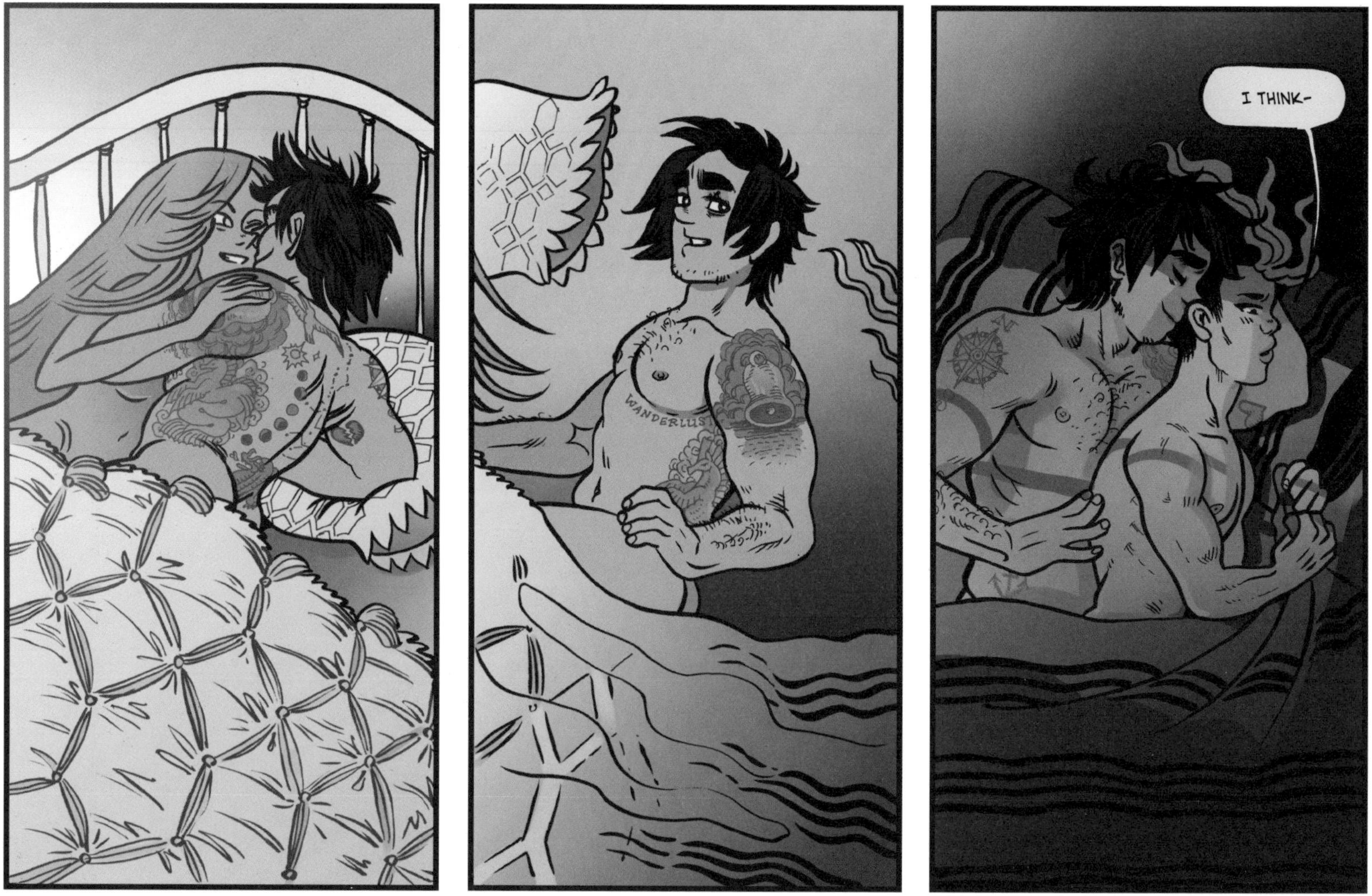
WANDERLUST
I THINK-

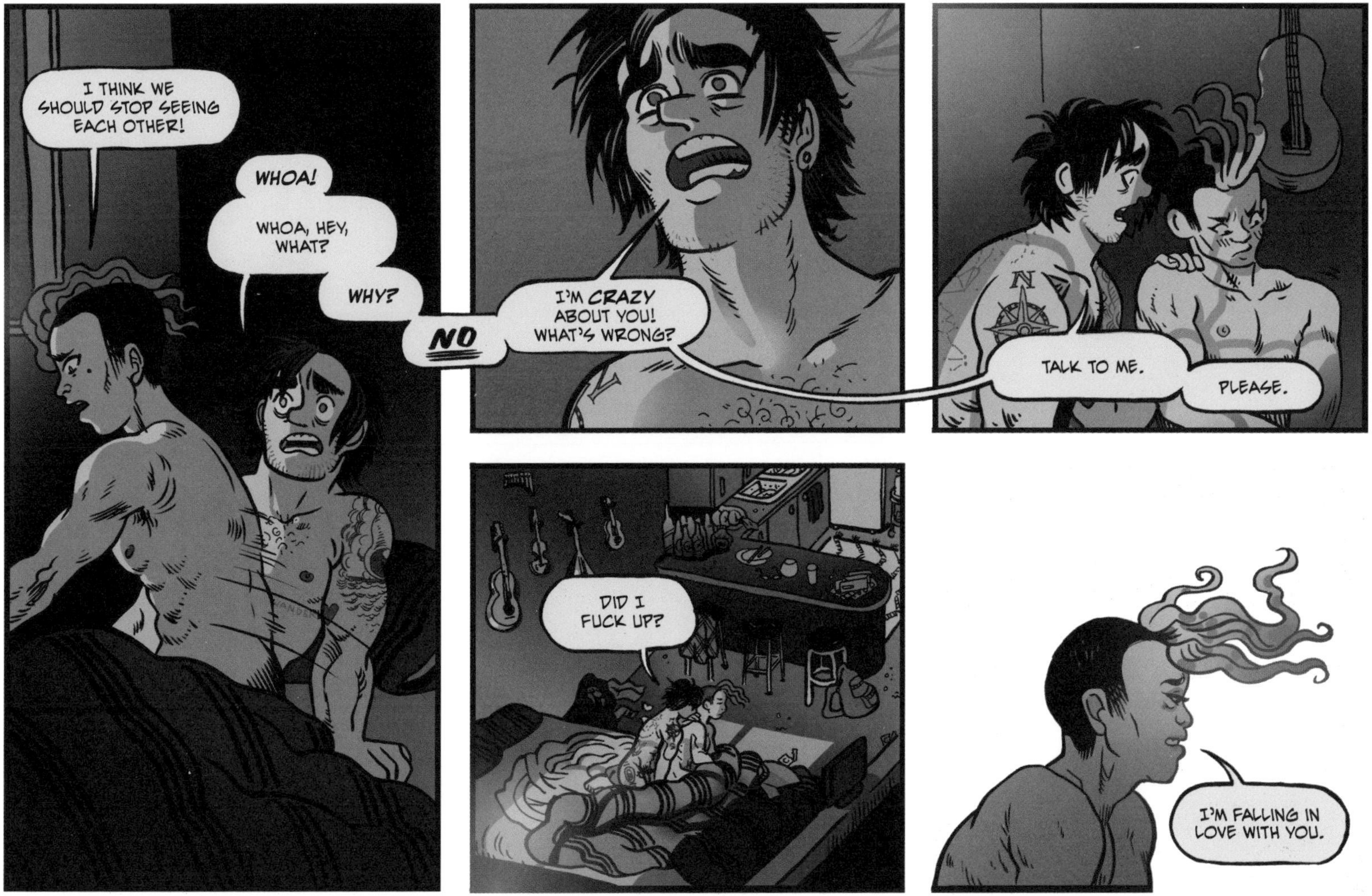

I THINK WE SHOULD STOP SEEING EACH OTHER!
WHOA!
WHOA, HEY, WHAT?
WHY?
NO
I'M CRAZY ABOUT YOU! WHAT'S WRONG?
TALK TO ME.
PLEASE.
DID I FUCK UP?
I'M FALLING IN LOVE WITH YOU.

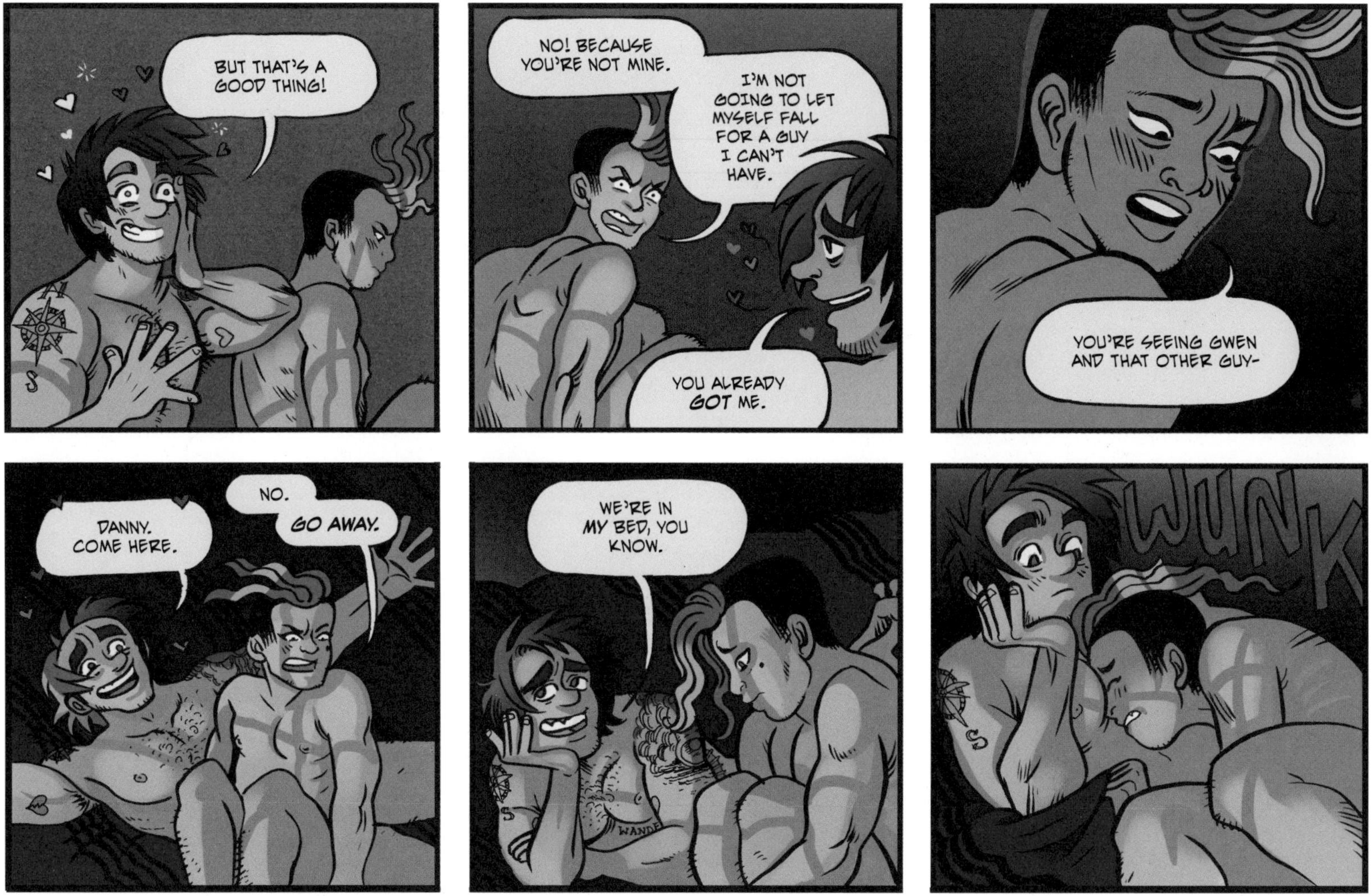
BUT THAT'S A GOOD THING!
NO! BECAUSE YOU'RE NOT MINE.
I'M NOT GOING TO LET MYSELF FALL FOR A GUY I CAN'T HAVE.
YOU ALREADY **GOT** ME.
YOU'RE SEEING GWEN AND THAT OTHER GUY-
DANNY. COME HERE.
NO.
GO AWAY.
WE'RE IN *MY BED*, YOU KNOW.
WUNK

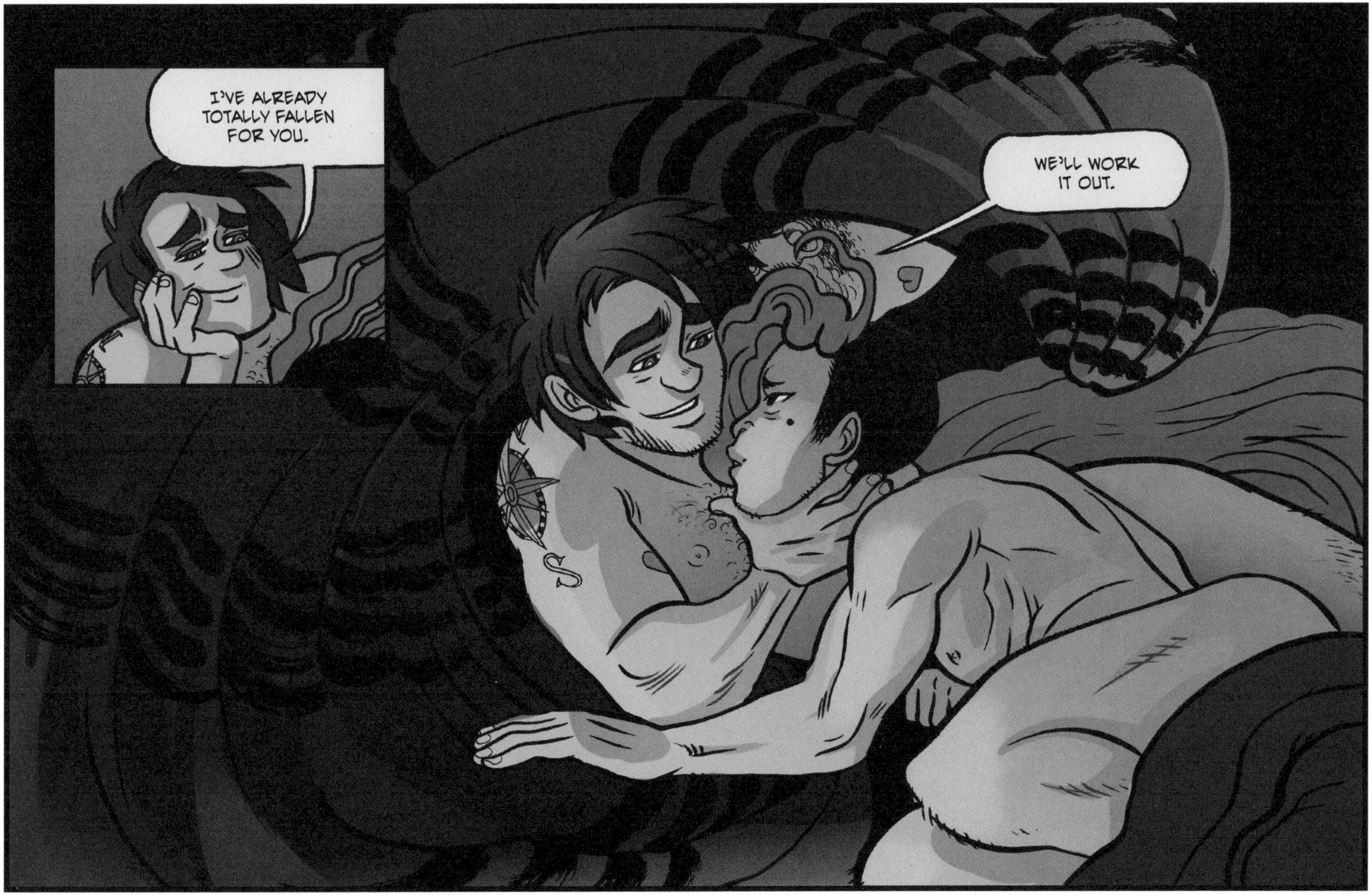
I'VE ALREADY TOTALLY FALLEN FOR YOU.
WE'LL WORK IT OUT.

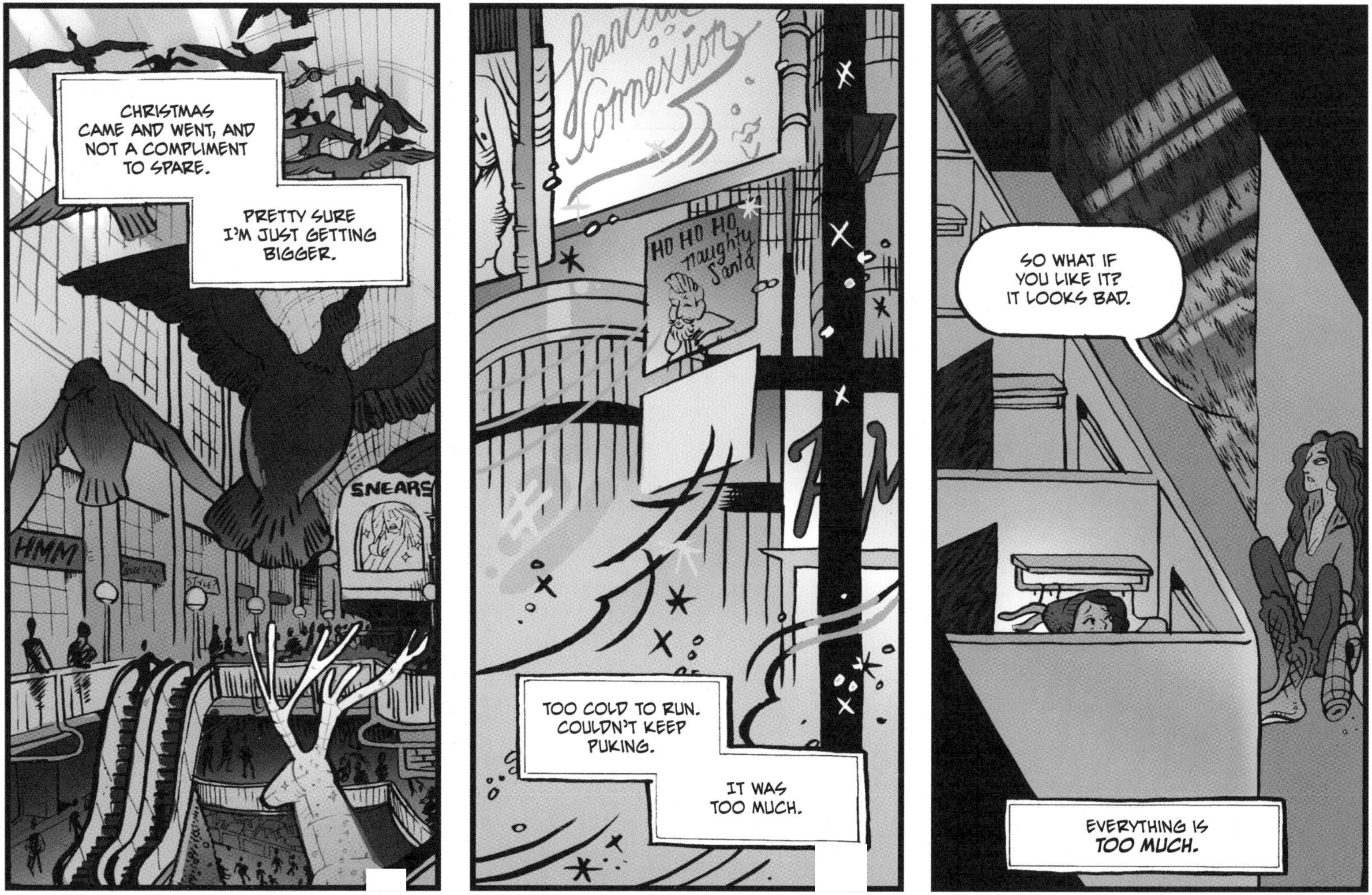
CHRISTMAS CAME AND WENT, AND NOT A COMPLIMENT TO SPARE.
PRETTY SURE I'M JUST GETTING BIGGER.
SNEARS
HMM
HO HO HO naughty Santa
TOO COLD TO RUN. COULDN'T KEEP PUKING.
IT WAS TOO MUCH.
SO WHAT IF YOU LIKE IT? IT LOOKS BAD.
EVERYTHING IS *TOO MUCH.*

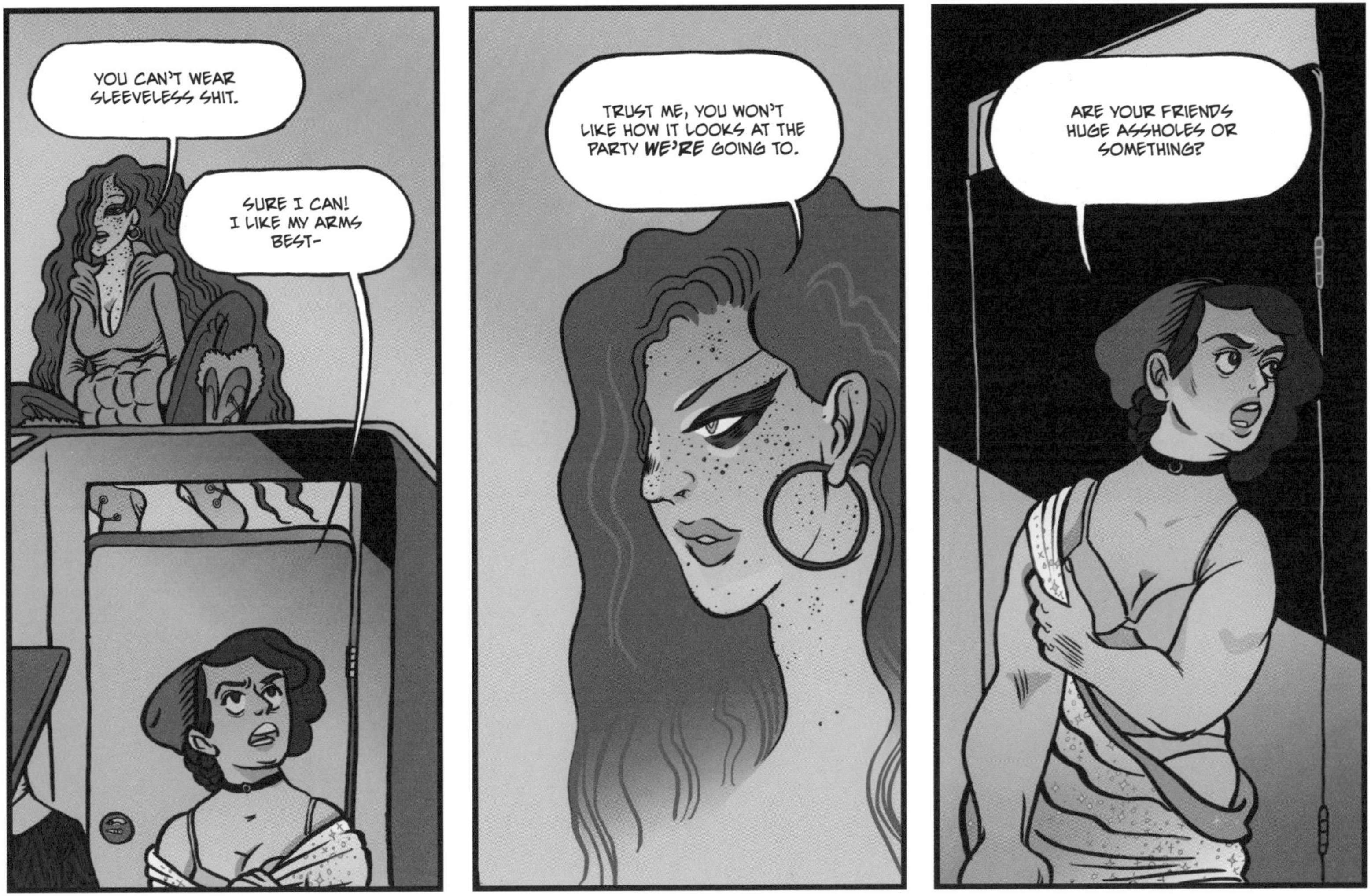
YOU CAN'T WEAR SLEEVELESS SHIT.
SURE I CAN! I LIKE MY ARMS BEST-
TRUST ME, YOU WON'T LIKE HOW IT LOOKS AT THE PARTY **WE'RE** GOING TO.
ARE YOUR FRIENDS HUGE ASSHOLES OR SOMETHING?

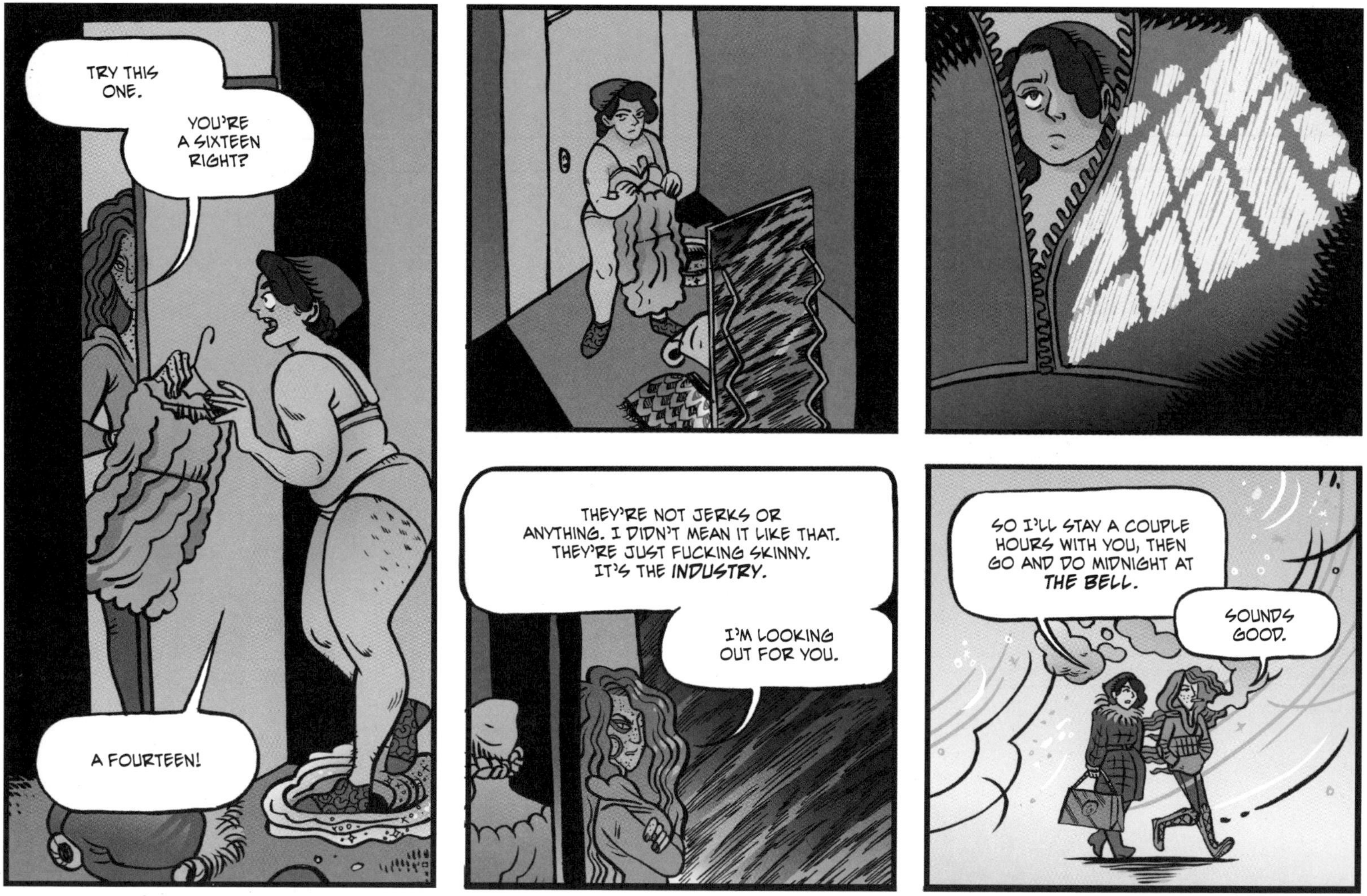
TRY THIS ONE.
YOU'RE A SIXTEEN RIGHT?
A FOURTEEN!
THEY'RE NOT JERKS OR ANYTHING. I DIDN'T MEAN IT LIKE THAT. THEY'RE JUST FUCKING SKINNY. IT'S THE INDUSTRY.
I'M LOOKING OUT FOR YOU.
SO I'LL STAY A COUPLE HOURS WITH YOU, THEN GO AND DO MIDNIGHT AT THE BELL.
SOUNDS GOOD.

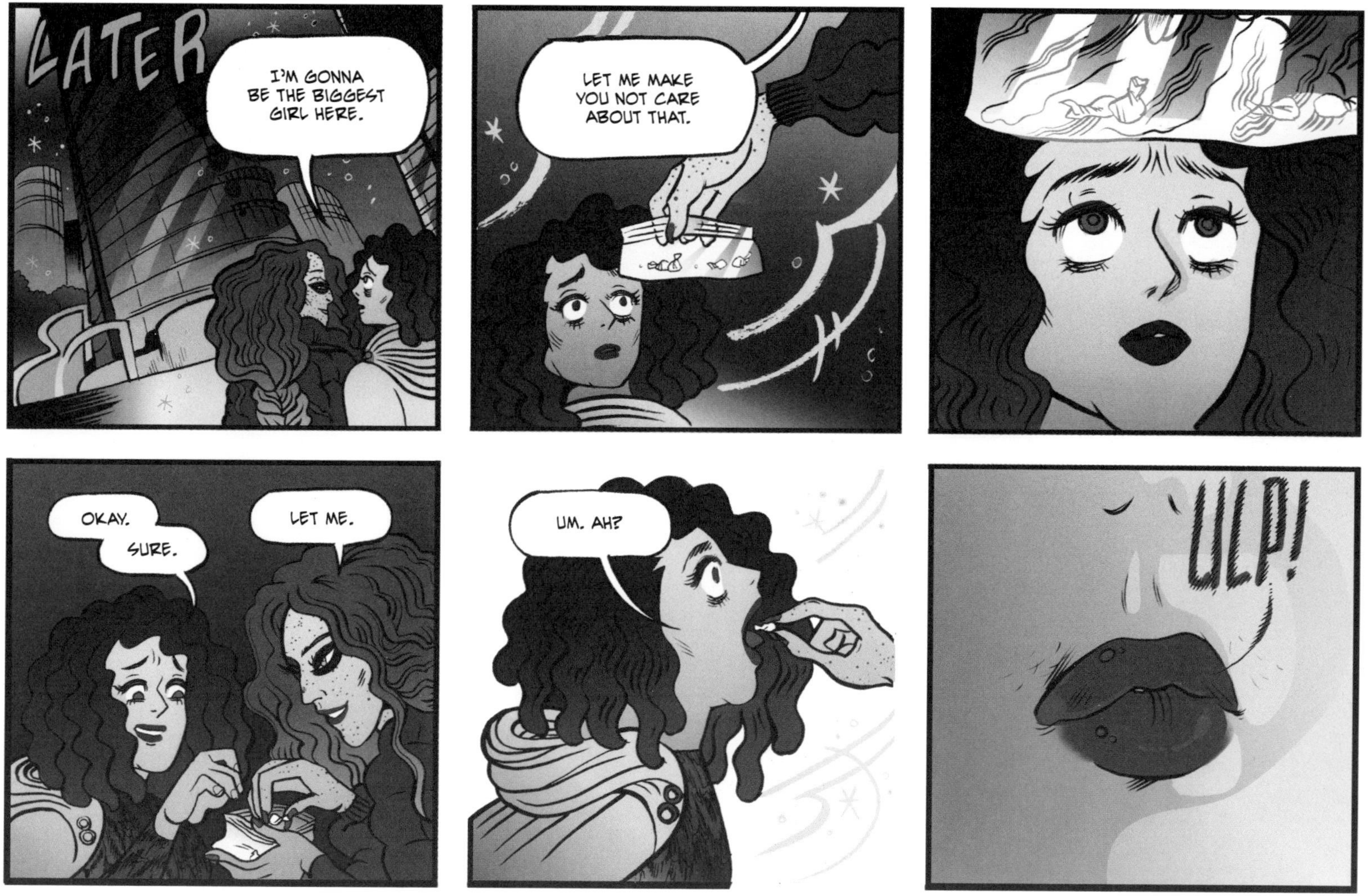
LATER
I'M GONNA BE THE BIGGEST GIRL HERE.
LET ME MAKE YOU NOT CARE ABOUT THAT.
OKAY.
SURE.
LET ME.
UM. AH?
ULP!

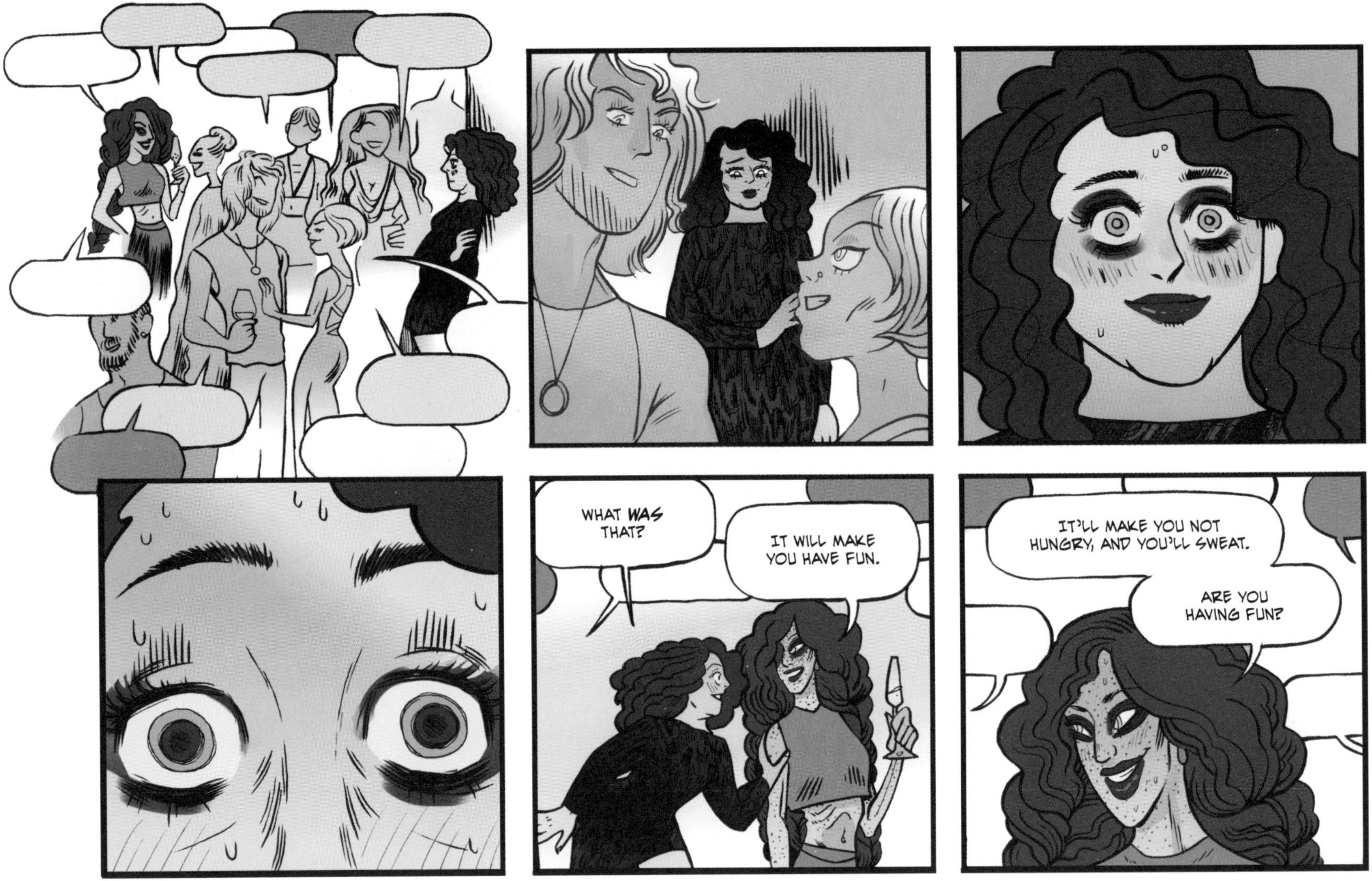
WHAT WAS THAT?
IT WILL MAKE YOU HAVE FUN.
IT'LL MAKE YOU NOT HUNGRY, AND YOU'LL SWEAT.
ARE YOU HAVING FUN?

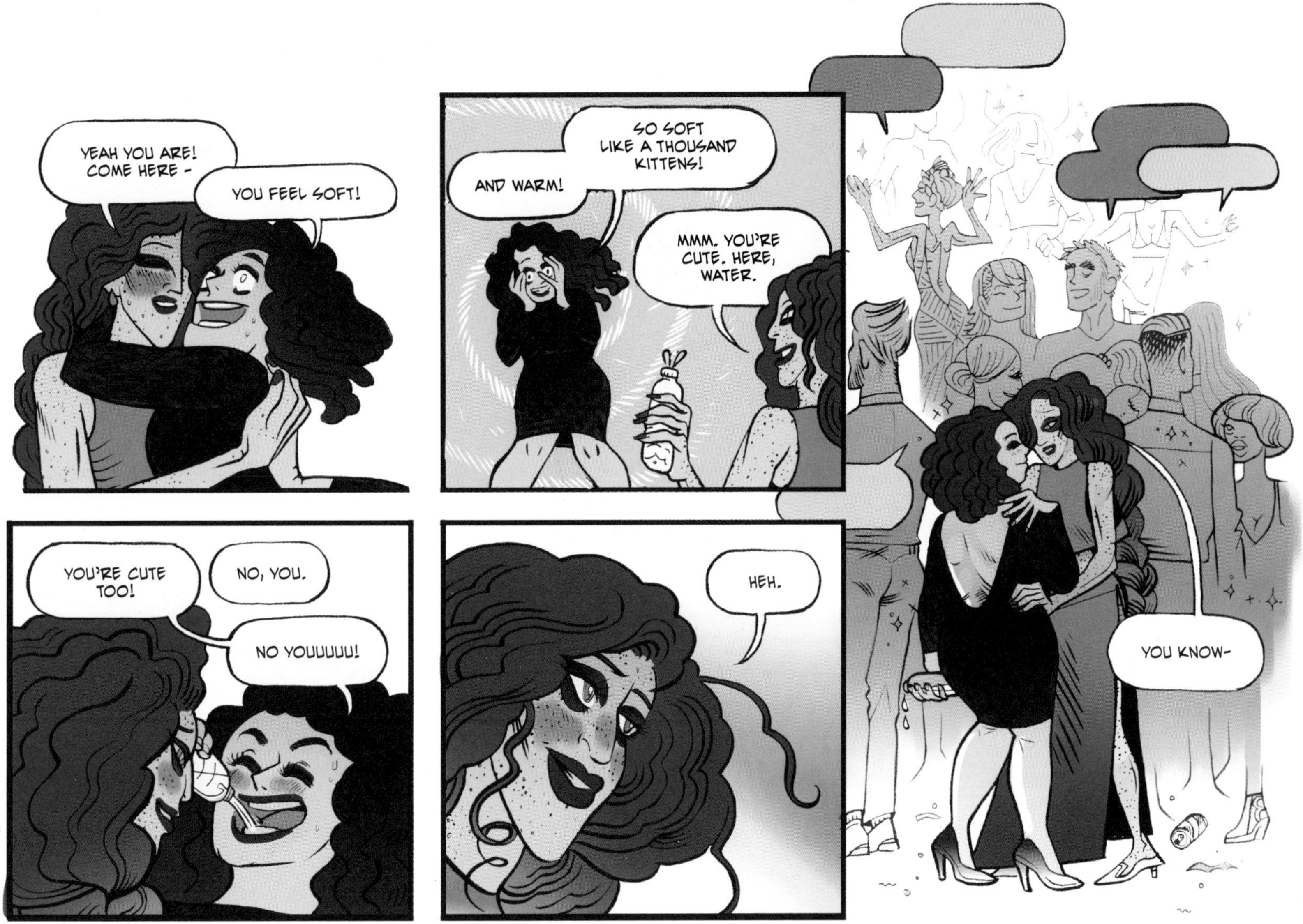
YEAH YOU ARE! COME HERE -
YOU FEEL SOFT!
AND WARM!
SO SOFT LIKE A THOUSAND KITTENS!
MMM. YOU'RE CUTE. HERE, WATER.
YOU'RE CUTE TOO!
NO, YOU.
NO YOUUUUU!
HEH.
YOU KNOW-

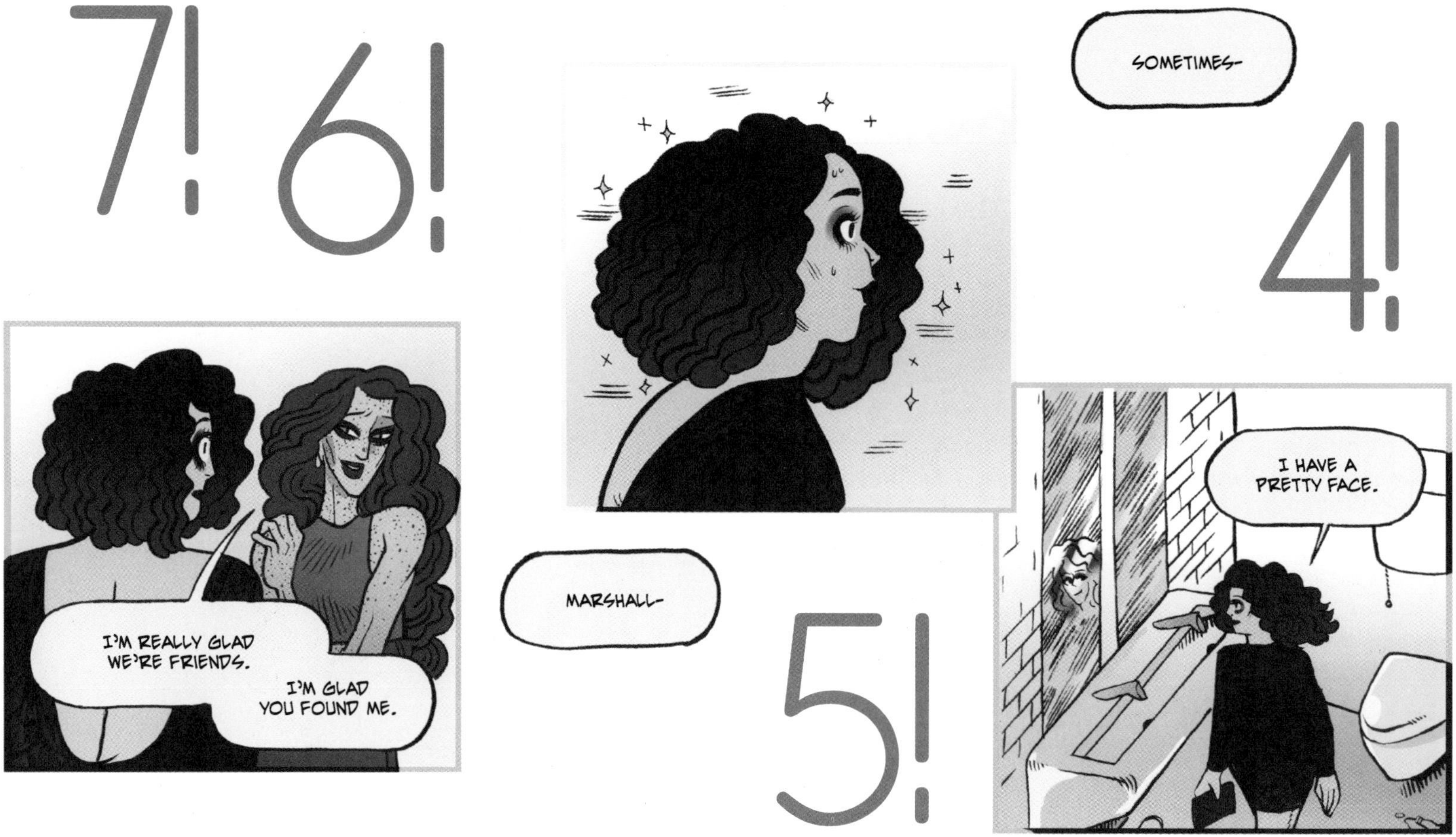
7! 6!
I'M REALLY GLAD WE'RE FRIENDS.
I'M GLAD YOU FOUND ME.
MARSHALL-
5!
SOMETIMES-
4!
I HAVE A PRETTY FACE.

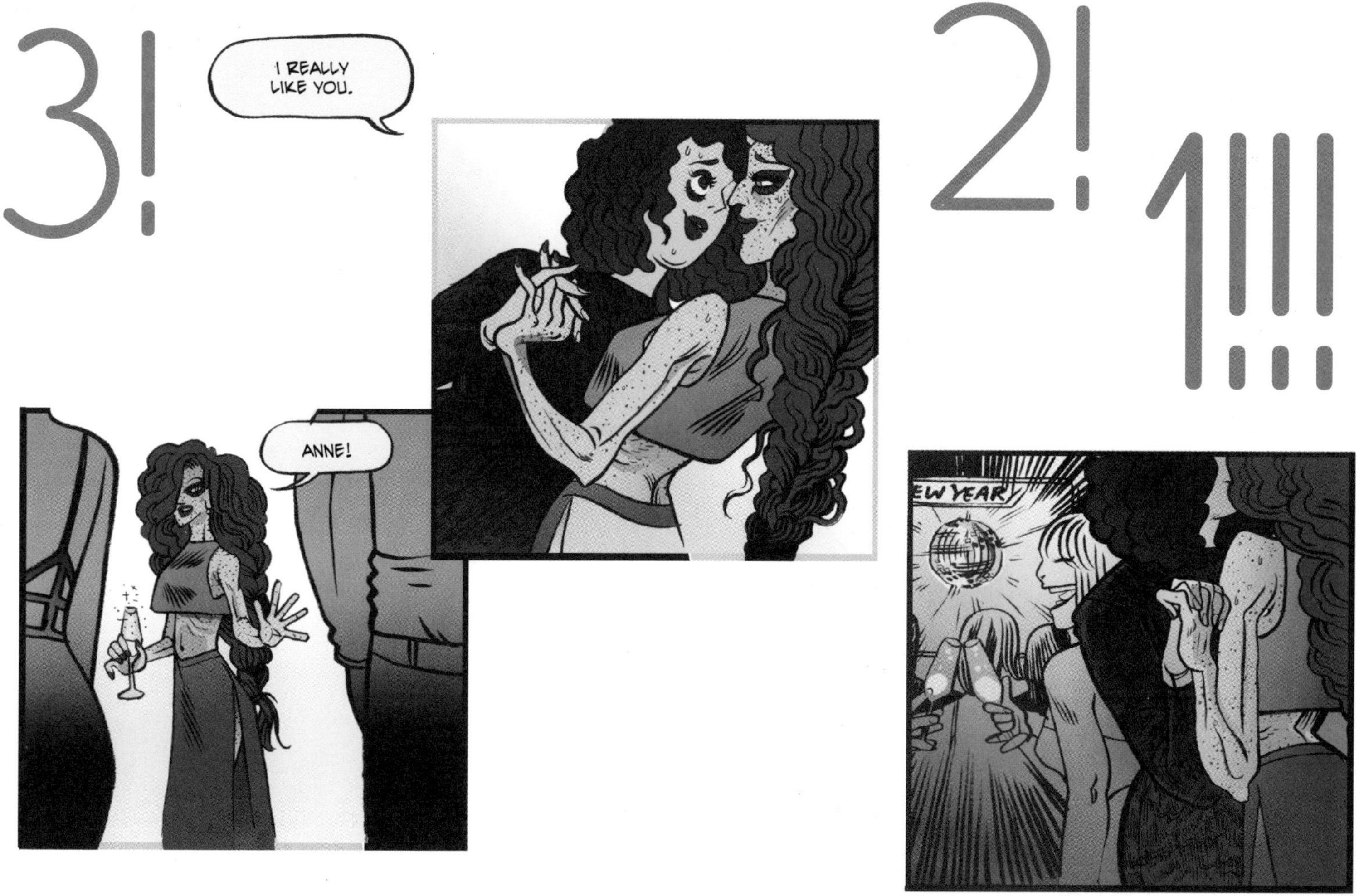
3!
I REALLY LIKE YOU.
ANNE!
2!
1!!!!
NEW YEAR

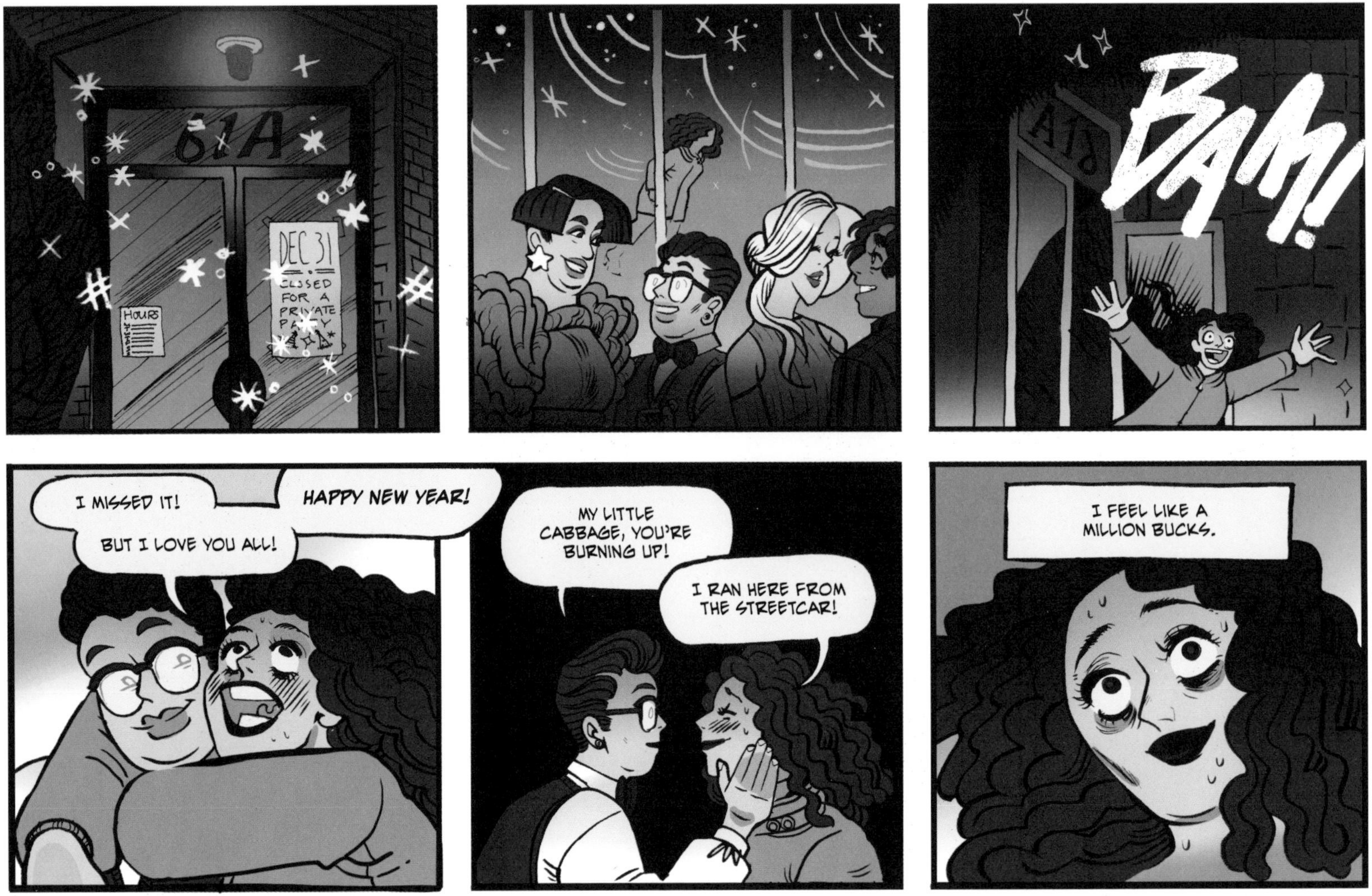
61A
HOURS
DEC 31
CLOSED FOR A PRIVATE
BAM!
I MISSED IT!
BUT I LOVE YOU ALL!
HAPPY NEW YEAR!
MY LITTLE CABBAGE, YOU'RE BURNING UP!
I RAN HERE FROM THE STREETCAR!
I FEEL LIKE A MILLION BUCKS.

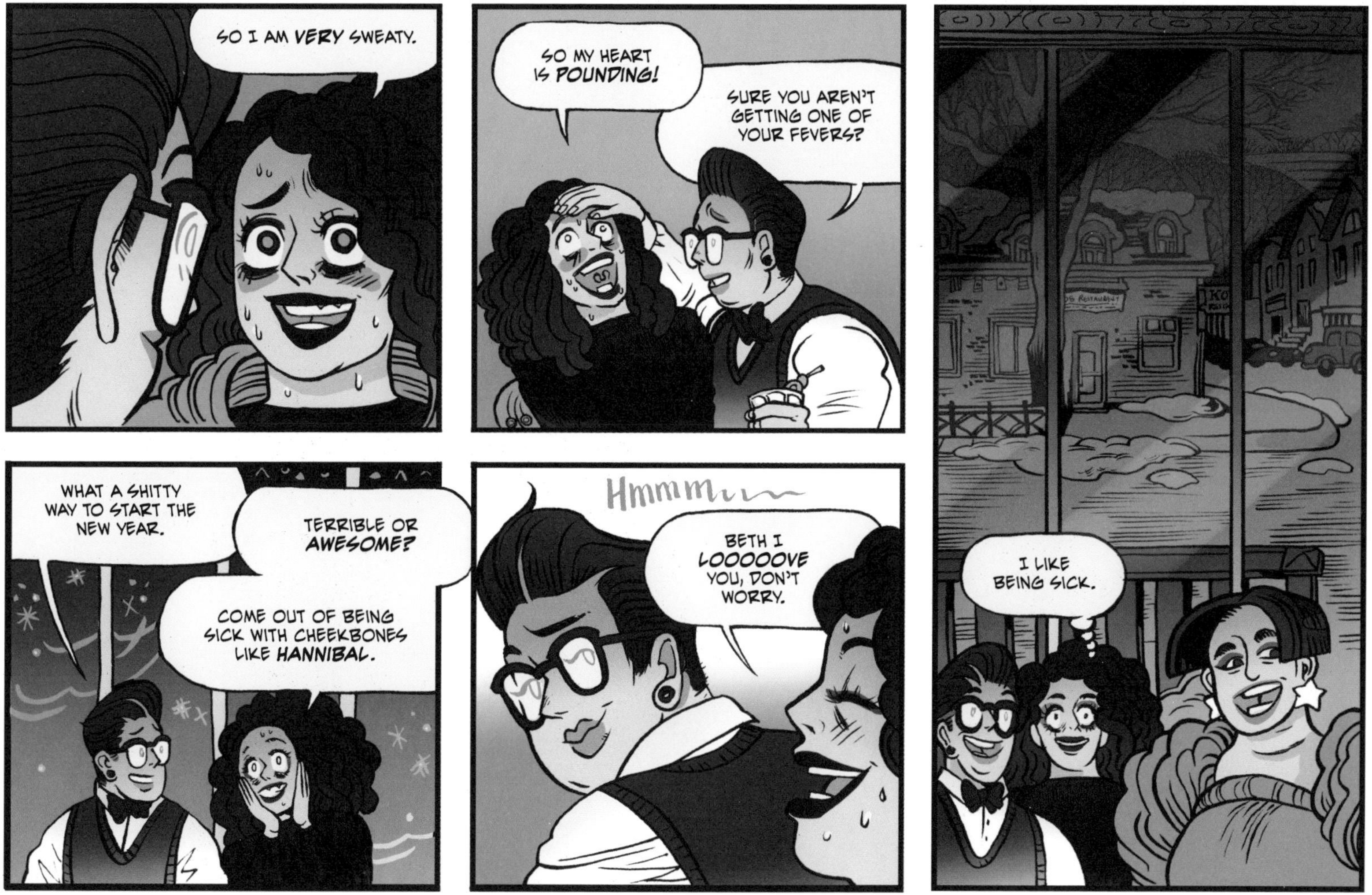
SO I AM **VERY** SWEATY.
SO MY HEART IS **POUNDING!**
SURE YOU AREN'T GETTING ONE OF YOUR FEVERS?
WHAT A SHITTY WAY TO START THE NEW YEAR.
TERRIBLE OR **AWESOME?**
COME OUT OF BEING SICK WITH CHEEKBONES LIKE **HANNIBAL.**
Hmmm
BETH I **LOOOOOVE** YOU, DON'T WORRY.
I LIKE BEING SICK.

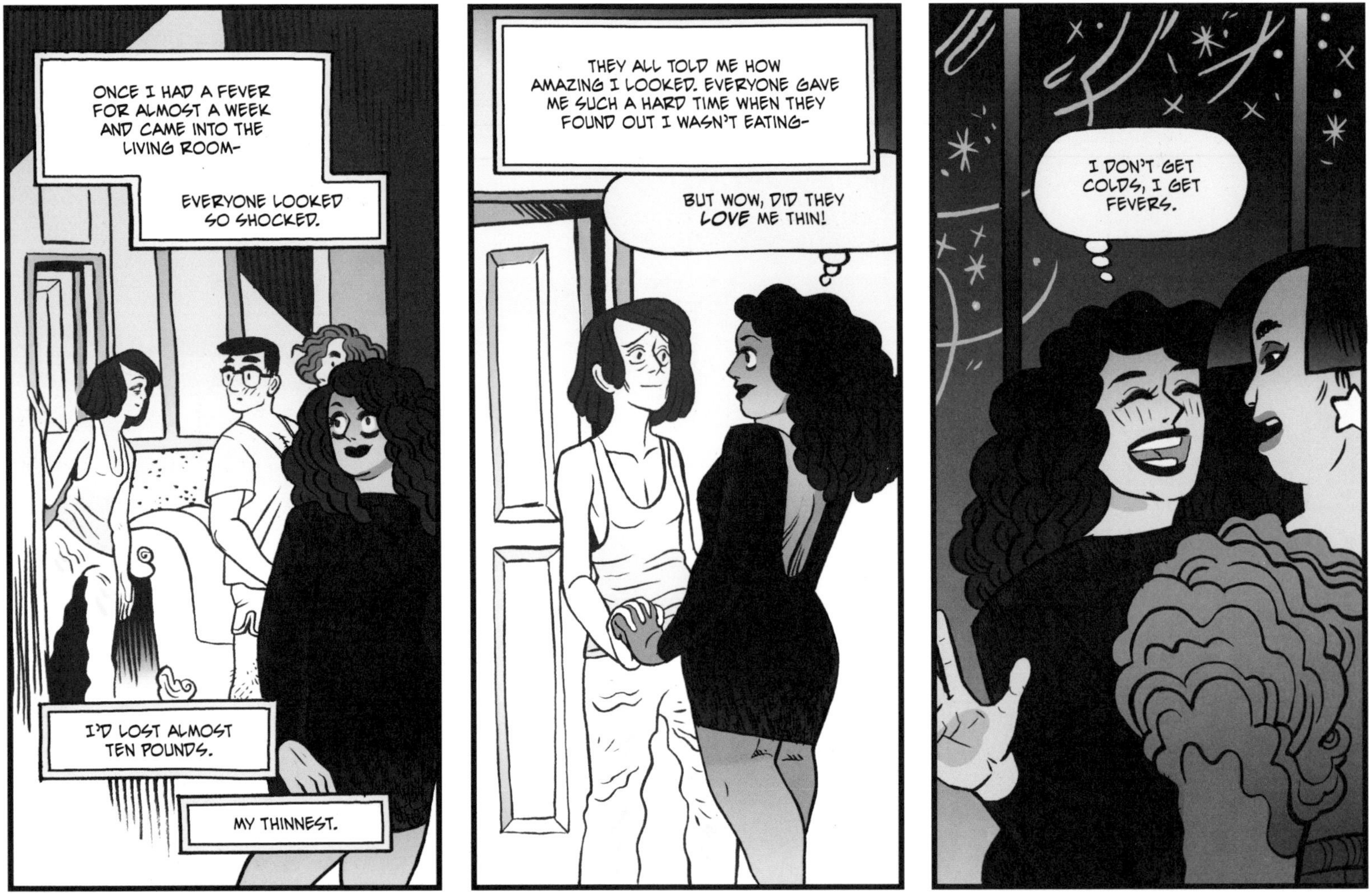
ONCE I HAD A FEVER FOR ALMOST A WEEK AND CAME INTO THE LIVING ROOM-
EVERYONE LOOKED SO SHOCKED.
I'D LOST ALMOST TEN POUNDS.
MY THINNEST.
THEY ALL TOLD ME HOW AMAZING I LOOKED. EVERYONE GAVE ME SUCH A HARD TIME WHEN THEY FOUND OUT I WASN'T EATING-
BUT WOW, DID THEY *LOVE* ME THIN!
I DON'T GET COLDS, I GET FEVERS.

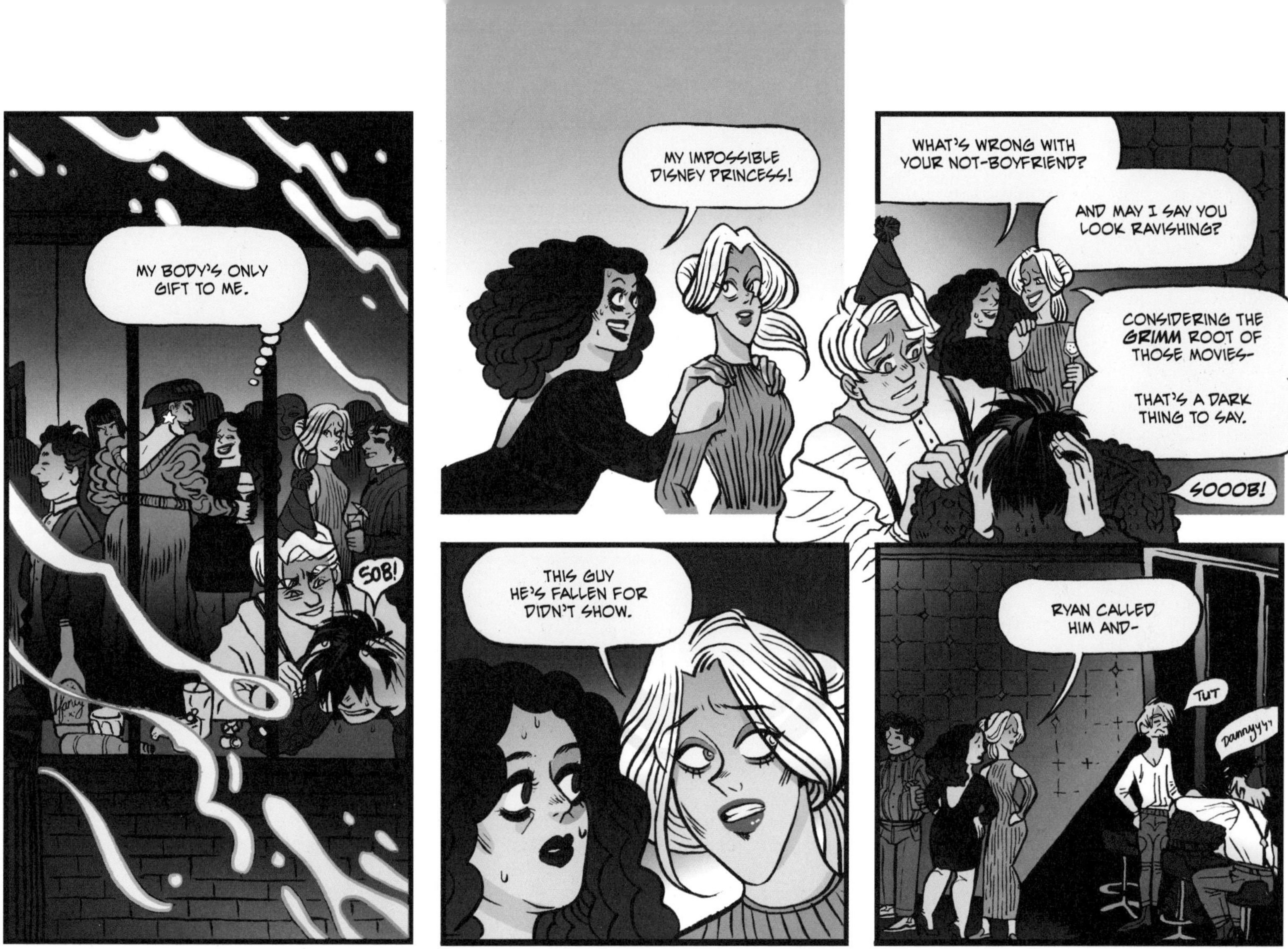

MY BODY'S ONLY GIFT TO ME.
SOB!
MY IMPOSSIBLE DISNEY PRINCESS!
WHAT'S WRONG WITH YOUR NOT-BOYFRIEND?
AND MAY I SAY YOU LOOK RAVISHING?
CONSIDERING THE **GRIMM** ROOT OF THOSE MOVIES-
THAT'S A DARK THING TO SAY.
SOOOB!
THIS GUY HE'S FALLEN FOR DIDN'T SHOW.
RYAN CALLED HIM AND-
TUT
Dannyyy

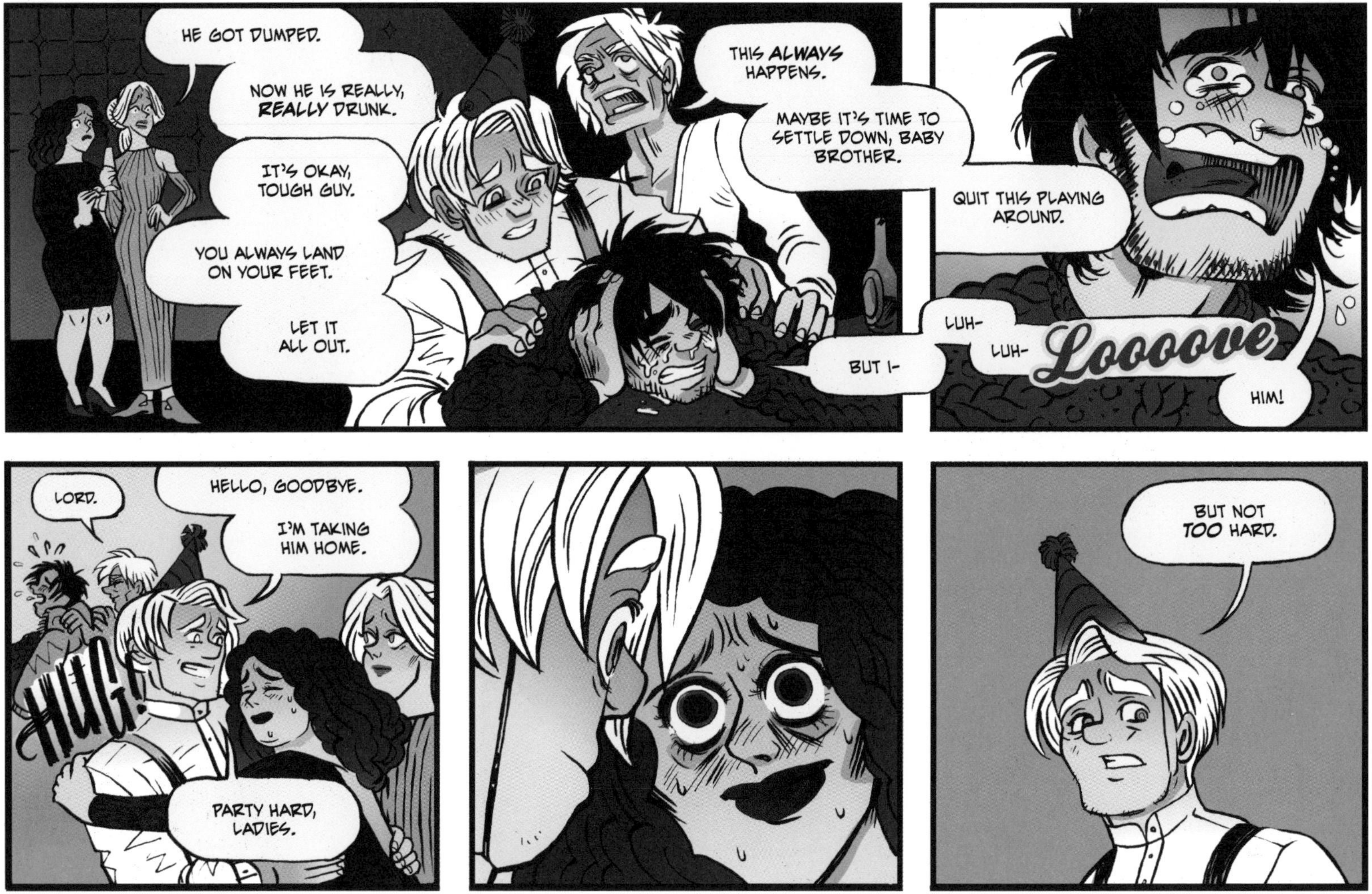

HE GOT DUMPED.
NOW HE IS REALLY, REALLY DRUNK.
IT'S OKAY, TOUGH GUY.
YOU ALWAYS LAND ON YOUR FEET.
LET IT ALL OUT.
THIS ALWAYS HAPPENS.
MAYBE IT'S TIME TO SETTLE DOWN, BABY BROTHER.
QUIT THIS PLAYING AROUND.
BUT I-
LUH-
LUH-
Loooove
HIM!
LORD.
HELLO, GOODBYE.
I'M TAKING HIM HOME.
HUG!
PARTY HARD, LADIES.
BUT NOT TOO HARD.

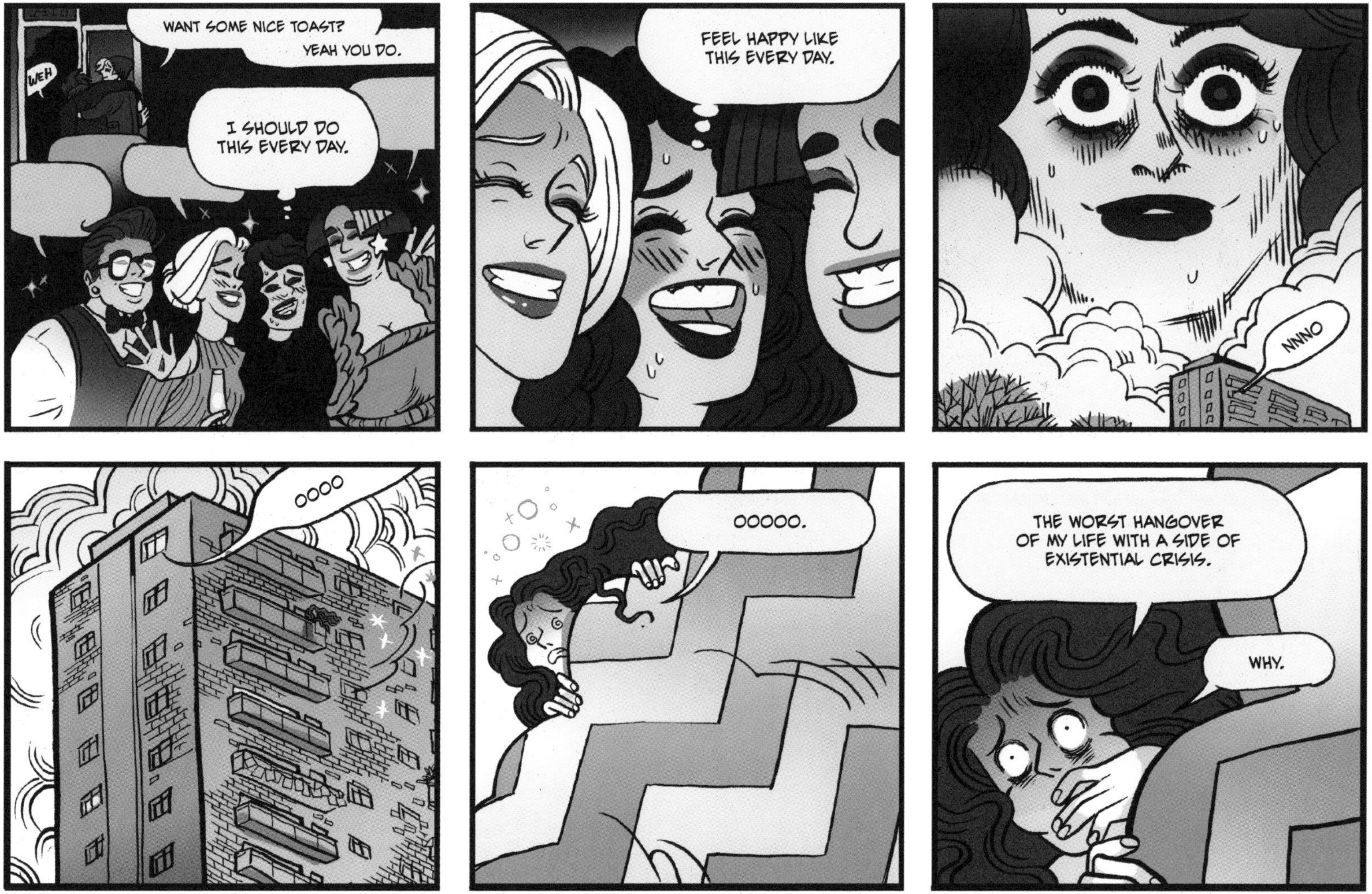
WANT SOME NICE TOAST?
YEAH YOU DO.
WEH
I SHOULD DO THIS EVERY DAY.
FEEL HAPPY LIKE THIS EVERY DAY.
NNNO
OOOO
OOOOO.
THE WORST HANGOVER OF MY LIFE WITH A SIDE OF EXISTENTIAL CRISIS.
WHY.

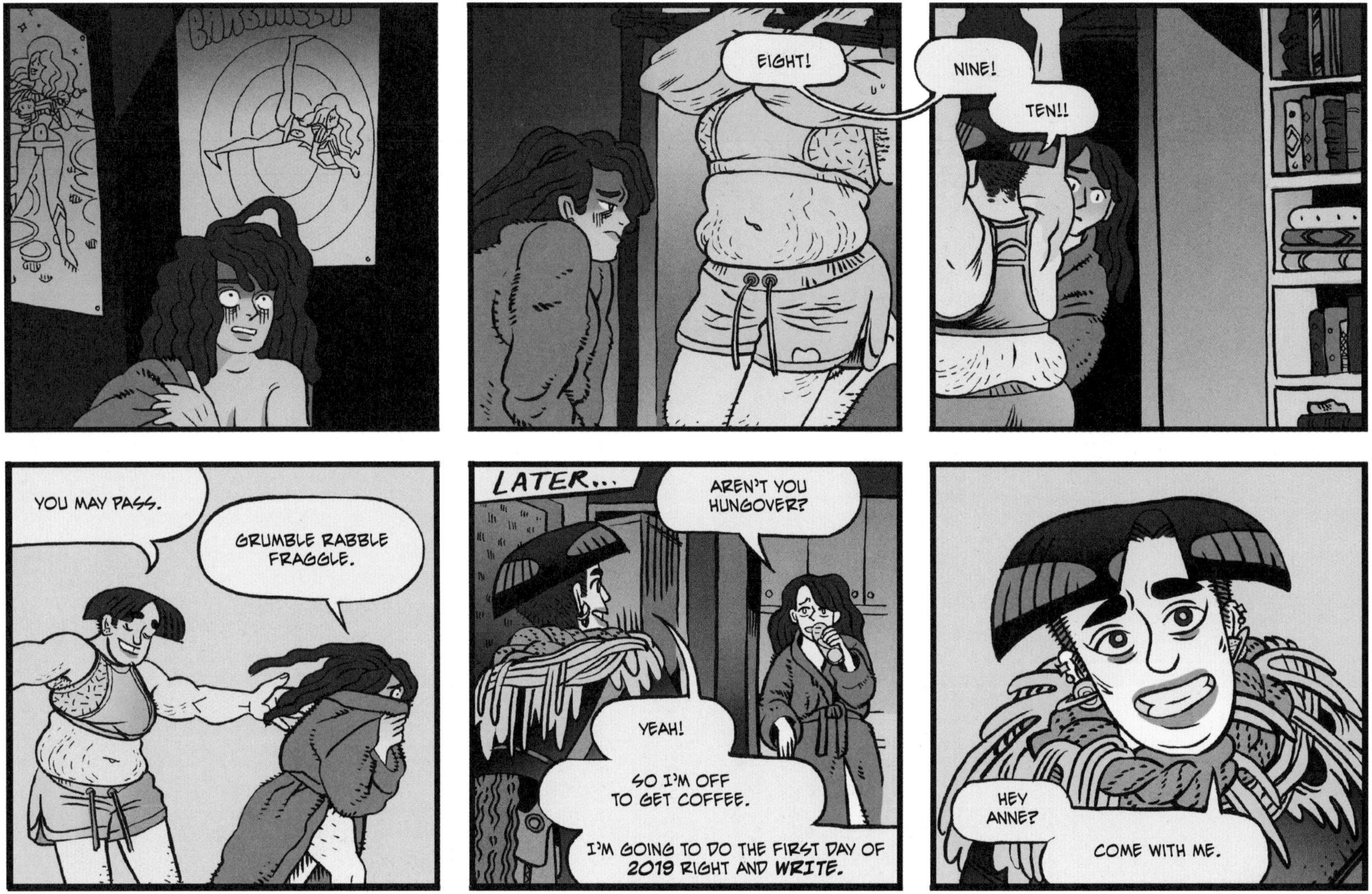
EIGHT!
NINE!
TEN!!
YOU MAY PASS.
GRUMBLE RABBLE FRAGGLE.
LATER...
AREN'T YOU HUNGOVER?
YEAH!
SO I'M OFF TO GET COFFEE.
I'M GOING TO DO THE FIRST DAY OF 2019 RIGHT AND WRITE.
HEY ANNE?
COME WITH ME.

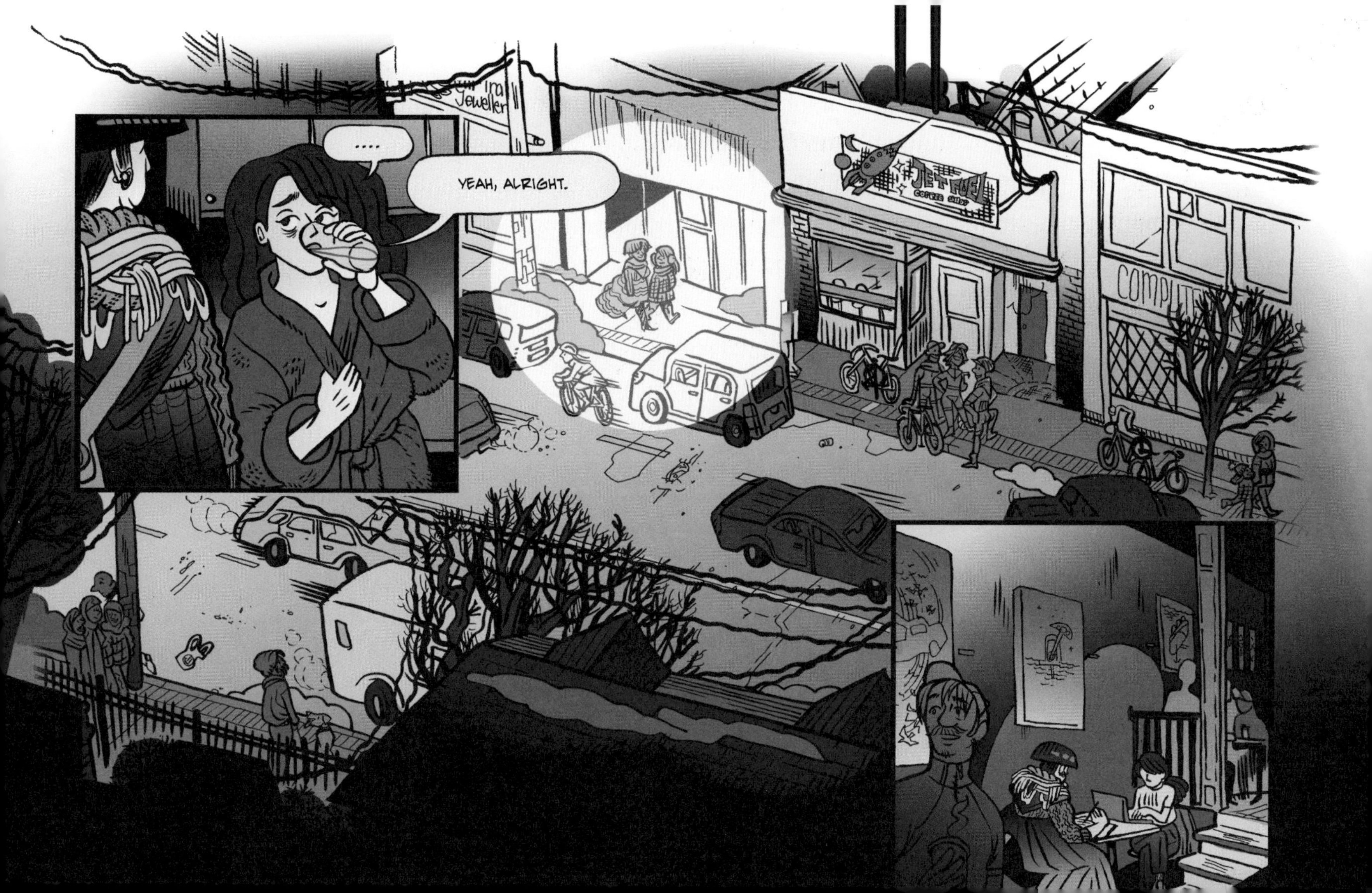

....
YEAH, ALRIGHT.
Jewellery
JET FUEL
COFFEE SHOP
COMPUTE

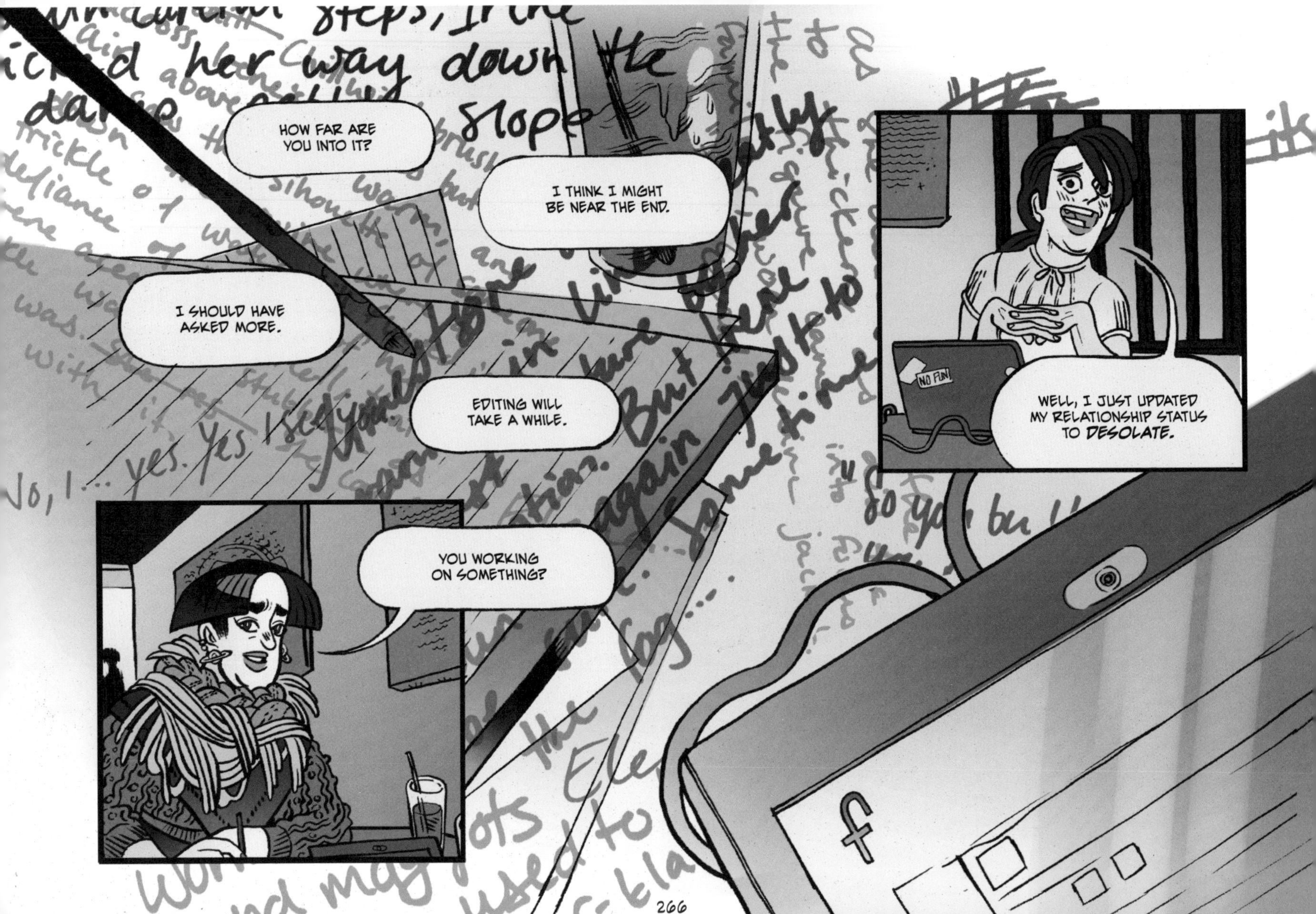

HOW FAR ARE YOU INTO IT?
I THINK I MIGHT BE NEAR THE END.
I SHOULD HAVE ASKED MORE.
EDITING WILL TAKE A WHILE.
WELL, I JUST UPDATED MY RELATIONSHIP STATUS TO DESOLATE.
NO FUN
YOU WORKING ON SOMETHING?

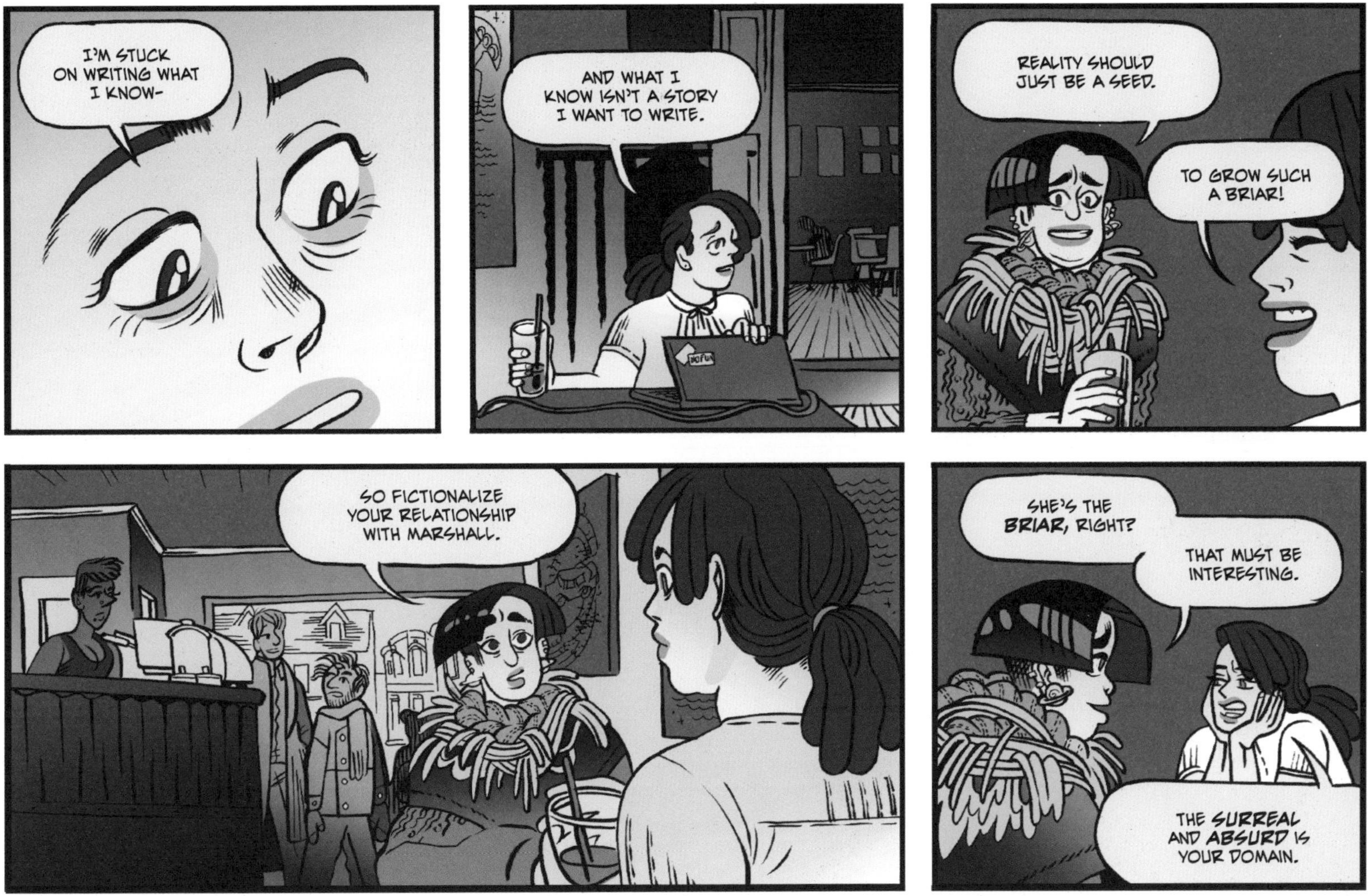
I'M STUCK ON WRITING WHAT I KNOW-
AND WHAT I KNOW ISN'T A STORY I WANT TO WRITE.
REALITY SHOULD JUST BE A SEED.
TO GROW SUCH A BRIAR!
SO FICTIONALIZE YOUR RELATIONSHIP WITH MARSHALL.
SHE'S THE **BRIAR**, RIGHT?
THAT MUST BE INTERESTING.
THE **SURREAL** AND **ABSURD** IS YOUR DOMAIN.

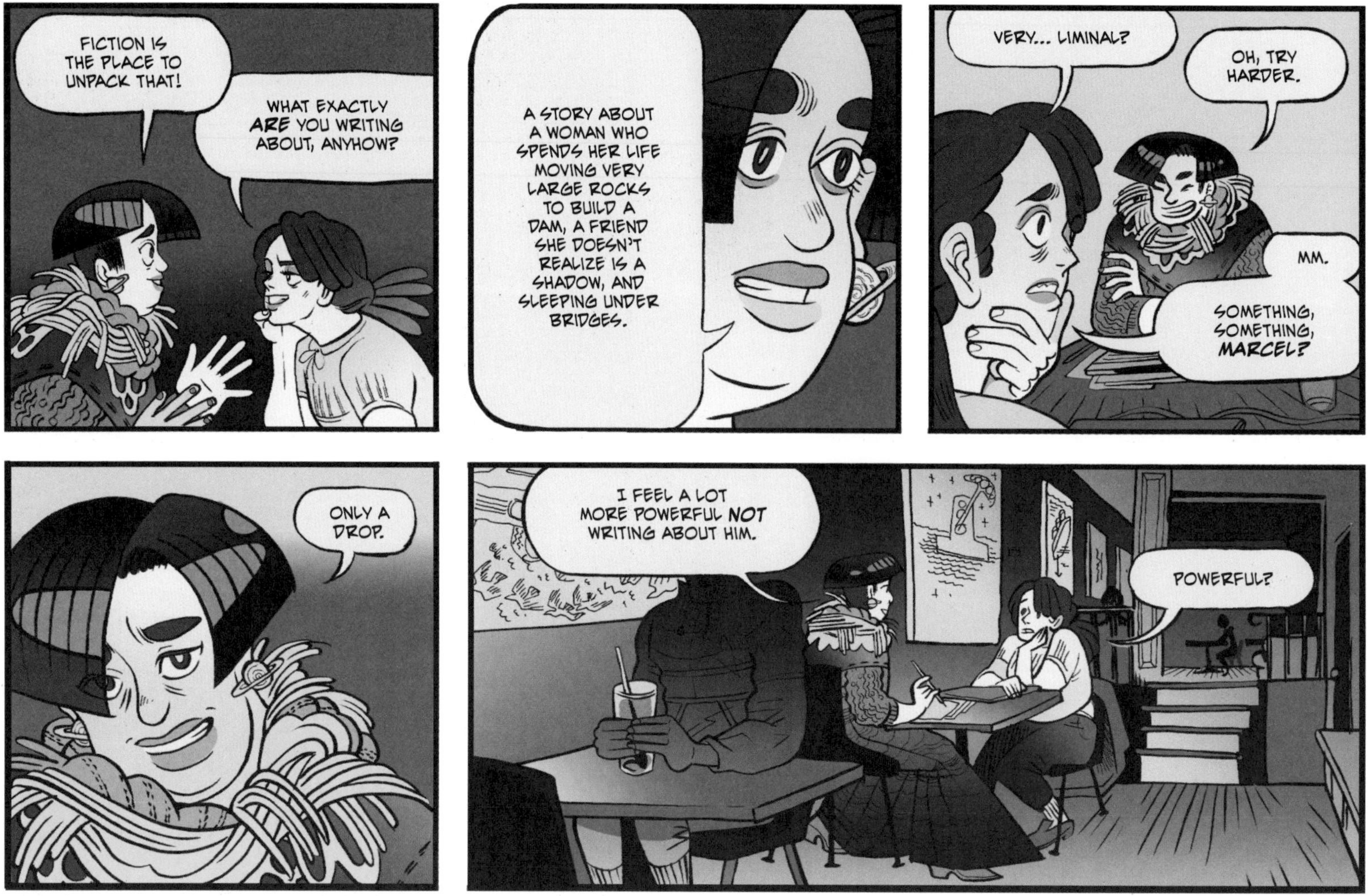
FICTION IS THE PLACE TO UNPACK THAT!
WHAT EXACTLY **ARE** YOU WRITING ABOUT, ANYHOW?
A STORY ABOUT A WOMAN WHO SPENDS HER LIFE MOVING VERY LARGE ROCKS TO BUILD A DAM, A FRIEND SHE DOESN'T REALIZE IS A SHADOW, AND SLEEPING UNDER BRIDGES.
VERY... LIMINAL?
OH, TRY HARDER.
MM.
SOMETHING, SOMETHING, **MARCEL?**
ONLY A DROP.
I FEEL A LOT MORE POWERFUL **NOT** WRITING ABOUT HIM.
POWERFUL?

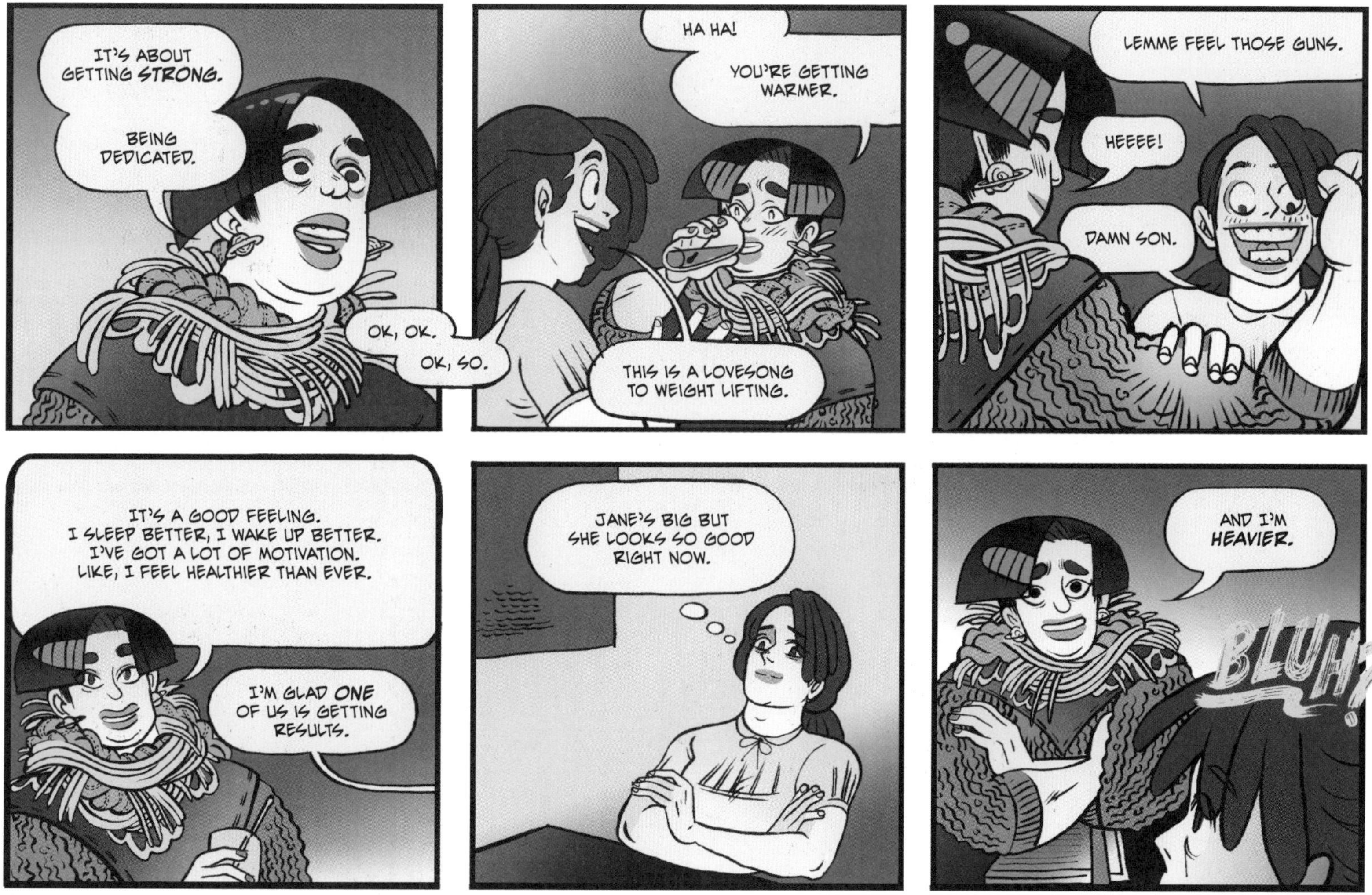
IT'S ABOUT GETTING **STRONG.**
BEING DEDICATED.
OK, OK.
OK, SO.
HA HA!
YOU'RE GETTING WARMER.
THIS IS A LOVESONG TO WEIGHT LIFTING.
LEMME FEEL THOSE GUNS.
HEEEE!
DAMN SON.
IT'S A GOOD FEELING. I SLEEP BETTER, I WAKE UP BETTER. I'VE GOT A LOT OF MOTIVATION. LIKE, I FEEL HEALTHIER THAN EVER.
I'M GLAD **ONE** OF US IS GETTING RESULTS.
JANE'S BIG BUT SHE LOOKS SO GOOD RIGHT NOW.
AND I'M **HEAVIER.**
BLUH!

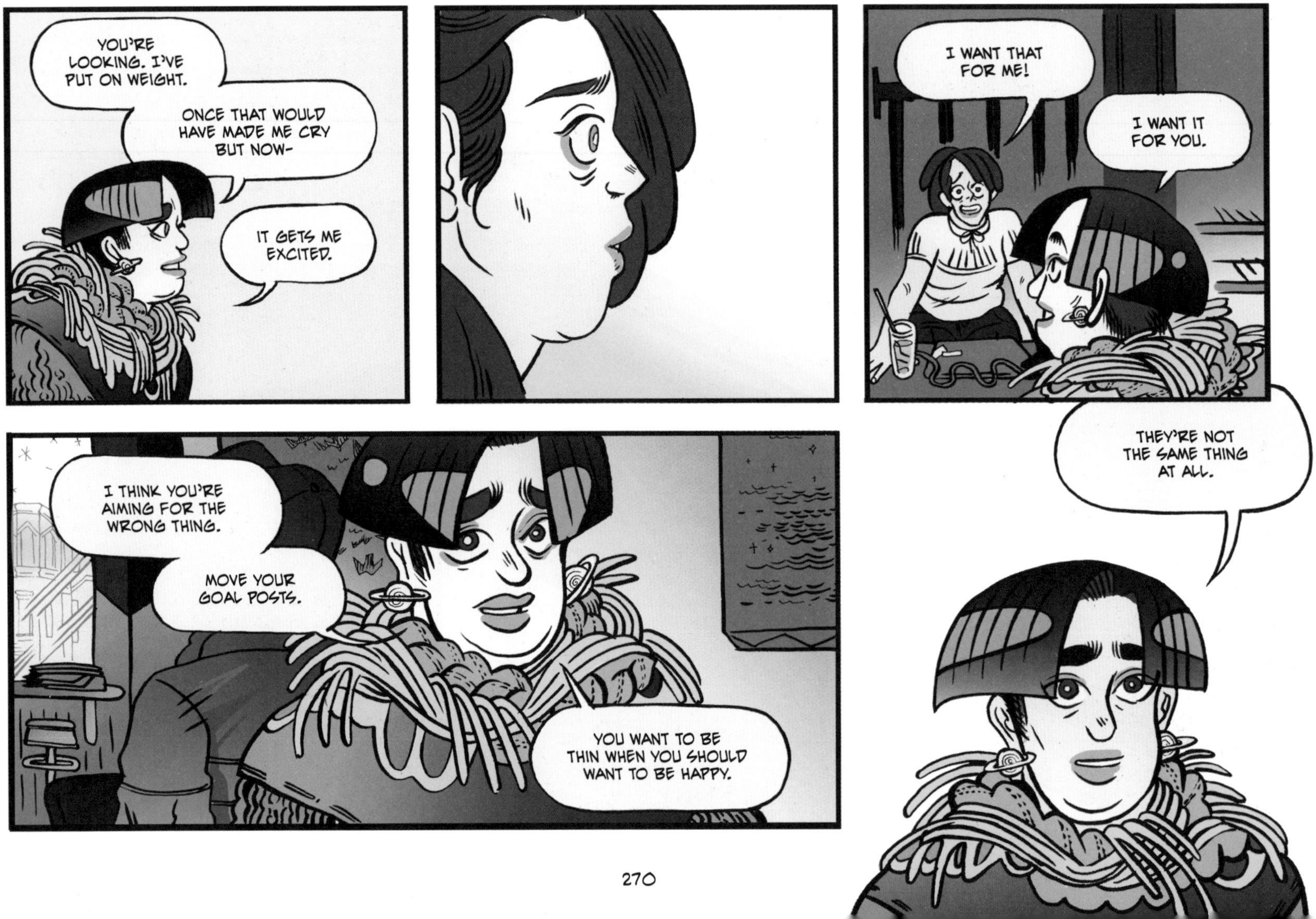
YOU'RE LOOKING. I'VE PUT ON WEIGHT.
ONCE THAT WOULD HAVE MADE ME CRY BUT NOW-
IT GETS ME EXCITED.
I WANT THAT FOR ME!
I WANT IT FOR YOU.
THEY'RE NOT THE SAME THING AT ALL.
I THINK YOU'RE AIMING FOR THE WRONG THING.
MOVE YOUR GOAL POSTS.
YOU WANT TO BE THIN WHEN YOU SHOULD WANT TO BE HAPPY.

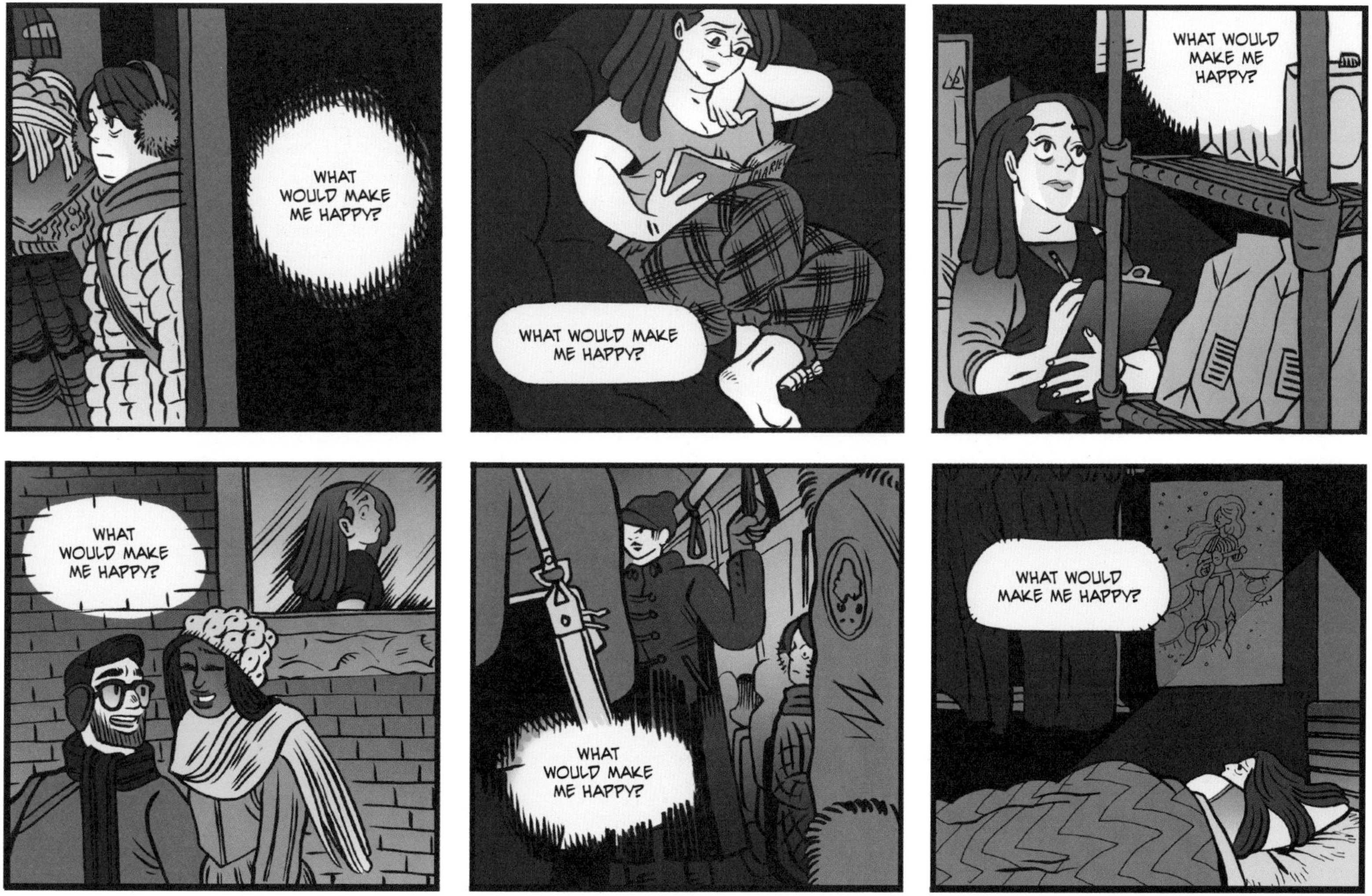
WHAT WOULD MAKE ME HAPPY?
CLARICE
WHAT WOULD MAKE ME HAPPY?
WHAT WOULD MAKE ME HAPPY?
WHAT WOULD MAKE ME HAPPY?
WHAT WOULD MAKE ME HAPPY?
WHAT WOULD MAKE ME HAPPY?

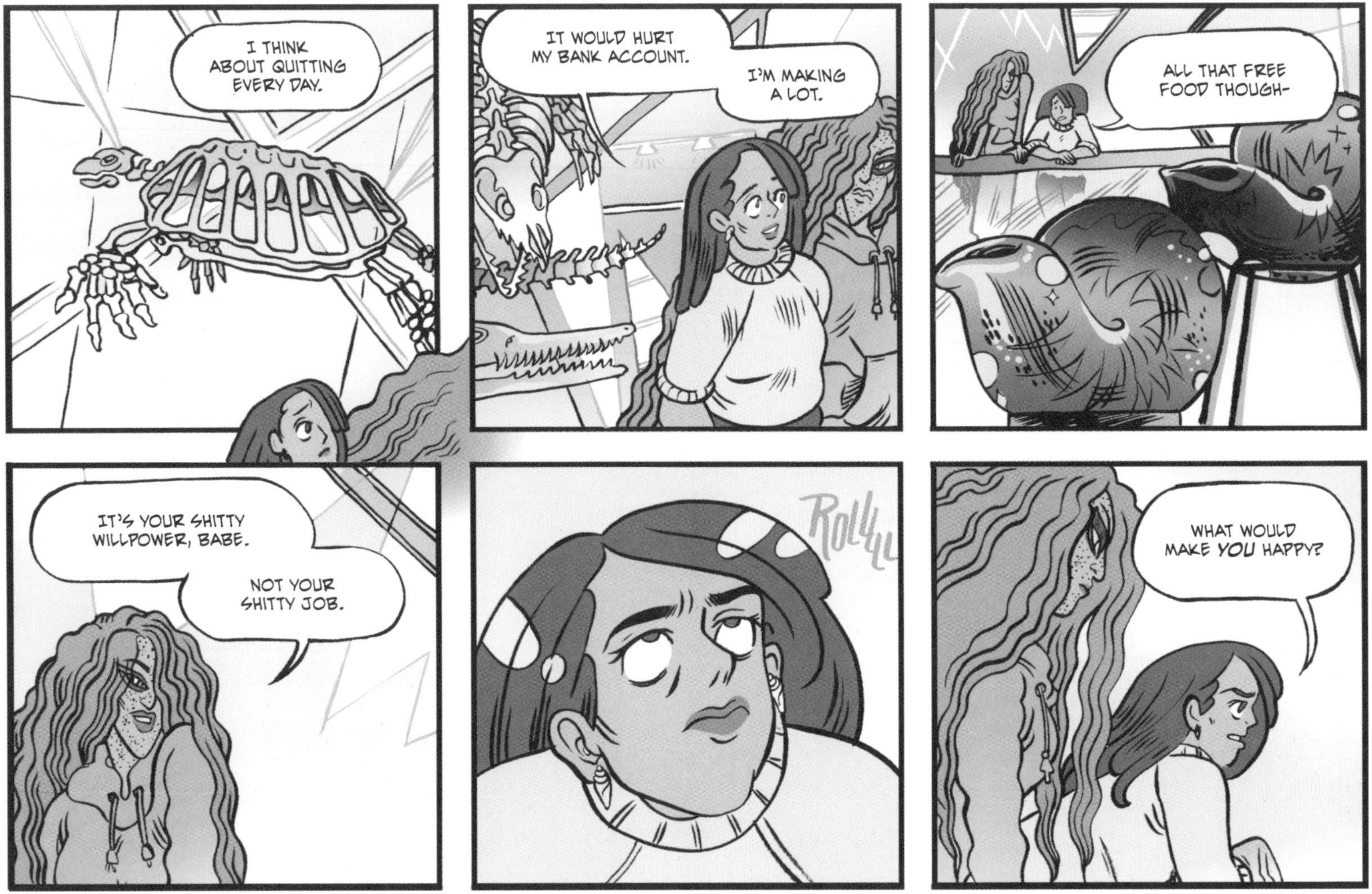
I THINK ABOUT QUITTING EVERY DAY.
IT WOULD HURT MY BANK ACCOUNT.
I'M MAKING A LOT.
ALL THAT FREE FOOD THOUGH-
IT'S YOUR SHITTY WILLPOWER, BABE.
NOT YOUR SHITTY JOB.
ROLLLL
WHAT WOULD MAKE *YOU* HAPPY?

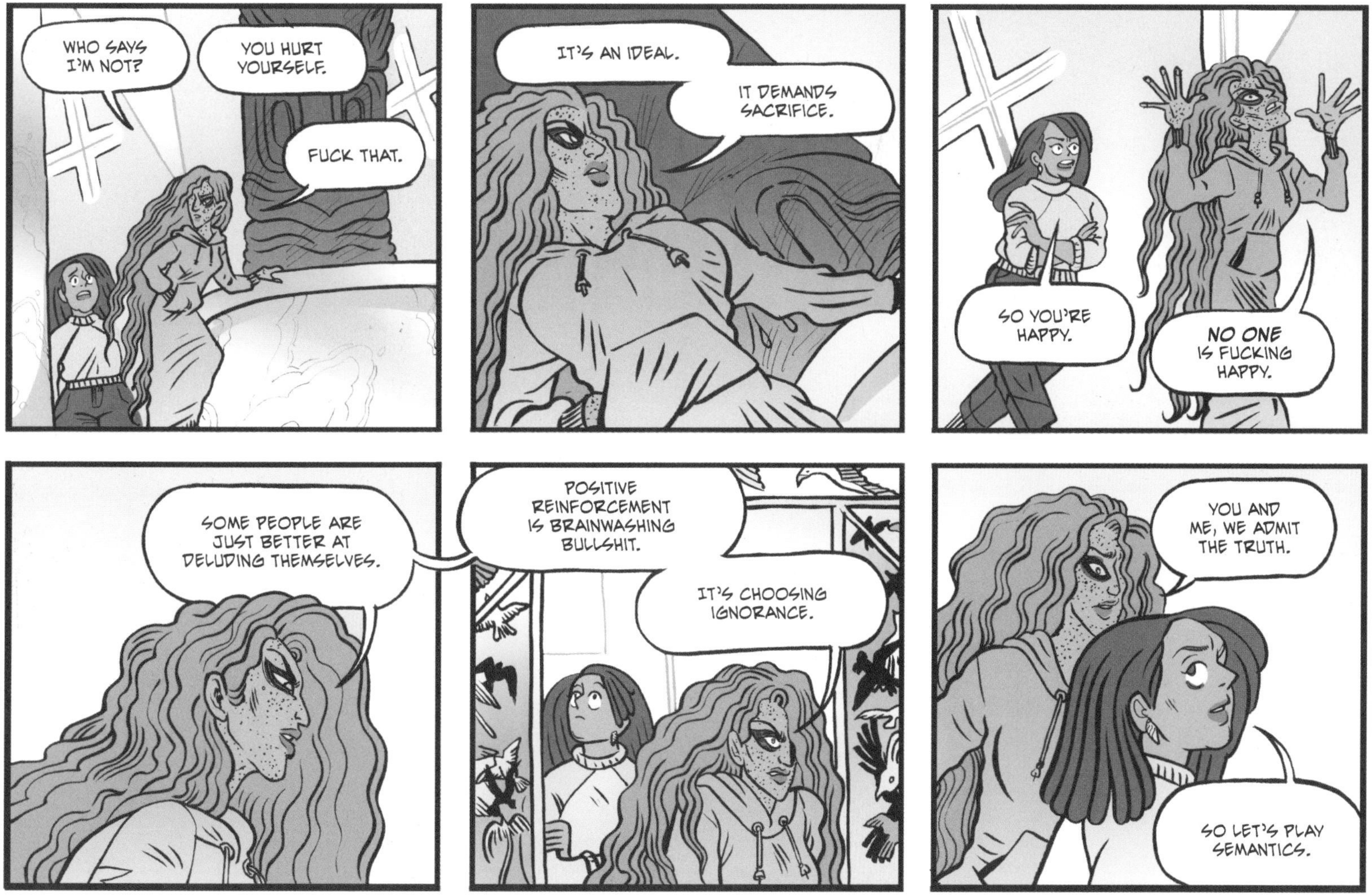
WHO SAYS I'M NOT?
YOU HURT YOURSELF.
FUCK THAT.
IT'S AN IDEAL.
IT DEMANDS SACRIFICE.
SO YOU'RE HAPPY.
NO ONE IS FUCKING HAPPY.
SOME PEOPLE ARE JUST BETTER AT DELUDING THEMSELVES.
POSITIVE REINFORCEMENT IS BRAINWASHING BULLSHIT.
IT'S CHOOSING IGNORANCE.
YOU AND ME, WE ADMIT THE TRUTH.
SO LET'S PLAY SEMANTICS.

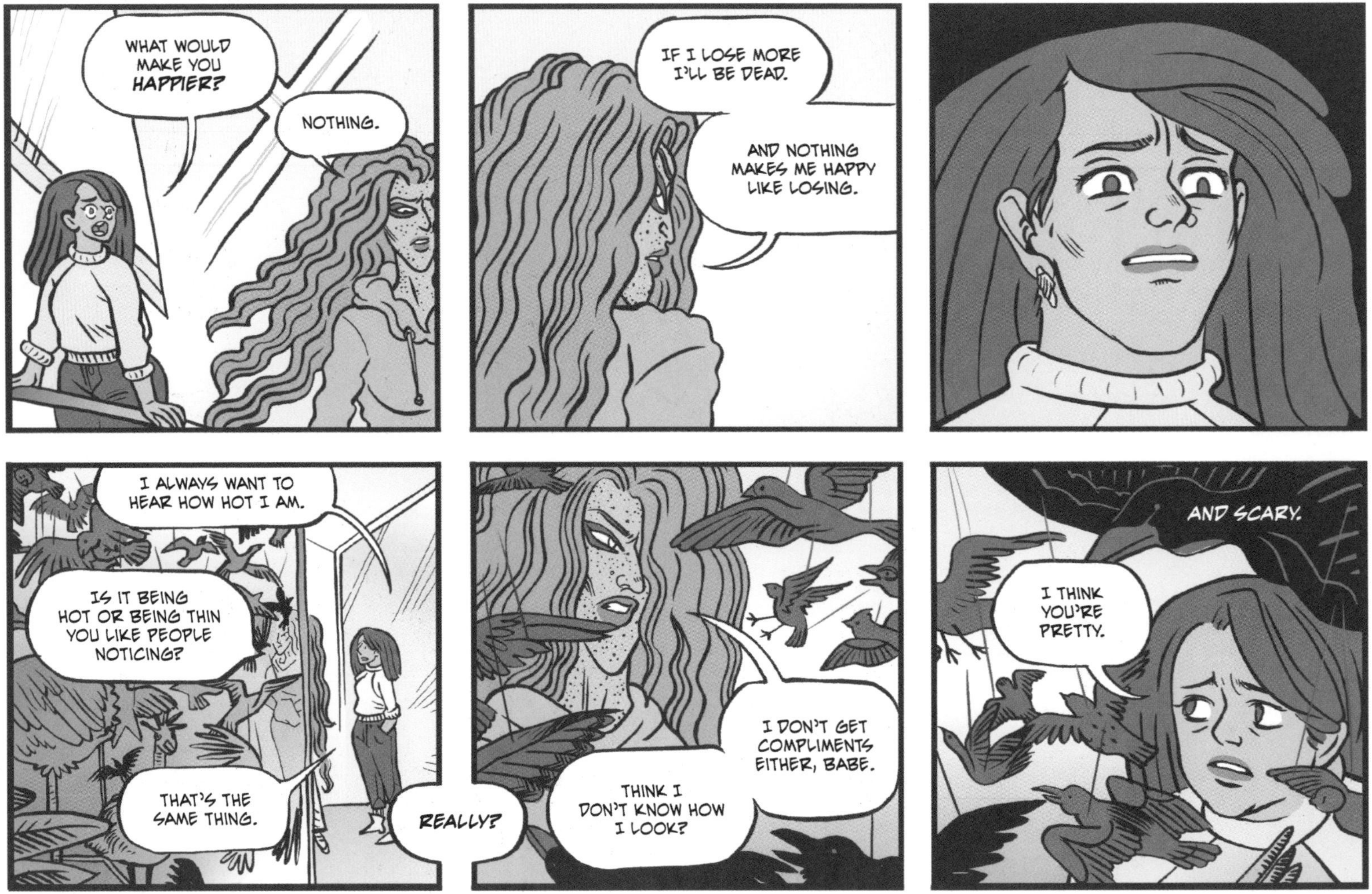
WHAT WOULD MAKE YOU HAPPIER?
NOTHING.
IF I LOSE MORE I'LL BE DEAD.
AND NOTHING MAKES ME HAPPY LIKE LOSING.
I ALWAYS WANT TO HEAR HOW HOT I AM.
IS IT BEING HOT OR BEING THIN YOU LIKE PEOPLE NOTICING?
THAT'S THE SAME THING.
REALLY?
THINK I DON'T KNOW HOW I LOOK?
I DON'T GET COMPLIMENTS EITHER, BABE.
I THINK YOU'RE PRETTY.
AND SCARY.

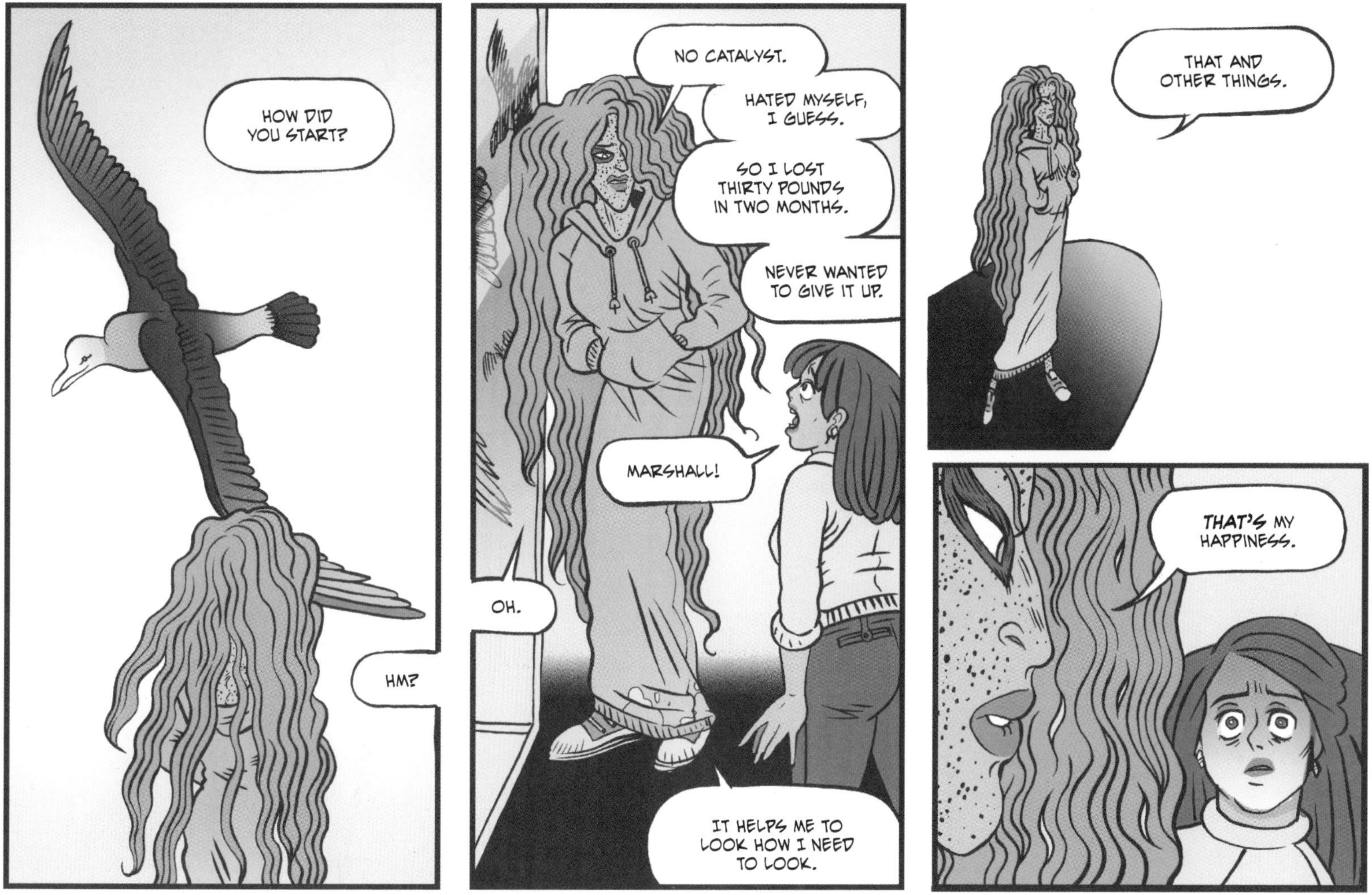
HOW DID YOU START?
HM?
NO CATALYST.
HATED MYSELF, I GUESS.
SO I LOST THIRTY POUNDS IN TWO MONTHS.
NEVER WANTED TO GIVE IT UP.
MARSHALL!
OH.
IT HELPS ME TO LOOK HOW I NEED TO LOOK.
THAT AND OTHER THINGS.
THAT'S MY HAPPINESS.

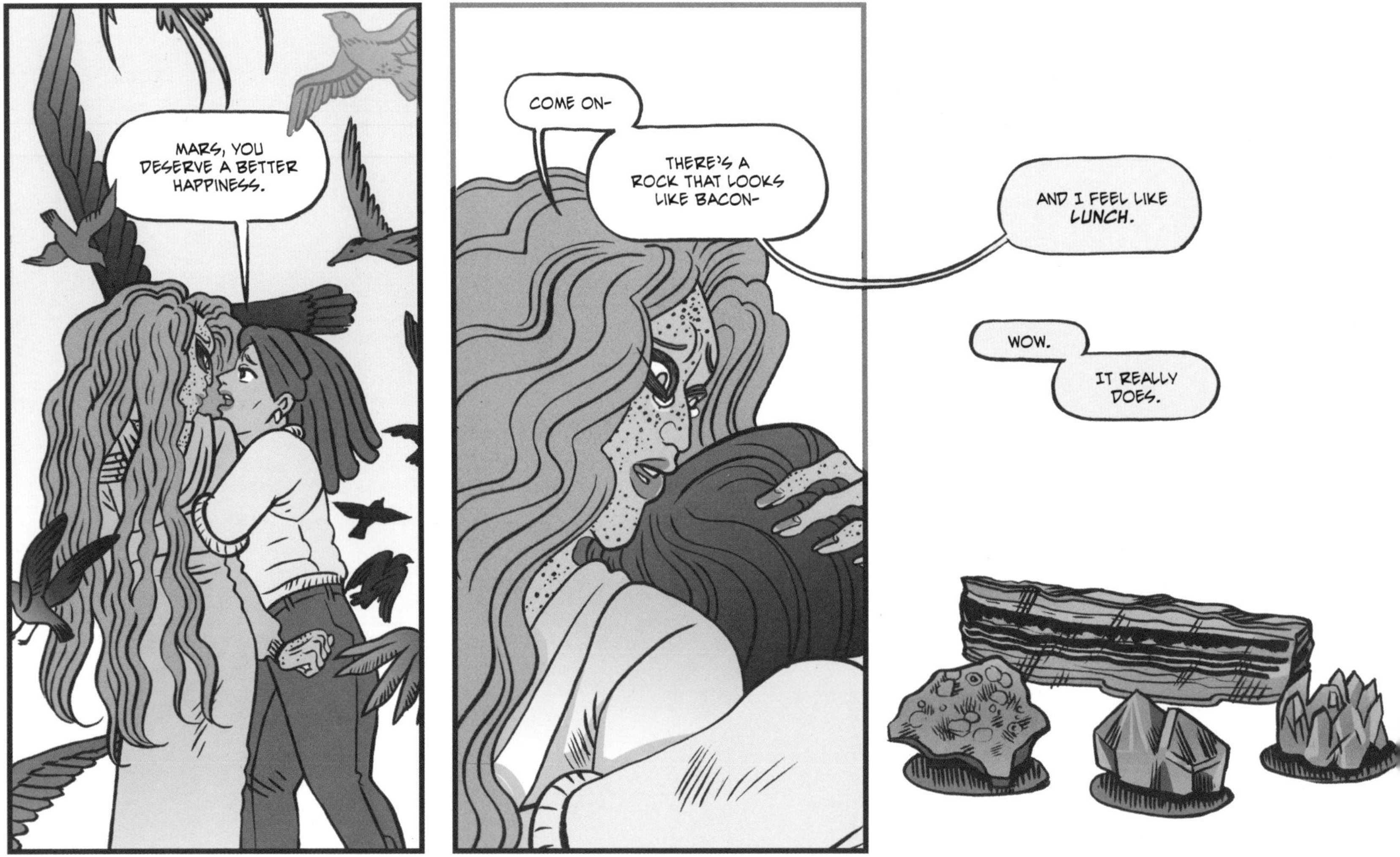
MARS, YOU DESERVE A BETTER HAPPINESS.
COME ON-
THERE'S A ROCK THAT LOOKS LIKE BACON-
AND I FEEL LIKE **LUNCH**.
WOW.
IT REALLY DOES.

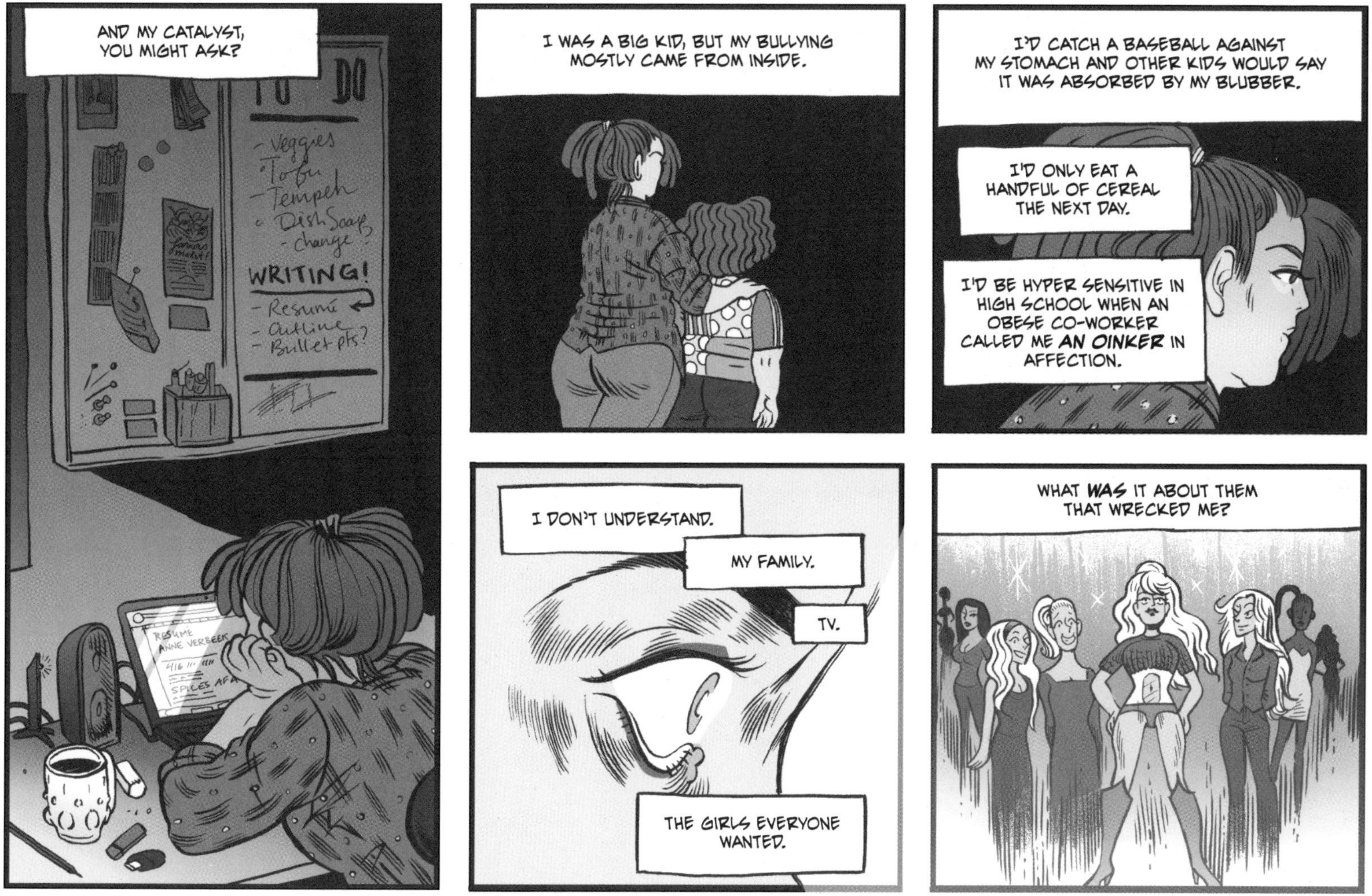
AND MY CATALYST, YOU MIGHT ASK?
TO DO
-Veggies
-Tofu
-Tempeh
-Dish Soap
-change?
WRITING!
-Resumé
-Outline
-Bullet pts?
RESUME
ANNE VERBEEK
I WAS A BIG KID, BUT MY BULLYING MOSTLY CAME FROM INSIDE.
I'D CATCH A BASEBALL AGAINST MY STOMACH AND OTHER KIDS WOULD SAY IT WAS ABSORBED BY MY BLUBBER.
I'D ONLY EAT A HANDFUL OF CEREAL THE NEXT DAY.
I'D BE HYPER SENSITIVE IN HIGH SCHOOL WHEN AN OBESE CO-WORKER CALLED ME **AN OINKER** IN AFFECTION.
I DON'T UNDERSTAND.
MY FAMILY.
TV.
THE GIRLS EVERYONE WANTED.
WHAT **WAS** IT ABOUT THEM THAT WRECKED ME?

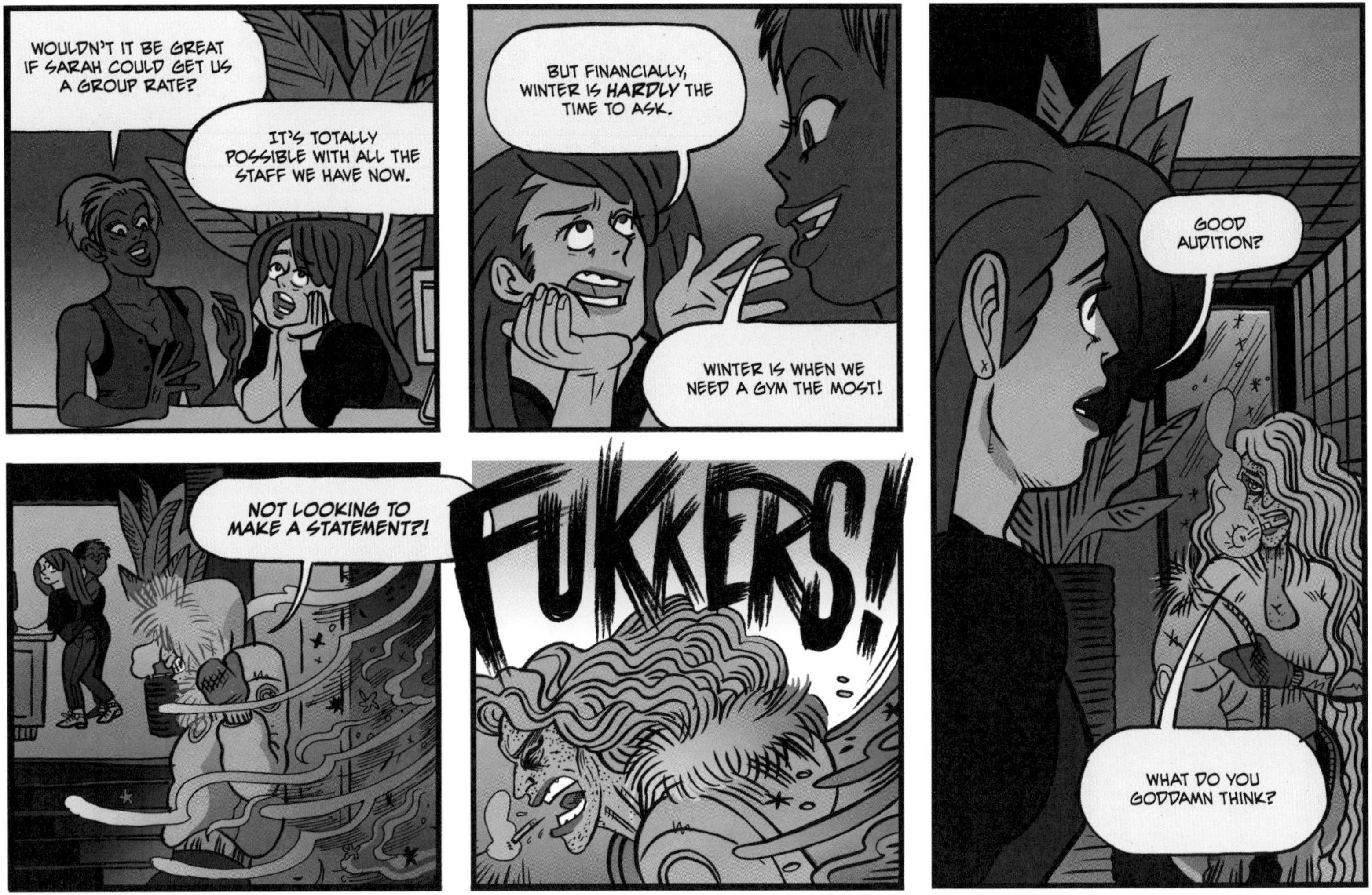
WOULDN'T IT BE GREAT IF SARAH COULD GET US A GROUP RATE?
IT'S TOTALLY POSSIBLE WITH ALL THE STAFF WE HAVE NOW.
BUT FINANCIALLY, WINTER IS HARDLY THE TIME TO ASK.
WINTER IS WHEN WE NEED A GYM THE MOST!
NOT LOOKING TO MAKE A STATEMENT?!
FUKKERS!
GOOD AUDITION?
WHAT DO YOU GODDAMN THINK?

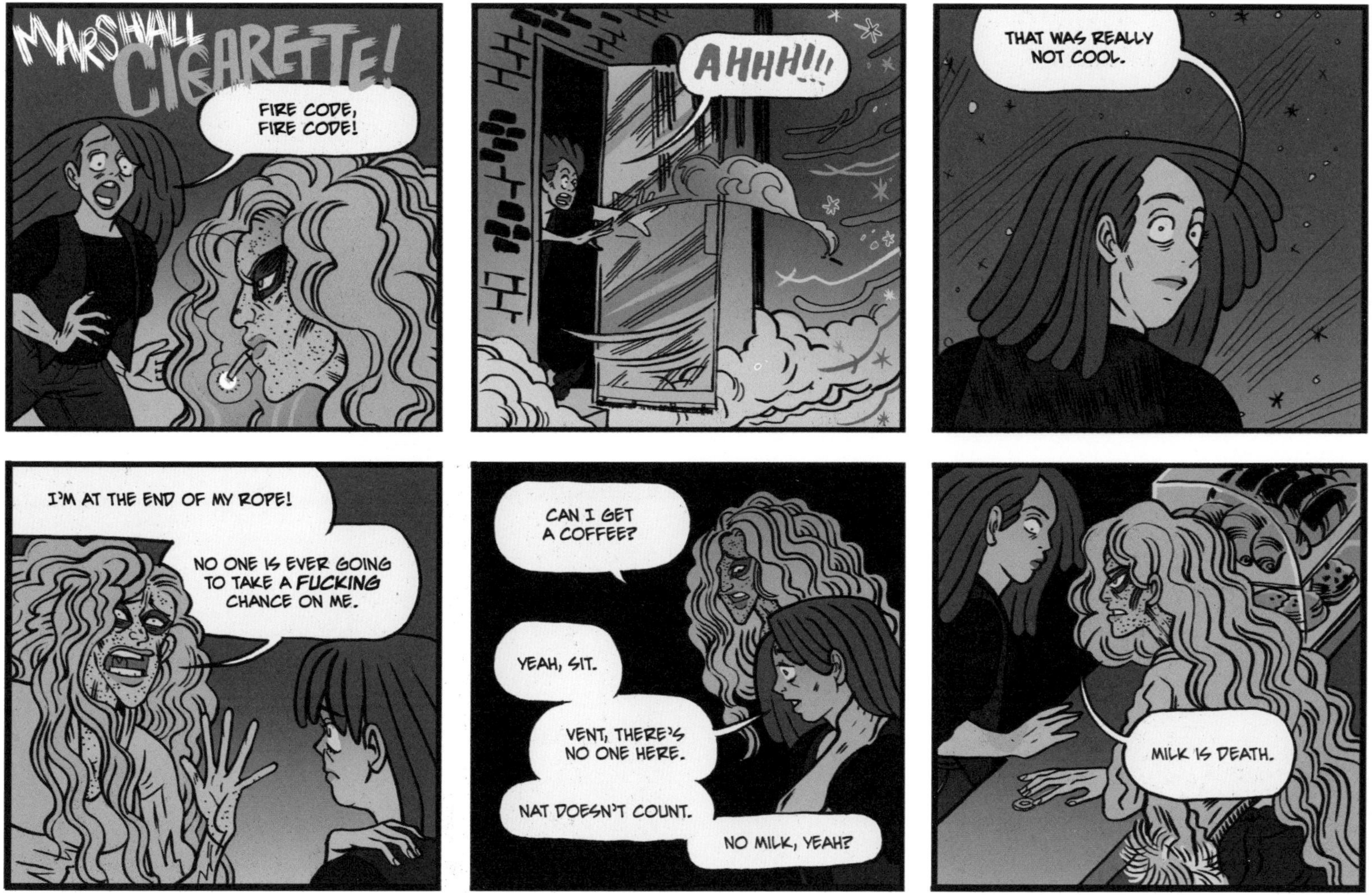
MARSHALL
CIGARETTE!
FIRE CODE, FIRE CODE!
AHHH!!!
THAT WAS REALLY NOT COOL.
I'M AT THE END OF MY ROPE!
NO ONE IS EVER GOING TO TAKE A **FUCKING** CHANCE ON ME.
CAN I GET A COFFEE?
YEAH, SIT.
VENT, THERE'S NO ONE HERE.
NAT DOESN'T COUNT.
NO MILK, YEAH?
MILK IS DEATH.

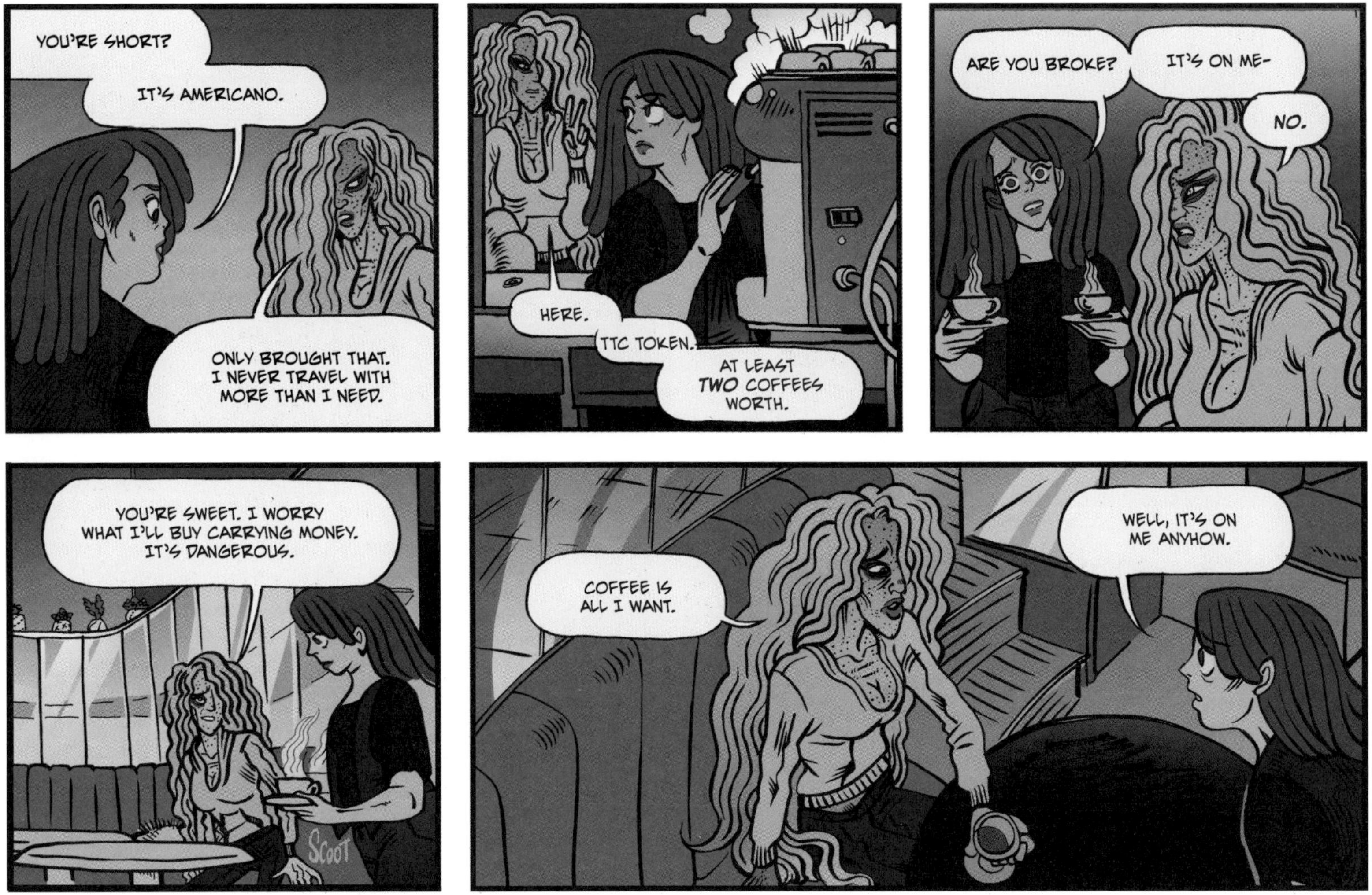
YOU'RE SHORT?
IT'S AMERICANO.
ONLY BROUGHT THAT. I NEVER TRAVEL WITH MORE THAN I NEED.
HERE.
TTC TOKEN.
AT LEAST TWO COFFEES WORTH.
ARE YOU BROKE?
IT'S ON ME-
NO.
YOU'RE SWEET. I WORRY WHAT I'LL BUY CARRYING MONEY. IT'S DANGEROUS.
SCOOT
COFFEE IS ALL I WANT.
WELL, IT'S ON ME ANYHOW.

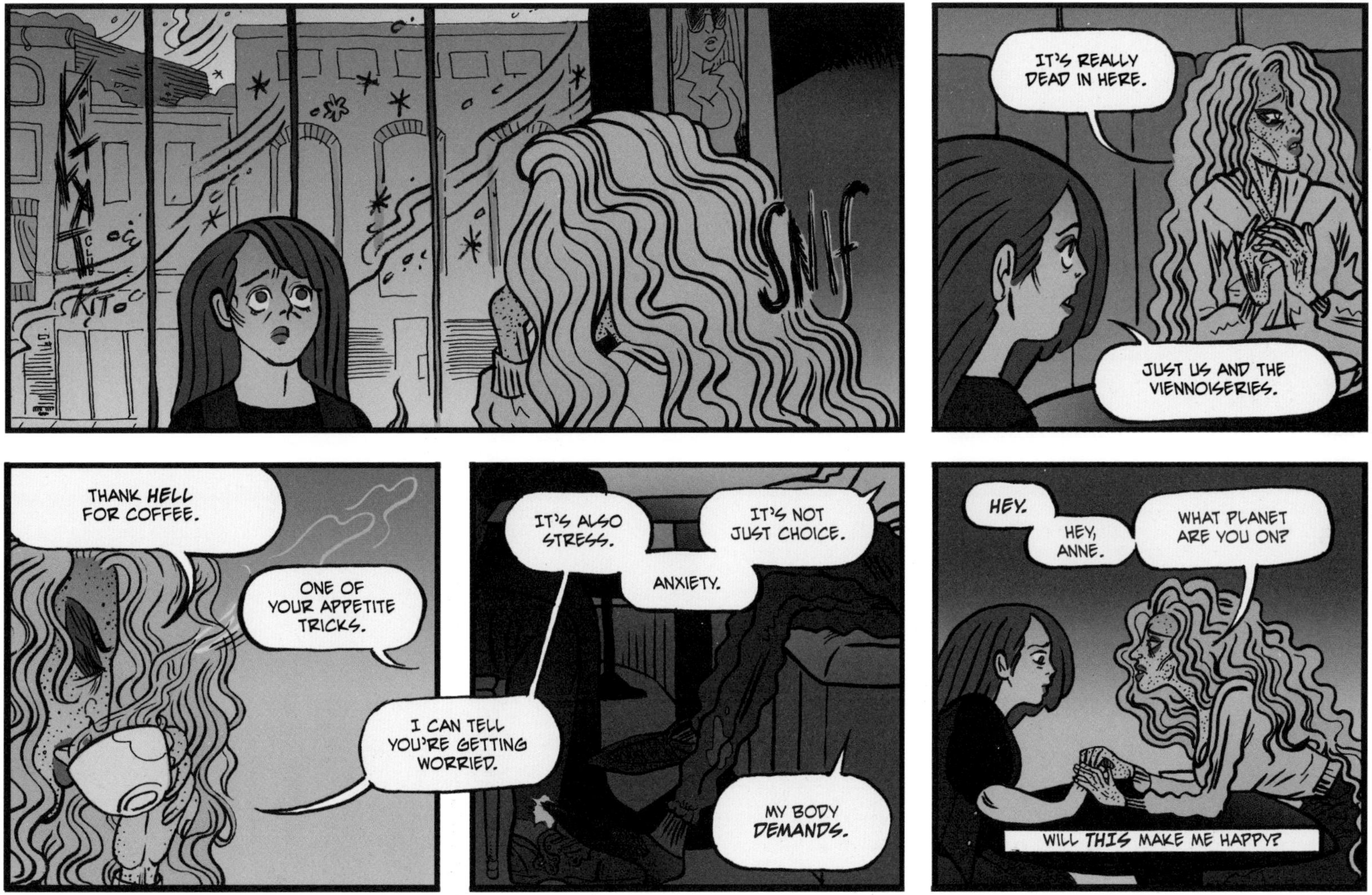
SNIF
IT'S REALLY DEAD IN HERE.
JUST US AND THE VIENNOISERIES.
THANK **HELL** FOR COFFEE.
ONE OF YOUR APPETITE TRICKS.
I CAN TELL YOU'RE GETTING WORRIED.
IT'S NOT JUST CHOICE.
IT'S ALSO STRESS.
ANXIETY.
MY BODY **DEMANDS**.
HEY.
HEY, ANNE.
WHAT PLANET ARE YOU ON?
WILL **THIS** MAKE ME HAPPY?

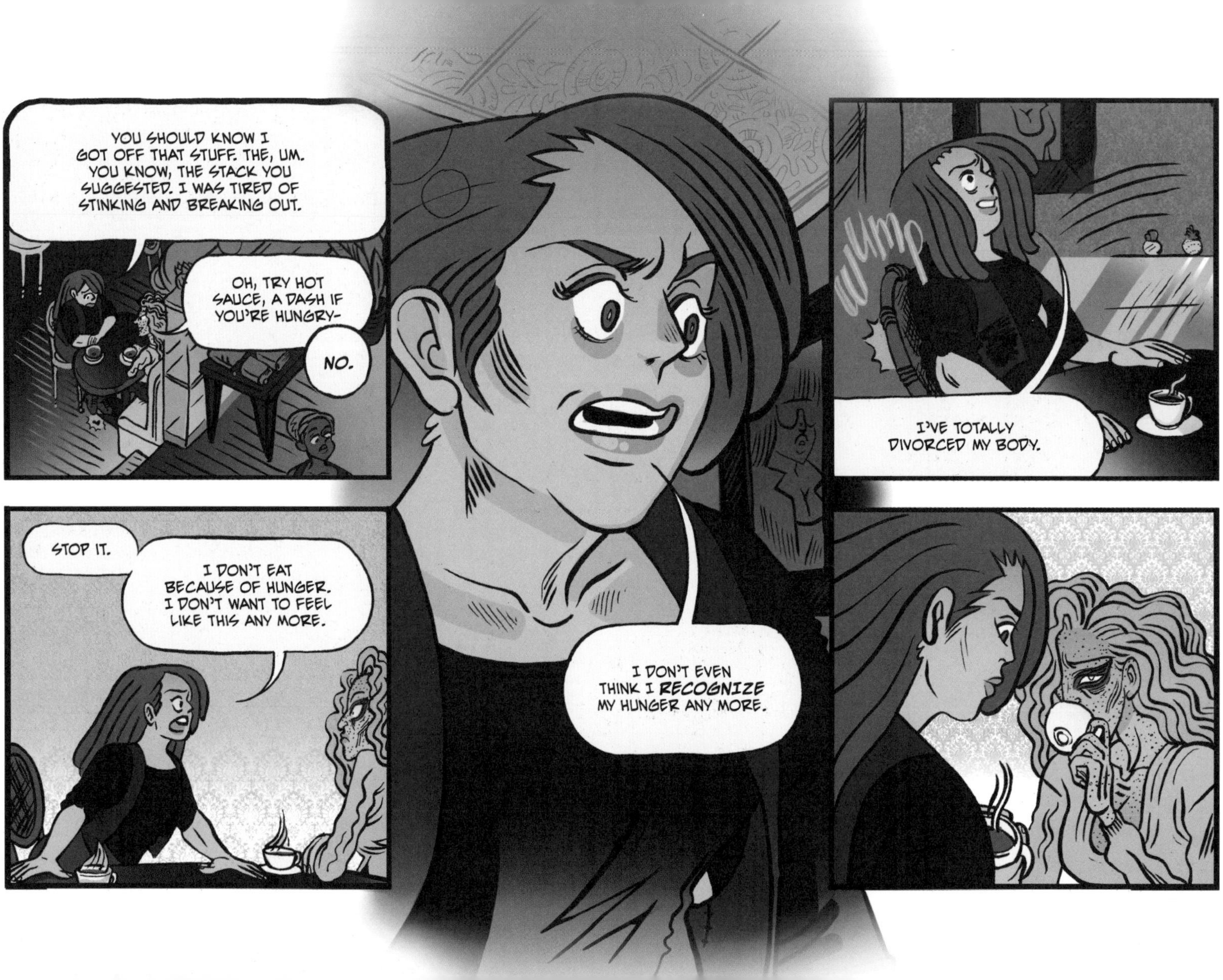

YOU SHOULD KNOW I GOT OFF THAT STUFF. THE, UM. YOU KNOW, THE STACK YOU SUGGESTED. I WAS TIRED OF STINKING AND BREAKING OUT.
OH, TRY HOT SAUCE, A DASH IF YOU'RE HUNGRY-
NO.
WUMP
I'VE TOTALLY DIVORCED MY BODY.
I DON'T EVEN THINK I RECOGNIZE MY HUNGER ANY MORE.
STOP IT.
I DON'T EAT BECAUSE OF HUNGER. I DON'T WANT TO FEEL LIKE THIS ANY MORE.

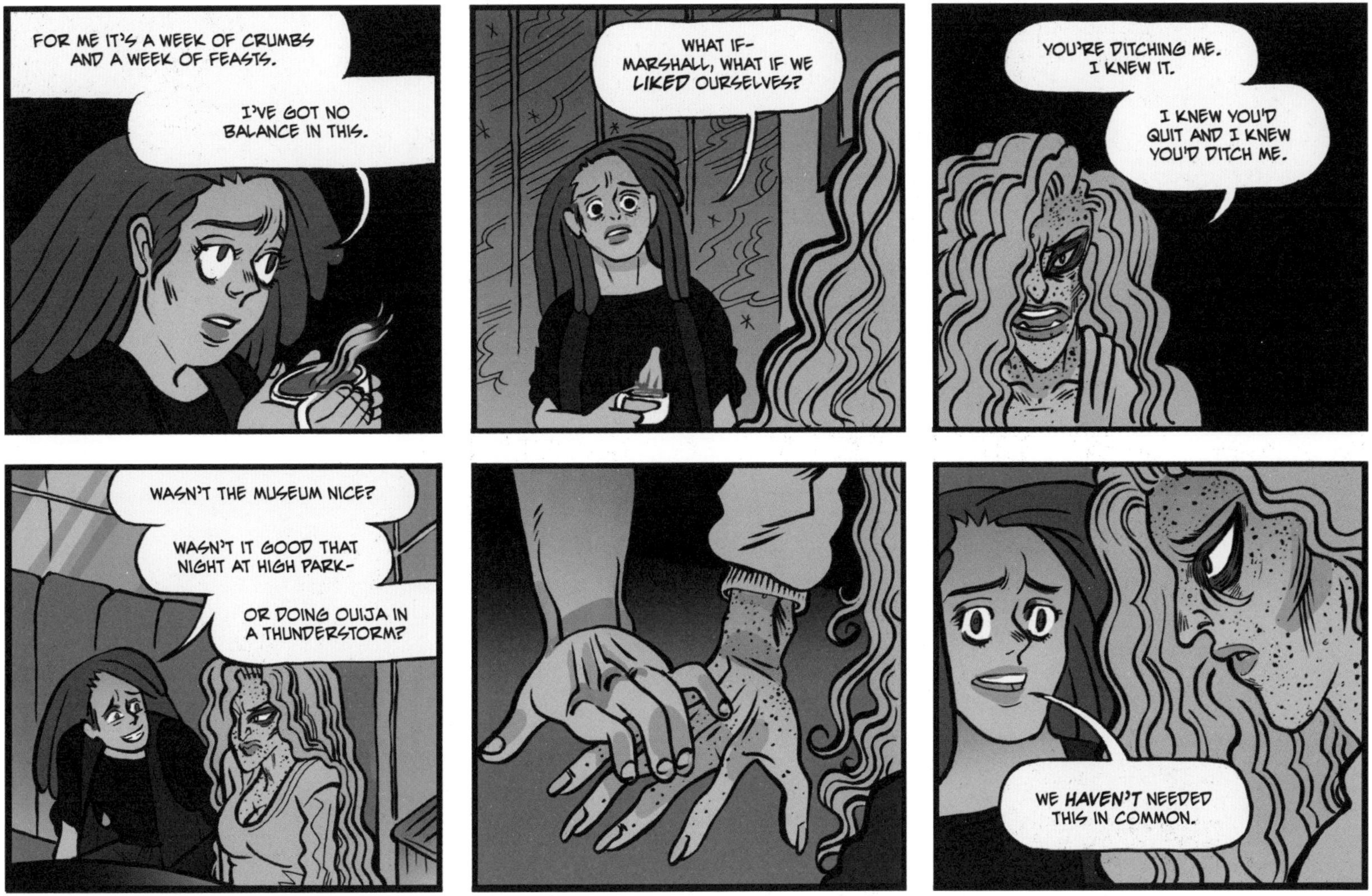
FOR ME IT'S A WEEK OF CRUMBS AND A WEEK OF FEASTS.
I'VE GOT NO BALANCE IN THIS.
WHAT IF- MARSHALL, WHAT IF WE *LIKED* OURSELVES?
YOU'RE DITCHING ME. I KNEW IT.
I KNEW YOU'D QUIT AND I KNEW YOU'D DITCH ME.
WASN'T THE MUSEUM NICE?
WASN'T IT GOOD THAT NIGHT AT HIGH PARK-
OR DOING OUIJA IN A THUNDERSTORM?
WE *HAVEN'T* NEEDED THIS IN COMMON.

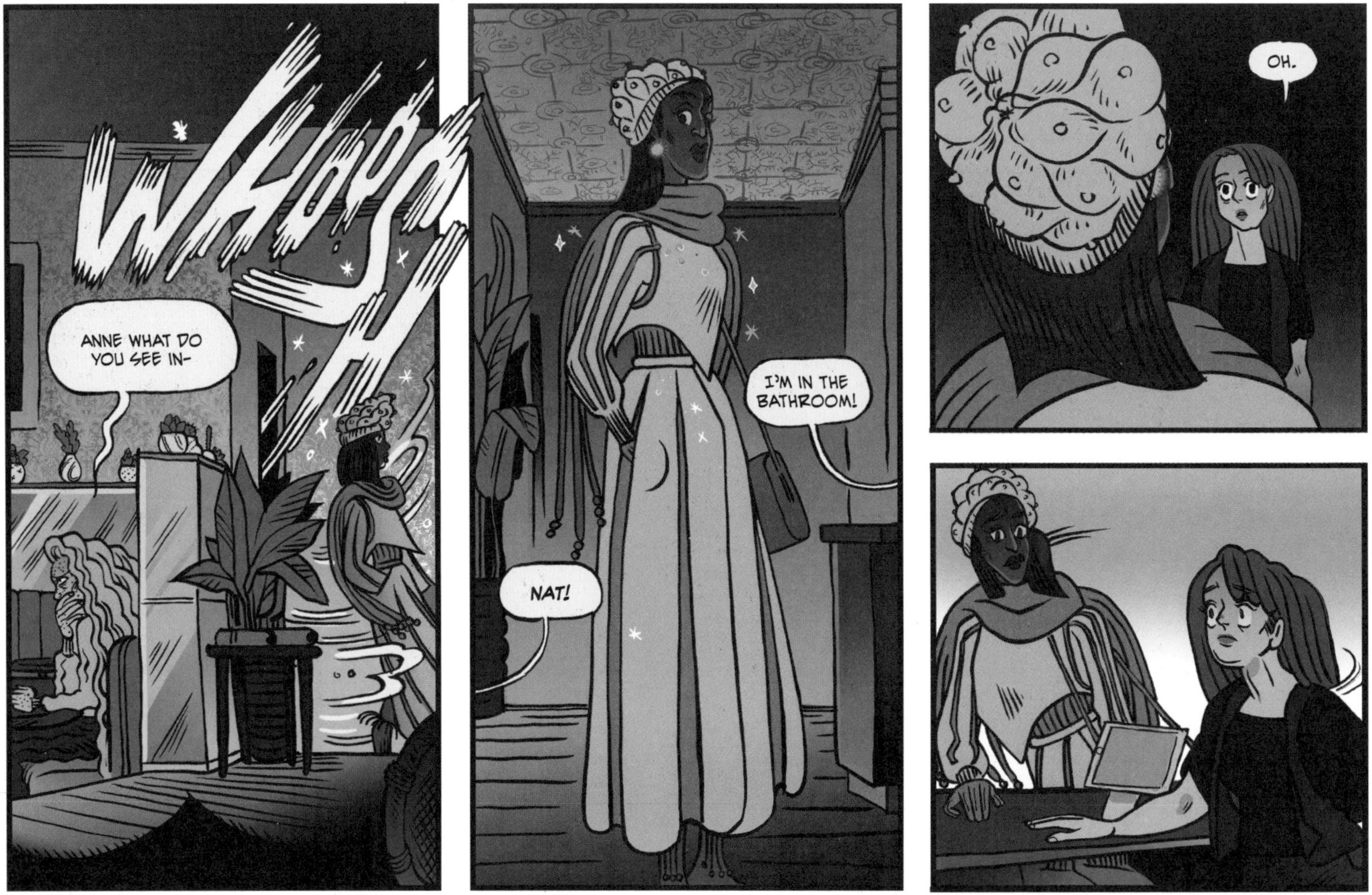
WHOOSH
ANNE WHAT DO YOU SEE IN-
NAT!
I'M IN THE BATHROOM!
OH.

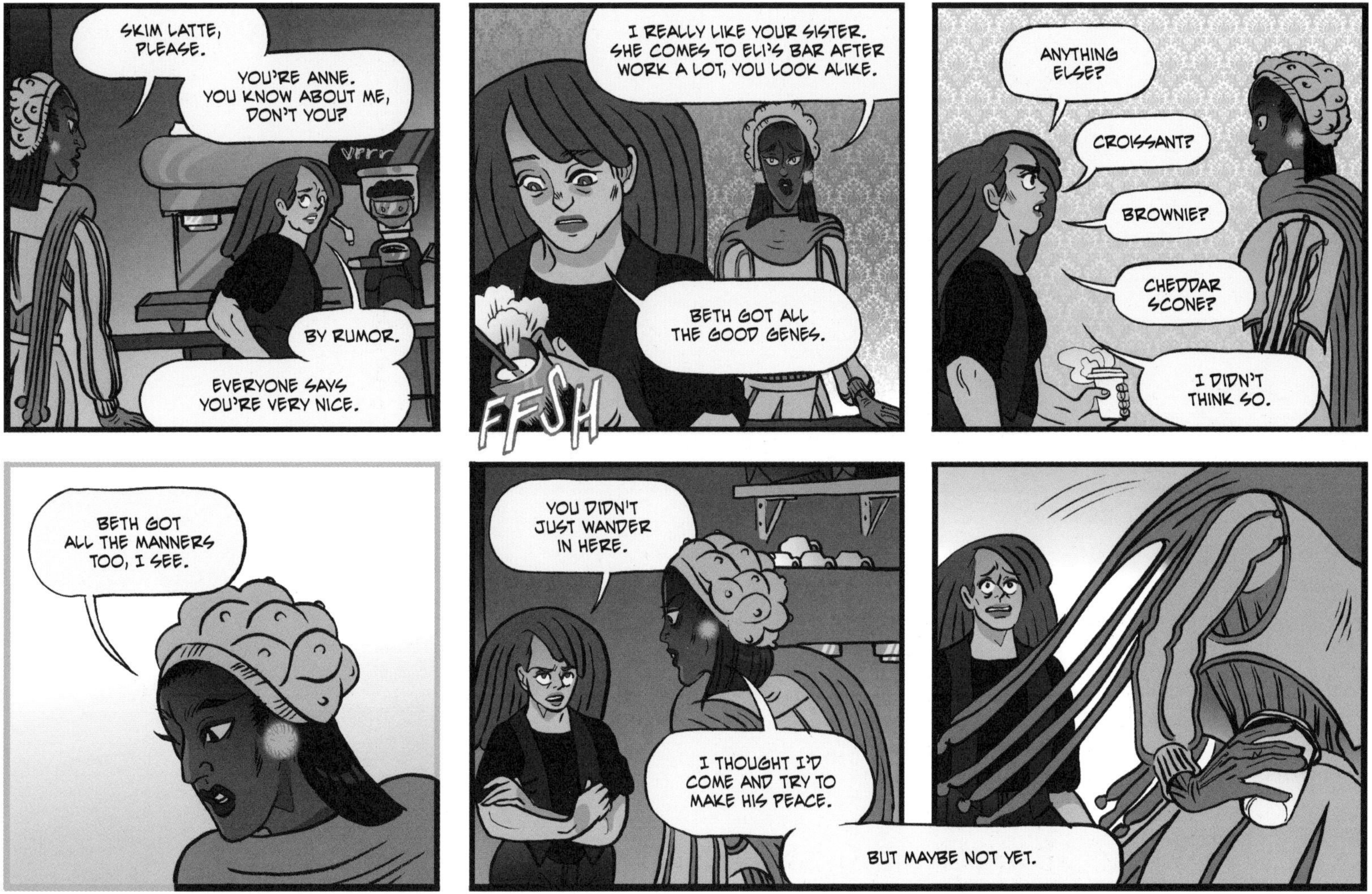
SKIM LATTE, PLEASE.
YOU'RE ANNE. YOU KNOW ABOUT ME, DON'T YOU?
VPRR
BY RUMOR.
EVERYONE SAYS YOU'RE VERY NICE.
I REALLY LIKE YOUR SISTER. SHE COMES TO ELI'S BAR AFTER WORK A LOT, YOU LOOK ALIKE.
BETH GOT ALL THE GOOD GENES.
FFSH
ANYTHING ELSE?
CROISSANT?
BROWNIE?
CHEDDAR SCONE?
I DIDN'T THINK SO.
BETH GOT ALL THE MANNERS TOO, I SEE.
YOU DIDN'T JUST WANDER IN HERE.
I THOUGHT I'D COME AND TRY TO MAKE HIS PEACE.
BUT MAYBE NOT YET.

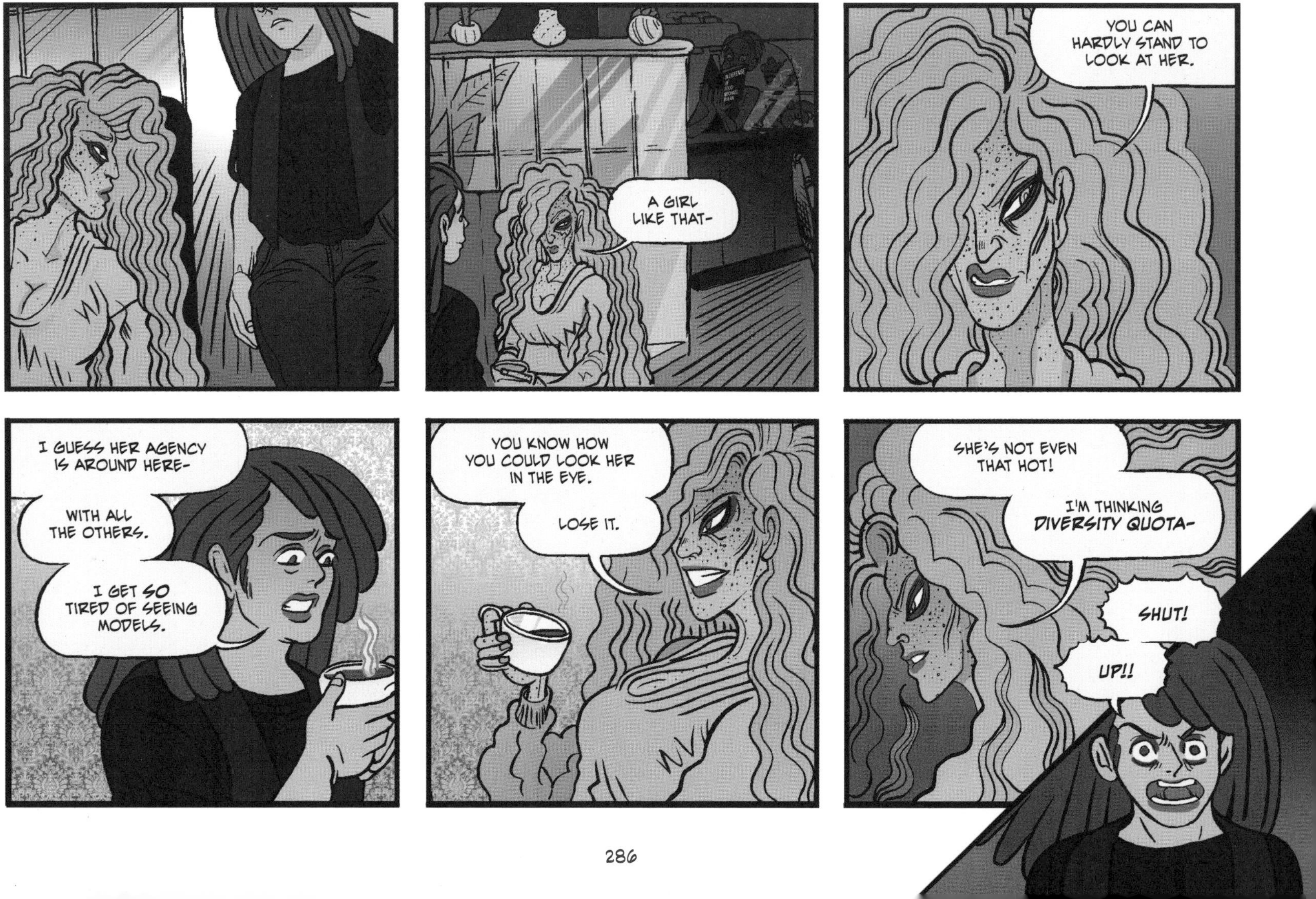
A GIRL LIKE THAT-
YOU CAN HARDLY STAND TO LOOK AT HER.
I GUESS HER AGENCY IS AROUND HERE-
WITH ALL THE OTHERS.
I GET SO TIRED OF SEEING MODELS.
YOU KNOW HOW YOU COULD LOOK HER IN THE EYE.
LOSE IT.
SHE'S NOT EVEN THAT HOT!
I'M THINKING DIVERSITY QUOTA-
SHUT!
UP!!

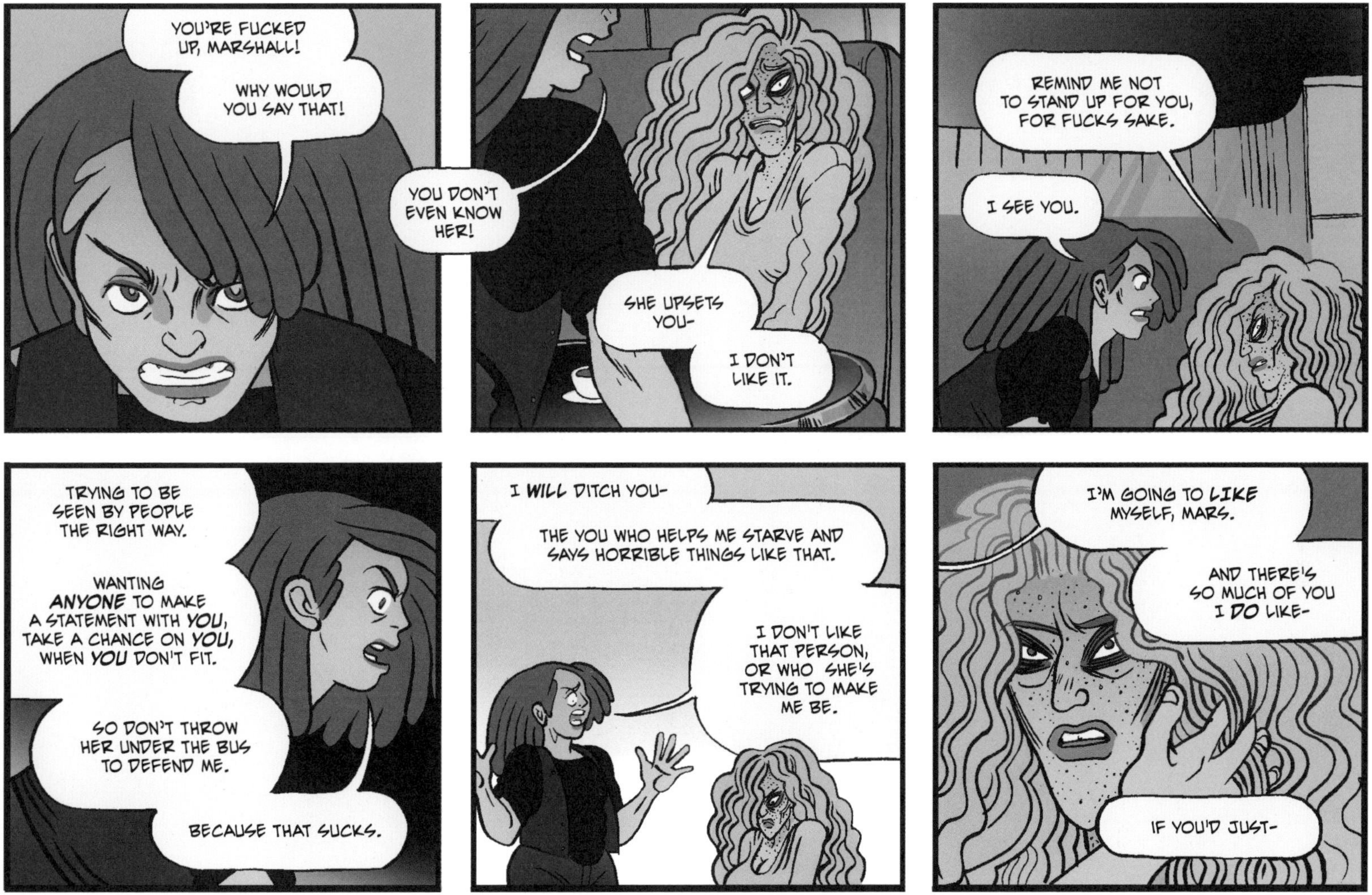
YOU'RE FUCKED UP, MARSHALL!
WHY WOULD YOU SAY THAT!
YOU DON'T EVEN KNOW HER!
SHE UPSETS YOU-
I DON'T LIKE IT.
REMIND ME NOT TO STAND UP FOR YOU, FOR FUCKS SAKE.
I SEE YOU.
TRYING TO BE SEEN BY PEOPLE THE RIGHT WAY.
WANTING ANYONE TO MAKE A STATEMENT WITH YOU, TAKE A CHANCE ON YOU, WHEN YOU DON'T FIT.
SO DON'T THROW HER UNDER THE BUS TO DEFEND ME.
BECAUSE THAT SUCKS.
I WILL DITCH YOU-
THE YOU WHO HELPS ME STARVE AND SAYS HORRIBLE THINGS LIKE THAT.
I DON'T LIKE THAT PERSON, OR WHO SHE'S TRYING TO MAKE ME BE.
I'M GOING TO LIKE MYSELF, MARS.
AND THERE'S SO MUCH OF YOU I DO LIKE-
IF YOU'D JUST-

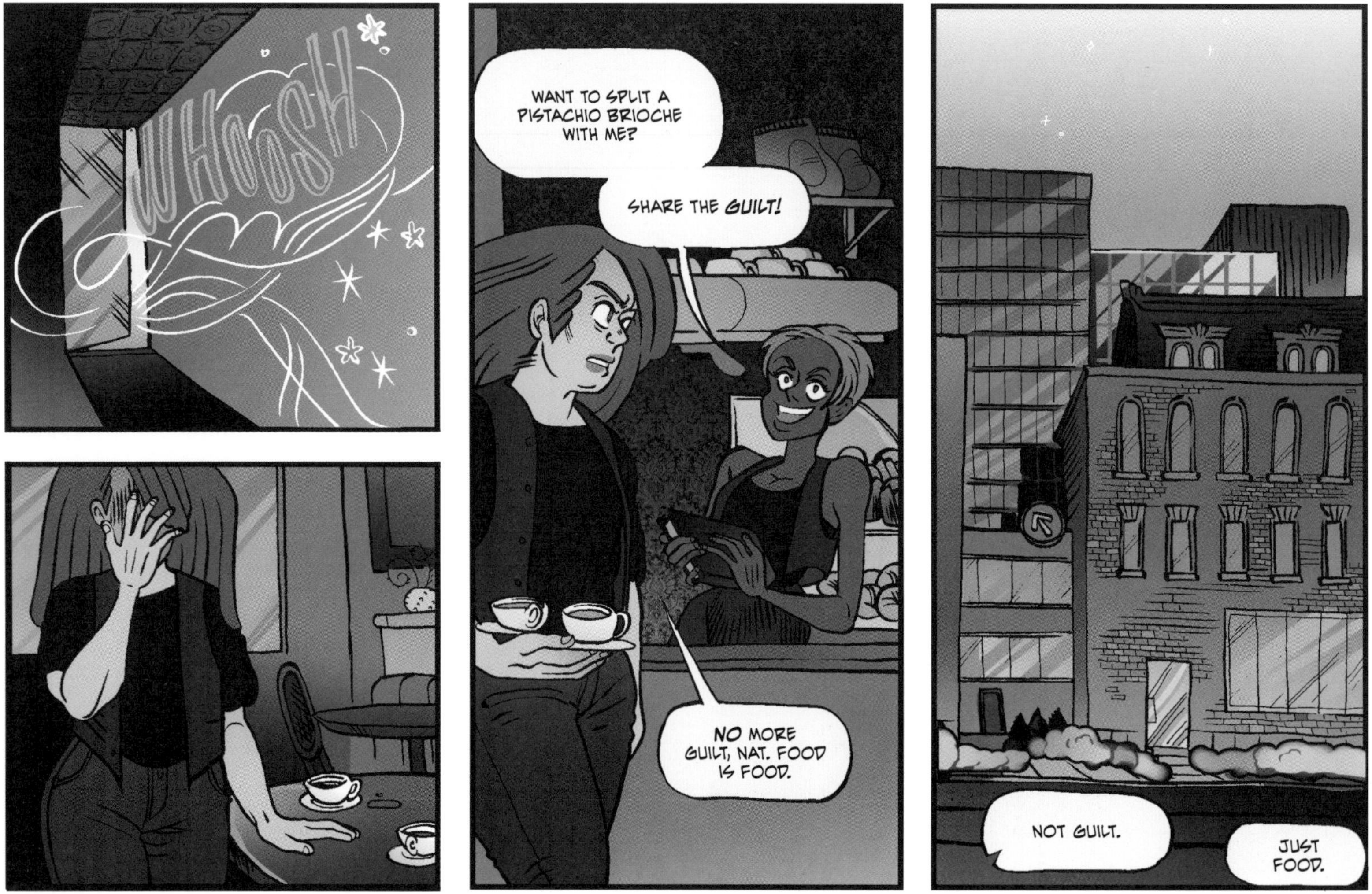
WHOOSH
WANT TO SPLIT A PISTACHIO BRIOCHE WITH ME?
SHARE THE GUILT!
NO MORE GUILT, NAT. FOOD IS FOOD.
NOT GUILT.
JUST FOOD.

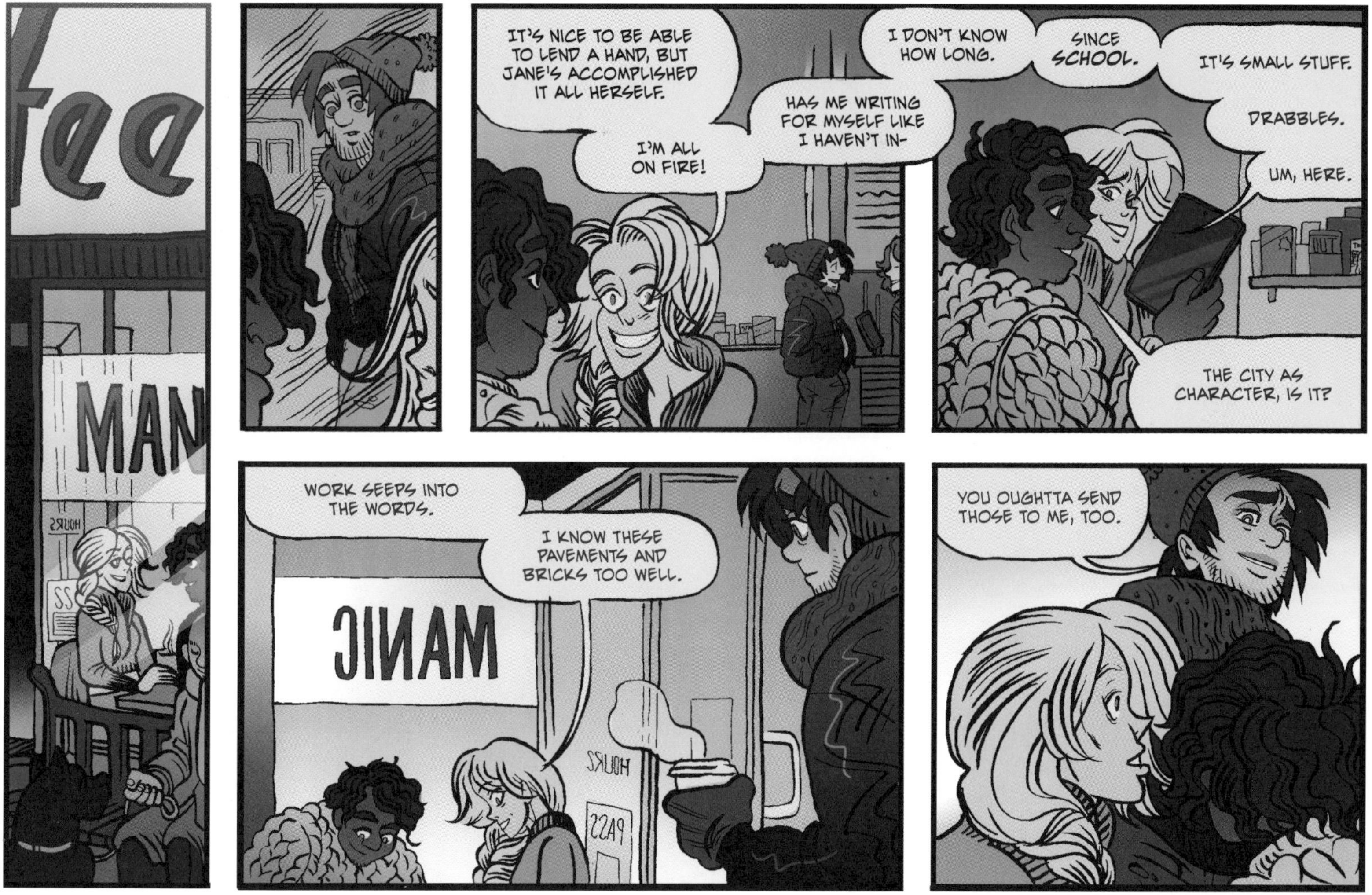

IT'S NICE TO BE ABLE TO LEND A HAND, BUT JANE'S ACCOMPLISHED IT ALL HERSELF.
I'M ALL ON FIRE!
HAS ME WRITING FOR MYSELF LIKE I HAVEN'T IN-
I DON'T KNOW HOW LONG.
SINCE SCHOOL.
IT'S SMALL STUFF.
DRABBLES.
UM, HERE.
THE CITY AS CHARACTER, IS IT?
WORK SEEPS INTO THE WORDS.
I KNOW THESE PAVEMENTS AND BRICKS TOO WELL.
MANIC
YOU OUGHTTA SEND THOSE TO ME, TOO.

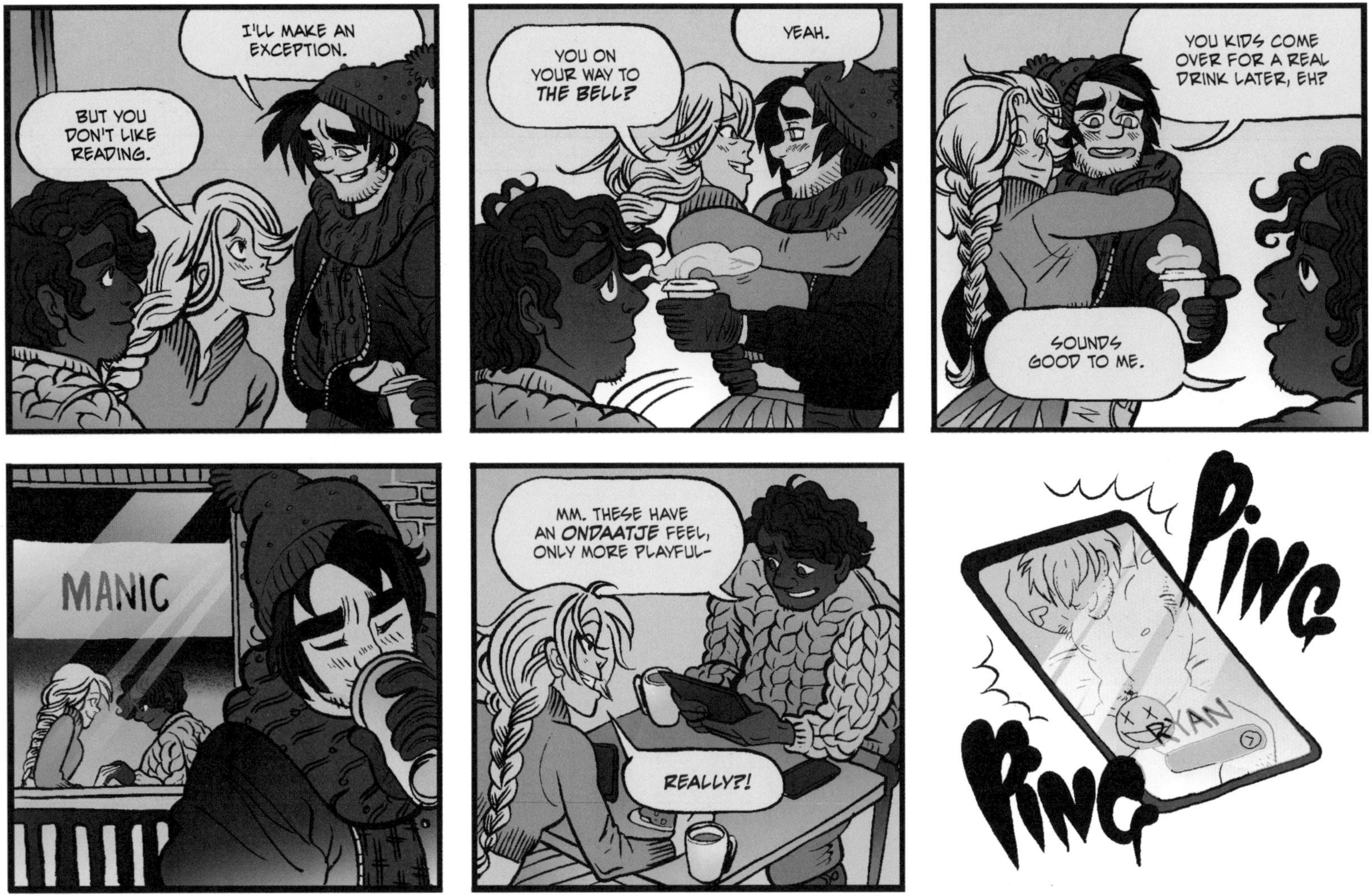

BUT YOU DON'T LIKE READING.
I'LL MAKE AN EXCEPTION.
YOU ON YOUR WAY TO THE BELL?
YEAH.
YOU KIDS COME OVER FOR A REAL DRINK LATER, EH?
SOUNDS GOOD TO ME.
MANIC
MM. THESE HAVE AN ONDAATJE FEEL, ONLY MORE PLAYFUL-
REALLY?!
PING
PING
RYAN

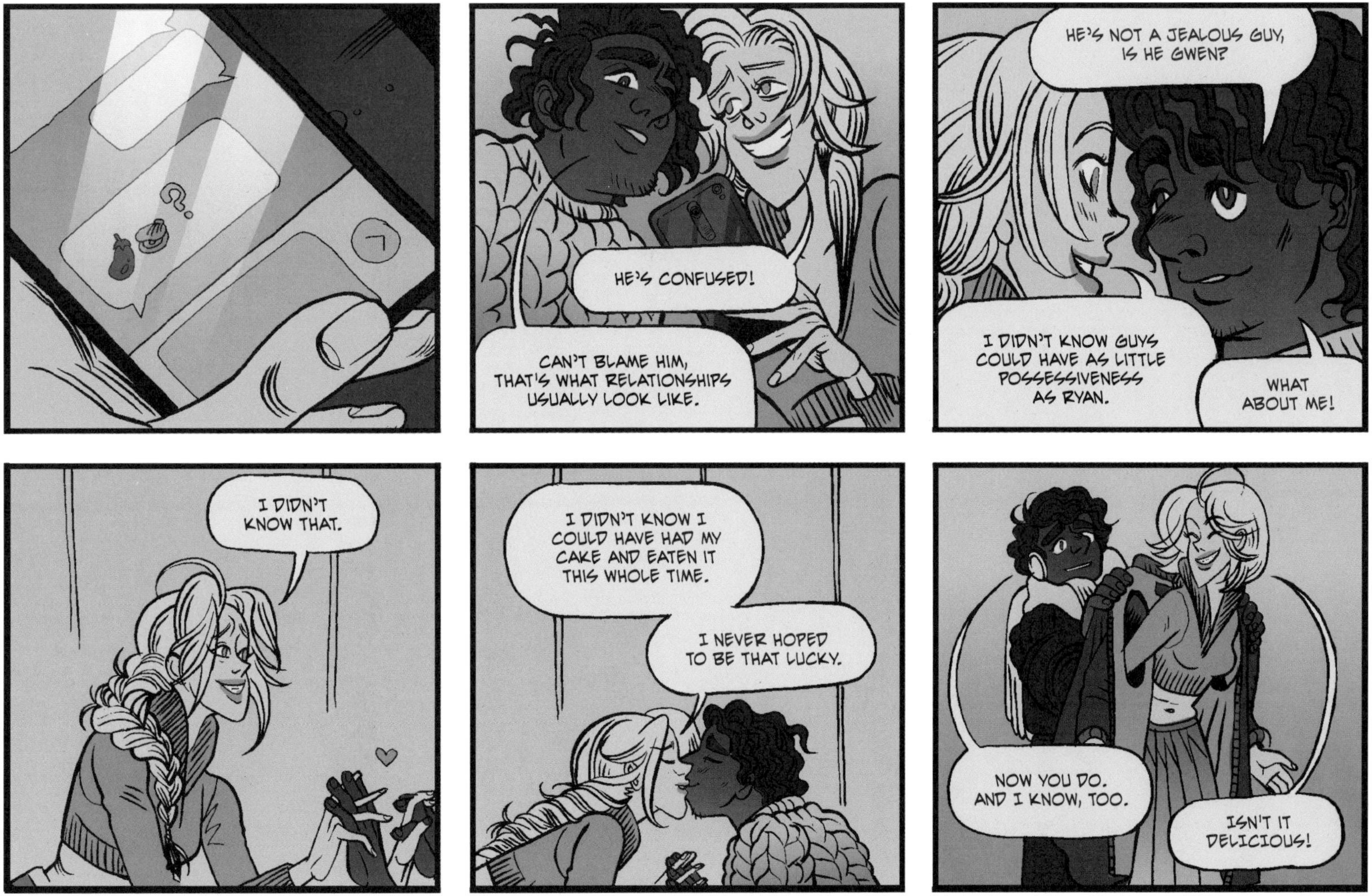

HE'S CONFUSED!
CAN'T BLAME HIM, THAT'S WHAT RELATIONSHIPS USUALLY LOOK LIKE.
HE'S NOT A JEALOUS GUY, IS HE GWEN?
I DIDN'T KNOW GUYS COULD HAVE AS LITTLE POSSESSIVENESS AS RYAN.
WHAT ABOUT ME!
I DIDN'T KNOW THAT.
I DIDN'T KNOW I COULD HAVE HAD MY CAKE AND EATEN IT THIS WHOLE TIME.
I NEVER HOPED TO BE THAT LUCKY.
NOW YOU DO. AND I KNOW, TOO.
ISN'T IT DELICIOUS!

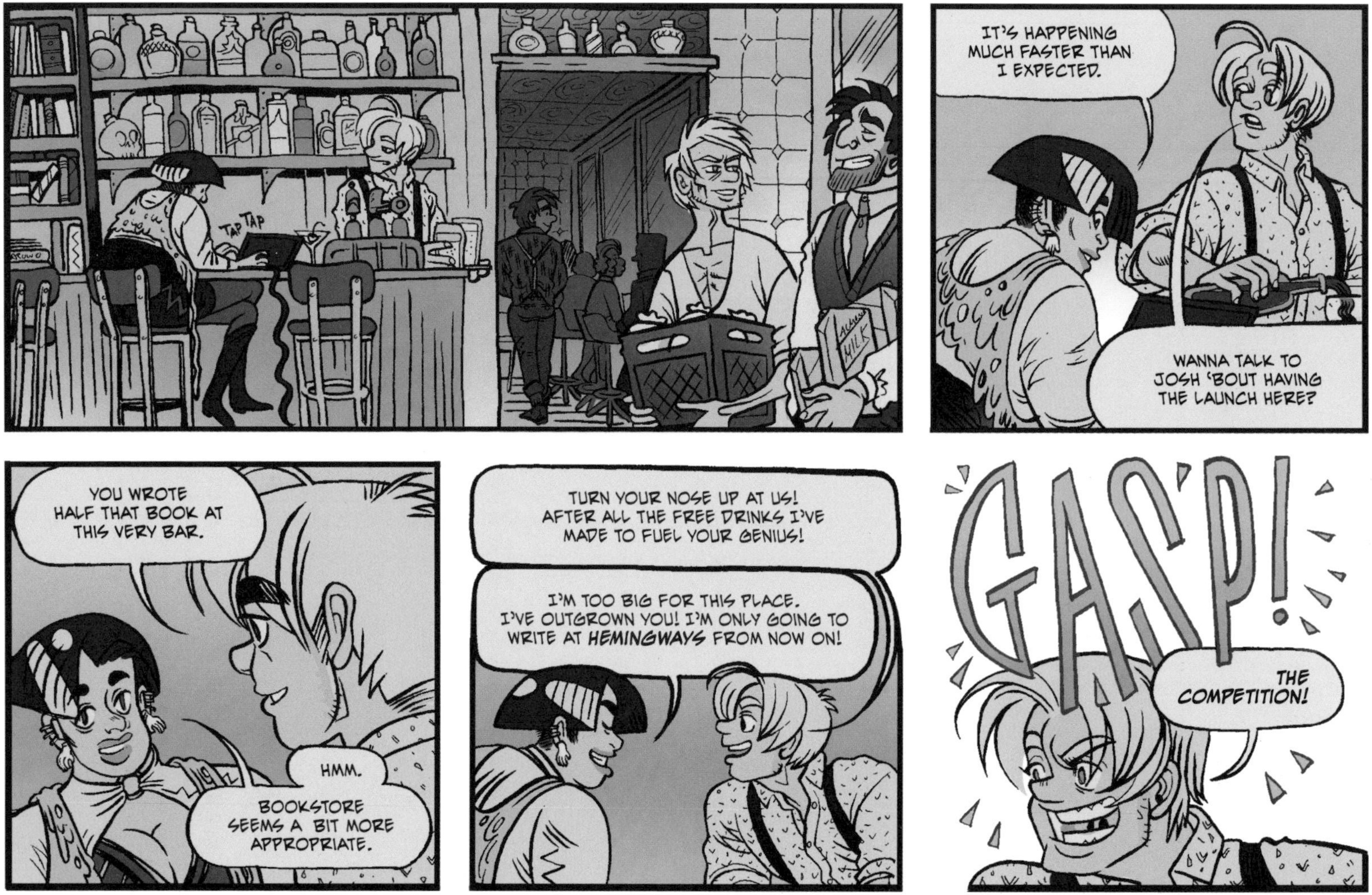
TAP TAP
IT'S HAPPENING MUCH FASTER THAN I EXPECTED.
WANNA TALK TO JOSH 'BOUT HAVING THE LAUNCH HERE?
YOU WROTE HALF THAT BOOK AT THIS VERY BAR.
HMM.
BOOKSTORE SEEMS A BIT MORE APPROPRIATE.
TURN YOUR NOSE UP AT US! AFTER ALL THE FREE DRINKS I'VE MADE TO FUEL YOUR GENIUS!
I'M TOO BIG FOR THIS PLACE. I'VE OUTGROWN YOU! I'M ONLY GOING TO WRITE AT HEMINGWAYS FROM NOW ON!
GASP!
THE COMPETITION!

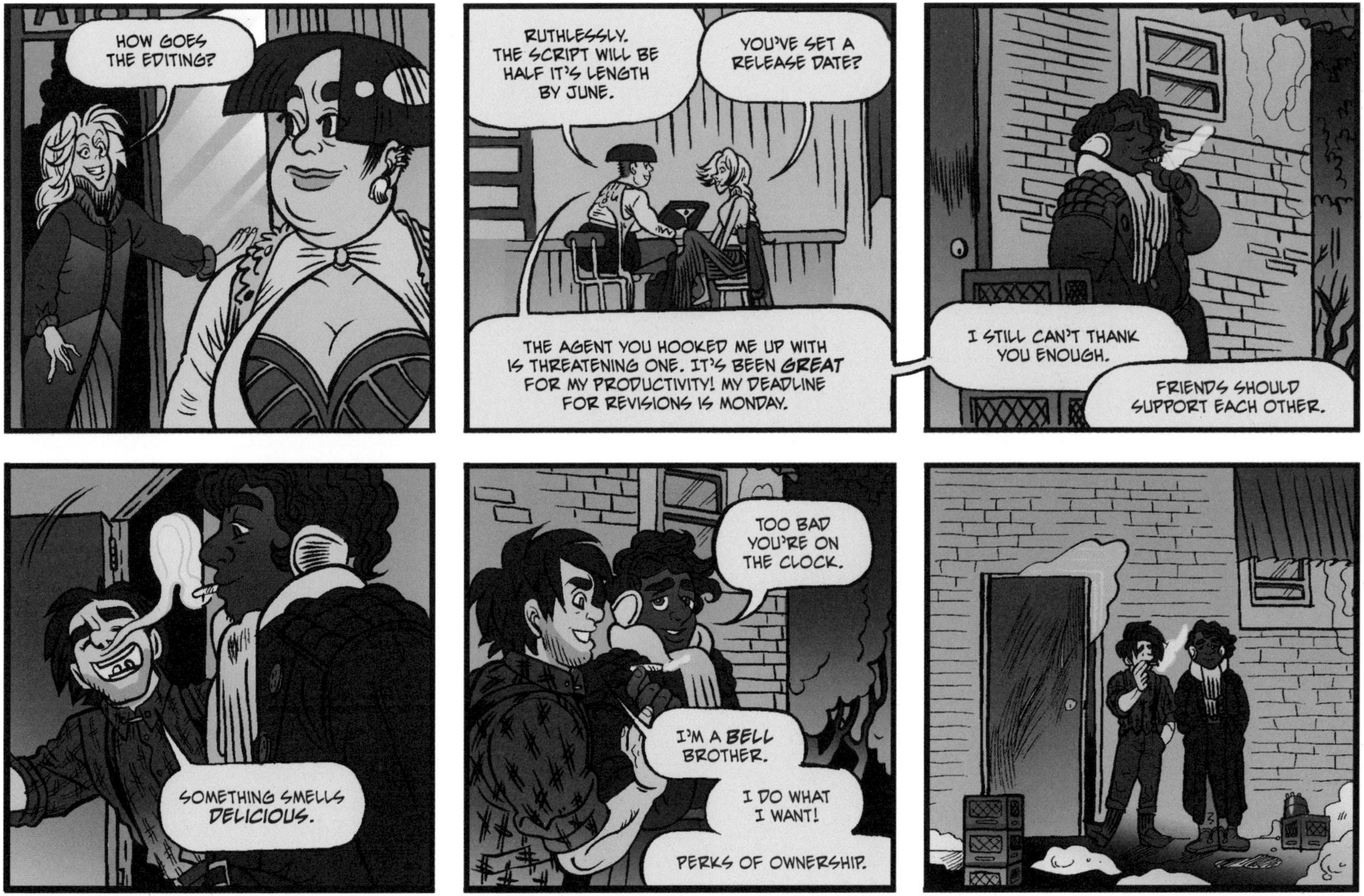
HOW GOES THE EDITING?
RUTHLESSLY. THE SCRIPT WILL BE HALF IT'S LENGTH BY JUNE.
YOU'VE SET A RELEASE DATE?
THE AGENT YOU HOOKED ME UP WITH IS THREATENING ONE. IT'S BEEN GREAT FOR MY PRODUCTIVITY! MY DEADLINE FOR REVISIONS IS MONDAY.
I STILL CAN'T THANK YOU ENOUGH.
FRIENDS SHOULD SUPPORT EACH OTHER.
SOMETHING SMELLS DELICIOUS.
TOO BAD YOU'RE ON THE CLOCK.
I'M A BELL BROTHER.
I DO WHAT I WANT!
PERKS OF OWNERSHIP.

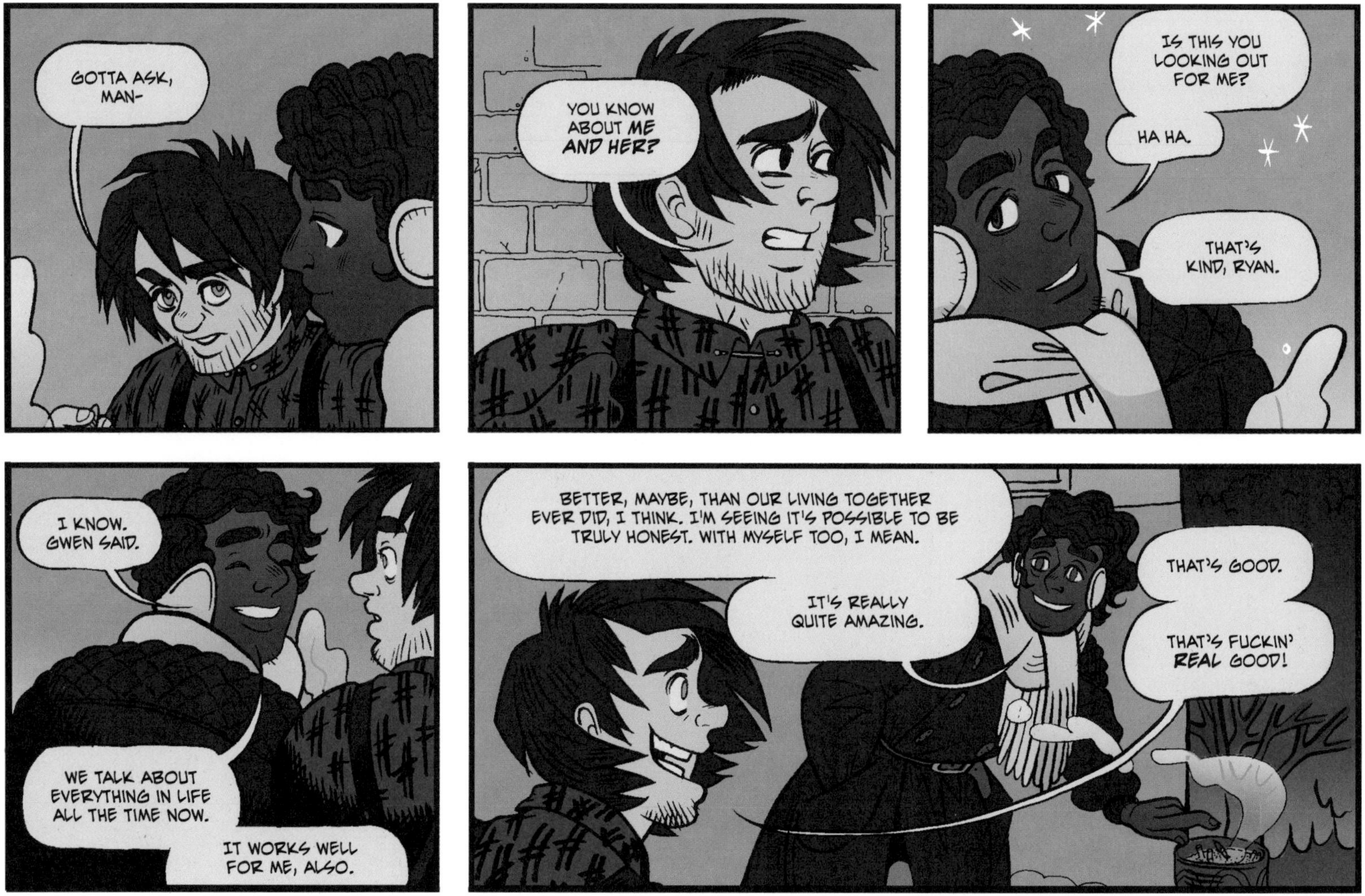
GOTTA ASK, MAN-
YOU KNOW ABOUT ME AND HER?
IS THIS YOU LOOKING OUT FOR ME?
HA HA.
THAT'S KIND, RYAN.
I KNOW. GWEN SAID.
WE TALK ABOUT EVERYTHING IN LIFE ALL THE TIME NOW.
IT WORKS WELL FOR ME, ALSO.
BETTER, MAYBE, THAN OUR LIVING TOGETHER EVER DID, I THINK. I'M SEEING IT'S POSSIBLE TO BE TRULY HONEST. WITH MYSELF TOO, I MEAN.
IT'S REALLY QUITE AMAZING.
THAT'S GOOD.
THAT'S FUCKIN' REAL GOOD!

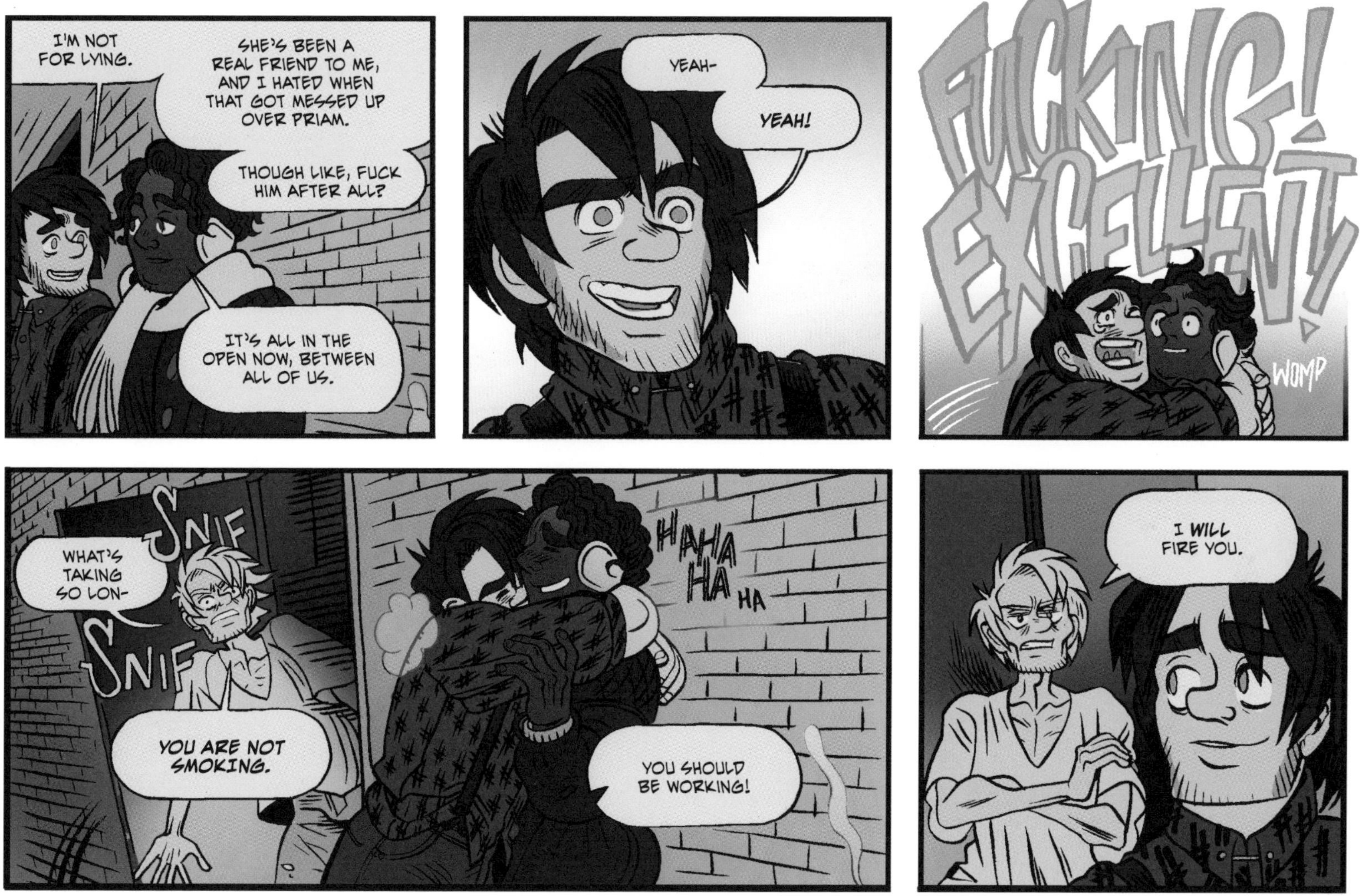
I'M NOT FOR LYING.
SHE'S BEEN A REAL FRIEND TO ME, AND I HATED WHEN THAT GOT MESSED UP OVER PRIAM.
THOUGH LIKE, FUCK HIM AFTER ALL?
IT'S ALL IN THE OPEN NOW, BETWEEN ALL OF US.
YEAH-
YEAH!
FUCKING! EXCELLENT!
WOMP
SNIF
WHAT'S TAKING SO LON-
SNIF
HAHA HA HA HA
YOU ARE NOT SMOKING.
YOU SHOULD BE WORKING!
I WILL FIRE YOU.

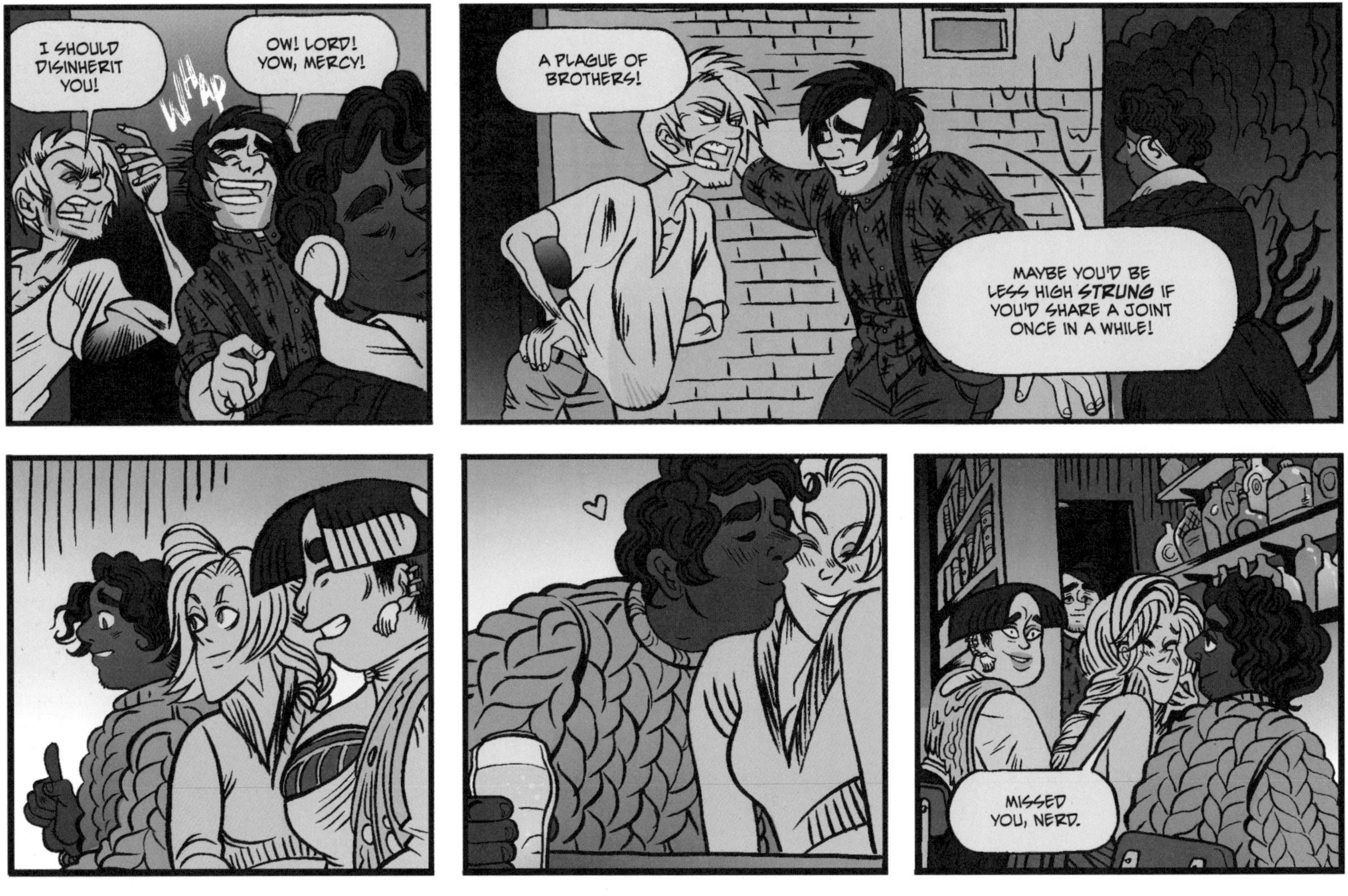
I SHOULD DISINHERIT YOU!
WHAP
OW! LORD! YOW, MERCY!
A PLAGUE OF BROTHERS!
MAYBE YOU'D BE LESS HIGH STRUNG IF YOU'D SHARE A JOINT ONCE IN A WHILE!
MISSED YOU, NERD.

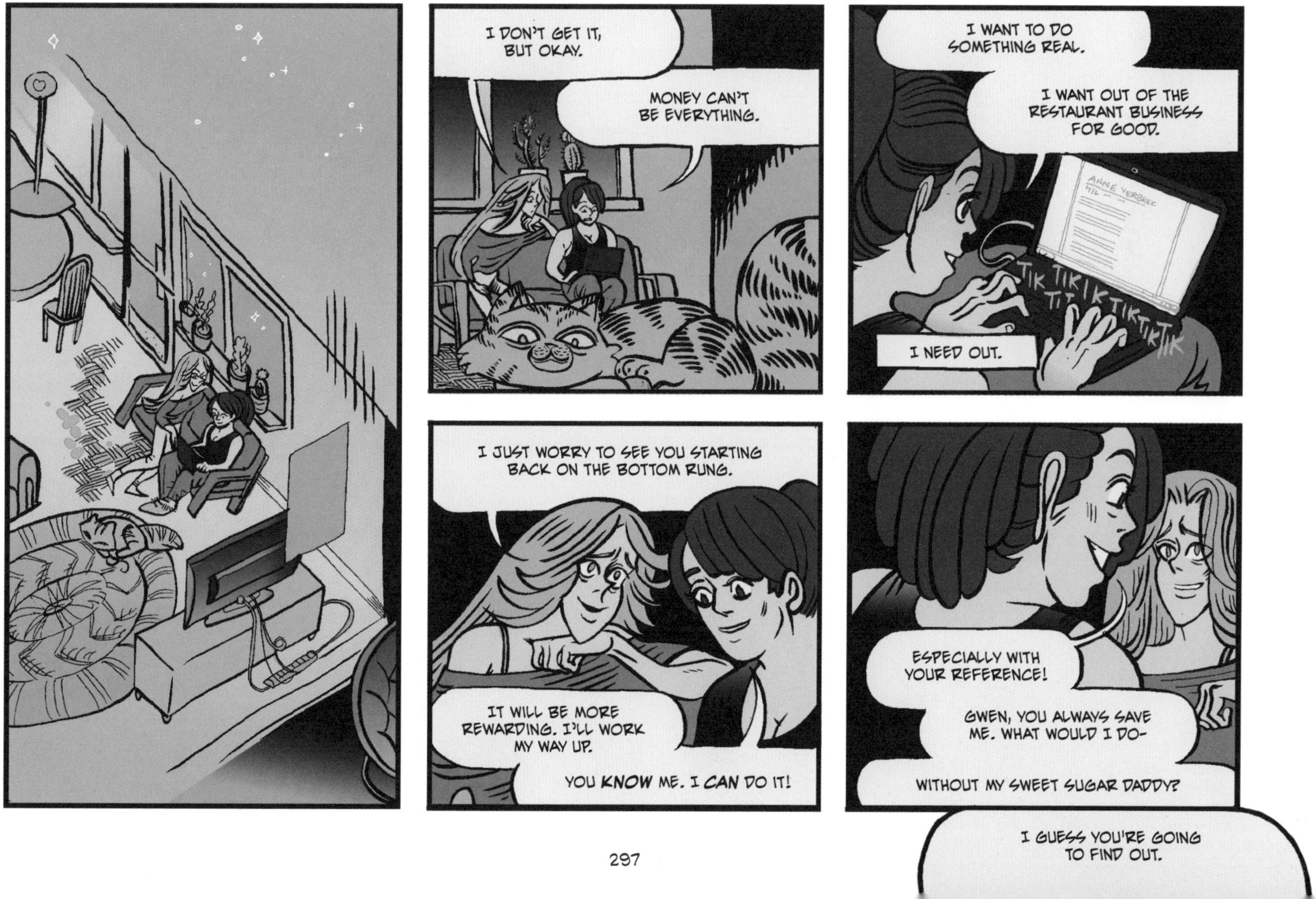
I DON'T GET IT, BUT OKAY.
MONEY CAN'T BE EVERYTHING.
I WANT TO DO SOMETHING REAL.
I WANT OUT OF THE RESTAURANT BUSINESS FOR GOOD.
ANNE VERBEEC
TIK TIK TIK TIK TIK TIK TIK TIK
I NEED OUT.
I JUST WORRY TO SEE YOU STARTING BACK ON THE BOTTOM RUNG.
IT WILL BE MORE REWARDING. I'LL WORK MY WAY UP.
YOU KNOW ME. I CAN DO IT!
ESPECIALLY WITH YOUR REFERENCE!
GWEN, YOU ALWAYS SAVE ME. WHAT WOULD I DO-
WITHOUT MY SWEET SUGAR DADDY?
I GUESS YOU'RE GOING TO FIND OUT.

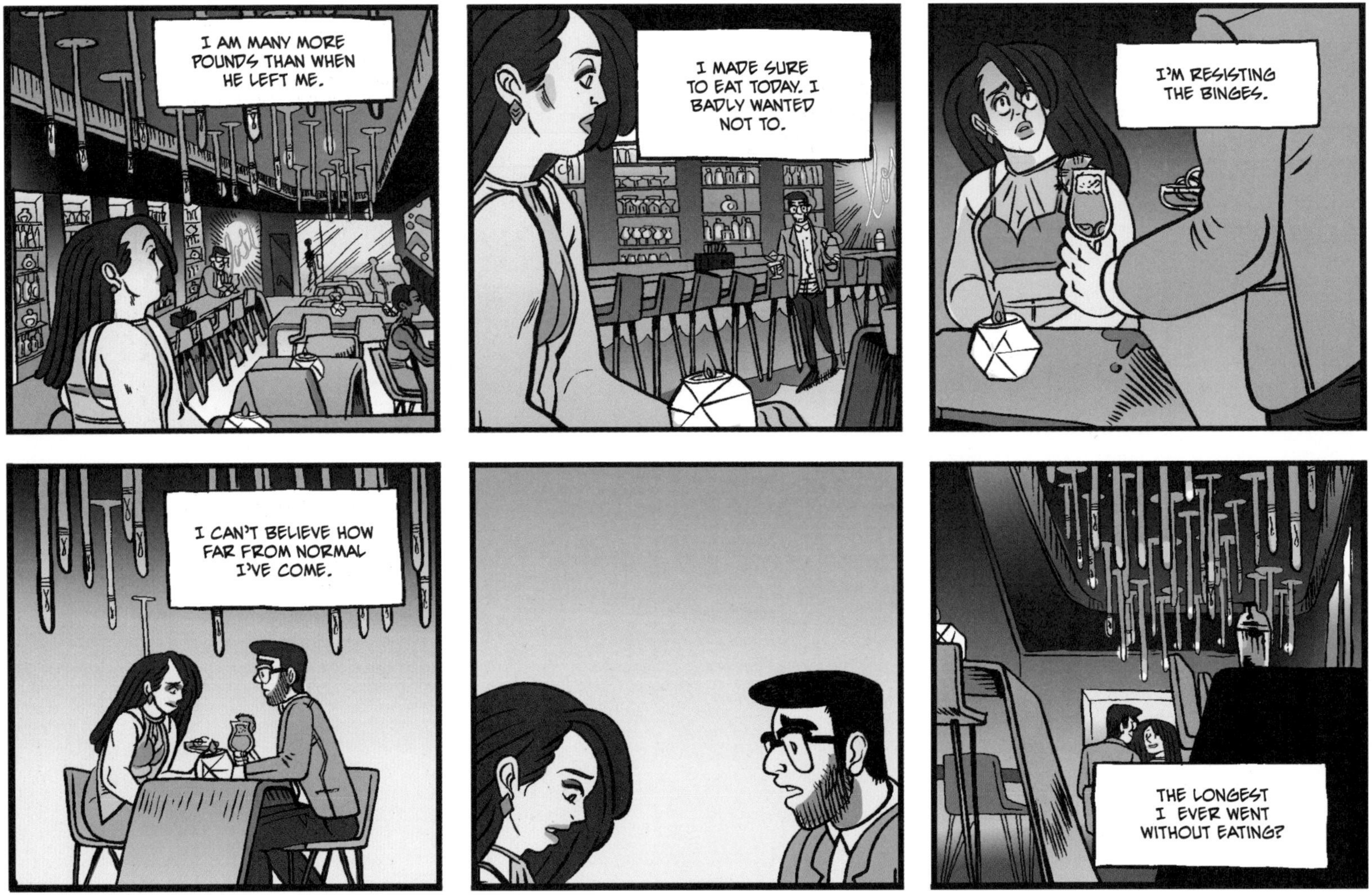
I AM MANY MORE POUNDS THAN WHEN HE LEFT ME.
I MADE SURE TO EAT TODAY. I BADLY WANTED NOT TO.
I'M RESISTING THE BINGES.
I CAN'T BELIEVE HOW FAR FROM NORMAL I'VE COME.
THE LONGEST I EVER WENT WITHOUT EATING?

FOURTEEN DAYS IN A ROW.

I'VE REPEATED THIS PATTERN SO OFTEN I CAN'T EVEN SAY WHEN IT WAS.

I STOPPED GETTING MY PERIOD FOR SIX MONTHS.

THE DOCTOR RULED OUT ANOREXIA IMMEDIATELY BECAUSE OF MY SIZE, HA.

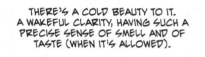

THERE'S A COLD BEAUTY TO IT. A WAKEFUL CLARITY, HAVING SUCH A PRECISE SENSE OF SMELL AND OF TASTE (WHEN IT'S ALLOWED).

THE REST IS VERY UGLY.

I CAN'T ENJOY THOSE ACUTE SENSES WHEN EATING WITH MY FRIENDS CAUSES A *PANIC ATTACK.*

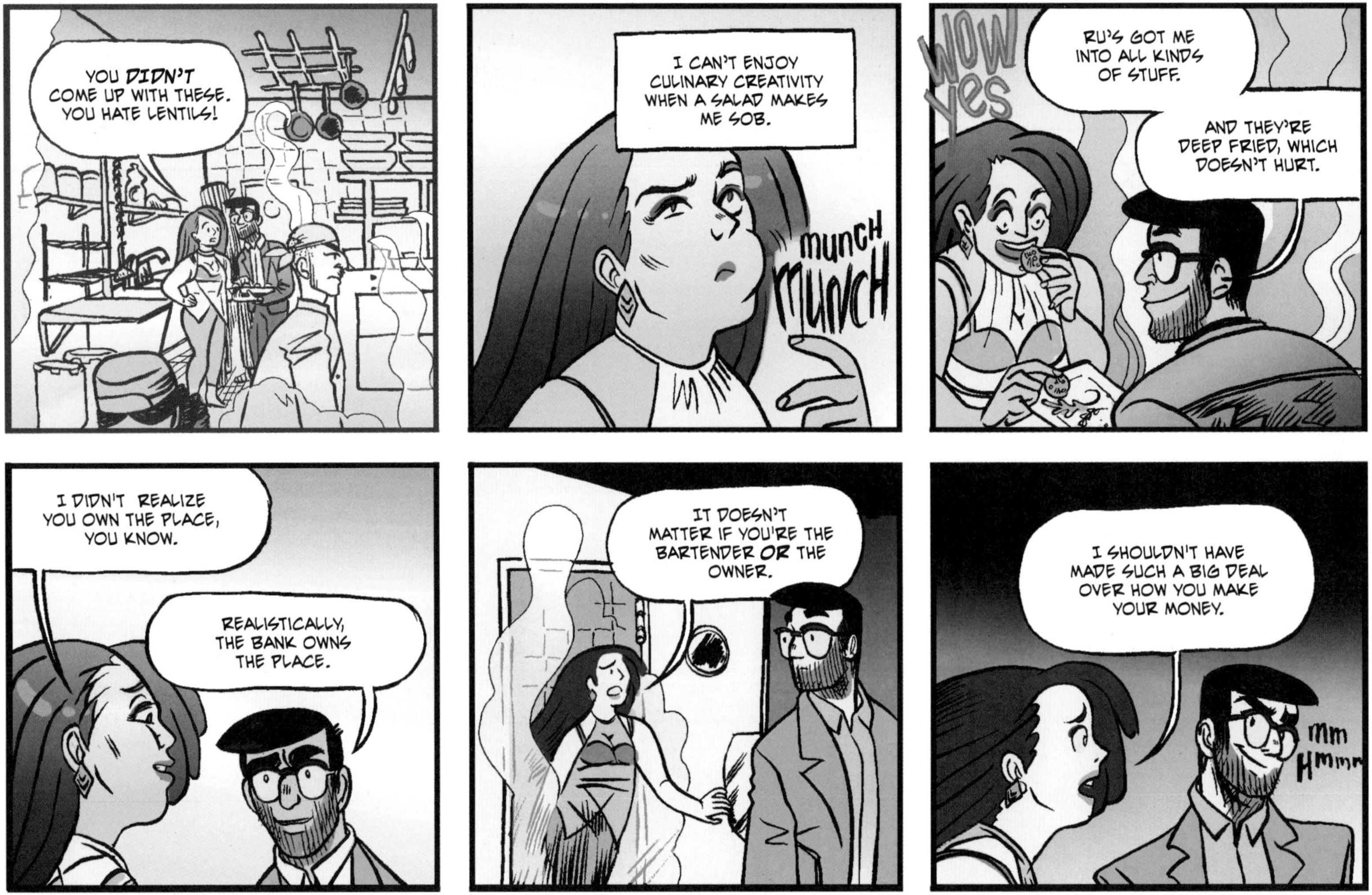
YOU **DIDN'T** COME UP WITH THESE. YOU HATE LENTILS!
I CAN'T ENJOY CULINARY CREATIVITY WHEN A SALAD MAKES ME SOB.
munch
munch
WOW
yes
RU'S GOT ME INTO ALL KINDS OF STUFF.
AND THEY'RE DEEP FRIED, WHICH DOESN'T HURT.
I DIDN'T REALIZE YOU OWN THE PLACE, YOU KNOW.
REALISTICALLY, THE BANK OWNS THE PLACE.
IT DOESN'T MATTER IF YOU'RE THE BARTENDER **OR** THE OWNER.
I SHOULDN'T HAVE MADE SUCH A BIG DEAL OVER HOW YOU MAKE YOUR MONEY.
mm Hmmm

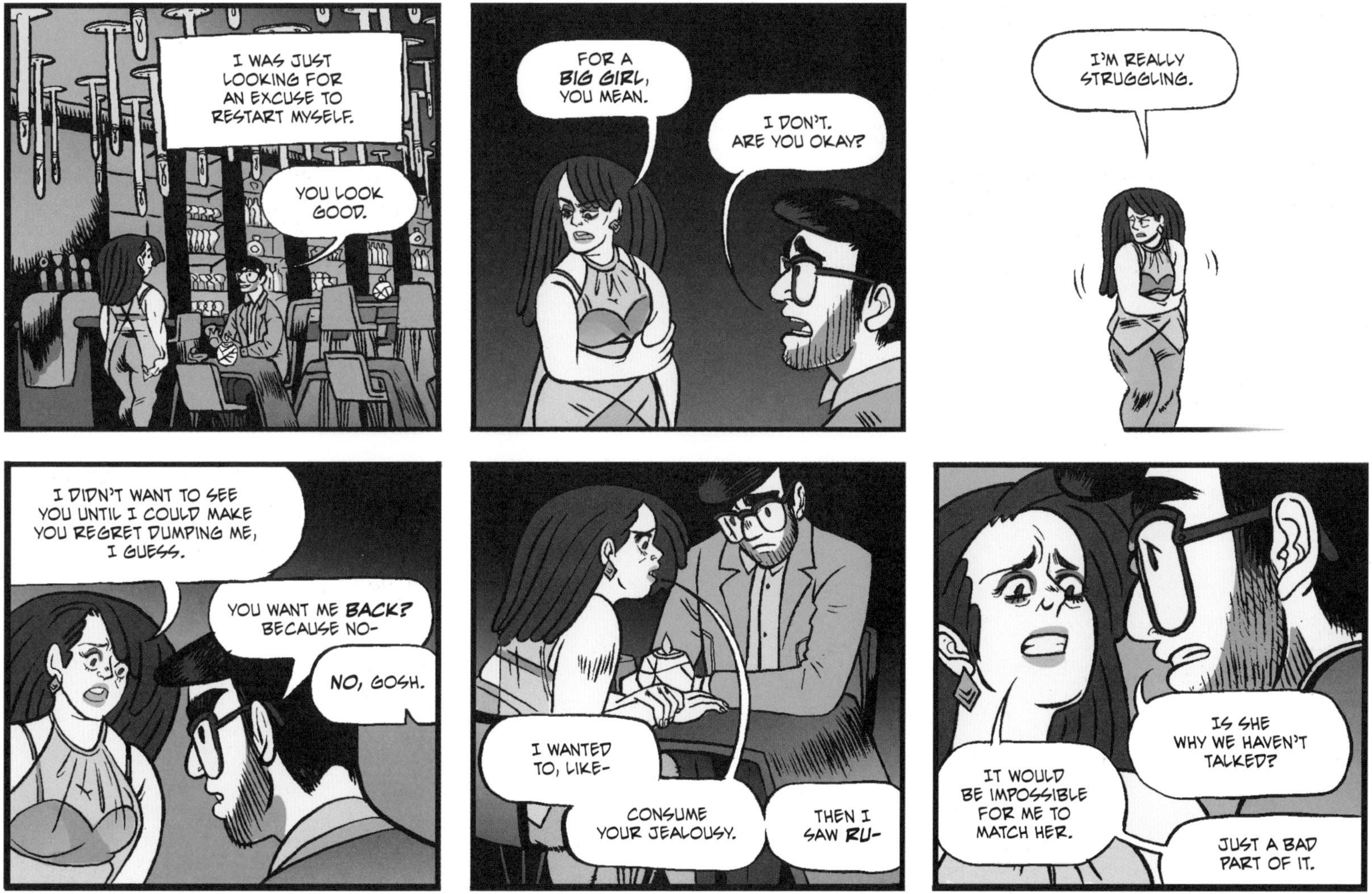
I WAS JUST LOOKING FOR AN EXCUSE TO RESTART MYSELF.
YOU LOOK GOOD.
FOR A BIG GIRL, YOU MEAN.
I DON'T. ARE YOU OKAY?
I'M REALLY STRUGGLING.
I DIDN'T WANT TO SEE YOU UNTIL I COULD MAKE YOU REGRET DUMPING ME, I GUESS.
YOU WANT ME BACK? BECAUSE NO-
NO, GOSH.
I WANTED TO, LIKE-
CONSUME YOUR JEALOUSY.
THEN I SAW RU-
IS SHE WHY WE HAVEN'T TALKED?
IT WOULD BE IMPOSSIBLE FOR ME TO MATCH HER.
JUST A BAD PART OF IT.

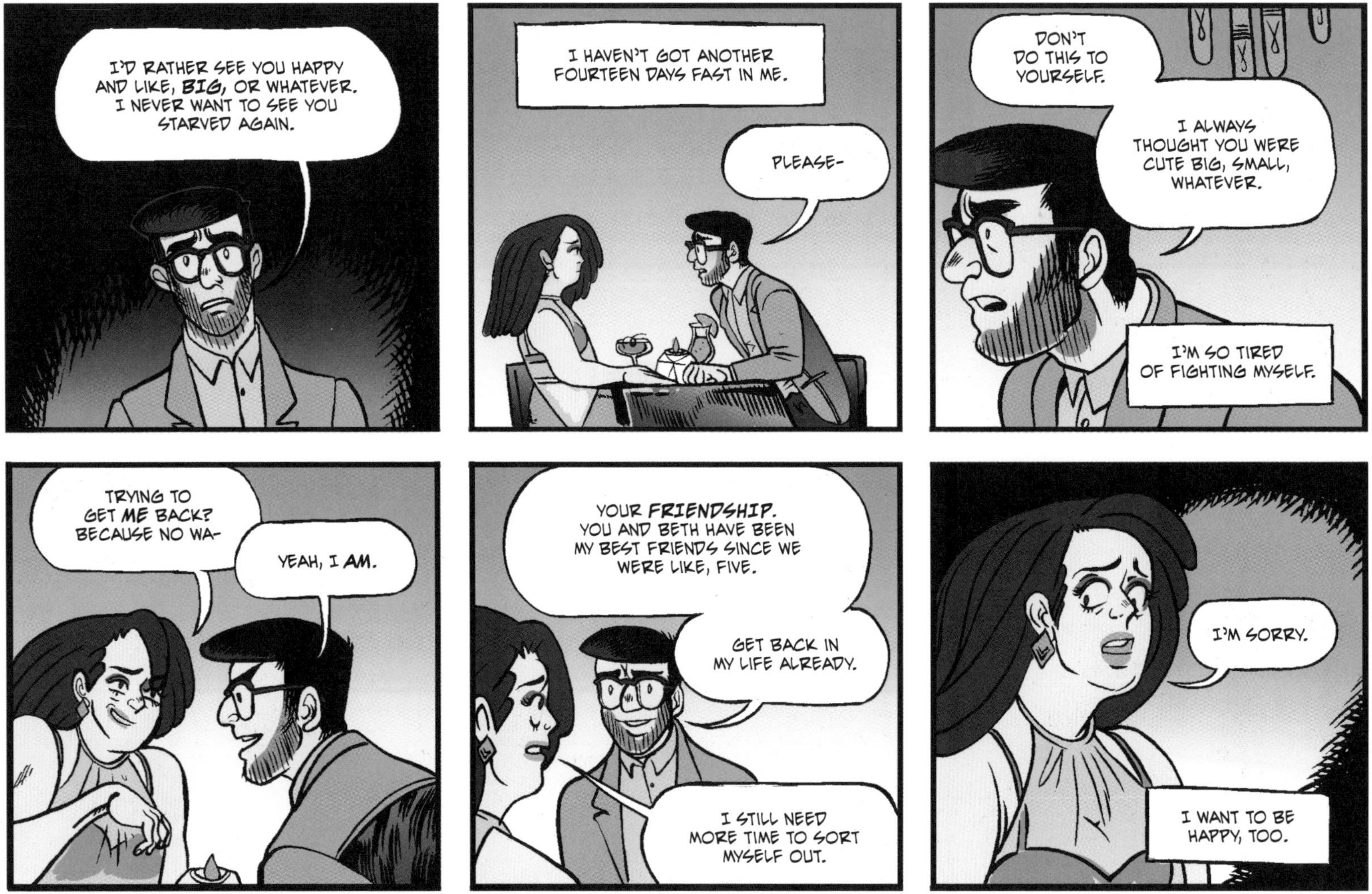
I'D RATHER SEE YOU HAPPY AND LIKE, **BIG**, OR WHATEVER. I NEVER WANT TO SEE YOU STARVED AGAIN.
I HAVEN'T GOT ANOTHER FOURTEEN DAYS FAST IN ME.
PLEASE-
DON'T DO THIS TO YOURSELF.
I ALWAYS THOUGHT YOU WERE CUTE BIG, SMALL, WHATEVER.
I'M SO TIRED OF FIGHTING MYSELF.
TRYING TO GET **ME** BACK? BECAUSE NO WA-
YEAH, I **AM**.
YOUR **FRIENDSHIP**. YOU AND BETH HAVE BEEN MY BEST FRIENDS SINCE WE WERE LIKE, FIVE.
GET BACK IN MY LIFE ALREADY.
I STILL NEED MORE TIME TO SORT MYSELF OUT.
I'M SORRY.
I WANT TO BE HAPPY, TOO.

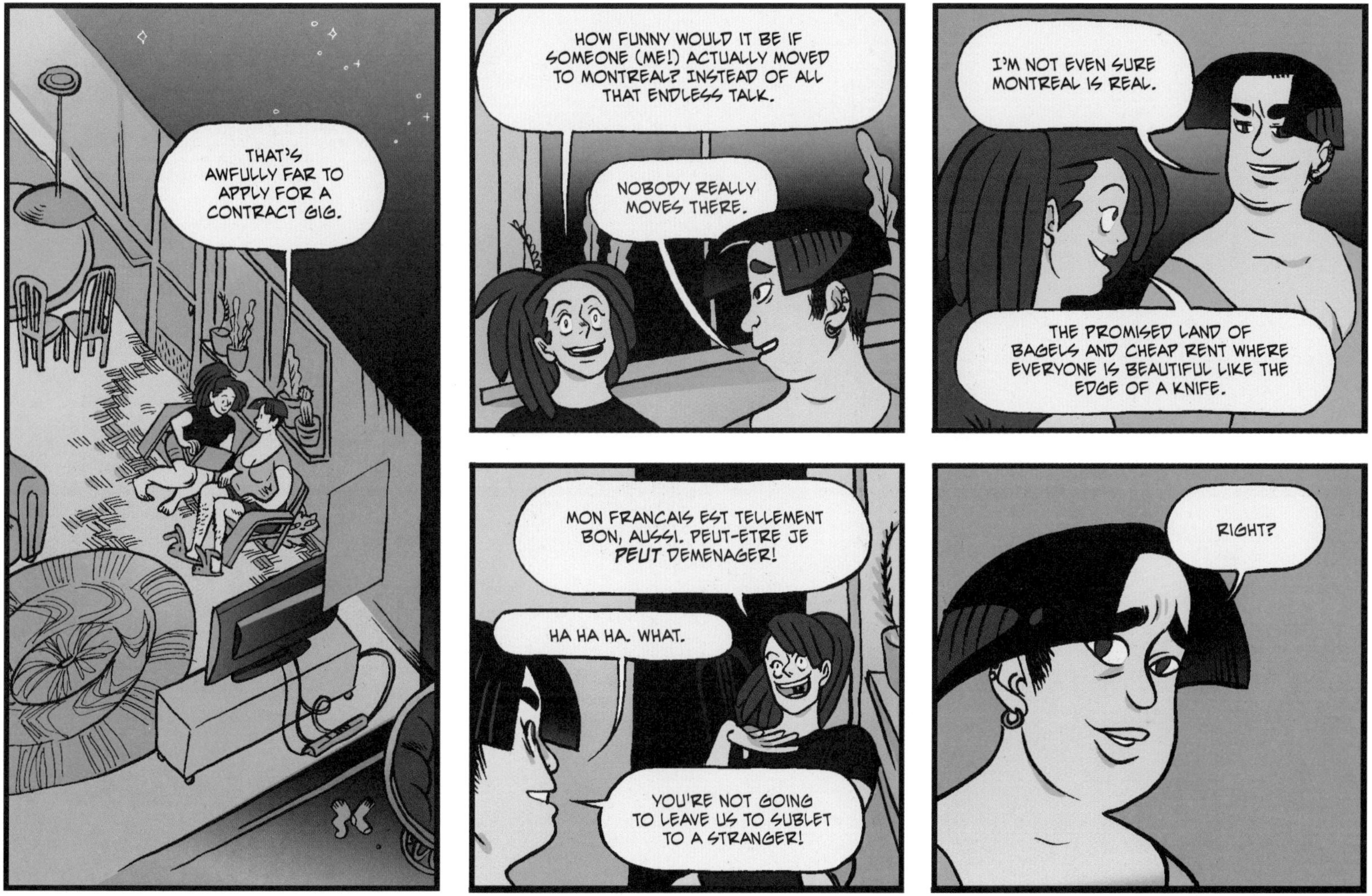
THAT'S AWFULLY FAR TO APPLY FOR A CONTRACT GIG.
HOW FUNNY WOULD IT BE IF SOMEONE (ME!) ACTUALLY MOVED TO MONTREAL? INSTEAD OF ALL THAT ENDLESS TALK.
NOBODY REALLY MOVES THERE.
I'M NOT EVEN SURE MONTREAL IS REAL.
THE PROMISED LAND OF BAGELS AND CHEAP RENT WHERE EVERYONE IS BEAUTIFUL LIKE THE EDGE OF A KNIFE.
MON FRANCAIS EST TELLEMENT BON, AUSSI. PEUT-ETRE JE *PEUT* DEMENAGER!
HA HA HA. WHAT.
YOU'RE NOT GOING TO LEAVE US TO SUBLET TO A STRANGER!
RIGHT?

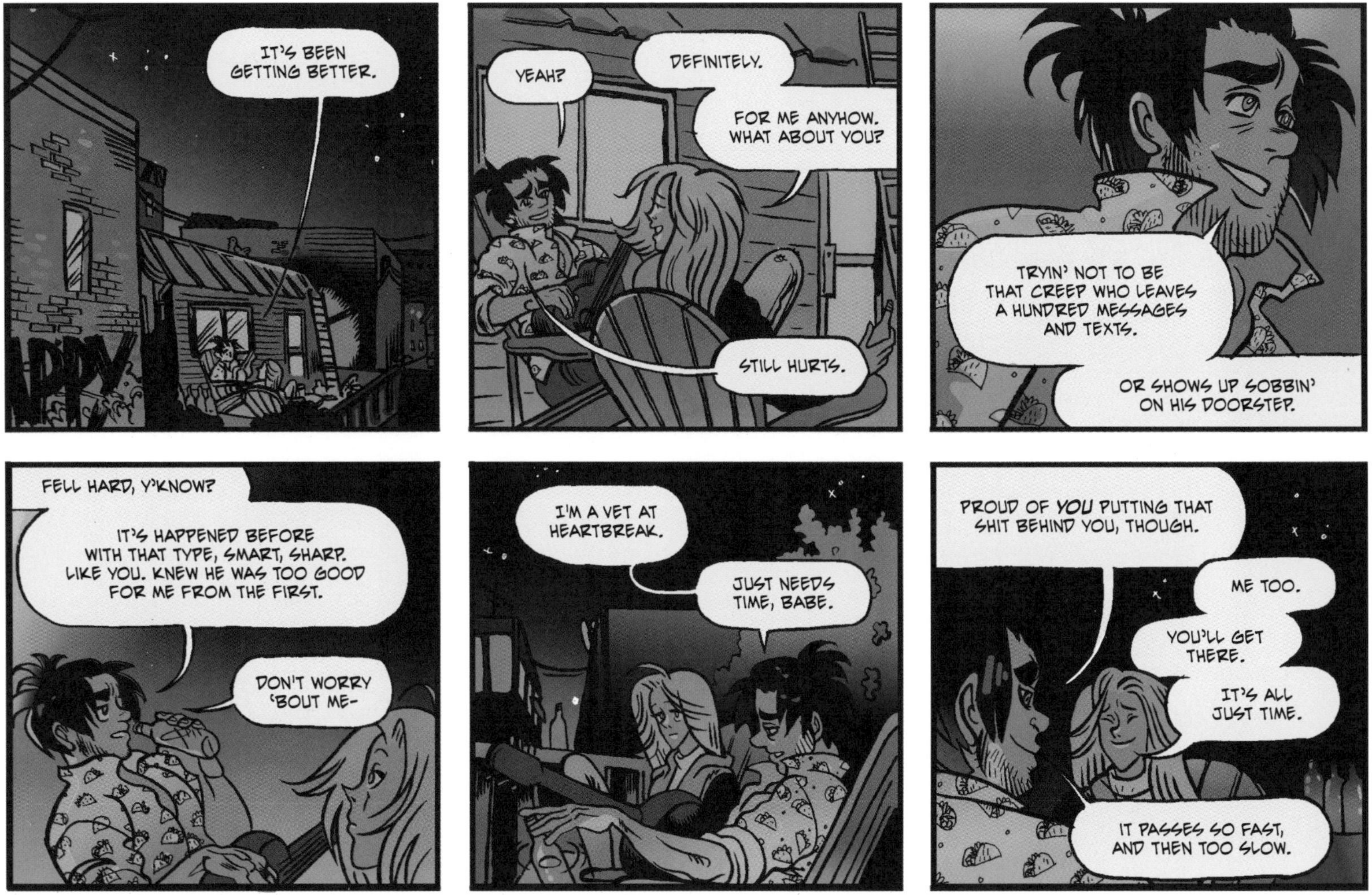
IT'S BEEN GETTING BETTER.
YEAH?
DEFINITELY.
FOR ME ANYHOW. WHAT ABOUT YOU?
STILL HURTS.
TRYIN' NOT TO BE THAT CREEP WHO LEAVES A HUNDRED MESSAGES AND TEXTS.
OR SHOWS UP SOBBIN' ON HIS DOORSTEP.
FELL HARD, Y'KNOW?
IT'S HAPPENED BEFORE WITH THAT TYPE, SMART, SHARP. LIKE YOU. KNEW HE WAS TOO GOOD FOR ME FROM THE FIRST.
DON'T WORRY 'BOUT ME-
I'M A VET AT HEARTBREAK.
JUST NEEDS TIME, BABE.
PROUD OF *YOU* PUTTING THAT SHIT BEHIND YOU, THOUGH.
ME TOO.
YOU'LL GET THERE.
IT'S ALL JUST TIME.
IT PASSES SO FAST, AND THEN TOO SLOW.

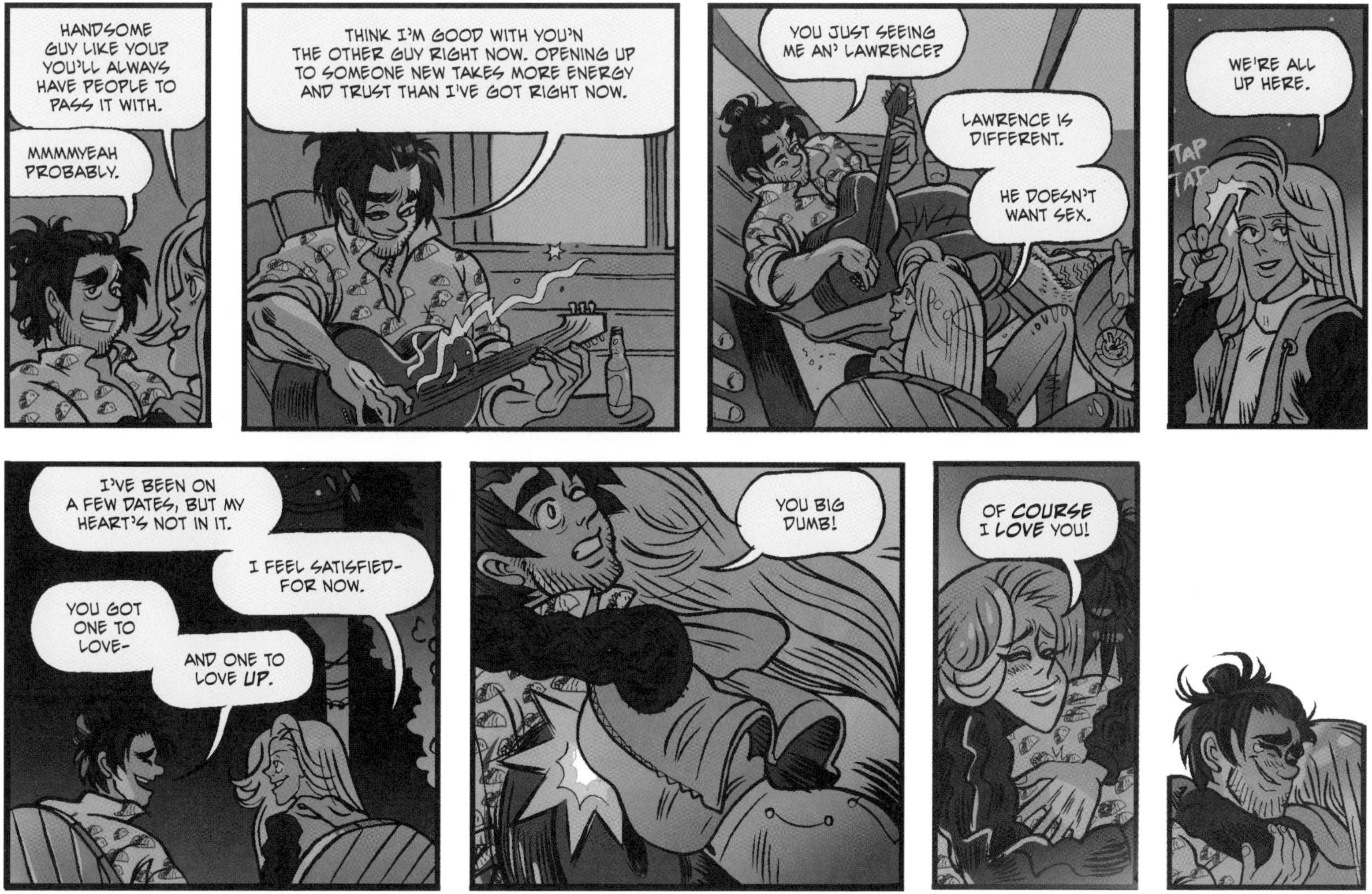
HANDSOME GUY LIKE YOU? YOU'LL ALWAYS HAVE PEOPLE TO PASS IT WITH.
MMMMYEAH PROBABLY.
THINK I'M GOOD WITH YOU'N THE OTHER GUY RIGHT NOW. OPENING UP TO SOMEONE NEW TAKES MORE ENERGY AND TRUST THAN I'VE GOT RIGHT NOW.
YOU JUST SEEING ME AN' LAWRENCE?
LAWRENCE IS DIFFERENT.
HE DOESN'T WANT SEX.
WE'RE ALL UP HERE.
TAP TAP
I'VE BEEN ON A FEW DATES, BUT MY HEART'S NOT IN IT.
I FEEL SATISFIED- FOR NOW.
YOU GOT ONE TO LOVE-
AND ONE TO LOVE UP.
YOU BIG DUMB!
OF COURSE I LOVE YOU!

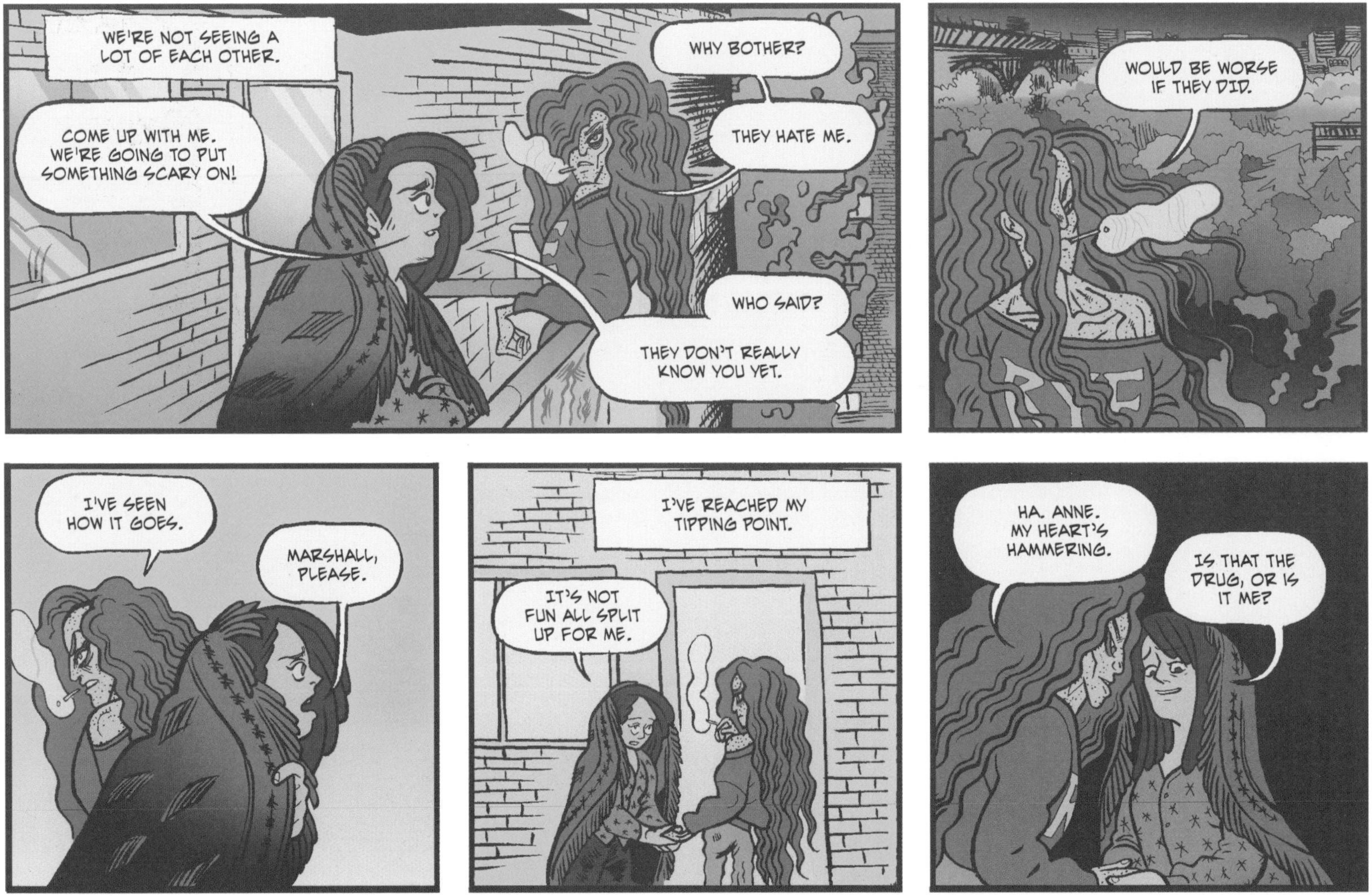

WE'RE NOT SEEING A LOT OF EACH OTHER.
COME UP WITH ME. WE'RE GOING TO PUT SOMETHING SCARY ON!
WHY BOTHER?
THEY HATE ME.
WHO SAID?
THEY DON'T REALLY KNOW YOU YET.
WOULD BE WORSE IF THEY DID.
I'VE SEEN HOW IT GOES.
MARSHALL, PLEASE.
I'VE REACHED MY TIPPING POINT.
IT'S NOT FUN ALL SPLIT UP FOR ME.
HA. ANNE. MY HEART'S HAMMERING.
IS THAT THE DRUG, OR IS IT ME?

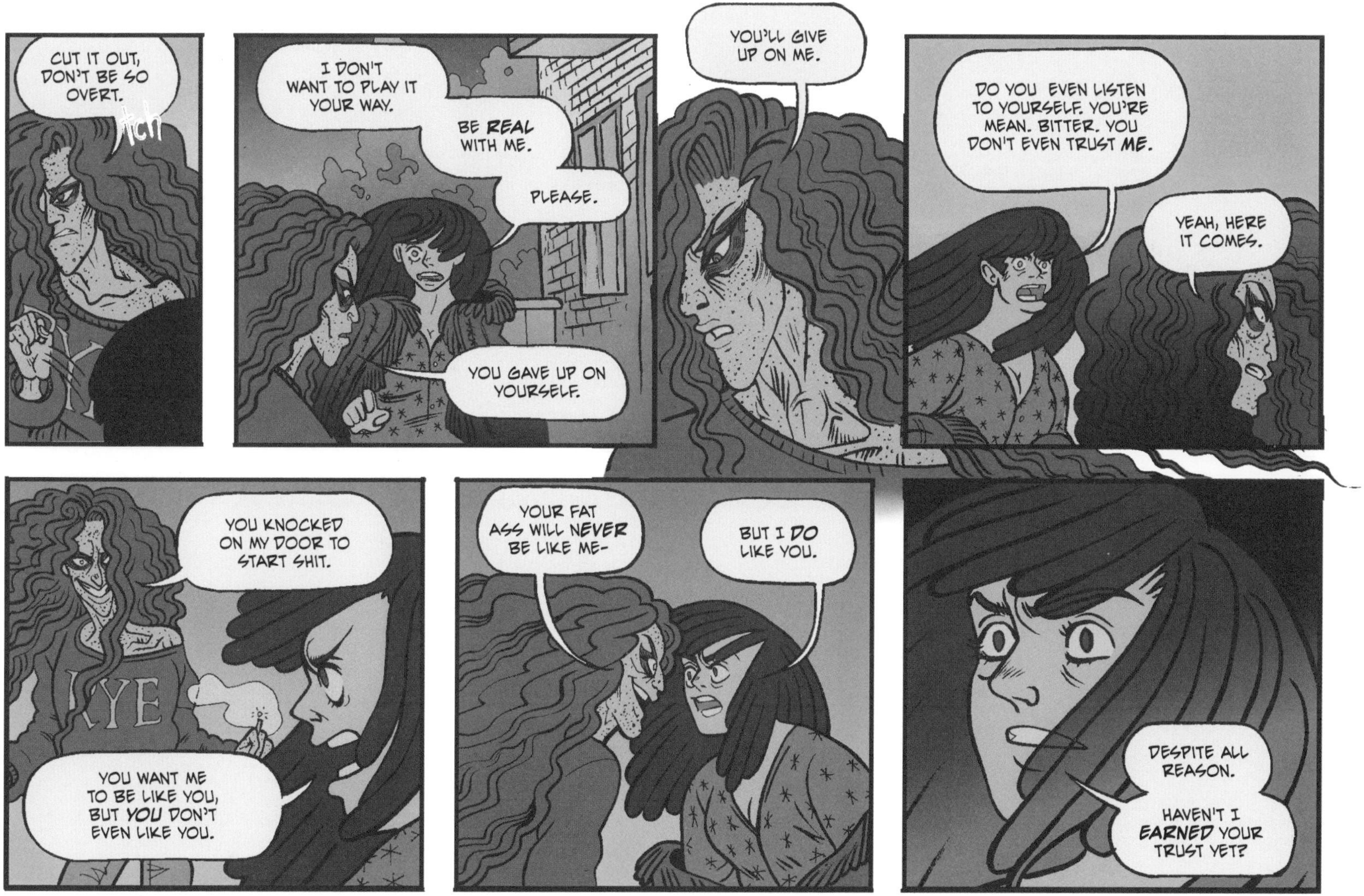
CUT IT OUT, DON'T BE SO OVERT.
tch
I DON'T WANT TO PLAY IT YOUR WAY.
BE REAL WITH ME.
PLEASE.
YOU GAVE UP ON YOURSELF.
YOU'LL GIVE UP ON ME.
DO YOU EVEN LISTEN TO YOURSELF. YOU'RE MEAN. BITTER. YOU DON'T EVEN TRUST ME.
YEAH, HERE IT COMES.
YOU KNOCKED ON MY DOOR TO START SHIT.
YOU WANT ME TO BE LIKE YOU, BUT YOU DON'T EVEN LIKE YOU.
YOUR FAT ASS WILL NEVER BE LIKE ME-
BUT I DO LIKE YOU.
DESPITE ALL REASON.
HAVEN'T I EARNED YOUR TRUST YET?

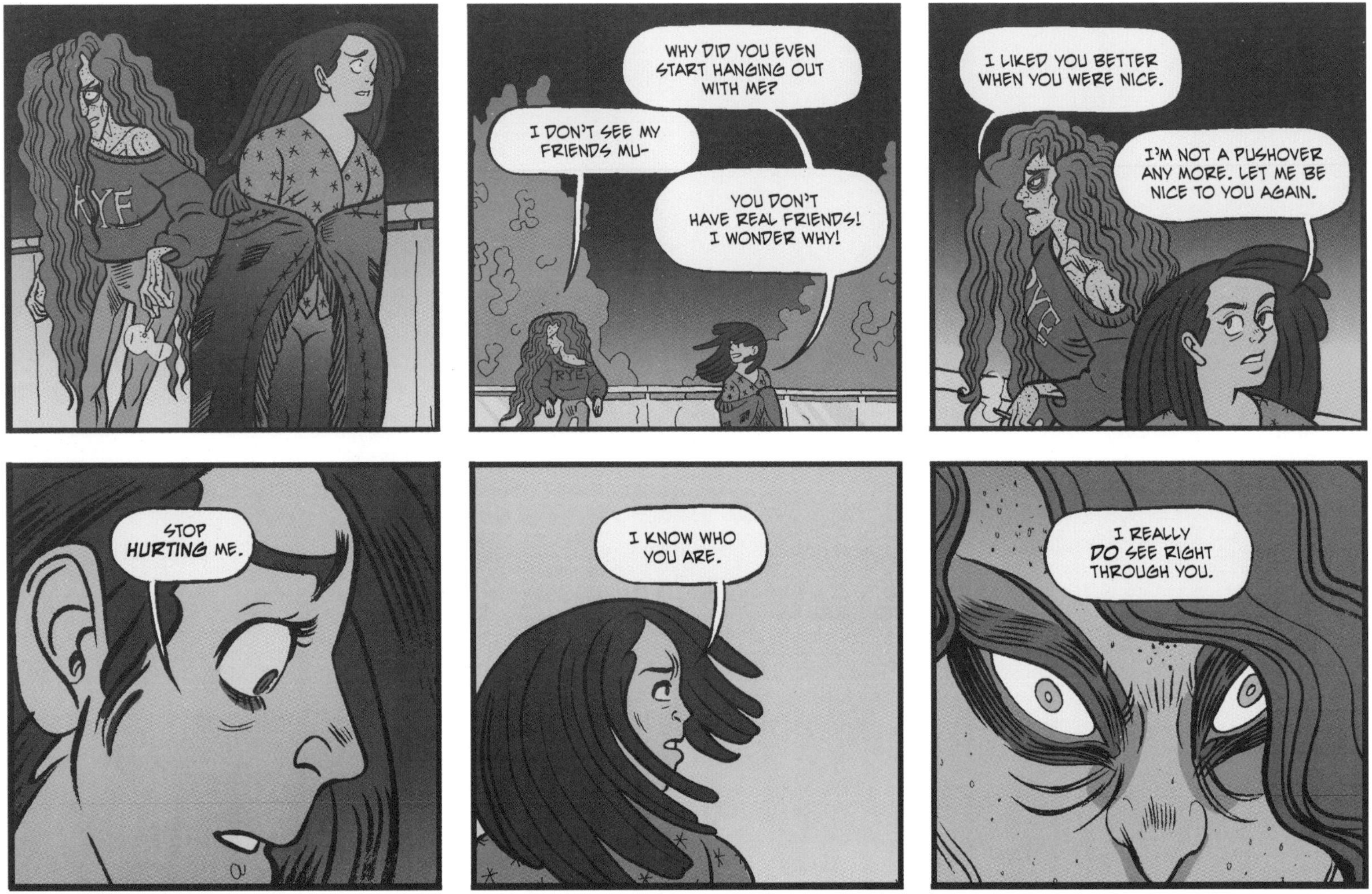
WHY DID YOU EVEN START HANGING OUT WITH ME?
I DON'T SEE MY FRIENDS MU-
YOU DON'T HAVE REAL FRIENDS! I WONDER WHY!
I LIKED YOU BETTER WHEN YOU WERE NICE.
I'M NOT A PUSHOVER ANY MORE. LET ME BE NICE TO YOU AGAIN.
STOP **HURTING** ME.
I KNOW WHO YOU ARE.
I REALLY ***DO*** SEE RIGHT THROUGH YOU.

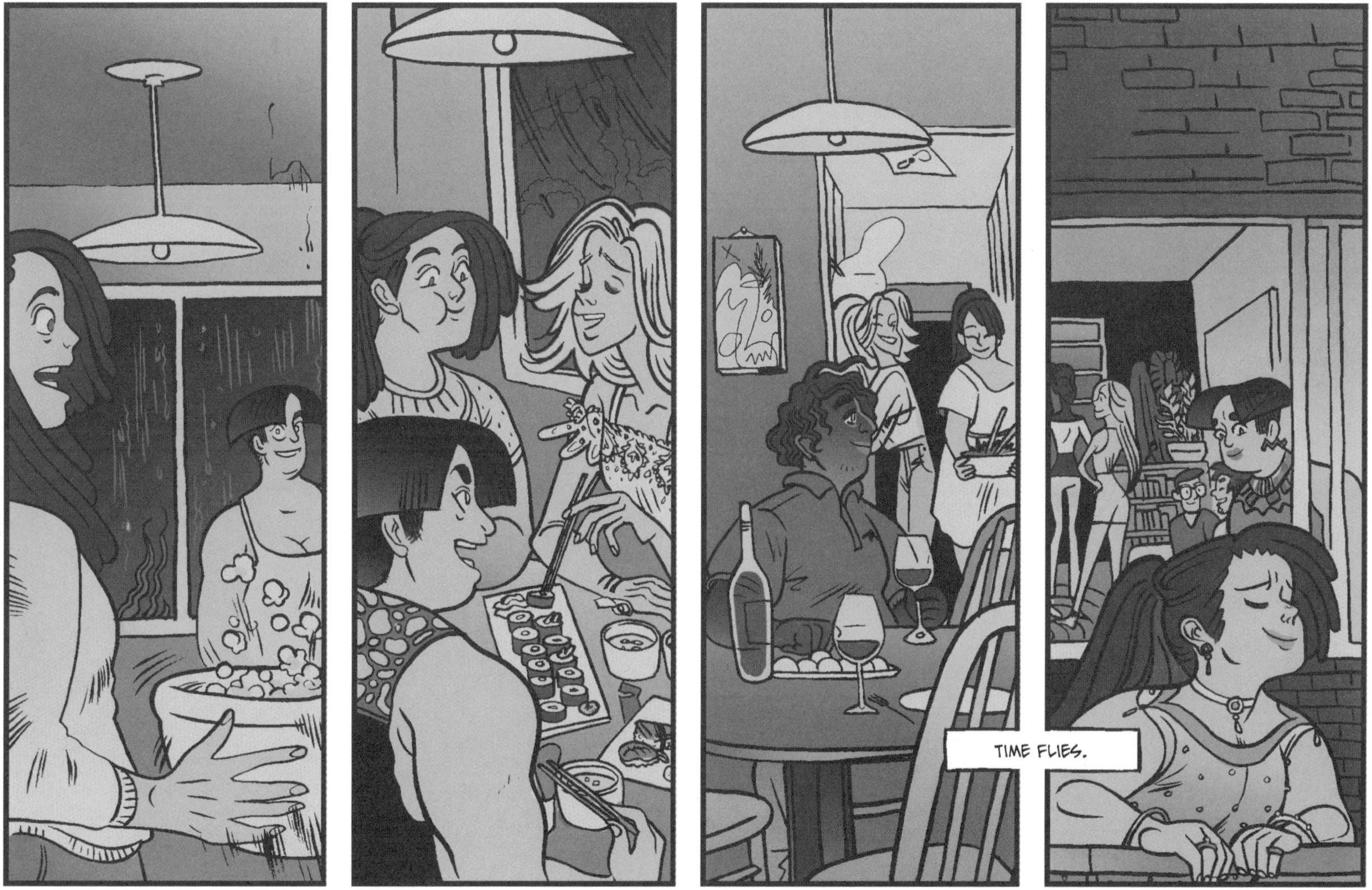
TIME FLIES.

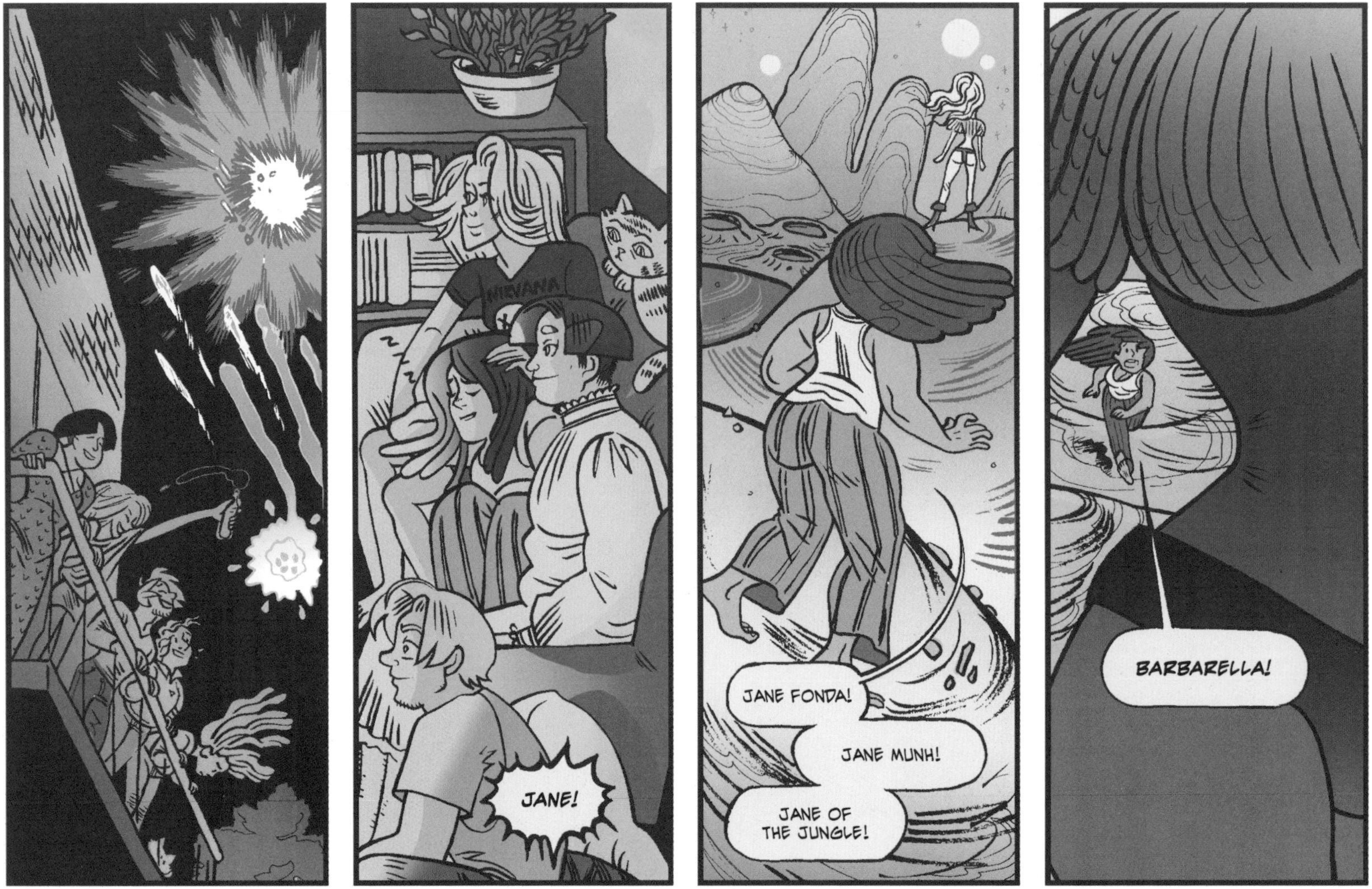
JANE!
JANE FONDA!
JANE MUNH!
JANE OF THE JUNGLE!
BARBARELLA!

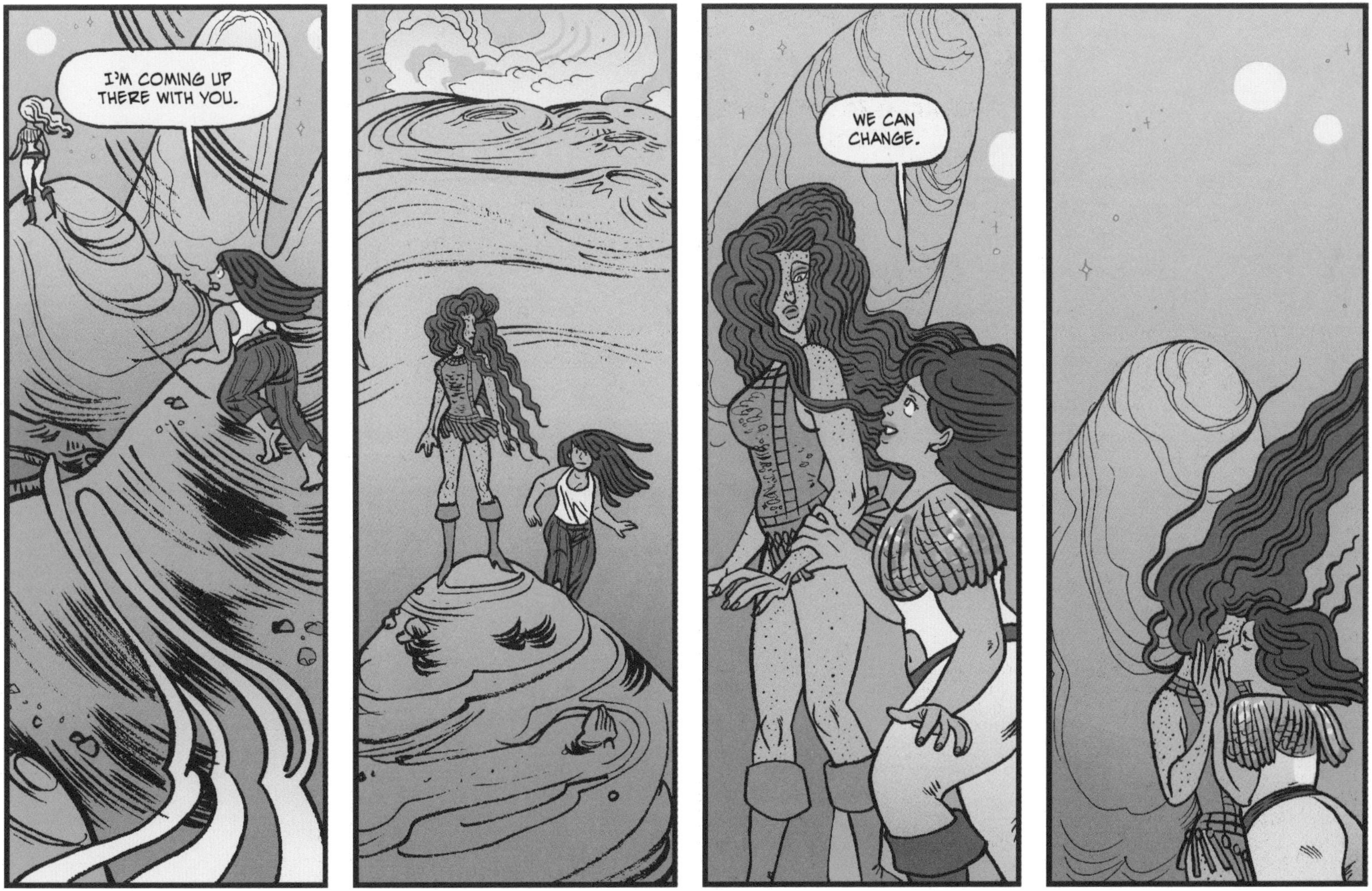
I'M COMING UP THERE WITH YOU.
WE CAN CHANGE.

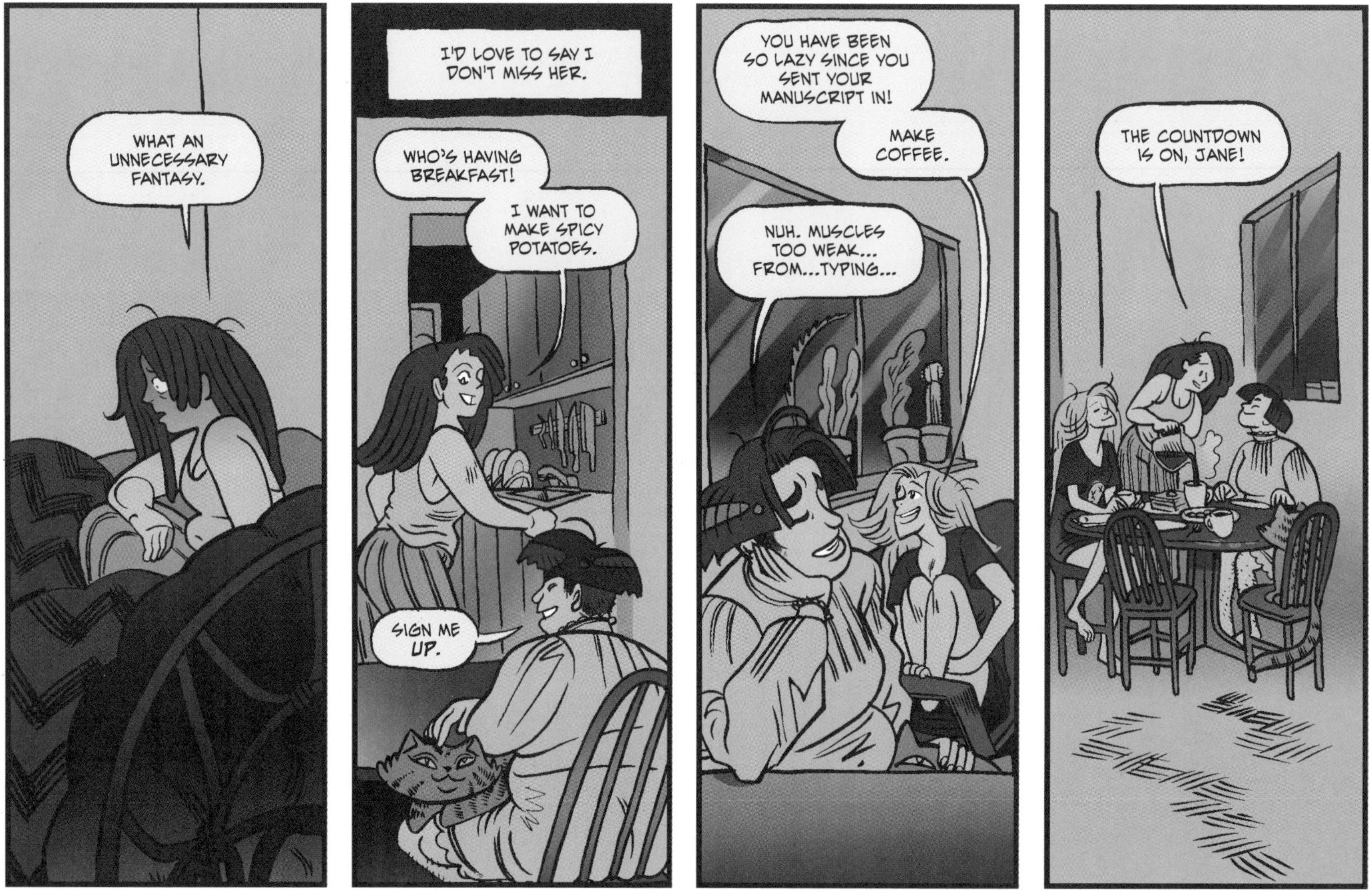
WHAT AN UNNECESSARY FANTASY.
I'D LOVE TO SAY I DON'T MISS HER.
WHO'S HAVING BREAKFAST!
I WANT TO MAKE SPICY POTATOES.
SIGN ME UP.
YOU HAVE BEEN SO LAZY SINCE YOU SENT YOUR MANUSCRIPT IN!
MAKE COFFEE.
NUH. MUSCLES TOO WEAK... FROM...TYPING...
THE COUNTDOWN IS ON, JANE!

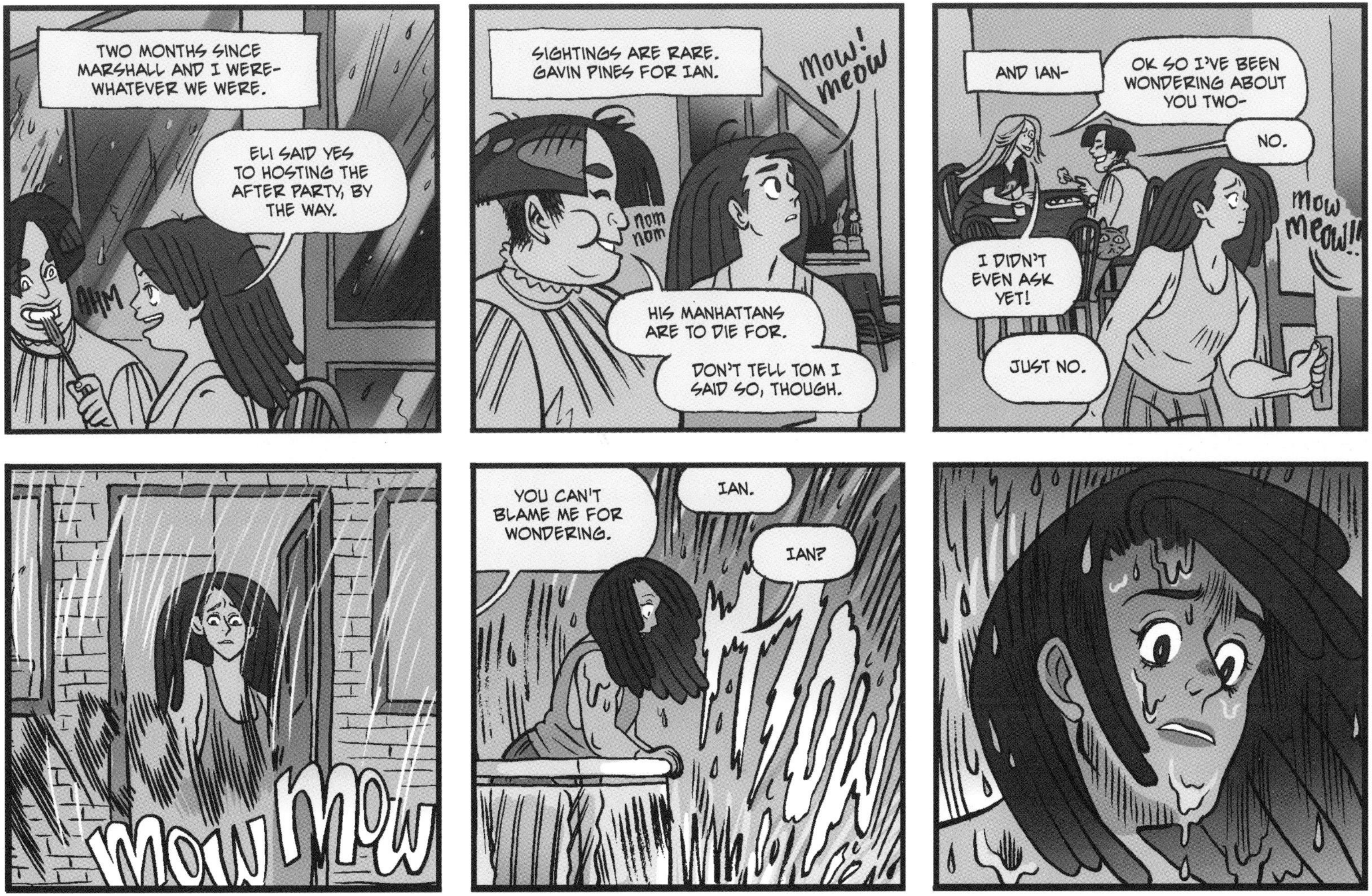
TWO MONTHS SINCE MARSHALL AND I WERE- WHATEVER WE WERE.
ELI SAID YES TO HOSTING THE AFTER PARTY, BY THE WAY.
AHM
SIGHTINGS ARE RARE. GAVIN PINES FOR IAN.
MOW! MEOW
NOM NOM
HIS MANHATTANS ARE TO DIE FOR.
DON'T TELL TOM I SAID SO, THOUGH.
AND IAN-
OK SO I'VE BEEN WONDERING ABOUT YOU TWO-
NO.
MOW MEOW!!
I DIDN'T EVEN ASK YET!
JUST NO.
MOW MOW
YOU CAN'T BLAME ME FOR WONDERING.
IAN.
IAN?

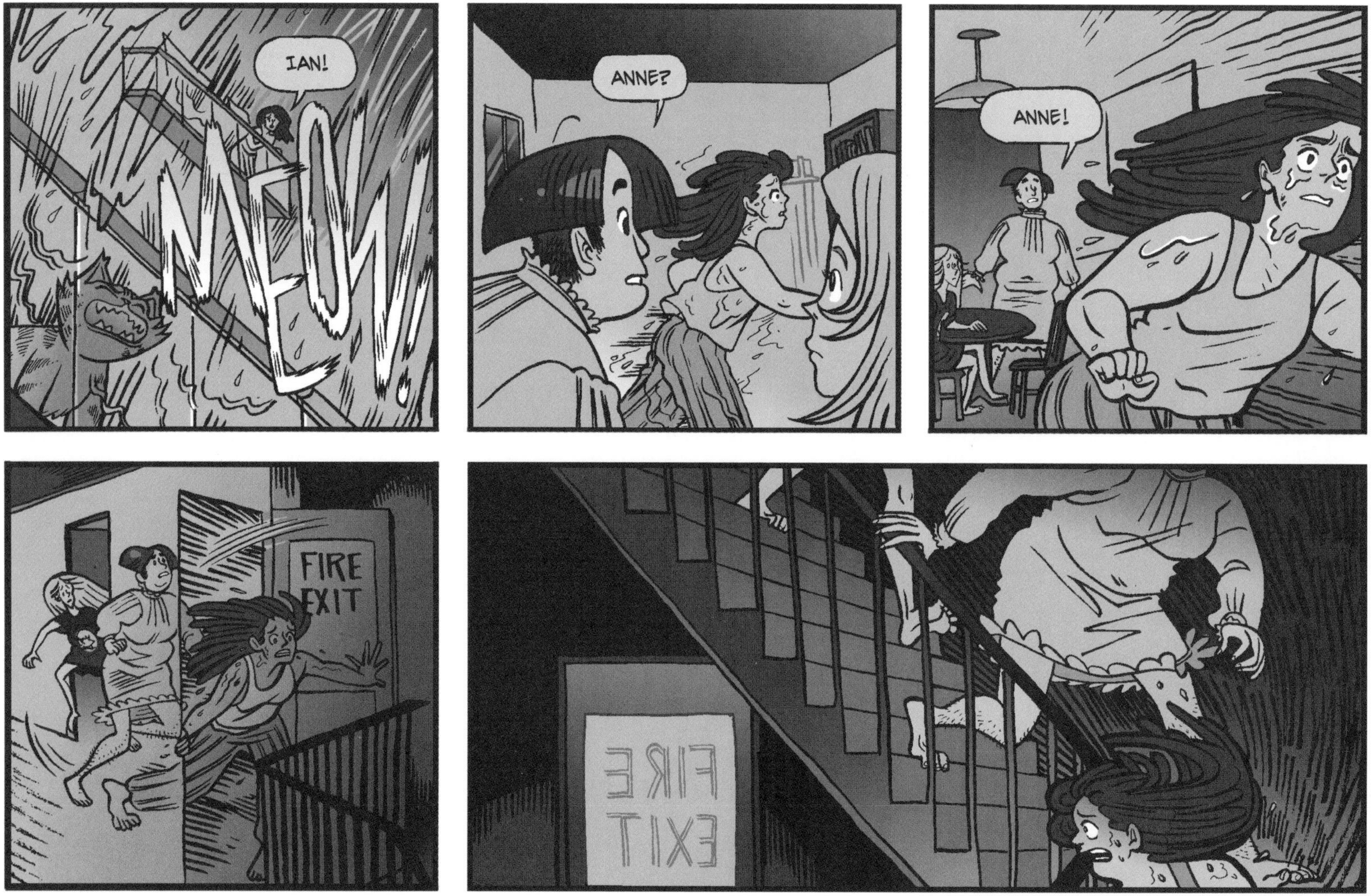
IAN!
MEOW!
ANNE?
ANNE!
FIRE EXIT
FIRE EXIT

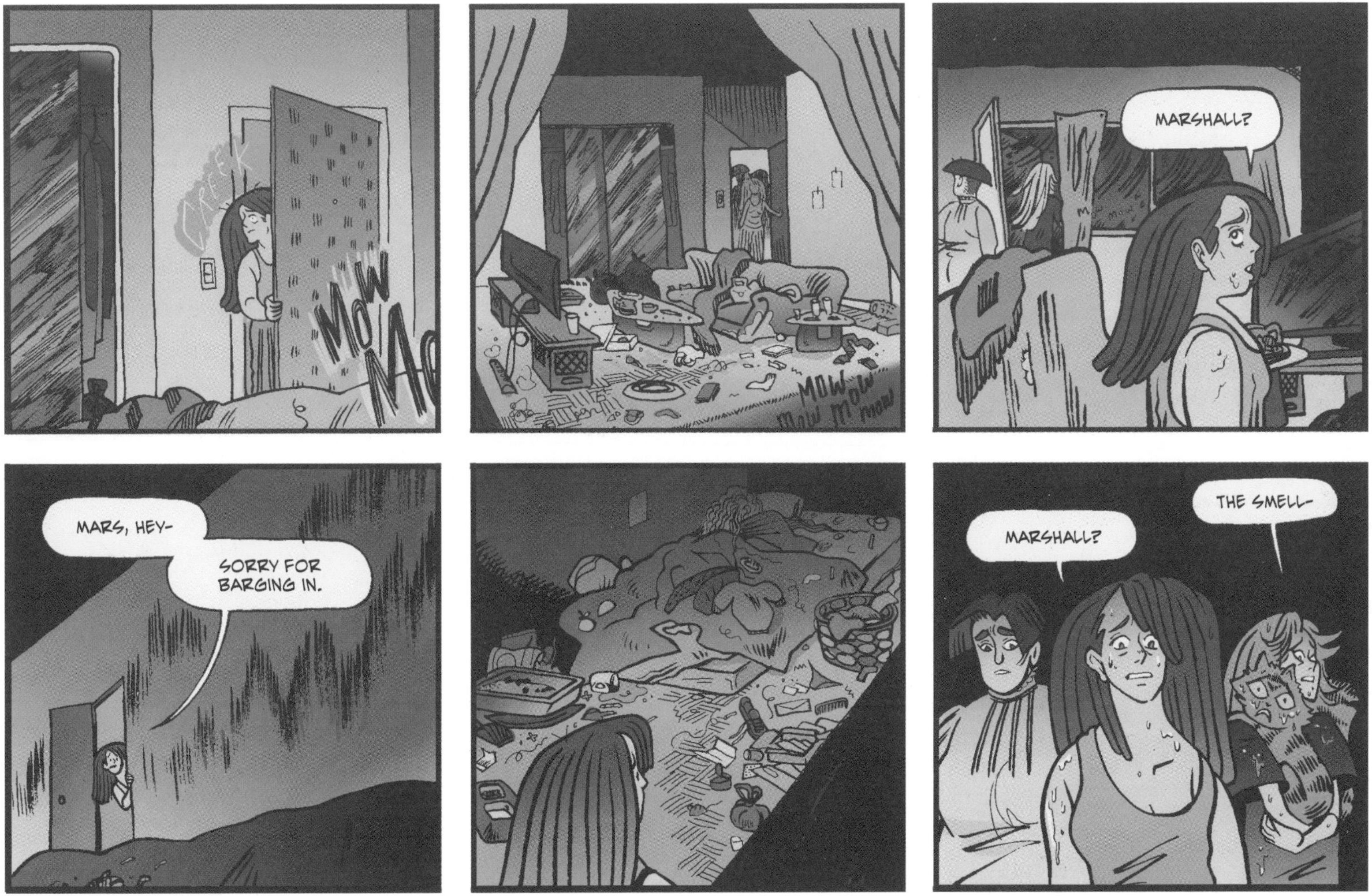
CREEK
MOW
MOW MOW MOW mow
MARSHALL?
MARS, HEY-
SORRY FOR BARGING IN.
MARSHALL?
THE SMELL-

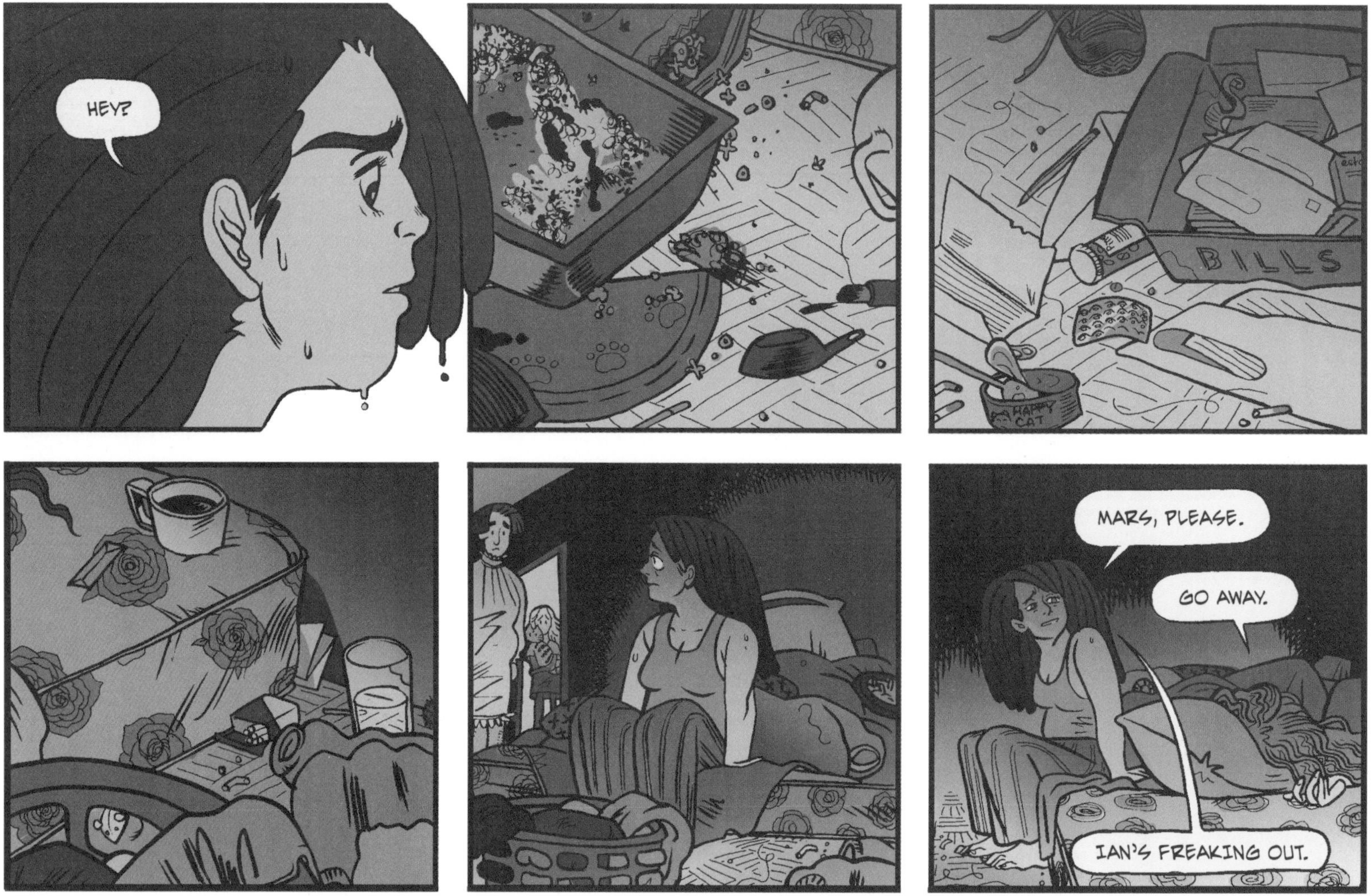
HEY?
BILLS
HAPPY CAT
MARS, PLEASE.
GO AWAY.
IAN'S FREAKING OUT.

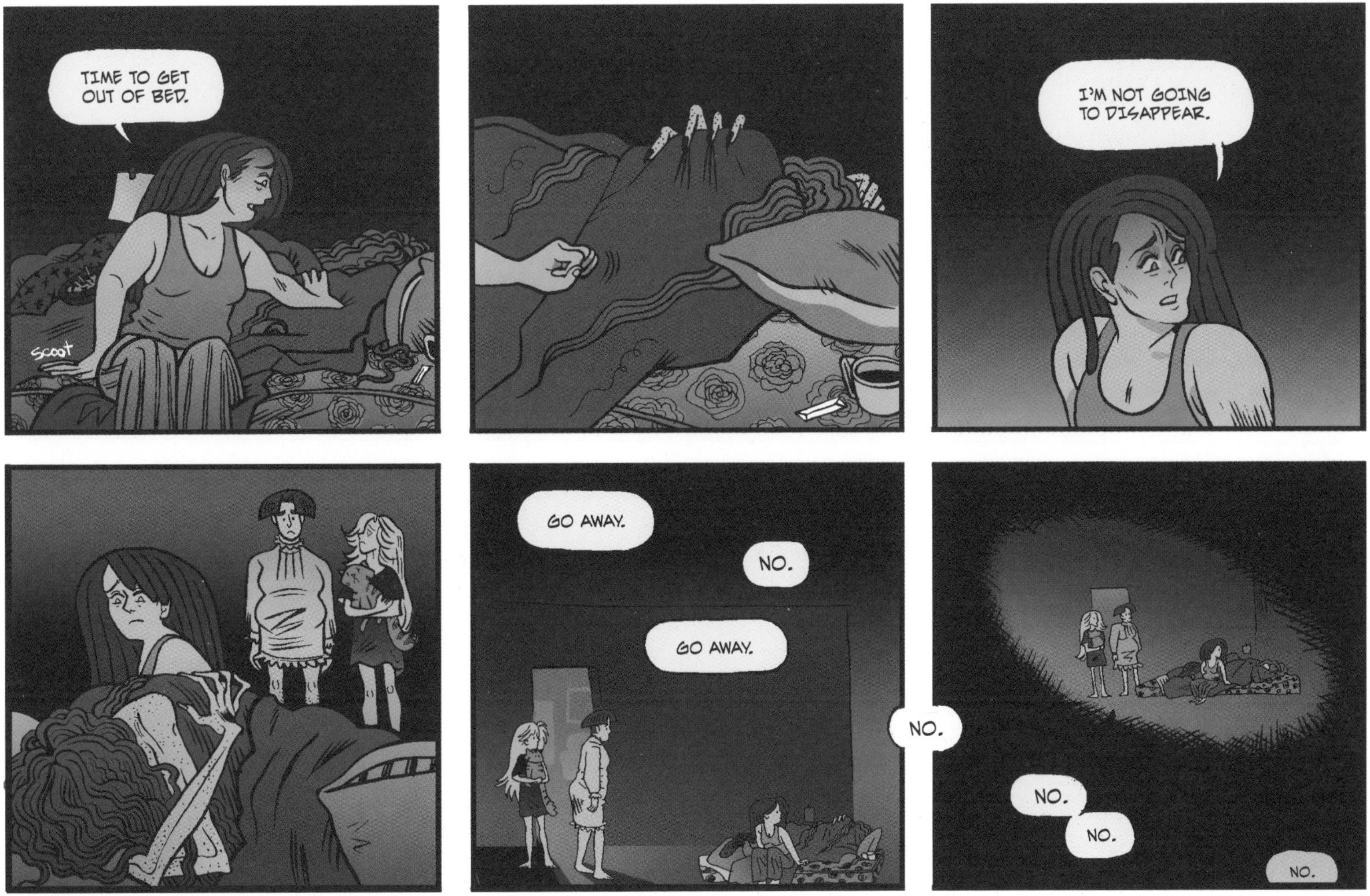
TIME TO GET OUT OF BED.
SCOOT
I'M NOT GOING TO DISAPPEAR.
GO AWAY.
NO.
GO AWAY.
NO.
NO.
NO.
NO.

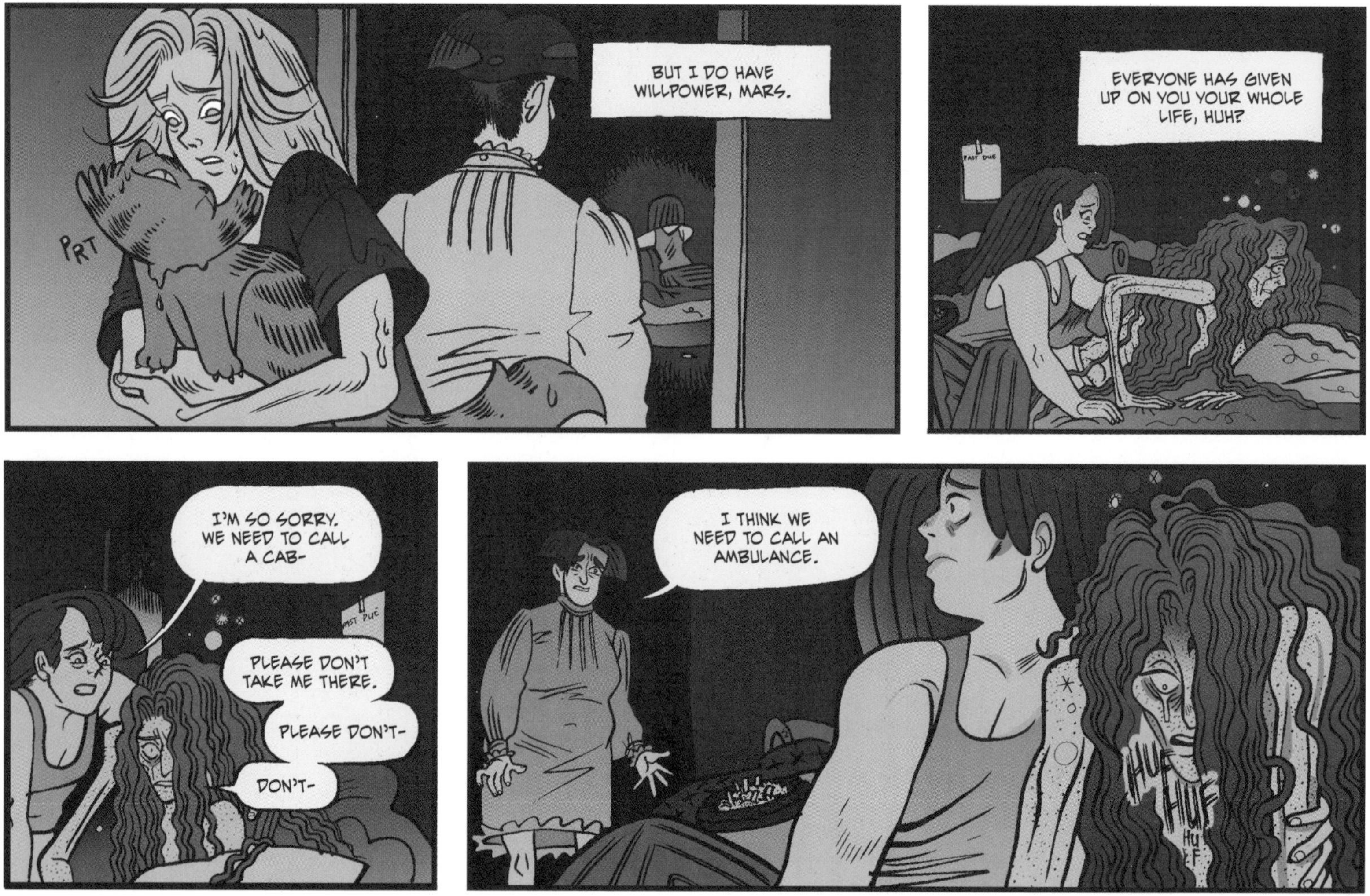

PRT
BUT I DO HAVE WILLPOWER, MARS.
EVERYONE HAS GIVEN UP ON YOU YOUR WHOLE LIFE, HUH?
PAST DUE
I'M SO SORRY. WE NEED TO CALL A CAB-
PAST DUE
PLEASE DON'T TAKE ME THERE.
PLEASE DON'T-
DON'T-
I THINK WE NEED TO CALL AN AMBULANCE.
HUF
HUF
HUF

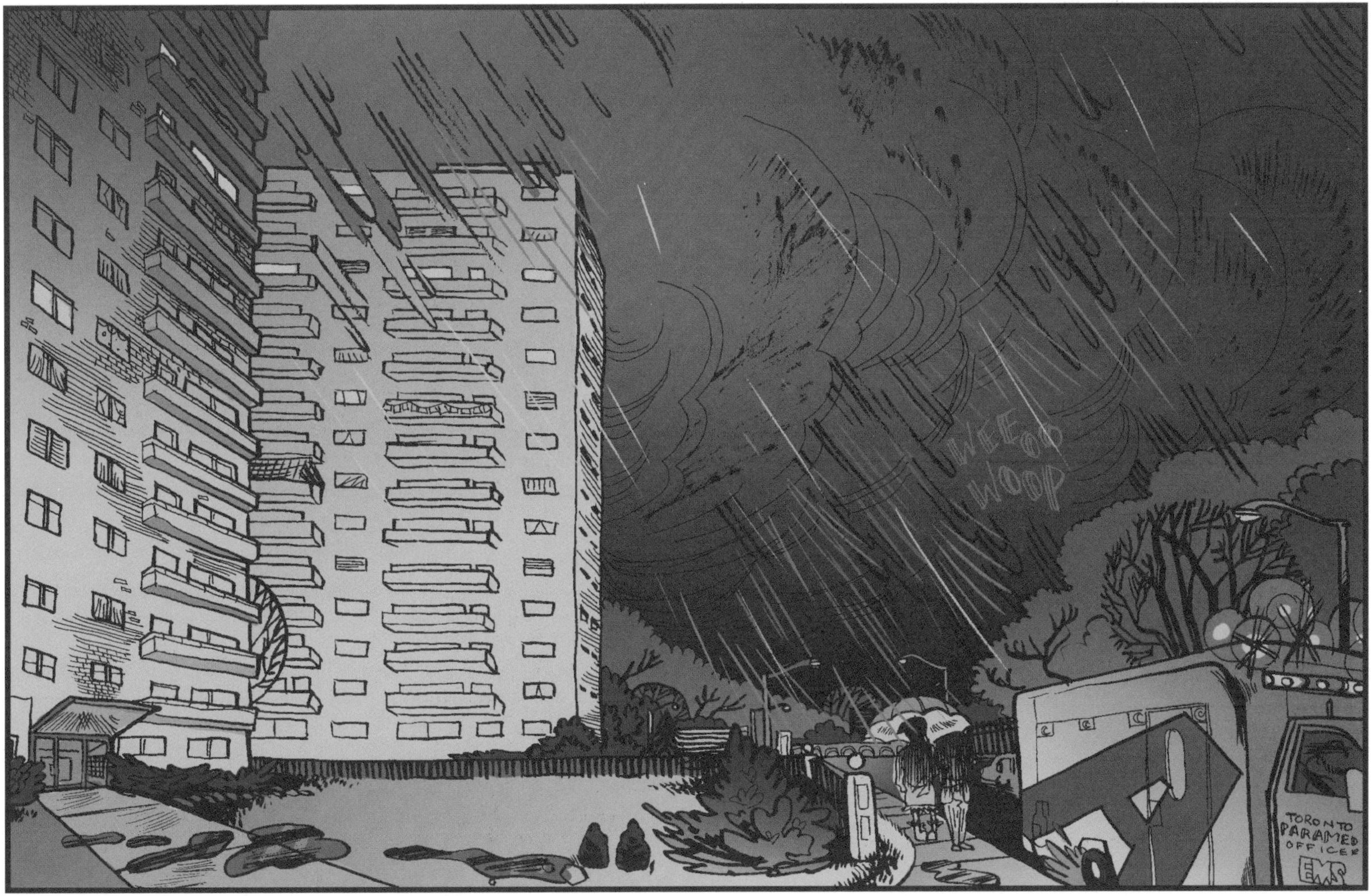
WEEOO WOOP
TORONTO PARAMED OFFICER

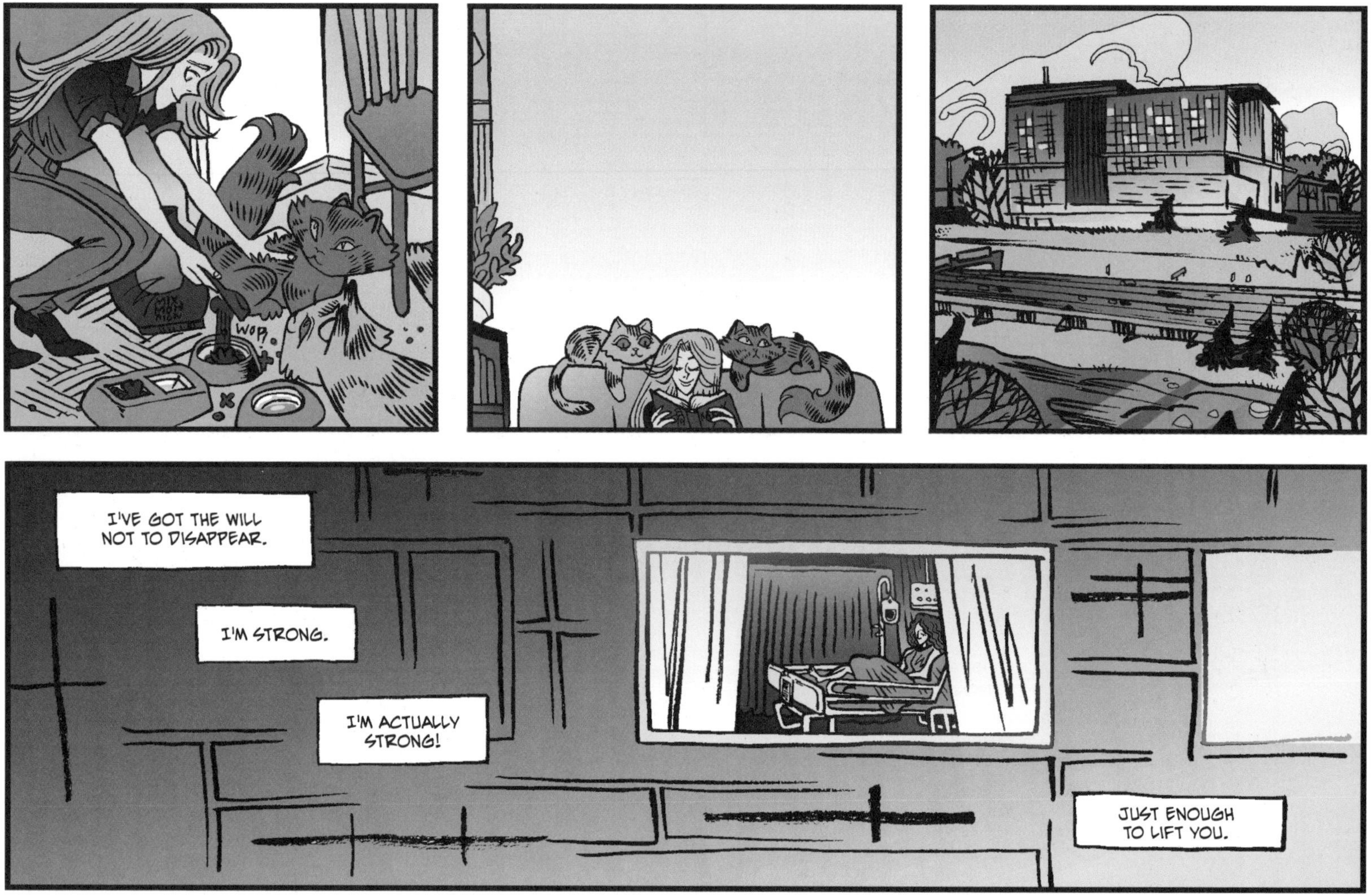
WOP
I'VE GOT THE WILL NOT TO DISAPPEAR.
I'M STRONG.
I'M ACTUALLY STRONG!
JUST ENOUGH TO LIFT YOU.

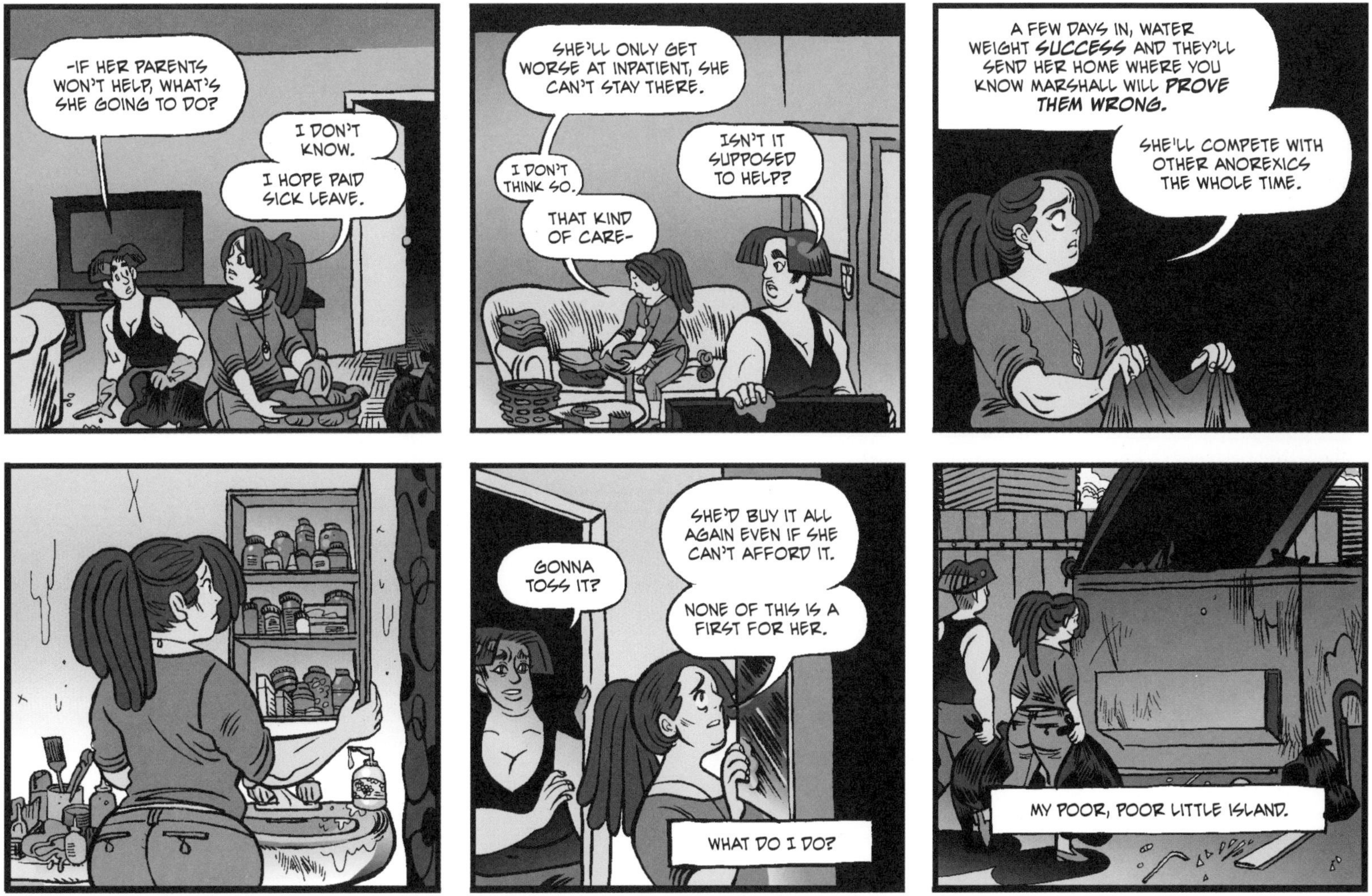
-IF HER PARENTS WON'T HELP, WHAT'S SHE GOING TO DO?
I DON'T KNOW.
I HOPE PAID SICK LEAVE.
SHE'LL ONLY GET WORSE AT INPATIENT, SHE CAN'T STAY THERE.
I DON'T THINK SO.
THAT KIND OF CARE-
ISN'T IT SUPPOSED TO HELP?
A FEW DAYS IN, WATER WEIGHT **SUCCESS** AND THEY'LL SEND HER HOME WHERE YOU KNOW MARSHALL WILL **PROVE THEM WRONG.**
SHE'LL COMPETE WITH OTHER ANOREXICS THE WHOLE TIME.
GONNA TOSS IT?
SHE'D BUY IT ALL AGAIN EVEN IF SHE CAN'T AFFORD IT.
NONE OF THIS IS A FIRST FOR HER.
WHAT DO I DO?
MY POOR, POOR LITTLE ISLAND.

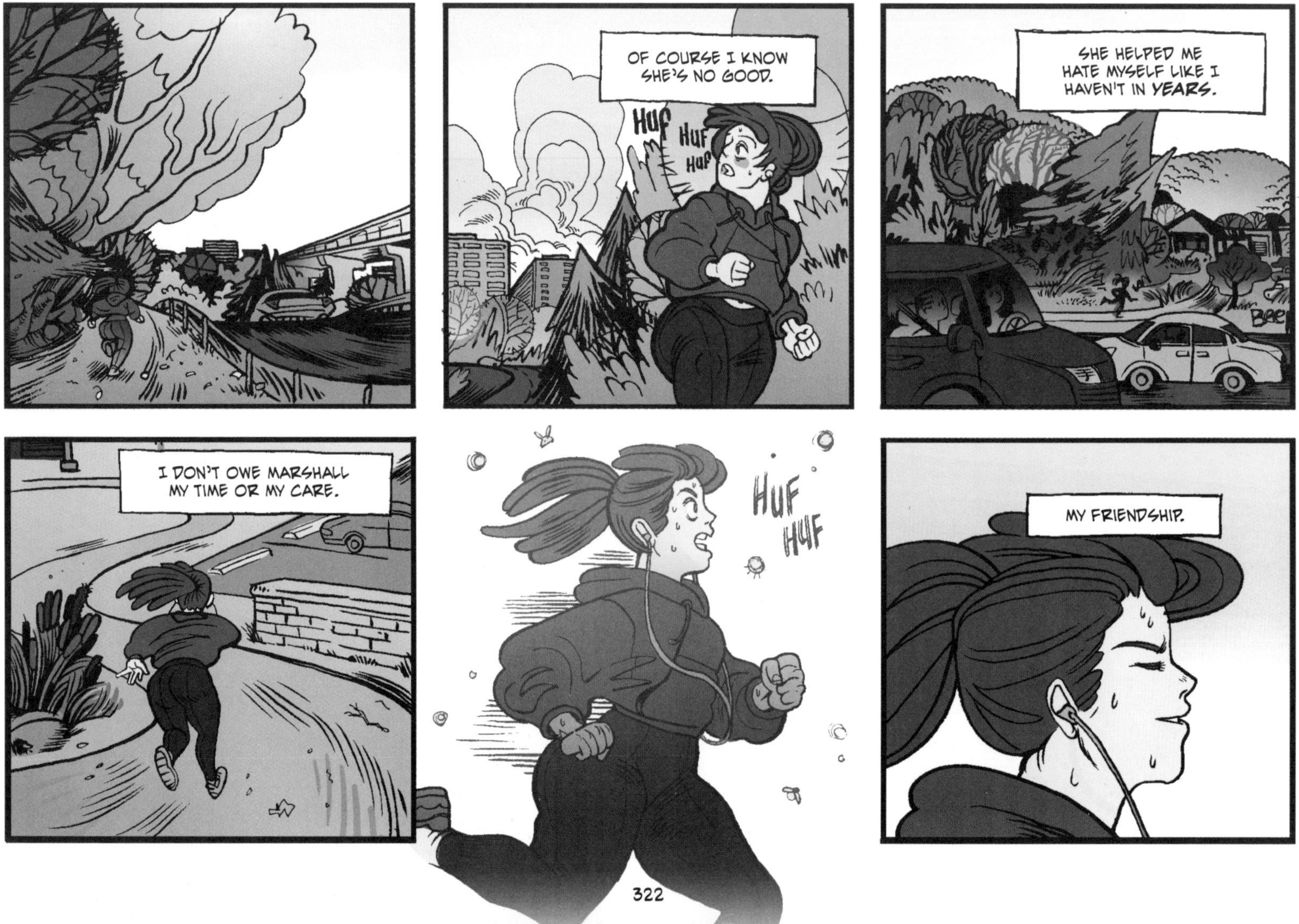
OF COURSE I KNOW SHE'S NO GOOD.
HUF HUF HUF
SHE HELPED ME HATE MYSELF LIKE I HAVEN'T IN YEARS.
I DON'T OWE MARSHALL MY TIME OR MY CARE.
HUF HUF
MY FRIENDSHIP.

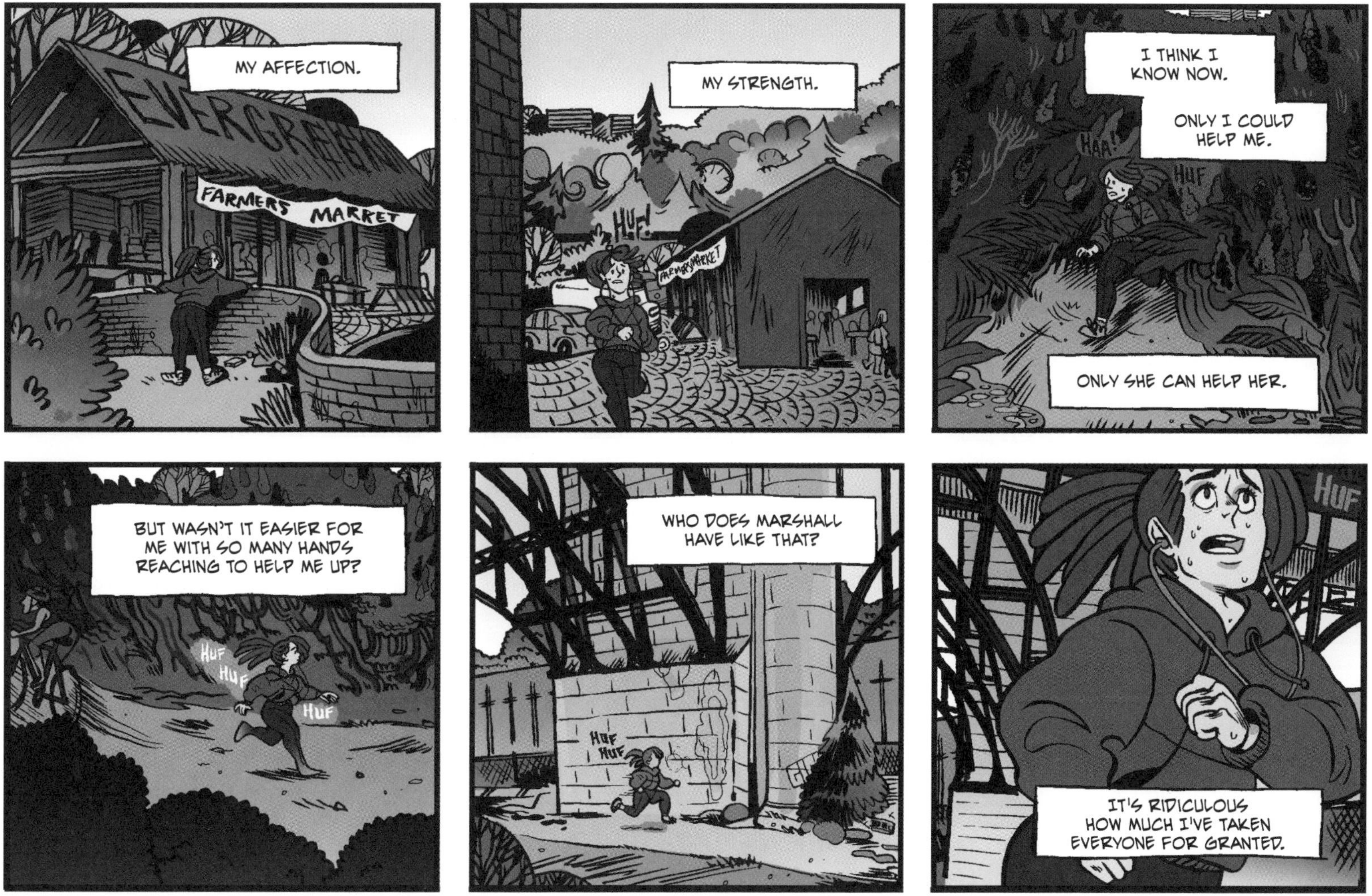
MY AFFECTION.
EVERGREEN
FARMERS MARKET
MY STRENGTH.
HUF!
FARMERS MARKET
I THINK I KNOW NOW.
ONLY I COULD HELP ME.
HAA!
HUF
ONLY SHE CAN HELP HER.
BUT WASN'T IT EASIER FOR ME WITH SO MANY HANDS REACHING TO HELP ME UP?
HUF
HUF
HUF
WHO DOES MARSHALL HAVE LIKE THAT?
HUF
HUF
HUF
IT'S RIDICULOUS HOW MUCH I'VE TAKEN EVERYONE FOR GRANTED.

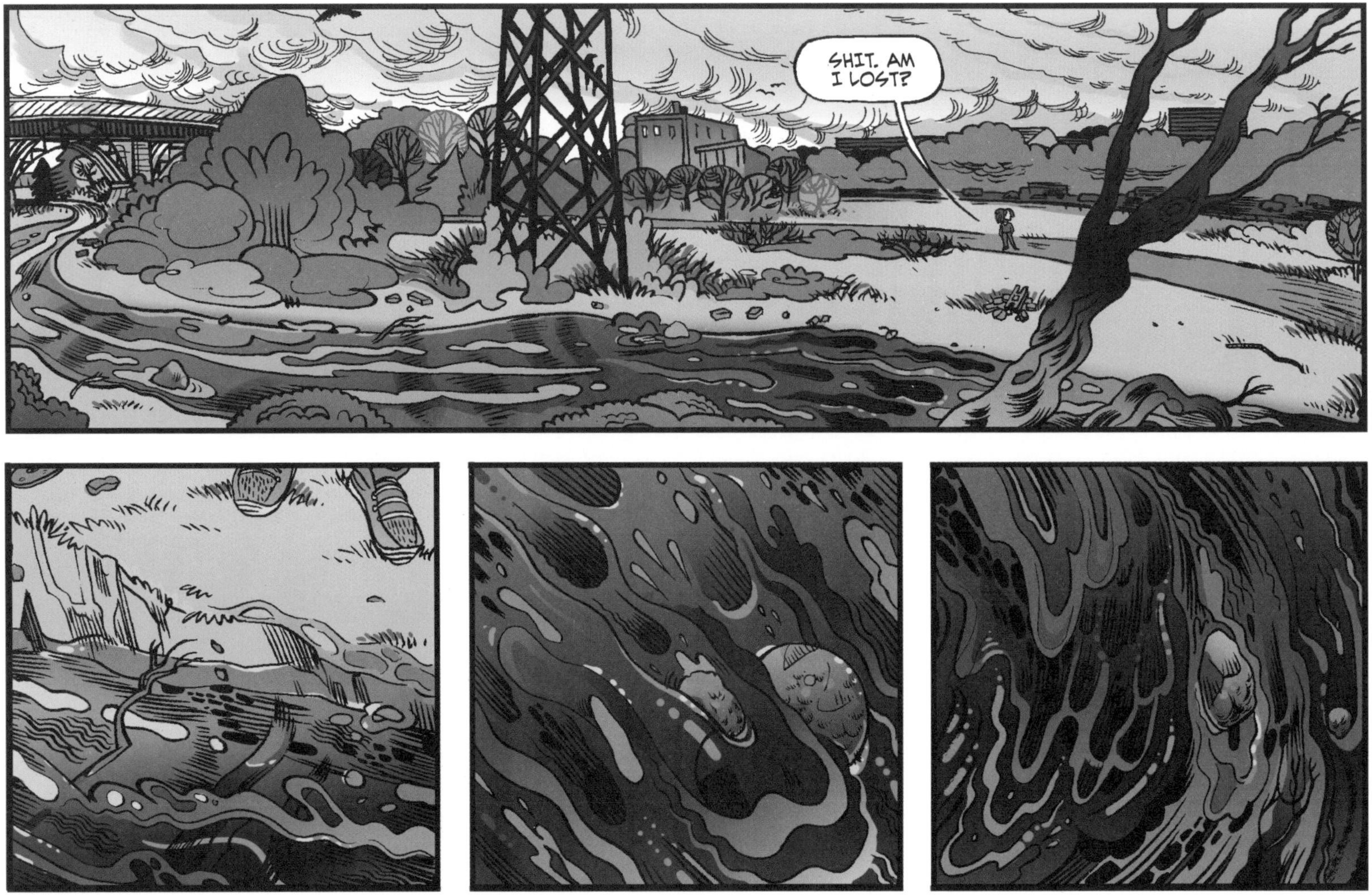
SHIT. AM I LOST?

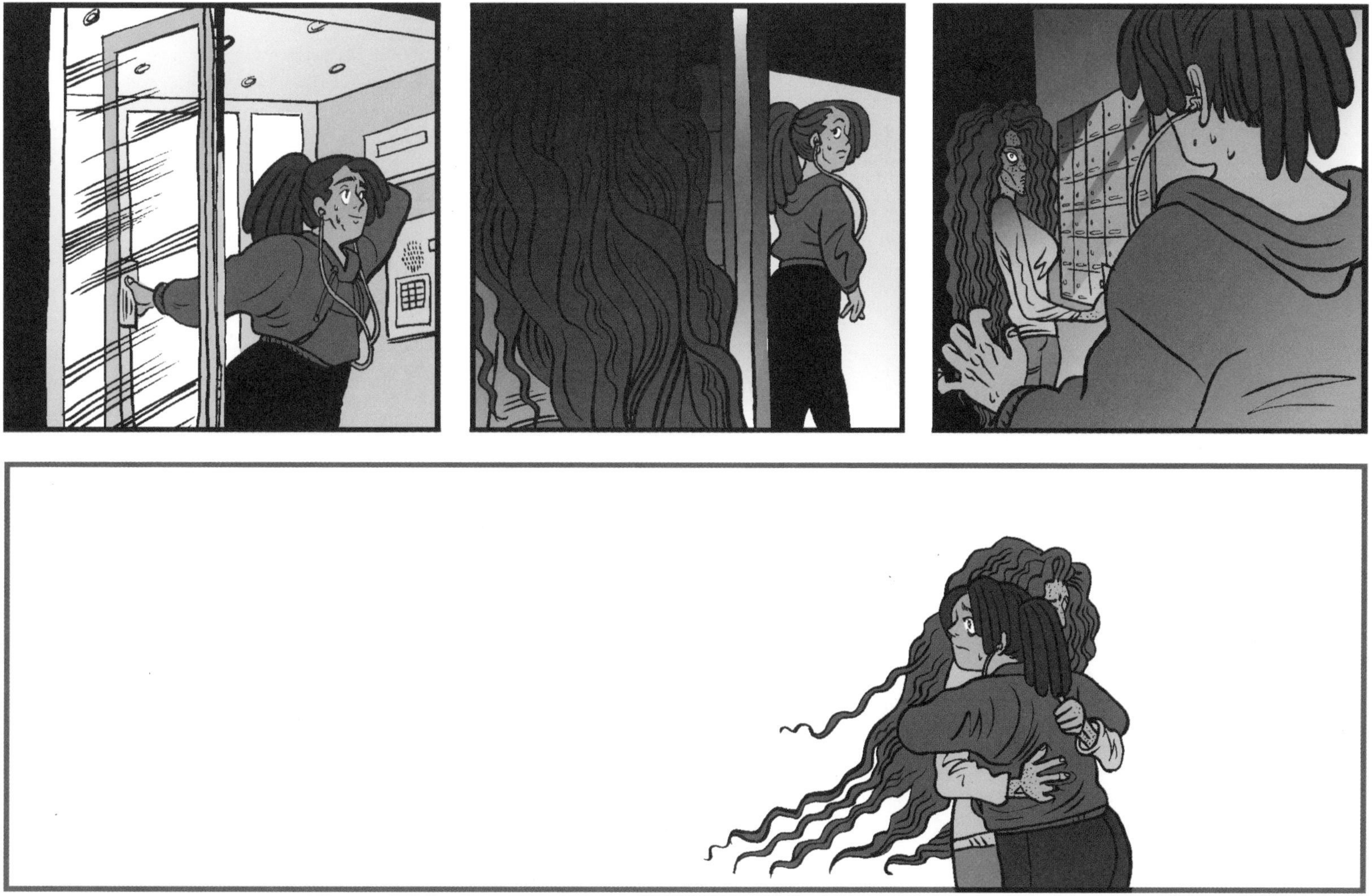

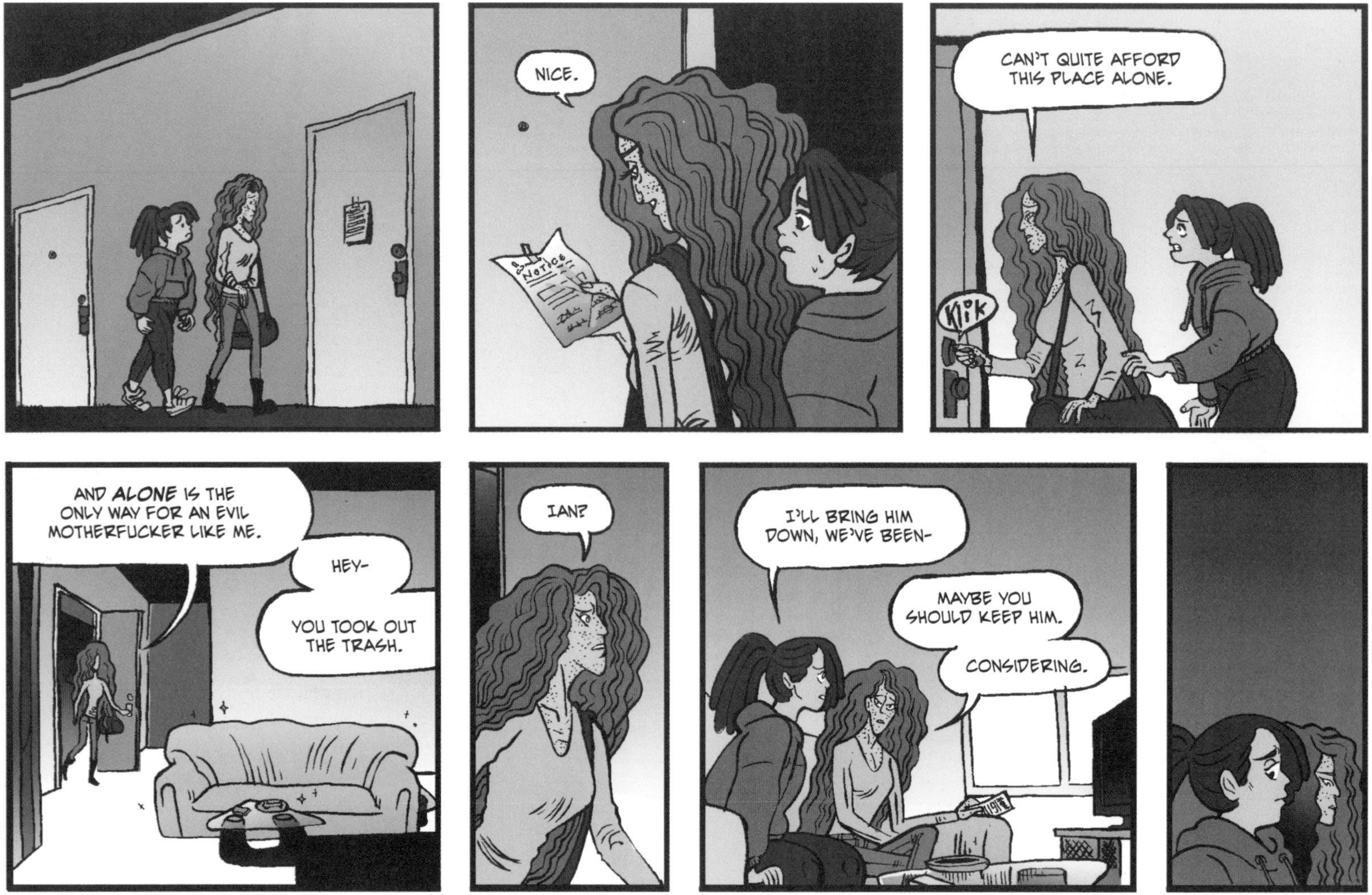
NICE.
CAN'T QUITE AFFORD THIS PLACE ALONE.
KLIK
AND ALONE IS THE ONLY WAY FOR AN EVIL MOTHERFUCKER LIKE ME.
HEY-
YOU TOOK OUT THE TRASH.
IAN?
I'LL BRING HIM DOWN, WE'VE BEEN-
MAYBE YOU SHOULD KEEP HIM.
CONSIDERING.

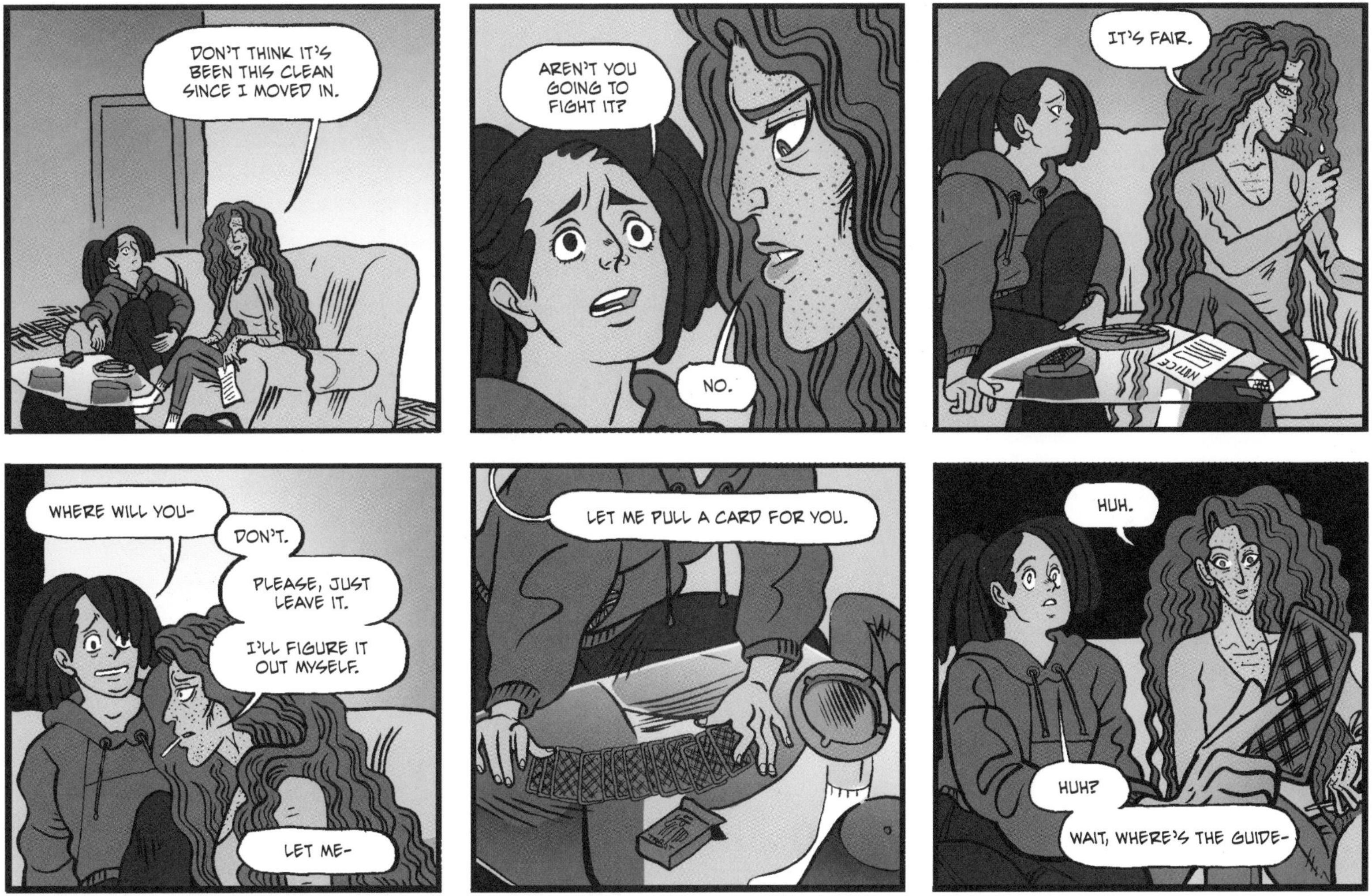
DON'T THINK IT'S BEEN THIS CLEAN SINCE I MOVED IN.
AREN'T YOU GOING TO FIGHT IT?
NO.
IT'S FAIR.
NOTICE
WHERE WILL YOU-
DON'T.
PLEASE, JUST LEAVE IT.
I'LL FIGURE IT OUT MYSELF.
LET ME-
LET ME PULL A CARD FOR YOU.
HUH.
HUH?
WAIT, WHERE'S THE GUIDE-

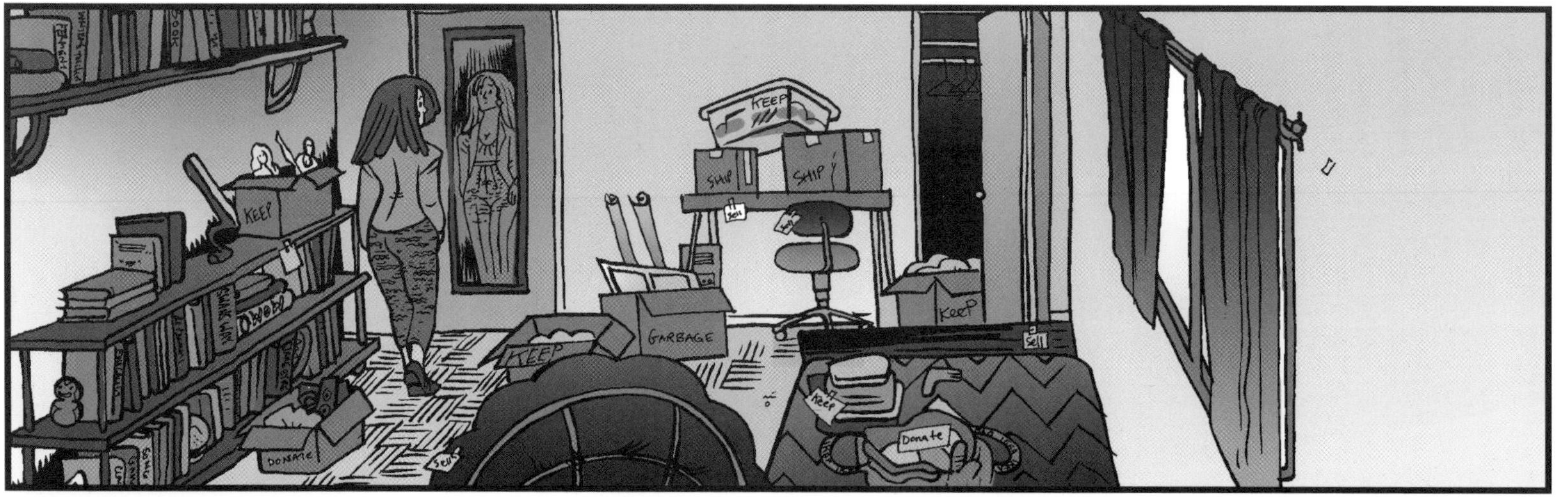
KEEP
KEEP
SHIP
SHIP
KEEP
GARBAGE
KEEP
DONATE
Donate

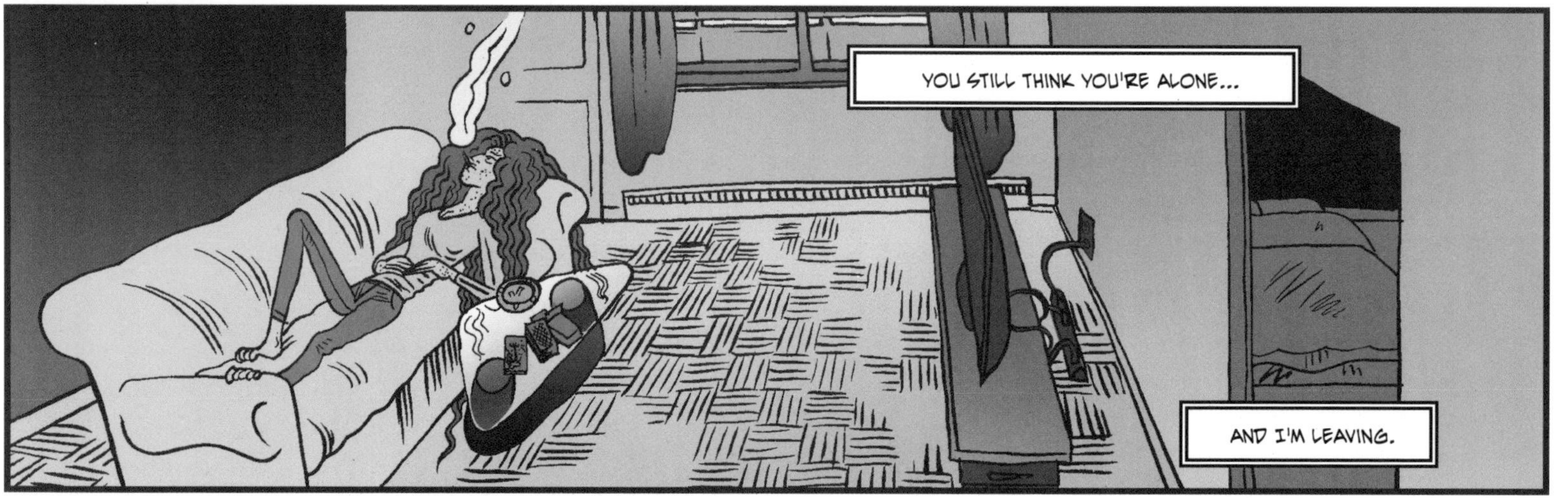
YOU STILL THINK YOU'RE ALONE...
AND I'M LEAVING.

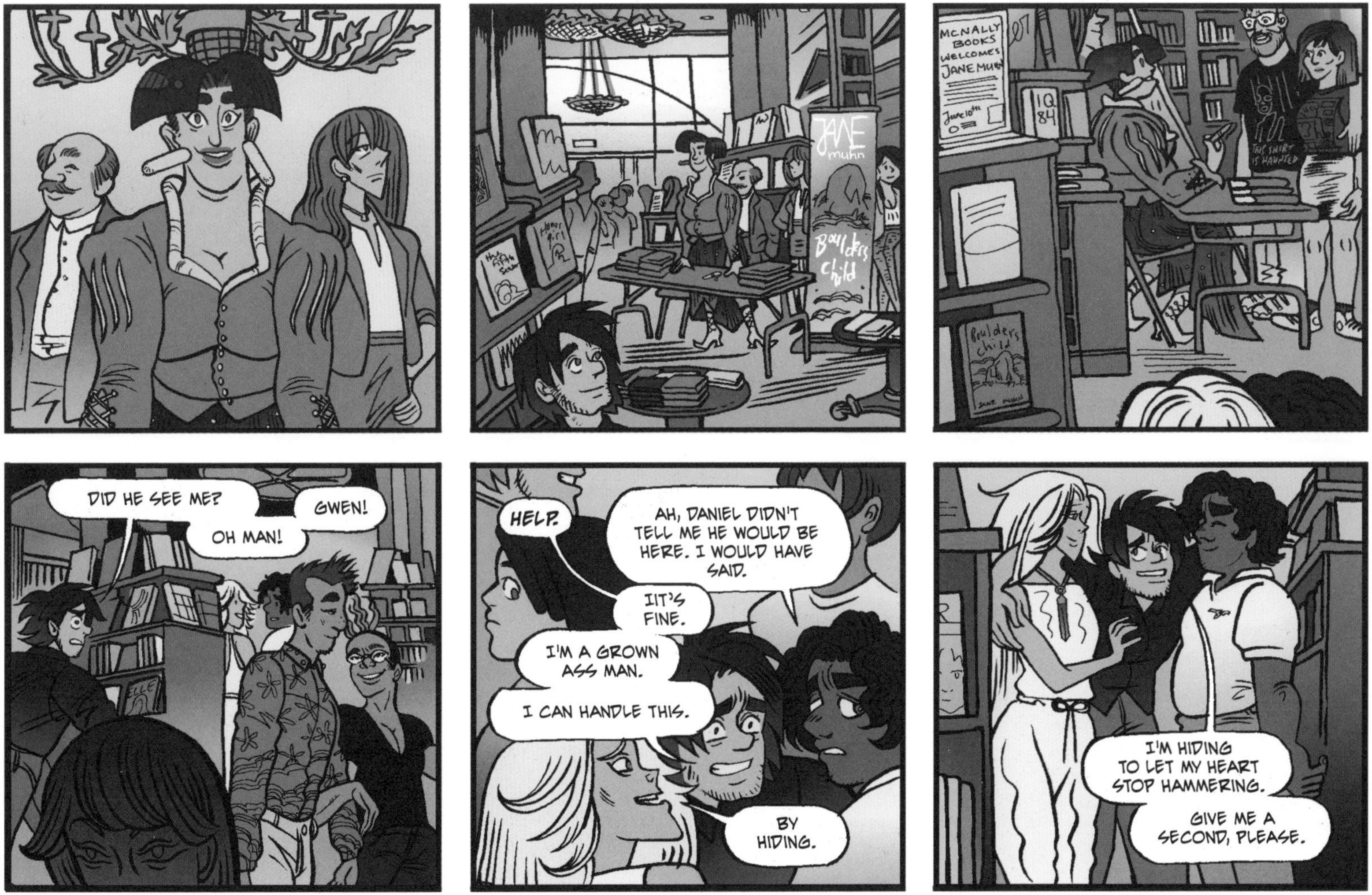
JANE
muhn
Boulders child
McNALLY BOOKS WELCOMES JANE MUHN
1Q 84
THIS SHIRT IS HAUNTED
DID HE SEE ME?
OH MAN!
GWEN!
HELP.
AH, DANIEL DIDN'T TELL ME HE WOULD BE HERE. I WOULD HAVE SAID.
IIT'S FINE.
I'M A GROWN ASS MAN.
I CAN HANDLE THIS.
BY HIDING.
I'M HIDING TO LET MY HEART STOP HAMMERING.
GIVE ME A SECOND, PLEASE.

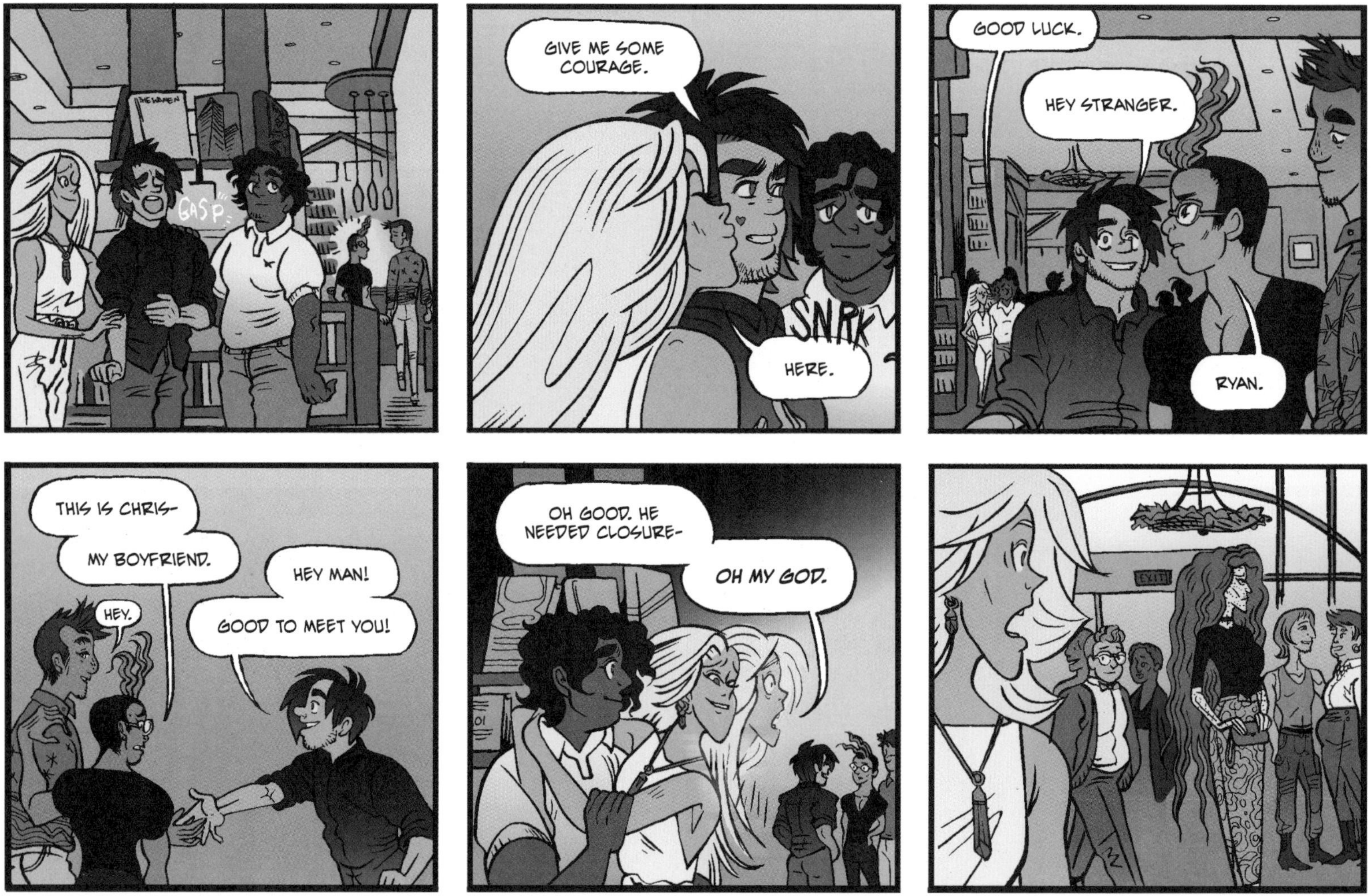
GASP!
GIVE ME SOME COURAGE.
SNRK
HERE.
GOOD LUCK.
HEY STRANGER.
RYAN.
THIS IS CHRIS-
MY BOYFRIEND.
HEY.
HEY MAN!
GOOD TO MEET YOU!
OH GOOD. HE NEEDED CLOSURE-
OH MY GOD.
EXIT

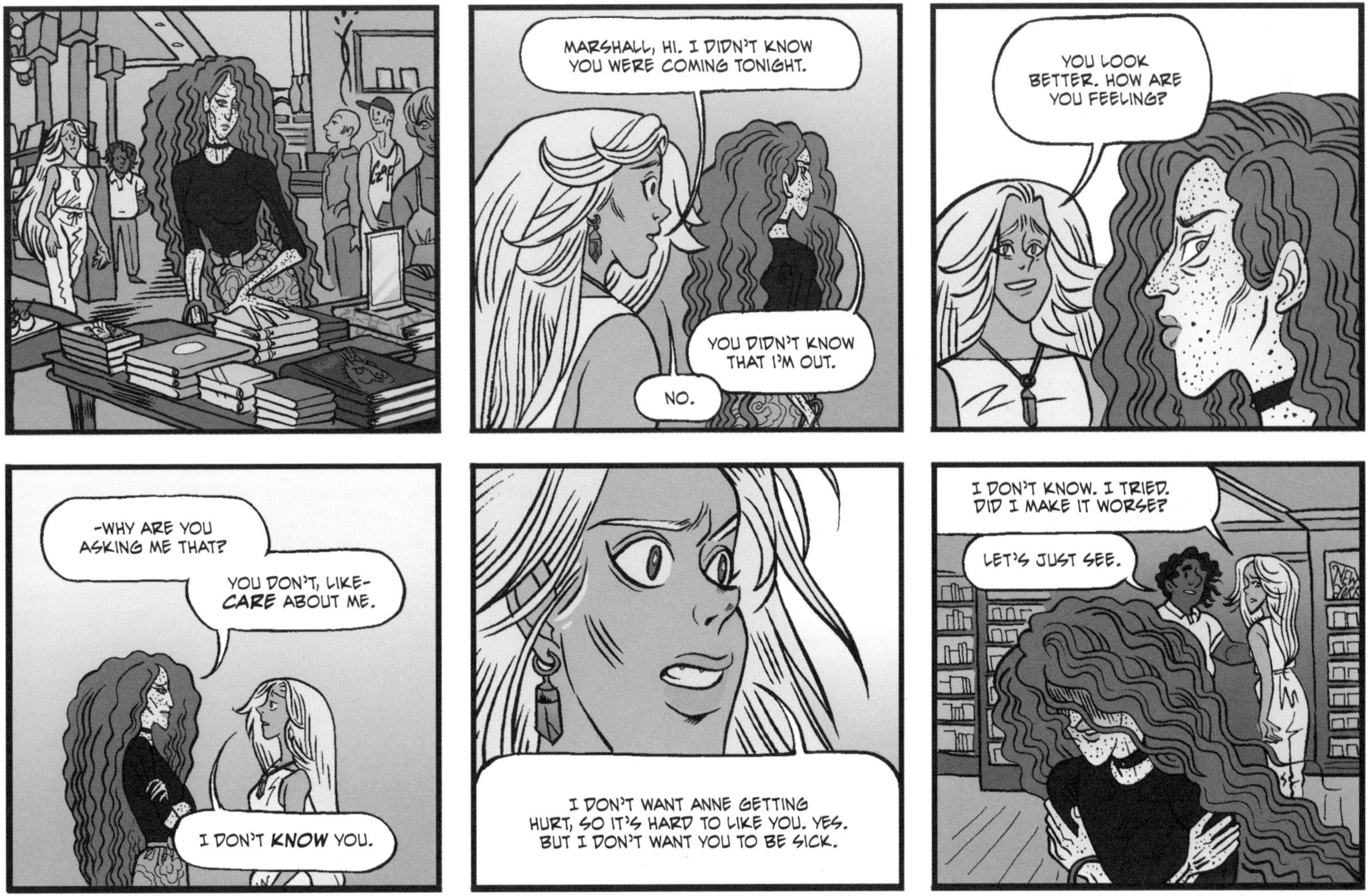
MARSHALL, HI. I DIDN'T KNOW YOU WERE COMING TONIGHT.
NO.
YOU DIDN'T KNOW THAT I'M OUT.
YOU LOOK BETTER. HOW ARE YOU FEELING?
-WHY ARE YOU ASKING ME THAT?
YOU DON'T, LIKE- CARE ABOUT ME.
I DON'T KNOW YOU.
I DON'T WANT ANNE GETTING HURT, SO IT'S HARD TO LIKE YOU. YES. BUT I DON'T WANT YOU TO BE SICK.
I DON'T KNOW. I TRIED. DID I MAKE IT WORSE?
LET'S JUST SEE.

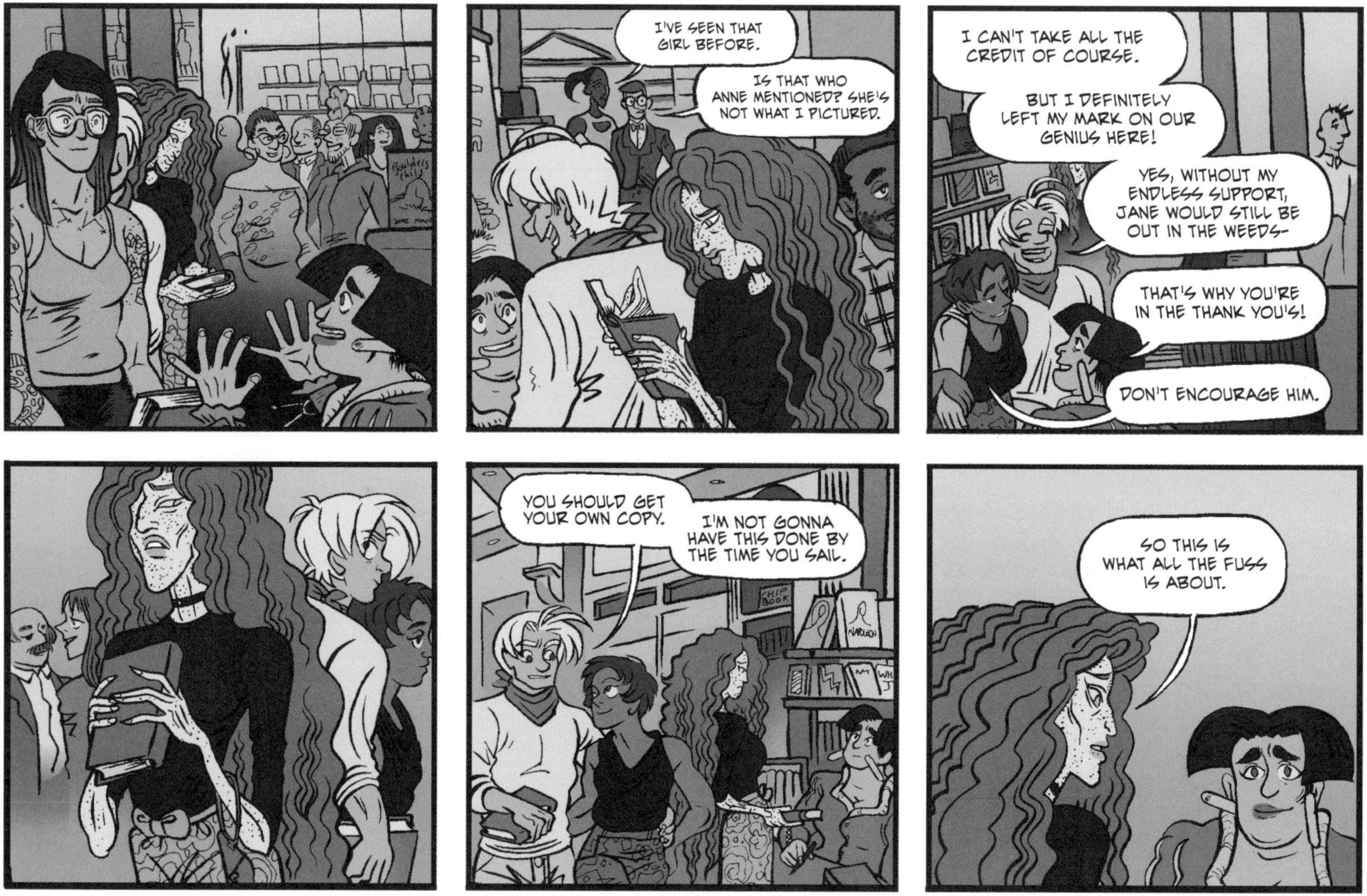
I'VE SEEN THAT GIRL BEFORE.
IS THAT WHO ANNE MENTIONED? SHE'S NOT WHAT I PICTURED.
I CAN'T TAKE ALL THE CREDIT OF COURSE.
BUT I DEFINITELY LEFT MY MARK ON OUR GENIUS HERE!
YES, WITHOUT MY ENDLESS SUPPORT, JANE WOULD STILL BE OUT IN THE WEEDS-
THAT'S WHY YOU'RE IN THE THANK YOU'S!
DON'T ENCOURAGE HIM.
YOU SHOULD GET YOUR OWN COPY.
I'M NOT GONNA HAVE THIS DONE BY THE TIME YOU SAIL.
SO THIS IS WHAT ALL THE FUSS IS ABOUT.

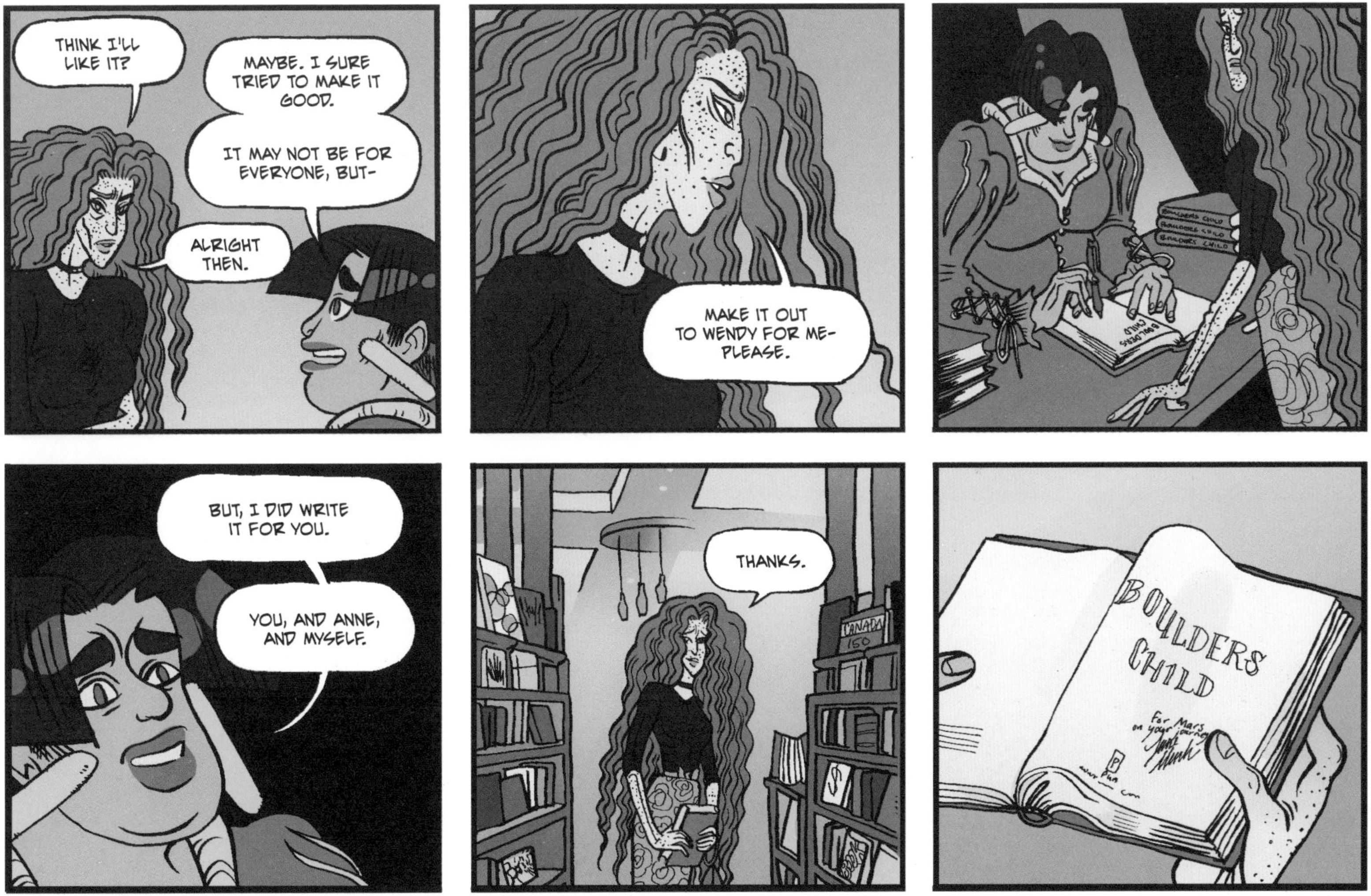
THINK I'LL LIKE IT?
MAYBE. I SURE TRIED TO MAKE IT GOOD.
IT MAY NOT BE FOR EVERYONE, BUT-
ALRIGHT THEN.
MAKE IT OUT TO WENDY FOR ME- PLEASE.
BOULDERS CHILD
BUT, I DID WRITE IT FOR YOU.
YOU, AND ANNE, AND MYSELF.
THANKS.
CANADA 150
BOULDERS CHILD
For Mars on your journey

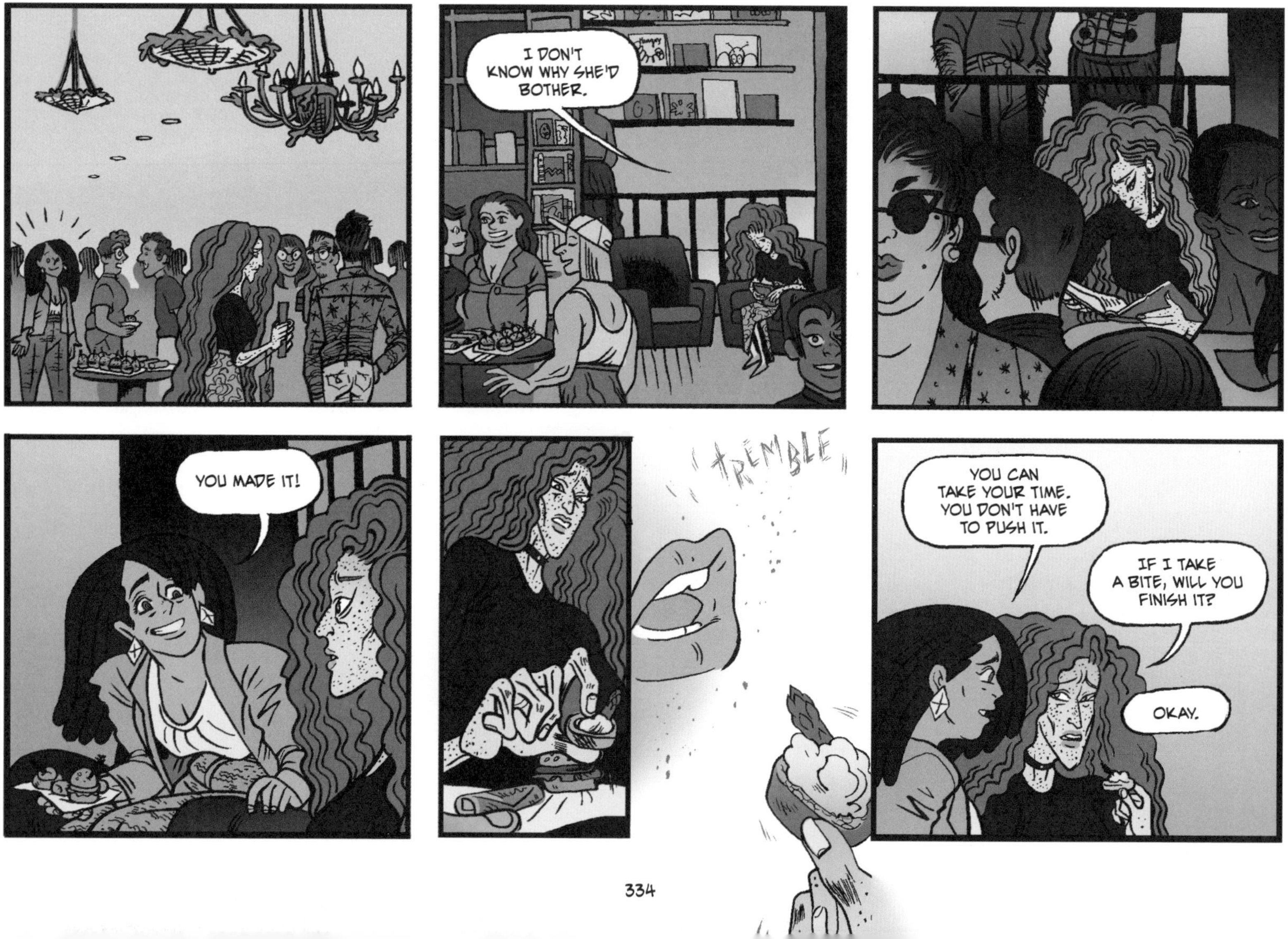
I DON'T KNOW WHY SHE'D BOTHER.
YOU MADE IT!
TREMBLE
YOU CAN TAKE YOUR TIME. YOU DON'T HAVE TO PUSH IT.
IF I TAKE A BITE, WILL YOU FINISH IT?
OKAY.

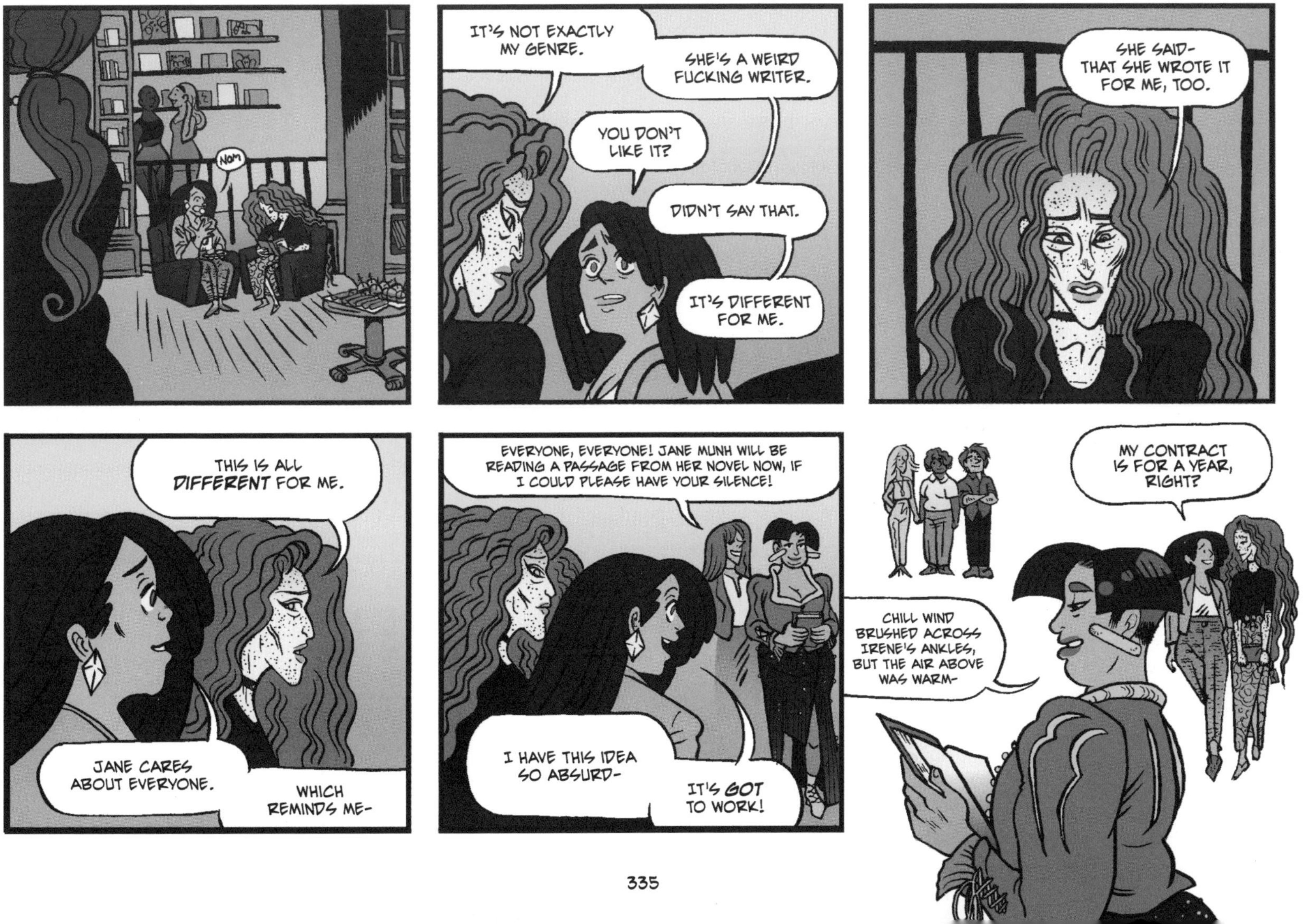
NOM
IT'S NOT EXACTLY MY GENRE.
SHE'S A WEIRD FUCKING WRITER.
YOU DON'T LIKE IT?
DIDN'T SAY THAT.
IT'S DIFFERENT FOR ME.
SHE SAID- THAT SHE WROTE IT FOR ME, TOO.
THIS IS ALL DIFFERENT FOR ME.
JANE CARES ABOUT EVERYONE.
WHICH REMINDS ME-
EVERYONE, EVERYONE! JANE MUNH WILL BE READING A PASSAGE FROM HER NOVEL NOW, IF I COULD PLEASE HAVE YOUR SILENCE!
I HAVE THIS IDEA SO ABSURD-
IT'S GOT TO WORK!
MY CONTRACT IS FOR A YEAR, RIGHT?
CHILL WIND BRUSHED ACROSS IRENE'S ANKLES, BUT THE AIR ABOVE WAS WARM-

IT WRAPS EVERYTHING UP NICELY, DON'T YOU THINK?

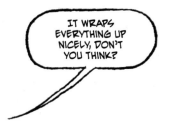